# HOOPING IT UP

# HOOPING IT UP

## THE COMPLETE HISTORY OF
## NOTRE DAME BASKETBALL

## TIM NEELY

DIAMOND COMMUNICATIONS, INC.
NOTRE DAME, INDIANA
1985

# HOOPING IT UP

Manufactured in the United States of America

Diamond Communications, Inc.
PO Box 94
Notre Dame, IN 46556

Library of Congress Cataloging-in-Publication Data

Neely, Tim, 1961–
  Hooping it up.

  1. University of Notre Dame–Basketball–History
2. Basketball–United States–Records. I. Title.
GV885.43.U55N44  1985    796.32'363'0977289  85-25324
ISBN 0-912083-05-0

# Contents

This book is dedicated
to my brother, Chris Neely

# Acknowledgements

I have always been a believer in the adage, "If you want something done right, you have to do it yourself." But without the help and guidance of many others, I could not have done this "myself."

First and foremost was all the help I received at Notre Dame. Herb Juliano, a true Notre Dame man, who for most of the research process was working for the sports information office, was invaluable throughout and was a continuing source of encouragement and support. John Heisler, Eddie White, and Roger Valdiserri of the sports information department opened up the vast season and player files to me and allowed me to make changes and corrections to their already outstanding basketball media guides as new information on old seasons became available. Help on the very sketchy "club" days of women's basketball came from Rich O'Leary of the Office of Non-Varsity Athletics and Astrid Hotvedt, coordinator of women's athletics since women began competing intercollegiately at Notre Dame. Further help came courtesy of *The Observer*, ND's student paper, which covered women's basketball long before anyone else cared about it. Also of assistance was the staff of the University Archives, and Jethroe Kyles of the International Sports and Games Collection, where it all began.

Thanks are also in order to the staff of the newspaper/periodical section and the interlibrary loan department of the South Bend Public Library for its cooperation. I spent hundreds of hours poring over hundreds of microfilm reels from South Bend newspapers to confirm dates, scores, and statistics of games played before Notre Dame's files began. Everyone's friendliness and courtesy was much appreciated.

Much of the research was done through the mail. Response to my requests for information on long-forgotten contests, often against long-forgotten teams, was gratifying. And while not all could supply everything I needed, most were as thorough as possible. So, with apologies to anyone I may have forgotten, I wish to thank the following:

*Sports Information Offices*—Ball State, Goshen, Grace, Lewis, Marion, Marquette, Michigan State, Northern Illinois, Northwestern, St. Francis (IN), St. Joseph's (IN), Toledo;

*Newspapermen*—Mark Brattain of the Logansport (IN) *Pharos-Tribune*, Bill O'Brien of the Dubuque *Telegraph-Herald*, Dave Schultz of the Huntington (IN) *Herald-Press*;

*University/College Libraries and Archives*—Bradley, Cornell, Creighton, Dayton, Denison, DePauw, Earlham, Franklin, Grove City, Hope, Indiana, Marquette, Marshall, Nebraska, Niagara, Syracuse, Valparaiso, Wabash, Western Michigan;

*Public Libraries*—Allen County (Fort Wayne, IN), Anderson (IN), Buffalo and Erie County (NY), Carnegie (Pittsburgh), Chicago, Dayton and Montgomery County (OH), Detroit, Dixon (IL), Fairfield (IA), Gary (IN), Grand Rapids, Indianapolis-Marion County, Jefferson County (Birmingham, AL), Marion County (KY), Milwaukee, Mobile, Nashville-Davidson County, New Orleans, Odell (Morrison, IL), Omaha, Onondaga County (Syracuse, NY), Peoria (IL), St. Louis, Tiffin-Seneca (OH), Tippecanoe County (Lafayette, IN), Toledo-Lucas County (OH);

*Others*—Alabama Department of Archives and History, Alabama Public Library Service, Kentucky Historical Society, NCAA Statistics Service, Nebraska State Historical Society, Shelby County (IL) Historical and Genealogical Society.

Several basketball players and coaches of both recent and distant past offered recollections and supplied helpful background: Johnny Dee, Chet Grant, John Jordan, Jenny Klauke Moose Krause, and Dick Rosenthal. Also thanks to Claude Renshaw, Jill Langford of Diamond Communications (for patience beyond the call of duty), Mike Riccardi, Chuck Freeby, Mike Sullivan, Karen Chavis, Tracy Reimer, and Roban Bottei.

Last but definitely not least, thanks are in order to my parents, William B. and Judith U. Neely of Telford, PA for their support, both financial and moral. Without them this book would not have been possible.

# Section I
## *The Story*

# Introduction

In the eyes of many basketball fans, the history of Notre Dame basketball began on January 19, 1974, when a young, flashy coach and his band of upstarts ended the longest winning streak in college basketball history. Or perhaps a few years earlier, on January 23, 1971, when a talented scoring machine helped put the other bookend on that winning streak.

Actually, Notre Dame has a long tradition of basketball excellence, dating back to its first game in 1897 against the Fort Wayne YMCA. Since that victory, the Fighting Irish have won over 1,200 games and lost only a few more than 600. In fact, Notre Dame is ranked in the top ten among all Division I NCAA schools in both wins and winning percentage.

Of course, the reason why Irish basketball exploits, though generally successful, remained obscure is because of the overwhelming tradition of Notre Dame football. Many books—over 50 by at least one count—have chronicled the great coaches, the great comebacks, legends, lore, and history of the fall sport at ND. But even with the team's success, no such book existed on Notre Dame basketball.

Until now.

What you are now reading may be the most comprehensive book ever composed on a single college in a single sport, including Notre Dame football. How this work is set up will be explained below. First, a few basketball-related facts that you may not have known before.

Notre Dame is the only Division I-A school ranked in the all-time top ten in both basketball and football. First in football winning percentage and second (behind Michigan) in wins, the Irish rank eighth and seventh, respectively, in basketball. Here are the top ten (through the end of the 1983-84 season):

3

| Basketball Wins | | Won-Lost Percentage | |
|---|---|---|---|
| 1. Kentucky | 1358 | 1. Kentucky | .7625 (1358-423) |
| 2. North Carolina | 1317 | 2. North Carolina | .7280 (1317-492) |
| 3. St. John's | 1277 | 3. St. John's | .6986 (1277-551) |
| 4. Kansas | 1270 | 4. UCLA | .6952 (1106-485) |
| 5. Oregon State | 1258 | 5. Western Kentucky | .6913 (1115-498) |
| 6. Pennsylvania | 1239 | 6. Kansas | .6727 (1270-618) |
| 7. NOTRE DAME | 1202 | 7. DePaul* | .6723 ( 950-463) |
| 8. Washington | 1185 | 8. NOTRE DAME | .6681 (1202-597-1) |
| 9. Temple | 1180 | 9. Syracuse | .6637 (1131-573) |
| 10. Duke | 1176 | 10. Duquesne | .6606 ( 979-503) |

| Won-Lost Percentage | | | |
|---|---|---|---|
| 1. Kentucky | .7625 (1358-423) | | |
| 2. North | .7280 (1317-492) | | Carolina |
| 3. St. | .6986 (1277-551) | | John's |
| 4. UCLA | .6952 (1106-485) | | |
| 5. Western | .6913 (1115-498) | | Kentucky |
| 6. Kansas | .6727 (1270-618) | | |
| 7. DePaul* | .6723 ( 950-463) | | |
| 8. NOTRE | .6681 (1202-597-1) | | DAME |
| 9. Syracuse | .6637 (1131-573) | | |
| 10. Duquesne | .6606 ( 979-503) | | |

Such men as Louis Salmon, Gus Dorais, Knute Rockne, and George Gipp are among the early legends of Notre Dame football. But did you know that those four also either played or coached basketball at Notre Dame? How about half of the fabled Four Horsemen, and half of Notre Dame's Heisman Trophy winners? Many Notre Dame gridiron giants also played the winter sport on a varsity level. Elsewhere in this book you will find a list of Notre Dame first-team football All-Americans who also spent some time on the hardwood. The length of the list may surprise you.

On a national scale, Notre Dame's basketball reputation actually preceded its football reputation. Here are some excerpts from newspaper articles, which I offer as proof:

" . . . the visitors rank among the half dozen best teams in

---

*DePaul's record dates only from the 1923-24 season, though the school played basketball for many years before that, at least back to 1909. So that percentage may actually be worse . . . or better.

the country and it was plainly evident that they were playing their best." (Fairfield, IA)

"The Notre Dame team is one of the best equipped teams of any college five . . . " (Morrison, IL)

"Notre Dame . . . fairly dumbfounded the locals by the quickness of their passes, accuracy of judgment and rapidity of movement." (Montgomery, AL)

"Each player is a star, but it is as a team that they tantalize and nearly always succeed in putting their opponents up in the air." (New Orleans, LA)

"Notre Dame had everything and was everywhere. Hardly a member of the crowd had any idea that that such a well-balanced basketball team existed . . . " (Dayton, OH)

Lavish praise indeed! But would you believe that all of these were excerpted from newpaper articles which were written in the above cities during the *1908-09* season after visits from Notre Dame? This was nearly five years before the football team's 1913 upset of Army. And, as is obvious from the datelines, the basketball team was "rambling" long before Knute Rockne's well-traveled gridiron squad earned the nickname "Ramblers."

How about those for starters? And there's much more where that came from.

The first section of this book tells the story of Notre Dame basketball from its traceable beginning—one year earlier than previously assumed—all the way to the present. You will meet many great players here, from Justin Moloney to John Paxson and dozens in between. Many great coaches, both friend and foe, will be met, and many great games reviewed. Also included, since they are part of the Notre Dame basketball story, are sections on the up-and-coming women's basketball program from its barely documented beginnings.

Next up is a statistics-lover's dream. Included here are year-by-year season records of coaches, a list of every game ever played by Notre Dame (college opponents only after 1950), and the playing records, as completely as currently possible, of every man or woman who ever saw action in at least one game of basketball representing Notre Dame. Much of the latter data is newly compiled for this volume and is unavailable from any other source.

There is something in here for the casual fan who knows next to nothing about Notre Dame's rich basketball past and for the die-hard who knows most of it. So enough of the pre-game introductions. Let's start the game!

Tim Neely
South Bend, Indiana
Winter, 1985

# 1

## Starting Out

Exactly when Notre Dame men first passed or shot a basketball on the campus is lost to posterity. It likely wasn't long after Dr. James Naismith invented the game at the Springfield, Massachusetts YMCA in December 1891, as the sport spread rapidly from coast to coast. It is certain, however, that men within Brownson Hall on campus were playing pick-up games among themselves by October 1895, and that the first interhall match took place between Brownson and Carroll Halls in January 1896. Obviously the men were still novices, as the score of this game was Brownson 5, Carroll 0. It was not for another year that basketball began to be played in an organized fashion at Notre Dame, and then primarily through the efforts of one man.

Frank Hering came to Notre Dame after spending his undergraduate years under the tutelage of Amos Alonzo Stagg at the University of Chicago. Once he arrived, he became ND's first paid football coach in 1897 after one prior year as player-coach, and he remained until he completed his law degree in 1898. Along with his football expertise, he brought with him a greater knowledge of basketball than anyone else at ND had—Stagg had introduced the game to UC in 1893, and Hering had picked it up—and, as a result, became Notre Dame's first coach of the sport.

What Hering did early in 1897 was to organize the three undergraduate dorms into an interhall league. Once each hall had its teams, the best players from each were selected and molded into ND's first varsity.

The first game was scheduled for early February against the South Bend Commercial Athletic Club but was cancelled. Not

7

until the 24th did the varsity officially take the court for the first time, against the Fort Wayne YMCA in a five-on-five game. (The number of players on the court at the same time had yet to be standardized.) At that time the YMCAs were the hotbeds of basketball; while quite a few colleges were playing the game, very few were playing each other. Not until the early 1920s did Notre Dame play its last game against a YMCA as part of the official schedule.

But the Fort Wayne YMCA was the first. As many students as possible (roughly 200) crammed into the old Carroll Hall gymnasium to witness this historic event. And with the advantage of playing by "collegiate rules" rather than "YMCA rules," Notre Dame won its initial contest, 26-11.

Almost a month passed before the second game was played. This one was ND's first road game, against the same Fort Wayne YMCA team that had come to ND. Although playing by different rules, including the only time Notre Dame ever played seven-on-seven, another victory was at hand early, the final score 21-5.

The scoring star of both these games was the team's "elder statesman" and first-ever captain, John Shillington. He had been at Notre Dame for some time, leaving in 1894 to join the US Navy and returning in 1896. He was an excellent athlete; he also starred as a shortstop on the Notre Dame baseball team and was awarded a retroactive monogram for his work on the 1897 team. However, he did not live to receive his award. Midway through that 1897 baseball season, he left the campus again and rejoined the Navy. Less than a year later, on February 15, 1898, Shillington went down with the battleship *Maine* at the start of the Spanish-American War. A monument to him—a mounted shell taken from the sunken ship—was erected in front of Brownson Hall, his last campus home. It has remained there ever since, secluded in a nook on the south of what is now the east wing of the Administration Building.

Shillington, as basketball team captain, was involved in Notre Dame's first court controversy in the third—and last—game of 1897. The opponent was the powerful Central YMCA from Chicago, and, as was custom at the time, a representative of the visiting team (Central) served as referee, and a ND man was umpire. Apparently Shillington, his teammates, and the partisan home crowd felt that the ref was unfairly favoring the visitors. Finally, midway through the second half, Shillington took matters into his own hands. He called time, went to Coach Hering, and declared that the team could no longer play under these conditions. The Central men agreed to let a Notre Dame man be moved to referee, out only if a YMCA representative remained as umpire. Shillington would not agree, and that was the ball game. It ended 25-22 in favor of the Central squad—Notre Dame's first loss, and a rather bitter one at that.

The Central loss started a three-game losing streak which lasted until Notre Dame played its first-ever collegiate opponent, Rush Medical of Chicago, in the last varsity game in the Carroll Hall gym. The second of those losses was the first of the 1897-98 season, against the First Regiment team of Chicago. Notre Dame had lost the scoring punch of John Shillington (9 points per game) and had not found a suitable replacement. Because of this, a hopelessly outmanned squad was utterly destroyed, 64-8. (Official records for years listed this score as 35-8; a re-check of the only known boxscore of this game, in a February 1898 edition of the Notre Dame *Scholastic*, revealed that First Regiment's field goals had incorrectly been credited for only one point each, thus the error.) Not until 1971 would ND lose a game by more than the 56-point difference in this one.

Another Chicago team, the independent Clybornes, came into Carroll Hall and left with a win, this one a more respectable 19-13. And finally, the win against Rush Medical closed the season; the final record was 1-2.

Meanwhile, a spacious fieldhouse which could accommodate all four major sports (football, basketball, baseball, and track) plus a plethora of intramural sports was under construction. When it was completed in the winter of 1899, it was one of the largest collegiate gymnasiums in the United States, and the basketball team took advantage by having its first—and only —undefeated season. This should, however, be taken with a grain of salt; only two varsity games were played.

Frank Hering was no longer around, having left to pursue a career in law, so Fred Powers took the role of both coach and team captain. At the end of the short season, he also ended up as leading scorer, as he had been in 1897-98 despite playing in only two of the three games. (And after leaving ND, he became the first basketball coach at Holy Cross.) Also helping matters were three other returning starters and the awesomeness of the new gym, the likes of which it is likely neither opponent had seen before.

After 1899, even Notre Dame came close to never seeing it again. In 1900, the one-year-old fieldhouse burned down, effectively rendering the fledgling varsity program dead. Fire had played a large role in the history of Notre Dame, as it seemed that after every one, a more grandiose building replaced the old. The gymnasium was no exception. Even though the building was reopened in 1901, there was no varsity basketball again until 1908 with one brief exception to be mentioned later.

In the interim, interhall basketball captured the fancy of the campus. In fact, the four interhall teams—Brownson, Carroll, Sorin, and later Corby—were good enough individually to defeat off-campus competition and often did. South Bend and Mishawaka teams, as well as those from elsewhere, usually suffered defeat at the hands of Notre Dame's dorm teams. It is probably not too great an overstatement to say that some of the most intense basketball competition in Indiana took place in the Notre Dame interhall circuit in the 1900-1907 years. Yet only once in this period did another group of interhall all-stars form a team representing the entire campus, and that only after a challenge from another Indiana school.

Purdue was claiming the basketball championship of Indiana in 1902 and offered to take on any and all comers. Notre Dame accepted, and the two teams arranged a game at the neutral site of Logansport, Indiana. The problem: ND needed a team. That became the responsibility of Dominic Groogan, Brownson Hall's team captain. A seven-man squad representing the three campus teams was formed. One of the men was Louis "Red" Salmon, a Hall of Fame football player and the first from Notre Dame ever mentioned on an All-American team (Walter Camp's 1903 third team). With a limited amount of practice, the squad went on the first extended road trip for ND basketball.

As tune-ups for the big game with Purdue, Notre Dame lost one to the Indianapolis YMCA and defeated the Anderson "Y" team twice. While these preliminaries were taking place, reports in both the Notre Dame and South Bend press claimed that at least two men on the ND team were academically ineligible to play (the accuracy of this is difficult to determine today). Of greater concern to the team was a serious injury Groogan sustained in the Indianapolis game which rendered him unable to play the rest of the trip. Another player was sent to Logansport for the Purdue game as a replacement.

When Notre Dame arrived for the Saturday, February 22 game, they found out that Purdue, for reasons claimed to be injury-related, had been unable to show. Instead, a team of men from Logansport Commercial College stood in so that the ticketholders could still see a game. The LCC team literally did not exist 24 hours before the game and thus had never practiced as a unit, yet Logansport won the game, 17-14, in a very slowly-played game reflective of the two teams' relative unfamiliarity with teamwork. This game, played under another set of rules (there were many in those confused early days), had each field goal worth three points instead of the familiar two. Even if the scores had been registered in today's fashion, ND still would have lost. The disappointed men returned to campus with a 2-2 record.

After that, there was talk of forming another varsity, but nothing came of it. Not until 1908 and the arrival of Bert Maris as a coach did Notre Dame field a campuswide team again.

# 2

---

# Take Two

Bert Maris came to Notre Dame ostensibly to take charge of gymnasium operations and to coach track, both of which he did successfully. In the meantime, he resuscitated basketball just as successfully. The interest in a varsity team existed again, and interest grew such that during Maris' tenure, the number of men to see action grew to 18 in his last year from eight in 1907-1908.

Before the first Maris season, a group of athletes, most of whom would comprise the nucleus of the early varsity teams, formed a barnstorming squad (not officially representing Notre Dame, but calling itself the "All Collegiate Basket Ball Team") which spent the Christmas vacation of 1907 playing some of the top collegiate and independent teams of the Midwest. Their record was a respectable 5-3, thus setting a pattern of winning which would continue throughout the early years of Notre Dame basketball.

Maris picked his varsity squad not long after the holidays. Shortly thereafter, a schedule of approximately 16 games was announced. Even in those early times, Notre Dame feared no challenge; they scheduled anyone and everyone who would agree to a date, and usually defeated them.

"Modern" Notre Dame basketball history began with two of the most utter annihilations ever dished out by ND squads. Admittedly, neither the South Bend Commercial Athletic Club nor the Kalamazoo YMCA were top-notch competition. They were expected to provide at least token resistance, however, but they failed miserably. The CAC lost 66-2 and the YMCA fell 78-8, the latter still a record for ND in one-game scoring margins. The main cogs in the Notre Dame juggernaut were forwards John Dubuc and Justin Moloney.

Dubuc, who pitched nearly a decade of major league baseball after leaving the university in 1908, scored 20 and 18 points in those two games, and had a season high of 28. Moloney, a freshman, tallied 26 against the CAC and 34 against the Kalamazoo team, the latter a record for nearly 50 years. In his four-year career, he scored about 1,000 points. During that time, if an opponent could shut down Moloney, it usually could stop Notre Dame. That didn't happen very often.

Wabash, the mythical "Champions of Indiana" at that time, was the first to do so. Moloney had only nine points, Dubuc but seven (only one field goal) as Notre Dame lost its first game under Maris in the Fieldhouse. After a convincing win over Hartford City, Indiana, ND went on its first road trip of the season.

The team returned 1-2, with the sole win coming over Michigan Agricultural College (now Michigan State) at the "neutral" gym of the Lansing YMCA. The Aggies were played twice on consecutive days. The first game (the loss) was played at MAC's home gym, a band box which featured a ceiling so low that there were only a few spots from which a team could take a shot and not be rejected by a beam. By their familiarity with the court, MAC could stop nearly anyone from getting to those spots. As a result, the Aggies had a phenomenal home court advantage. Notre Dame won but once there before a new gymnasium was erected in 1915.

Back at home, Notre Dame won four straight, including a victory over Baker University of Baldwin, KS. Under the tutelage of a future coaching legend, Forrest C. "Phog" Allen, Baker had gone undefeated in 1906-1907. Allen was still coaching Baker in 1907-1908, but was also coaching his alma mater Kansas on the side. In one more year, he added Haskell to them and led three teams at once! During those two years of multiple duty, Allen's five teams lost a total of 16 games, two to each other. One other of those 16 — probably the most convincing — was to Maris' first Notre Dame team. Baker couldn't stop Dubuc and Moloney — John had 10, Justin 22 — and ND breezed, 46-13.

The only other loss of the season came on the team's other road trip, to southern Indiana and northern Kentucky. After

defeating Indiana, 21-20, on a late-game free throw by Dubuc,
Notre Dame tried to avenge the early-season loss to Wabash,
but failed on the Little Giants' court. The season ended aptly,
with ND taking the rubber game of the three-game series with
MAC on the Fieldhouse floor to end with a 12-4 mark.

A .750 won-lost percentage against some pretty ambitious
competition for a first-year team. How does one top that in the
second? Well, how about by playing 40 games—believed to be
a record for a college team—and winning 33 of them? That was
the astounding record of the 1908-09 Notre Dame five.

What makes it even more astounding is that 30 of the 40
games were played on the road under often adverse conditions—
differing rules, "homer" referees, hostile crowds, and exhaus-
tion. But the teamwork and uncanny skill (for the time) at canning hoops usually elicited applause from the crowds and praise
from the local papers, some of it quite lavish. Only Chicago (12-0)
and Kansas (26-3) had records to surpass Notre Dame's in
1908-09; neither played against anything like the competition ND
faced. In fact, ND tried to set up a game against Chicago but
was rebuffed. And Kansas didn't try, perhaps recalling what had
happened to Phog Allen's Baker team one season earlier.

The credit—or blame, depending on point of view—for this
suicidal schedule must not go to Bert Maris, but to the team's
manager, Fay Wood. Until the arrival of Jesse Harper in 1913,
schedules for each sport were drawn up by the team's student
manager. Wood, who had been starting guard a year earlier, saw
action in 1908-1909 only under emergency situations because of
a nagging football injury. He, however, knew what basketball
teams were considered among the best and corresponded in
hopes of forming a schedule for the two university breaks which
occurred during the season. He was able to compile a southern
and eastern road trip. (A third slate of western teams was con-
templated but never carried out.) While this team certainly got
to see much of the country east of the Mississippi, it was scheduling like this which soon led to the necessity of a full-time athletic
director.

Everywhere the team went, there was more than just praise,
there was controversy. Several times the ND traveling squad was
accused of professionalism. Once, it led a team (the Rochester

Athletic Club) to cancel a game at the last minute—ND had already arrived in the city—because they claimed that by playing the Buffalo Germans, a professional team, Notre Dame had lost its amateur status. There was no such rule. It is more likely that Rochester did not want to be embarrassed in front of its home fans. (Instead, they were embarrassed at the Fieldhouse, 60-15, the next season.)

Most of the "professionalism" controversy, however, revolved around the man who replaced John Dubuc—who had left ND for a pro baseball career—as the second scoring punch to Justin Moloney. He was Robert "Pete" Vaughan, a standout in both football and basketball at Crawfordsville (IN) High School (as Moloney had been) before coming to Notre Dame. Pete was already a legend at the University because of his football exploits as a fullback. He scored ND's touchdown in a 12-6 loss to Michigan and generally stood out. But sometime during the southern trip, rumors began to circulate that Vaughan was actually a "ringer," i.e., a professional who played college ball under an assumed name and was not even enrolled at the school. In fact, the Detroit Athletic Club tried to claim victory over ND because they claimed that Vaughan had played pro ball in 1906. Well, in 1906 Pete was at Crawfordsville High—and never played any professional ball. He had the misfortune of resembling a known "ringer," and that led to the problems. After leaving ND in 1910, he returned to his hometown and was a long-time coach and athletic director at Wabash College during that school's glory days in athletics in the teens and twenties.

Finally, there was a controversy involving Wabash. This one had nothing to do with professionalism, but with, in a way, excess amateurism. After leaving the Fieldhouse floor the year before covered with dirt, Wabash team officials threatened to call off the Notre Dame trip for 1908-09 unless another site was found. It wasn't the last time there would be complaints about the dirt (actually clay, like a clay tennis court) floor from opponents and from ND players and coaches as well. Wabash finally did agree to return—and lost twice.

They weren't the only ones to lose to Notre Dame. At one point, 22 consecutive games ended in victory, a skein ND has never been able to surpass. (It was equalled once, but not within the confines of one season.) Two feats make this streak look even more impressive. One, it was compiled against many of the top independent, college, and YMCA teams in the South and Midwest. And two, 18 of the 22 contests were road games! The losses were few and far between. The first, to Chicago's Central YMCA in ND's first overtime game, was avenged later in the year. Two others were to the Buffalo Germans, the most dominant pro team of its day, a team few professional, much less college, teams could beat. They were later inducted into the Basketball Hall of Fame as a unit. Two more losses were definite surprises, to Tiffin of Ohio and to the same Detroit AC team that claimed victory in an earlier encounter (This time they won for real.) Both of these, however, were at the end of the team's second road trip. A battered and weary five took the floor in each game and could not keep up with fresh players.

Because of the first team's condition, Maris played nothing but reserves in the second-to-last game of the season, a 21-8 victory over Armour Institute, to save his "stars" for the all-important Wabash game. And his top players were ready—ND won 33-24, in a game which wasn't that close.

Years after that game closed the 1908-1909 season, the Helms Foundation chose an "All-America" team for that year and selected as one of the guards Notre Dame's Ray Scanlon. Captain and starting guard for two seasons, the 5-11 senior didn't score many points. That, however, was not his primary task. In the early days of basketball, a "guard" did just that—guard the basket and force the opposition to take bad shots while seldom venturing beyond center court. In that role, Scanlon was extremely successful, and his efforts were rewarded by Helms in 1957.

Scanlon and Vaughan did not return to the team in 1909-10, but the other three starters—Moloney, James Fish, and new captain Chet Freeze—did, and formed the solid nucleus of another successful team. Replacing Vaughan at center was a problem never adequately solved, although it could have been had Robert Vance stayed in school. In Notre Dame's first two wins—29-17 over Lewis Institute and that 60-15 drubbing of the Rochester AC—Vance scored 16 and 20 points, respectively. He did not return to South Bend after Christmas, and the team was without a real center or a bona fide second scoring punch. As a result, the 1909-10 team went 10-4—certainly respectable, but not up to the standards set by the last two.

Two of the four losses were at the hands of the Michigan Aggies. The first of these, 28-21 at the Fieldhouse, was without Moloney, who was injured and unable to play, and the second, a worse drubbing, was in MAC's low-ceilinged gym. A close loss at Wabash (avenged at home later in the season) and a surprise by Hope College of Holland, Michigan rounded out the negatives.

On the positive side were the aforementioned 60-15 thrashing of the Rochester team (after the RAC had refused to play ND at Rochester on the 1909 Eastern trip) and a 49-16 destruction of Butler, a game in which 12 men saw action for Notre Dame, an extremely rare occurrence in the "iron man" days of early basketball. In a rare upstaging of his front-court companion Moloney, James Fish scored 20 to Justin's 16. In a later 35-15 pasting of Olivet, things reverted back to normal, as Moloney had 19 of those 35 points.

But going beyond the wins and losses, the most obvious change in the 1909-10 season was the severely truncated schedule. From two long (in both distance and duration) road trips in 1908-1909 to two shorter trips (one four-game stint covering southern Indiana and Dayton, Ohio and two games in Michigan); from a schedule befitting a barnstorming professional team to the more typical regionalized slate of a college team—that is what occurred. Most likely the "professionalism" charges affected any plans for elongated road trips. Even then Notre Dame seemed very conscious of its reputation; perhaps they feared becoming known as a "basketball factory" (long before the unjustified charges of "football factory" came about in the 1920s and since).

The schedule was reduced even further in 1910-11—to a measly 10 games. Only during World War I did the slate drop to fewer contests, and then only because of wartime limitations. All of the home games (five) were played on Saturdays, and four of the away games were contested on one four-day trip in late February. One of the reasons the home schedule was so short was Bert Maris' increasing involvement in the more prestigious indoor/outdoor track program. Meets were scheduled as early as February, and the team was unquestionably "best in the West" at the time. Of the four major sports at Notre Dame in 1910, basketball had certainly slipped to number four and was treated as such for years.

A mixture of young and old took the court for ND's truncated 1910-11 season. Fourth-year players Moloney and Fish, forwards, were joined in the starting lineup by another senior, Clem Ulatowski, and two newcomers, sophomore Bill "Peaches" Granfield and freshman Al Feeney. Moloney finished with the lowest scoring average of his four years because defenses were keying on him. Fish and, to a lesser extent, Granfield helped take up the slack. But they weren't always able to, as ND finished 7-3. Two of the losses were on the road trip—back-to-back, season-ending losses to St. Mary's of Ohio (now the University of Dayton) and the Dayton Turners, a club team. The other one was a 39-21 thrashing on the Fieldhouse clay by Wabash, a loss avenged at Crawfordsville later in the season.

Most of the wins were by less than 10 points, a reflection of both a smaller, tougher schedule and the defense, both by and against ND. Feeney was such a defensive stalwart that he overcompensated by seldom shooting the ball. He scored no points in 1910-11 despite his starting role and scored only a handful his entire career. He preferred to pass the ball to his forecourt mates and emphasize his defensive skills—perhaps the epitome of the selfless player. His career individual stats aren't that impressive—but only four times in his three years in the backcourt did any team score more than 25 points, and all four resulted in Notre Dame losses.

And speaking of ND losses, there were only two in 18 games the next season (1911-12). It was Maris' best season under the Dome, and also his last. After the track season had been completed in the spring of 1912, Maris announced his resignation after five ND years to move on to greener pastures; at the time Notre Dame was not held in high esteem by the college coaching fraternity as it is now. Maris served as either coach or athletic director at Michigan, Armour Institute, and Northwestern for many years after leaving ND.

Considering that Maris lost his two starting forwards to graduation, the 16-2 record is even more admirable. Center Granfield, who was elected captain as a junior, took over as primary scoring threat, ably aided by Dan McNichols, a senior seeing regular action for the first time; Jim Cahill, a sophomore forward who was injured much of January but came on strong in February; and Joe Kenny, a freshman who started in place of Cahill when he was injured.

But it was defense where the 1911-12 team stood out. Al Feeney again was the bulwark at guard, with sophomore Bill Kelleher, and Paul "Curly" Nowers, a freshman with amazingly accurate long shots, taking turns at the other guard. Their effectiveness can be measured by Notre Dame's stinginess on defense. Allowing an average of less than 18 points per game and not more than 25 in any one contest, ND needed only minimal offense to win most of the time.

There were those times when the team did far more than necessary. For example, the average score of Notre Dame's first three games was 27-7. The most noteworthy— and devastating— of those was against the All-Collegians, a barnstorming group of former college stars based in Chicago which included ND alumnus Chet Freeze. They served as a last-minute replacement for Marquette, which had cancelled its basketball program for 1911-12 after a schedule had already been formed. And after what Notre Dame did to them, the All-Collegians probably wished they had never offered to fill the open date, or wished they had stayed in the lake-effect snowstorm which struck northwest Indiana the night of the game. The All-Collegians were demolished, 36-5.

At least three other events of the season were notable. First was the renewal of the extended road trip after two seasons without one. Beginning at the South Bend Commercial Athletic Club and extending into Ohio and Michigan, the Irish went 5-1, including a one-point win over Ohio State. In addition to the six games played, three others had to be cancelled: a February 22 contest against Hope College was snowed out and games against St. Mary's and Miami (both of Ohio) were inadvertently scheduled on dates where games were booked earlier. Also noteworthy were the first games against DePaul. The Blue Demons' team still was very loosely organized, and that showed when ND demolished them twice in a home-and-home series,

58-11 and 32-20, the latter while using only reserves. The two teams didn't play again until Ray Meyer became DePaul coach in 1942-43. Finally, there was what may have been the greatest upset of a Notre Dame basketball team in history.

Notre Dame lost only two games in 1911-12. One was to the South Bend CAC, which had improved substantially since 1907-08 and the 66-2 game and was now one of the better teams in the state; however, ND beat them twice, the second one a "post-season" game to determine who was "champion of Indiana." The other loss that season, the major upset, was to little Northwestern College of Naperville, Illinois (now North Central College) in the fourth game of the season, and at the Fieldhouse, no less. The team and the local press took this game so lightly that all involved considered it a "practice game" for the more "important" clashes with Wabash and the teams on the road trip. Some practice. Northwestern took the game 23-19 while holding Granfield to a mere two baskets. How quickly ND had forgotten that this same school fell only 16-9 one season before. Notre Dame, however, would get its revenge in 1912-13 by defeating the Napervillians, 34-17.

Other than the win over Northwestern College, an eight-games-in nine-days road trip which included two embarrassing losses—the only two of the season—and 13 wins overall which included 10 wins by 10 or more points, the most interesting part of the 1912-13 season was the coach. As mentioned, Maris had resigned. In May 1912 he was replaced by Frank Gormley, who had coached the New Orleans YMCA team that ND defeated in its 1908-09 southern tour. Gormley never coached a game at Notre Dame. In his role as assistant football coach, he apparently did not get along too well with head coach John Marks and left the school in late September. The Faculty Board hurriedly hired and approved one Bill Nelson, about whom little is known except that he had been successful in the East before his tenure under the Dome. And after one game, he became a lame-duck coach.

In a budget-cutting move possibly aimed at de-emphasis—long before the 1950s—Notre Dame hired one man to serve both as coach of all four sports simultaneously and as full-time athletic director (a role served by student managers before this time) in December 1912, Wabash College's Jesse Harper. He was ostensibly to replace Marks, who had resigned as grid coach, but in a sweeping move the Faculty Board added the baseball, track, and basketball teams to his duties, all four effective in September 1913. This made Nelson, the track and basketball coach, a victim of circumstance—but if it affected him any, it wasn't reflected on the team.

Five of the top six players from the 1911-12 squad returned. For his senior year Granfield was moved to forward, and a newcomer, Rupe Mills, became center, a mutually beneficial arrangement. Granfield went wild in his scoring, several times hitting the 20-point barrier, tallying 28 points on 14 field goals against Rose Polytechnic in a 54-10 pasting. Offensive production was up overall, and with rare lapses, the stalwarts on defense—captain Feeney and Nowers—kept the opponents away, four times holding teams to 10 or less points.

Twice, however, the defense faltered and the offense was ineffective. These were on the road trip, where Notre Dame lost big twice—one a 47-13 loss to Denison which snapped a 17-game win streak over two seasons, and the other a 40-7 embarrassment by MAC in its infamous gym. The seven points marked an all-time low in ND point production, a record which will probably stand forever. But it was the victories which really stand out.

Most of the time, when ND won, it *really* won—52-8, 38-5, 36-11, 31-12 were typical final scores. And the team did not treat its future mentor, Harper, very nicely. It defeated Wabash twice, 28-21 and 33-24, as Harper concluded his reign in Crawfordsville like Nelson in South Bend, aware he'd be somewhere else in another year.

During his brief stay, Bill Nelson did make one important move. He began to take his squad off campus—to the South Bend YMCA, the Commercial Athletic Club, South Bend High School —for some practice sessions. All three of those places had wooden basketball courts, as did the vast majority (if not all) of ND's foes. Playing on the fieldhouse clay was beginning to become a liability not only for opponents, but to the home team as well, and ND needed practice on a hard court before hitting the road. (As it turned out, some of the scrimmages against the local high school five were better contests than those against "real" competition.) This was a problem the university would have to face eventually if it wanted to maintain some sort of passable basketball program.

# 3

## Cruising

In his five years as a Notre Dame coach, Jesse Harper continued the winning tradition established by his predecessors. The feats of the basketball team in his first four years continued to be outstanding, but it seemed as if the team was on cruise control, not slowing down, but not accelerating, either.

A large part of this stagnation was because of Harper's multiple duties, and especially the growing national prominence of the Notre Dame football team. It was in Harper's first year that the football team defeated Army at West Point, stunning much of the football world and putting a new name in the spotlight. Over the next several years, Harper's football activities began to dominate his time at the expense of the other three varsity sports at ND. Harper finally dished off the track team to his protégé and assistant, Knute Rockne.

That's getting a little ahead of the story, however. On the basketball side, things did get off to a decent start under Harper — the 1913-14 aggregation won its first seven games on the way to an 11-5 slate, despite one major in-house change in eligibility rules: at Harper's urging, freshmen became ineligible for varsity competition.

Many returning players made life easier for the new coach as he took over the team. Center Rupe Mills was back, as were forwards Jim Cahill (the team captain) and Joe Kenny and guard Paul Nowers. Four other men saw a great deal of action: sophomore Freeman Fitzgerald, who had played two games in 1912-13; Charles Finegan, a junior who had seen limited action his freshman year and spelled Nowers and Al Feeney at guard the next;

Bill Kelleher, a junior who did not play at all his sophomore year because of a football injury; and junior Alfred "Dutch" Bergman—the first of three different "Dutch" Bergmans who played varsity football at ND from 1910 to 1923—who had not played varsity basketball before, yet proved a valuable second-teamer for the 1913-14 squad.

This basically eight-man team started off very well. Of those seven season-opening victories, the closest were two seven-point decisions against Harper's old school, Wabash—the only time he was able to coach ND to a sweep of that season series. Of the other five, two were especially notable: the second win of the year, 35-9 over Beloit at the Fieldhouse, was Notre Dame's 100th, and the fourth, against Lake Forest (33-15), would be the last over that college for another three seasons.

In the second Wabash game, captain Cahill was injured and supposedly out for the season—at quite an inopportune time. Notre Dame was about to start a week-long road trip to the East for February break, and he was the team's second-leading scorer and one of two free throw specialists. Cahill did play later in the season, but was not at 100 percent, especially in two road blowouts in which he forced himself in—he couldn't sit by and watch while the team was being destroyed. Those were a 41-14 destruction by Cornell and an even worse 50-14 slaughter by Syracuse.

After those first seven victories, and the injury to Cahill, ND finished out at 4-5. On the long road trip, Notre Dame went 3-3; one of these was historic because it was ND's first overtime win, 25-23 over St. Lawrence. But more typical was the 44-22 defeat at the hands of MAC in the Aggies' old ballpark. Kenny had five field goals and Fitzgerald made 12 foul shots in a game more reminiscent of football than basketball—and that was *all* the scoring by ND.

This "split season" finally ended at home against West Virginia Wesleyan, and the Wesleyans gave ND all it could handle. Joe Kenny, Bill Kelleher, and Dutch Bergman all were unable to play, so Harper called on Herbert "Rip" Kelly, a senior who had seen little action the two previous years and was not even on the 1913-14 roster. Instead, he had led his interhall team to the campus championship. With interhall season over, he was asked to *start* for the hurting squad. This one-day wonder scored 10 points in ND's 35-34 win over WVW.

Despite missing the last game, Kenny led the team in scoring with 102 points; Mills was second with 93. No one scored quite as many points as Moloney and Granfield had in years past. The highest one-game total by anyone was Mills' 14 against Polish Seminary; the highest team total was 38 against the same. Most of the time, these lower totals were enough to win. Just to make sure, those figures went up in 1914-15.

With four out of five starters returning again (only Cahill had graduated), prospects looked good for Harper's second season. Those hopes were fulfilled as well as could be expected, for Notre Dame finished 14-3. One contributing factor to that record was an abundance of home games, more than at any time in the past. The longest road trip was two days at the end of the season, both in Indiana. The reason for so few road games (only five of 17) was Harper's involvement with all the other sports at ND. Because of that, long road trips created a conflict with the baseball and track teams, which began practices right after the holidays. There also were many multiple-sport participants at Notre Dame, and being away meant missed sessions with the other sports.

This team was the epitome of versatility, as two men on the squad did what only one man has done since: won monograms in four sports in one academic year. Rupe Mills and Alfred Bergman performed this amazing feat in 1914-15, even though the latter played only four games for the basketball team. (Bergman had also won four monograms in 1913-14, thus becoming the only man ever to do it twice.) Several other members of the team monogrammed in other sports as well—Joe Kenny in baseball, for example.

Despite—or maybe because of—this versatility, this was Harper's best squad. The team outscored its opponents by an average of 13.9 points per game, a great figure even by today's standards but amazing in the low-scoring days of the sport. This margin was buttressed by many shellackings of suspect competition, like a 36-14 decision over Lewis Institute, a 29-10 drubbing of Arkansas, 42-21 over Beloit (Fitzgerald had 17 to lead ND), and the two worst—59-30 over the South Bend YMCA and a 70-13

annihilation of a pathetic team from Indiana Dental School. The
last of the great slaughters was a 25-point romp over West Virginia Wesleyan, as if to pay it back for the one-point scare from
a year earlier. In most of those games the Notre Dame machine
was so well oiled that four different men traded off as team scoring leader—Fitzgerald, captain Kenny, Mills, and newcomer
sophomore Rich Daley.

When necessary, the team was also capable of strong defense. The Michigan Aggies were held to 14 and 19 points in
the home-and-home series (unfortunately, in ND's visit to MAC,
the team managed only 13) and Wabash to 17 in the Fieldhouse.
Overall, only twice did teams score more than 30 points against
this Notre Dame team. One of those was the only home loss of
the season, a 34-24 upset by Lake Forest College.

The only other loss of the season (after MAC and Lake
Forest) was a heartbreaker. Harper returned to Wabash on February 19 for the second clash of the year against the Little Giants
and left with a 29-25 double-overtime loss, the first time Notre
Dame had lost to Wabash since 1908. Fitzgerald had 10 to lead
ND, with Kenny—who led the team in scoring for the second
straight year overall—adding eight, but there was no offensive
support from their teammates. However, the spark was back the
next night in Terre Haute as Notre Dame closed out a most successful season with a 47-38 decision over Rose Poly. Mills scored
19 points—his career high output in this, his last ND basketball
game.

Mills, Kenny, Finegan, and Bergman were lost to graduation for 1915-16. As usual, though, there was no shortage of incoming sophomores and reserves to replace them. Freeman Fitzgerald was back, as was Rich Daley, the new captain and the
third junior so named since 1907-08. Most of the rest of the squad
was made up of newcomers: Joe Meyers, Tom King, Joe Mc-
Kenna, Pete Ronchetti. Added to them were former reserves Clifford Cassidy and Emmett Keefe, both of whom saw much action. This relatively inexperienced team performed well on a
mostly home-dirt schedule (only two of 12 games were away from
ND); the final won-lost record was 9-3.

The season began with two wins—a 56-19 no-contest over
Lewis Institute (Fitzgerald had 22, Daley 18 in the easiest game

of the year) and a 23-21 squeaker over Kalamazoo College, costly because Daley was injured and out for two weeks. As a result, senior Fitzgerald began to account for a disproportionate number of ND points, a situation which continued even upon Daley's return to the lineup.

After a loss — for the second straight season, and at home — to Lake Forest (30-24), Notre Dame reeled off seven straight wins. Only one of these was on the road, but it was a big one: for the first time since the anomalous 1908-09 season, MAC went down at ND's hands on the Aggies' home court, 24-23. Fitzgerald scored 22 of those points to end the East Lansing jinx. Earlier, ND had defeated the Aggies, 19-18, in the Fieldhouse, thus sweeping the season series. Fitzgerald had "only" 12 in that game. Two of the other more interesting victories were a 31-16 defeat of Dubuque, which was coached by former ND quarterback Gus Dorais in his first coaching job, and the seventh of the seven straight, 24-15 over St. Viator, in which Harper rested his starting five (Daley, Fitzgerald, Meyers, King, and McKenna) in preparation for the all-important Wabash series.

Harper's squad was 9-1 going into the Wabash games. Eight days later, it was 9-3. The Little Giants showed no mercy, blowing out ND at the Fieldhouse, 41-19. Wabash held Fitzgerald to five points, his season low, and the Notre Dame defense, which had but once given up more than 25 points in any one game, could not contain the attack. Notre Dame managed to close the gap in the return match at Crawfordsville, but still came up short. It was a disappointing end to what had started as a great season. Ten years would pass until there was another season as good, though.

One might have expected a fine year in 1916-17. Nine men on the 12-man squad had seen varsity action before, four on a regular basis (Joe Meyers was to see very limited action, however, in 1916-17). But the team's "designated scorer," Freeman Fitzgerald, the last of the early-day four-year players, had graduated, leaving a giant hole in the offense. It was filled ably by sophomore Frank McDermott, as he took over the bulk of the team's offense. This resulted in a lack of offensive diversity for the second straight year, and with a schedule missing many of the pushovers of years past, the team finished 8-5, the worst since

Notre Dame resumed varsity basketball competition in 1907-08.

For the first time since then, ND opened on the road, against a first-time—but not last-time—opponent in Purdue, with its young but soon-to-be-legendary coach, Ward "Piggy" Lambert. And for the first time since Bert Maris resuscitated the program, the Irish returned home 0-1, victims of a 21-18 nailbiter. What hurt ND's chances most in the game was McDermott's inability to sink foul shots, canning only two of 10.

The rest of the season was a series of mostly convincing wins—although never more than two in a row—and mostly close losses—though not more than one in a row. Of the wins, one of the most satisfying was the 17-11 defeat of Lake Forest, as the Irish had lost to them each of the last two seasons. McDermott was beginning to adapt to his role of designated scorer with Rich Daley out with an injury for the second straight year; he scored 11 of ND's points. Team captain Joe McKenna, sophomore Chet Grant, and junior Tom King contributed a field goal apiece, and the combined defensive effort held Lake Forest to fewer points by any ND opponent since Arkansas on December 16, 1914. More typical of the team's wins were a 37-16 pasting of West Virginia Wesleyan, 42-26 over St. Viator, and 33-19 over MAC at home. Resuming tradition, Notre Dame lost at MAC and lost twice to Wabash—ND's fourth and fifth consecutive losses to the Little Giants. The season's other loss was to a surprising Kalamazoo College five, 32-30, at the Fieldhouse. This season closed on the road against downstate Indiana teams which would prove thorns in the side of future Notre Dame teams—DePauw, Wabash, and Franklin—and ND defeated two of them.

On this up note, Notre Dame concluded its least successful season in 15 years, but with hope for improvement in 1917-18. Little could anyone realize that world events and a few other factors would make that 1916-17 season look awfully good for the next six years.

# 4

# The Dark Ages

The next six years, for the most part, ranged from the merely mediocre to the absolutely *awful*. During those years of infamy, the Irish lost nearly twice as many as they won. Three different coaches, the archaic Fieldhouse floor, a proliferation of football players using basketball to stay in shape rather than as an end in itself, and lack of support from the top man in Notre Dame athletics, Knute Rockne, all played a role in the decline of one of the most consistently good Midwestern basketball teams.

The beginning of the slide, however, was beyond the control of anyone at Notre Dame.

In 1917, the United States finally entered "The War to End All Wars," which had been raging in Europe for three years, and much of ND entered with it. Needless to say, Jesse Harper had a tough time putting together a basketball team for the winter. Only two players who had seen action in 1916-17 returned, and one of them—pre-season captain Tom King—did not practice with the squad because he knew his call to serve the country was long overdue. Pete Ronchetti, the only other player with varsity experience, was named acting captain before the opening game against powerful Purdue.

Harper was unable to accompany the team to West Lafayette, as his presence was requested at a football coaches' conference, so his assistant, Rockne, served as acting head coach. Perhaps Knute's disdain for basketball resulted from his initial coaching effort in the sport: the Irish trailed 37-2 at halftime and eventually lost 48-12.

After the New Year, the Irish played a severely curtailed schedule because of wartime restrictions. Five more games were contested—a scheduled contest with Valparaiso was snowed out on January 12 and never rescheduled—and the Irish ended up 2-4 including the Boilermaker debacle, their first losing season of the twentieth century. The two wins, both at home, came against Western State Normal (now Western Michigan) and MAC and both were close, low-scoring affairs (17-14 and 25-23, respectively). Meanwhile, Harper's losing streak to Wabash rose to seven with two more losses to the Little Giants. The other loss was at East Lansing to MAC as usual.

If the first war year had been bad, the second and last was worse. In fact, it was the worst season in Irish history based on percentage. Harper had resigned from his Notre Dame duties the year before. Rockne became football coach and continued in track, while Gus Dorais, the quarterback on the fabled 1913 Notre Dame team which defeated Army, returned to his alma mater to coach basketball and baseball. And while Rock became a coaching legend, Dorais didn't. He stayed under the Golden Dome for only two years before moving on.

Dorais' first team, despite having four returning starters and three returning subs, finished 2-10. Other than for its utter awfulness, this team was noteworthy because, for the first and only time ever, tradition was broken and Leonard "Pete" Bahan served as captain of both the football *and* basketball teams in 1918-19. It was also noteworthy for the little-known fact that George Gipp played four games for the squad early in the season. Gipp had played basketball in high school and was actually a decent player, but this brief stint was his only foray into the court game at ND.

This gridder-dominated team was actually 1-1 at one time. After the annual loss to Purdue, the Irish defeated Kalamazoo in their home opener, 23-12. Bahan with 10 and Gipp with six led the scoring in a good defensive effort. But after that start, things quickly deteriorated. An 18-point effort by Bahan against Western State Normal (MI) was wasted as ND fell, 31-29, and MAC, Wabash, and DePauw all came onto the Fieldhouse dirt and beat the Irish by progressively worse margins.

Notre Dame then hit the road and the wooden floors of opponents' gyms—and except for a narrow victory at MAC, the losing continued. Five more contests came on the trip, and the Irish, probably the worst college team in Indiana in 1918-19, lost all five—to Western State Normal, DePauw, Wabash, Franklin, and Indiana—by an *average* margin of 20 points. It's no wonder that this and future Irish squads until 1923 were sarcastically known by players and fans alike as "Victory Fives."

For 1919-20, Dorais returned, but no one else did, quite literally. Even though most of the men on the last team were underclassmen, all of them passed up basketball. Two men eventually did return—Leo Ward and Joe Brandy—but too late to make a whole lot of difference in the general direction of the season. With a sophomore-dominated lineup, there was slight improvement over the 1918-19 disaster. Then again, how could things get much worse? The Irish finished 5-13 as they contested a full schedule again with the end of World War I.

There was only one legitimate basketball player on the squad; without his presence, that 5-13 could have been even worse. Harry Mehre was his name. He was a standout at Huntington (IN) High School in basketball, and he fully intended to specialize at Notre Dame. Knute Rockne, however, talked him into playing football, although he had not played the sport at all in high school, and by his senior year he was the starting center. But it was his first love in which he excelled. Mehre scored a disproportionate number of ND's points in 1919-20 (about two-thirds). But because of a lack of a supporting cast on defense, it usually wasn't enough.

As usual, the Irish started off with a loss to Purdue, then followed it with a loss to the Fort Wayne Knights of Columbus, both before Christmas. After the holidays, Dorais became ill and was forced to bed, which forced Rockne to again stand in as head coach, as he had for Harper two seasons earlier.

Things started better for Rock in this substitute stint. ND clobbered Kalamazoo, 44-17, as Mehre scored 20 and Roger Kiley and Gene Kennedy each added 10. After that, things weren't so great for the great football coach, as his basketballers lost four in a row, twice to Western State Normal and once each to MAC and the South Bend YMCA. With each loss, Knute became more and more frustrated in his attempts to coach a hoops team. Much to Rockne's relief, Dorais finally became well enough to take over again on January 31. Rockne's basketball coaching career ended with a 1-5 record. (When Notre Dame suffered its fifth loss under

Rockne on the gridiron, the year was 1925, and 61 wins and three ties had preceded it!) Only once thereafter did Rockne do anything to support basketball at Notre Dame willingly, although he was often forced into doing other things.

Even with Dorais' return and the return of Joe Brandy to add some stability to the young team, the losing continued, against Marquette (the first time the Hilltoppers, as they were known then, played the Irish) and, again, the South Bend Y. Then the team actually won three straight. Two of them were particularly satisfying: the first, a 24-14 defeat of Wabash, was Notre Dame's first win over the Little Giants since 1915, and the second avenged an earlier-season loss to MAC, 30-23. Mehre carried the Irish scoring attack as usual, with 16 and 18 points, respectively. The third win was against one of Dorais' future employers, the University of Detroit.

Notre Dame closed its home season with—what else?—a loss, against DePauw in overtime, then hit the road for five games. Dorais returned to Dubuque, from whence he had come to ND, and defeated them 29-18. From there the Irish closed the season the way it had begun. Two losses at Nebraska (scheduled as a result of the football series which had begun in 1919) and defeats at DePauw and Wabash ended another dismal year.

By this time ND had quite a road-court disadvantage. In 1919-20 the Irish went 1-10 on the road, primarily because of unfamiliarity with wooden courts. (At home they played at a respectable 4-3 clip.) Most teams looking to play Notre Dame balked at coming into the Fieldhouse, with its 1899 version of a multipurpose floor. Unfortunately, the dirt didn't lend itself to an increasingly important part of basketball strategy—dribbling. The Irish home site was antiquated for the rapid advances in the game.

Gus Dorais left ND after the 1920 baseball season to take a coaching job at Gonzaga, where he was able to coach football as well. His replacement at Notre Dame was Walter Halas, brother of National Football League pioneer George Halas, who in 1918-19 coached Somerset (KY) High School to state championships in all four major sports, in the process setting the coaching world on fire. Halas tried to turn things around at ND, but failed, although he did better than his predecessor (which isn't saying much, admittedly).

Two pre-World War I starters had returned for 1920-21, and both landed starting berths again—guard Chet Grant and forward Frank McDermott. McDermott, who had led the team in scoring as a sophomore, and junior captain Harry Mehre formed quite a one-two scoring punch. In fact, the team outscored its opponents over the course of the season. Again, though, the Irish were hurt by their inability to win on the road; while they went 6-2 at home, they only managed a 3-12 ledger on the road for a 9-14 total. Included in that were two major upsets and too many close losses.

Halas took his team on a five-day, five-game trip to open the season. Two colleges and three independent teams were played, and the Irish went 1-4. The team, however, lacked offensive punch as McDermott was unavailable on the trip. Twice ND could manage but 11 points, and the one win was by 27-25 over Mount Union College.

A second brief road trip was much more successful, as ND won the last away games it would win this season, one of which was a stunning upset of one of Indiana's best teams. Valparaiso, coached by future legend George Keogan, finished the 1920-21 season 19-5. One of those five losses was to Notre Dame, and at the Valpo home gym. (One of the 19 wins was also against ND, as Valpo won the return match at the Fieldhouse.)

As the Irish returned home, the winning streak grew to five, and for the first time in four years ND had a winning record (6-4). Notre Dame was able to play its "offense" and the opponent unable to work its because of the surface of the gym. Three straight opponents were blown out as the Mehre-McDermott combination clicked for 84 points in the three contests.

Unfortunately, the streak didn't last. The five-game win skein was followed by a six-game slide as the Irish hit the road again. The first four losses were away—to Wabash and DePauw (the latter by only one), and then to Western State and MAC. Returning home, they lost again to DePauw, and then to Marquette at Milwaukee. Mehre and McDermott continued to score the bulk of ND's points, but it became clear they couldn't carry the team.

This downturn ended with another home-court win, avenging a loss to Western State, 24-19, and was followed by ND's offensive and defensive high point of the season, a 59-15 thrashing of Armour Institute. In the Armour game, Halas benched three of his starters—Eddie Anderson, Roger Kiley, and Chet Grant—because of some sort of disagreement. Throughout the landslide, the three men sat on the bench watching substitutes like sophomore Les Logan score 23 points and others who had seen little action play strong games. Anderson and Kiley both returned to the lineup after this one-game suspension, but Grant stayed home on the next road trip and never played basketball for Notre Dame again.

This streaky Irish squad lost four more in a row, three on a western road trip to Creighton and Nebraska, and the other to a vengeful Valpo squad. But ND managed to salvage some pride by closing the season with a win over powerful Wabash on a buzzer-beater, 31-30. This was ND's second major upset of the season and a complete reversal from the 30-15 thrashing the Little Giants had dished out in Crawfordsville. It was also the first season-ending win for Notre Dame in four years.

Nearly everybody returned from the 9-14 squad for 1921-22, and an improved season seemed to be in the offing. Actually, though, things regressed. Many factors contributed to a disappointing 6-13 record. Chief among them were an improved schedule which included several outstanding teams, a split home schedule and two football-related incidents.

Among the new teams on Notre Dame's schedule (i.e., not on the schedule in 1920-21) were two Western Conference schools, Illinois—Halas' alma mater—and Northwestern, Butler of Indianapolis, and a stronger-than-usual Kalamazoo College. Add to these the usual home-and-home matches with DePauw and Wabash, and it equals many sound defeats. The Irish record against these teams was 1-11.

This split home schedule was a harbinger of things to come. Notre Dame had used the floor of the South Bend YMCA for years to prepare for road games. For the first time, ND began playing some of its home games there as well, mostly in deference to visiting teams. As mentioned earlier, it had become increasingly difficult to schedule quality teams for home games because of the Fieldhouse's dirt floor. Moving bigger games to the YMCA was a stopgap measure in an attempt to upgrade the home slate.

Finally, the two football-related incidents—always a risk when over half the hoops team played the sport—related to three returning starters, Harry Mehre, Eddie Anderson, and team captain Roger Kiley, all seniors. The first was a football injury to Mehre which rendered him unable to play the first half of the season. His scoring punch and floor leadership were sorely missed. In the eight games he missed, the Irish went 1-7, the one win coming over whipping-post Armour Institute. The other incident surfaced in January 1922, and it involved the young—and generally scorned—sport of professional football.

Mehre, Anderson, and Kiley, along with several other Notre Dame football players and a group from the University of Illinois, participated in a pro game in Illinois under assumed names—not an uncommon occurrence in the early, shadier days of play-for-pay. Most of the time the players didn't get caught because there was no surefire way to prove involvement, and those who did usually weren't found out until after they had graduated from college. In this case, a player from the U. of I. team was asked to join in this game, and he declined the offer. He then was responsible for turning in every collegian who did play. The three ND basketballers were immediately dropped from the team, and Kiley's vacated captaincy was awarded to Frank McDermott.

The two weeks after the players' suspensions was when the 1921-22 squad played its most inspired basketball. What was basically a seven-man squad went 3-1 in those two weeks, scoring victories over MAC, Columbia College of Iowa (formerly Dubuque), and Northwestern, the latter avenging an early-season loss, and losing only a heartbreaking two-point decision to Wabash at the YMCA. A team of seven men coud not keep up the pace, however; the last four games ended in defeat, and the season had ended on a downer. But then, with all that had already happened in 1921-22, it was to be expected.

Three of the men who had become starters after the football incident returned for Walter Halas' third attempt at a return to respectability—senior captain Mickey Kane, senior Les Logan, and junior Gene Mayl. Joining them were seven newcomers, three of whom did not play football but four of whom did—sophomores Rex Enright, Noble Kizer, Elmer Layden, and Don Miller, the latter two later to gain fame as one-half of the "Four Horsemen" backfield of the 1924 championship football team. This young squad faced a schedule at least as difficult as that the year past and performed well enough to spark some local interest again. For the first time in years, fellow students showed such support that a split-ticket system had to be used for those games played in the YMCA because of its small capacity (2,000). The problem in 1922-23 was that the Irish couldn't win there.

Notre Dame went 4-0 at the Fieldhouse and its dirt floor, where the Irish played the lesser lights on the home slate. ND had its best record on the road in years (6-8). But at the "Y," the Irish went 0-4, and that was the difference in another disappointing season — 10 wins, 12 losses.

Eleven of the first 12 contests were played on the road, and the team actually had a 7-5 record during that time. In the process, the Irish blew out MAC (40-15), defeated both Illinois Wesleyan and Bradley by 11, and pulled back-to-back shockers by beating Northwestern (20-13) and edging Iowa, a first-time opponent scheduled because of a football rivalry (again), 24-23. The losses were to Michigan in the first meeting between the two schools in any sport since 1909, Millikin, Illinois in overtime (41-39), Butler, and Purdue.

When the squad returned home after the holiday break, there was a great deal of anticipation among the students and townsfolk. With nine of the last 11 games played at Notre Dame or in downtown South Bend, an end to the long dry spell of winning seasons seemed assured. It looked even better as ND won its first two of the nine, against Armour Institute and Western State, to up its record to 9-5.

Then came the disaster.

As hard as the Irish tried, they could not keep their record above .500. Butler destroyed them at the "Y," Indiana did likewise at Bloomington, DePauw pulled out a close one in Greencastle, IN. The losing streak was snapped with a one-point win over Kalamazoo in the Fieldhouse. But the Irish found winning at the "Y" an impossible proposition. They lost by five to Wabash and by one each to DePauw and MAC. The last was the most frustrating, as ND had defeated the Aggies 40-15 in East Lansing in December. This time, however, Noble Kizer, who had become ND's top foul shooter, was sidelined and unable to play, and that was the ballgame. And speaking of 40-15, that was the score when Wabash put the crunch on the Irish to close a gut-wrenching season.

Kizer was the first guard ever to lead the team in scoring, mainly because of his free-throw proficiency. At this time, one player usually took all a team's foul shots, which were awarded for both personal and "technical" (i.e., violations such as double-dribbling or running with the ball) fouls. The rules people, decrying the slowdown in action which resulted from what had become a parade to the foul line, eliminated shots on the so-called technical fouls in 1923-24. Instead, the ball was awarded to the other team out of bounds. At the same time, the rules committee ended the days of the free-throw specialist; henceforth, all fouled players had to take their own free throws.

Halas never got a chance to implement these changes at ND, as he resigned after three years. As a replacement, Knute Rockne suggested, and the Faculty Board approved, George Keogan, a one-time dental student who had earned the nickname of "The Doctor" early in his successful coaching career which dated back to 1909. He had first come to Rockne's attention in 1920, when the Irish had an unexpectedly tough time on the gridiron with a Keogan-coached Valparaiso team; only with a fourth-quarter burst after trailing 3-0 did the Irish win, 28-3. Rockne did not forget that when it came time to hire a new coach for Our Lady. He knew who he wanted, and he got him. It may have been the last time he directly supported basketball while athletic director, but it certainly was the best. The beginning of the end of the Dark Ages was near.

# 5

## The Doctor Is In

George Keogan's first move as Notre Dame coach was to move *all* the basketball practices and games off campus to the South Bend YMCA, barring conflicts (and the "Y" people made sure there were few). He explained this controversial decision matter-of-factly, "I won't have my boys playing on any dirt floor."

There was no doubt that the ND gymnasium was obsolete for basketball and had been for years. For some time there had been talk of building an addition capable of housing a removable, wooden floor. By moving the team to South Bend Keogan more or less forced the hand of the administration. The new section was eventually built with funds from a somewhat ironic source to be explained later. Until then, for two years the basketball team representing Notre Dame played no games at Notre Dame. During those two years, however, "The Doctor" began to cure the ills of the Irish basketball program.

Six players with experience returned—Noble Kizer, Don Miller, Rex Enright, Phil Mahoney, Tom Reardon, and captain Gene Mayl (the only senior among the returnees). They were joined by two outstanding sophomores: Joe Dienhart, who did not play until the second half of the season but quickly found a niche in and near the starting lineup, and Clem Crowe, a football player also, the first and best of seven brothers who played basketball for Notre Dame from 1923 to 1938. With this experienced and talented squad, Keogan went 15-8 in 1923-24, the first Irish winning season since before the war. Had there been such an award at the time, he could have been named Coach of the Year.

It quickly became easy to tell that things were changing. The "new" Irish stayed in games by relying on tenacious defense. In only five of the 23 games did an opponent score more than 25 points; ND went 1-4 in those contests. Thanks to that defense, the Irish quickly gained some Midwestern respect by defeating Minnesota in the second game of the season, 16-14, in a rare home loss for the Gophers. It was no coincidence that ND had opened the season in Minnesota with a two-game series; Keogan was born and raised in the state and, in fact, had attended some classes there in the early years of his coaching career, which began at age 19.

From there, Notre Dame returned to South Bend for two home-away-from-home games and won both. Loss number two came at the hands of Illinois in Champaign, 29-21, but three days later the Irish returned to the YMCA and did something they hadn't done in nearly ten years.

They won an overtime game.

February 14, 1914 had been the last ND extra-period victory, over St. Lawrence. In the interim, loss after frustrating loss resulted when the score was knotted after 40 minutes. Wabash, DePauw, Illinois—all had taken advantage of this overtime jinx over the years. Finally, on January 5, 1924, the Irish turned the tables, and Michigan was the victim. Noble Kizer scored 11 points to lead ND to a 29-25 thriller win. And as if that nailbiter wasn't enough, the next two South Bend games were equally intense— 22-21 over Western State and 24-23 over Loyola of Chicago (the Irish also defeated them in the Windy City four days later).

At this early stage of the season, the team was an amazing 7-2 going into the first of two games against mighty Franklin. The Indiana school featured the *real* "Victory Five," the Franklin High team which included future Hall of Famer "Fuzzy" Vandivier. They had won the high school championship of Indiana in 1920, 1921, and 1922, the only time any school has ever captured "Hoosier Hysteria" three years in a row. All five went across town to play at Franklin College, and they more than held their own. In 1922-23 they did not play varsity because of freshman eligibility rules, but began a two-year success story as sophomores. Franklin would prove quite an opponent for Notre Dame over the next four years, beginning with a 19-12 defeat of the Irish at the South Bend YMCA.

Seven straight "home" contests closed with a decisive win over Michigan State (35-17) in which Rex Enright scored as many points as the entire MSC squad after having to sit out the Franklin contest, and a tough loss to Wabash, 27-22, in which ND shot a miserable 4-for-12 from the free throw line. Now the Irish had to play nine of their last 11 games on the road. There was definitely some worry on the home front considering the horrible traveling record from years recently past.

However, this was the present.

Other than a lackluster two-game stint with Creighton in Omaha, Nebraska (the Irish lost both), Notre Dame more than held its own on the road, losing only a tough one to Indiana by one point and to Franklin in Notre Dame's poorest defensive showing of the year (40-29). The "Victory Five" were hot and ND wasn't, and the Irish had a season-closing loss for the third straight year.

Before that, ND won at Wabash, avenging the earlier home loss. Clem Crowe had 10 points to lead the Irish cause, and the guards (Mayl and Kizer) played stellar defense as the tide was turned, 23-16. Other road wins came against Concordia, Michigan State, Western State, and Wittenberg, the latter by the lopsided margin of 39-16. Balanced scoring—Crowe and Kizer had nine, Dienhart eight—and tough defense did it. Finally, in the two non-road games, the Irish defeated inferior opposition (Adrian and St. Viator) convincingly. In the not-too-distant future, that would become routine. First, however, Keogan had to suffer through his sophomore jinx.

Notre Dame could only hit .500 (11-11) in 1924-25, and that only because two games which were added to the originally-announced schedule resulted in Irish wins. There were several reasons why. Youth was one, as Keogan was forced to use four sophomores in key roles. All four, though, adjusted well to varsity play, and two of them finished one-two in scoring. The primary reason, however, was football.

See, 1924 was the year Grantland Rice of the *New York Herald Tribune* immortalized Notre Dame's backfield in perhaps the most famous opening paragraph in sportswriting history: "Outlined against a blue-grey October sky, the Four Horsemen rode again." For the first time, Fighting Irish football began to take on legendary status. The resulting publicity—and an undefeated and untied season—led to the Irish accepting an invitation to the Rose Bowl, then the only bowl game. Preparations for the bowl extended the football season more than a month, and this did not make Keogan very happy.

At the time, there were still multi-sport varsity men at ND, and two of Keogan's best players from 1923-24, Clem Crowe and captain Noble Kizer, were part of the "Seven Mules" offensive line for the "Four Horsemen" and were tied to football until at least January 2. (Kizer, as he was hoops captain, did make one road trip with the hoops squad before then, but he saw little action.) In their absence, however, they were hardly missed, as Keogan's young team went 5-1 before the triumphant footballers returned, and the one loss was to Minnesota in the one game Kizer entered on the road trip. Although both men were good basketball players, they never quite fit in with the 1924-25 squad. A certain chemistry had developed, and upon their return, it was destroyed. It didn't help any that Kizer, once back, became mired in a scoring slump from which he was never able to escape (his high game total was six points). With the gridders, ND went 6-10 on the way to what turned out to be Keogan's worst season under the Dome.

It was a strange 11-11. Ten of the wins were convincing . . . but so were eight of the losses. The one close win was a 27-26 squeaker over a school Keogan had once coached, St. Thomas of St. Paul, Minnesota. All the others ND won by eight points or more. Two of the losses—both games against the Franklin "Victory Five," all now juniors—were by four points, and one other was by five; the rest were by nine points or more.

As mentioned earlier, the season opened auspiciously. A 34-13 thrashing of Armour Institute marked the varsity debut of the first of Keogan's great centers over the years, South Bend's own John Nyikos. Only 5-10, short for a center even in those days, he scored 18 in his first game and went on from there to become the team's leading scorer for three years.

After a split in Minnesota, Notre Dame renewed the annual duel with Northwestern. But starting this season and continuing for many decades, the two schools began playing each other twice a year. At Evanston, Ray Dahman, another of the sophomores, led a balanced scoring attack as the Irish won, 22-13, and back at the YMCA on December 30, Nyikos scored 19 as ND destroyed the Wildcats, 36-15. Finally, the 5-1 pre-return of the gridders skein ended with a 44-17 thrashing of Mercer.

The roof fell in, however, as ND won only three of its next 13 games. Butler, Franklin, Creighton, and Wabash each won twice from a disorganized squad that lacked the unity which existed among the former sophomore-dominated lineup. The other two losses were to Penn State and Carnegie Tech (both first-time opponents) on a western Pennsylvania road trip. All three of the wins were at "home" and all were convincing—by 23 over Michigan State, by 19 over Loyola (IL), and by 11 over Illinois.

As the team closed out its YMCA schedule, with a tough 31-27 loss to Franklin, it was 8-11 with three road contests left. But the Irish didn't collapse. Nyikos had three consecutive stellar offensive efforts, and for the only time in 1925's portion of the season the squad won three in a row. John had 16 in a 42-10 rout of a hapless Michigan State squad. In the dedication game of a new fieldhouse at Iowa's Columbia College (now Loras), Nyikos had 17 to ruin ND alumnus Eddie Anderson's attempt to defeat his alma mater, 44-26. And in a rather slow game, the 5-10 center had nine points in a 19-11 Irish win over Loyola of Chicago. The last two games had been the contests added during the season, and the latter was Notre Dame's 200th basketball win. Interestingly, ND's 200th football win had occurred in the recent grid season.

Years later, the Helms Foundation selected All-America teams for the early years of basketball, before national attention was focused on the sport. On its 1924-25 squad, the Helms people inexplicably named Noble Kizer as one of the guards. The selection must have been based on his overall college career more than on his performance that season, as 1924-25 was his worst offensively and most spotty on defense. The latter problem, however, plagued most of the ND squad after January 5.

Even though the Rose Bowl and its ramifications had had a short-term chilling effect on Keogan's rebuilding efforts, two things resulted which paid long-term dividends. First, Notre

Dame officials adopted a no-post-season-play policy. Such an elongation had proven detrimental to the organization and performance of the victim of such a season extension. It also seemed to favor one sport over another. From here on out, football-playing hoopsters would miss no more than a couple of basketball games; Keogan solved that problem by scheduling light early-season competition. The post-season ban lasted long after its original inspiration had become obsolete through athletes' specialization and was not completely rescinded until 1969. And second, the Irish share of the bowl receipts were used not to begin a new, larger football stadium as Rockne had assumed they would, but to build that sorely-needed addition onto the Field-house which would both bring the building into the 20th Century and return the basketball team to campus. The Rock was not happy with either of these administrative decisions. But football had both prestige and a decent place to play on campus. Basketball in 1925 had neither . . . but that was about to change.

# 6

---

# A New Gym Means More Wins

The addition to the fieldhouse, in which new locker rooms and the removable, raised basketball floor were located, was about half the size of the older section. The annex had benefits for other sports as well, track in particular, as the indoor track was increased in length to a more reasonable lap-per-mile ratio. But it was George Keogan's charges who enjoyed their new home the most.

In the first two seasons in the new gym, the Irish went 22-0 there. Few of the 22 were even close. In the process, Notre Dame put together the most successful back-to-back basketball seasons in its history and gained some national recognition for its exploits. At the same time, student attendance at home games increased, and so did participation. Keogan was able to establish freshman and junior varsity squads which went through the same paces in practices as the varsity, a previously unheard-of luxury. This system hoped to perpetuate the success ND was having.

Of the eight regulars in 1924-25, five were back for 1925-26. One of the non-returnees, Joe Dienhart, had been appointed captain after the end of the last season, but was unable to return to the team for his senior year. Vince McNally, a junior forward, received the nod as Dienhart's replacement. Now things were ready for the beginning of a near-dynasty in Midwestern basketball.

Aided by a 13-game home schedule, the first time in years Notre Dame played more games on campus than off, the Irish went an incredible 19-1 and were considered the class of the region in 1925-26. In the process, the Keoganites held the op-

44

position to an average of 21.5 points per game and scored an average of 34.3. Ten times ND held opponents to 20 points or less —and 13 times ND scored 30 or more.

The Irish began their blitzkrieg through a decent schedule with a home win, the debut on the brand-new wooden floor at Notre Dame, the first game played on campus in almost three years, and the first time ND opened at home in ten years. Armour Institute was a 53-26 victim as 13 men saw action and Clem Crowe and John Nyikos each scored 13 points. Five days later, an overflow crowd crammed into the campus basketball showplace for the dedication game against Minnesota, a team Keogan wanted at home as much as later coaches would want UCLA to "visit" the ACC. The front line of Crowe, McNally, and Nyikos provided balanced scoring, and guards Ray Dahman and Lou Conroy helped keep the Gophers' front line from doing the same. A delirious home crowd saw the Irish paste 'em, 36-14.

Following a 10-point win at Northwestern, the mighty Iowa Hawkeyes came to the new and improved Fieldhouse for the first time. Another tough defensive squad, the Hawks held the Irish triumvirate to only four field goals. But Iowa fouls and the resulting accuracy from the line (9-for-11) helped the Irish edge out the Hawkeyes in what was considered quite an upset at the time, 17-16. Almost routine wins against Northwestern, Mercer, and first-time visitor Kansas State put Notre Dame at 7-0 as it left the extremely friendly confines of its new home for a game against nemesis Franklin.

This was a classic matchup in its symbolism. The "Victory Five" of the past had fallen on some hard luck. All were now seniors, but injuries had reduced their effectiveness. The rising star of Notre Dame faced the setting sun of Franklin on this day, and the twilight won out. Franklin defeated the Irish, 33-22, and ended a 10-game winning streak as the defense faltered for the only time all year.

The team next played in Detroit for the first time since January 1921. The opposing University of Detroit coach was none other than Gus Dorais, who had done such "wonderful" things as an ND coach several years earlier. And Dorais and Detroit were beaten badly in front of a sellout crowd, 31-14, to begin a new Irish winning streak. City College of Detroit and Wabash were the next road victims, 24-17 and 41-29, respectively.

Returning home, two surprise stars shone in the last game before semester exams, a 33-14 drubbing of Michigan State. Ted Ley, a senior used as "sixth man" all season, started in place of an injured Clem Crowe and scored eight points, and John Viktoryn, another second-teamer, put in seven to lead the scoring thrust.

After the exam period, the Irish had a welcome addition to their team. Mike Nyikos, older brother of John and a senior, completed his second semester in residence and was beginning his third, and thus became eligible to play. He had transferred from Indiana, where he had, ironically, played a role in the Hoosiers' 21-20 defeat of ND two years earlier. One of the few transfer students ever to play varsity basketball, he provided some added scoring punch as ND continued to win.

Detroit nearly got revenge on a sluggish post-exam Irish team, but Notre Dame pulled one out in overtime thanks to the newcomer. After his younger brother fouled out, Mike scored five points in OT to pace the win. Illinois was a 26-14 road victim; the Irish then returned home and squeaked past Wabash, 25-23, as Keogan used his starting five the entire game.

Again, unlikely heroes helped in a win against Michigan State. Keogan used mostly second-teamers against the down-and-out Spartans. Mike Nyikos scored 10 points, seldom-used Don Harvey eight in a 40-25 rout, the last road game of the year. And all four remaining home games were against teams which had defeated the Irish in their last meeting:

—One year past, a young Notre Dame team traveled to western Pennsylvania and lost to Carnegie Tech by five. A year later, a junior-dominated ND squad utterly dominated the rematch. McNally's 14, John Nyikos's 11, and Crowe's 10 led the team, which had a total of 60, the most points by an Irish team since 1914; the outmanned Tech had but 26.

—The most anxiously-awaited contest of the year, a sellout weeks in advance, was Notre Dame's rematch with Franklin. By this time, the "Victory Five" was but a shadow of its old self, and an emotionally-charged Irish squad made their only vanquisher look bad, 40-19.

—Two games with Creighton ended the season, that team's first visit to Notre Dame. The Irish were no gracious hosts: Crowe scored 13 of ND's 23 in the first game, and McNally scored 17 of ND's 29 in the second, and Creighton as a team could muster but 17 and 18 in each game, in that order.

Not only had Notre Dame finished with a 19-1 record, but they did something almost never achieved: they lost fewer games than the football team of the past fall! (Rockne's year-after-the-Four-Horsemen team went 7-2-1.) With almost all the key players returning, coming close to a similar feat, even with a tougher schedule, seemed a cinch. And it was. For the second year in a row Keogan's charges went 19-1. This time, in addition, Notre Dame was generally considered the class of not only the Midwest, but the entire nation, as determined by the research of the Helms Foundation.

The team's solid foundation consisted of four seniors: John Nyikos, the team captain, who for the third season in a row led the team in scoring and was later named by the Helms people to their 1926-27 All-America team; Vince McNally; Ray Dahman; and Lou Conroy. These four were reinforced by three outstanding sophs: the third of the seven Crowe brothers, Frank; footballer John Colerick; and Joe Jachym. One of the many reasons Keogan was able to coach ND to winning season after winning season was his use of sophomores in key roles to provide a continuum from year to year. Seldom did he ever have to completely rebuild.

Another Keogan trademark was reinforced on opening day of the 1926-27 season. As mentioned previously, ND intentionally scheduled relative lightweights at the start of the season so those basketball players who also played football (there were still several each season) would not be missed too much and could gradually work themselves into a basketball groove before the first "tougher" game, usually against a Big Ten opponent. Most of these games were no contest from the start, so Keogan used as many healthy players as he could. In Game One, a 51-14 drubbing of Armour Institute, 17 men saw action, 11 of whom scored.

Again, tough defense combined with a relatively potent offense was why Notre Dame lost only once. These statistics tell the tale: 12 times ND held the opposition to 20 points or less,

19 times to 26 or less— and 15 times the Irish scored more than 26. Just as in 1925-26, the one defensive breakdown resulted in the one Irish loss.

For the second straight year, the Irish began 7-0, increasing the team's winning streak over two years to 19. This start was far from suspect. Hard-fought wins over Minnesota in Minneapolis and Iowa in Iowa City, plus a two-game sweep of Northwestern, were highlights of this stretch. Then for the second straight season, a potentially unbeaten season was marred by a loss— against the same school and in the same gym as the year before, with an almost-identical final score, almost exactly a year to the day.

A very different Franklin team took the floor in 1926-27. No more were the vaunted "Victory Five" around. The end of Franklin's days as a major basketball force was near. But in front of frenzied fans, the upset of the year in the sport took place. Franklin took advantage of an injury to Nyikos which sidelined him for the only time in his collegiate career and defeated the Irish, 34-22.

Most of the rest of Notre Dame's season was relatively routine. The average victory margin was better than 11 over some quality competition, including Wabash twice, Creighton twice in Omaha, Marquette twice, Michigan State twice, and a tough defensive struggle in Wisconsin which the Irish won, 19-14.

Included in this 12-game string of wins was another vengeance match against Franklin. Again a complete sellout filled the Fieldhouse for the rematch, and again the true colors of the Irish showed. Nyikos and Conroy each scored 11 as ND put 'em away early. Keogan then put in an entire second team to mop up, the final ending up 36-16. Also noteworthy was Notre Dame's first encounter with Pittsburgh. During the Keogan years, the ND-Pitt series became the most intense Irish rivalry, with two future Hall of Fame coaches matching wits, ND's George "Doc" Keogan and Pitt's Clifford "Doc" Carlson. This first game saw ND win, 33-17, as the Panthers couldn't stop Nyikos, who scored a season-high 17 tallies.

Three days after Pitt couldn't stop John, the Gus Dorais-coached Detroit Titans did, in the only close call of the 12 post-Franklin-at-Franklin wins. For the only time in his three years,

Nyikos scored no points; Keogan shuttled in 12 different men as the Irish had all kinds of trouble. Notre Dame finally won, 24-23, to keep the skein alive.

And before the season-ending trip to Omaha, Notre Dame students and fans said their collective goodbyes to the four seniors who, along with their coach, had led the Fighting Irish back to basketball prominence. Five and a half thousand partisans packed the Fieldhouse for the last home appearance of McNally, Dahman, Conroy, and Nyikos on February 26, and Marquette was the victim by a 33-13 count. And after the almost anticlimactic road trip which secured ND's two-year ledger at 38 wins and two losses was over, the question became: would all of Keogan's planning for the future pay off, or would success be a two-year fluke?

# 7

## Etc.

During the next four years, the Keogan system became firmly implanted in the Notre Dame Fieldhouse. While none of his 1927-31 squads was quite as victorious as the 1925-27 national champions, they still didn't lose very often, and by the early thirties Keogan was becoming widely known and respected in college coaching circles.

He made two major contributions to college basketball. First, he had become one of the first college coaches to adopt the offense of the famed professional team The Original Celtics, an aggregation so successful that it, like the earlier Buffalo Germans, was inducted into the Hall of Fame as a unit, and also, unlike the Germans, was broken up by officials of the American Basketball League, of which it was once a member. With John Nyikos at center working the "pivot play" – probably a Celtics invention and revolutionary for its time – the Keoganites had had little trouble blowing through the opposition, as adequately described earlier. Second, he designed a defense to combat the pivot play, which he correctly assumed would eventually become commonplace.

The most common defense in the early 1920s was the "standing zone," which is exactly what its name implies – the five men literally stood still in the forecourt in a 3-2 alignment. Such a defense was no defense against a pivoting team. What Keogan did was combine elements of the very unpopular man-to-man defense with it, thereby making the zone move. The result became known as the "shifting man-to-man," although it was really a zone defense. Echoes of this innovation are seen today in the styles of any coach who uses a zone defense, as most of today's variants are merely modifications of the Keogan system.

As practiced by its inventor and his charges, the defense was so successful that in the 1927-31 period, only five times in four seasons did Notre Dame give up more than 30 points in any game. It was this strong, consistent defense which became the hallmark of Notre Dame's offensive strategy, as they had no one able to run the pivot play like Nyikos had done.

What the 1927-28 team had was experience, even with four seniors graduated. Juniors dominated the fifth Keogan team: captain Joe Jachym, Frank Crowe, and John Colerick, regulars from the 1926-27 team; and Bob Newbold, Bob Voglewede, and Jim Bray, who added some talented depth. Three sophomores worked their way into the regular rotation: Ed Smith, Clarence "Red" Donovan, and John McCarthy. Nine of the top 10 players on this team were underclassmen; even so, the young Irish stretched their all-time Fieldhouse-addition record to 32-0. All of the ND losses came on the road, four in all—but there were 18 wins to counteract that.

Notre Dame opened the season with five straight wins, two of them without its head coach. Keogan was forced to Indianapolis for a week because of the death of his brother, so his assistant, Mike Nyikos, took over for victories over Illinois Wesleyan and Iowa. As usual, the Hawkeye clash was hard-fought. ND used only five men, but committed only four personal fouls, which aided in the 23-20 win. After Keogan returned, victories over Northwestern and Minnesota followed.

The series had started a few years earlier, but the semiannual tussles with Northwestern became another of the great matchups of the Keogan years. The Wildcats were entering their glory years in basketball under another Hall of Fame coach, Arthur "Dutch" Lonborg. An indication of that was the first Irish defeat in 17 games, at Evanston, 25-23, the first time in nearly three years that Notre Dame lost to an out-of-state opponent.

Five straight wins followed, including what were becoming increasingly routine games against Franklin and Wabash—both would be dropped from the schedule in the not-too-distant future—and a couple of somewhat anomalous contests, one a New Year's Eve victory over a traveling Princeton team, 35-24, and a 29-19 win over Drake at Des Moines, Iowa, another team scheduled by virtue of a football series.

Of the five wins before semester exams, none was more significant than the "W" on January 7. The opponent was the University of Pennsylvania in Notre Dame's first basketball visit to one of the major Eastern cities (Philadelphia). The big event featured the team considered the class of the Midwest against one of the East's traditional powers, staged in a brand-new, 9,000-plus-seat gymnasium called The Palestra—and it was all it was billed to be. A see-saw battle went into overtime, with Notre Dame the eventual winner at the end, 30-28.

A revived Michigan State team came into the Fieldhouse as ND's first post-exams opponent. After the game, the reason for the closeness of the battle was generally assumed to be the post-exam sluggishness, but perhaps not: the Spartans took the Irish into three overtimes—the longest game in ND history to this time—until the Fieldhouse win streak survived, 29-25. But six days later, the same two teams met in East Lansing, and MSU gave the Irish their second setback, 26-16.

Notre Dame went 7-2 the rest of the season. In that span, the team tallied victories over Marquette (twice), Wabash and Drake (for the second time each), as well as Wisconsin and Carnegie Tech. The two losses were to Pittsburgh and Doc Carlson, who finished 18-0, 24-22, and Butler, which the Irish had beaten at home earlier. Again, this split was the commencement of a hard-fought Notre Dame series of the Keogan era. At Indianapolis, Butler, coached by another future Hall of Famer, Tony Hinkle, defeated the Irish, 21-13, for a season-ending loss and the end of the Keoganites' reign as mythical Indiana and Western champions.

All of the key elements of the 1927-28 team returned in 1928-29, though because of closer games only seven of them played anything like the role they had the prior year. For the first time, the Irish had co-captains during the season (Joe Jachym and Frank Crowe). Also, for the first time under Keogan, no newcomer cracked the starting or top-reserve lineup. Again, the emphasis was on tough defense and balanced scoring. Crowe, the team's leading scorer, had only 106 points during the season, but the defense held 19 of 20 opponents under 30 points, so usually it didn't matter. Nonetheless, a lack of scoring punch occasionally hurt; the 1928-29 record slipped slightly to 15-5.

After two straight wins over relative patsies Armour Institute (54-14 with 17 from Crowe, both figures being highs for the season) and Albion (15-8 in a very slowly played game), Northwestern rolled into the Fieldhouse and did something no team before had been able to accomplish. They defeated Notre Dame in the new Fieldhouse. The Irish still were not together; they were missing John Colerick because of a football injury, and he would continue to recuperate until January. His absence had an effect on the team's scoring, and this would be borne out by his average after his return, which ended up higher than anyone else's on the team. As a result, the Wildcats were able to hold ND to only 14 points to NU's 18.

And to add insult to injury, three days later Indiana played the Irish in the Fieldhouse, and they too came out winners, 29-17. This was the Hoosiers' first visit to Notre Dame for basketball — the lack of acceptable facilities had kept them away until this time — and it wouldn't be the last, although the visits were sporadic until the late 1960s. But this loss left the Irish at 2-2, and a two-game trip to "neutral" Kansas City, Kansas to play Phog Allen's KU Jayhawks loomed ahead.

In this case, however, the Keoganites had the edge. Before the season had even started, Kansas had suffered a great blow to its season. Allen, ever the innovator, was grooming a seven-foot freshman as a potential dominating force in a game still played by six-footers, and expected him to be in the lineup in 1928-29. During the off-season, however, the young man drowned in an accident, a tragedy which cast a pall over the entire team and ruined the season. Notre Dame didn't help matters too much, sweeping the series, 32-21 and 29-17.

Colerick returned to the lineup for the January 5 home Detroit game and the January 9 tilt at Wabash, and the spark to the offense was immediately noticeable. The Irish had two of their best combined offense-defense efforts of the year as the Titans fell, 49-14, and the Little Giants, 42-19. Then ND fell at home for the third time, losing to a first-time, but certainly not last-time, opponent — Kentucky.

Later to become Notre Dame's most controversial series, this was strictly a one-shot deal. Adolph Rupp wasn't even Wildcat coach yet, and not until the mid-1930s did the ND-UK matchup become a yearly series. Still, under coach John Mauer, Kentucky was a successful team in its home state and in the South, and was beginning to make itself nationally known. By holding Frank Crowe scoreless and the Irish to only four field goals, the Wildcats pulled off the upset, 19-16.

ND's second trip to Penn's Palestra proved profitable as the Irish beat the Quakers, 31-19; then, returning home, they defeated Michigan State. They ended the first semester attempting to avenge the earlier loss to Northwestern, this time failing at Evanston, 27-24.

Following exams, the Irish were finally able to win consistently, emerging victorious seven times in a row. All of them were tough defensive battles, and most were close. At the Fieldhouse, Wabash played much closer than they had in the earlier contest, mostly because Keogan used 12 men, but the Irish won, 26-23. Eleven men saw action as Marquette fell next at Milwaukee, 29-17. In the other five wins, Keogan used for the most part only six players; consecutive tough games made this necessary.

Ever-tough Pitt, while not quite at the level of the unbeaten squad of the year before, was still formidable. But John Colerick canned 14 points as the Irish coasted, 33-23. At Indianapolis, Butler went down at ND's hands to only its second defeat of the year, 24-21. Michigan State was the next stop, and after two overtimes, the Irish had won a squeaker, 28-27, for their first double-overtime victory. Again in enemy territory, an earlier rout became a close contest. This time Detroit played tough defense to hold ND to a 19-16 win. And win seven in the streak, by an identical 19-16 score, was the home rematch with Marquette.

For the second straight year, though, Notre Dame closed its season with a loss. The same Butler team which the Irish had defeated in Indianapolis entered the Fieldhouse to make sure they would finish their season 18-2, and boy, did they! Butler won by what was at the time the worst drubbing ever handed a Keogan-coached ND team, 35-16.

Once the season was over, the Christy Walsh Syndicate selected Notre Dame junior guard Ed Smith as an All-American. This was the first time any ND man had been chosen to a contemporary all-star team. (The earlier Helms Foundation mentions were all retroactive.) His play at guard was a key reason why only Butler had cracked the 30-point mark against the Irish. He was also elected by the same group to the same honor in 1929-30 to become ND's first two-time honoree.

Along with Smith, Keogan had John McCarthy and Red Donovan (the 1929-30 captain) back from the starting lineup. Behind them there was a dearth of returning experience. Joe Gavin, who had played sparingly in 1928-29, was back as a junior, but otherwise there wasn't much. Three sophomores, two of whom were younger brothers of former Irish hoopsters, formed the rest of the top seven. The one who wasn't related to a prior Keoganite was center Ray DeCook; the other two were forwards Bill Newbold (brother of Bob) and Norb Crowe (fourth of that clan to play for Keogan). This both young and experienced team finished 14-6 against, as usual, some formidable competition.

After getting past the early-season pushovers (this time Kalamazoo, Lake Forest, and Albion) easily, so easily that Keogan used 19 men in each of the latter two games, the "real" season began with Northwestern again. Predictably, Dutch Lonborg's charges came ready to play, and the result was ample evidence: NU 30, ND 28, the third straight Irish loss in the series.

Iowa was next. The Hawks were not as good as they had been been earlier in the decade, and they went home losers, 32-19. Then Keogan's men went off to Columbus, OH to play Ohio State; the offense was cold, and the Irish came back with their second loss, 29-22.

The return match with Northwestern, Notre Dame's next game, began a tradition which continued nearly unbroken until World War II. The annual Irish-Wildcat showdown in Evanston became a New Year's Eve special, the beginning of a festive evening for Evanstonians. In this first December 31 matchup, ND forced Wildcat fans to keep the celebration capped until midnight. Aided by Newbold's 10 points, and the usual stellar defensive effort, Northwestern's three-game hex over ND ended with a 22-18 Irish win.

They defeated Indiana, 30-29, despite going 0-for-7 from the charity stripe, and then coasted over Marquette in preparation for Pitt. Doc Carlson's team this time was as good as his 18-0 team two years past, although they did lose a couple this time—

but not to Notre Dame. This marked the first time the teams played twice during the season, which was the custom until the late 1930s, and the Panthers destroyed the Irish in each, 33-13 and 25-16, the former an even worse blowout than the Butler game one March ago.

A strange game was on the schedule next, as for the only time during the regular season the Irish played a foreign team, the FAL team of collegians from Mexico City. Keogan knew they weren't in ND's class, so he started a team of second- and third-stringers. Such seldom-used men as Marshall Kizer (brother of Noble), Dennis Heenan, and Paul Host showed their talents while the regulars, for the most part, had a rest. For some other places, FAL might have been good competition, but not for Notre Dame, as the reserves won, 29-23. Two days later, the regulars were back in action in East Lansing — and lost to Michigan State, 28-21, to close the pre-exam schedule.

Immediately following the break, for once Notre Dame was ready. Instead of the usual sluggish performance following the layoff, the team tackled Wabash with a vengeance. The Little Giants were not the great team they had been a decade earlier, and the Irish illustrated that graphically with a 26-10 shellacking. In Milwaukee, Marquette played ND close in the return battle. The Irish used four-of-five shooting from the line to pull it out, 20-18.

After the previously-mentioned second loss to Pitt, two more wins followed — a 28-20 defeat of Butler at Indianapolis, a little revenge for the seaon-ending drubbing dealt ND a year past, followed by a little more revenge, a 29-17 home defeat of Michigan State. In a rough game, the Irish made 15 foul shots, and John McCarthy hit seven-of-eight of his to clinch it. Then there was a little revenge in reverse.

Wabash was not in Notre Dame's class in sports anymore by 1930. They had, however, been utterly embarrassed in the ND gym earlier in the season, and wanted to reverse the score in Crawfordsville. The Irish were without Bill Newbold, who was unable to play because of a slight injury, but his absence shouldn't have made a difference with Keogan's "team" concept. To put it simply, Notre Dame was overconfident going into the game, and the lesser Little Giants pulled a *big* upset, the biggest of an

Irish team in almost 20 years, 21-16. The Irish closed the season with two wins, a satisfying 29-16 home defeat of Butler, in which Smith, McCarthy, and Donovan made their last appearance before the home fans, and a 24-17 win over Penn at the Palestra.

The 1930-31 season turned out what is euphemistically called a "rebuilding year," although in the case of Notre Dame, "inter-regnum" might be more descriptive. This team had no captain during the season (the lone senior, Joe Gavin, was named "honorary captain" after the last game); it had its worst offensive year since the immortal "Victory Fives" of post-World War I infamy (only 24.3 points per game); and it had the least effective defense since 1924-25. Despite that, the team still finished 12-8.

Ray DeCook and Bill Newbold were the returning regulars. DeCook's 131 points were the most by any Irishman since John Nyikos, and Newbold was second with 93. But beyond that, scoring was minimal. Both were juniors, as were Norb Crowe and Tom Burns, two more starters in 1930-31. Joining them were Gavin and sophomore John Baldwin, and Al Schumaker and Clay Johnson served as seventh and eighth men. It was a young and fairly inexperienced squad; this showed in the one "patsy" game before the "regular" schedule, as the Keoganites won over Kalamazoo by only 26-15. This season was obviously going to be different.

Actually, the first five losses of the season (as compared to 10 wins in the span) were to superior teams. Keogan, however, could not have been pleased with the non-performance of the defense in the home game against Northwestern. The Wildcats, who won their only Western Conference title ever and were also named Helms Foundation national champions with a 16-1 record, their most wins in a season until 1982-83, outpointed ND, 44-29, in the worst defensive performance by an Irish basketball squad since the 1921-22 season.

The coach was no happier against another first-division Big Ten team, Purdue, as the Irish lost, 34-22. This was the first Irish-Boilermaker clash of the Keogan era, and it became by far the stormiest athletic relationship of the era. Keogan and Purdue coach Ward Lambert respected each other but eventually got to the point where they couldn't be in the same gym at the same time. Neither one was particularly passive on the bench during a game, and in later tilts between the two schools the coaches often yelled more at each other than at their respective teams. In this ND-PU contest, the star was South Bend product John Wooden, a junior who became a three-time All-American and the only man so far named to the Hall of Fame as both a player and a coach. For three years he tore apart the competition as Purdue's top man; Notre Dame was no more successful at stopping him than anyone else, even with a specially-designed defense.

During the season, the Irish defeated some good teams — and some bad — but didn't really blow anybody out. For example, they could muster no more than a 10-point decision over Wabash in Crawfordsville; and in the Giants' visit to ND, the Irish won by only one as the teams played each other twice in a season for the last time. The widest victory margin of the year was achieved over Penn in the Quakers' first visit to the Fieldhouse. The two teams played home-and-home in 1930-31, and in the return match at the Palestra, ND only escaped by one point. Other Irish wins came against Illinois Wesleyan (24-17) and Indiana (25-20) at the opposition's court, and in the friendly confines, Ohio State (27-24), Marquette (30-23), and Butler (27-19). But they lost a little more often than usual, and all were interesting — and close — games which could have resulted in Irish victories in other years.

In the Northwestern rematch at Evanston — this time on January 3 — Notre Dame vastly improved its defense, but the offense couldn't come through. The Irish surrendered but 20 points, but the Wildcats, only 17.

Two better games were the home-and-home series with Pitt. This time, the games could not get much closer, *both* going into overtime. But ND could not hold the Panthers back in the extra period. There is what may be an apocryphal tale which Pitt coach Doc Carlson liked to tell about the first of these games, which was played at the ND fieldhouse. In these days, the official time was kept at the scorer's desk, and when a half was over, the timer let everyone know by firing a starter's gun. As it happened, Pittsburgh was ahead by two points with time running out, and Notre Dame was frantically working for a good shot. The timer raised the gun and prepared to pull the trigger. Just at that moment, a little old lady tapped him on the shoulder and admonished him to wait. By the time the timer had fought off the distraction and fired the gun, the crowd had erupted in glee as the Irish had scored the tying basket! Pitt did go on to win the OT, and the game, 28-20, but this incident illustrates that even when everyone except the lucky few was playing in fairly small, close gyms, there was somewhat more of a home-court advantage at Notre Dame. Nothing quite so bizarre happened at Pitt, except that ND had its top offensive output of the season (32), aided by Crowe's 12 points. However, the Panthers scored 35 to win another OT thriller.

After the February 21 Butler game, the last home tilt of the year, the Irish played five straight road contests and went only 2-3. Both wins were by identical scores—26-25 over first-time hoops opponent Army at West Point and Marquette. The three losses were the third overtime setback of the season, 28-23 to Syracuse; 20-15 to Butler as the Irish went 3-for-13 from the line; and a season-ending 23-17 loss to Iowa as Joe Gavin closed his collegiate career with a team-leading six points.

Despite the 12-8 record, Keogan was not too worried. Not only were nearly all the regulars returning in 1931-32, but he had an outstanding crop of freshmen moving up, including the man who would become one of the great players in Notre Dame basketball history.

# 8

# A Man Called Moose

It could be very easy to say that the 1931-34 period in ND basketball history was dominated by one man, but that would be oversimplification. Many other men contributed to the overall 54-12 record in those three years. But certainly Edward "Moose" Krause was a big reason for the resurgence of the Irish offense from its late-1920s doldrums.

He had been a schoolboy star at De La Salle High School in Chicago before coming to Notre Dame, and he continued to excel in college. During his three years at ND, he became the most prolific scorer since the days of dirt floors, 40-game schedules, and Justin Moloney. Also, in 1932-33 he became the first ND player since the days of free-throw specialists to average more than 10 points a game. He became so dominant that the three-second rule was concocted to stop him and others of his ilk. In addition to his basketball exploits—which were to lead him to his selection to the Hall of Fame—Krause also monogrammed three times in football and once in track, and played a year of baseball as well; he was so popular among his fellow students that they voted him a trophy, the only ND student ever so honored.

But one player does not a team make, and this was certainly the case during Krause's years on the ND varsity. He had ample help from quality teammates who could take over the scoring if a team guarded Moose a little too closely. And of course, since games cannot be won if the other team scores more points, the defense played an important role in Notre Dame's .818 percentage during the Krause years.

In his sophomore year there was a stellar supporting cast, featuring most of the 1930-31 starting lineup. Captain Norb Crowe, Bill Newbold, and Ray DeCook were the team's next three scorers after Krause, and Tom Burns played a tough guard. All were seniors, and the first three were third-year starters. Added to them were two more sophomores who entered with Moose: Leo Crowe—the 1931-32 season was the only time two Crowes played major roles on the same team, though not the only time two played on the same ND team—and Joe Voegele, who alternated with Krause at center until Keogan moved him to forward. Finally, there was John Baldwin, the only junior of note on this squad, who missed the second half of the season with pneumonia. This team, after a shaky start, put together one of those long winning streaks typical of Keogan-coached teams, finished 18-2, and were considered the best or near-best team in the nation by many sports authorities.

Things were pretty much as usual in the early-season warm-up games. Kalamazoo (37-7) and Adrian (37-13) were the patsies, and four different men were the top two scorers. In the Kazoo game, DeCook had 10 and Baldwin had eight; against Adrian, Newbold had 10 and Voegele had eight.

Notice that the name Krause did not appear on this list. Because of football season, he had not seen much work with the basketballers at that point. Even when he did get into the early games, he was ineffective as a scorer: in his first three games, he scored three field goals and three foul goals and ended up watching the next two games from the best seat in the house.

The older center, Ray DeCook, was seeing most of the action at the pivot at this time, but even three years of game experience couldn't help the Irish defeat Indiana or Purdue as ND's record fell to 2-2. In the Hoosier game, Tom Burns had a rough day, fouling out without scoring, and neither DeCook nor Krause could muster any offense as IU won, 23-18. And in Purdue's first visit to the Fieldhouse, John Wooden again ran roughshod over ND (and Burns fould out again) as the Boilermakers won, 32-24. (Purdue was to finish the season 16-1.)

But from this point on, there was no stopping the Irish in 1931-32.

While Krause continued to watch from the bench, his team-mates led Notre Dame to the 300th win in its basketball history with a 32-25 decision over Northwestern to close a five-game home stand. Ten days after that December 21 game, the Irish went to Evanston to take on the Wildcats again. In front of a festive New Year's Eve crowd, ND spoiled the evening for NU, 22-21. Moose finally got a chance to show his stuff; he came off the bench to score 12 of the Irish tallies to lead ND to victory.

A sparse home crowd saw ND defeat St. Thomas, 34-19, and an upset attempt by Michigan State was thwarted, 28-25, in East Lansing. Then the Hilltoppers of Marquette invaded the Fieldhouse, and for the first time the home crowd got to see the real Moose Krause in action. Before fouling out late in the game, long after the outcome of the game was in question, he scored seven field goals—as many as he had scored all season before that—and three free throws for 17 points in Notre Dame's top scoring output of the season, 43, to Marquette's 31, one of the only three teams to score more than 30 points against the Irish in this successful season.

One of those three was *not* Pennsylvania. In Notre Dame's annual trip to the Palestra, Krause fouled out again—this time with only four points—but Norb Crowe had eight and Baldwin six in his last game of the season as the Irish won, 32-25. Then there was a week off until the long-awaited home match against Pitt.

The Irish had lost four straight games to Doc Carlson's Panthers, and there was revenge on the students' minds. As many as could pack into the Fieldhouse were there, and as many townspeople as could get tickets were there too. This time they did not leave disappointed. Keogan used only six men to defeat Pittsburgh, 25-12.

After the exam period, the Keoganites coasted past Iowa in preparation for the return game against Pitt. The game in Panther country was very rough and eventually turned into a free-throw shooting contest. The Irish were held to six baskets, but, spearheaded by Krause's 8-for-10 at the charity stripe, continued the win streak with a 26-19 decision.

Syracuse went down by eight in the Orangemen's first trip to Notre Dame. Next it was a trip to Cleveland to face Western Reserve, a first-time opponent; Krause scored 13 and Voegele added nine to pace ND's 32-25 victory. And traveling to Indianapolis, Voegele scored 15 to carry the Irish over Butler, 37-32.

By now Krause had firmly established himself as not only the Irish starting center, but as one of the premier pivotmen in at least the Midwest. In the last four games he continued to impress as he led the Irish in scoring in all four. He shared the honors with Voegele as ND defeated Michigan State for the second time; in the last road game of the season he tallied eight to lead Notre Dame over Marquette for the second time. But it was the final two home games in which Moose was at his most imposing. Army came into the Fieldhouse in the return game for the 1930-31 Irish trip to West Point, and little short of a Sherman tank was going to stop Ed. Nineteen points on seven field goals and 5-for-9 from the line—his best performance to date—led ND to a 41-23 victory (compared to a one-point ND victory one year earlier). And in the return match against Butler, won by ND, 28-23, Krause scored 10 on three field goals and 4-for-4 from the line.

Notre Dame's win streak was 16, and it was because of the emergence of Krause as a major offensive force and the solidification of a senior-sophomore lineup which continued to play tough defense while scoring more points than any prior Keogan-coached ND team. Krause's contribution to the Irish surge was recognized by several All-American selection committees, making him the first ND sophomore to receive such honors.

A strong nucleus returned for the 1932-33 campaign, but a lot was lost as well, and Keogan didn't have a really spectacular sophomore class to replace the graduates. Back for more were Krause and Voegele, along with Leo Crowe and captain (and lone significant senior) John Baldwin. Through the season, Keogan went for the most part with six men; added to the returnees were Eddie Alberts, a junior who had seen very little action as a sophomore, and sophomore John Jordan, who landed a starting berth.

The best way to view this season is to split it at the January exam break time. Before finals, the Irish were 6-6 and just an average Midwestern squad. Afterwards, ND closed 10-0, including three defeats of teams lost to earlier, for a respectable 16-6 final record.

The season began with three wins to stretch ND's victory

skein to 19, tying Keogan's best with the Irish so far. Notre Dame defeated Albion, 41-20, without Krause, who was still with the football team as it took on Southern Cal on the West Coast. So Joe Voegele took over the pivot and scored 20 points, the top performance for any ND player in 1932-33. Illinois Wesleyan went down next, and then Northwestern, as Moose scored 11 in a 28-25 win.

Then Notre Dame backers had to suffer through the longest losing streak in eight years. Four times ND took the court against some rough competition, and four times the Irish ended up on the short end. Purdue (36-31), Ohio State (30-24), and Northwestern on New Year's Eve (33-29) defeated the Irish on each school's respective home court, and Marquette pulled out an overtime victory in the ND Fieldhouse, 35-32, as both Krause and Voegele fouled out.

The losing streak finally ended with a 36-19 victory over Michigan State. But Tony Hinkle's Butler team ended the new Irish win streak with a 27-25 decision; Krause hit only one of 11 field goal attempts and Voegele only two of 12 to "aid" in this one. Another win streak began with a 30-22 win over Minnesota, and it was halted just as quickly by another tough Doc Carlson-coached Pittsburgh squad. Even though Krause and John Baldwin canned 12 points each, the defense faltered as ND lost, 39-35. That was to be Notre Dame's last basketball loss in 364 days.

As the Irish closed strong for the second straight year, the offense averaged 37.6 points per game in an 11-game, end-of-season streak while Moose Krause and Joe Voegele fought it out for the team scoring honors; Krause finished with 213, Voegele with 198. It began right before the exam break when a frustrated Irish team took out its loss to Pitt on the way home, destroying Toledo, 42-14.

After the break, the season was all Notre Dame—but there were some close calls, beginning with an unexpectedly close tussle with Carnegie Tech, which the Irish won 37-35 thanks to Krause's 17 points. A surprise offensive source emerged at the University of Chicago (the last Western Conference team to have never played Notre Dame); John Jordan scored 17 to lead the 37-26 ND win. And then it was time for Pitt again. This time, in front of the home crowd, the Irish got their revenge by a 38-31 count.

A trip east yielded two more wins: the annual defeat of Penn at the Palestra, and an unexpectedly close battle with Western Reserve in Cleveland, 40-35. Three different Irishmen (Krause, Voegele, and Baldwin) scored in double figures in the latter game, which helped to counteract foul trouble. And, returning home, the Irish knocked off Michigan State for the second time, 30-25.

It looked as if the Irish win skein was going to come to an end in Indianapolis. Butler had already defeated ND once—at the Fieldhouse—in 1932-33, and with time running out, the Bulldogs held a two-point lead in this one. And it looked even better after Notre Dame missed a shot with less than a minute left which would have tied it, and in the scramble for the rebound, Moose Krause had been knocked down. Yet somehow he ended up with the ball and, while still on his back, heaved the ball up—and it went through the net just as regulation time ran out. But it took a tip-in by seldom-used Jim Newbold, the third of three Newbold brothers to play for Keogan, to win it for the Irish in overtime, 42-41. It was Jim's only basket of the season. In his post-game talk to the squad, Coach Keogan used Krause and his miracle shot as an example of the kind of basketball he liked to see. The next day, back at Notre Dame, Keogan was only mildly amused to walk into practice to the sight of his players practicing shooting baskets while lying on their backs!

The rest of the season was almost anticlimactic. The Irish closed out the home slate with an easy victory over Wabash, and then eked out a couple of road wins. The first, over Marquette in Milwaukee, avenged an earlier loss as Krause, Voegele, and Baldwin all hit double figures in a 36-34 win. And Minnesota went down for the second time, 31-27.

Certainly the Irish had become the nation's elite team by the end of the 1932-33 season, but because of the slow start, they were ignored by most when it was time to decide who the best team was. But Moose Krause wasn't—for the second straight year he garnered All-America mention. And he still had one more year left.

Four starters returned from the streaking Irish for 1933-34. Krause (now team captain), Voegele, Leo Crowe, and John Jordan were back. Three top sophomores aided in the cause: guard George Ireland and forwards Marty Peters and John Ford. Just as two years earlier, Keogan had essentially a senior-sophomore starting lineup. And just as two years earlier, Notre Dame had a fine season. For the first time under Keogan, and for only the second time ever, the Irish won 20 games. Only four losses were rung up; two were to teams ND had also defeated in 1933-34, and the other two were to an old nemesis.

First, Notre Dame got off to the best start in its history so far. Five straight home wins increased ND's win streak to 16. Included in this were two biggies: a 28-24 win over Northwestern which featured balanced Irish scoring, and Notre Dame's first win over Purdue since the two schools began playing in the cage sport in 1916, 39-28.

Three relatively easy wins followed to tie Keogan's all-time win streak: over Bradley at Peoria, Illinois, 34-27; the return trip to Northwestern, 37-21 (Krause had 13); and a win at the Fieldhouse over a traveling Arizona team, 46-24, as Keogan used 13 men in the romp.

Win number 20 was most difficult. At East Lansing, the Michigan State team gave the Keoganites all they could handle. Voegele fouled out with but four points, and three other ND men had three fouls, one short of disqualification, at the end of the game. As it turned out, Krause's 11 points and Crowe's 10 were what carried the Irish to victory in a nail-biting, three-overtime thriller, 34-33. Notre Dame did not play such a long game again until 1959.

Another tough one followed, as a strong Marquette team which eventually finished 15-4 came to take on the undefeated Irish. And Moose Krause again proved the difference; his 11 tallies led ND to its 10th win of the season by a 30-28 margin. Four days later, Butler proved a surprisingly easy opponent as the Irish won number 22 in a row, 37-17, to tie the Notre Dame win streak record. All they had to do was beat Pittsburgh in Pittsburgh to set a new standard.

All they had to do . . . A fired-up ND squad led the Panthers at halftime, and expanded the lead to 27-16 as the second half drew toward the 10-minute mark. But, of course, there are 40 minutes in a game, and in the last half of the last half the Irish defense must have been in Forbes Field. Pitt put on a furious 23-7 spurt as both Voegele and Crowe fouled out, ending the ND win streak and also handing the Irish their first loss of the season, 39-34, almost a year to the day that Notre Dame had last lost—in this same arena to the same school by an almost-identical score (39-35 one year earlier).

Well, when one winning streak ends, what now but—of course—start a new one! This the Irish did, as Leo Crowe (11 points) and Marty Peters (10 points) led ND to a 37-26 win over Chicago just before finals.

After exams, Notre Dame extended the new win streak to six and the season record to 17-1. Except for the first one, the five second-semester openers were fairly easy. A scrappy Valparaiso squad—probably the second-best team in Indiana in 1933-34—gave the former Valpo coach Keogan all he could handle. The Indiana school held Krause to two points—his lowest point total of the season thus far—but other Irishmen compensated in a 27-25 win. An easy victory at Detroit (36-17) followed, and then came an awe-inspiring, one-man show on February 6 in the Fieldhouse.

Minnesota was the guest, and the showman was the amazing Edward "Moose" Krause. In front of an enthusiastic crowd, he scored 10 field goals and went 2-for-5 from the free throw line for 22 points, the most by an Irish player since Clem Crowe scored a like number of points against Adrian a decade earlier. The home team won, 43-34, but Moose was the story of the day. Ironically, the next coaching opponent for Keogan was none other than Clem Crowe, who was leading Xavier; the Irish beat the Cincinnati school, 25-15. And in the annual trip to Philadelphia, this time against Temple, ND won by 42-33. Anticipation of the next game, the Pitt rematch, began to grow.

In front of as many students and townspeople as could be crammed into the local gym, Notre Dame played a tough defensive game, holding the vaunted Panthers to but 21 points while at the same time no Irishman garnered more than two personal fouls. But the Irish shooting was cold—Krause had only two points, the team's collective foul shooting was 7-of-13—and they could only manage 17, the lowest output since the no-offense days of 1930-31. Notre Dame had its second loss—and both were to the same team.

The Irish had three more relatively easy wins to increase the record to 20-2. Keogan gave walking-wounded Jordan and

Voegele a rest against Michigan State and let the others carry the team to a 28-19 win. A 34-24 win at Butler was next, and then Krause, Crowe, Voegele, and Jim Newbold played their final home games to a thunderous ovation. The seniors went out in style; Moose tallied 10 and Joe added 12 as the Irish defeated Ohio State.

But there were still two road games left, and ND lost both — by a total of three points. Krause, who had scored 11 against Marquette earlier in the year, found himself unable to operate against a Hilltopper double-team in the rematch. Usually, when a defense used this tactic, the guards and forwards would pick up the scoring slack, but except for Joe Voegele, the offense was cold. Moose fouled out for the only time all year and had only two points, and Marquette closed its 15-4 season with a 21-20 victory. And Minnesota, against whom Krause had his 22-point game earlier, let Moose score as often as he could. He tallied 14 in his last collegiate game, Leo Crowe hit 11, and defensive stalwart George Ireland fouled out as the Irish fell in overtime, 43-41.

Those two losses cost Notre Dame another national championship. But *two* regulars received All-America mention—Moose Krause for the third year in a row, and George Ireland, the sophomore guard who had helped keep opponents in check.

The Irish would need all the defense they could get in 1934-35, as most of the scoring punch was gone. This season was another "interrregnum" between great classes, Keogan knowing he had a tremendous freshman team for 1935-36 varsity play, and he tried to make the best of it by trying to re-emphasize the defensive. He had some success, but the offensive spark was missing, and the 1934-35 Irish lost an awful lot of close games, ending up 13-9.

Some of the close losses were: 26-25 to Northwestern at home; 30-28 at Minnesota, as two Irishmen fouled out late in the game; 27-26 at Illinois; 26-22 at Pittsburgh; and 27-25 to Pittsburgh at home. (This game was noteworthy for another reason to be explained later.) But one of the not-so-close games was much more significant, because it marked the beginning of college basketball's move to the Big Time.

Way back in 1930-31, Notre Dame and Army played each other in basketball at West Point. Originally, the officials at both schools wanted to play the game in the huge indoor arena in New York City known as Madison Square Garden. But Garden officials were skeptical of basketball's drawing power at the time, so they nixed the idea. Enter a newspaperman named, appropriately, Ned Irish, who, after fighting crowds to get a seat at city games in old armories, thought that collegiate hoops *would* draw in the Garden. He managed to arrange some benefit doubleheaders between New York area schools to aid victims of the Great Depression. As many as 19,000 people attended these extravaganzas, and so Irish thought about inviting some good outside teams and setting up a regular slate of these doubleheaders. The first of these was on December 28, 1934. Game One featured Westminster (PA) vs. St. John's; the nightcap and main attraction, Notre Dame vs. New York University (NYU). The night was financially (if not athletically) a rousing success as a full house witnessed the twin bill. Doubleheader fever began to spread, first to Philadelphia, then all over the country; the intersectional rivalries which these fostered helped to end certain regional variations in the sport which still existed in the 1930s. But the MSG bills were the classics; New York became known as the Mecca of college basketball, and remained so until the early 1950s. And it all started with a 25-18 defeat of Notre Dame by an undefeated NYU squad.

A couple of Irish wins this season were significant. One was a 29-19 defeat of Stanford—a game everyone would have liked to have seen had it taken place two years later because of events transpiring at both schools. Notre Dame's first trip to Boston, after the loss at the Garden, was a 45-19 slaughter of Holy Cross, in which Marty Peters tallied 17 points; HC cancelled its basketball program for several years after the 1934-35 season thanks to too many games like this. Other noteworthy wins were two over Butler, and one each over Northwestern, Marquette, and Minnesota. But somehow it is the losses which stick out in the 1934-35 season.

On January 31, Keogan had to stay behind because of illness, so assistant football coaches Joe Boland and Tom Conley accompanied the team on a one-game road trip to Ohio State. It is likely that team captain John Jordan did much of the actual coaching; even so, the Irish fell to the Buckeyes, 31-22.

Then there was a game at Philadelphia's Convention Hall, part of a doubleheader; the Irish lost to Temple in ND's first loss ever in Philly, 34-26.

But oddest of all was the aforementioned 27-25 loss to Pittsburgh at the Fieldhouse. This game was another example of "Notre Dame time," which had played a role in a 1930-31 ND-Pitt game. But this time, time stood still. Official time was kept by a timekeeper at the scorer's desk, and as the second half began to get interesting, referee Frank Lane asked the ND manager who was in charge of the official watch how much was left, and he replied, "Twelve and a half minutes." About 10 or 12 minutes later, Lane asked again, because he felt the game was nearing its end. The timer looked at his stopwatch and saw that it hadn't moved an inch. It still said 12½ minutes left. No one was sure how much time had really expired since the last time out, so after much discussion, Lane felt the only fair thing to do was to restart the watch as if 12½ minutes were still left. In that time, the trailing Panthers managed to come from behind and win the game, the low point of what was one of Keogan's roughest seasons as Irish head man. After the game, Keogan made sure that he would never be vexed by that stopwatch again; he took it from his manager and furiously slammed it against a wall in the Fieldhouse, effectively rendering that timepiece defunct.

Even though the team was not up to the standards of the recent past, there was still enough action to keep Irish fans interested. Probably the most excitement was generated by the duel for the season scoring honors between senior Joe O'Kane, who because of illness and injury had seen little action his first two years, and junior Marty Peters. Although O'Kane closed fast, Peters hung on to win, 137-134—a far cry from the one-two punch of Krause and Voegele. But with an amazing group of newcomers from the Class of '38 coming in, even the Krause-Voegele totals would look small.

# 9

## 62 Wins, 8 Losses – and 1 Tie

The title says it all. During 1935-38, Notre Dame enjoyed its finest three consecutive basketball seasons ever (except 1925-28). Three straight years the Irish won 20 or more games, a feat unmatched at ND for almost 35 years. Three straight years someone came away impressed enough to declare the team national champions. Three straight years two Irishmen were acclaimed as All-Americans, an unprecedented and unduplicated feat. Yet, for the most part, Notre Dame's success in this period tends to be overshadowed in basketball histories by a trendsetter from the West Coast.

See, this was also the era of Hank Luisetti, who set the basketball world on fire with his rediscovery of the one-handed set shot and the resulting New York media superstardom. It's not that he did not deserve the acclaim, because he was a high scorer and his Stanford team was a legitimate mythical national championship contender his junior and senior years. What has happened is that Notre Dame's fine teams of the era have been forgotten or glanced over as a result.

But there was no doubt in 1935-36 as to who was on top. Nearly everybody considered the Irish the best team in the nation. They defeated almost all the good teams they faced and destroyed the not-as-good while allowing 26 men to play at least once. And Keogan did it with another of those senior-sophomore teams which had been so great in 1931-32 and 1933-34.

Once the patsies were pasted, Keogan settled on a 10-man lineup (reduced to eight in the second half of the season because of nagging injuries). Five who saw some action in 1934-35 – all seniors – and who performed regularly in 1935-36 were Keogan's co-captains Marty Peters and John Ford, guard and two-time All-American George Ireland, Frank Wade, and John Hopkins. Added to that quintet was a great fivesome of sophomores unmatched at ND until 1968-69. Tom Jordan, younger brother of John, saw the least action of the five. The other four were Ray Meyer, a splendid two-handed set shot artist; Tom Wukovits, a South Bend product who eventually became a starting guard; Paul Nowak, a 6-6 center, another local boy and the tallest player Keogan ever used regularly; and the biggest surprise of all, a forward from Buffalo named John Moir, who had never played organized basketball before entering Notre Dame! This was a very talented squad with the luxury of great depth, and they generally rolled over all comers, to the tune of 22 wins, two losses, and one tie.

The first five games were incredible displays of awesome offense and tenacious defense against outmanned opponents. Four of them were even more amazing because they were parts of two doubleheaders. The one that was a single game, a 62-26 rout of Albion, featured 20 men in action. In Game One of the December 4 doubleheader, Keogan used 10 second- and third-teamers to defeat Moose Krause's St. Mary's (Winona, MN) team, 45-22. Using his big guns in Game Two, Keogan and his charges ambushed Kalamazoo, 65-17. Thirteen men saw action in that "contest," and no one played in both. Three days later, the Irish played another doubleheader and again had no problem (Moir scored 21 as Millikin went down, 58-30, and Keogan again used 20 men as ND utterly decimated St. Joseph's of Indiana, 71-22).

Those two games merit extra attention because of the site of the twin bill. For the last time, Notre Dame played within the city limits of South Bend. In the early twenties, the Irish played many of its home games in the South Bend YMCA before the Fieldhouse had a standard floor. In this case (December 7, 1935) the basketball court had been taken up to make arrangements for a visit from President Franklin D. Roosevelt. The two games, therefore, were moved to the Studebaker Athletic Association gym in downtown South Bend. Obviously, the site had little effect on ND's performance.

Taking to the road for the first time, ND defeated Washington University of St. Louis, and then returned home to beat

Northwestern, 40-29. Even though the prodigious scoring pace of earlier was not maintained, there was still plenty of offensive firepower; Moir scored nine points in each game, and Nowak and Meyer also contributed substantially to the point totals. But something rare for the season happened next – Notre Dame lost. And something rare at any time followed – a tie.

In another of the classic George Keogan vs. Ward Lambert shouting matches, Purdue defeated the Irish 54-40. Both Moir and Nowak were disqualified on fouls after each had contributed eight points to the losing cause. Twenty-one fouls were assessed on the Irish in all – a very high figure for the day – and neither coach was particularly satisfied with the officiating.

Much more unusual was the New Year's Eve game with Northwestern at Evanston. The Irish had already defeated the Wildcats once in 1935-36 and were looking to sweep the series. But they didn't expect the tough time they had. Notre Dame was down, 20-14, with less than 10 minutes left, and had apparently fallen one point short of catching up as the teams retreated to the locker room at the presumed end of the game.

Both the ND and NU scorekeepers at the scorer's desk, as well as the gym scoreboard, said Northwestern 20, Notre Dame 19. But there was, immediately after the game, a flurry of activity on press row. All the sportswriters had on their scorecards Northwestern 20, Notre Dame 20. (And despite the scoreboard tally, most of the fans had remained, expecting an overtime.) What had happened was that Ray Meyer had made a foul shot near the end of the game that the scorers had neglected to record. By the time the courtside controversy had been settled in ND's favor, both teams had been showering; there was no way to get them back on the court to finish the game. After Northwestern officials conceded the tie, the two schools tried to set up a date to finish the game, but no mutually agreeable date could be found. So the game went into the books as a 20-20 tie – an extremely rare, but not unique, occurrence.

The 1936 part of the season, by comparison, was almost routine. The Irish went 15-1 the rest of the way, losing only to an inspired Ohio State team in the Fieldhouse finale, 28-23, as John Moir had a season-low three points. In the process, for the first time ND became a "point-a-minute" team, averaging 42.1

points a game, and at the same time giving up only 27.1 each game for a scoring margin of 15.0, an utterly phenomenal differential in those relatively low-scoring days.

While ND was rolling up the victories, John Moir, the man who never played before entering college, was rolling up the points. He was difficult to stop, and few teams were successful at it—and even if they were, there was always Paul Nowak or John Ford or someone else to pick up the slack. His most impressive moment was his single-game 25 points against, of all teams, Pittsburgh at the Fieldhouse in a 43-27 rout. But he also had games of 18, 17, 16, and 14 points in the Irish stretch drive. Not only was Moir named a Helms Foundation All-American, but he was also selected by that organization as 1936's College Player of the Year—outstanding achievements for *any* sophomore, even more so for a newcomer to the sport.

Paul Nowak was also an All-American his sophomore year. On center jumps, he consistently got the ball to his waiting teammates thanks to his height advantage. And while he didn't score nearly as much as Moir, he was always a threat to do so. He scored 16 points to aid in a 43-35 defeat of Pittsburgh at Pitt, and several other times he cracked into double figures.

But it took more than two individuals to hold opponents to low scores. During the season, the *team* defeated Minnesota twice, Pitt twice, Marquette twice (a rare feat for ND), Butler twice, Penn at the Palestra, Syracuse in that city, Detroit in Motown, Illinois, and St. Benedict's, few of the games were close. Two other wins stick out above the others, though. One was a 38-27 defeat of NYU as Notre Dame began to make Madison Square Garden an annual stop. A year had passed since ND's first visit to MSG, and Keogan was now wiser of the ways of Eastern referees, who traditionally allow much less than Midwest officials. Notre Dame's team totals of 12 field goals and 14 foul shots—the latter taking advantage of what was at the time an Eastern rules aberration known as the blocking foul—certainly bear this out. The other was the commencement of the soon-to-be-controversial series with Kentucky. They had played once in 1929, but that was a one-shot deal. This was different; two coaching legends, Keogan and fifth-year UK mentor and mutual friend Adolph Rupp, arranged the series as a once-a-year, home-and-home (with "home" on the Wildcat side to be Louisville rather than Lexington because at the time the UK campus did not have a facility large enough to accommodate the anticipated throngs for such a game, even in comparison to the ND Fieldhouse). Keogan defeated Rupp at ND the first time with help from Moir's 17 points, 41-20. It would be some time until Rupp would win a game in this series.

Keogan didn't quite have the depth of his 22-2-1 team coming back. He did have his five returnees—Moir, Meyer, Nowak, Jordan, and Wukovits, all juniors—and two sophomores who entered the lineup: Eddie Sadowski and football star Earl Brown. This was still a young team—Keogan had a junior captain in Ray Meyer, who remained healthy the entire season for the only time as a collegian—but there was so much talent that the Irish still finished 20-3—and avenged all three losses later in the season.

Three wins over the usual early-season competition were a little closer than the abject blowouts from the 1935-36 season—41-27 over Kalamazoo, 39-27 over St. Mary's of Minnesota (Moose Krause returns again), and 37-22 over first-time foe Western State Normal of Illinois (now Western Illinois). Moir started out fast—in his first two games he had 17 and 13 points—but did not play against Western because of injury. Ray Meyer led the way in that contest with 11.

The "real" season did not start encouragingly. A good, but not great, Northwestern team entered the ND home gym and handed the Irish the incredibly lopsided defeat of 38-19, the worst defeat of the Irish at home since 1929. And things didn't get much better as ND traveled to Champaign and lost to Illinois, 44-29. Moir was still recovering from his injury, and it hampered his performance; he had five against NU and four against the Illini, and as the Irish turned the tables on Northwestern on December 31 by winning, 24-23, John still had only four. Fortunately, Eddie Sadowski had 10 to lead ND to the turnaround.

However, from the turn of the year to the end of the season—17 games—Moir went wild by the day's standards. In 15 of the 17 games he broke double figures and led the offense in Notre Dame's 16-1 record in that period. His high point came against Syracuse at ND. In a 52-31 rout of the Orangemen—an uncharacteristically lopsided score for this series—Moir had 10 field goals and 4-of-5 from the line for 24 points. He scored 21 points against Canisius in Buffalo, NY, as Notre Dame arranged a ballgame in his hometown (a tradition which continues to this day). And in the two games he didn't hit double digits? One was an eight-point performance against Pitt in one of the lower-scoring games of the season, a 29-18 win. (This had avenged the only loss of the 1937 portion of the slate, a hard-fought loss at the Panthers' gym, 34-31.) In the other, Moir scored nine points but deferred to reserves in the second half as ND mopped up on Butler in Indianapolis (after the two had played close at ND, the Irish eking out a 25-24 triumph) by a 42-17 count.

Big wins started to become the rule as the season wore on. The Irish defeated Adolph Rupp and Kentucky, 41-28, in front of a surprisingly small crowd at the Louisville Armory. Neither team was entirely comfortable there, for neither had had a chance to practice on the court, but the Moir and Nowak Show made life even more uncomfortable for the 'Cats, tallying 12 and 16 points, respectively. And after that loss to Pittsburgh, double-digit blowouts became the norm—by 32 over Western Reserve, 26 over NYU at the Garden, 17 at home vs. Marquette, 26 at home with Minnesota, and 18 at Detroit in addition to the previously-spotlighted Syracuse and Butler games. The most interesting games, however, were back-to-back home clashes with Purdue and Illinois.

The February 3 Boilermaker clash brought the long-running feud between Keogan and Piggy Lambert to a head. After PU had fallen to the Irish, 47-40 (aided by Moir's 15 points and Nowak's 13), in front of an even more raucous home crowd than usual, the two coaches ended the series amidst much animosity. It was definitely a mutual contempt, as opposed to the Adolph Rupp problem in the 1940s.

Three days after that, Illinois came into the "snakepit" in hopes of sweeping the season series. (The Illini had won the first, as discussed earlier.) But this time the Irish, with a healthy John Moir (he was still healing in the first meeting), were not to be denied. Moir had 19 points to lead ND's revenge, 41-33.

Despite the 20-3 record, the emergence of Stanford and Hank Luisetti as a national force overshadowed the Irish. Though both Moir and Nowak were both named All-Americans for the second straight year, the one-handed shot of Luisetti took the nation by storm, and the Helms Foundation considered the Indians the top team of 1936-37 and Hank as player of the year.

For 1937-38, two events took place which revolutionized college basketball and basically hallmark the "modern era" of the sport. First was the organization of the first sustaining all-collegiate post-season basketball tournament. This "national invitational tournament," organized by the Metropolitan Basketball Writers Association of New York, was to consist of six teams – the three best New York-area schools against the three of the best from the rest of the nation. It was a smashing success, so much so that the MBWA turned over the operation of the NIT to the Madison Square Garden authorities and the NCAA started its own copycat tournament the next year.

And second was the abolition of the center jump after each basket; instead, the team which was scored against received the ball out of bounds behind the opponent's basket. Keogan was an outspoken opponent of the no-jump rule until the day he died, and he lobbied to have the rule reverted. He felt that by awarding the ball to the opponent after a basket, the offensive team was unfairly penalized for scoring. Although an innovator, Keogan also felt strongly about the status quo: he was also an opponent of the 10-second backcourt penalty (he felt it made basketball into a half-court game) and, though he originally supported it, the three-second lane violation. It was natural he would feel this way, as he was one of the coaches whose exploitation of the existing rules (backcourt stall, Moose Krause, Paul Nowak) led to the rules changes.

Center jump or no, in the end there was no difference in Notre Dame's record in 1937-38. For the second straight year, the Irish finished 20-3. The three losses were to the Western Conference champ (Minnesota), a next-to-impossible team to defeat in its home gym (Marquette), and an overtime loss on the road (Illinois and future baseball Hall of Famer Lou Boudreau). At the end of the year, the Irish were again considered one of the best three teams in the country, along with Stanford (again) and NIT champion Temple.

Again ND had a deep team; no regular was gone from the 1936-37 squad, although Ray Meyer – captain for the second

straight year, an honor not given to anyone solo since Ray
Scanlon in 1907-08 and 1908-09—was injured early in the season
and out of actin for almost six weeks. Again, Moir, Nowak,
Wukovits, and Jordan, seniors along with Meyer, saw much action, along with Sadowski and Brown. Add to these Mike Crowe,
a senior who had been a reserve for two years, and several
sophomores—Paul Ducharme, Rex Ellis, and Gene Klier the most
prominent—and one of the deepest teams in Notre Dame history
results. If one of the players wasn't performing to standards,
there was someone else of near-equal quality to spell him. And
Keogan was not afraid to bench any of his "stars" when he felt
he wasn't playing to capabilities. Nor was he averse to trying
some psychological ploys.

When the Irish faced Wisconsin in the first "real" game of
the year at the Fieldhouse, they trailed a mediocre team at halftime. Questioning his own motivational abilities, Keogan turned
the team over to injured captain Meyer at halftime, and Keogan
watched the rest of the game from the stands. ND rallied to win
the game, 33-31—it can be said that this was the beginning of
Meyer's successful coaching career. And after another sluggish
performance five days later against Northwestern (a 30-27 win
at home), well  . . . Keogan may have considered watching the
rest of the season from the stands.

The other 15 wins (after those above and three over patsies), however, were much more satisfying. All 15 were by 10
points or more; this included some big wins over tough teams
like Kentucky (Moir scored 20 in a 47-37 decision) and NYU (again
Moir led the way in a 50-38 win at the Garden). But the most
satisfying win may have been on February 5 against Pitt in the
home gym.

Because Pittsburgh was temporarily giving up big-time
athletics, it decided to discontinue athletic relations with ND after
1938, and this was to be the final game in Notre Dame's most
consistently interesting series of the past decade. Already ND
had beaten Pitt in the Steel City this season (51-41), but no one—
not Pitt, not the over 5,000 fans shoehorned into the Fieldhouse,
and perhaps not even the Irish themselves—was prepared for
what happened in the return match. They scored early and often,
and the Panthers couldn't buy a bucket. Keogan was able to use

12 players against a demoralized Pitt squad without losing anything. The final? Notre Dame 51, Pittsburgh 17 – in the eyes of many Irish fans, a fitting end to what at times had been a frustrating series for the home team.

Otherwise, things were pretty routine. The Illinois win over ND on December 28 ended another 19-game winning streak, and the loss to Minnesota was a case of Irish sluggishness to a better team. And a win at Canisius – another showcase for John Moir, who canned 19 in front of the hometown folks for a 57-33 win – ended a six-game road trip during the Christmas holidays similar to those the Irish now take.

With an 18-3 record and two games left against tough teams, the Irish had a chance for another "national championship." Marquette, a victor over ND earlier, had the tables turned on them in the seniors' farewell. Every healthy senior on the roster got into the game. John Moir scored 11, Paul Nowak 15 in their last home appearance – and the Irish won, 39-28. And Detroit, with a 16-3 record entering the game in the Motor City, fell to ND's hands in the last game as balanced scoring led the way.

Of course, as Notre Dame was considered the class of the Midwest, it was invited to the initial NIT. However, Notre Dame administration officials did not see fit to lift or modify the post-season competition ban in effect since the 1925 Rose Bowl. Stanford also declined a bid to the Garden extravaganza because of travel costs (the team already had made one long trek East in 1937-38). Therefore, the NIT did not have the two best teams in the country.

Even though no post-season play was permitted, the post-season honors came pouring in again. Moir and Nowak were named All-Americans for the third straight year – the first time contemporaries on the same team were so honored three consecutive seasons. And the two of them, along with Tom Wukovits, entered the new National Basketball League after graduation as a unit with the Akron Firestones and led the team to back-to-back championships in their first two seasons. But for the Irish and George Keogan, it was time to put these great years behind them and keep rolling on, as they always had under the tutelage of "The Doctor."

# 10

## "Off" Years

The next four seasons were trying times for George Keogan. It wasn't that his teams started losing; in fact, they continued to have fine seasons. Though the Irish basketball team was not under a microscope like the football team was, the pressure of nearly two decades without a losing season began to take its toll on the coach. By the end of his 19th season (1941-42), he was a sick man, under doctors' orders to restrict his coaching activity.

Before that turn of events, Keogan had expanded his involvement in college basketball beyond Notre Dame—for example, he was on the selection committee of the early NCAA post-season tournament. He was also able to maintain a winning program at Notre Dame as basketball's attraction as a spectator sport continued to grow.

Despite losing his all-star contingent from 1937-38, Keogan had much to work with in the new season. Seniors Eddie Sadowski, Paul Ducharme, and captain Earl Brown joined juniors Rex Ellis, Mark Ertel, and Gene Klier as returnees with experience. But it was a sophomore—Eddie Riska—who provided the scoring punch to (almost) replace John Moir and was the glue that helped construct another top-notch team in 1938-39. While not as outstanding at the last three seasons, the final 15-6 record was quite good.

As usual, the season began with overwhelming wins over underwhelming competition (64-13 over Kalamazoo and 70-30 over Ball State). Almost everyone except Earl Brown, who was still serving the football team as an All-American, got into the act; 14 different men scored at least once in either game. But, not quite as usual, the next four games—opening the "real" season—were not so overwhelming, as ND lost three of them. All three were close, and two were on the road—45-39 at Wisconsin and 43-39 at Northwestern on New Year's Eve, the latter a series which epitomized the saying, "You can throw the book out on this one." (The Irish had defeated the Wildcats, 48-30, at ND nine days earlier.) The other loss was to a school long absent from the Irish schedule, Michigan. Despite 19 points from Riska, ND lost a close one, 40-38.

The Irish had fallen to 3-3, but they then picked things up; they rattled off 10 straight wins after the Northwestern debacle.

Some of these wins were against suspect competition, and twice ND approached its record scoring output of 78 against the hapless Kalamazoo YMCA team in 1908. On a three-day road trip to Buffalo and Cleveland, Notre Dame defeated a Canisius team which won only one game all year, 72-36, as Rex Ellis scored 18, and then beat John Carroll, 74-37, with balanced scoring as many Irishmen had eight or nine points. But there were some big wins against very good teams as well.

One of Adoph Rupp's best pre-World War II Kentucky teams went up against the Irish in Louisville. And ND beat the Wildcats for the fourth straight year. The difference in the 42-37 victory over a UK team which lost only four times all season (and won 16) was the amazing accuracy of the Irish at the foul line: Notre Dame shot 22-for-24 from the charity stripe, phenomenal for the 1930s and a team record for years.

Also, the tremendous advantage ND enjoyed at home manifested itself against the Big Ten's two best teams, Minnesota and Illinois, as both fell to the Irish by wide margins. Keogan used 15 men in the Minnesota contest, which ended in a 55-33 win. Riska led the team with 13 points despite early relief. And in the Illinois game, Paul Ducharme led a 38-24 Irish win with his 10 points.

Finally, the win streak went to 10 with a thrilling win in Syracuse. Riska scored 11 as the Irish handed the Orangemen one of only four losses they suffered the entire season, in overtime, 35-34. But then along came Marquette.

For the first time in four years a team went 2-0 against Notre Dame. The Catholic school from Milwaukee pulled off the feat in back-to-back games a week apart. No Irishman scored more

than five points in a 47-22 *home* loss, ND's worst offensive showing since the 20-20 tie on December 31, 1935 and the worst defeat
for an Irish team since the Dark Ages. Then at Marquette, ND
fell, 58-50. The loss streak grew to three as Butler defeated the
Irish by eight at Indianapolis. It finally ended in the game which
usually marked the end of the season, against Detroit, 48-42.

There was still one more game; for the first time, NYU
traveled to Notre Dame to play in the Fieldhouse. The Violets
were having only a mildly successful year, and the Irish had
already beaten them in Madison Square Garden in 1938-39. But
the home team played with no less intensity; Paul Ducharme
ended his collegiate career with 11 points after tallying 17 against
Detroit and 10 against Butler. Notre Dame's hot hand led the
Irish to a 46-42 victory and a sweep in the only season the two
intersectional rivals played twice.

For the first time in eight years, the Irish had no All-
Americans, a reflection of the greater emphasis on team play and
a lack of real stars. The same thing happened in 1939-40 but,
as usual, many players with extensive game experience returned,
and a couple of reserves moved up. Not the usual was that only
one sophomore saw any regular action (George Sobek). Regardless, for the second straight year ND finished 15-6, although they
were probably better than a year earlier. Two of the six losses
were to the two best teams in the nation, and the other four were
to high-quality teams.

The initial four games of the season went into the "W" column convincingly, Kalamazoo fell, 62-34, behind Sobek's 12-
point debut; Valparaiso, which celebrated 20 years since "The
Doctor" had arrived there and led the school to back-to-back great
seasons, on "George Keogan Night" in the Hilltop Gym, lost
63-26 (Eddie Riska had 18); Cincinnati was 54-17 loser; and
Wisconsin fell, 51-33. None of those teams were particularly competitive this season.

Michigan, the next opponent, certainly was; it ended up
one of the Western Conference's best teams. But the Irish lost
that one, and the next three as well. Even 23 points from Riska
weren't enough to pull out the Wolverine game, as ND dropped
a 41-39 nailbiter. Southern California, the long-time football
nemesis, stopped into the Fieldhouse on the way to the East

Coast, and left with a convincing 55-38 win. The Trojans were arguably the best team in the nation in 1939-40 (the Helms Foundation selected them as such), and their win over Notre Dame buttressed their claim, although they were upset by Kansas in the finals of the NCAA West Regional. Illinois (at Champaign) and Northwestern (at Evanston on the night before New Year's Eve, since December 31 fell on a Sunday) were the others to contribute to the longest Irish losing streak in seven years.

But then along came January.

The first month of the year seemed to have therapeutic effects on Notre Dame through the years; the Irish were in the midst of a four-year, all-games winning streak and a 16-year home winning streak in January (1933-49). Sobek and senior Rex Ellis tallied 12 each to overcome one of Riska's poorest days (one field goal and 3-of-10 from the foul line) as Syracuse fell, 33-29. One week later, Keogan's charges made Adolph Rupp 0-5 against Notre Dame; Riska returned to form with 17 points in a 52-47 Irish win over Kentucky. Balanced scoring (Sobek and senior captain Mark Ertel 13, Riska 12) led to an easier-than-expected 55-39 defeat of Butler. Then the Irish returned to Philadelphia for their first Palestra visit in two years and drubbed Penn, 55-35.

Revenge was the motive as January ended and February began. To make the task easier, both rematches were in the raucous Fieldhouse before fired-up crowds. And boy, what revenge! Northwestern, a 47-37 winner in Evanston, was a 56-27 loser at Notre Dame. (The 29-point margin would have been even larger had not ND shot an abysmal 10-for-20 from the line.) And Illinois, a 42-29 victor at its home arena, was turned away by 18 at ND.

A superb NYU team ended the Irish streak at six. The Violets were the best team not to go to either tournament, finishing with an 18-1 mark. One of those was their first win over Notre Dame since the first game in the annual Madison Square Garden series. Although the New Yorkers couldn't contain Riska (17 points), they did a job on everyone else, and won, 52-43. But on the way back to South Bend, ND stopped off at Toledo and beat a decent team by 38-30.

Closing out the home schedule, the Irish beat John Carroll and Marquette convincingly. In the home finale, Riska tallied

17 and Ken Oberbruner, a senior who had been seeing limited action but gained a greater role with an injury to George Sobek, tallied 12 as ND won, 56-39. Oberbruner led Notre Dame in the first of the three season-ending road games with 11, but the Irish, who had beaten Butler at home by 16, found themselves on the losing end in Indianapolis in another very close one, 39-38. Balanced scoring led to a win at Marquette, ND's first there in three years, 36-32, and Oberbruner closed out his time at Notre Dame with 12 tallies as the Irish defeated Detroit, 47-40.

A significant change came as the 1940-41 season got under way—the hiring of Notre Dame's first full-time assistant basketball coach, ND alumnus and two-time captain Ray Meyer. In years past, volunteers—usually former players enrolled in graduate school or living in South Bend—served this function. The new assistant would be sorely needed; by the end of 1940 there were serious doubts as to George Keogan's coaching future. The stress of so many close games, the pressure of trying to continue his enormous success, and his own workaholic nature finally caught up with him.

Before another of those down-to-the wire games, a 41-39 overtime loss to Illinois (at home, no less), doctors discovered a heart ailment. It was serious enough that some felt he would be forced to retire after the Illinois game. After several days of tests and recuperation, he was given the OK to return to the job as long as he restricted his activity—advice which he promptly ignored. After a game against North Dakota on February 4, he took a short break to return home, ostensibly for his sister's funeral. But while there, Keogan checked into the Mayo Clinic in Rochester, Minnesota. While he was discharged promptly, upon his return to South Bend he was to stay in bed and away from any stressful activity, i.e., coaching, until further notice. For the last seven games of the season, Ray Meyer was, for all intents and purposes, Notre Dame's coach.

Even though the health of their mentor was a question mark, the Irish still had a great year. Had it not been for two late-season losses to teams they had beaten earlier, they would have been invited to one of the tournaments (although, of course, they would have had to decline the offer). Nevertheless, the final record of 17-5 was outstanding.

As usual, ND began with three wins over the light early season foes. The first two came on the same day, as for the fourth (and last) time the Irish played a twin-bill. Senior team captain Eddie Riska seemed ready for some more top scoring; he tallied 33 points in the two games. His mates were scoring as well; Monmouth fell, 81-34, and then Kalamazoo, 73-37. And in a game which was a bit closer, the Irish beat Illinois Wesleyan, 34-28. But the tide turned with three losses in four games to close out 1940.

In Madison, the Irish took on Wisconsin, the eventual Big Ten and NCAA Tournament champions, and lost by only one point, 44-43. Returning home, they then turned the tables on Michigan, 37-27. Then came the discovery of Keogan's heart problems, and the possible last game for the coach no doubt exacerbated his condition—the Illinois OT game mentioned earlier. But after a holiday break, there he was, back on the sidelines, leading his boys against Northwestern. It was not a good night for the Irish in Evanston, and Keogan shuttled in man after man to try and find some combination which would work. He never found it; the Wildcats won, 46-36, to drop ND's record to 4-3.

Cy Singer, a sophomore who had worked his way into the starting lineup at guard, notched 14 points in consecutive games to help get Notre Dame on track again. All his points, plus some more high-percentage shooting from the line (16-for-20), helped the Irish defeat Kentucky in the Louisville Armory, 48-47, and Wabash at the Fieldhouse, 53-38. Riska followed up with an 18-point performance in a 45-35 ambush of Butler at home, and Singer led with 15 in a 53-37 pasting of Penn in the first game of a two-game Eastern swing. The second of the two, at Syracuse, proved costly.

Notre Dame won the contest in overtime, 54-49, but suffered what would have been a crushing blow for almost any other team. Captain and high scorer Eddie Riska broke his foot in a rough game and was out for over a month. Yet ND won all five games he missed as some outstanding young players got to show their stuff. Sophomore Charlie Butler scored 17 points to help defeat Michigan State at the start of a four-game home stand, 46-39, and generally balanced scoring all around led the Irish to defeats of Marquette (58-40) and North Dakota (46-38). But for the rematch with Northwestern, not only was ND without its high scorer, it was also without its head coach.

Keogan was in Minnesota as Ray Meyer directed the Irish over the Wildcats, 47-36. But upon his return to South Bend, the elder statesman was forced to bed and his trusted assistant took over coaching duties on a full-time basis for the rest of the year. During practices, the two were in constant contact over a phone Keogan kept by his bedside, and Meyer has said that during this period of turmoil he was merely following orders and doesn't really deserve much credit for keeping the program on a successful track during Keogan's convalescence. However, there was no phone at the bench during games, so the young man definitely did some game-day coaching and had some decision-making powers. He would learn fast, as five of the last six games were on the road.

Behind 15 points by George Sobek and 14 by Cy Singer, Meyer won his first road game, in Madison Square Garden over a strong NYU squad, 41-38. And then, in the home finale, Riska made his obligatory farewell; even though not fully recovered, he got into the game against Georgia Tech and scored eight points as part of a balanced 53-42 Irish victory.

The baptism under fire for Meyer continued at Butler, as for the third year in a row the Bulldogs defeated the Irish in Indianapolis, 54-40, and then ND lost to Michigan State in East Lansing, 44-35. These gave Meyer his first two collegiate coaching losses, dropped ND's record to 15-5, and ended the possibility of a ceremonial post-season bid. But the season ended with a flourish with a 44-39 defeat of Marquette and a 56-42 win in the traditional season closer at Detroit. In the latter, Riska ended his college career strong, bowing out with 16 points, and Butler added 15 to increase his stock for the next season.

Exactly who would be Notre Dame's head coach in 1941-42? There was some doubt about Keogan's fitness to resume his familiar role. In fact, after head football coach and athletic director Elmer Layden resigned to become Commissioner of the NFL, and the rumors as to his replacement began to circle, the most prominent was that Frank Leahy would become football coach only, George Keogan would be honored for his longevity on the Irish sports scene (at the time, he had served as a coach longer than anyone in ND sports history) by an elevation in rank to the less strenuous post of athletic director, and his assistant, Ray Meyer, would take over fully the reins of the basketball team. Had this prognostication happened, history would have been changed in innumerable ways. But Keogan received clearance to resume some of his duties with the squad and preferred to stay with the team, and Leahy upheld the ND tradition of the football coach also serving as athletic director.

One of the restrictions placed upon " The Doctor" was that he was not allowed to travel with the team. So Meyer was retained as assistant and served as acting head coach on all the road trips except one. Even though the team basically had two men at the helm off and on, the Irish still finished at 16-6.

The two men quickly decided, based upon the talent and height of the underclassmen, to go with a young team. They realized the early going might be tough, but they reasoned that things would work out in the long run (which they did). A 6-5 sophomore, Bob Faught, beat out senior Frank Quinn for the starting center spot, and another soph, John Niemiera, knocked George Sobek from his starting forward role. The other senior of note, Art Pope, although captain, was not a starter in the past and wasn't in 1941-42, either. Charlie Butler, the junior who had come on in Eddie Riska's absence a year earlier, held down the other forward spot, and Cy Singer and Bob Rensberger, two more juniors, were starting guards. Several other young men – John "Buster" Hiller, Ray Kuka, Orlando Bonicelli – also subbed when needed. It was a young, deep, talented team, but the kinks had to be worked out first.

The Irish easily beat Franklin, 49-30, but then had to face a rough first-time opponent in Great Lakes. Because of the wars in both Europe and the Pacific, the United States was preparing for what was seen as inevitable conflict with either Japan or Germany. As part of that preparation, a peacetime draft was instituted for the first time in the nation's history. This obviously nabbed some great athletes from colleges and the pro ranks, and many of them ended up at Illinois' Great Lakes Naval Training Center. To help out the cause, many colleges agreed to play service teams in sports; Notre Dame was no exception. This December 3 game would be the Sailors' only trip to ND, because only four days later the invasion of Pearl Harbor plunged the US into World War II. But for now the only wars were on the court, and the youthful Irish had the experienced Great Lakes team by 10, but they blew the lead in the second half and lost, 54-46. The Irish closed the three-game home stand with a lopsided win over St. Louis, and then they hit the road.

Notre Dame outscored Wisconsin from the floor, but an excess of fouls in Ray Meyer's first game of the season as head coach helped the Badgers extend a win streak to 18, 43-35. Charlie Butler tallied 14 in the next game as Meyer fooled around with the lineup until he found one he liked, in time for ND to defeat Michigan, 46-40. Then Illinois simply blew out the Irish in Champaign, 48-29, and the team's record dropped to 3-3. But then the young squad began to jell, and it promptly streaked to a 12-1 record over the next 13 games, nine of which were at home.

The loss was to a good Butler team at Indianapolis. The Bulldogs jumped to an 11-1 lead at the outset, and after that Meyer tried 13 men in a futile comeback try as the Irish fell short by six. But other than that, the Irish were outstanding. They defeated Northwestern twice, 40-36 at Evanston and 61-43 at ND, and the latter would have been even worse had not Otto Graham of football fame tallied 18 points for the losers. Two teams tried to pack in a zone in attempts to cut off ND at the pass with no success. Harvard, coached by ND alumnus Earl Brown (who led Dartmouth to a second-place NCAA finish in 1944), managed to stay in the game for over 25 minutes with a zone, and Brown refused to take his team out of it despite a vicious verbal tongue-lashing from his old mentor Keogan about the non-virtues of straight zone defense, but the Irish won, 39-31. And Washington University of St. Louis held the score down to 34-31 using the same game plan.

One of the great assets of this team was that different people were capable of taking the scoring lead. Charlie Butler began hot, giving way to Cy Singer in early January, and Bob Rensberger got hot late. But none was hotter than Bob Faught on January 31 and February 14. He scored 25 against Marquette in a 66-42 win, and then set what was a Madison Square Garden record of 26 in a 55-42 defeat of NYU. This team also could come from behind; Adolph Rupp thought he had his first win ever over ND, as Kentucky led 22-15 at the half. But behind 17 points by Rensberger, the Irish continued their jinx over "The Baron," 46-43.

There were a couple of romps in the streak. Syracuse fell, 51-35, and later a hapless Western Reserve squad fell victim to an onslaught of Irish offense, 70-39. And they also could pull out tight ones, taking Michigan State, 52-49.

Finally, ND dished out some revenge. In a rough game which resulted in two Irishmen (Ray Kuka and Orlando Bonicelli) landing in the hospital, Keogan—who received clearance to travel with the team this one time only—led his charges to a 46-43 victory over Great Lakes in Chicago Stadium—ND's first game there—in a Navy Relief Fund benefit. And the close of the 12-1 skein was a 57-54 win over Butler, in which the Irish built a huge lead and watched the visitors nearly wipe it out.

The last three games were on the road, and none were real classics. The team lost back-to-back 46-43 contests against teams already beaten once, Marquette and Michigan State. But the season ended on an up note; Frank Quinn closed his career with 10 points in the second half to lead a 43-41 ND win over Detroit.

The season-ending win was Ray Meyer's last at Notre Dame. He heard of a head coaching opening in his hometown of Chicago, at DePaul, and, with help from a glowing recommendation from Keogan, he got the job for the 1942-43 season—and for 41 more years as well. He closed his coaching career at Notre Dame with an "unofficial" 9-7 record, all but two of the 16 games on the road, and he contributed in his assistant's role to many of the Keogan-led wins of the past two seasons.

Meanwhile, someone at the *South Bend Tribune* noted the eerie re-occurrence of the number 43 in Irish scores in 1941-42. Nine times, including the last three games and five of the last seven, either Notre Dame or its opponent scored that number of points, and the paper's sports editor mused in a post-season column that there might be some significance to that. Little would he realize that there was, for 1943 turned out to be a year of great change in the Notre Dame basketball program, in a way no one really expected.

# 11

# And Suddenly, An End

George Keogan's 20th Notre Dame team may have been his best. Consider these credentials: six of the regulars and top reserves, and seven team members in all, played in the growing, ever-more-important professional leagues after World War II. Four men paced one of the most balanced scoring attacks in Notre Dame history: Bob Faught led the team again with 196, but added to his totals were 186 by Frannie Curran, 185 by Bob Rensberger, and 180 by the team's captain, Charlie Butler. This four-pronged scoring attack made it impossible to completely shut down ND's offense. And overall, the team finished 18-2; both losses were to extremely good teams—one of them under unusual circumstances—by a total of nine points.

Most importantly of all, this was also Keogan's last team.

On February 17, 1943, he had returned to his South Bend home after leading his 12-1 team through its daily practice and had just sat down with the evening paper when a massive heart attack killed him. He was not yet 53 years old. Earlier that very day, he had done something he had not done all season: he actually went onto the court and helped out with drills, a job he usually left to his assistant. Ironically, the greatest coaches in three different sports at ND had now met untimely deaths: Knute Rockne in 1931 (plane crash), track coach John Nicholson in 1940 (heart attack), and now Keogan.

Even though he had been given a clean bill of health to resume most of his coaching duties, including leading the team on road trips, he was still not completely healthy. Still, the loss shocked Notre Dame and the entire basketball world because of its suddenness. Moose Krause, the new assistant basketball

90

coach, who had revived Holy Cross's dormant program before returning to his alma mater, took over as head coach and completed the season.

Keogan's death overshadowed the fine year of the Notre Dame team. The dramatic events both at ND and elsewhere (World War II restrictions were beginning to take effect) were the main reason why the administration did not end its postseason tournament ban after the Irish were invited to the NCAAs at the end of the season. But the probable top team in the nation, Illinois' fabled "Whiz Kids," also declined a bid; and for the first time in some years, the Irish and Illini did not play each other during the season, although efforts were made to schedule a game late in the season to benefit the war effort.

A major change in the schedule was the participation in four Chicago Stadium doubleheaders. Gradually, since the advent of the major-arena college twin-bill in late 1934, other big venues began hosting them, with very profitable results. The move out of the campus band boxes to the large arenas presaged the basketball boom of the late 1940s. Notre Dame, as one of college basketball's top programs and as a big draw in the alumni-rich Chicago area, became a fixture at Stadium doubleheaders, playing at least two games a year at its home-away-from home for almost 30 years, even for several years after the Athletic and Convocation Center opened. Keogan's move to the profitable and more visible Chicago games spelled the beginning of the end of the Notre Dame Fieldhouse as a viable basketball venue, although because of other priorities, the Irish continued to use the obsolete structure for another quarter of a century.

Between the two sites, this outstanding team won its first six games. Two of them were over Northwestern at Chicago Stadium; two others were over Ball State and Western Michigan. The closest of these was a two-point overtime win over Wisconsin, 61-59, in which Faught tallied 18 points, and a 46-43 defeat of Purdue and Piggy Lambert. The last of these games came about in an interesting manner. Keogan and Lambert had long had little use for each other, in fact, had hardly communicated since the schools' last meeting on the court in 1936-37. But "The Doctor's" illness must have had a mellowing effect on him. One day, he just picked up a phone, called the Purdue coach's office, and offered to resume the series . . . and that was that. All bygones became bygones on that day. In fact, ND and PU enjoyed a long continuing basketball series which lasted until 1965-66, but—to the chagrin of many fans in Indiana—hasn't been contested since.

Saturday, January 23 was the date of Keogan's last loss as a coach, in the Louisville Armory against Kentucky. The 60-55 win of Adoph Rupp's charges was not only "The Baron's" first win over Keogan, but it also marked the end of Irish domination in the series. Only once since has ND been able to win two in a row over the Wildcats, and since John Jordan's ascension to the helm in 1951, Notre Dame is an awful 4-24 in the series.

On the way back to campus, ND beat a Butler team without its longtime coach Tony Hinkle and a season away from dropping basketball for the duration of the war, 45-34. This was the start of another six-game winning steak which, as it turned out, closed the book on Keogan's coaching career. Two of the other five were against teams which appeared in the NCAA tournament at season's end (only eight teams appeared in the tourney in those days).

First was against DePaul, which ND had not played in over 30 years. This was another teacher vs. student contest: Keogan, who had never lost to any of his former players-turned-coach, against Ray Meyer, the first-year head man who owed his job in no small part to his mentor's glowing recommendation. The elder statesman won in this Stadium clash, but the younger man gave Keogan a real scare—the final was 50-47. Notre Dame needed all 17 of Bob Rensberger's points to clinch the victory and overcome the Blue Demons' gawky, 6-11 freshman whom Keogan had looked at but turned down, thinking he was a hopeless case, George Mikan. Ray Meyer has said that one of the great disappointments of his long coaching career was that he only had one chance to go up against Keogan, and did not defeat him.

After Keogan's last two wins in the Fieldhouse (50-45 over Marquette and 45-34 over Michigan State), the Irish pulled off their second win against an NCAA tourney team—NYU. And this one, at Madison Square Garden, wasn't even close. The Violets were utterly demolished, 74-43. Frannie Curran had 21 points and Rensberger 20, and 13 men saw action in this, Notre

Dame's 500th basketball win. And Keogan got his 327th—and last—coaching win two nights later against Canisius, 55-37.

Keogan's fatal heart attack occurred during preparations for a game at the Stadium against the Great Lakes Naval Training Center, a team which worried him because of all its great current and former collegiate talent, including former ND stars Eddie Riska and George Sobek and on-leave Butler head coach Tony Hinkle. One day before the coach's passing, Ray Kuka, one of the super subs on ND's deep squad, was called to duty in WW II, which didn't help matters any. The day after, both Notre Dame and Great Lakes officials considered cancelling the game because of the turn of events, but Ruby Keogan, the late coach's wife, swayed them from doing so, feeling George would have wanted the game to go on. So the players were faced with the unenviable situation of serving as pallbearers for the funeral on the morning of February 20 and playing against the toughest team on the schedule in Chicago that night. Under such emotional conditions, how could the Irish win? Yet they hung tough, taking the vaunted Sailors into overtime, but they lost in the overtime, 60-56. And it was just whom Keogan had feared most—Riska and Sobek—who hurt ND most.

Under interim head coach Moose Krause, the team regrouped and ended the season with six more victories. Every player in uniform but one—15 in all, including a couple who hadn't seen game action under Keogan—got into a 64-32 drubbing of Butler. Michigan State fell at East Lansing by three; Wabash went down by 27 (69-42); and Marquette was a 49-47 Irish victim in Milwaukee. The big one came next, another overtime game against Great Lakes, this one in front of an extremely partisan crowd of sailors at the training base's small gym. And this time, the result was in ND's favor: Curran and Faught each scored 11 points as the Irish won, 44-42. And finally, for the first time since 1929 Detroit came to the Fieldhouse, and this phenomenal ND team bowed out, most of it playing for the last time in an Irish uniform, by making the Titans very unwelcome, 52-43.

Graduation and the war broke up this team; only one of the 10 top men on the 1942-43 squad ever donned a Notre Dame uniform again. Yet the phenomenal success of this squad certainly proved that George Keogan, even with all the despised rules changes, didn't let what he saw as the ruination of a great game get in the way of building a great team. Of course, the challenge would be keeping success going without the great coach, who was elected to the Hall of Fame in 1961. But the greater immediate challenge would be to keep the program going, period.

# 12

## Getting Through the War

World War II was a disruptive influence on college basketball. Many schools abandoned their programs for the duration; those that didn't were plagued by fluid rosters and coaching staffs as call-ups continued even after V-E and V-J Days. Notre Dame was no exception. In three years, four men served as coach and 43 played at least one game. In addition, the University loosened its requirements by lowering the average needed for eligibility and allowing transfers and freshmen to play immediately without the one-year wait. Even with all that going on, the team continued its string of consecutive non-losing seasons and by 1946 was beginning to rival the football team in popularity.

A tough task awaited Moose Krause, now permanent coach, as the 1943-44 team began practices. He had no returning lettermen and only two players who had seen any action at all a season past. Bob Faught, Frannie Curran, Orlando Bonicelli, John Niemiera, and Tom Brennan, all of whom would have been seniors in a normal time, were at various military bases or already in combat.

Almost everyone on this roster was in the University's naval or marine training program, as the Navy essentially took over the campus for the duration of the war. By doing this, college-age men could serve the war effort while continuing to receive an education and compete in athletics. As an added incentive, those in these V-12 programs could play varsity sports and not have V-12 seasons count against athletic eligibility. But because these trainees could be called to duty at any time, teams loaded up with either very young (under the draft age) or very tall (higher than the height restrictions) players.

In ND's case, it was the very young who took precedence, as two freshmen saw extensive action in 1943-44. Carl Loyd, a local product, started eight games at forward until he received his draft notice in late January; and Johnny Lujack, the man who had so ably filled in for Angelo Bertelli when the latter was called to duty during the 1943 football season, started nearly every game after football season ended and went on to win four monograms in 1943-44—the first to pull a "grand slam" since 1914-15. (His other two sports were baseball and track.) The only new varsity man who had been a Notre Dame freshman one year earlier was John Kelly, who started all but one game at forward or guard. In addition, two sophomore transfers—Marko Todorovich from Washington University of St. Louis and Ernie Kivisto from Marquette—played key roles.

The two "leftovers" from the 1942-43 team were factors as well. Bernie Rutledge—the team's only senior and captain almost by default—generally played a decent game and could even score a few points every once in a while when he didn't foul out. In his 18 contests, he fouled out eight times. And finally, junior Leo "Crystal" Klier became the team's star. In three games as a sophomore, he went 4-for-4 from the floor. In his second season of eligibility, he scored more than twice as many points as any teammate and set a record for a normal-length season in that category. In the process, Klier was accorded All-America status after the season. But with so many inexperienced main players, it was no wonder that the Irish could muster but a 10-9 record.

The way it was compiled was certainly odd. In the first 14 games, Notre Dame went 7-7, winning every odd-numbered game and losing every even-numbered one! Such consistent inconsistency earned the Irish the nickname of "Finnegans" in the local press (after the "in-again, out-again" saying). They then managed to lose another one, then actually put together a three-game win streak (including two major upsets) before losing the final one.

The Irish opened the season by beating Alma easily—but lost to Western Michigan when WMU outscored them 22-9 in the second half. This was to be ND's last home loss for a long, long time.

They knocked off Wisconsin behind balanced scoring—but lost badly to a good Northwestern team in the first of five Chicago Stadium doubleheaders. Otto Graham, the future Hall of Fame quarterback, was the main cog in the Wildcat attack.

They defeated Purdue by seven in what was considered an upset—but lost to Wisconsin after defeating the Badgers earlier in the season. Although Klier scored 23 in the New Year's Eve contest in Milwaukee, a last-second field goal defeated ND, 47-45.

They again defeated Purdue, this time in West Lafayette, behind a 16-7 edge in the second half, 35-32—but Kentucky pulled out a one-point victory, 55-54, behind the almost single-handed attack of Bob Brannum. His foul shot capped a furious Wildcat rally which resulted in seven points in less than two minutes. The Irish had led, 54-48, and seemed to be at the end of their "Finnegan"-ism—and on the verge of a major upset (UK finished 19-2).

They put down Marquette at home—but again lost to Northwestern at the Stadium. This one was a bit closer, but again Otto Graham led the way for the winners.

They used their youth to outrun a veteran Valparaiso team, as Loyd scored a career-high 15 in the last game before his call-up—but they lost the return match with Marquette by 17; the Irish were behind all the way this time.

They beat Bunker Hill, a late stand-in for surprising, V-12-laden DePauw, behind John Kelly's 18 points—but Ray Meyer and DePaul drubbed ND, 65-41, beginning a streak of eight straight seasons where the Blue Demons beat the Irish at least once.

Finally, the up-one-game, down-the-next squad ended its unusual streak; Great Lakes utterly destroyed the Irish in the naval base gym, 84-48. But Notre Dame rebounded with three straight wins: 59-53 over NYU at Madison Square Garden for the George Keogan Memorial Cup, contributed by Ruby Keogan and to be presented to the ND-NYU winner annually; and two of the greatest upsets anywhere in the country all year.

Just 10 days earlier, Great Lakes had defeated ND by 36 points. The seamen had a 28-3 record and a 21-game winning streak when they came up against the Irish in Chicago Stadium, but behind the two-pronged attack of Klier (18 points) and Rutledge (17 more), Notre Dame pulled a big surprise, 54-51. And a week later, in the last game in the Fieldhouse in 1943-44, the all-civilian Iowa team, which was leading the Big Ten and finished 14-4, was crushed, 66-42.

A game scheduled against Detroit was cancelled, so the Irish closed their season on March 3 against Camp Grant—without the head coach and two starters. Moose Krause, Marko Todorovich, and Bernie Rutledge all reported to active duty on March 1. Wally Ziemba, Krause's assistant, took over temporarily, and center Frank Kaufmann, another freshman who had made some appearances with the team, moved to a starting role. Despite 22 points from Leo Klier, ND ended the season with a loss. The main cog in Camp Grant's offense was a former teammate of Klier's, John Niemiera; he led the way in the 63-47 CG win.

Not only had 1943-44 been subpar on the court, but in the stands as well. Wartime rationing of tires and gasoline, lousy weather, and a location too far away for easy walking held down the South Bend attendance, and a 7:30 P.M. curfew imposed by the military on weeknights kept non-civilian students away. (The number of home games was restricted also by Navy edict, thus the five games at Chicago Stadium.) The biggest Fieldhouse crowd of the year was about half its capacity against Purdue. That, however, would soon change.

Notre Dame graduate Clem Crowe, who had coached for over a decade at Xavier and was available because that school had suspended its basketball program, became Moose Krause's official fill-in, theoretically for the rest of the war years. He stuck around the Dome for only one season, however, but his short tenure was positively amazing.

For the second season in a row, the Irish had not one returning letterman. But an outstanding crop of freshmen and V-12's managed to coalesce into a high-scoring machine built around one of the greatest players in college basketball, and finished with a 15-5 record, quite a remarkable showing for a team with almost no experience. But this was no ordinary team.

Six men saw a great deal of action in 1944-45. The only one who had had any prior play at Notre Dame was Frank Gilhooley, a guard who had played in seven games in 1943-44. George Ratterman, a V-12 who eventually became better known for his exploits on the football field, gradually gained a starting berth at forward. A couple of transfers aided the cause: sophomore Johnny Dee, from Loyola of Chicago, already somewhat of an Irish legend because during the 1944 football season he had literally been selling programs one Saturday and was starting quarterback the next in a bizarre wartime twist of fate, and junior Billy Hassett, from Georgetown, who had played on the NCAA runner-up squad from 1942-43. And two players too young for the draft rounded out this miracle team: Paul Gordon, who saw some spot starts but served primarily as a sixth man, and a 17-year-old from East Chicago, Indiana, who, had he stayed at Notre Dame all four years, would probably still hold many Notre Dame records—Vince Boryla. He became a prolific scorer and ended up shattering all the records Leo Klier (now in the Navy) had set a year earlier. But Dee and Ratterman contributed over 10 points a game to the cause, too.

This team rolled through its first five games with almost unprecedented ease. Kellogg Field fell by the lopsided score of 89-28, a new Irish offensive record; ND outscored Miami of Ohio 22-0 at the start of a 68-34 romp; Boryla and Dee each scored 18 in a 71-30 pasting of Alma; in the first road game of the year, in Madison, the freshman phenom put in another 18 to aid in a 57-46 defeat of Wisconsin; and the 13-day-old scoring record fell again behind 23 points from Boryla, 91-44 over Loras (which ND had played in the past in its two previous incarnations—Dubuque and Columbia College). But the game was costly because Hassett, who was playing superbly at guard, strained ligaments in his knee and was forced to sit out the next game, at mighty Iowa.

Without Hassett, the defense faltered. The Hawkeyes lost only once all year, and it wasn't to Notre Dame. Even though Boryla tied the modern ND scoring record with 26 points, the Irish as a team scored only 46; Iowa scored 63. The 17-point romp was Notre Dame's worst defeat of the season. And they were still sluggish on December 30 when Hassett returned to the lineup. Purdue— which had asked that the game be moved from its original December 27 date—was the tormentor, and the Irish barely won, 49-47. And then, two days later, the offense got lost on the way to West Lafayette for a return match. For the first time as a collegian, Boryla was held below double figures (he had but seven) and Ward Lambert's boys won big, 44-32. And the Irish losing ways continued at the Great Lakes Naval Training Center; a buzzer-beater by the Sailors spoiled a fine effort by Johnny Dee (25 points), and ND had its third loss in four games, 59-58.

Things got back on track with four straight wins, three of them upsets. First, the Irish returned to Iowa City, but this time to play the Iowa Pre-Flight team. And, like many other teams, the Seahawks had all kinds of problems stopping Vince Boryla. The 17-year-old had 25 points in ND's 49-44 upset. This seemed to get the Irish over the hump; Marquette went down at the Fieldhouse next, 79-56, and then ND avenged its loss to Great Lakes behind another 25-point performance by Dee, 55-51. And then there was Kentucky.

The Wildcats were to finish 22-4 and lose in the first round of the NCAA tournament. On this day, Adolph Rupp's team suffered one of those four setbacks at the Louisville Armory. The Fighting Irish used the same five men the entire game, Vince Boryla led a balanced ND attack with 18 points, and Johnny Dee scored the winning basket in overtime in Notre Dame's 59-58 upset. Certainly the memory of his role in beating the vaunted Ruppians this season continued to inspire Dee as a head coach; there was no team he took greater delight in defeating (except UCLA in 1971).

On February 2 and 3 the Irish played on back-to-back nights in Chicago Stadium, and in the first, the win streak ended. DePaul came back from a 14-point deficit in the second half to win going away, 56-52; the Irish had simply fallen apart. So the next night Clem Crowe pulled a chapter out of the Knute Rockne book of tricks and started a team of reserves against Northwestern, all of whom stayed in the game most of the first half. As a result, NU led at the half, 26-24. But once Crowe unleashed his starting five, ND coasted to a 32-11 second-half edge and won, 56-37.

Boryla and George Ratterman each tallied 24 points in an Irish attack on NYU at the Garden, 66-60. And then Iowa Pre-Flight entered the Fieldhouse and left with its second loss to Notre Dame and only its fourth all season, 51-38. But the three-game streak came to a crashing halt in Milwaukee.

Against Marquette the second time, Notre Dame played sluggishly and rough. Three Irishman fouled out— and that was with the new rule giving players an additional foul (a fifth) before disqualification. ND's lack of quality depth hurt in the end, and Marquette scored a 56-55 upset win. But the Irish, returning home, closed the season with two wins—almost a guarantee at the Fieldhouse. First Northwestern fell by 71-66, and then Detroit felt the Irish sting.

Before the last game against the Titans, Vince Boryla was named "honorary captain" for his exploits throughout the season, and he promptly celebrated the award on the court. He needed but three points to top Leo Klier's modern scoring record for a season; the freshman far surpassed that and set another modern record. Boryla scored 31 points and ND coasted, 87-43.

Billy Hassett's exploits as a guard earned him consensus All-America honors after the season ended, but Boryla's as a scorer did not, primarily because of his freshman status. And not long after the basketballs stopped dribbling for the year, rumors began to circulate about Clem Crowe's future. He finally confirmed them by taking a head football coaching position at Iowa.

Replacing Crowe at the helm for the duration was a proven winner, Elmer Ripley, even though he, in serving as interim coach at Columbia, had had two consecutive losing seasons. He had taken a young Georgetown team to the final game of the NCAA tourney in 1942-43, after which the Hoyas suspended their program for WWII. Not long after he was hired, the war ended, though not soon enough for most schools to re-activate programs and most student-soldiers to re-enroll. Regardless, Ripley still had an excellent team—he really didn't need any help. Not only were five of the top six players—to be exact, the usual starting five (only Paul Gordon was lost to the draft)—returning, but Leo Klier was back as well, and freshman Ray Corley was available as a seventh man when needed. For the most part, Ripley didn't use any other players, started the same lineup every game, and had one of the greatest teams ND ever fielded.

In Ripley's lone season at Notre Dame, the Irish went 17-4. In the process they were ranked Number One for six weeks running by AP on its then informal poll, and broke attendance records in every city they visited. Records for a basketball game in Louisville, East Lansing, St. Louis, Detroit, Chicago, and New York were set by the traveling ND squad, and it was impossible to get tickets to any of the home games after the first two. The attention paid Notre Dame basketball was unprecedented; the 4,200 seats then in the Fieldhouse could have been filled three times over considering the demand for ducats. In fact, the *South Bend Tribune* of February 21, 1946, contained this brief item: "Preliminary sketches have been drawn for a new Notre Dame fieldhouse which will seat close to 10,000 spectators . . . " But the postwar boom in student population and Fr. Theodore Hesburgh's athletic "de-emphasis" of the 1950s put those sketches in mothballs for an excruciatingly long time, a move which severely hurt the program during especially the latter part of that decade. But that's a saga for later.

First, though, the Irish of 1945-46 began their season more successfully in the won-lost column than any before or since; ND went 13-0 and soared straight to the top. The season began with five straight home games; oddly, none of them resulted in real blowouts. Fitting Klier in with his returning teammates proved a sticky proposition, and the chemistry necessary for a successful team took a long time to form. Both of the "patsy" games were too close to make mass substitutions (56-37 over Camp Atterbury and 52-45 over Chanute Field), and other games they played just well enough to win. Things began to mesh with wins over Wisconsin (65-51) and St. Louis (60-45), but a close home win over Purdue (49-47) raised some doubts again.

After the turn of the new year, the Irish went on the road for the first time to face the Boilermakers again. In front of a large Purdue crowd, the home team hung on tough, but Klier scored the winning basket with little time left for the second straight ND two-point win over Purdue, 50-48. The next game was arguably the most exciting in many years.

For the first time, Ray Meyer entered the Fieldhouse as coach of DePaul in the first of two games between the Irish and the Blue Demons—a semi-annual home-and-home series unbroken through 1968-69. Meyer really wanted the win in this, George Mikan's final year, and in one of the most difficult gyms for a visitor anywhere, and it appeared he had it. Notre Dame played one of its worst games, hitting a combined 3-for-18 from the foul line—perhaps the worst in post-center jump ND history—and trailed the entire game. Tough defense from Billy Hassett and company held the 6-11 Mikan down, however, and kept it close. Finally, Hassett, who hadn't made a field goal in 11 tries, threw one up just before the buzzer sounded with ND trailing 42-41—and when it went in, the crowd went crazy! The unbeaten record had been preserved, and Meyer had been thwarted in his first attempt to win in the "snakepit." The win put Notre Dame atop the Associated Press poll of sportswriters.

From here on out, 11 of the remaining 14 games were away from the oh-so-friendly confines of the Fieldhouse, and this eventually became too much of a handicap to overcome. But not so in the beginning. The Irish went to Great Lakes for the last time, and defeated the trainees, now coached by future pro football coaching great Weeb Ewbank, 72-50. A win at St. Louis with its freshman phenom, Ed Macauley, followed, and then, to close the books on an always-interesting wartime series, the Irish defeated Great Lakes again, this time at Chicago Stadium. Behind 30-23 at halftime, ND came up with its usual one good half per game to pull it out, 56-54 , for a season sweep—the only time either team had done that.

Back at home, Notre Dame won a not-as-close-as-the-final-score 69-67 decision over Marquette, and then it was back to Louisville for the annual Kentucky game. Both teams were about equal; it was one of the top games in the nation all season, and a record crowd filled the Armory to the rafters to see it. And the Irish kept their unbeaten record intact behind phenomenal streak playing by Vince Boryla and George Ratterman, 56-47. Boryla scored ND's first 14 points and Ratterman the last 11 to seal it. Kentucky continued on to win 28 games and the NIT title.

Home again—for what would be the last time in almost a month—the Irish knocked off a decent Michigan State team, 62-57, for a 13-0 record. But then Northwestern ended all the dreams of an unblemished record on a Saturday night in Chicago Stadium. NU's star on one of its best teams ever (second in the Big Nine and an overall 15-5 record), Max Morris, scored with a minute left to put the Wildcats ahead, 56-55, and a minute of frantic attempts to score failed.

Originally Notre Dame had a February 4 home game with Iowa Pre-Flight scheduled, but the Seahawks cancelled out; Ripley tried to get Kentucky as a replacement, but the Wildcats were in the midst of their Southeastern Conference schedule and had a tough game coming up in two days, so Rupp declined. So next it was a trip east for the Irish, where they defeated Canisius, 69-47; but then, in the annual MSG game in New York, NYU once and for all demoted ND from the top spot in the poll by building a huge lead from which the Irish never recovered. The 62-58 loss to the Violets was their first to NYU in six years.

For the third straight Saturday, ND lost—and this time to a team already beaten once by the Irish—68-59 to Marquette, in the process blowing a 37-30 halftime lead. A very close game in front of a record crowd in the new Jenison Fieldhouse ended the two-game Irish loss skein (56-54 over Michigan State), but then the Saturday night jinx struck again. DePaul, looking for revenge after ND had pulled out the miracle in the Fieldhouse earlier, got it. An all-time Chicago Stadium record throng of 22,822—a crowd no longer possible today because of fire regulations—showed up for the doubleheader, the first game of which pitted Ohio State and Northwestern for the Big Nine title (OSU won). In the nightcap, George Mikan, whom Notre Dame had usually been able to hold to a minimum of points, ran roughshod in his last Stadium appearance as a collegian. He scored 33 points, a new record by an Irish opponent, and the Blue Demons coasted, 63-47. Interestingly, although DePaul went 19-5 and had won the 1945 NIT, Meyer and Co. were snubbed by both the NCAA and the NIT—there were simply too many good teams in the Mideast and Midwest in 1946 in a day when the word "regional" meant something.

Finally, the Irish played another home game, which had been sold out for weeks and was a tougher ticket to get than one for any football game. Revenge was the motive, for Northwestern was the guest—the team which had begun ND's Saturday night fever 24 days earlier. And this time, Notre Dame won, 57-50. And the finale, *another* Saturday night road game, ended better than the last four had. Detroit was the victim, convincingly, 66-39.

Because of the late-season slump and the plethora of excellent Midwestern teams, Notre Dame didn't receive a post-season bid to reject this time, but Leo Klier was named a consensus All-American, and *True* magazine named Klier and Billy Hassett to its first team and Vince Boryla on its second. "Crystal" had broken the modern season scoring mark again, and Boryla came within one point of tying his old record.

While all this had been going on, Ed Krause had returned from his tour of war duty and had seen most of the games on the home floor, and was eagerly anticipating his return to the sidelines in 1946-47. With most of the Irish talent he was watching of undergraduate status, and some other previous monogrammers returning, Krause felt that he was going to have some great years ahead.

# 13

## Riding Out the Forties

Over the next half decade, college basketball reached new peaks of popularity which fell precipitously in 1951. While Notre Dame was not generally one of the great teams in the nation at the time, the Irish still fielded representative teams capable of a major upset now and then.

One of the reasons ND's pre-eminence in basketball began to slip was that the coach, Moose Krause, gradually spent less and less of his time with the team. He also served as an assistant football coach in 1946 and 1947, was elevated to assistant athletic director in 1948, and became athletic director, replacing Frank Leahy, in 1949, a job he retained through 1980. He decided to devote all his energies to the administrative end of ND sports as of 1951, realizing by then that in order for Notre Dame to remain competitive, it had to have a full-time coach.

He had started out very well, though. The 1946-47 season was outstanding, but not because Krause had everyone back like he thought he would. In fact, the only monogram winner to return was George Ratterman. Leo Klier, although with a year of eligibility remaining, decided to graduate with his class; Ray Corley and Tom O'Keefe followed Elmer Ripley back to Georgetown; Johnny Dee returned to Loyola of Chicago for his senior year. The biggest loss, though, was Vince Boryla, who left ND for the Army. Krause expected him to return, first for 1947 and then for 1948, but he never did, which may have hurt in trying to build for the future.

But for 1946-47, the future was now thanks to a great deal of youth. Sophomores dominated the top spots: John Brennan, Leo Barnhorst, Paul Gordon, Jim O'Halloran. Senior captain

Frannie Curran, a veteran of prewar George Keogan teams, held down one forward spot, and another senior, John Kelly, started at the other. But there was much juggling; 13 men saw action in at least half the games, not the least of whom was a freshman from San Francisco, Kevin O'Shea, generally regarded nationally as the best West Coast prospect since Hank Luisetti. With all this, the Irish couldn't help but be successful, finishing 20-4, and as per school policy, receiving but declining a bid to the NCAA tournament.

The team started out by absolutely obliterating two vastly inferior teams—Franklin, 86-38, and Ball State, 80-31. The big story, however, was not the games but the crowds. The influx of students into Notre Dame after World War II resulted in a new situation: there were now more students than seats in the Fieldhouse. Because of this, no places could be guaranteed for members of the general public. If any space was left as of 7:30 P.M., general admission tickets were made available—but there was no assurance that any would be. This made it very difficult, if not impossible, for most members of the Michiana community ever to see the local college team play at home, and therefore for the team to make money at home, since students were admitted free. This, combined with the fact that good teams were growing reluctant to come to Notre Dame only to be victimized by ND's incredible home-court advantage, forced the Irish to play more than half their games away from home—a situation unrectified for over two decades. (Eventually, ND officials did set aside about 500 seats for local residents, but that step was a few years away.)

Of course, that didn't mean the Irish couldn't *win* on the road, for they did just that against Indiana behind the two-pronged attack of O'Shea and Curran, 70-60. But at Wisconsin, despite more heroics from O'Shea, who scored the basket to take it into overtime, the Badgers handed ND its first loss, 53-49.

Two bizarre games began the next Irish victory streak. They defeated Drake at the Fieldhouse, 59-56, but the real story was that this game was three decades ahead of its time. Through a scheduling mistake, three referees instead of the usual two showed up. Since the error was evidently Notre Dame's, all three would have to be paid anyway, so the two coaches agreed to

play with three officials on the court. The performance generally received favorable notices but did not become commonplace
until the late 1970s. Following this, the Irish went to Cleveland
to play Dartmouth. Cleveland was trying to become a major
league basketball town; to go along with its new professional
team, the Ironmen, the Arena began scheduling college doubleheaders. Both were colossal flops. The Cleveland Ironmen were
gone by the next season, and even with a draw like Notre Dame,
many empty seats were in evidence as ND beat Dartmouth,
66-55.

A scheduled game—which would have been a classic—
against Illinois and its reunited "Whiz Kids" at Notre Dame was
cancelled because the Illini coach wanted to take a long holiday,
so the Irish had to wait to extend the win streak until a January
3 game at St. Louis. And that they did. John Brennan and Leo
Barnhorst double-teamed the Billikens' sparkplug, Ed Macauley,
and made him a non-factor as ND won, 48-46.

Notre Dame upped its record to 7-1 with an abject blowout
of Butler at home, 86-40, but Purdue ended the latest ND win
streak at four at West Lafayette in a 60-56 upset. Four more wins
followed, all of massive poportions; the average score was 79-50.
The most ridiculous was 81-40 at Detroit, but the most satisfying was the 79-43 avenging of the loss to Purdue; the Irish
streaked to a 17-3 lead in front of a loud student-body crowd
and coasted home. With a record now at 11-2, ND had risen to
the third spot on the informal Associated Press poll and was
beginning February with a contest against top-ranked Kentucky
at the Louisville Armory. Sportswriters pointed to this as one
of the big games of the season. However, it wasn't even close.

The mighty Wildcats absolutely destroyed the Irish, 60-30.
Alex Groza scored 20 and Ralph Beard added 17 to outscore the
outclassed ND team all by themselves. Notre Dame could manage only nine field goals the entire game. Certainly there was
no question as to who was number one now. On the way home,
the Irish regrouped at Butler, completing a sweep of the Bulldogs
for the season, 73-60. In quick succession, the Irish knocked off
Michigan State at home and Northwestern at Chicago Stadium,
the latter of which saw Kevin O'Shea reinjure an already shaky
knee, and then really put it to DePaul, 80-45. The convincing

win over a good opponent moved ND back to number two behind—of course—Kentucky with the annual trip east next.

Nothing happened to diminish ND's standing there; wins over Canisius and NYU pushed the Irish up to 17-3, and some speculated that ND might end its post-season ban to accept either an NCAA or NIT bid—or both. During World War II, both the golf and tennis teams had won NCAA titles in the post-season tournament; before, individual fencers, for example, had competed in the NCAA championships. In fact, the only varsity teams still prohibited by university policy from competing in post-season play were the football and basketball teams. Krause, for one, favored accepting a bid, but that decision was up to the good fathers under the Golden Dome.

Meanwhile, the Irish played on back-to-back nights against Chicagoland teams in the Stadium with mixed results. A fired-up DePaul squad, hoping to prove it was better than that earlier flogging in the Fieldhouse, certainly succeeded. Ed Mikan, younger and lesser-known brother of George Mikan, scored 31 points, and the Demons coasted, 61-50. The next night, it took a miracle buzzer-beater from the top of the key by the durable Kevin O'Shea to supplement Leo Barnhorst's 19 points and put the Irish over Northwestern, 55-53. They closed the home agenda with a second win over St. Louis, this one 65-43, and the season ended with win number 20, the first time that plateau had been reached in nine years, over Marquette in Milwaukee, the first ND win there in four years, 73-68.

Well, the NCAA did put out its bid to Notre Dame. And, just as when the NIT offered in 1938 and the NCAA in 1943, the Irish declined it, citing the overextension of the season. At that time the NCAA and NIT took place one after the other, as both tournaments' finals were held in New York, and the NCAA took place last. Also, the two post-season eliminations were seen as much as exhibitions as they were true championships. In fact, until the early 1950s, more often than not the nation's best team gravitated toward the NIT. Which champion, if either, was the real one was often the subject of much debate. Notre Dame did not receive another bid from either post-season classic until 1953, and by then the attitude of the administration toward the NCAA tournament had changed.

The 1947-48 team, with a number of breaks, could have been a contender. Instead, it finished 17-7. Had there been as many teams making the tournament in 1948 as in more recent times, ND could have been invited, but only eight teams made the entire NCAAs at that time. What made that 17-7 more frustrating was that five of those seven losses were by four points or less.

Krause had lost Frannie Curran and John Kelly to graduation, so he moved Leo Barnhorst to forward and penciled Jim O'Halloran into his usual starting five. Joining second-team All-American Kevin O'Shea at guard was junior Paul Gordon. John Brennan, the 1946-47 leading scorer, was Moose's pivot man again. Also seeing early-season starting action was captain John Hiller, who had been one of Keogan's top men six years earlier but had seen only spot action in 1946-47. This group got off on the right foot with a 66-49 defeat of Indiana State in ND's only home game of the 1947 portion of the season. An interesting feature of this game was its coaching matchup. Since Krause, in his role of assistant football coach, was in California helping lead the Irish to a 38-7 drubbing of USC and a second consecutive national championship, his basketball assistant, Tom Brennan — John's older brother and a victim of the often confusing eligibility rules after World War II which caused his ineligibility for 1946-47 — took over the reins. On the visitor's bench was a man considered one of the best young college coaches in the country, John Wooden.

Krause returned in time for a trip to Champaign to face Illinois, finally. But the Illini held Kevin O'Shea to only five points and the Irish to 38, their lowest output of the season, in a 40-38 squeaker. Northwestern went down by six in the Stadium, and then ND went west, or at least as far west as an Irish basketball team had yet traveled. And while in Denver, Notre Dame suffered a triple whammy. Not only did the University of Denver upset the Irish thanks to a Roy Nelson field goal with 15 seconds left, 61-60, resulting in what was then and what probably still is the biggest win in the school's history, but in the game John Brennan fractured his right arm and was sidelined until late February. And further yet, Denver became the winner in the Vince Boryla sweepstakes, as the young man, who was then playing AAU ball with the old Denver Nuggets, decided to stay in the Colorado city when he returned to college for 1948-49. The Irish did win one on the way home, 51-49 over Kansas. Brennan's replacement at center, sophomore John Foley, scored 18 in his debut in the starting lineup to lead the way.

The next two games on the schedule were a first in ND basketball history. After much behind-the-scenes negotiations, Indiana's Big Four schools—Indiana, Purdue, Notre Dame, and Butler—got together in what was a growing trend in a basketball-hungry country, the holiday tournament. This double double-header was dubbed the Hoosier Classic and was to be held annually at what was then the largest indoor venue in the state, Butler's fieldhouse in centrally-located Indianapolis. However, an opposed to most other "classics," the Hoosier Classic was not designed to crown a champion. It was set up so that on one night Butler played Purdue and Notre Dame, Indiana and on the next Notre Dame played Purdue and Butler, Indiana. Since Notre Dame-Butler and Indiana-Purdue already were well-established home-and-home rivalries, those matchups were intentionally avoided. Interestingly, in most of these Classics one team won two games and thus was "champion." In the inaugural tourney, the "winner" was, surprisingly, Butler. Notre Dame ruined its chances by being blown out by a worse Indiana team, 72-46, on opening night, but then, thanks to a last-minute hoop by Jim O'Halloran, the Irish topped Purdue, 42-40. (In the first five Classics, the story for ND was the same: though not always in this order, it lost to Indiana and defeated Purdue.)

After a month of traveling, Notre Dame played three straight games in the extremely friendly confines of the fieldhouse—an easy way to continue the momentum gained by that last-minute Purdue win. It was reunion day when Georgetown came in; Elmer Ripley, who had spent one glorious year as Irish head coach, was the Hoyas' head man, and two ND expatriates, Ray Corley and Tom O'Keefe, were the team's mainstays. And while Corley scored 12 and O'Keefe 11 to pace a balanced Hoya attack, Kevin O'Shea tallied 19 and the Irish won, 77-69. This win was also significant because it marked Notre Dame's 35th consecutive win at home dating back to 1943, topping the 34-0 mark set after the new Fieldhouse wing opened in 1925. In short order, the skein climbed to 36 with an overwhelming defeat of the Butler team which "won" the Hoosier Classic and then to 37 with a 52-46 over DePaul.

Back on the road again, the Irish seemed on the verge of a major upset in Kiel Auditorium against St. Louis. They led, 32-21, with 14:30 left in the game. But the rest of the way, ND was outscored 21-8, with much of the damage coming from Easy Ed Macauley, and the Billikens had triumphed by two. A week's layoff followed, after which the Irish had a tough time with Northwestern. The stubborn Wildcats forced the game into overtime, but ND finally won with a 13-2 margin in the extra period, 59-48. It was not a particularly impressive performance considering that ND's next opponent was mighty Kentucky.

The 1947-48 Kentucky squad may have been the greatest in modern (since 1937) college basketball history. Adoph Rupp's juggernaut was built around juniors Alex Groza, Ralph Beard, and Wallace "Wah-Wah" Jones, plus a remarkable supporting cast of Cliff Barker and Kenny Rollins, among others; this team rolled to a 36-3 record which included an NCAA championship and for the five aforementioned players, a 1948 Olympic Gold Medal. Of its three losses, one was to Temple in Philadelphia by one point; one was to the top AAU team, the Phillips 66 Oilers, in the Olympic Trials by four points. And then there was February 2, 1948 at the Notre Dame Fieldhouse, a.k.a. "the snake pit," or "the bandbox," or various unprintable terms (to Kentucky fans).

To put it mildly, this was one of the shockers of this, or any, season. For the Fighting Irish defeated the Wildcats, 64-55, extending the home court win streak to 38 and giving coach Krause a wonderful 35th birthday present. Most felt before the game that it couldn't be done. But the Irish played a perfect ballgame and beat the unbeatable convincingly. This one game had far-reaching implications, both on and off the court, after its conclusion.

For one, Kevin O'Shea led all scorers with 25 points, mostly from close range. He was able to work free so often because of a new offense installed by Krause for this game specifically. Krause stationed his two tallest men, Leo Barnhorst (6-4) and John Foley (6-5), at the foul line in order to keep Groza and Beard from setting up for rebounds under the basket. This setup also cleared the baseline for O'Shea rather effectively; two different

UK defenders fouled out trying to contain him. On defense, although the two all-stars tallied 23 and 19, respectively, the rest of the Wildcat team could garner only 13. Rupp had never seen this "high post" setup before; soon after this night, he adopted it himself and used it the rest of his career. Of course, there was a little outside help, too, and for that this game has become one of Krause's all-time favorites.

Anticipation was so high among the students that ND officials warned the public not to expect any tickets to be made available. Consequently, the place, jammed to the rafters with students, became so incredibly loud that Rupp found it impossible to communicate with his team. This "problem" was amplified by the placement of the Notre Dame band—directly behind the Kentucky bench—and by the presence of from 300 to 400 members of the Holy Cross community in their black robes—directly across from the Kentucky bench. Following the game, Rupp claimed that under those circumstances it was impossible to win at Notre Dame, where he was now 0-5, and that he would never bring his Wildcats back as long as he was coach. Unfortunately for "The Baron," the ND-UK contract still called for one more visit to the fun house in 1950.

After such an incredible high, a letdown was inevitable two days later at Butler; the Irish hung on to defeat a team which had lost to ND by 24 earlier, 53-52. The next day Detroit fell easily, 55-30. Notre Dame had won eight of its last nine games and was 11-4 overall; now another fanatic home crowd was preparing to "welcome" the second-best team in the nation, St. Louis, which had won by only two at the Gateway City earlier in the year. After the amazing performance against Kentucky, could lightning strike twice?

No. The 38-game home winning streak came to a crashing and convincing end behind Ed Macauley's 21 points. The Irish were never really in the 68-51 loss. And the Billikens, with first-year coach Eddie Hickey pulling the strings, were well on the way to a final 24-3 record and the NIT championship (they wisely avoided Kentucky in the NCAAs). For the Irish, they quickly fell out of contention for a post-season bid. At Chicago Stadium, a late rally fell short against DePaul; the Blue Demons beat the Irish in the Windy City for the fifth straight year, 50-46. And considering the considerable home court advantage ND enjoyed, the back-to-back contests against Michigan State were decidedly odd. The Irish won in East Lansing, 51-44, but lost at home, 54-50, blowing an 11-point lead in the process. Now ND had lost two in a row at the Fieldhouse for the first time since Coach Krause was a junior (1932-33)!

John Brennan, the regular center, returned to the lineup for the last five games after his Denver injury had healed—and the Irish won all five. The day after the MSC loss, they closed the home slate with, finally, another win, 72-55 over Marquette. To commence a three-games-in-five-days road trip, Brennan's 22 helped defeat Canisius in Buffalo, 64-55. And then came another major upset.

The annual Madison Square Garden clash with New York University took on added significance because the Violets were Number One and the only unbeaten team in the nation (19-0). In a closely-fought game which included 17 lead changes, the Irish ended the longest undefeated skein in the country, 64-59. Featured in this game was a strong defensive effort which restricted NYU star Dolph Schayes to eight points, and an incredible comeback in the late going with two ND starters out on fouls. This streak-breaking loss, which some historians erroneously credit to St. Louis in the NIT final, led to a severe slump for the Violets; NYU closed the regular season from here 1-2 and then won its first two tourney games before the loss to the Billikens. This wasn't the last time that the late-season end of an unbeaten season at the hands of Notre Dame had this effect on the victim. Two wins, over Penn and Marquette, closed the season almost anticlimatically. But the play of sophomore Kevin O'Shea was impressive enough, particularly in the big games, to garner a first-team All-America mention on six different teams.

Because Moose's top six players were back for 1948-49, he had high hopes for the year. The schedule he put together certainly reflected that. Gone were the early-season patsies; all 24 games were against traditional or respected opponents, comprising perhaps the most challenging schedule in the country. According to Krause in a pre-season interview, so many places and teams put out attractive offers to Notre Dame that he scheduled contests forgetting about home games, and some last-minute scrambling and postponements had to be done to get nine Field-house games squeezed in. With this schedule, which took the "New Ramblers" from New York to Dallas to San Francisco and numerous places in between, it was no wonder that Notre Dame could muster "only" a 17-7 record for the second year in a row. Those seven losses were to the class of the nation; the combined won-lost record of the teams which defeated ND (counting St. Louis twice, once for each ND loss) was 145-39 (.788).

One of the setbacks was in the opener against Illinois (eventually the third-place NCAA team with a 21-4 final record). For the first time in exactly 25 years, Notre Dame went into its second game 0-1. The Irish were unable to hold a 27-20 halftime lead, and the Illini were able to come back to win it in overtime, 59-58.

Krause had found satisfaction, despite the loss, with a four-senior, one-junior starting lineup (Jim O'Halloran, Leo Barnhorst, John Brennan, team captain Paul Gordon and Kevin O'Shea), and this crew turned things around quickly with five straight wins, over Northwestern at the Stadium (55-44), Wisconsin (60-54), Pennsylvania (55-42), Navy at the Stadium (70-62), and Purdue in the opener of the second Hoosier Classic, thanks to a late free throw by Barnhorst (51-50). But, in what was becoming the norm, the Irish dropped the mythical championship game to Indiana. This one was quite a bit closer than the 1947-48 blow-out, but the 50-47 defeat was still a loss.

In a way, the next two contests were like a vacation which was interrupted for a few hours each of two nights for a basketball game. The Irish left the Indianapolis home of the Hoosier Classic and immediately headed for Dallas—ND's first hoops trip to Texas—for a December 30 tussle with Southern Methodist, which was won fairly easily, 58-45. From there, the team was off to another place where no ND basketball team had gone before—San Francisco. This was a "home" game for Bay Area product Kevin O'Shea, and in the Cow Palace, he helped the Irish to a 70-66 defeat of nearby St. Mary's, a more worthy opponent in 1949 than it was in 1981 when the Gaels traveled to Notre Dame for the first time.

Fortunately there were eight days until the Irish had to play again, because they were delayed in their return to campus by a snowstorm in the Rockies. Unfortunately, the first opponent for ND on its three-game home stand was ever-ready DePaul. Ray Meyer was still looking for his first win in the Fieldhouse as Blue Demon head coach. And even though his seventh DePaul team was not his best (16-9), it was his day. The Irish were annihilated, 59-38, their worst home loss in nearly ten years. Another week passed, and ND beat a tough Butler team, 60-58. But it was a costly win. O'Shea did not play because of another injury, but he would return soon. John Brennan would not. For the second year in a row, an injury curtailed his season; this one, torn ligaments in his left knee, ended his career. Krause would have to do some juggling for the Denver game.

He inserted John Foley at center—the second year in a row that Foley had inherited the pivot after serious injury to Brennan; little-known senior Dick Kluck started at one forward with Barnhorst; and O'Halloran and Gordon held down the guard spots. With this somewhat patchwork lineup, the Irish defeated Denver, 49-46. What made this game intriguing was the return to South Bend of Vince Boryla, the former Irish standout who now was garnering All-America status in the Colorado capital city. But ND was up to the challenge. Barnhorst put on a show worthy of All-America mention, scoring 20 points and holding Boryla to only five—one field goal and three foul shots—for his collegiate low mark. What a way to make up for the tough loss out there a season ago!

Exam time gave ND a week off and got O'Shea back into playing shape in time for a game expected to be tough—a trip to Louisville to face Kentucky. Had it not been for some off-court shenanigans which ended in an unexpected loss to Loyola (IL) in the NIT after winning the NCAAs again, this Wildcat team would rank as greater than the one which preceded it: with Groza, Beard, and Jones now seniors, this edition of Ruppians went 32-2. No one realized it at the time, but some of those 32 were tainted along with that Loyola loss and an NIT loss to Utah in 1946-47. One of those was UK's revenge on ND's stunning 1947-48 upset, 62-38. (Why these games were odd will be discussed later.) To make matters worse for the Irish, on the way home from the massacre they lost to Butler in Indianapolis, 68-54.

The easiest way to break a losing streak was to play at home, and that's how this one ended. Because of a continuing injury to Paul Gordon, sophomore Marty O'Connor earned a start against Michigan State and performed well in the streak-breaking 63-47 triumph. A victory at mediocre Marquette (71-64) followed; then the Irish headed into St. Louis and gave another great Billiken team a great scare. Krause tried to shake up Eddie Hickey's team by throwing a zone defense at it, ND's first use of this tactic all season. The scheme worked for a half; St. Louis led only 24-23 at intermission, but halftime adjustments and cold Irish shooting turned a close one into a rout, 61-44.

Six straight wins followed, including five straight away from home. First the Irish swept the season series from Marquette, winning at the Fieldhouse, 59-42. Next at Chicago Stadium, the tables were turned on DePaul, which had so demoralized ND earlier; a balanced scoring attack led by O'Halloran's 15 and Barnhorst's 13, and 22-of-26 accuracy from the line, catapulted the Irish to a 54-49 victory. Notre Dame won its 600th all-time basketball game at East Lansing, but just barely; despite a 32-17 Irish lead at halftime, Michigan State chipped away, and chipped away, and held the frustrated Irish to just 11 second-half points, but the visitors held on, 43-41. (Thirty-four years would pass before ND won a game with so few points again.) As the Krausemen headed east, they stopped off at Buffalo and beat Canisius, 59-51, and then, in front of the usual enthusiastic Madison Square Garden crowd, the Irish erased a six-point halftime deficit despite having all five starters saddled with four fouls and defeated NYU going away, 71-66. Back at its home away from home, Chicago Stadium, ND upped its record to 17-6 with a hard-fought 59-56 win over Northwestern.

To close the season, St. Louis visited the Fieldhouse. And while the game was closer than the one in Kiel Auditorium, the Irish still fell short, 68-59. Although Paul Gordon closed his college career with 22 points, Leo Barnhorst closed his with an early exit via disqualification on fouls, which hurt considerably. John Foley's five-foul performance didn't help, either.

Two weeks after the final game, Moose Krause was elevated to the athletic director's chair, replacing Frank Leahy, who decided to concentrate on football only. He had already served a year as Leahy's assistant to prepare him for a job he would hold for over three decades. For the first two years he retained the reins of the basketball team as well, but decided to stick to one position when he found he was unable to spend the kind of time with the hoops squad he would have liked.

Even barring his new job, there were tough times ahead. Schedules weren't getting any easier, and the talent pool wasn't what it had been. The 1949-50 Irish had to rebuild after losing many seniors to graduation, and the replacement horses were not of the same breed as the ones which had moved on. The team, therefore, dropped a couple of notches to a 15-9 final record.

Kevin O'Shea was back for his senior year, and regained the form which was evident when he was a sophomore. He was given the captain's role, and time and again he was counted on in the clutch. John Foley, another senior, finally earned the center spot on his own and not through injury to the front-line man. Also in the starting lineup the first day were three men who had not played a varsity minute: sophomores Don Strasser and Leroy Leslie and junior Dan Bagley, who missed his first year of eligibility because of subpar grades. Both Leslie and Bagley averaged in double figures but displayed an annoying tendency to land in foul trouble; Bagley, in fact, set a record which has not been eclipsed (though tied twice) by fouling out 11 times. The fact that two-thirds of the top scorers were often on the sidelines during the stretch run may have played a role in most of the losses; none was by more than 10 points.

A 57-50 win over Creighton, back on the ND schedule after two decades, got things started at home, but four straight losses — to Wisconsin, Northwestern, Iowa, and Indiana in the Hoosier Classic opener — weren't particularly encouraging. The defeat by the Hawkeyes was the most frustrating, for it was at the Fieldhouse, and the Irish led at halftime, 35-32, only to fall, 64-62. The 1-4 start was ND's worst since 1921-22. But, as opposed to that Dark Ages season, the Irish quickly turned things around by winning five in a row.

As usual, they closed the Hoosier Classic by upending Purdue (59-41); back at Notre Dame, Butler fell, 54-33; in East Lansing, behind 21 by O'Shea, the Irish topped Michigan State, 76-65; they took a convincing 28-14 halftime lead and — again led by O'Shea—knocked off DePaul, 58-53; and at the beginning of a two-games-in-two-days road trip, John Carroll, now coached by the ubiquitous Elmer Ripley, fell in Cleveland, 73-66. The streak ended, however, in Buffalo, with ND's first-ever loss to Canisius, which was having a good season in 1949-50 (17-8), 53-50. But that losing skein ended at one with a 71-65 defeat of Michigan State at home, in preparation for what was to be the last visit to Notre Dame by an Adolph Rupp-coached Kentucky team.

Today, this game could not have taken place as scheduled. It might have been the only way Rupp would fulfill the contract for one more game at the Fieldhouse, for the ND-UK match was on January 23—right in the middle of Notre Dame finals week. (Current policy prohibits any ND sports participation during exams.) If the venerable Wildcat coach thought this maneuver would keep the students away, he figured wrong. In many ways this game was similar to the 1948 game at ND, although the cast of characters on both sides was substantially different. For Kentucky, Alex Groza, Ralph Beard, and Wallace Jones had joined the National Basketball League as a unit called the Indianapolis Olympians. (This coup by a dying league led to the NBL's merger with the stronger Basketball Association of America into the National Basketball Association.) Now the big gun for the Ruppians was seven-foot center Bill Spivey, who was perfect for the high-post offense which "The Baron" had adopted after ND had used it on him two years earlier. But the greatest similarity was in the final result.

The Irish easily defeated UK, 64-51. Figuring that stopping Spivey would be difficult at best, Krause didn't try to; instead, he had his team swarm on everyone else. The Wildcat center scored 27 points—which meant everyone else on the team had only 24 combined. Meanwhile, ND's top three scorers led a balanced attack; O'Shea had 18, Bagley 16, and Leslie 14, and the crowd played its part again, making Rupp feel very uncomfortable. Again the band was seated behind his bench, and he couldn't hear himself think, much less direct his team. For the students, they couldn't think of a better, or more appropriate, way to send the coach away for the last time than to show up despite their exams.

Another sendoff, this one much more cordial from the ND fans at the Stadium, was awarded Arthur "Dutch" Lonborg, long-time Northwestern coach who was stepping down at season's end. Lonborg almost bowed out against his traditional non-conference rival with a season sweep, but the Irish tallied 15 points in the last five minutes of the game and emerged victorious, 64-57. Butler dropped ND's record to 9-6 with a 63-57 win at its fieldhouse, quite a reversal from the earlier Irish 21-point win. But two more victories followed: 79-61 at home over an awful Marquette team, and 56-41 over Loyola of Chicago, back on the ND schedule for the first time in 25 years.

Old thorn in the side St. Louis proved to be one again. A major factor in Notre Dame's 55-45 loss—the low offensive output for the 1949-50 Irish—was that four starters, all but O'Shea, fouled out. And speaking of O'Shea, all eyes focused on him as his collegiate career neared its end, for he was approaching two ND milestones: the modern season scoring mark (held by Leo Klier) and the 1,000-point career mark (held by no one). He got close to the latter in a home 67-60 win over Loyola, and then scored number 1,000 against DePaul in the Chicago Stadium. But—again—the opponent avenged a loss in the Fieldhouse. DePaul's 68-58 trimph was particularly satisfying to Ray Meyer because his Demons were doomed to a losing record for the first time since he took over (12-13).

For the second year in a row, ND closed its home schedule against St. Louis. And now that Adolph Rupp had been tormented in the "pit" to the point of repulsion, the Irish began to do the same to another future Hall of Fame coach, Eddie Hickey. Three years had passed since the Billikens had lost to ND, but behind 15 points by Leroy Leslie and some clutch foul shooting by—you guessed it—Kevin O'Shea, the Irish ended their drought, 55-52. To end the season, the team traveled to the East Coast, topping Navy in Annapolis, 65-59, and finding itself the victim of an upset by NYU, 66-63. Nearer to home, Kevin O'Shea, who needed 21 points to eclipse the season scoring standard, scored 23 to lead ND over Marquette for the eighth straight time, 65-58, to end this up-and-down season on an up note.

To the surprise of few, Moose Krause announced that the 1950-51 season would be his last. But the timing of his announcement was unusual; he told his team right before tipoff of the first game of the season, against Franklin. This wasn't the only surprise this season offered to the college basketball world at large.

On January 17, 1951, a Manhattan College player, Junius Kellogg, reported an offer of a bribe—which he turned down but several teammates did not—to college officials. That started a snowball rolling which, by October 21, 1951, had enveloped the entire sport and made any on-court mistakes, even when—as in the vast majority of cases—they were honest, look suspicious. When the whole tale was told, 32 players from seven schools were discovered to have "shaved" points in 86 games played in 23 cities in 17 states during a four-year span (1947-1950). Included were some of the nation's top teams and stars: Long Island University, a school which had built its entire reputation on successful basketball teams; City College of New York, the Cinderella story of 1950 with its unprecedented feat of winning both the NCAA and NIT; and, most shocking of all, the greatest of all teams during this period, Kentucky—and both Alex Groza and Ralph Beard had been on the take several times, including both those upset losses in the NIT and the 1949 Kentucky-Notre Dame game in Louisville, which UK had won despite everything.

In most cases, however, the point was not to "throw," i.e., intentionally lose, a game, but to make sure that the team did not "beat the spread," or win by more points than bookmakers thought a team would win by. In basketball, this was a relatively easy proposition; since there are only five men on the floor at a time, if one or two of them were influenced by crooked gamblers' money, the effect would be much more profound than, say, to try the same in football or baseball, the other big-bettor team sports. All a gambler had to do was, when no one was looking, offer a player large sums of money, more than could be obtained otherwise, and try to convince him that to win by less than the spread this way, i.e., point shaving, was not wrong because the team was still winning. Then he would bet a bundle on the underdog and cash in on the setup . . . until he was caught.

As a result of the scandals, several actions were taken. Fearing for its own shaky existence, the NBA immediately banned any player implicated and forced Groza and Beard to sell their stock in the Indianapolis Olympians; without them, the team folded within two years. Bill Spivey, the seven-foot center coveted by many NBA teams, was prohibited from playing in the league for his role, however slight. Most, if not all, of the players still in school were expelled. Most of the schools made their own internal reforms; LIU, for example, dropped basketball for five years and resumed only with stringent controls on its operation in force. Kentucky, however, was different. Thanks no doubt to some Adolph Rupp comments such as "The Chicago Black Sox threw games, but these kids only shaved points," and an unwillingness to reform on its own (e.g., to fire Rupp), a full-scale investigation of UK's activities was launched. As is its wont, the NCAA, though, in its own ruling treated the symptoms but not the causes of the problems. Since much of the activity was centered at Madison Square Garden, the association banned post-season games in the arena and tried to discourage its members from playing any games there.

So on a national scale, the sport ended 1950-51 in turmoil. Some might call Notre Dame's play that season a scandal as well.

Many times, a coach's pre-season announcement of his retirement will spur a team on to lofty heights. This did not happen in Krause's case. His last team as head man finished 13-11 and fell two wins short of giving him 100 at Notre Dame.

The 1950-51 Irish had three major problems. One was an inability to play up to the competition. With one noteworthy exception, the best major-college team they beat all year was Northwestern, which finished 12-10. Another was difficulty playing well away from home, a major hindrance to any ND team which wanted to be successful. The Irish were 9-0 at the Fieldhouse, but 4-11 outside its friendly home. Finally, this team had a propensity for fouling. A total of 665 personals (nearly 28 per game) were whistled on Irishmen this season, a dubious ND record which teams playing as many as nine more games a season have been unable to touch. Worse, 53 times Notre Dame men were forced to sit because they had five personals. In 41 of these cases the usual members of the lineup (forwards Dan Bagley and Leroy Leslie, center Norb Lewinski, and guards Marty O'Connor and Jim Gibbons) were disqualified, and 10 different men fouled out at least once. It was no wonder this team had problems winning—

it almost never had its top players on the court at the end of the game. At least there was enough of a bench that ND always had five players on the floor.

A deceptively auspicious 4-0 start, over such competition as Franklin, Anderson, Wisconsin, and Northwestern, was tempered by a major loss. Don Strasser, a starting guard, broke his ankle against the Badgers and was out for the season. Gibbons and sophomore Jerry McCloskey alternated in his spot the rest of the year. Exactly what effect Strasser's loss had is hard to gauge, but he had gone through his sophomore season fouling out only once, so he might have helped hold down that total.

The bubble finally burst at Iowa. The Hawkeyes outrebounded the Irish, 71-31 (in one of the first ND games in which rebounding stats were kept) en route to a 63-60 win. Continuing a tour of the Western Conference, in the fourth Hoosier Classic ND held to form—Purdue fell and Indiana won. Before returning home, the squad stopped at Northwestern—actually Evanston High School, since NU had torn down its Patten Gym to make room for a new academic building and didn't build a replacement for another half a decade—and edged the Wildcats, 76-73. At the Fieldhouse, an abysmal Butler team fell, 55-48. Two days later, ND lost to another good St. Louis team there, 56-47. And in a foul-marred contest—the Irish alone were whistled 42 times—Notre Dame defeated Loyola of Chicago, now coached by ND graduate and Krause teammate John Jordan, 78-67. At this point, the team's record was still a good 8-3. But the worst was yet to come.

The complexion of the season began its decided turn in the wrong direction during a two-game road trip before exams. First, in Cincinnati, Xavier upended ND, 60-52. Two days later, the controversial Kentucky series resumed. For the first time, the contest was played in Lexington, in UK's brand-new, 12,000-seat arena. However, the move to the new building didn't change the Wildcats' own phenomenal home-court advantage which made Notre Dame's look nonexistent. Kentucky smashed ND 69-44, for its 92nd win in a row in Lexington, a streak destined to hit 127 before it finally ended (ND's longest streak was 38). The Irish cause was not aided by a second-half field goal "accuracy" of 4-for-25, either.

After semester exams, the Irish continued their downturn with a 60-43 loss to Michigan State, then finally broke out of it with their last road win of the season at Butler. In light of the betting scandals which had just begun to break, Indianapolis police, acting on rumors that there had been large amounts of money exchanged at illegal bookie joints on this game, searched the Butler Fieldhouse for any open gambling but made no arrests.

The win began a 5-1 streak, the last hurrahs for Moose Krause as a coach. The one loss was at Chicago Stadium to DePaul, which was avenged six days later at the Fieldhouse. With the exception of that road loss, ND was playing its best basketball of the season. Marquette fell convincingly, 82-56, and in the last home game, a payback for the loss at Michigan State was received, 76-65; but no greater illustration can be made than to look at the home rematch with St. Louis.

Eddie Hickey had another great squad; it finished 22-8 and went to the NIT. But Notre Dame, riding an emotional high, streaked to a nearly-ludicrous 46-20 lead at halftime and, spurred on by the partisans, held on to win, 77-70. Dan Bagley tied the post-1923 scoring record with 31 points to play a major role in this stunning upset. The Billikens did not return to the Fieldhouse until 1961; two straight upset losses there certainly played a key role, though Hickey later would claim otherwise.

Four games remained, and Krause had 98 wins at his alma mater. But his team dropped all four of them, the last of them to the same Marquette squad which finished only 8-14 and had been such an easy Irish victim earlier—an embarrassing way to bow out. The other losses were on an Eastern trip of three games in four days, to Canisius, 60-53 (four Irishmen fouled out), NYU, 87-72, and Penn, 71-60.

The NYU game was held at Madison Square Garden as usual. But the arena had become the scapegoat in the betting scandals, and even though neither team had been affected by the revelations, there was guilt by association in the eyes of the fans. The Violets were having a fine season, and Notre Dame was usually the best out-of-town draw in New York, but only 6,022 fans—less than a third of capacity—showed up, at that time a record low for college basketball at the Garden.

Before the season had mercifully ended, February 20 to be exact, ND announced the results of its coaching search. Not coincidentally, all the serious candidates were former Irish players. Ray Meyer was the first choice, but DePaul, not taking any chances, signed him to a long-term contract not long after Krause's resignation. Others considered for the job were George Ireland, a successful Chicago high school coach, and John Brennan, Krause's assistant. But the winner was John Jordan, who had spent years coaching winners at Chicago Mt. Carmel High School and had a year of college experience at Loyola. He was relatively little known outside of Chicago and South Bend, but the selection of Jordan proved most beneficial to the slumping Irish basketball fortunes.

# 14

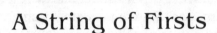

# A String of Firsts

During John Jordan's first five years at Notre Dame, many firsts for Irish basketball occurred. Some of these were of great consequence to the current and future progress of the program, while others were merely trivial. Several of these firsts came during Jordan's first—1951-52. And they started from the time the Irish first took the floor in a game that season, in St. Paul, Minnesota, against St. Thomas.

That day—December 1, 1951—marked the first time a black played basketball for Notre Dame. In fact, *two* of them played—started, even—and they both made major contributions to ND's 71-37 destruction of St. Thomas.

Blacks had never been banned from the University; there simply weren't many black Catholics, and those that were could not afford or could not get into Notre Dame, or never considered it in the first place. The first to matriculate at ND was Frazier Thompson in 1944; he also became the first to win a monogram, as he was an outstanding track athlete. Six years later, the first black basketball players participated on the freshman team; a year later, both of them—South Bender Entee Shine and Joe Bertrand—were good enough to start in their first varsity game. Despite their ground-breaking status—a photo essay on the two young men appeared in the February 1952 *Ebony* magazine, a reflection of the national attention they received—the players and students at Notre Dame generally treated them no differently than any other athlete. But ND officials realized the rest of the world was not so tolerant; although invited, no trips to the South were scheduled as long as the two were eligible. (The farthest south ND went in those years was Louisville in 1951-52, and that came about mainly through the efforts of a strong ND alumni club in that city.)

While at Notre Dame, Bertrand was a standout; he scored over 1000 points while starting nearly every game for the Irish for three years. Shine, after a frustrating first year, transferred to Tennessee State. One of the reasons Shine had such a tough time was that he had to watch the last 11 games in his street clothes. For the first time in Irish history, key players were lost during the season because of academic deficiency.

Notre Dame always has had fairly rigorous academic standards for its athletes. From the time a faculty board in control of athletics was established in 1898, athletes have had to maintain the same academic standards as any other student. For many years this presented little problem; even though exam time usually fell in the middle of basketball season, George Keogan never lost an important player during the season because he dropped below the 77 (of 100) necessary to stay eligible. But the potential was there.

Before February 1, 1952, Jordan's team was a very respectable 11-4. Then the first semester grades came out . . . and sophomore Shine, freshman Jack "Junior" Stephens, and senior Don Strasser were placed on academic probation, ineligible for the rest of the season. Strasser and Shine had been starters, and Stephens a top substitute.

For Strasser, it was not the way he had hoped to end his career at ND. A starter as a sophomore, he played only three games as a junior because of an ankle injury. He also was captain of the 1951-52 team, but had to relinquish that role to the only other senior, Leroy Leslie. Stephens was one of three freshmen on the 1951-52 varsity under a temporarily-reinstated freshman eligibility rule (rescinded at the end of the academic year and not to return until 1972), and the only one to see anything resembling regular game action.

As could be expected, the trio of probations had a devastating effect on the rest of the season. The Irish staggered in at 5-6 afterwards, finishing 16-10. Had the three lost men played three, or even two, different positions, ND might have been able to absorb the jolt and continue on. All three, however, were guards—

the two starters and the top sub at the position—and that position became the major Irish weakness the rest of the year.

But as mentioned, things had started so well. In fact, the Irish had won their first six games, doing it with an old standby—the senior-sophomore starting five. Sophomores Bertrand and Shine, along with center Dick Rosenthal from St. Louis, and seniors Strasser and Leslie led the way; a defeat of Wabash in the home opener was the end of an archaic series, and a home 83-78 win over Penn had been a battle of unbeatens.

Ah, but the Irish then lost three of their next four. The Hoosier jinx continued in the Hoosier Classic, and an old bugaboo (and a new one) led to Indiana's 67-54 win. Four Irishmen fouled out (the old one), and Hoosier freshman Don Schlundt of Washington-Clay High School in South Bend (the new one) scored 17 to lead IU. ND then did what they had done in each previous Hoosier Classic—beat Purdue.

After back-to-back setbacks to Michigan State (at home) and Louisville, and a too-close home win over Butler, Jordan shook up the troops by benching Shine and starting freshman Stephens against Marquette—and the Irish won, 74-56, behind 23 by Rosenthal. Then they beat Michigan State at Jenison Fieldhouse to make up for the earlier setback.

Exam time came next, but the probations didn't take effect until February 1. Meanwhile, Bertrand led ND to its fourth straight win, 72-59 over Canisius, with 26 points. Number five in a row looked good against Pitt in the first meeting of these classic opponents since 1938. The Irish led by 15 at the half; then foul trouble reared its ugly head again. Five men were forced to retire as the Panthers came from behind to win, 62-55.

The triple disaster had struck just in time for the annual Kentucky game. For the first time, the clash was being staged in Chicago Stadium, Notre Dame's "neutral site," in a compromise move to keep the series going. For the first time also, the band accompanied ND to a game away from the campus. But the psychological ploy didn't quite work. Jordan had to start his fourth and fifth guards (Jerry McCloskey and Jim Gibbons), yet somehow the undermanned Irish stayed in the game until the end, finally losing, 71-66. After beating Northwestern again—this time in Evanston—the Irish lost another home game; poor free throw shooting (14-for-31) led to Marquette's 57-50 revenge.

On a two-game road trip, St. Louis blew them out, 80-58, and it looked as if Butler was about to do the same. But a 20-6 spurt in the fourth quarter (the NCAA had temporarily joined the high schools and pros in adopting the four-quarter system) gave the Irish a 52-48 win. Then again ND trailed after three quarters, this time at home against DePaul, but a 21-11 spurt in the final stanza resulted in a 76-70 win. And the Irish closed out the home slate with their third loss on the Fieldhouse floor, a 62-60 heartbreaker against Pitt in Doc Carlson's last game against ND.

A three-games-in-four-days road trip didn't start well, with a loss to Navy—ND's first loss ever to the Midshipmen in basketball—and an overtime game with NYU—a first in that series. Notre Dame's already-decimated team was further handicapped by a back injury to Bertrand, who had been moved to guard after numerous combinations there weren't working; he wasn't even on the road trip, and was replaced by sophomore football player John Lattner. Aptly, it was the new man who provided the heroics in the NYU game.

In front of a paltry 7,111 at the Garden—an after-effect of the scandals which had surfaced in 1951—NIT-bound NYU was leading by three with little time left in the OT. Dick Rosenthal scored to bring ND within one, and then Leroy Leslie fouled out with :26 left. Lattner replaced him. The Violets elected to waive the free throw and freeze the ball, but they turned it over, and the future Heisman Trophy winner scored the winner with nine seconds left, 75-74.

One-point decisions quickly became habit. A night later, Penn used 19-of-20 free-throw accuracy to win at the Palestra, 67-66, to split the season series and to end the Eastern swing on a down note. But at Chicago Stadium, ND, for the first time since the Ray Meyer era began at DePaul, swept the season series. Senior Leroy Leslie, who finally led the team in scoring after finishing second two straight seasons, bowed out with 32 points, but it was Norb Lewinski who was the hero with the winning basket in the 78-77 ND victory.

Toward the end of the season, Notre Dame received a bid to a post-season tournament in Hawaii, a predecessor of today's

Rainbow Classic, but the Irish declined because of the travel costs involved (although Moose Krause recommended the bid be accepted). And not long after the season ended, there was talk of a basketball version of the minor-sport Central Collegiate Conference; negotiations were begun but eventually broke down. The eight-school league would have consisted of Notre Dame, DePaul, Marquette, Loyola, Drake, Bradley, Louisville, and Butler, all well-established basketball schools. It would have been a pretty good challenger to the Big Ten's Midwest dominance of conference hoops—but it was not to be.

A major rules changes, however, had a major effect on the Irish for 1952-53. The "Hack Incorporated" teams were to disappear forever because it was no longer profitable to foul late in the game—the two-shot foul returned to the game and the "waiver rule" was canned. Never again would two players foul in triple digits in the same season (Rosenthal 104, Leslie 100) and only once would anyone tie the disqualification record of 11 which Leslie had tied in 1951-52. The resultant re-emphasis on "real" defense paid immediate dividends with two great seasons and Notre Dame's first post-season play. In the process, Jordan disproved the commonly-held theory that a team couldn't win in the 1950s without a "big man"—ND's tallest player was 6-5.

In the hopes of keeping everyone eligible, the schedule was reduced from 26 to 22 (later 21; a March 5 game with Alabama and its new coach Johnny Dee—Jordan's assistant in 1951-52 and a new graduate of the ND Law School—which was scheduled for the new Fort Wayne Coliseum had to be cancelled because it conflicted with the SEC tournament). Among those dropped from the schedule was Kentucky, for the NCAA had put its entire program in suspended animation after the incredibly numerous violations discovered in the wake of the betting scandals. But the slate was still outstanding; 15 of the 21 games were against teams with eventual winning records. And the Irish were up to the task, finishing with their best regular-season mark in six years—17-4.

Jordan was aided immeasurably in that all the key men stayed eligible all season, so he used, for the most part, only six men on his first NCAA Tournament team. With the graduation of Leroy Leslie, Dick Rosenthal was moved from center to forward, joining Joe Bertrand, and captain Norb Lewinski regained his starting center berth. Jack Stephens filled one starting berth at guard, and senior Jim Gibbons and junior Bill Sullivan shared the other spot. This combination, particularly the first four, was a potent scoring machine; the Irish averaged 72.4 points per game, by far a new record.

They started right off with an 80-59 home win over Creighton, which wasn't much of a tune-up for a key game against one of the nation's best—Indiana. This was the Hoosiers' first visit to Notre Dame in over 20 years, a result of the temporary suspension of the Hoosier Classic, which bit the dust because of the Big Ten's new round-robin home-and-home schedule and allowance of only four outside games. And it was a classic. It was a back-and-forth affair all game, and not until Stephens' hoop with four seconds left put the Irish into the win column, 71-70, did anyone leave the gym. Lewinski scored 28 to lead the victors, and at the same time put a clamp on Indiana's sophomore center Don Schlundt. This was not the last ND heard from the Hoosiers this season; they were to meet again with higher stakes.

Following a road win over Marquette and a home win over Loyola of Chicago, the Irish took to the road, playing eight straight contests away, spanning almost a month. They started off in East Lansing, Michigan at their first holiday tournament other than the discontinued Hoosier Classic. The Michigan State Spartan Classic was set up much like the Indianapolis tourney in that the games were set in advance to avoid matching up Notre Dame and Michigan State, who already had a game scheduled; the purpose was to see two great nearby teams against two great teams from elsewhere. In this case, the foes were Kansas State, unbeaten at the time, an 80-64 winner over ND for the Jordanians' first loss, and UCLA, beginning its rise to prominence under John Wooden. This game was strictly a one-shot deal without a great deal of buildup; the name "UCLA" did not yet have the magic it would attain in another decade and a half. The Bruins were decent, however, and Notre Dame's 68-60 win, behind 20 points by Rosenthal, was considered a mild upset at the time.

That began a six-game winning streak which continued at Butler (63-49), at Northwestern (62-57), and at Boston against Holy Cross (73-71). The fifth win was the closest shave, the 20th consecutive year ND traveled to Madison Square Garden to face NYU. This one, like the last one, went into overtime, but 8-of-9 shooting from the stripe in the OT led the Irish to a 78-77 win. Number six was at West Lafayette; Dick Rosenthal scored 30 points against a dismal Purdue team in the 71-55 victory. But a trip to Rosenthal's hometown, St. Louis, proved not so kind to either Dick or his teammates—he scored only four points, and the Billikens dropped ND to 10-2 with an 86-81 win. The Irish finally returned home, and promptly nearly lost, but a fourth-quarter spurt overcame a good Bradley squad, 74-64, just before semester exams.

Two things worked to Jordan's advantage from here on: one, everyone stayed eligible, and two, of the eight games remaining, six were at home and two were in Chicago Stadium. And the only two losses were at the Stadium. The sluggishness which often plagued post-exam ND teams struck again against DePaul, and resulted in an 83-56 loss; the other was a close 78-77 loss to St. Louis, the last game of the continuous series.

The villain in the St. Louis case was its coach, Eddie Hickey. Undeniably a great mentor (he is in the Hall of Fame), he, however, had his troubles with Notre Dame. He claimed it wasn't fair financially to play ND home-and-home because Notre Dame received a much larger check for its visits to St. Louis' Kiel Auditorium than SLU did for its games at the Fieldhouse, a true statement but a picky reason for wanting to end an athletic relationship. He wanted any future Notre Dame "home" games played at the Chicago Stadium so that St. Louis would get its fair share of money. More likely, however, was that Hickey, like Adolph Rupp, had found it extremely difficult to win in ND's band box and used the money as a convenient excuse to avoid future trips there. Irish officials agreed for one year (1952-53) to accede to Hickey's demands, but after that, they told him basically to find his money somewhere else. Hickey was to rear his head again at another school later in the decade and singlehandedly end one of Notre Dame's longest continuous series using the same line.

Away from the politics, the Irish won their six games on the home floor, and the closest was 74-68 over Marquette. Butler, Louisville, Michigan State, Northwestern, and DePaul were the other victims. The most interesting of these was the 73-62 defeat of Louisville because, for the first time, a Notre Dame game was affected by television; the starting time was pushed up not because the game was being aired, but because there was a world championship fight on the tube that night (February 11) and Notre Dame feared attendence would suffer if the two events intersected. The victory over DePaul was also important; it was a 93-67 romp, a 53-point turnaround from the Stadium debacle and a new ND record for points in a game. It also earned the Irish their first trip to the NCAA tournament.

The main reason Notre Dame ended its post-season ban in basketball was the institution of the four-regional system. Games were closer to home and did not require lengthy stays in, or long travels to and from, any one city; in fact, in the first NCAA regional, ND day-tripped to both sites (Fort Wayne and Chicago). As the closest major college to the former site, the Irish even served as hosts at the new Coliseum. In front of the "home" crowd, they beat Eastern Kentucky, 72-57, and at the Stadium for the semis, they knocked off Pennsylvania—which had been absent from the regular schedule—69-57. But in the Mideast Regional finals, Indiana was the foe, and the Hoosiers, denied by one point in the Fieldhouse on December 6, weren't going to be on March 14. Don Schlundt set an opponent individual record by scoring 41 points in the IU 79-66 win—another step on the Hoosiers' road to their second national championship. For the Irish, the season was over at 19-5, but they had lost to a better team, a rarity for ND in future post-season play.

During the 1952-53 season, Jordan had made some attempts to get a big center—perhaps the only element missing at Notre Dame. In one of ND's few attempts at recruiting outside a 100-mile radius during the Jordan era, the Irish nearly nabbed one Gary Nelson, a 7-1 prospect from Oregon, but he never got to South Bend. (They did manage to get a seven-footer during this period, but from all reports he was so uncoordinated that he made the early George Mikan look like a ballerina, and he never played varsity ball at ND.) Nonetheless, Jordan looked forward to another great season, with four of his top six men back, but no one expected one *this* great. During the regular season, ND went 20-2, the best since 1935-36.

Again Jordan did it with basically a six-man squad, again with no one taller than 6-5. He moved Rosenthal back to the center spot, which he had occupied in the first part of 1951-52. Bertrand was back for his senior year at one forward, and sophomore John Fannon ably filled the other spot. Stephens returned at one guard, Bill Sullivan at the other, with senior Ed McGinn, little used in the past, as a sixth man when needed. This sextet was incredible, again breaking all scoring records while doing a yeoman's job on defense. A reflection of the success of the potent combination was this: even in the higher-scoring 1950s, no team scored more than 74 points against Notre Dame, and out of 20 regular-season wins, only five were decided by less than ten points!

The only two regular-season losses were against the defending NCAA champions and the eventual NCAA runners-up. Against Indiana in Bloomington, the defense did what it could. It held All-American Don Schlundt to nine points, but relatively unheralded Bob Leonard took up the slack with 21, and the Hoosiers played a little defense of their own; they held the Irish to what would be their lowest point total of the year (55) while IU scored 66. And the other one, at Peoria, Illinois, against Bradley, was a case of too little, too late. The Braves built a huge lead, but ND came fighting back in the fourth quarter. Alas, the comeback fell just short, and the Irish lost, 74-72. The rest of the season was nothing short of fantastic.

Of the 20 wins, the most significant, and one of the most convincing, had to be on January 15 in the Boston Garden against Holy Cross. In the midst of a 16-game end-of-season winning streak, the Irish blew out the Crusaders, 83-61. This loss was one of only two suffered by Holy Cross all season (26 wins), as the Crusaders went on to win the 1954 NIT. Another big one was at home against Louisville, another NIT participant; the high-scoring Cardinals fell to the Irish defense, 72-53. That 53 was the least scored by Louisville in over four seasons. And in the very next game, the Irish offense came up against NYU at the snakepit and broke its record for points by tallying 99 to the Violets' 64. Earlier in the season, Joe Bertrand had set a new individual scoring record with 35 (finally breaking Justin Moloney's 34 scored in 1908) against Loyola at home, as the Irish rolled to an 81-65 victory. And one day after the Holy Cross romp, Dick Rosenthal nearly duplicated that with 34 in a 78-59 Irish win at Canisius.

After that, the machine was put into overdrive; there were only three close calls in the last 11 games. Pesky Ray Meyer and DePaul were having only a so-so season (11-10), but in the contest at Chicago Stadium, the Demons stretched ND to the limit before the Irish came out on top, 59-54. (At Notre Dame, there was no contest—86-71 Irish.) Michigan State came within three points three days after the DePaul game, at Jenison Fieldhouse (74-71). And Loyola came back at the Chicago Stadium to give ND a scare late in the season, 71-65. By that time, however, Notre Dame's place in post-season play had been assured.

In the eyes of most observers, the Irish clinched their bid on February 20 in Annapolis, Maryland, against Navy, which was to come within one game of making the Final Four from the East Regional. For the first time, television focused on Notre Dame basketball, as the ABC network beamed the ND-Navy game to a nationwide audience. (This was also the year that the NCAA final game was telecast live for the first time, on the Dumont network.) And the Irish didn't disappoint their many fans; they defeated the Midshipmen, 84-72. After closing with wins over Penn and Marquette (twice) in addition to Loyola, it was NCAA tourney time again.

Again the Irish "hosted" the first-round game at Fort Wayne, and again they moved on, defeating Loyola of New Orleans, 80-70. This win gave ND, 21-2 and ranked in the top ten, the "honor" of playing Indiana, 19-3 and also firmly planted in the top ten. Prognosticators predicted a close one in this game in Iowa City, and that it was. For the second time Notre Dame's intense defense stopped Don Schlundt, holding him to but one field goal and ten points, while his opponent at center, Dick Rosenthal, scored 25, hauled in 15 rebounds (this was one of the few ND games before 1956 in which rebound stats were kept), and put up the eventual winning basket in a 65-64 thriller.

Not only was that game a slice of revenge, but it also put the Irish in an unusual position: they were now favored to win the entire tournament as they were the highest-ranked team left. But Penn State—the last team invited to the NCAA's—thwarted them. The Nittany Lions pulled a stunning upset in the Mideast Regional finals, catching ND on the emotional downswing the day after the big Indiana upset and throwing a zone press at the Irish—the first time ND had seen one all year. The final was 71-63, marking the first of a not-so-glorious Irish tradition of upset after frustrating upset in post-season play.

Nevertheless, it had been a great year. Jordan was named Coach of the Year by the Metropolitan Basketball Writers Association, the first ND coach so honored. Rosenthal had become the first player in ND history to average more than 20 points per game, and was selected to a couple of All-America teams. But the real story was the team. There had been not one outstanding member of the 1953-54 team, but many. The great success of Jordan in his first three years, compared to the relative lack of it in Moose Krause's last three, caused the athletic director to quip to anyone who would listen, "My first good move as athletic director was to fire the basketball coach."

But there were tough times ahead for the 1935 Notre Dame graduate.

Jordan had lost three-fifths of his starting lineup to graduation, and because he had fielded basically six-man squads each of the last two seasons, most of those left had limited varsity experience. He decided early on that he was going to revolve his 1954-55 squad around Jack Stephens, the only significant senior on the team and in his fourth year on the varsity. He was the captain, leading scorer, and a second-team All-American at season's end, and he seldom fouled, so he was almost always in the game when needed. He was the leader of a starting lineup which, in addition to himself, consisted of three juniors and a sophomore.

John Fannon was back from regular duty in 1953-54, Bill Weiman back from semi-regular action, and Lloyd Aubrey, a junior with limited game experience, became the new regular center replacing Dick Rosenthal, and proved a surprising source of alternate scoring punch, averaging nearly 17 points per game. The final spot in the starting lineup was filled by sophomore John Smyth; he also averaged in double figures, and led the team in rebounding. Depth was hard to find, again. When Jordan needed a substitute, he called on two more sophomores, Lee Ayotte and, during the second semester, footballer and another future Heisman Trophy winner Paul Hornung. The team was both less experienced and less talented than its immediate predecessors, and that showed in the overall 14-10 record and no tournament bid (though the NIT was interested for a while).

Inconsistency was the hallmark of the 1954-55 Irish; they never won more than two in a row, but only once lost as many as three consecutively. All but one of the losses was to a team with an eventual winning record: the one that wasn't was the first.

The December 11 game versus Indiana was a first in another way. For the first time, national TV cameras entered the Notre Dame Fieldhouse to televise a game, in the debut of the CBS-TV "Big Ten Game of the Week," a weekly spotlight for what was generally considered the best conference in the nation. And the Irish and Hoosiers gave the audience a good show. Notre Dame led most of the way, but IU took the lead in the last 44 seconds of the second half (the college game had returned to the half system) and held it for a 73-70 triumph.

The Irish closed the four-game start-of-season home stand at 3-1. After the heartbreaker to Indiana, they beat Loyola of Illinois after having earlier topped Wisconsin and Northwestern. But then they hit the road—and promptly lost three in a row to Big Ten opposition. The downfall for ND in the 78-58 loss to Purdue, a 66-57 decision by Illinois, and the 77-66 loss to Minnesota, particularly in the two closer games, was poor free throw shooting. With the new bonus rule, making the first foul shot late in the game became of great importance, and the Irish had all kinds of problems down the stretch.

But there were no problems as Notre Dame took its first trip to the Deep South since 1908-09 for the Sugar Bowl tournament. The Irish had been invited to the 1953 tourney, but declined the offer because of an already-full schedule (although the fact that there would be problems in the still-segregated South with a black on the squad may have played a role as well—there were no blacks on the ND roster in either 1954-55 or 1955-56). They did agree to enter the 1954 tournament, the first tournament ND entered to have a definite winner instead of predetermined matchups. And the Irish were that definite winner. They rolled over Loyola of New Orleans, a rematch of both teams' first-round NCAA game last March, 66-45, and then upset Holy Cross, behind Mr. Reliable, Jack Stephens, and his 24 points, which helped to counteract 30 by Tom Heinsohn of HC, 74-69.

The two-game winning streak ended quickly. Despite 29 more from Stephens, Louisville defeated the Irish in the Louisville Armory, 73-69. Then for the next nine games, the Irish won two and lost one, in that order, three times to increase both their record to 11-8 and the talk of a possible post-season bid.

First they knocked off Butler in a rare home game during the students' vacation. This gave South Benders their best chance in years to see Notre Dame in action, and also gave Butler athletic officials a pleasant surprise—a percentage of the gate receipts. Next stop for the team was Madison Square Garden and NYU. For the 22nd straight year, the Irish and the Violets were playing each other, but this appeared to be the last as the contract was not renewed for 1955-56. ND decided to end the series with a flair; the team came out in new green jerseys and, thus inspired, easily won, 93-74. But a trip up the coast to Boston was not so easy. Holy Cross was ready after ND had won in the Sugar Bowl; Tom Heinsohn scored 35 points while the Irish were cold, and the Crusaders rolled, 93-57, Notre Dame's worst defeat since 1944 when it lost by a similar 36-point margin to Great Lakes.

After an 82-74 defeat of Northwestern in Evanston on January 15, the team had three weeks off for exams—an unusually long break—and for the last 10 games the team was able to have Hornung, who added some needed depth. Upon the resumption of the season, the Irish defeated Loyola in Chicago, but then lost again. A lost nemesis—foul trouble—reappeared on the ND scene; four men fouled out in a 93-79 loss to Michigan State.

Two more wins followed (Bradley and Butler), and then ND, for the first time, traveled to the state of Oklahoma for a game. It wasn't a really good trip, as Tulsa knocked off the Irish, 74-59. But two nights later in Manhattan, Kansas, Notre Dame won its 700th lifetime game by defeating Kansas State, 76-74.

The win over K-State made ND 12-8, and if the Irish could have won their last four games, the NIT (or even the NCAA) would have made the phone call. Whether Notre Dame would have accepted he bid to the New York classic is unknown, because ND promptly played itself out of that chance. Admittedly, both Marquette and DePaul were very good, but the Irish had beaten only one very good team all year (Holy Cross, which later turned the tide). They tried at home against the powerful Hilltoppers, but the Milwaukee team rolled to its 21st straight win, 84-74. Then DePaul beat ND at Chicago Stadium, 81-77. So much for post-season play. But the Irish did have return matches with each of their Catholic counterparts to try and even the score.

That they did. First they topped the Blue Demons, who finished 16-6, in the Fieldhouse to make Ray Meyer 1-9 on his alma mater's home floor. And then ND pulled one of the big upsets of the season by defeating Marquette in Milwaukee, ending the Hilltoppers' 22-game winning streak. A two-pronged Irish attack led in the incredible 85-64 pasting of the eventual second-place team in the Mideast Regional of the NCAA; Jack Stephens, in his last game at Notre Dame, scored 35 to tie the Irish record, and Lloyd Aubrey added 28 as the up-and-down Irish ended on an up note.

The momentum from the two big wins at the end of the season didn't carry over into the 1955-56 season. Very little carried over from the last campaign, not even Irish tradition. For the first time in 33 years, the Notre Dame basketball program suffered through a losing season. Needless to say, the natives got restless; more than once during the year, scattered boos and pennies (along with other debris) littered the hallowed Fieldhouse halls. Notre Dame fans were not used to losers— especially not at home. For the first time since 1918-19 (the worst team in Irish history) and only the second time ever, ND dared to have a losing record at the venerable building. And when the long, frustrating season was over, the Irish stood 9-15. But they sure deserved better.

Almost every game was close. Many were not decided until late in regulation time, and a record five went into overtime. Fourteen of the 24 games were decided by six points or less, but the Irish lost 10 of them. And it all started in the opener at Detroit; the Titans' star, Bill Ebben (father of a future ND women's basketball player), scored 32 points to lead the home team to a 77-71 win, Detroit's first win ever over Notre Dame.

With the exception of a one-week period around New Year's Day, the Irish could not win consistently no matter how they tried. That one week was one of great team and individual achievement, starting with a return trip to the Sugar Bowl. Notre Dame was a decided underdog to even finish third after its poor 2-5 start and with two other tournament teams ranked in the top 20. But a record-tying (for the second time this season) 35 points by Lloyd Aubrey and another 21 by John Smyth got the Irish into the finals over Alabama, 86-80. This was the first and only time the two schools played in men's hoops; the Tide coach was still Johnny Dee, in his fourth year and easily his best as a college mentor. The loss to ND made Alabama 5-3, but it was the last regular-season loss for the Crimson Tide in 1955-56. Dee's team of fourth-year players (eligible by SEC but not by NCAA rules, thus ineligible for the tournament) won its last 16 games, including a big win over hated Kentucky to clinch the league title. But for post-season play, Dee sent the 21-3 Tide into the AAU tournament, where they were no match for the semipro industrial-league men. The fourth-year coach then left for the AAU Denver Truckers.

Seventh-rated Utah had defeated Marquette to become ND's finals opponent. And again the Jordanians put together a superb effort and defeated the Utes, 70-65, the second upset victim in as many nights. While Smyth had 27 points and sophomore Bob Devine added 21, the real story was the defensive job Aubrey did on Utah's All-America candidate Art Bunte. The high-scoring center was held to 15 points and was forced out on fouls with 10 minutes left. Notre Dame had become the first team to repeat as Sugar Bowl champions.

And five days after the greatest team effort of the season, the greatest individual effort took place at the Fieldhouse. Lloyd Aubrey, who had tied the ND record twice already, finally shattered the points-in-a-game mark, at the expense of Butler. The 6-5 senior center scored 43 points to lead the Irish over the Bulldogs, 83-69.

Otherwise, there wasn't much to cheer about in 1955-56. Notre Dame did defeat Northwestern twice—but the Wildcats went 2-20 overall. Marquette was also a two-time Irish victim, a more significant achievement. The other wins were a road victory over Navy and a home overtime win over Loyola of Illinois, 86-85, thanks to Bill Weiman's field goal with 23 seconds left.

But at the Chicago Stadium, ND lost the return match to the Ramblers, 71-65, the only time Loyola has defeated Notre Dame in 23 meetings. And so many of the other losses were heartbreakers. The Irish took Michigan State to overtime, but Julius McCoy's 45 points—a record for an Irish opponent which still stands, even withstanding the NBA-style scoring of the 1960s—cinched the Spartans' win. Louisville, the eventual NIT champ, was another team ND took to overtime before falling short. And in Notre Dame's first trip to Rhode Island, Providence won thanks to a 44-foot desperation heave by a substitute, Gordon Holmes, in the first overtime, 85-83. It was just that kind of a season, and when the Irish returned from Peoria after a March 3, 69-63 loss to Bradley, almost everyone was glad to see the worst season since 1921-22 end.

# 15

## Comes the Hawk

Well, John Jordan had a task ahead of him. After the debacle of 1955-56, he needed to turn things around—fast. But what was nice was that he had the catalyst ready to move up to the varsity for 1956-57—Tom Hawkins.

A product of Chicago's Palmer High School, "The Hawk" was one of the most sought-after prep stars in the country in 1955, but he chose Notre Dame—an increasingly rare decision for blue-chippers. But even though he was a black man in a white man's world at ND, he never regretted his decision. He always admired the character of his fellow students; years later, he used the following story to illustrate his point.

He once took a date into a popular student hangout not far from campus; however, he was not allowed to be seated because of his race. He had become somewhat accustomed to such treatment, and calmly left with his girl. But he didn't expect what happened afterwards: there were a number of fellow students in the joint at the time, and when Hawkins left, all the Notre Dame men followed him out and didn't return. An effective word-of-mouth boycott of the place among ND students began and didn't end until it reversed its no-black policy.

Of course, Hawkins was better known for his wizardry on the basketball court. Before he was done, the record book had been completely rewritten. He broke records for game, season, and career points, and game, season, and career rebounds (the latter of which he still holds). At the same time, he helped lead Notre Dame to consecutive 20-win seasons for the first time since the 1930s.

Because Hawkins was so outstanding, often overlooked was his supporting cast, all of which was capable of pouring in the points as well. The offense shattered ND scoring records in the process of compiling an 18-7 regular-season record in 1956-57 by averaging 84.4 points per game.

Jordan experimented with several lineups while using eight players regularly. Hawkins held one forward spot, and John McCarthy eventually won the other after splitting time with senior Joe Morelli. Another senior, captain John Smyth, moved to center with the graduation of Lloyd Aubrey. Junior Bob Devine nailed down one guard spot, with the other one alternately held down by Ed Gleason and Tom Sullivan, the latter back on the team after three years in the military, until Jordan found his spark plug. Little 5-7 sophomore Gene Duffy, with his passing ability and quickness on defense to compensate for his lack of height, began to start at guard midway through the season, and after that there was no turning back on the way to Jordan's third NCAA bid. But things did get off to a slow start.

There was little doubt as to this team's potential offensive prowess after ND posted consecutive blowouts over weaker teams, St. Joseph's of Indiana (98-55) and at Wisconsin (75-55). But in the third game of the season, the Irish, none of whom was over 6-5 (a familiar theme), had to meet a Northwestern squad which *averaged* about that height. Notre Dame lost, 75-60, and then fell to another taller team, Purdue, at West Lafayette, 85-72. Welcome relief came at the hands of Valparaiso, 86-74, but Louisville, behind 40 points by its All-American, Charlie Tyra, defeated ND, 85-75, in a contest played at the new Fairgrounds Coliseum instead of Louisville's normal home site, the Louisville Armory, because of the anticipated throngs. (The Coliseum is better known under the name Freedom Hall.)

The Irish then went east, to the East Coast Athletic Conference (ECAC) Holiday Festival, an eight-team tournament hosted by Madison Square Garden. And what school did they face in Round One but NYU, the old opponent with which ND had been having trouble coming to terms in attempts to revive the traditional series. The game was a tough one, and the Irish almost got sent home early, but Bob Devine came through at the buzzer with a layup, and the Violets fell, 72-71. The semifinal game, ND's first encounter with Brigham Young, was no contest: Jordan used only six men, and all six tallied in double figures as BYU fell, 91-66. This, for the third straight year, put ND into the finals of a holiday tournament. This time, though, the Irish fell to a fine Manhattan team, 86-79, despite Tom Hawkins' 35 points. Back in front of the home folks, the Irish appeared to be streaking through Butler; they tallied 53 points in the first half and appeared to be coasting. But there was a little too much Ted Guzek for ND. He had 38 points, including the tip in of a missed basket at the buzzer. He, in combination with a stiffened Bulldog defense (ND scored only 31 in the second half), counteracted 37 points by John Smyth and dropped the Irish to 5-5, 86-84.

It was about this time that Gene Duffy, the 5-7 sparkplug, began to see much more action, finally entering the starting lineup for good. Not coincidentally, the revitalized lineup streaked to a 13-2 record the rest of the season, and tourney talk, which had been mum for three years, became hot and heavy again as ND streaked to nine straight wins to close the season.

The only two losses were to Illinois, again a problem for the Irish (in 1955-56, the Illini became the first team to score in triple figures against Notre Dame in a 103-93 win which, appropriately, was the high point total for ND that year), which won, 99-81, and Canisius, which finished a strong 22-6, 94-89 in two overtimes. The Irish led 89-88 in the second overtime, but then, as they tried to hold the ball for the win, had the ball stolen twice in consecutive possessions for easy Canisius layups.

Otherwise, the big question the rest of the way was not whether ND would win or lose, but whether this team could break 100 points. Seven times the Irish hit 90 or better, but every time they fell just shy, mostly because subs couldn't hit the "key" basket. Five of the seven were at home, with the student crowds pulling for the century mark which never came. Loyola went down, 90-76 (and later, at Chicago Stadium, after a 52-29 first half, went down again, 96-64); Indiana was stomped upon, 94-82; and in each of the last three home games, the triple-digit barrier was in jeopardy. Detroit fell, 99-88, and then DePaul, 95-80, and finally Marquette to end the season by the lopsided tally of 94-55. In the latter game, Jordan used a host of reserves who had not seen much action and Jack Bedan, a seldom-used senior, led all ND scores with 22. The one other game on the road was a 99-82 thrashing of Holy Cross behind the left-handed push shots of John McCarthy. His shooting style, in stark contrast to the smooth jump-shot technique of Tom Hawkins, earned the junior the nickname "Shot-Put John."

Only two of the wins were decided by 10 points or less. Michigan State, the eventual winner of one of the tightest Big Ten races in years (Illinois, Indiana, and Purdue—all Irish opponents—were in the hunt as well), fell by only 10, 86-76, at the Fieldhouse, and stingy Butler was the victim of Irish revenge, 70-65. In the tradition of "turnabout is fair play," the Bulldogs led, 63-53, with five minutes left, and ND outscored them down the stretch, 17-2.

With the nine-game win skein at the end of the season, there was a good chance that Notre Dame would break with tradition and accept an NIT bid, which was almost certain to come. But to nearly everyone's surprise, the Irish instead received an at-large berth to the NCAA playoffs. As that happened, ND appeared in the wire service polls for the first time all season—17th in AP, 19th in UP.

The Irish opened strong with an 89-77 win over Mid-American Conference champion Miami of Ohio at Ohio State's St. John Arena. But in the Mideast Regional semifinal, at the University of Kentucky's Memorial Coliseum, surprising Michigan State, the eventual Final Four representative from the Mideast, shocked the hot Irish, 85-83. The Spartans did it by generally containing Tom Hawkins, though the multi-talented sophomore still registered 19 points. Of course, what made the loss even more difficult to swallow was ND's 10-point win over MSU in the regular season. That, however, had been at the Fieldhouse. The Irish came back to salvage third place—and a 20-win season—by defeating Pittsburgh, 86-85.

Jordan had reason to be optimistic as preparations for 1957-58 began. He lost only one of his final 1956-57 lineup to graduation (John Smyth). Returning were both forwards (Hawkins and McCarthy) and both guards (Devine and Duffy), but filling the center spot was a sticky problem until the beginning of the second semester. Tom Reinhart, a junior, started the year there, but sophomore Mike Graney, academically ineligible the first semester, got his grades up in time to help the Irish in the stretch run. While those six men saw the lion's share of playing time, seniors Ed Gleason and Jim Williams and junior Mike Ireland, the son of former ND great and Loyola coach George Ireland, also contributed at times. This team had the second-best record in Jordan's collegiate coaching career; after the regular season, its ledger stood at 22-4. There was no doubt as to ND's participation in post-season play.

With the graduation of Smyth, Hawkins became a much bigger part of the offensive picture. During 1957-58 he scored 730 points, by far the largest one-season total up to that time in ND history. Very seldom were defenses able to contain the junior. Even when they could, there was plenty of alternate scoring punch available; both McCarthy and Devine also averaged in double figures and Graney almost did.

For all the scoring potential, defense was the byword in Notre Dame's first three wins, 82-63 over St. Ambrose, 75-53 at Wisconsin, and 69-56 over Nebraska, the Cornhuskers' first visit to Notre Dame and the first time the two had played since the early 1920s. But then the Irish took their 3-0 record into Milwaukee . . . and left 3-1. Marquette, which was 0-4 before the game, upset ND, 78-64, despite 31 from Hawkins. The team continued its eternal mastery of Loyola of Chicago next, 82-63, but then it went to Michigan State and lost there, 79-72. Larry Hedden of the Spartans scored 21 points in the second half, and the Irish had foul troubles, both of which contributed to the ND loss.

December 27-28 saw the renewal of the Hoosier Classic for the first time in six years. Because the Big Ten altered its scheduling policy, Indiana and Purdue were free to resume relations with Butler, which led to the resumption of the popular tourney. The Hoosier State's "Big Four" again were paired such that the traditional opponents would not meet (ND-Butler, Indiana-Purdue). And in this first resumption of the Classic, Notre Dame, for the first time, won both its games and the unofficial tourney championship. First the Irish knocked off Purdue, 68-61, and then Indiana (for the first time in six Classic meetings), 89-74.

Four more wins followed the Hoosier Classic triumphs. A pesky Northwestern team held Tom Hawkins to his season low, nine points, and almost came back from a 38-23 halftime deficit as ND held on for a 71-66 decision. Returning home for the first time in three weeks, the Irish knocked off Butler, 83-72, and then did the same to Valparaiso and DePaul. The Valpo game was unusual because it was played in Fort Wayne, the first regular-season college game played in the Coliseum since its opening. The Indiana city had lost the Fort Wayne Pistons, there since 1941, to Detroit, and was hoping big-time Indiana college basketball could help fill the void. In the case of ND-Valpo, it didn't work, for a small crowd showed up, but Fort Wayne would serve as another Notre Dame "neutral site" in the early and mid-1960s.

Not only did the winning streak end at Louisville—a spurt just before the half by the home team put the game out of reach—but coach Jordan was forced to leave the game in the second half with a nosebleed. He ended up in the hospital for two weeks, and while there, his top assistant, Jim Gibbons, took over the reins. He hardly missed a beat, as a week after falling to Louisville, the Irish knocked off Illinois in Chicago Stadium, 81-67, in Mike Graney's first varsity appearance, behind 39 points by Hawkins and 18 more by McCarthy. Just as important to the win was the ND defensive job on Illinois' Don Ohl; the All-American managed only three points. Equally, if not more, satisfying was the reception when Louisville entered the Fieldhouse for the return match after the defeat down there. The fired-up Irish showed no mercy, earning revenge, 73-53. But in Gibbons' third and last game as fill-in head coach, another strong Bradley team (an NIT participant in 1957-58) topped ND at the Stadium, 81-70—Notre Dame's fourth loss, all on Saturday nights away from home. But it was to be the last of this great season.

Upon Jordan's return to the bench, the Irish won their last ten games in preparation for their second straight NCAA trip. In this stretch, their average victory margin was an incredible 17.6. The addition of Graney on defense and the continued phenomenal scoring pace of Hawkins were the catalysts to the strong finish.

Hawkins really turned on the afterburners in the late going. He scored 24 against Navy (85-63), 25 against NYU (93-77), 35 against Butler (90-81), and tied the team record of 43 against Air Force, another "disappointing" game for the home fans because ND just missed 100 with a team of subs (98-70). But the big game was at Chicago against first-time opponent and defending national champion North Carolina. His 33 points helped lead the Irish to a massive win over the Tar Heels, 89-70. Notre Dame had been blessed with a schedule primarily composed of usually-tough teams on off seasons, and this win added some badly-needed respect to a fine record.

After the aforementioned Air Force game and the century-mark near-miss, the Irish tried again two days later. And on February 10, 1958, Notre Dame passed the 100-point mark for the first time. Marquette, which had defeated ND earlier in the season, was the unwilling victim of a 106-74 barrage which could have been even worse if not for some little-used subs playing out the string. The Irish topped 100 again at Detroit, but this time the defense almost gave up the same amount in an NBA-style 102-96 contest. Much tighter was the season finale at DePaul's Alumni Hall, the Blue Demons' two-year-old home. Thanks to a spark from Jim Williams, who scored four key points late, ND took its win streak into the tournament intact, 75-71.

The Mideast opening round was at Northwestern's McGaw Hall; while there, the Irish annihilated Tennessee Tech, 94-61, to earn another trip to Lexington, and a rematch with Indiana. Jordan's men sent the Hoosiers into the consolation round, 94-87. Unfortunately, the next rung to a Final Four berth was Kentucky.

One of the most controversial practices of the NCAA selection committees over the years, especially in recent years when the word "regional" is almost meaningless, has been to place tournament teams so that they will, or could, play on their home courts. Proponents say this is necessary to spur local interest and avoid massive numbers of empty seats; opponents, however, point to the unfair advantage of home teams that no team deserves in a tournament of this type, especially when most games are in neutral sites. And in the 1950s, no team had a greater home edge than Kentucky, which had, earlier in the decade, the longest home winning streak in NCAA history and had only cooled off slightly since. The Wildcats, on their way to the NCAA title, took advantage in the first meeting of the two schools since 1952 and utterly destroyed the Irish, 89-56, ND's worst loss ever in post-season play. This blowout did have a fringe benefit of sorts: the

Irish and Wildcats resumed the dormant basketball series on a yearly basis starting in 1958-59.

Again Notre Dame had fallen short of the Final Four by one game. Twenty years would pass before ND got so close again, and 11 years before the Irish even got beyond the first round again. With the graduation of Bob Devine and John McCarthy, the often-overlooked co-captains of the 1957-58 team, decline came quickly.

# 16

## The Long Slide

The six seasons from 1958-59 through 1963-64 were not particularly satisfying for Irish faithful. Four of those seasons yielded a losing record, and in the other two, the Irish responded to NCAA tournament berths with first-round losses. Most of Notre Dame's trouble in fielding competitive teams during this era can be traced to one source—the aging Fieldhouse.

For years the Irish had been playing nearly 60 percent of their games away from home, and these years were no exception. The problem now, however, was finding any school willing to play ND at home. There was no money in it except a small guarantee, since most patrons were non-paying students—a discouraging factor for most new teams. And the old ones—well, many had had enough of sending fine teams into the snakepit and having them leave snakebitten, from the Kentucky of Adolph Rupp to the Indiana of Branch McCracken and many others like them. As a result, most home schedules consisted of traditional opponents (e.g., Butler, DePaul, Detroit) padded with college-division opponents out of necessity. Nearly all of ND's toughest games against big-name opponents were away from the Fieldhouse, which led to (usually) a wide disparity between home and road records.

Another problem in maintaining ND's strong basketball tradition was in recruiting. The small gym, high academic standards when many schools had literally none, no recruiting budget apart from road trips, and Notre Dame's reputation as a football school where basketball was lost in the shuffle all played roles in the fact that few national-caliber players even considered Notre Dame, much less came. The majority of ND's players from

1958-64 came from three areas: Chicagoland, Northern Indiana, and the New York metropolitan area, all of which had strong alumni and subway alumni contingents. Unfortunately, the Irish were not often landing the best players from these very good basketball areas, particularly from New York, where Frank McGuire generally lured the best down to North Carolina, and John Jordan—a close friend of McGuire—got to pick from the leftovers.

Theoretically, poor recruiting should not have been a problem in 1958-59, because three-fifths of the starting lineup, including the immensely talented co-captain Tom Hawkins (the first black to hold that position), were back from the 24-5 team of a year earlier. In fact, the Associated Press panel thought so highly of this edition of the Irish that it ranked them number three in pre-season, ND's highest placement since the polls became regular in 1949. But the formerly high-powered offense missed sorely the scoring punch of its two graduated seniors (Bob Devine and John McCarthy). Defenses were able to key on Hawkins much more effectively; he still scored a lot, but there was no other real Irish scoring threat (he scored almost twice as many points as anyone else on the team). This, plus awful shooting (barely better than one in three—34 percent—for the season), combined for a marked decrease in production and a 12-13 record.

This disappointing season began with a win over Bellarmine, a small Catholic school in Louisville coached by ND grad Gene Kenny, 87-55. In it, Hawkins tallied 39 points to break Jack Stephens' career scoring mark, to which he added all season. But things steadily worsened. For the first time in Jordan's coaching career, the Irish lost four in a row, the first time this had happened since Moose Krause's last four games at the ND helm.

Northwestern, Wisconsin, Michigan State, and North Carolina were the culprits. The most ignominious of these had to be the 56-54 loss to the Badgers at Madison, for Wisconsin had lost 11 straight games over two seasons and finished 3-19 this time—a horrible team by any standards. And in the game against the Tar Heels, the Irish led Frank McGuire's New York refugees 34-23 at one point but lost in this, the opening game of the Bluegrass

Festival, 81-77. They then beat the home team, Louisville, for third place and an end to the losing stretch.

A week later ND was in another holiday tournament, the only time the Irish played in two the same season. This, of course, was the Hoosier Classic, of which they were defending "champions." They aimed to make it two in a row by defeating Indiana, 73-67, but were blown out by Purdue, 74-59, despite Hawkins' 31 points. That started *another* four-game losing streak which, with the season less than half over, all but dashed any hope of a third consecutive playoff appearance.

The worst of these was the second, a New Year's Eve rematch with Northwestern. This was a very special day for John Jordan, for his first child was born that afternoon. But that night, Notre Dame shot even worse than usual, 25-for-103 for 24 percent, and were mauled from the opening tip in the 102-67 pasting. Just as bad in another respect was the 69-54 loss in another game with North Carolina, this one at "neutral" Charlotte in a rare trip south for ND. Substitute Don McGann fractured his collarbone to end his season early, and the franchise, Tom Hawkins, tallied only six points and left the contest with a sprained ankle that sidelined him for two weeks.

During that time, the Irish dropped an embarrassment at home to Butler by blowing a 19 point lead in the 62-60 game, topped Detroit behind double-figure performances from five players, 73-62, and lost for the first time in DePaul's Alumni Hall to the Demons, 69-66. Before the new losing trend became entrenched, Hawkins came back and Loyola came to town. He scored 26 points as Notre Dame continued its mastery over George Ireland's Ramblers. That was followed by two games in Chicago Stadium, in which ND beat Illinois but lost to Xavier.

Three straight wins followed to raise ND's record to 9-10 and keep hopes of a winning record alive. A new opponent, St. John's—the one in New York—did something rare; it came to the Fieldhouse to initiate the series, and then kept coming back on a regular basis for more than a decade, well into the ACC years. During these less-than-stellar times for Irish basketball, two truly major upsets came courtesy of the visiting Redmen. In this case St. John's, which won the 1959 NIT, fell victim to both the Fieldhouse crazies and Tom Hawkins' hot hand. The

Hawk scored 36 points in the 72-70 upset. Not nearly so monumental, but important wins nonetheless, came on an Eastern trip, over Canisius and Army, the latter of which saw both co-captains, Hawkins and 5-7 Gene Duffy, top the 20-point mark.

Of the last six games, three were played at the Fieldhouse and three elsewhere—and ND won all three at home, lost all three on the road. After the box-office success of the ND-Kentucky NCAA game in 1958, the two sides agreed to resume the yearly series on a Chicago Stadium-and-home basis (Adolph Rupp still hadn't changed his mind about the ND Fieldhouse). At the Stadium, the Wildcats, ranked number one at the time, didn't make the Irish feel at "home;" Kentucky held ND to its lowest score since December 31, 1953 in a 71-52 win. More heartbreaking was a 92-89 loss at Butler which wasted a marvelous 36-point effort by Tom Hawkins and wasn't decided until after the third overtime, one of the three longest games in Irish history. And in the last road game, which followed a revenge win at home over DePaul, a great Marquette team scored 54 points in the second half to doom ND to its sub-.500 mark, 95-76. But in 11 days the two would meet again at Notre Dame.

Coming off its biggest offensive burst of the season (93 vs. Valparaiso), ND was ready for Marquette this time. But Eddie Hickey, in his first year at the helm of the Warriors, was also "ready" for the Irish. Remembering that his last two visits to the venerable building with St. Louis resulted in upset losses, he wanted to make sure it didn't happen again. When Marquette won the opening jump ball, a stall ensued. And ensued. As it turned out, the delay had the opposite effect. The Irish bided their time, and finally after 10½ minutes of this ultimate in over-coaching, Tom Reinhart scored the first points of the game for either team to give ND a 2-0 lead. At the half, the game was tied at 16; after that, Tom Hawkins, in his last collegiate game, came alive. He tallied 18 points in the second half to lead the Irish to a 51-35 victory—a major upset. It is entirely likely that had Marquette played its normal game it would have won, but Hickey's misguided stalling tactics gave the Irish the game. The repercussions of this game lasted long beyond the final buzzer.

Again, just as he did when he was at St. Louis, Hickey wanted the home-and-home series changed so that the Notre

Dame "home" game was at Chicago Stadium, but he wanted
*his* home game left where it was. Just as before, he claimed financial reasons, but the fact that his team lost in the Fieldhouse and
then lost in the NCAA Mideast Regional after a 22-3 regular-
season mark undoubtedly played a part. And again, Notre Dame
refused his demands—the series had been going fine with no
problem for 33 years, the longest continuous series on the
schedule in fact, so why change? Thus ended another great
series, not to resume until 1969, when a new and more diplomatic
coach was leading Marquette.

The Marquette Warriors weren't the only element missing
in the 1959-60 Irish season; three starters, including Tom
Hawkins, had graduated. So Jordan, looking at the poor season
he had just experienced trying to play run-and-gun, changed to
a ball-control offense. His team responded with a 17-8 regular-
season record and an NCAA berth it probably didn't deserve.
(An NCAA rule prohibited more than one team from a conference
from participating in the playoffs, a restriction which existed until
1975; without this blatantly pro-independent rule, Indiana, which
went 20-4 in 1959-60 but finished behind Ohio State in the Big
Ten, would have been a strong team in the tournament. The same
probably holds for 18-6 North Carolina and 16-7 Illinois.)

Despite that, it still was a pretty good team and might have
been better had it not been for a key injury in the backcourt which
made the team very vulnerable to a zone press. Captain Mike
Graney, a very good player who was invited to the 1960 Olympic
Trials and was also drafted in the 17th round of the NFL draft
by the Philadelphia Eagles despite having played only two minutes of college football, and Emmett McCarthy, another senior
and younger brother of John, held down the forward spots.
Junior Bill Crosby and senior Bob Bradtke, whose season-ending
injury in the 12th game of the season took away some quickness
in the backcourt, were the starting guards, and junior Mike Tully,
the tallest regular in Irish history to that time at 6-7, alternated
with sophomore John Dearie (6-6) at center. After Bradtke's injury, Jordan tried three different men in his spot without finding a suitable replacement: Don McGann, another senior; Mickey
Bekelja, still another fourth-year man who was capable of scoring at will when he wasn't out of control; and sophomore Ar-

mand Reo. Also of note was Eddie Schnurr, who was only eligible in the second semester but averaged nine points a game in his nine appearances.

The senior-dominated squad got off to a fine start, winning seven of its first eight games. The only loss in this streak was to Michigan State at East Lansing in overtime after the Irish had made up four points in the last 37 seconds of regulation, 61-56. And while none of the wins were against outstanding opposition, three straight wins on the road against Northwestern (in two overtimes, buoyed by 30 from Graney and 25 from McCarthy), Air Force, and Nebraska (ND's first victory ever in Lincoln) were impressive. Also of note was a 67-45 defeat of Chicago Loyola at the Fieldhouse because this marked the end of another fairly long-running series; ND grad George Ireland never again coached against his alma mater.

Seventh in the 7-1 beginning was a win over Purdue in the opening game of the Hoosier Classic, 82-79, in which Graney had 21 points while playing all of the second half with four fouls. But mighty Indiana, mentioned earlier as a victim of NCAA injustice, kept ND from a mythical tourney championship by winning, 71-60. After the game, IU coach Branch McCracken put the future of the Hoosier Classic in jeopardy by announcing that the Hoosiers were not returning in 1960-61; they had been invited to a prestigious West Coast tournament taking place at the same time as the all-state tourney and planned to accept. Also, McCracken felt that host Butler was no longer of the same caliber as his school, Purdue, and Notre Dame. An insulted Tony Hinkle, Butler coach, said that despite Indiana's pullout, the show would go on with a comparable replacement for the Hoosiers.

After the loss to Indiana, the Irish broke up for the holidays but were delayed in reuniting thanks to fog at several cities. So ND was rusty when it resumed action at Charlotte against North Carolina, and it resulted in a 75-65 loss in which Mike Graney was held to but six points. But a return home helped the Irish begin a new four-game winning streak. High school teammates Graney and Bob Bradtke (from Bishop Noll of Hammond, Indiana) tallied 22 and 21, respectively, to lead a 76-51 romp over Butler, and Detroit, ranked 15th behind a multi-talented sophomore sensation named Dave DeBusschere, fell easily, 75-63, but

Bradtke suffered his season-ending knee injury in the contest to put a damper on the ND win. Thirty points from John Dearie helped the Irish defeat DePaul in Alumni Hall, 73-70, and balanced scoring—Emmett McCarthy 20, Mike Graney 18, Mickey Bekelja, who had scored two points all season before insertion as Bradtke's replacement, 16—led to a convincing win over new opponent St. Francis of Pennsylvania, a school run by the same order of priests as Notre Dame and which had its greatest basketball glory when Maurice Stokes was there in the mid-1950s.

But the win streak would be challenged at Detroit. The question was: could ND make Dave DeBusschere a non-factor again as it had earlier? The answer: no. He scored 30 points while Graney was held to only five, and the Titans came out on top, 68-61, in another step to a 20-6 regular season. And then Bradley, ranked second and on the way to an easy NIT championship, turned on its fearsome zone press against the Irish at Chicago Stadium and turned what had been a close game into no contest, 86-65. After exam break, Illinois did the same number to ND, 71-67, for the team's third straight loss. Even a mediocre Canisius team tried to play a zone press and a tough forecourt defense, and the Irish had fits. Had they not shot 55 percent from the floor, they would have lost embarrassingly at home. As it was, the team took only 44 shots, but still won, 71-65. Finally ND broke out of its doldrums by routing Army, 87-55, just in time to face Kentucky in Lexington.

This was a rare occasion in which a Notre Dame victory over the Wildcats would not have been a total surprise, for UK was also in a temporary slump (it stayed home at playoff time). But Adolph Rupp took advantage of his troops' own home-court advantage to eke out a 68-65 triumph, the last time until 1982 that this annual game took place at either school. On the way home, the Irish finished their sweep of Butler, 79-62, and then did likewise at home against DePaul, a game with tournament implications, 70-58. Two days later, the Irish accepted a bid to the NCAA Mideast Regional while DePaul was sent to the Midwest.

Three games remained until tourney play, and none were easy. Evansville, which replaced the road game with Marquette on the Irish schedule, was no slouch even though a College Division team; it was number-one ranked and defeated most University Division schools it faced. Notre Dame was no exception; the Irish fell to 15-8 with the 92-87 setback. But back-to-back wins over Louisville (at Chicago Stadium) and Creighton, the other replacement for Marquette on the slate and soon to become ND's regular season-ending home opponent, got things on track again.

In the opening game of the NCAA tournament, played at Lexington, the Irish, which many believed did not belong there, faced Ohio University, the winner of the Mid-American Conference. The game was close in the first half, but the Bobcats blitzed ND with a potent fast break in the second half, and the Irish never recovered. Ohio won, 74-66, to end ND's season abruptly. Even so, this would be great compared to the next two years.

Jordan's 1960-61 team was decimated by graduation—Graney, McCarthy, McGann, Bradtke, and Bekelja all received their degrees. Unfortunately, there wasn't a great deal of comparable talent replacing them. Bill Crosby, Mike Tully, and John Dearie were back in the starting lineup, and Armand Reo and Eddie Schnurr had some prior experience, but there wasn't much depth. Despite featuring what was then the tallest starting lineup in ND history, the team's inability to win away from home led to a 12-14 record.

The disparity between home and road marks was the most marked since the days of the dirt floor in the Fieldhouse. The Irish went 10-2 in their cozy quarters; the two losses came after they had stretched a long home winning streak to 24, third longest in ND history. But on the road, the team fell to a dismal 2-12, the only wins coming in the city of Indianapolis. Some were close, others were not, and at least one was controversial.

After two impressive season-opening wins, including one over Evansville, 83-68, in which Notre Dame led by an incredible 50-22 after a half, the Irish traveled to Louisville to face Kentucky. The series was still on less than solid ground, but after ND received its share of the take from this "neutral site," the foundation became much firmer; the two teams filled, or came close to filling, Freedom Hall each of the next 21 years as well. This was a chance for Notre Dame to do to Adolph Rupp what had not been done to him since he became Wildcat coach in 1930: drop him below .500 at 1-2. Alas, it didn't happen. Rupp kept his never-a-losing-record streak alive with a 68-62 win which showed that this neutral site might not be as neutral as the term suggested. The Irish stayed close, but two separate times when ND tried to make its move, very controversial offensive foul calls wiped out Irish baskets to break the back of a valiant effort.

Bowling Green was the next home victim, followed by a unique but disastrous six-game road stretch during the holidays. It began with Notre Dame's first trip to the West Coast since 1948-49 about which the best that can be said was that the plane didn't crash. The games in the Los Angeles Sports Arena were put together with the help of Butler University; the two schools pooled resources, traveling in the same craft and then playing Southern Cal and UCLA on alternating nights. This joint venture, at least in ND's case, was neither an artistic nor financial success. The Irish were badly beaten on both nights, first by UCLA, 85-54, after trailing by only two at the half, and then by USC, 93-63; they were forced into a run-and-gun game in both and shot 26 and 29 percent respectively from the floor, contributing mightily to the first back-to-back 30-or-more-point blowouts in ND history. In the stands, the games were even less a hit, for less than 5,000 showed up in the Sports Arena for each session; those small crowds didn't portend a future for this cooperative venture.

Returning to the Midwest, Notre Dame next was victimized by two members of the juggernaut known as the 1960 Olympic basketball team. First, as big-time college basketball returned to the Fort Wayne Coliseum, Walt Bellamy scored 29 points for Indiana in its 74-69 win. Then, a week later, Terry Dischinger of Purdue registered 32 for the Boilers in the opening game of the ninth—and last—Hoosier Classic in an easy one, 78-58. The Irish did extend its streak of winning at least one game in every Classic by edging Tony Hinkle's "comparable replacement," Illinois, 69-66. Unfortunately, the absence of Indiana kept Hoosier basketball fans away from the Butler Fieldhouse; attendance was way down, and try as he might, Hinkle could not lure the most popular team in the state back to the tourney again. Although the venerable Butler coach claimed there would be a Hoosier Classic the next December, the turnstile count told a different story, and this time the well-intentioned tournament ended for good. (There is today a "Hoosier Classic" in Indianapolis with, ironically, Indiana as the host team, but the only resemblance it bears to its more fascinating ancestor is its name.) The six-game road trip came mercifully to an end when ND blew a nine-point lead and lost to Northwestern, 59-56.

The Irish, now 4-6, turned around and won four of their next five. Of course, those four were all at home. Butler (72-56), St. Francis of Loretto, Pennsylvania (76-54), Detroit (66-62 behind 23 points by Armand Reo and a strong second-half comeback), and DePaul (61-58 in the Demons' first loss of the season—but every prior DePaul game had been at home) were the victims in the cozy confines. The win over the Demons marked the 23rd straight in the Fieldhouse for Notre Dame, a statistic which made the home-court advantage that much clearer and made the road all the more frustrating. Another illustration of those woes was at Charlotte, where the Irish had Frank McGuire's last North Carolina team down, 71-68, with less than a minute left. However, an unnecessary technical foul and the resulting free throw, two more foul shots, and a last-second tip-in gave the Tar Heels the win, 73-71. But ND's record at semester break was 8-7, and the squad still harbored hopes of a winning season.

Those hopes continued for a while; although Illinois, an ND victim in the Hoosier Classic, evened the season thanks to cold Irish shooting, 77-62 at the Stadium, the squad bounced back to pull out a road win over Butler and then spring another upset upon St. John's.

The Irish-Redmen game was originally slated for St. John's new fieldhouse in Jamaica, New York. A trip there would have been something of a homecoming, as four of ND's five starters hailed from the New York metro area. The only problem was that the building wasn't finished yet, and since Madison Square Garden wasn't available on short notice, coach Joe Lapchick agreed to return to Notre Dame's band box instead. In the end, St. John's had only one of four regular-season losses when, with 10 seconds left, Armand Reo canned a basket and the Redmen were unable to answer in kind. The big Irish win, 64-63, was marred, however, by boorish and unsportsmanlike fan behavior which eventually led to the end of pre-game introductions for several years. Notre Dame students had never been particularly kind to visiting teams, but their actions at this game went beyond the bounds of good taste.

Despite their fans, the Irish had won an emotional victory, but it was all downhill from there. They struggled in at 2-6 the rest of the way, and only a couple of those six losses were close: a 79-72 loss at the hands of Canisius in Buffalo and a very tough 84-81 defeat to Bradley in overtime at Chicago Stadium which wasted a tremendous off-the-bench performance by Karl Roesler, who scored 19 points—15 percent of his entire season total—in the upset bid. Otherwise, forget it. The 24-game home winning streak came to an ugly end "courtesy" of 4-12 Michigan State, 89-74; the Spartans shot an ungodly 23-for-24 at the foul line, and Dick Hall, a sophomore, scored 34 points to fuel the upset. A loss to Detroit there (82-71, 26 by Dave DeBusschere) preceded the Bradley toughie.

An easy win over sister school (also run by Holy Cross priests) Portland broke the losing streak, but St. Louis, back on the Irish schedule after almost a decade, and at the Fieldhouse no less, started a new one on the way to the NIT final game, 74-60. At Alumni Hall, DePaul made a complete reversal of an earlier loss to ND and ensured a losing record for the Irish, 78-57. Thankfully, the team avoided further embarrassment in front of its home crowd by defeating an 8-16 Creighton team, 61-54, to close the door on Jordan's tenth edition of Irishmen.

Before the 1961-62 season began, history repeated itself when another college basketball point-shaving scandal was discovered, this one even more widespread than its 1951 counterpart. Twenty-two teams and 37 players were involved this time, and games were found to have been fixed all the way back to the mid-1950s. The operation this time was designed to insure its perpetuation—of course, until the New York district attorney's office stepped in. Gamblers studied teams, looked for players who might be in need of quick cash because of their personal situations, and preyed upon them; for example, several players with wives and children and trying to make ends meet were easy targets. They even offered "softening-up" money to freshmen, who couldn't play, in preparation for bigger payoffs when they became eligible as sophomores. Finally, as opposed to the 1951-era fixes, most of the players were paid to lose by more than the spread rather than to win by less.

With 22 teams affected, some were hurt more than others. Seton Hall, for example, banned any post-season play for its basketball team, a prohibition which lasted until 1974. Easily the most serious blows were dealt North Carolina and St. Joseph's of Pennsylvania. Tar Heel coach Frank McGuire emigrated to the NBA Philadelphia Warriors, and the entire program was de-emphasized and slowly re-emphasized under his replacement, a young man named Dean Smith; UNC did not return to post-season play for six years. And St. Joe, a Cinderella team in 1960-61, was forced to give up its third-place trophy from the NCAA tournament because of three players' involvement with gamblers.

Since 1961, there have been several isolated incidents of point shaving involving such schools as Seattle and Boston College, but nothing as widespread. Unfortunately, many of the same problems which led to the previous scandals still exist. One of the most tempting of these is the regular publication of point spreads in major newspapers, a practice which Bobby Knight, a player in 1961 and today one of the game's great coaches, has likened several times to publishing the phone numbers of prostitutes. Perhaps the greatest reason why something like the betting scandals could happen again is the potential for the attitude of some schools to rub off onto their recruits. If a school cheats and tries to get away with it, is it too much to think that players might copy the example?

Anyhow, under the pall that more fixes cast over college basketball, the 1961-62 season went on despite the cries of skeptics who thought the sport was now dead. At Notre Dame, however, it essentially was, but because of the way the team played. It could have been worse—there could have been a full slate of 25 games instead of the 23 on the final schedule. As it was, ND's final record of 7-16 was the school's worst in 42 years, when the home court was made of clay and most of the players had first allegiance to football.

So why did the Irish suffer back-to-back sub-.500 seasons for the first time since 1921-22 and 1922-23? The top six players in 1961-62 each played at least 16 games the prior season, but it is hard to call any of them top-line compared to prior ND stars. A further sign of the deterioration was that only 11 men played at all and but 10 in the second semester, the smallest roster since

World War I. Notre Dame now lagged far behind its counterparts in recruiting. Then consider a schedule of which 16 of the last 18 games were played against teams which finished with winning records. All of these added up to problems.

A misleading 3-2 record, of which two wins were by one point (one in overtime, 59-58, when Northwestern did an Eddie Hickey and stalled the ball for the last five minutes of regulation and the five in OT, only to be outscored 2-1) and the other over Bellarmine, inspired 3,500 local residents to go to the Fieldhouse to see longtime foe NYU, back on the schedule temporarily, in the students' absence. What they saw was the beginning of the longest losing streak since, well, those dark ages of the early 1920s.

Six times the Irish took the court during the next three weeks, and six times they left with losses. The worst of it was a three-game stretch of routs. Kentucky overwhelmed ND, 100-53. Indiana did the same, 122-95, the 122 marking an Irish defensive futility record which still stands. And North Carolina, which was on a self-imposed probation after the aforementioned fixes, did very little traveling, played few schools outside the South, and finished 8-9, added to the Irish woes, 99-80.

Notre Dame finally won again on January 13, the 800th in school history, over Detroit by using only five men, and even won a second straight, over DePaul, by missing only 2-of-30 foul shots for a dramatic turnaround. But just as ND was gaining a little momentum, it was lost somewhere in semester exams. After the break, the Irish were 2-8.

Most of the games were reasonably close, and the lack of depth hurt in some of the losses. Also a factor was that the last home game took place ridiculously early (February 10 vs. Creighton, a 74-71 loss) and, therefore, ND's last six contests were on the road. The two positives were at home over Canisius, 88-72 (the Irish outrebounded their foe 71-46 to help immeasurably), and — surprise — at Evansville's home court, always a tough place for visitors, 99-91, which featured an 81-foot field goal by the Aces' Buster Bradley at the final buzzer for some excitement as the Irish were rolling up their highest point total in four years. Otherwise, a noteworthy "almost" against St. John's (the attempt at a third upset over the Redmen in four years fell six points short after two overtimes) was about it. After the Creighton setback, losses to Butler, Detroit (and Dave DeBusschere's 33 points and 23 rebounds), Purdue, and Bradley followed in short order until the win over Evansville. And to end this disaster, a player named M.C. Thompson canned 37 points for DePaul as the Blue Demons avenged their earlier loss to ND, 87-80. After this season, John Jordan knew that the only way things could go from here was up. In fact, he already had made plans for just such an inevitability.

He had his first semblance of a good sophomore class since 1957 thanks to some Indiana residents who might have gone to Bloomington had not IU recruited Indianapolis's Van Arsdale twins, Tom and Dick. Another Indianapolitan, Walt Sahm, Goshen's Jay Miller, and LaPorte's Ron Reed, who was also an outstanding baseball pitcher, formed three parts of a high-scoring foursome. The other was a Troy, New York product, ND's first black basketball player since Tom Hawkins and only the fourth ever, Larry Sheffield. To go along with this heralded quartet was another sophomore, Larry Jesewitz, and two seniors who were rewarded for coping with their first two dismal years with the co-captaincy, John Andreoli and John Matthews. This was a classic George Keogan-style senior-sophomore lineup, and of all of Jordan's teams during The Long Slide, this one could have been great.

It didn't turn out that way, and the reason can be summed up in one word: academics. In a crushing blow reminiscent of the one that hit Jordan's first ND team, both Reed and Sheffield were declared ineligible for the second semester stretch run, eliminating 30 points per game from the offense. Before exams, the Irish were 12-4 and one of the surprise teams in the nation. After exams, they crawled in at 5-4 and became again a beneficiary of the unfair NCAA at-large bid rules with a 17-8 mark.

Ironically, the 1962-63 season began just as the probation-riddled 1951-52 team had — with a 6-0 record. In the process, the newcomers helped roll up some impressive numbers; right off the bat Ron Reed scored 35 points in his varsity debut against St. Joseph's of Indiana. But just three days later, the Irish rolled up a 70-49 lead over an inept Michigan State team only to see the Spartans tie it at 83; ND finally won, 92-85. After that, for the first time the squad topped the century mark in back-to-back contests (101-70 over St. Francis (PA), 102-90 at Valparaiso). Two more of the super sophs, Sheffield and Sahm, combined for 51 points to beat Western Michigan. But the game which opened some eyes nationally, resulting in ND's first UPI top-20 ranking since 1958 (tied for 16th with UCLA), was a 74-48 crushing of Creighton in which CU's high-scoring Paul Silas was totally shackled by the Irish defense, Jay Miller in particular, who heretofore had been the least heralded of the Big Four sophomores. Because of his defensive skills, and Reed's lack of same, Miller soon replaced the higher scorer as a starting forward.

After this auspicious start, the Irish dropped out of the top 20 as quickly as they had risen to it by losing two in a row, to an inspired Butler team which was only 1-6 coming in but went 15-4 the rest of the way (66-59) and then to—who else?—Kentucky at—where else?—Louisville (78-70). ND gave up 20 points to the Wildcats' star, Cotton Nash, in the first half, but held him down after putting Jay Miller on him. But less-heralded Don Rolfes matched Nash's first-half output in the second stanza, which made the difference.

But two exciting comeback wins in neutral sites against name teams really stirred up the fans' interest in South Bend. In Chicago Stadium, third-ranked and unbeaten Illinois found itself down to ND by 11 at one point, then bounced back to lead by eight. But the Irish weren't through; they came back impressively for a 90-88 upset. Over in Fort Wayne the day after New Year's, Indiana streaked to a 19-point lead in the first half, and led, 46-30, at the halfway point. However, the second half was another story. After the two teams traded baskets twice, ND went on a tear, outscoring the Hoosiers, 23-3, over the next ten minutes and going on to win, 73-70.

Well, for the first time in three years Notre Dame had a bona fide exciting team in one of the two major sports, and the winner-starved students, and the locals as well, wanted to see the games in person instead of merely watching them on TV (all home games were televised locally to help hold down the Fieldhouse crowds). So when a four-game home stand began with North Carolina's first and only trip to ND, students and townies migrated to the old barn in droves. For the first time in some years, spectators had to be turned away because there was simply no more room into which to shoehorn anyone; as it was, the turnstile count was 4,230 for the game in a 4,000-seat gym. And then the Tar Heels had to ruin everything by winning.

More than a few wondered about Dean Smith when he agreed to play the Irish in the old noise box, bucking the prevailing trend. But he proved the doubters wrong. When Jay Miller tipped in a Ron Reed miss with :06 left to put ND up, 63-61, most of the delirious students began celebrating. But Billy Cunningham cut them short by canning a desperation 40-foot heave as time ran out to sent it into overtime. Thus imbued with the momentum, the Tar Heels went on to a 76-68 triumph.

Notre Dame athletic officials made special arrangements for the other three home games in hopes that the anticipated throng of students could be accommodated. Enough, however, had been scared away to actually result in a few empty seats around the place when ND easily defeated DePaul, 8-0 before the game, (82-62), Detroit (105-70), and Butler (80-54). With a record of 11-3, the Irish had moved back onto the UPI survey and up to 14th with two games left before break. But only a week after ND had beaten DePaul by 20, it lost to the Demons by 14 in Alumni Hall, the worst loss of the year. Then at the Fort Wayne Coliseum, Walt Sahm scored 30 points to help defeat Purdue and give the Irish a sweep in Fort Wayne for the season, 96-86.

Even with four losses, ND had looked awfully good in the first semester. Six different players had finished a game as the leading scorer, no one more than three times, a display of unusual scoring balance. But with the disqualifications of Reed and Sheffield, the scoring balance was distributed among fewer people; thereafter, a team which had been averaging 82 points a game fell to a per-game mark of 71.

One of the men forced into a great role, junior Sam Skarich, help Notre Dame defeat Boston College at Chestnut Hill, but then the Irish, finally playing at the new arena at St. John's after a two-year delay, found themselves on the short end of a 57-52 upset—repayment for what ND had done to two highly-touted Redmen teams of the recent past.

Through the efforts of two recent ND alumni, an Erie, Pennsylvania sports broadcaster and the opponent's new sports information director, tiny Gannon College ended up on the Irish schedule as cannon fodder, 82-47. The two chief seniors, Andreoli and Matthews, were the vital elements of a win over Navy, 68-56, in which famed Midshipman quarterback Roger Staubach made a brief appearance. But the two-game winning streak ended as soon as the Irish went on the road again. They lost to Bowling Green, 67-58, and NYU, in ND's first game in Madison Square Garden in five years, 80-79.

Between the two games, Notre Dame received a bid to the NCAA tournament, one which, again, might not have been tendered had every good team in the country been eligible to participate. Jordan considered turning down the offer because his team was obviously not at full strength, but reluctantly decided to accept in fairness to the other players—after all, there was more to this team than Reed and Sheffield.

Like Sam Skarich, for example. His six free throws in the last 40 seconds made the difference in a second win over Detroit, 83-79. Then a win over ever-tough Evansville in the final home game and a tough 72-66 loss to Bradley at the Stadium after leading by 12 at the half closed the books on the regular season.

At Evanston the Irish had to face Mid-American Conference champion Bowling Green again. They had already lost to BG once—but that was at the Falcons' home court. Unfortunately for ND fans, the result wasn't much different this time. While the Irish tried, and generally succeeded in the effort, to neutralize big center Nate Thurmond, that left Harold Komives free for 34 points in BG's 77-72 win. Despite the loss, the season had been very exciting, at least for a semester, and all looked forward to having nearly everyone back for 1963-64.

Call it bad luck, or something, but John Jordan's 13th season at the helm turned out an absolute disaster. It also turned out to be Jordan's last, for after a particularly disheartening loss to DePaul at home about which more will be said later, he announced his resignation effective March 1, 1964. Not only that, but Ron Reed again ended up on probation for the second semester. By then, his absence made little difference, for this team that was supposed to be superior to its predecessor plummeted to a 10-14 record.

What happened? Injuries, the key one an early-season back sprain suffered by 6-10 center Walt Sahm, the tallest player ever listed on an Irish roster thus far, which forced him to the sidelines for six games, were a factor; Jordan used 10 different men in starting lineups at one time or another. A good team, though, would have overcome that. One problem here, like another supposedly great Jordan squad had in 1958-59, was that its unheralded senior losses were too much to overcome. The coach's offense didn't have a quarterback, so to speak (a charge also leveled at the 1963 Irish football team, which used six in nine games en route to a 2-7 mark), and thus it often degenerated into some sort of run-and-gun. That would have been fine if the 1963-64 team had known the meaning of the term "defense," for even though it scored 84.5 points per game, a new Irish record, and had two men averaging 20 or more points a game, an Irish first, it also gave up 83.9 per contest for a more dubious new team mark. When ND held its opponent under 70—it actually happened five times—it was 5-0. But defense usually took a back seat, with often dire results. Notre Dame scored over 100 points in four games— another new record—but *lost* three of them!

All of the wins in ND's 4-3 start resulted by holding the foe under 70. The most satisfying was the 79-65 defeat of Bowling Green, the school which had defused Irish hopes for advancement in the previous year's NCAA playoffs. Even though Howard Komives scored 41 points, the Irish held the rest of the team to only 24 and outrebounded the outmanned Falcons, 63-33. (Reed and Sahm finished sixth and seventh nationally in rebounds despite probation and injury, respectively; they were the top rebounding tandem in the country in 1963-64.) The others were over Christian Brothers of Memphis, Valparaiso (in which ND set a Fieldhouse scoring record with 107), and Northwestern (at McGaw Hall). As for the losses, Larry Sheffield scored 41 against Indiana, but Tom and Dick Van Arsdale combined for 76 (42 for Dick, 34 for Tom) as the Hoosiers outran ND at Fort Wayne, 108-102. At Illinois' new Assembly Hall, the Irish shot 30-for-91 from the floor in losing, 79-68. And at Kalamazoo, Western Michigan, which finished with an identical 10-14 record, upended ND, 92-89.

From there, things rapidly fell apart. Six straight losses would set the tone from here on out. First, second-ranked Kentucky took advantage of poor second-half Irish shooting to coast, 101-81. (Jordan finished 0-for-Kentucky as a result.) Next, in a rematch at Chicago Stadium, Illinois again won, 87-78. Then, at Greensboro, North Carolina, which was only average this year, canned ND, 78-68, after roaring to a 26-point lead. During this period, Sahm was watching from the bench because of his back problem, and his dominance on the boards was sorely missed. He was replaced at center by Larry Jesewitz, who was simply not the rebounder Sahm was.

But Sahm was back, the Irish were at home for the first time in nearly a month, and DePaul, at 9-0 one of the nation's surprise teams, was the guest. Notre Dame had knocked the Blue Demons out of the unbeaten ranks a year earlier, and hopes were high that it would happen again. Instead, DePaul easily triumphed, 86-73.

As the result became clear, the score came very close to being recorded as 2-0. In an utterly classless, though typical, display of student frustration, the crowd, having been subjected to football seasons of 2-8, 5-5, 5-5, and 2-7 the last four years and basketball seasons of 12-14, 7-16, and 17-9 with this one rapidly going downhill, began throwing pennies and wads of paper onto the court. If any coin had hit a referee, at least one of the two was prepared to award the game to DePaul on the spot. (Had that happened, Notre Dame *really* might have needed a new fieldhouse—fast.) Meanwhile, a group of students in the end zone began chanting "Jordan must go! Jordan must go!" more in frustration than in malice—John Jordan was probably the best-liked coach among fans, players, administrators, and opponents in Irish history. This fan action, however, proved to be the final evidence he needed to convince himself that an idea he had been considering for some time was timely. On January 10, two days after this debacle, John Jordan announced his resignation.

He didn't admit it, but the fact that the students had turned on him hurt. Just as significant to Jordan, he did admit later, was his age. He was now 53, older than his mentor, George Keogan, had been when he died, and, remarked Jordan, "I didn't want to be carried off the court." The coach had been involved in basketball all his adult life; now was as good a time as any to bow out.

Not even this announcement could spur on this team. In front of a record crowd at Creighton, Paul Silas, held down a year earlier, scored 37 to help his team win, 95-81. And then

Detroit uncorked its second-ranked offense. The score was 100-100 at the end of regulation, and 114-104 in favor of the visitors at the end, Detroit's first win ever at the Fieldhouse. There was too much going on this time for the fans to start throwing things, like a Notre Dame record 47 points for Larry Sheffield, a mark since topped by only two others. On a two-game road trip before exams, the Irish finally won one, over Michigan State, and then in another shootout at the Fort Wayne Coliseum, Purdue handed ND another high-scoring overtime loss, 112-103, this one in two extra stanzas.

Right after semester break, the Irish were back on the road. Accurate shooting (53 pecent from the field) and—for a change—tenacious defense helped Notre Dame defeat Butler, 72-64. But two losses quickly followed, to DePaul and Detroit, both for the second time in 1963-64. In the latter, the Irish were hanging tough with the Titans until Ron Reed, in his last game before his probation took effect, fouled out with 15 minutes to play. From then on Detroit had it easy.

Now was the part of the schedule where pre-season prognosticators thought the Irish would gather momentum for playoff action—six games left, five at home. Instead, ND had to win all six just to finish 12-12. Five out of six would give the retiring coach 200 wins at his alma mater. Alas, neither happened; but hopes were high after the Irish won three straight for the only time all season, all at home, over St. Louis (82-73 behind 33 points and 21 rebounds by Walt Sahm), St. John's (89-83, 79 of them by Sheffield, Miller, and Jesewitz), and Butler (90-73). But Bradley spoiled the bid for a .500 season at Chicago Stadium with an 82-72 victory. Hope still existed for a five-for-six, even more so when the Irish upset Evansville, 20-2 coming in, behind Sahm's 29 and Jay Miller's 25, 91-75. But the bid for John Jordan's 200th win at ND failed against Creighton, 84-71. Though he didn't hit that milestone, he still managed to win more than 60 percent of his games while playing 60 percent away from home.

Probably the best news to come out of this season came from above. As part of its "Challenge II" fund-raising drive, Notre Dame decided that a new athletic facility was of high priority. In fact, the blueprints were unveiled early in 1964. The name to be given the new double-domed structure was "The Athletic and Convocation Center," though there was some sympathy in the local press for naming the building after slain president John F. Kennedy, a common trend in early 1964, and because of the awkwardness of the name—and its initials (ACC, which, of course, already meant "Atlantic Coast Conference" to sports fans).

Meanwhile, about the same time, the man who would lead the team into its new quarters was being interviewed for the opening head coaching position. On March 7, it became official: Johnny Dee, who had played for ND during World War II and had been a successful coach on every level (Chicago St. Mel's High School, University of Alabama, the AAU Denver Truckers, and the Kansas City Steers, the last champion of the defunct American Basketball League), became Notre Dame's new head coach on a four-year contract. Under Dee, who had been Jordan's first assistant at ND while he was earning a law degree, with help from a new fieldhouse, a necessity since at least World War II, Notre Dame finally began to move back to the big time.

# 17

# Dee-fense

Immediately, Johnny Dee set out to make changes. First, he spruced up the old Fieldhouse. Banners were hung from the rafters for each opponent, similar to the flags which flew at Notre Dame Stadium; an American flag was hung over the old manual player-by-player scoreboard; and pre-game introductions were revived. This time, opponents were given the gold carpet treatment, courtesy of American Airlines; the rug was rolled out from the bench to center court, then set off with railings as if the players were entering a swank hotel rather than one of the most feared fieldhouses in college basketball. And when the Irish took the court, they did so in new uniforms for the first time in years.

Off the court, Dee managed to get the administration to push up its timetable for the new athletic building by a year for a December 1968 opening, so he could use the lure of playing on a brand-new court their senior year as a recruiting tool. And, as a recruiter, he became the first ND basketball coach to have a real budget for the purpose above and beyond travel to road games. Also, he looked nationwide to nab players and heavily recruited qualified blacks—the latter a controversial (but necessary) move. He also made moves to change the schedule to include more teams outside the Midwest and as many of the best teams as could be squeezed into a 26-game schedule without ignoring such traditional foes as DePaul, Detroit, Butler, Kentucky, and Indiana.

Speaking of tradition, he recognized ND's rich basketball past by instituting an annual homecoming game and a Homecoming Award to be given to an Irish basketball monogram winner who had distinguished himself after graduation. To heighten community interest (remember, he would have to fill three times as many seats in a new arena), he later began a freshmen-vs.-varsity series and took it on the road to such places as Elkhart, Indiana and Niles, Michigan. The radiocasts of ND games did not reach to some of these outlying areas, so Dee played a role in allowing WSBT-AM (5000 watts) to share local rights with WNDU-AM (250 watts). And in the summer of 1968 and each of the next two summers, with the cooperation of the City of South Bend, ND basketball players became involved in "Operation Reach-Up," which brought basketball to the poorer neighborhoods to help keep the kids off the streets.

But most important was the new philosophy on the court. Dee basically ditched his predecessor's patterned offense for a run-and-gun, freelancing game which, when it worked, was tremendously exciting and, when it didn't, looked terribly disorganized. The result of this philosophy was decidedly mixed.

Dee's first team, 1964-65, was without question the most wildly inconsistent in Notre Dame history. There was no way to know from one game to the next what to expect from it. For example, the team had an offensive production range from a high of 116 to a low of 54; it destroyed a team by 30 points on the opponent's home court but on a neutral court lost by one; it played well against some good teams but poorly against some bad ones. In the end, the Irish did make the NCAA Midwest Regional with, believe it or not, a 15-11 record, but earned the bid in a most unusual fashion.

Upon the start of the new season, ND fans got to see the Runnin' and Gunnin' Irish score points at a pace which would make an NBA team envious. The four-senior, one-junior starting lineup obviously was having a good time as it scored 99 vs. Lewis, 116, a team record, against Ball State, 100 against Michigan State, and 107 against a very good Detroit team. In the Ball State game, the Irish landed six players in double figures, and Mr. Rebounds, Walt Sahm, hauled in 30 for an ND record on the way to his third straight finish in the national top 10 in that statistic. Defense in these games was another matter; Lewis had 87, Ball State 82, Michigan State 93, and Detroit 86. But Dee's philosophy seemed to be "the best defense is a strong offense," and not only did that get ND out at 4-0, but it also resulted in a feature article in *Sports Illustrated* after the Detroit game on the "resurgence" of Notre Dame basketball.

Though they weren't on the cover, some variation on the legendary *SI* cover jinx may have rubbed off, for the Irish lost their next three in a row. Evansville, St. John's, and Indiana all defeated ND; the first two were close games, but Indiana took advantage of the long-standing Irish weakness against the press and pounded them into submission, 107-81. In the Evansville game, ND fouls hurt, because the Aces made 29-of-34 from the line and the Irish only 6-of-10, a big factor in the 89-82 final.

Then, only eight days after the Irish had looked so bad against the Hoosiers, they put on an onslaught against Kentucky the likes of which the school had never seen before and hasn't seen since. Ron Reed scored 34, Jay Miller 23, and Larry Sheffield 21 to lead ND to a 111-97 drubbing of the Wildcats at Louisville. The Irish outrebounded UK, 81-44, as they became only the third team to hit triple figures against Kentucky. (Coincidentally, all three were coached by Notre Dame graduates—Johnny Dee twice, the first while at Alabama, and George Ireland of Loyola.) No other team has ever scored so many points against the Wildcats and won. (In December 1966, Northwestern scored 116 against UK, but lost in OT, 118-116.) Two nights after this great victory, the Irish made up 14 points in the last six minutes against Bradley but still lost, 74-72.

Up and down, up and down . . . Notre Dame hit the 110 mark in two consecutive games and took the national lead in team scoring in the process. First, Western Michigan fell at the Fieldhouse, 115-87, and next, at Houston, the Irish blew out the Cougars, 110-80. But next, in what Dee termed at the time "our worst game of the season," they scored only 67 to St. Louis's 75. Notre Dame then breezed to a 49-19 halftime lead en route to a home 94-57 defeat of Butler, but wheezed to 32-for-98 field goal shooting (33 percent) as the team lost at Purdue, 78-74. And in a game which was both up *and* down, ND easily defeated Toledo, 113-65. But Johnny Dee had benched two of his seniors, Walt Sahm and Larry Jesewitz, for three games. They would be sorely missed when the Irish resumed the season after finals.

Notre Dame's second semester season began exactly opposite to the first-semester season; the squad lost the first three and then won four in a row, putting the Irish at 13-9 and still, if Johnny Dee was to be believed, in the running for an NCAA bid, though most outsiders thought he was overly optimistic. Illinois, Wisconsin, and Detroit consecutively defeated ND, but Butler, DePaul, Ohio University, and Bowling Green all became Irish victims. Appropriately, the DePaul game was the first homecoming, and also appropriately, Ray Meyer was the first recipient of the Homecoming Award, explained earlier. But the Blue Demons almost spoiled the day for the returning Irish monogram winners; they fell by only three, 62-59. In the Ohio contest, the Irish jumped to a 24-point lead only to have it shrink to five, but Larry Jesewitz, back out of Dee's doghouse, scored 10 points in a five-minute period late in the game to preserve the Irish victory, 94-86. And after another win over Bowling Green, 88-72 — certainly the seniors still remembered 1963! — the Irish were ready to take on Duke at Chicago Stadium.

The Blue Devils, 17-2 entering the game, finished the season 20-5 but, because they lost the Atlantic Coast Conference tournament, stayed home at playoff time. The Irish actually stayed with Vic Bubas' squad for awhile, but eventually fell, 101-88. Then ND traveled to Madison Square Garden, which they did every year without fail through 1980; for now, it agreed to play NYU every year until the new arena opened, at which time the Violets would return to ND. Without a doubt, Notre Dame played its worst game of the year in losing, 60-54. The Irish missed their first 19 shots from the field and only had 17 points at the half, but NYU was almost as bad this night, thus the low score. Those two losses dropped Notre Dame to 13-11 and out of contention for an NCAA bid.

Or so everyone thought.

This was an especially mediocre year for teams eligible for at-large berths, and one spot was still open in the NCAA field. So the selection committee stood up and paid attention when the Irish broke DePaul's 17-game home court winning streak behind a record 25-for-26 from the foul line, 83-67. By now, Dee was using an all-senior starting lineup of Walt Sahm and Jay Miller at forwards, Larry Jesewitz at center, and Ron Reed and Larry Sheffield at guards; junior Bucky McGann, who had started most of the season at guard, and sophomore Jim Monahan and

Kevin Hardy, the latter of whom in 1964-65 became the last three-sport letterman in one academic year at Notre Dame (football, basketball, baseball), came off the bench for relief. Now the seniors had a chance to return to the NCAA playoffs.

Before the last game, at home with Creighton, the PA announcer read a message from the NCAA: the winner between CU, 13-9, and ND, 14-11, would become the elusive last team for the playoffs. That was all the motivation the Irish needed. All five senior starters hit double figures, and the basketball-playing yo-yo known as the 1964-65 Fighting Irish were on their way to Lubbock, Texas and the NCAA Midwest Regional with their 92-79 victory. But one annoying tradition didn't change with a new coach; again the team failed in the first round. This time, Houston, which ND had beaten by 30 points in January, came back from a 49-40 halftime deficit to tie it at 88 and almost win it in regulation, but Larry Sheffield's block of a last-second Cougar shot sent it into overtime. Then three Irishmen fouled out and a Houston sub, Art Winch, gave his team an insurmountable lead with two key free throws. With Sheffield's uncontested layup at the buzzer, the final was 99-98. But the Irish were genuinely lucky to have played that game in the first place.

In all his years as a coach on all levels, Dee never had a losing season. But for 1965-66, nearly everyone was gone, and one of the returnees, Kevin Hardy, was unavailable because of a football-related back injury and never played another varsity basketball game. Because of his late arrival at ND in 1964, he hadn't a chance to do any substantial recruiting, so he was left with two returning lettermen (Jim Monahan and captain Bucky McGann) and a collection of odds and ends. He hoped beyond hope that the 1965-66 Irish would at least break even, but with a suicidal schedule, that seemed impossible. And it was—to the tune of a 5-21 record. Only the 1918-19 team, with a 2-10 record, had a worse winning percentage in Irish basketball annals.

Deceptively, Notre Dame started off the season 3-2 and even set a couple of team records in the process. In a 97-79 loss to Wisconsin at Madison, ND's first loss of the season and a harbinger of things to come, the Irish made 39 free throws, and in a 110-77 walloping of St. Norbert, they hauled in 91 rebounds. The other two wins came against Lewis and Bowling Green. Then the roof caved in.

Thirteen times the Irish took the court from December 18, 1965 through February 5, 1966, and 13 times they lost. Only one of them was close, and that was the first one, a 93-89 home loss to NIT-bound Boston College. All the others ND lost by 10 points or more; six were lost by more than 20. Overall, the average margin of defeat, including the BC game, was 18.4 points.

February 9, therefore, became a day of great rejoicing at the old Fieldhouse. On that day, Notre Dame finally won again! The team did it in the most satisfying way possible—it defeated a team which already had beaten the Irish once. Butler, which had won by 23 (90-67) at Indianapolis, lost by 23 at Notre Dame, 84-61. And three days later, the Irish won their second in a row, this time on the road, over a team which had beaten them in the Fieldhouse! Detroit was the embarrassed victim by a 76-67 count. As far as winning goes, that was it in this horrid season. ND did take Bradley to two overtimes before losing in a stalling match, 55-44, and the margin of defeat in the last three games got progressively closer (eight, six, and four), but the Irish still lost their last six to clinch their first-ever 20-loss season.

Well, Johnny Dee already had made plans not to let that happen again. Coming up from the freshman ranks were his first three top-line recruits, all of whom played major roles in the rebuilding task: Bob Arnzen, from Fort Thomas, Kentucky by way of St. Xavier High in Cincinnati; Dwight Murphy, from Kansas City, Kansas; and Bob Whitmore, of DeMatha High near Washington, DC. The recruitment of Whitmore was the beginning of a tradition of Washington-area Catholic high school blue-chippers heading to Notre Dame which, though the funnel has narrowed lately, has had a profound effect on the Irish program.

This "DC Connection" actually began with Brian Keller, from St. John's High, the second leading scorer on the 1965-66 Irish squad but who saw less and less action when more talented players supplanted him. Whitmore of DeMatha was next, and from there the lineup is a veritable Who's Who of recent Irish basketball history: Austin Carr (Mackin), Collis Jones (St. John's), Sid Catlett (DeMatha), Chris Stevens (St. John's), Adrian Dantley (DeMatha), Don Williams (Mackin), Tracy Jackson (Paint Branch, Maryland, actually a suburban public school, but the coach had connections to the Washington Catholic schools), Cecil Rucker (Mackin), Tom Sluby (Gonzaga), and Joe Howard (Carroll). The catalyst behind Notre Dame's amazing success in recruiting from the nation's capital is an anonymous bank executive who was a friend of Dee's dating from the time they spent in the service together in the early 1940s. Even after Dee left ND, he continued to point great basketball talent in the direction of South Bend, much to the delight of Digger Phelps, who called the man "The Ambassador."

Dee decided from the start that his 1966-67 team was going to sink or swim with the three sophs in the starting lineup. Before the end of December, he added a fourth – Jim Derrig of Villa Park, Illinois. As might be expected, the team had a tough time in the early going but ended the season with a 14-14 record, or is that 14-12, or is that 15-14?

The confusion in ND's final record resulted from the way the school's appearance in the Rainbow Classic was treated. The NCAA allows teams to play games in Hawaii without having them count against the allowable limit of games (in those days 26). For some years after the season, Notre Dame listed the team's record as 14-12 for that reason, although the official stats included 28 games. The 15-14 record results if a game ND played in Hawaii against a non-collegiate team, opponents which the NCAA has considered unofficial since the early 1950s, for seventh place in the tourney is included. But for practical purposes, the 1966-67 team record will be recorded as the NCAA records it: 14-14.

The best way to look at this season is to split it into its 1966 and 1967 components. During December, the sophomore-dominated team struggled to a 2-9 official record. After New Year's Day, it had begun to find itself and finished strong at 12-5. Both early-season wins were at home against College Division opponents – Lewis (100-77) and St. Norbert (97-72). Of the nine losses, six were by six points or less. Against Detroit, the Irish had numerous chances to put the Titans away, but blew all of them to allow UD to leave the Fieldhouse with a 74-73 win. Against Evansville, four starters fouled out during a 105-99 overtime loss in the two schools' last meeting. Then, on the start of a long road trip, St. John's pulled one out, 65-62, and then Indiana by the same margin, 94-91, despite Arnzen's 38 points. Still, Notre Dame had trouble with its guards when the opponent threw a press up on defense; nowhere was this more evident than in the next game.

This contest came about because of a recruit Johnny Dee didn't get. He, like so many others, tried to get New York Power Memorial's seven-foot wonder, Lew Alcindor, and like everyone else except UCLA's John Wooden, failed in his attempt. Dee realized that with Alcindor, the Bruins were going to be nearly impossible to beat. He also realized that they would be *the* attraction to open the new arena. In 1965, Notre Dame and UCLA signed a five-year agreement to play each other. The first two had to be at the Uclans' own new venue, Pauley Pavilion, but Dee was willing to sacrifice two wins for a chance to get the Bruins to open Notre Dame's new fieldhouse in 1968. Games four and five were scheduled at UCLA and ND, respectively. The series has continued on at least an annual basis ever since and developed into one of the top intersectional rivalries in the nation. The first game was all UCLA and its press, as could be expected. The Irish did hold Alcindor to less than his season average, but not by much; the Bruins were loaded and won easily, 96-67.

As inferred earlier, Notre Dame's first and only trip off the mainland during the season to play basketball was not successful. The state of Hawaii had been trying to get ND to come to the islands for a basketball tourney since 1952; finally, the Rainbow Classic was successful in nabbing the Irish for its eight-team show. Even with Notre Dame there, only six of the eight teams were college – the other two were service teams. But because the Irish gave the tournament its tacit blessing, the Rainbow Classic became a top holiday tourney, and the organizers announced near the end of this one that eight colleges had signed up for the next one. All Notre Dame got out of it were two close losses, to California, the eventual champion, 69-63, and to Montana, 70-69. The game which didn't count in the standings or the statistics but saved ND from finishing last in the Classic was an 88-67 defeat of the Hawaii Marines. Just two days later, the Flying Irish were in Louisville to play Kentucky and lost, 96-85, to Adolph Rupp's worst team (13-13) for their sixth official loss in a row.

At this point, the Irish got a well-deserved week off to start 1967. When the team resumed play, it ran off six straight wins, the longest ND win streak in four years. The Irish finally defeated a University Division school in Air Force, 68-56, and then beat up on King's College, which agreed to fill two gaps in ND's home schedule in consecutive years in exchange for an Irish trip to Wilkes-Barre, Pennsylvania to dedicate its new gym in 1968. The next four wins were all on the road, ND's longest win skein away from the Fieldhouse since 1959. DePaul (76-72), Detroit (87-71), Illinois at Chicago Stadium (90-75) and Butler (101-80) were the victims. The Butler game was extremely impressive; Bob Whitmore scored a career-high 43 points, and the Irish as a team shot 42-of-58 from the floor for a .724 percentage, best one-game mark in Irish history.

Michigan State in overtime, 85-80, and Georgia Tech, 102-87, both defeated the Irish to drop them to 8-11, but a four-game home stand loomed, and the possibility of going above .500 now existed. They almost did it. Hawaii, paying back Notre Dame for its journey to the Rainbow Classic by visiting the Fieldhouse, became an easy Irish victim, 90-58. Then DePaul surprised ND with a tough defensive effort, 56-49, the second lowest point total by any Irish team under Johnny Dee and the Demons' last win at Ray Meyer's alma mater until the 1977-78 season. Maybe the Irish were looking forward to the next game, against Houston and its superstar Elvin Hayes.

The legendary Fieldhouse crazies made life impossible for the visiting Cougars, and Bob Arnzen helped out by doing the same to Hayes. The all-star missed his first eight shots, and Arnzen was red-hot. Before anyone realized what was happening, Notre Dame had an incredible 42-18 lead and Houston hadn't a prayer. When all was done, the Irish had an 87-78 win, Arnzen had 37 points, and although Hayes recovered somewhat in the second half, he was thoroughly rattled by the students; late in the second half, he completely missed everything while shooting a one-and-the-bonus to cap off an overall frustrating day for the Cougars. Two years would pass before Houston lost another regular-season game; all three of its losses from here through the end of the 1967-68 season were in the NCAA Final Four, two of them to UCLA. Butler closed out the home stand by falling, 57-48.

At the Stadium, Bradley did its usual thing by winning, 94-89. Two straight wins finally evened the Irish record at 13-13, over Western Michigan, 73-68, and NYU, 79-66. Down at Charlotte, North Carolina, Duke topped ND, 77-65, which meant that Notre Dame had to beat Creighton at home to salvage the .500 record. It did, easily, 84-59. Thanks to the strong finish, the 1967-68 season became anxiously awaited.

This version of the Irish was probably Johnny Dee's best Notre Dame team. Later squads had more talent, but this one was handled better than any of those. With any luck at all, it could have finished 24-2 in the regular season rather than the 18-8 it did finish. Yet with that record, the school's best in a decade, Notre Dame, in order to play post-season basketball, had to make its first appearance in the National Invitational Tournament.

Basically, ND used a seven-man team this season, anchored by the four sophomores of 1966-67, now juniors. The other starter was sophomore Mike O'Connell, the only top-rung newcomer, a fact which began to lead to claims that Johnny Dee recruited only every other year, especially after something similar happened two years later. Coming in as subs were two seniors, George Restovich and Jim McKirchy, each of whom was important to the Irish success. But the most publicized parts of this squad were the offense stalwarts, Bob Arnzen (the team's first junior captain since Ray Meyer and later a 1968 Olympic Trials invitee) and Bob Whitmore. Their scoring exploits—each averaged over 20 points a game, only the second such combination in ND history and the first on a winner—and their take-charge attitude on the court put them in the headlines so often that they soon were referred to as simply "A & W." As the restaurant chain of that name was known for its root beer, so these two players were known for their scoring points.

Atypically for a Dee team, though, the 1967-68 Irish also were strong defensively. Had it not been for several anomalous games, they would have given up fewer than 70 points per contest, but as it was, the 72.1 average was the best in five years. It also was one of the best free-throw shooting teams in the nation, finishing 18th with a .742 percentage. Ironically, most of the losses this season resulted from late-game defensive lapses and missed one-and-one free throw attempts at key moments.

Another aid to the 1967-68 Irish was that after almost 70 years, the old Fieldhouse was to close its doors to basketball at the end of the season. Almost appropriately, as if to say, "and just in time!," ND had its worst home slate in memory. Six of the 12 teams visiting the gym in its last season were in the NCAA College Division—St. Joseph's of Indiana, Lewis, St. Norbert, Villa Madonna, King's, and Valparaiso; an independent schedule-rating service ranked the Irish slate 112th among major colleges.

As if to offer proof, Notre Dame streaked to a 5-0 start, four at home, three against the first three teams named in the last paragraph. The only close one was the solitary road game, 81-73 over Wisconsin at Madison, in which three Irishmen scored in the 20s. A three-game trip promptly brought the team to earth. Still vulnerable to a press defense, the Irish blew an early lead when Indiana turned its on late in the first half; they never fully recovered and ended up losing in their farewell to Fort Wayne, 96-91. Two nights later, a hot streak from Bob Arnzen, who scored 23 of his 29 points in the second half, and clutch foul shooting from Jim Derrig, who hit 4-of-4 in the final 28 seconds, pulled one out at Utah State, 73-72. And then, in ND's second game in Pauley Pavilion, the Irish played like Murphy's Law personified. Everything that could have gone wrong did: they shot 40 percent from the floor (to UCLA's 56), were outrebounded, 58-41, were down by the ridiculous score of 57-22 at half, couldn't penetrate the Bruins' press if their lives depended on it, and lost badly, 114-63, ND's worst loss since the 1897-98 team lost 64-8, to First Regiment. Oh, and Bob Whitmore, thoroughly intimidated by Big Lew Alcindor, scored only six points. Something had to be done if this weakness in the Irish offense of taking eight or nine of the allotted 10 seconds to get the ball upcourt wasn't to be exploited by even the smallest school on the schedule.

Like Villa Madonna.

In front of a paltry holiday crowd of less than 2,000, the tiny Covington, Kentucky school from which former ND assistant coach Larry Staverman was graduated nearly pulled off an upset of nuclear-bomb proportions. The Irish, still shellshocked after the UCLA debacle, trailed for 32 minutes, and even though they did win, it was by only five, 64-59. Two nights later, ND was looking to pull its own great upset in Louisville against Kentucky. With under nine minutes to play, the Irish led by 10; their defense promptly left Freedom Hall, and the Wildcats streaked back and won going away, 81-73. Notre Dame would not lose again for nearly a month.

A combination of a tenacious defense which went five straight games without giving up more than 68 points, the always-dependable A & W offense tandem, and a new attack against the press designed by the new assistant coach Gene Sullivan over the original skepticism of his boss which got the ball upcourt twice as fast as in the past and curtailed the backcourt turnover problems, led to six straight wins, over King's (105-68), Air Force at Denver (58-45), Creighton at Omaha (72-63), Detroit (83-63), DePaul at Alumni Hall (75-68), and Butler (82-77). Against Butler, the A & W team combined for 67 points (Arnzen 27, Whitmore 40) to keep the Irish ahead, even though, relatively speaking, the defense was off. The victory against the Bulldogs put the Irish at a stellar 13-3 going into finals week, but because of the ludicrously easy home slate, they weren't ranked although other teams with worse records were.

All realistic hope for an at-large NCAA bid disappeared with the opening of the second semester, as five of the six post-break games ended in Irish losses. To make things more frustrating, four of those were by a total of 12 points. The Irish shot 15-of-21 from the line, but three of the six misses came on crucial late one-and-one attempts, and Illinois defeated them at the Stadium, 68-67. At Jenison Fieldhouse, ND looked awful in losing to Michigan State in the one blowout, 89-68. At the UD Memorial Building, Detroit avenged its earlier loss to the Irish, 82-79. Finally, the team won again, but the hard way. After leading DePaul at home, 75-68, ND allowed the Blue Demons to score seven unanswered points to send the game into overtime, but finally won, 91-85. Duke, another 1967-68 NIT participant, upended the Irish at Chicago Stadium, 73-67, and St. John's handed them their only home loss of the season and, therefore, their last loss in the Fieldhouse, when John Warren followed up a missed Redmen shot with :03 left, 83-81. Notre Dame made 23-of-36 foul shots, but in one stretch in the second half missed eight of nine.

Bids for the national championship tourney began to be offered, and, thanks to the ND slump, the NCAA looked elsewhere, although the 14-8 record at this point would have been fine enough to go in most prior years. This development led to rumors that, contrary to prior policy, Notre Dame would accept an NIT bid if offered. Only once before had ND received a formal invitation to the New York classic, and that was for the first one, 1938. Now, 30 years later, Madison Square Garden was likely to call again. Such a possibility became even more certain when the Irish topped Bradley for the first time in 13 years, 64-61, in preparation for the annual trip East to play NYU.

February 8, 1968 marked the end of an era: the old Madison Square Garden hosted its last college basketball doubleheader that night. But several nights later, a new building elsewhere in New York with the same name took its place. That is where, on the 20th, Notre Dame defeated NYU, 70-67, and then, after winning, said "yes" to the NIT, the first tourney to be held in the new Madison Square Garden. Why did the Irish break their "ban"? Simply, as one more step in the re-emphasis of ND basketball. There were some hard feelings about being snubbed by the NCAA, and with its own new arena nearing completion, Notre Dame felt the added exposure would be beneficial. No doubt that this first trip to the NIT helped open the door to the lifting of ND's long-standing and controversial football bowl ban a year and a half later.

Before the ringing in of the new, the Irish closed the doors of its own antiquated facility. After an 87-75 defeat of Valparaiso behind A & W again (Arnzen 35, Whitmore 28), Notre Dame ended its regular season—and the historic Fieldhouse's use as a basketball venue—against Creighton. Naturally, this day was the annual homecoming, and naturally also, Moose Krause was given the Homecoming Award in this, the last game in the building where he had played, coached, and witnessed so many games. But the Irish had to come from behind at the half to defeat the Omaha school, 73-68. The last basket in the last game in the band box, ND's 474th victory there against 91 losses since 1899, was scored by George Restovich—in fact, he scored the last two. After the end of the season, several possible uses for the building were discussed, including as a home for Irish intramurals, but Ellerbe Architects, the University's official firm, won out with their desire to have it torn down. Student protests saved the building in the early 1970s after pep rallies were forced, under threat of law, to the newer Stepan Center; it then became a unique home for ND's art department. But no maintenance was done on the aging structure, and it soon became a decrepit eyesore. Finally, on March 12, 1983, the old Fieldhouse fell to the wrecker's ball 15 years after Restovich's curtain-closing field goals.

For their first NIT game, the Irish found themselves underdogs to surprising Army, which turned down an NCAA bid to remain in its own back yard. Much of the credit behind the Cadets' showing belonged to their third-year head coach who, when hired, was the youngest top man in the country—Bobby Knight. Bucking the prevailing national trend toward high-powered offense, Army emphasized defense; in fact, with the stingiest defense in the country in 1967-68, Knight led the U.S. Military Academy to its first 20-win regular season ever (20-4). Ironically, it was defense which led to Knight's earliest departure ever from a post-season tourney. Notre Dame held the Cadets to only 20 points in the second half to win, 62-58.

Again ND was the underdog in the second round, against Long Island University, which was making its first appearance in post-season play since the 1951 scandals. LIU, now a College Division team, had posted a 21-1 regular-season mark and bypassed the NCAA College Divison playoffs in hopes of repeating Southern Illinois' 1967 feat of winning the NIT as a second-level team. But the Irish ended that dream. George Restovich was the late-game hero, scoring two key baskets to preserve the 62-60 win.

Now in the semifinals, Notre Dame had to face Dayton, another team which, with better luck, could have made the NCAAs. Again the Irish defense played well, but not quite well enough. The Flyers, on their way to the championship, dodged their closest bullet in front of a surprising sellout (the crowds for the entire NIT were far above expectations), 76-74 in overtime. This sent ND into the consolation game against St. Peter's, a small New Jersey school which had become a sentimental favorite. But behind 33 from Arnzen, 19 from Dwight Murphy, and 17 from Whitmore, "big, bad" Notre Dame triumphed, 71-68, for third place.

Not only was ND's first trip good for Madison Square Garden (sellouts in both Final Four doubleheaders), but for the Irish as well. The momentum from the surprisingly strong showing was expected to carry over to the new season, what with the entire starting lineup back for 1968-69. Just as importantly, the week at the Garden played a big part in improving future schedules; never again would ND have such a lousy one if Johnny Dee had his way. Thanks to the 1968 NIT, Notre Dame gained seven new opponents within the next two years: Dayton (champion), Kansas (runner-up), St. Peter's (fourth), Duquesne, Fordham, Villanova, and West Virginia.

Also boding well for the future was the best freshman class in ND history. Dee had outdone himself by snaring seven—count 'em, seven—blue chippers: Jim Hinga, Jackie Meehan, John Pleick, Tom Sinnott, Austin Carr, Collis Jones, and Sid Catlett. One writer called the recruitment of the last three, the best Catholic-school trio in Washington, DC if not the best three in the city, period, "a bigger heist than the Brink's Job." Catlett sat out his freshman year to get his academics in order, but the other six combined for a 6-1 record, the only loss coming at Marquette, which the freshman avenged in the Fieldhouse. The excitement over this crew, which also had defeated the varsity seven out of eight times during the Traveling Road Show referred to earlier, led to bigger crowds than for some of the varsity games; on February 8, over 2,500 people showed up to see the freshmen play Michigan State's frosh. They saw a sign of things to come that night. The highly-touted Austin Carr (unofficially) broke the Fieldhouse scoring record with 52 points as the Irish easily won. Boy, did the future look promising. A new arena, loads of talent, momentum. But maybe the future looked *too* promising.

# 18

# The Austin Carr Coliseum

After Notre Dame's success in the NIT, Johnny Dee was given a three-year extension on his four-year contract. In those three seasons, Irish basketball returned to the national spotlight. The new arena was finally opened after over 20 years of planning and construction, giving ND a legitimate home court for the first time since the 1930s. National television appearances increased. And also, the Irish had three more 20-win seasons for four in a row, the most consecutive years that had been done.

With the return to national attention, however, came some of the same pressures that made life for an ND football coach so difficult. In fact, the first season in the new home proved to be one of great turmoil which on the football side could only be equalled by that during Ara Parseghian's final season as head coach (1974).

With every starter back, plus all those incredible sophomores, the 1968-69 season promised to be very good. Most experts felt that the Irish had the potential to be one of the three best teams in the nation, and *True* magazine selected ND Number One — over UCLA — in its pre-season analysis. Because of all the advance ballyhoo, the resulting 20-7 season was seen as a major disappointment to players, coaches, and fans alike. The main fault of the 1968-69 team was that it never really was a whole, merely a jumbled collection of high-quality parts. And the beginning of the problems can be traced to the second game of the season.

After a somewhat lackadaisical win at the dedication of a new gym at King's College, the Irish came home to dedicate their own new arena in the culmination of "Performance Maximus," the opening week of events in the Athletic and Convocation Center, soon to become better known as the ACC, the Convo, or the Austin Carr Coliseum (take your pick). It had facilities for the rapidly expanding Notre Dame sports program far beyond the long-since-inadequate Fieldhouse's. Of course, it also was the home of the basketball team, and what better way to usher in a new era in the team's long history than by bringing in the nation's top attraction, UCLA?

Notre Dame players and coaches had been planning for this game for, in essence, three years. Dee and assistant Gene Sullivan had scouted the Bruins and their center, Lew Alcindor, extensively, and thought they now had the game plan—and the talent—necessary to knock them off. They called it "The Grand Design," and it worked. Unfortunately, there were a couple of flaws in the blueprint. For one, Alcindor played a marvelous game, scoring 29 points. But that didn't hurt as much as two substitutes, Don Saffer and Terry Schofield, did. While the Irish were able to limit UCLA's starting guards effectively, the two subs were the real difference in the Bruins' 88-75 victory. In fact, it was Saffer who was fouled while scoring the basket which obliterated the early Irish lead and put the Uclans ahead for the first time late in the first half. Then he missed the free throw, and Alcindor tipped it in. UCLA never looked back.

Finally, Notre Dame was unable to penetrate effectively because of Big Lew's presence in the middle, and the pullup jumpers UCLA was giving stopped popping consistently; also, the Irish failed to used their supposed bench strength, making no substitutions until it was too late to make a difference. This loss seemed to affect the team's play for some time afterwards.

The Irish picked up their first win in the ACC against Wisconsin, but it wasn't easy. A very down ND team needed a free throw from sophomore Tom Sinnott with 10 seconds left to defeat the Badgers, 57-56. After that squeaker, the Irish rolled up three consecutive wins, including—for the first time since January 2, 1963 and the first time at home since 1956-57—a win over rival Indiana, 104-94. The usual loss to Kentucky at Louisville in one of the worst defensive "efforts" in Notre Dame history, 110-90, ended the winning streak. A trip to the Baltimore Arena, then the only sizable venue in the Washington, DC, area, served as a homecoming for the four DC recruits. Carr, Bob Whitmore, Collis Jones, and Sid Catlett all garnered starts in a 92-67 whomping of American University.

But as 1969 got under way, things began to disintegrate.

First, there was Carr. Along with his senior teammates Whitmore and Bob Arnzen, he was pacing the potent Irish scoring machine. But in practice on January 2, he suffered a stress fracture of his left foot and was out of action for six weeks. It was the first major injury of his basketball-playing life, and it wasn't easy for him to sit on the bench. Yet without Carr in the lineup — and with the use of four different men in his place at shooting guard — the Irish went 9-2, including six straight wins before semester exams.

Those wins before the break made the Irish 12-2, and hopes were still high that this team, which really hadn't jelled but won most of those games on superior talent alone, could go down in history as one of the all-time great Notre Dame teams. About the only thing this team did from here was to go down.

The Irish played four of their first five post-exams contests away from the ACC and lost two of them. Illinois, a first-division Big Ten team, beat Notre Dame by the incredible margin of 34 points at Chicago Stadium, and a post-Elvin Hayes Houston team which didn't appear in either tournament defeated ND in the cavernous Astrodome, 89-82. Georgia Tech at home, plus DePaul and Detroit (with 1968 Olympian Spencer Haywood) in return trips, went down to defeat; the win over Detroit also marked Notre Dame's 900th all-time victory.

The faithful, however, weren't satisfied with the 15-4 record and let Dee and the team know how they felt when they returned home to face a mediocre Michigan State squad. The boos started early, and even though the Irish led, 28-25, at halftime, they had played poorly in the process, and the catcalls continued. After the half, things got worse, both on and off the court. Even with Austin Carr back (in the only game of his career which he played but didn't start), the Irish fortunes fell, and each Dee substitution was greeted with a fresh chorus of boos. When it ended, Notre Dame had lost, 71-59, thanks to 22-for-68 shooting from the floor, and needless to say, the near-capacity crowd let the team know how it felt on the way back to the locker room. Even though this disaster was over on the court, off the court it had only just begun.

With 5:58 left in the game, Dee inserted Bob Whitmore for Bob Arnzen, at the time the team's high scorer, and an unusually loud chorus of boos rang out. For the first time in Notre Dame history, five blacks were on the court at the same time: Whitmore, Carr, Jones, Sid Catlett, and Dwight Murphy. The next day they made it clear that they felt the strong reaction at that point was racially motivated. They wanted an apology from the student body for its actions; to get it, they threatened to quit the team—an action which would have hurt but not completely decimated the squad's talent because of its great depth, though the effect on the team mentally likely would have been devastating. What it certainly would have done is reflect badly on Notre Dame, particularly on University president Father Theodore Hesburgh, a nationally respected spokesman for civil rights.

Most insiders and outsiders—mostly white—felt the blacks' charge of racially motivated booing was absurd. Others felt they were being used, possibly by a campus group of black radicals who had earlier threatened demonstrations at the UCLA game. But the blacks claimed otherwise on both counts, and wanted their opinion respected. What ND officials wanted most was to get the mess straightened out as quickly as possible to avoid further damage to the school's reputation in a sensitive area—and because the next Irish game (Utah State) was on regional television and the University didn't want any fallout from the incident to reach the airwaves.

Finally, the student body president apologized on behalf of the booing students (whatever their true motivation) to the five blacks in front of cameras and reporters. But the soap opera wasn't over yet. When the five left the press conference and went to practice, they were greeted by a ranting and raving Johnny Dee—and they began to walk out. Quick action by cooler heads and a team meeting managed to save the day.

Meanwhile, the University was taking no chances for any demonstrations from the student body before the TV game on Saturday: it ordered no pre-game introductions. Happily to say, it didn't matter. For the first time all season, the great group of players played as a team, blasting a good Utah State team,

108-82—and the students were cheering as lustily as they had booed four days earlier. The damage from this week, however, had merely been bandaged. The wounds were still there, ready to be opened at the slightest aggravation.

(As a footnote to this whole affair of five blacks on the court at the same time, five years later, when Notre Dame ended UCLA's amazing 88-game winning streak, the team outscored the Bruins 12-0 at the end. All five players on the court during that entire streak were black. And nobody booed!)

After a thrilling 71-67 overtime victory over St. John's at Jamaica, New York, the Irish received their first NCAA bid in four years. They had won five in a row since the MSU debacle, and were now 20-5 with one home game left on the slate. Everything seemed to be together, but it wasn't. Creighton University, a lesser team, upset the Irish at the ACC, 79-74, to end the regular season on a downer. They didn't play very well, and the assumption was that this was a case of post-bid and pre-tournament letdown. Actually, that wasn't the case at all.

Notre Dame's first-round game was expected to be easy; the oddsmakers had the Irish as heavy favorites to defeat Mid-American Conference champion Miami of Ohio. But ND had an incredibly lousy week of practice before the game, partially as a result of a well-intentioned but bungled series of articles in the two-year-old student daily *The Observer* on "The Black Athlete at Notre Dame." The group of articles, which was never finished, made everyone on the team, not just the blacks, a bit uptight. Had the series run to its conclusion, there is little doubt that the booing incident would have been analyzed again, and no one on the team wanted that. But the sports editor ended the series before it could get that far, admitting that he had goofed in trying to see Notre Dame's black athletes and their concerns from a white man's perspective.

The psychological damage, however, had been done. Notre Dame rolled into Carbondale, Illinois, site of the first-round game, unprepared and probably overconfident. And Miami took advantage. In a game which assistant coach Gene Sullivan later admitted he felt was lost before it ever began, the Redskins upset the Irish, 63-60, to end what should have been the greatest season in ND history. Instead, it ended in confusion and disarray—

and, according to newspaper reports, in Dee's resignation, effective in two years. He later took back his remarks, but that, and the racial problems, hurt recruiting for several years, even into the tenure of the next coach.

Most notable of the non-recruiting years was 1969-70; not a single blue-chip freshman arrived in South Bend, and the first-year-men's team was composed primarily of walk-ons, with a couple of sophomores who had no prayer of seeing any varsity action thrown in for good measure. (Dee was prohibited by University policy from redshirting them, though he tried.)

But the real story of the new season was the emergence of Austin Carr as one of the, if not *the*, top player in the country. Elected captain at the end of the last season (the first black to solo at that spot), he started on the way to breaking every scoring record in the ND books, and a few in the national books as well. With Notre Dame's new "isolation" offense, or, as it was better known, the "double stack," Gene Sullivan, who designed and implemented it for 1969-70, took advantage of Carr's natural skills and his ability to work without the ball. Out of it, the Irish played 58 games; in them, Carr scored in the 20s 12 times, in the 30s 23 times, in the 40s 14 times, in the 50s eight times, and in the 60s once, and averaged 38 points a game.

At the same time, the offense of Carr was countered by a lack of defense overall (while in 1969-70 ND averaged 93.5 points a game for a school record, it also gave up 86.1 ppg for another school record) and an unbelievably tough schedule which at one point included three games in eight days against teams ranked in the top five, all away from home. The new arena and Johnny Dee's desire to play as many of the best teams in the country as possible aided in compiling this slate. Despite both, Notre Dame finished with an identical regular-season record as in 1968-69 (20-6).

The Irish won their first five games, including a big 87-86 win over Michigan and its scoring star Rudy Tomjanovich. During those contests, Carr got warmed up for later triumphs. He put in 37 against the Wolverines and 42 against Northern Illinois, the latter the biggest single-game scoring burst from an Irishman since January 1967. Another Austin Carr trademark began to emerge: when he was really on, his jersey would end up untucked from his shorts—a signal for the opponent to watch out.

After ND's first loss, and only home loss, of the season (to Kansas), the team went on a five-game Christmas-holidays road trip and played five high-quality teams. Indiana went down to defeat, 89-88, in a closer-than-expected battle in Bloomington. But it was the eight days from December 27 to January 3 that saw Notre Dame play three different top-five-ranked teams in what must rank as the toughest week in Irish basketball history.

—First, Kentucky was the opponent in "neutral" Louisville. And Carr put on one of many clinics he would conduct over the next two seasons. He shot 20-for-27 from the floor and tallied 43 points despite playing the last 15 minutes saddled with four fouls—the closest he came to fouling out in his junior and senior years. (One of the most amazing facets of Carr's ability was that he seldom landed in foul trouble; in his three years he averaged less than two personals a game.) But Adolph Rupp's UK squad still beat ND, 102-100.

—Next, the Irish traveled to the Sugar Bowl Tournament. Notre Dame had won two straight Sugar Bowls in 1954 and 1955, but hadn't been there since. The team was scheduled to go in 1956, but a new Louisiana law mandating segregation at athletic events forced ND (along with Dayton and St. Louis) to pull out. A possible 1964 trip was also thwarted by the same inane statute. But the Jim Crow laws had long since been thrown out by the courts in 1969, which allowed northern and western teams to return, including Notre Dame. The Irish defeated West Virginia in the first round, 84-80, which then put them into the finals against South Carolina, which under Frank McGuire had become a national power. Again Austin Carr had an unbelievable game, hitting on 19-of-24 field goals, including 14 in a row at one point, and tallying 43 points. But again the Irish lost, this time an 84-83 overtime thriller.

—Finally, it was off to Pauley Pavilion to play UCLA, still right near the top of the charts even with the loss of Lew Alcindor to graduation, a loss expected to take its toll. Well, it didn't; UCLA eventually won its fourth consecutive national championship, and a down Irish team offered little resistance in a televised 108-77 blowout.

Notre Dame returned home from its suicide mission 7-4, but the students had found a hero in Austin Carr. When in a convincing defeat of Fordham, Carr was removed once the outcome was no longer in doubt, the fans began to boo. Austin had become the first really exciting player at ND in some time, and the faithful wanted to see him break all the scoring records. And two games later, against DePaul, Carr was closing in on one of them—the one-game mark of 47 by Larry Sheffield in 1964— when he was relieved. The pressure from the crowd became relentless, and finally Dee bowed to the wishes of the paying customers and re-inserted his one-man team (he later would remark that he could pull three students out of the crowd to play with Carr and Collis Jones, the latter of whom was on his way to becoming a scoring threat in his own right, a statement which, obviously, didn't make the others on the squad very happy). Well, Carr broke the record with 51, and the Irish won, 96-73, both of which made the students happy; but Ray Meyer of DePaul wasn't, feeling he was a victim of Johnny Dee running up the score. This wouldn't be the last time a coach felt that way.

The Irish won one over new opponent Duquesne at Chicago Stadium, and then were upset by Michigan State for the second year in a row just in time for final exams. Another surprise awaited after the break; starting center John Pleick became academically ineligible. This forced Dee to alternate between Sid Catlett and senior football player Jay Ziznewski as his starting pivotman (both already had seen much playing time); at the same time, Doug Gemmell, the only sophomore on the junior-dominated squad, earned a starting berth at forward. The result of all this was nine straight wins, the longest Irish win skein since 1958. While winning these nine, the team *averaged* over 103 points a game.

It started with a little revenge for last season's worst defeat; ND upended Illinois in the annual Chicago Stadium duel between the two schools, 86-83. What followed when the Irish returned home were three of the most impressive wins of the year.

All the offensive guns were fired up for St. Peter's. Carr scored 44, Jones 27, Gemmell 13, seniors Mike O'Connell and John Gallagher 10 each, and the team as a whole 135, a Notre Dame record likely to stand for years and years. The victim of the Irish onslaught, who hasn't played Notre Dame since, tallied 88. A sense of the dramatic came along against Marquette, which had returned to the schedule for the first time since Eddie Hickey's tirade in 1959. (And while the Warriors' coach since 1965, Al McGuire, certainly was capable of explosions, he usually reserved them for on the court.) The Irish were down by two with :04 left, Marquette ball out of bounds. Tom Sinnott and Mike O'Connell stole the inbounds pass, got it off to—who else?— Austin Carr, who drove in for a layup to send the game into overtime and the crowd into delirium. A newly fired-up ND squad finally won out over the eventual NIT champions in double overtime, 96-95. And just three days later, St. John's, Marquette's final-game opponent in that NIT, went down relatively easily, 90-76.

Another OT battle ensued at Detroit as ND stretched its win streak to five, 95-93. That was followed by another record-breaking performance by the one and only Austin Carr. He shattered his one-month-old single-game record with 53 in a 115-80 pasting of Tulane. As in his last record-setting game (vs. DePaul), Carr was left in the game long after his presence was really necessary, but the pressure was on Dee to keep him in to set another record.

After a 77-65 win at the Garden against NYU, it was back to the ACC for the last home game, against West Virginia, already an Irish victim in the Sugar Bowl. And again Carr was permitted to set a one-game scoring record. The Mountaineer coach was not happy after the game and promised in no uncertain terms that when ND made the return trip in 1970-71, it had better watch out. Carr poured in 55 points as ND rolled, 114-78. Of as great significance to the team, however, was that the catalyst behind the Irish win skein, Doug Gemmell, suffered a broken ankle in the game and was out for the rest of the season.

A testament to the way basketball had changed over the years was the next game, against Butler in Indianapolis. That school's legendary coach, Tony Hinkle, was retiring after over 40 years at the helm. Just how much the sport he loved differed from when he began was demonstrated in a who-needs-a-shot-clock-to-score-like-they-do-in-the-NBA game. Another Irish record was set, this one for most points scored by two players in the same game, as Carr scored 50 and Jones added a career-high 40 in the 121-114 victory. When Hinkle began coaching, scores

100 points less per team were closer to the norm. (In the first game ever played at Butler, now Hinkle, Fieldhouse, in 1928, the final score was Butler 21, Notre Dame 13.)

Finally the Irish bubble burst. A fired-up Dayton squad which, along with Notre Dame, was NCAA tournament bound, upended ND, 95-79, in the University of Dayton Arena, a venue which time and again proved unkind to visiting Irish teams. But now it was tourney time, and for the fourth time in their last five playoff trips the Irish were matched against the champion of the Mid-American Conference in Round One (this time, Ohio University). Carr and Company were determined not to let the upset bug strike again.

It didn't.

Austin Carr treated the Ohio Bobcats as if they were a pick-up team at the campus emporium for pick-up games, the Rockne Memorial building. He broke the ND scoring record one more time; in the process, he also smashed the NCAA playoff record for points in a game, a record which still stands. The amazing Austin hit on 25-of-44 field goals and 11-of-14 foul shots for 61 points, a game total few collegians have hit since. And by the way, for the first time since 1958 the Irish advanced to the regional semifinals with a 112-82 win. In their next game, they had to face old nemesis Kentucky again.

Again Carr had a simply incredible game, scoring 52 points. This time, though, the Irish lost, 109-99. Exactly how disappointing the early departure from the tournament was could not be better illustrated than in the consolation game against Iowa. The Hawkeyes scored 75 points *in the first half alone*—an ND opponents' record likely to stand for a long time—and from there, well, even Carr's 45 points couldn't stop the eventual 121-106 defeat.

Believe it or not, Carr received only a handful of first-team accolades on All-American teams, though he did receive second-team honors on most of the others. Although he finished second in the nation in scoring and 25th in both field goal percentage and free throw percentage—amazing feats for such a prolific scorer—he was somewhat overshadowed by three M's, all of whom were first-teamers: Pete Maravich of LSU, Calvin Murphy of Niagara, and Rick Mount of Purdue. But, as opposed to all of the above, Carr was but a junior; undoubtedly he was the leading pre-season pick for player of the year for 1970-71.

The man would live up to his advance publicity. Like two years earlier, however, the team wouldn't.

Notre Dame was an up-and-down team in this, the senior year of the Magnificent Seven freshman class from 1967-68. Austin Carr did his thing, and Collis Jones bloomed into an effective alternative. Unfortunately, the rest of the squad was too psychologically dependent on the two stars, and their own individual play suffered. This squad had all kinds of trouble against a zone defense, and never really developed its full potential. As a result, the final regular-season record fell to 19-7, and the NCAA tourney bid was in doubt until very late in the season.

All began well with a 94-81 win at Michigan. But the home opener was a bungled opportunity to beat one of the nation's elite and avenge a loss from 1969-70, against South Carolina. The coaching staff felt that the Irish could effectively deter special defenses designed to stop Carr and Jones if one other player could become an effective scoring threat. But they picked the wrong game in which to experiment. Notre Dame found itself down by 10 at the half, mainly because the team tried too hard *not* to get the ball to its star (Carr was only 2-for-4 from the floor at half), and no one else could buy a basket against the Gamecocks' zone. Abandoning the let's-pretend-he's-not-there approach in the second half, Austin had 23 in the next 20 minutes, but it wasn't enough: USC's John Roche hit a sterling 16-of-16 from the foul line to key South Carolina's 85-82 win.

Two close road victories (Northwestern and St. Louis) followed, and then ND returned home for the annual encounter with Indiana. The game marked, once and for all, the end of any attempt to find another scoring possibility. Austin Carr had a field day, popping 54 points on every kind of shot imaginable, but the defense was missing, and the Hoosiers won, 106-103, for ND's second straight loss at home.

After a break for finals—moved from late January to before Christmas for the first time as academic calendar reform finally came to the campus—it was time for the annual "neutral site" encounter with Kentucky. The contest started with a touch of controversy; Johnny Dee delayed the start of the game because the official game ball was an Adolph Rupp autographed model. "The Baron," claiming executive privilege or something, wouldn't change balls. But it didn't matter to one Austin Carr, who on this day could have played with a George Keogan-era laced basketball. Again Austin found the Wildcats to his liking; he scored 50 points to lead ND to its first win in Louisville since 1964, 99-92. Carr continued his hot streak in the next two contests, tallying 43 in a New Year's Eve overtime win over Santa Clara, 85-83, and adding 45 against Minnesota as ND won, 97-73.

From January 10 to January 18, the Irish played four games, but except for one half of one of them, the team seemed to be looking forward to the January 23 home showdown with UCLA. Air Force proved an unexpectedly stubborn opponent on a Sunday regional telecast, ND's first Sunday game ever; Carr had 34 in a too-close 75-71 verdict for ND. Two days later, Marquette defeated the Irish in Milwaukee, 71-66, and held Austin to "only" 22 points, his low for the season, without using a gadget defense; the Warriors beat Notre Dame at its own game with a straight man-to-man setup. Two more days later, Detroit came into the ACC and looked ready to pull off one of the biggest upsets of the season; the Titans led by 13 at the half, and Carr was only 3-of-15 from the floor. But after a halftime tongue-lashing by assistant Gene Sullivan, he had a tremendous second half, the best half of his career, with 38 points; ND outscored Detroit by 27 in the final stanza and won going away. Finally, relatively unheralded Duquesne zoned Notre Dame and keyed on Carr and Jones—and also took advantage of Irish preoccupation with UCLA—to defeat ND in overtime, 81-78. The team was down, and the coaches and players knew it.

Ah, but for the Bruins they were ready.

UCLA had not lost to a non-conference opponent since the near-legendary showdown against Houston in the Astrodome three years earlier, 48 games in all. But on this day a sellout crowd and national television witnessed one of the big wins in Notre Dame history. Although the ever-powerful Bruins were favored, the game was probably decided in favor of the home team before it ever started.

Dee, on the day before the game, decided to lighten things up a bit. He had managers place tape on the court approximately the length of a free throw away from the basket and ordered that the next day, no one except Carr and Jones was to take a shot from outside that zone. The players seemed to joke around about it—they'd always been told they were a two-man team, anyway—but Sullivan sensed there was something wrong. He met with the eight top players and soon found he had a verbal free-for-all on his hands. Dee was quickly called in to join the fray. Before all was over, a great deal of pent-up emotion and frustration, mostly relating to the "two-man team" stuff, came out into the open. When it was over, the team was more united than at any other time during this long and frustrating season. It couldn't lose now.

From the opening tip, the Irish were in control. Collis Jones scored the first points to make it 2-0 Irish, and they never looked back; UCLA did not lead at any time. Notre Dame went right at the Bruins, easily breaking its zone press and not allowing UCLA to set up its offense. At halftime, the Irish went into the locker room leading, 43-38.

Foul trouble soon plagued ND; both Sid Catlett and John Pleick picked up their fourth personals early in the second half, and assist-man Jackie Meehan was assessed his third. Soon thereafter, the Bruins tied the game at 47. But a Jones free throw and two quick Carr field goals changed the momentum back ND's way. Next Pleick, a Californian rejected by the Bruins and who had played the game of his life, fouled out. Doug Gemmell replaced him and responded with four key boards and two baskets. Tom Sinnott, who had replaced Meehan when the latter got his third foul, also kept the motor running. But the Bruins were stubborn—you don't become number one by rolling over and dying. Twice more they closed to within two points, at 62-60 and 72-70. Then Austin Carr took over.

In the greatest individual performance ever against a John Wooden-coached team, he scored 46 points—17-of-30 from the floor, 12-of-16 from the charity stripe—and thwarted all Bruin attempts to defend him. Finally, Wooden had his All-American and only other serious candidate for Player of the Year, Sidney Wicks, guard Carr late in the game. All Austin did was tally 15 of the last 17 Notre Dame points and force a frustrated Wicks out on fouls. That, in effect, was the ball game. The place erupted as the first Big Upset in the history of the "Austin Carr Coliseum" was complete. With the two foul shots, the final was Notre Dame 89, UCLA 82. Whatever psychic student had composed the banner which read "Wooden Barriers Can't Stop An Irish Carr" had called this one correctly. The players, surrounded by a sea of students, cut down the nets in celebration of the greatest victory of Johnny Dee's coaching career.

Alas, this was not the NCAA final, which UCLA was to win again. Thirteen games remained on the schedule before the playoffs. After eight of those had been played the Irish had almost ended their chance at a tourney bid, as this supposedly great team had fallen to 14-7.

Some of the euphoria from the big win carried over to a 24-point defeat of Michigan State three days later, the first ND win over the Spartans since 1964. But Illinois exploited the Irish problems against the zone and upset them at the Stadium in overtime, 68-66. Returning to the ACC, ND victimized Creighton and Butler; but in the first Irish appearance in Philadelphia's Palestra since 1954, the Villanova team which later made the finals of the NCAAs shut down Notre Dame, 99-81, with a lot of help from Howard Porter, who was the reason for much of the Wildcats' success—and for their ultimate downfall when their accomplishments were stripped from them because he had prematurely signed a pro contract. Notre Dame's first road win in over a month finally came against Ray Meyer's worst DePaul team, 107-76, and another win came against College Division neighbor Valparaiso (100-75, Carr had 46). The Irish seemed all set to rev up the engines for the stretch drive to the NCAAs, but they stalled in New York in a game which ultimately cost Dee and Sullivan their jobs.

An unprepared and disorganized group of players which had to put up with hounding fans and reporters (mostly seeking Austin Carr) and some supposedly bad press which surfaced in the days preceding the game relating to the three DC seniors (as it turned out, the allegedly negative articles weren't that at all) lost to a fired-up and hot Fordham squad in front of over 19,000 fans in Madison Square Garden—the first regular-season sellout in the new Garden—by 94-88. The Rams, who had finished 10-15 one year earlier, became one of the miracle teams of 1970-71. They ended the regular season 24-2 under first-year coach Dick Phelps, who soon became better known by his boyhood nickname "Digger." This loss dropped the Irish to .667; later, Father Edmund P. Joyce, University executive vice-president and chairman of the faculty board in control of athletics, admitted that after this loss he had made up his mind to ask Dee to resign at the end of the season. But the team's late-season drive was almost enough to change his mind; the Irish won five in a row to close the regular slate and to—barely—receive a bid to the NCAA Midwest Regional.

Most interesting of these was a 107-98 win at West Virginia, the promised "tough game" after ND had run up the score a year earlier. This time Carr was needed until the end and scored 47. NYU in the last game in this oldest intersectional rivalry, St. John's, and Dayton all fell, and in an emotional farewell, the seven seniors received a sendoff unlike any in Notre Dame basketball history in an easy 110-79 win over Western Michigan. The ovation crescendoed as each senior was lifted individually; when Carr left, the noise was deafening and remained so for over 15 minutes. With :25 left in the game, the five starters were re-inserted, and the crowd went berserk. When it was all over, no one wanted to leave; the students wouldn't let Carr leave until the greatest player in ND history had spoken over the PA at the arena. Few who were there will ever forget that experience.

The season, of course, wasn't over yet; in the first round of the NCAA Midwest Regional, Carr again had a field day with 51 points in a 102-94 defeat of Texas Christian. Again, though, things went sour in the semifinals. Upstart Drake scored a bucket with three seconds left in regulation to send the game into overtime. With momentum on its side, the Iowa school pulled off the upset, 79-72, after five more minutes of play. In the consolation game, Carr again displayed his ability to bounce back from adversity with 47 points in the 119-106 loss to Houston. (Curiously, both Dee's first and last losses as a coach in NCAA tourney play were to the same team.)

After the bitter taste of this disappointing 20-9 season had begun to fade slightly, the expected accolades for Austin Carr poured in. He was Player of the Year by a wide margin for both AP and UPI voting; he was named a first-team All-American on every known survey; he had become only the second player in NCAA history to score over 1,000 points in two different seasons (Pete Maravich was first); despite four-year eligibility today, he still is among the NCAA leaders for points and scoring average in a career. Finally, he was selected first in the NBA draft and signed a big-money contract with the Cleveland Cavaliers. Collis Jones was named to a couple of All-American teams as well, and played a few seasons in the ABA, and Sid Catlett appeared briefly with the old Cincinnati Royals. But for Johnny Dee, the end was near.

He went to Fr. Joyce asking for a one-year extension on his three-year extension. But Joyce suggested instead that Dee ought to get out while the getting was good. Thus Dee announced his resignation, officially this time, unlike two years earlier; he was finally going to use his Notre Dame law degree, he said, and return to his Denver adopted home. Many saw Dee as an opportunist in resigning when the returning talent was sparse, but up to this point he had been having a very good recruiting year; most of those recruits played key roles in Irish successes the next three years. But Dee really didn't jump until he was pushed.

Rumors flew as to the identity of his replacement, and it wasn't long before word leaked that Digger Phelps, the coach who essentially had caused Dee's resignation/dismissal, was to be the man. But Gene Sullivan refused to believe it. He felt he was the heir apparent to the job—he had become almost a co-head coach under Dee—and enlisted the help of influential alumni and the head coaches of several other colleges and every other varsity sport at Notre Dame (including Ara Parseghian, who seldom meddled in non-football matters) in his 11th-hour attempt to change the minds of the powers that be. All he managed to do was further alienate the athletic hierarchy at ND (Joyce and athletic director Moose Krause most specifically). Not until 1980, after serving as A.D. at DePaul and Loyola of Chicago for a few years, did Sullivan get a major-college coaching position (at Loyola).

But despite all the turmoil, Johnny Dee's contribution to Notre Dame's basketball resurgence cannot be denied. He had built a foundation for a winning program. But his teams, while loaded with first-class talent, seldom played to their potentials.

Digger Phelps was able to get a Fordham team to do just that, and probably more, as his one Cinderella 26-3 season illustrates. Now could he do the same at Notre Dame, where he had wanted to coach ever since he could remember?

# 19

## From Nothing
## to Nearly Everything

When Digger Phelps became coach at Fordham, he turned a moribund program into a miracle 26-3 winner—in one year. Even the most optimistic of pundits did not expect him to coach Notre Dame to anything close to a similar record after all the graduation losses and the alarming lack of returning experience.

Two events occurred between his ND arrival and his first game as coach which more or less sealed his fate for 1971-72. First, team captain and only returning regular Doug Gemmell destroyed his leg in a motorcycle accident, disabling him for the season. (This left John Egart as the only returning letterman.) And second, promising sophomore John Shumate developed blood clots in his leg, complications of which nearly killed him; he also was sidelined for the year.

Needless to say, it was a ragtag squad which took the floor of the ACC on December 1, 1971 to face Michigan—and lost 101-83, a score closer than expected. The starting five that day consisted of five sophomores: forwards Tom O'Mara and Chris Stevens, center Gary Novak, and guards Tom Hansen and Bob Valibus. This "green" lineup actually had a short-lived winning record after consecutive wins over Valparaiso and Western Michigan. No one expected it to last—and it didn't.

Without going into too many of the gory details, suffice it to say that Digger's first team finished 6-20, the third worst record (by percentage) in Notre Dame history. Included in that were three consecutive embarrassments—a 94-29 thrashing by Indiana at the dedication game of the Hoosiers' new Assembly Hall, the worst defeat ever for an Irish men's basketball team; a 114-56 drubbing at the hands of UCLA at Pauley Pavilion; and an 83-67 loss to Adolph Rupp's last Kentucky team, "only" a 16-point differential which led some Kentucky fans to wonder what Rupp did wrong to win by so few compared to IU and UCLA. Most of the other losses were by similar thrashings. After football season ended, two gridders—Willie and Mike Townsend—joined Digger's Don Quixote squad. Willie, in fact, managed to land a starting berth and finished third in scoring on the team.

Yet there were things to be happy about. One was a victory at Philadelphia's Palestra, always a tough place for out-of-town opponents, a 97-71 blowout of LaSalle—one of two 26-point victories during the year (Bowling Green lost by the same margin later at the ACC). There were also victories over Tulane and DePaul, the latter of which was having problems of its own. Then there was Digger himself, whose flashy style and even flashier clothes quickly endeared him to the Irish faithful. But more than any particular game or the man, it was the team as a whole. Despite the relative inexperience, perhaps even ineptitude, critics noticed a certain amount of organization which had been lacking in those Johnny Dee squads of the last three years. Even though there were difficulties implementing a new system, there were good signs out there. Probably not with these players, but eventually.

No one expected it would take but two years.

As opposed to that 1971-72 team, there was much impressive new talent on Digger Phelps' second squad: a healthy John Shumate; two of Johnny Dee's last recruits, guards Dwight Clay and Gary Brokaw; and Pete Crotty, whom Digger had recruited for Fordham and who had followed Phelps to Notre Dame. This squad also marked, temporarily, the end of a dying Notre Dame tradition, as three football players graced the Irish— the Townsend brothers and freshman Frank Allocco. (Although all were underclassmen, none were really needed the next year, so none returned. Over a decade would pass until another ND varsity footballer would also play hoops.) Also going into effect before the 1972-73 season was what became known as "the freshman rule," which allowed freshmen to compete immediately without the one-year wait for the first time since 1951-52. It had very little immediate effect on Notre Dame, as the only freshmen to play in 1972-73 saw very little action in their four years— Allocco, Roger Anderson, and Myron Schuckman.

The Irish of 1972-73 actually started with a worse record than the previous year's squad by losing six of their first seven. But a look at some of the scores indicates the lack of experience in close-game situations—81-75 in overtime (Ohio State), 60-58 (St. Louis), 69-67 (Indiana), 65-63 (Kentucky). What was more frustrating was that ND led at halftime in every one. It was a baptism under fire for a team with only one senior. In fact, when the basketball press guide went to print, no captains had been selected; the original intent was to elect game captains.

However, things began to click after that horrendous (on the won-loss ledger) start. The team finally won a close one— an overtime thriller at home against Kansas on January 7. On the road against DePaul, ND escaped from the Blue Demons' Alumni Hall with a five-point win. Then came a matchup against Marquette.

Under youthful firebrand Al McGuire, Marquette's basketball fortunes had resurged. Four of the last five years the Warriors had appeared in the NCAA tournament; the one year they didn't, 1970, they won the NIT after boycotting the Big Show. They had an 81-game homecourt winning streak going into the matchup with the young but surging Irish. When Notre Dame left Milwaukee the night of the 13th of January, the skein was no more. Digger's upstarts had beaten the top-10-ranked Warriors, 71-69. Brokaw had 28 and Shumate 21 to lead the Irish, but it was Dwight Clay who put up the winning basket from the right corner with :04 showing on the clock. This game began two new traditions: Notre-Dame-as-streakbreaker and Dwight-Clay-as-last-minute-game-saving-shot-artist.

Four days after he put away Marquette, Clay struck again. With the team down by two with little time left, he put one in against Pittsburgh to send the game into overtime. Buoyed by the shot and the partisan ACC crowd, ND put the Panthers away by nine. Those two shots earned Clay the nickname "The Iceman." He was to continue to live up to that moniker in the future.

Meanwhile, after a win over Dayton, ND's record stood at 6-6. By this time, Digger had discovered the winning formula for this particular squad, one he utilized the rest of the season. It was Clay, Brokaw, Crotty, Shumate, and Novak. Period. No substitutions unless one got into foul trouble. Then it was Don Silinski, the team's lone senior, or Willie Townsend. The same five men started every game; except in the blowouts, the rest of the team was only along for the ride.

Then came three straight losses. One, an 87-84 decision by traditionally difficult Illinois, was the last game Notre Dame was to play in Chicago Stadium, the site of numerous ND appearances since 1942. The next, an 82-63 loss to UCLA at the ACC, was the Bruins' 61st consecutive win dating back to ND's 89-82 win over them in 1971, breaking the all-time record of 60 set by San Francisco in the heyday of Bill Russell in the mid-fifties. After those disappointments, the "Iron Men" rattled off five straight wins again, and suddenly talk of the NIT began.

Actually, NIT talk had begun after the first four-game streak in January but had been quashed quickly after those three straight defeats. Now Digger and the Irish Iron Men had a chance to prove they belonged in a post-season tournament. In front of the Metropolitan Basketball Writers Association Notre Dame played Fordham to start a four-game road trip.

When Phelps had left Fordham, he was seen as a "turncoat" and "traitor" by many New Yorkers. One sportswriter went so far as to claim that Digger had broken a "solemn pact" when he left the Rams for the only head coaching job he had ever really wanted. Few times in the history of the modern Madison Square Garden were the boos as loud as when Digger appeared on the court. But when the Irish left the court at the end of the game, those same fans were cheering—because Fordham had upset the Irish, 70-69. A loss to Duke at the Blue Devils' "insane asylum" followed, 86-74. That was to be Notre Dame's last regular-season defeat.

The Irish closed the season with four straight victories, two of them over NCAA tourney-bound St. John's and South Carolina, and a final record of 15-11. The invitation to the NIT did come, probably not so much for the record as for the drawing power Notre Dame would have in New York. No one—perhaps not even the Irish—suspected that a miracle was nearly to be pulled off.

First the Irish Iron Men defeated traditional football opponent Southern Cal, then Louisville, then tourney favorite North Carolina—three straight upsets, the last against the Atlantic Coast Conference's regular-season champs who had lost to Maryland in the ACC tournament. Suddenly Notre Dame found itself in the final game of the NIT against equally-surprising Virginia Tech—the 15th and 16th-seeded teams in the tourney, respectively. ND led at the half, and most of the way, but Tech tied the game to send it into overtime. With time running out, the Irish held a tenuous one-point lead, mere seconds away from their first post-season basketball championship. Tech's last-shot attempt went up. It missed! But Bobby Stevens came down with the rebound and swished a 15-footer as the buzzer sounded. Virginia Tech had pulled off a miracle of its own, 92-91. Even with this season-ending shocker, Irish eyes were smiling, because almost everyone was back for the 1973-74 squad.

And what a team it appeared to be! With a returning starting lineup, only one graduating senior (Don Silinski), and six, count 'em, six freshman prospects of varying abilities and credentials to replace him, Digger would have the luxury of more depth in 1973-74. Most impressive of the newcomers was Adrian Dantley, one of the most sought-after prospects in the country and another of the "DC Connection" which had fed ND with quality talent from Washington for almost ten years. Yet Dantley wasn't the only one: among the others were Toby Knight, Ray Martin, Bill Paterno, and Dave Kuzmicz, all of whom would make contributions to Irish basketball over the next few years. There was a lot of talent here, but loaded teams were not rare in Notre Dame basketball's recent past; meshing the parts without the gears jamming was, however.

Valparaiso went down by 50 points in the home opener, but a tough road contest against Ohio State was up next. And guess who came through again? Dwight Clay, of course. He put up *another* last-second jumper to take OSU into OT for the second year in a row. Clay's heroics overshadowed a fine game by John Shumate as ND won the game, 76-72.

Two easy wins (Northwestern and St. Louis) followed, and then the Irish headed down to Assembly Hall in Bloomington,

Indiana, with memories of a 94-29 massacre in this venue two years earlier, and without Gary Brokaw, who was lost with an ankle injury. Phelps started two freshmen (Dantley and Paterno) against Indiana, which was undergoing a resurgence of its own under Bobby Knight and had won 19 straight on its home floor. But the streak breakers came through again. Shumate had 26 and the first-time starter, Paterno, added 16 in the 73-67 victory.

Phelps was concerned, however. It was finals time, and he was worried about his freshmen. He was not—and still isn't—in favor of freshman eligibility, but he knew he would be at a gross disadvantage in building a solid program if he didn't go along. This was his first major recruiting class, and happily all got the first-semester freshman minimum of 1.75 or better. Now it was back to basketball. Denver was the next easy victim, and in a rarity, Kentucky lost to the Irish in Louisville by 15. The Wildcats had only a mediocre (13-13) team in 1973-74 while Notre Dame had what was looking like a great one.

In a rarity at a non-exam time, the team had two weeks between games; many of the players, and Digger Phelps as well, went to New Orleans and took in the town before, during and after the Sugar Bowl, in which Notre Dame's footballers defeated mighty (and number-one ranked) Alabama, 24-23, for their first unbeaten and untied season since 1949. (Remember that margin of victory and the opponent for both come into play in this basketball season, oddly enough.)

Meanwhile, after the celebrating was over, the team regrouped to prepare for the next games, which ended up as two more convincing wins; Xavier and Georgetown were the Irish victims. Now all eyes in the sports world were focusing on South Bend, as a classic battle was shaping up—Notre Dame vs. UCLA.

As usual, UCLA topped the polls. But Notre Dame was number two. The Irish had a nine-game win streak, their longest in almost four years. The Bruins had an 88-game streak, the longest by anyone, ever. On the TVS independent network, a national television audience would be watching, and because of that the starting time was moved to 12 noon local time. (This was the year of the so-called "energy crisis," and the East was on daylight saving time while Indiana, as usual, remained on standard time.) Officials in South Bend declared January 19, 1974 "College Basketball Day." The stage was set for a game which lived up to all the advance hoopla.

This battle for top spot was a game of streaks. But it started as if it would be no battle at all. With 6:41 left in the first half, the Uclans led, 33-16, behind the inspired play of Bill Walton, their All-American center. Walton, who had missed the last two weeks with a back injury, shot 6-of-7 from the floor in the first half and 12-of-14 in the game in his return to the lineup. The Irish fought back and cut the deficit to five, but UCLA put together a streak of free throws and led at the half, 43-34.

Notre Dame, buoyed by the home crowd, closed to within two by scoring nine of the first 11 points of the second half. But UCLA quickly ended that threat with nine consecutive points to make the score 54-43. The Bruins continued to lead as the second half passed its halfway point, but ND did not give up. The margin was closed to 64-59 with 4:17 to go, and the 11,343 at the ACC were fired up again. But six straight points by the Uclans made the score 70-59 less than a minute later. With 3:22 left, Notre Dame called time.

Digger made three changes in a last-ditch effort to get back into the game. First, he inserted Ray Martin for Bill Paterno to add some quickness to the lineup. Second, he moved John Shumate to the front of the press so he could pressure the inbounds pass. Third and finally, he ordered "spurt time." Spurt time was a drill Phelps ran in practice in which he put a small amount of time on the clock and a large deficit on the scoreboard. The goal was for the starting five to come from behind before the time ran out. He hadn't had to use it in a game yet. This was the time.

The Irish quickly drove up the court, and at 3:07 Shumate put in a jumper to cut the Bruin lead to nine.

Immediately thereafter, Move Two in the timeout paid off. Shumate stole the inbounds pass and made the easy layup, and the score was 70-63. By this time the crowd, which had been in and out of the game all afternoon, was back in it, and this time for keeps.

UCLA tried to work the ball for a score, but Adrian Dantley

stole it and went in for another layup. The crowd was going crazy. 2:22 to go. 70-65.

The Bruins began to come back upcourt, but Tommy Curtis, who scored the last UCLA basket at 3:32, traveled. Irish ball. They got it inbounds and worked it to Gary Brokaw, who put up a 20-footer from near the foul lane. It went in. 2:01 to go. 70-67.

For the first time in a minute and a half, the Uclans got to take a shot. Dave Meyers tried to close the door on the Irish comeback attempt. He missed the shot, and the Irish controlled the rebound. Brokaw gets to take the shot again, from nearly the same spot as his last one, and again it goes in. 1:11 to go. 70-69.

Move Number One was about to pay off. Keith Wilkes of UCLA drives in for a layup. :45 to go, and UCLA . . . But wait! The whistle has blown. Ray Martin stood his ground. Offensive foul. No basket. UCLA coach John Wooden yells "You crook!" at the referee. It's likely he wasn't heard by anyone except TV lip-readers. The crowd is as loud as any since the "snakepit" days at the Fieldhouse.

Notre Dame inbounds, hoping to get Brokaw or Shumate open for an inside shot. But the Bruins clog the inside. On the TVS mike, Dick Enberg counts down the seconds remaining: "Thirty-five, thirty-four, thirty-three, thirty-two . . ." Brokaw passes off to Dwight Clay, "The Iceman," who is open in the right corner. He gets it off as a flying Curtis tries to block it. Bingo! 29 seconds left; Notre Dame 71, UCLA 70. Twelve straight points. Change number three, "spurt time," has worked; now can the Irish hold on?

UCLA gets the ball into the forecourt, only to nearly lose it in front of press row. Unable to get the ball to Walton, Curtis puts up a far-outside shot in hope that one of the big guns will get the rebound. One of them does; Dave Meyers misses the followup. Brokaw grabs it—but he can't hold it! Out of bounds, UCLA ball, six seconds left. Everyone in the place knows who the inbounds pass is going to if it can get there . . .

It does. But Bill Walton, who has not missed from the floor in the second half, does just that from close range . . .

Pete Trgovich tries to tip in the missed shot . . .

Meyers tries to do likewise as Notre Dame has all sorts of

trouble getting the clinching rebound; again the shot is missed . . .

Finally, Shumate grabs the rebound with one second left, cradles the ball, then heaves it high into the air! The game ends, but the roar is so deafening that the buzzer is inaudible.

"It's all over!!" shouts Dick Enberg to what was then the largest TV audience in college basketball history.

And so it was. Notre Dame 71, UCLA 70. A one-point win over the top-ranked team. The end of a dynasty and "the greatest game in Notre Dame basketball history," according to Phelps, an assessment hard to disagree with. Mobbed by admiring fans, the players cut down the nets. Interestingly, in practice the night before, Phelps had his men "practice" the ritual in anticipation of the next day's event. For the first time since the wire services began their weekly basketball polls, Notre Dame was Number One.

Alas, the position atop the world lasted but one week. The inevitable letdown led to a near-upset at Kansas three days later, and St. Francis made the Irish 12-0. But then ND had to play the Bruins again, this time at Pauley Pavilion, one week after The End. The Walton Gang went out and showed the "Kings for a Week" why the Bruins had been kings for nearly a decade with a 94-75 victory. And there wasn't much time to regroup before the next tough opponent, Marquette.

The Warriors gave the no-longer-undefeated Irish a fierce battle, and Al McGuire's men nearly ended Notre Dame's home winning streak which dated back over a year. The Irish survived the challenge in a defensive battle, 69-63. DePaul and Davidson were relatively easy wins, and the team was rolling again.

An unexpectedly close battle with Michigan State in East Lansing, a defeat of LaSalle at the Palestra, and a home win over Duke put the Irish at 18-1 in preparation for the annual trip to New York and the wrath of the fans at Fordham.

For three straight years—once with Digger at the helm of the Rams and twice with Digger the victim—Fordham had defeated Notre Dame. But this was the streakbreaker team; finally the Irish claimed a victory over the Rams, 79-69. Next up was South Carolina, which had won 34 straight games on its home court; after Shumate (26 points) and the Irish were through, the

Gamecocks had to begin a new one. Notre Dame won, 72-68, to break another opponent's streak.

Returning home, the Irish machine shifted into overdrive with big wins over Western Michigan, West Virginia (in which Dantley showed some of his future flash with 41 points), Ball State, and Villanova. After the defeat of the latter, Digger's squad had met its preseason goal by being named to the NCAA tournament, and was riding its second 12-game winning streak of the year. Also, for the first time since 1959-60, Notre Dame had not lost at home all year. Two days after the bid, the Irish closed their most successful regular season in 47 years in a venue in which they had never won against the home team, the University of Dayton Arena, and a fired-up Flyer squad handed ND only its second loss in 26 games.

The NCAA Mideast Regional started well, as Notre Dame defeated Austin Peay and its star Fly Williams convincingly, 108-66. But Phelps got a surprise. He and his assistants has expected to play Indiana in the semifinal round, but Michigan upset the Hoosiers to win the Big Ten, catching Notre Dame off guard. As it turned out, the Wolverines caught the Irish off guard in more ways than one.

Campy Russell ran roughshod over them, and ND picked an inopportune time to play its worst game of the year (for example, Adrian Dantley had only two points). Michigan pulled off the upset, 77-68, and the Notre Dame NCAA jinx continued. The Irish cause was not helped any by the crowd at the regional site of Tuscaloosa, Alabama. The locals, remembering what ND's football team had done to their Crimson Tide last New Year's Eve, were openly hostile toward the Irish. They would have cheered for the USSR over Notre Dame that night.

ND played the game it should have played against Michigan in the consolation game, a 118-88 drubbing of Vanderbilt. But it was no consolation to Digger and the team. It was even less of a consolation that, as it turned out, three of the Final Four had been ND victims during the season (UCLA, Marquette, and Kansas).

But the accolades began rolling in. The final NCAA stats had Irish players or the team as a whole listed among the leaders in eight different categories. Shumate and Brokaw were named All-Americans, and Phelps was named Coach of the Year by UPI, the Metropolitan Basketball Writers Association, *Basketball Weekly*, and *The Sporting News*. Even though the Irish had lost in the tourney, they had become a team to be reckoned with again in a very short period of time. Now the challenge was to make it last.

# 20

## Finally, the Final Four

The Irish did make it last, thanks to five consecutive recruiting years (1973 through '77) which ranged from good to fabulous. Once the new men gained experience, Digger had the luxury of talented depth. He could fashion lineups for whatever the situation warranted, and if a regular was injured, there was someone to fill in without a great drop in ability. By March 1978, the countless miles traveling the country spotting and signing top high-school talent finally paid off in Notre Dame's first trip to the NCAA Final Four. Before that, there were some good seasons, great upsets, consecutive trips to the tournament, and consecutive upsets in the semifinals. Also, there was Adrian Dantley. But when ND was in the Final Four, it was relative no-names who held center stage.

First, however, was the long building process, which resumed immediately after the 1973-74 season ended. To join the long list of returnees from the 26-3 team were four new faces: guards Jeff Carpenter and Don "Duck" Williams, and forwards Randy Haefner and Dave Batton. What a team—perhaps the greatest in Irish history—Digger could have had in 1974-75 had not both John Shumate (a senior academically in 1973-74 but a junior in eligibility) and Gary Brokaw entered the pro basketball hardship draft and signed big-money contracts in the NBA. Instead, the team was young (nine sophomores and freshmen and only two seniors—Dwight Clay and Pete Crotty—in key roles) and thus unpredictable. What happened was an 18-8 mark and a second consecutive trip to the NCAAs, thanks in no small part to ND's killer schedule and the team's phenomenal sophomore, Dantley.

Of the 26 games on the slate, 13 of them were played against eventual NCAA or NIT participants, this when the combined tourneys were half the size of today's. Of the other 13, some had fine records and/or home gyms notoriously difficult for visiting teams. And as for "A.D.," his escapades will be chronicled as the chapter goes on.

To open the season, Notre Dame played at Valparaiso's minuscule gym for the last time, and won by only 11, 91-80. Then the Irish opened the ACC slate with three straight wins to stretch the home victory streak to 24, over Northwestern (100-84, with 44 by Dantley, 32 in the first half), perennial Ivy League contender Princeton (80-66), and then-ninth-ranked Kansas (75-59) for Notre Dame's 1000th win ever. The four-game home stand—and the ACC streak—ended against third-ranked Indiana, 94-84. And if that wasn't bad enough, after the exam period ND had to face eight straight road games.

The longest road trip for the Irish since 1952-53 varied from tremendous to awful, but tended toward the latter, as Notre Dame came home 7-6 and out of the polls. The first stop was Pauley Pavilion, where UCLA had a 70-game homecourt streak going. And it looked as if the streak breakers would come through again; ND led by 19 points at one time, but fell apart down the stretch and lost by 13. Then a double whammy was suffered at Louisville: not only did Kentucky win the game going away, 113-96, but the pro-Wildcat press corps passed up A.D.'s 39-point performance and gave the Shively Memorial Plaque (player of the game) to UK's Larry Johnson.

Venerable Hinkle Fieldhouse proved good medicine for Irish ills, as in the first meeting between the longtime foes in four years, ND defeated Butler, 93-83. But the fifth top-10-ranked opponent of the year, Maryland, knocked off the Irish at Cole Field House, 90-82, as Dantley and Duck Williams had a homecoming of sorts (both from Washington, DC). ND's downfall was its 12-for-22 free throw shooting, several of them blown one-and-the-bonus attempts. The long march continued with games in Charlotte, and Philadelphia, and two big wins resulted: Dantley scored 38, and Dave Batton and Jeff Carpenter made strong contributions off the bench in a 89-75 defeat of Davidson; and then all hell broke loose at the Palestra against Villanova. Notre Dame set a new Palestra record for points in a half (75) and new Philadelphia Big Five opponents' records for field goals (52) and points (125). The game itself was no contest. Dantley stayed in long enough to score 37 points and remain atop the NCAA scorers' list, and then sat with 10:22 left. The 125-90 ND win marked the second-highest offensive production in the school's history. But Digger would have gladly taken some of that excess in the next two games.

Pittsburgh upset the Irish in "neutral" Civic Arena after coming from 15 points down, 84-77. The high point of a so-far frustrating season for the Panthers, the Pitt coach called this his team's "first road victory of the year." And then Marquette and ever-crafty Al McGuire sprang a triangle-and-two defense on ND, Dantley was held to 17, and the Irish couldn't hold a late lead, losing 71-68 to end the long road trip.

In a way, the month-long trek was a blessing because, of the 13 games left, 10 were at home, and two others were within 100 miles of home (Kalamazoo and Chicago). And ND took advantage of this scheduling, streaking to an 11-2 mark the rest of the way and into the tournament. This is not to say that the opponents were patsies. Far from it.

Notre Dame was nearly caught looking ahead to its rematch with UCLA against 13-2 Holy Cross. But a three-point play by Dantley and 4-for-4 from the line by sophomore Dave Kuzmicz down the stretch clinched a hard-fought 96-91 win. Kuzmicz's heroics earned him a start in that UCLA game—the only start in his four years. And in that UCLA game, the Irish topped the Bruins for the second year in a row at home. The stakes weren't as high as they had been a year earlier, but the 84-78 triumph was only slightly less exciting to the home folks. Dantley, as usual, led the way with 32 against the eventual NCAA champs in John Wooden's last season.

At Kalamazoo, Western Michigan nearly caught the Irish on the rebound. But Adrian Dantley, injured earlier in the game thanks to an elbow in the nose, returned to hit the winning free throws in the 73-71 victory. Back home, A.D. wore a face mask as ND romped over Xavier, and scored 31 points in the next game, against Michigan State. But the 12-5 Spartans left with the win, 76-73, thanks to five technical fouls. And then he man-

Varsity Basketball Team, 1897.

Notre Dame's first varsity basketball team poses for its official picture in March 1897. **Row 1:** team captain John Shillington, Frank Cornell, Joseph Naughton; **Row 2:** Thomas Steiner, Daniel Murphy, coach Frank Hering, John Donovan; **Row 3:** Martin O'Shaughnessey, Thomas Martin, William Kegler, Edward Herron, John Fennessey, Thomas Burns. (Courtesy University of Notre Dame Archives)

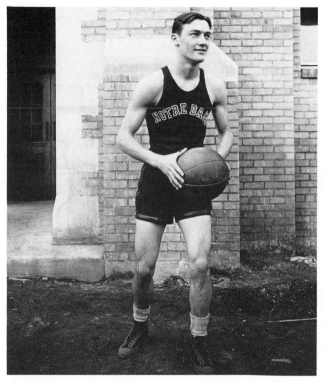

John Nyikos, center from 1924-27, leading scorer three straight seasons; All-American as a senior. (Courtesy Sports Information Department, University of Notre Dame) [NDSI]

Ed Smith, an outstanding defensive guard and ND's first two-time All-American in the late 1920s. (Courtesy NDSI)

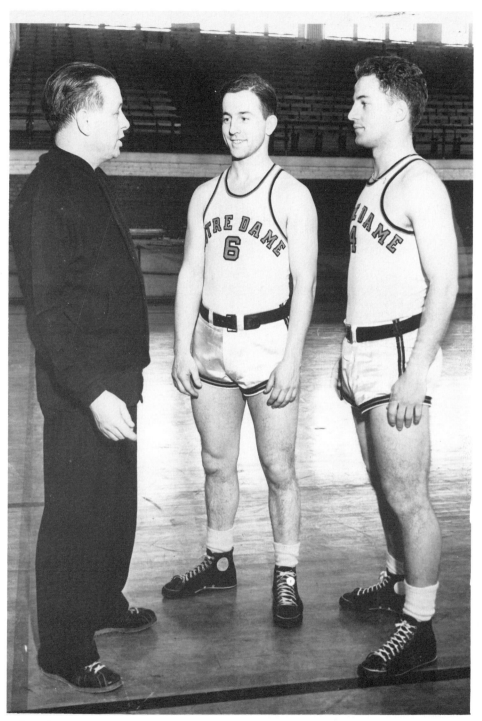

Irish coach, George Keogan, with Mike and Emmet Crowe, the last two of seven Crowes who played at Notre Dame in the '20s and '30s. This shot was taken around 1935. (Courtesy NDSI)

February 20, 1943: Notre Dame players bow their heads in tribute to their late coach, George Keogan, before playing Great Lakes at Chicago Stadium. The Irish lost an emotional game in overtime, the last of only two losses all season. (Courtesy NDSI)

Dick Rosenthal (1951-54) played center and forward on John Jordan's first three Irish teams. During his ND career the Irish went 57-18. (Courtesy NDSI)

Dale Barnstable (24) has just had a shot blocked by Jack Neumayr in Kentucky's last-ever visit to the Fieldhouse, January 23, 1950. Notre Dame won, 64-51. Also pictured: Dan Bagley (19), Leroy Leslie (17), UK's seven-foot center Bill Spivey (behind Leslie), Don Strasser (hidden in back of action), Jim Line (34), and All-American Kevin O'Shea (7). (Courtesy NDSI)

Tom Hawkins, one of ND's all-time greats, soars for two over Marquette's Jim McCoy in 1959 action, "The Hawk's" last ND game. The Irish upset the Warriors/Hilltoppers, 51-35. (Courtesy NDSI)

Johnny Dee, the successful but controversial coach who led the Irish on the first steps back to national prominence in the 1960s. (Courtesy NDSI)

Dee's job was made easier by "The Man," Austin Carr, here streaking past a Northern Illinois defender for two of his 2,560 career points . . . (Courtesy NDSI)

Austin Carr – An ovation for greatness. (Courtesy *Notre Dame Magazine)*

. . . and by Collis Jones, who developed into a strong offensive player. (Brother Charles McBride/Courtesy NDSI)

January 23, 1971: Austin Carr finishes cutting down the nets after he almost singlehandedly led ND to an 89-82 upset of UCLA in the greatest moment of the Dee years. (Courtesy NDSI)

January 19, 1974: Dwight Clay launches his ''shot heard 'round the world'' with 29 seconds left to cap a 12-0 spurt in the last 3:22 and end UCLA's amazing 88-game winning streak, 71-70. (Joe Raymond/Courtesy NDSI)

Richard "Digger" Phelps, architect of many great Irish "moments" in recent history.

Great players helped make Irish basketball exciting in the 1970s. Some of them include John Shumate . . .
(Courtesy NDSI)

Another Irish powerhouse of the '70s was Adrian Dantley. (Courtesy Paul Joyce)

Here AD muscles his way in for another two. (Courtesy Paul Joyce)

. . . and Kelly Tripucka, shown in ND's 81-78 defeat of UCLA in Pauley Pavilion in December 1978. (John Dlugolecki/Courtesy NDSI)

Tripucka counsels with "Digger" Phelps. (Courtesy *Notre Dame Magazine)*

John Paxson (1979-84), a two-time Irish All-American
and steadying force as a junior and senior on two of
Digger Phelps' most inexperienced teams. (Courtesy
Notre Dame *Observer)*

David Rivers came on in 1984-85 as the most exciting Notre Dame freshman in a decade or more.
(Courtesy NDSI)

Jenny Klauke, the first woman to receive an athletic grant-in-aid from the University, showed flashes of brilliance her freshman year, but was slowed by injuries for two years, which hindered her further advancement.

Maggie Lalley, the five-foot dynamo, listens attentively to Coach Mary D's directions (Courtesy *The Dome*)

Mary Beth Schueth, a four-year starter and two-time team captain, was the women's most productive scorer as a freshman and sophomore and stands second on the all-time Irish scoring list. (Courtesy NDSI)

Trena Keys, the North Star Conference Player of the Year as a junior, is prepared to become Notre Dame's career scoring leader in 1985-86 and could possibly become ND's first All-American in women's basketball. (Courtesy NDSI)

aged only 10 points against a swarming South Carolina defense, but behind a second-half starting lineup of three freshmen (Williams, Carpenter, Batton) and two sophomores (Bill Paterno and Dantley), the Irish pulled out a 66-65 overtime decision. Dantley was finally given clearance to shed the mask against Air Force, and he celebrated by scoring 49 points, his career high and the most by any Irishman ever (other than Austin Carr, of course) as ND rolled, 99-66.

A rarity in the Dantley era, balanced scoring (A.D. 18, Toby Knight 16, Paterno, 17, Williams 10), helped ND edge St. John's at Madison Square Garden in the last game between the two schools (they couldn't agree on where to play games on the St. John's end; Notre Dame wanted to play in the Garden or Nassau Coliseum, but the Redmen argued for their campus gym), 68-67. Dantley returned to pre-eminence against 19-3 LaSalle, scoring 36 in ND's 91-75 win. And in this season of the killer schedule, even St. Joseph's of Indiana entered with a 19-3 record; the Irish beat them by a close margin for the series, 97-81.

At Alumni Hall, DePaul laid a roadblock for the streaking Irish; a comeback in the last three minutes helped the up-and-coming Demons defeat ND for the first time since 1967, 75-70. But Notre Dame ended the regular season with two big wins in a row, 98-61 over Fordham and 102-69 over Dayton to prepare for a trip to the Midwest Regional.

The Irish had already defeated their first-round opponent, Kansas, once, and they did again, 77-71, to move into the semifinals against another team ND had faced already, Maryland. Just like the last time, though, the Terrapins defeated the Irish, this time 83-71, to end another trek to the Final Four before arriving there. In the last Midwest Regional consolation game, the Cincinnati Bearcats tied it to send it into overtime and then zapped the Irish for 19 points in OT to win, 95-87.

The most interesting off-season story was that of Adrian Dantley, who had been named nearly everyone's first-team All-American and was second in the nation in scoring average (though first in actual points scored). Originally, he enlisted in the hardship draft, but then—thanks to great internal pressure—he removed his name from the list just before the deadline. He would be back at ND for 1975-76, but probably not any longer.

Of all of Phelps' teams, the 1975-76 contingent is probably the most easily overlooked. Most observers felt this team, without a single senior in a regular position, was at least a year away, yet it went 22-5 in the regular season. Of those five defeats, four were by six points or less, and all were against highly-regarded competition. And no one could complain about the schedule, either that it was too grueling or too easy. Sixteen home games—the most in Irish history to that time—certainly made life easier, but not too much so, as there were few pushovers.

The regular season began with three straight home slaughters over Kent State (90-61), Valparaiso (117-83, with 39 more for A.D.), and Texas Tech (88-63). But worthy of mention is the preseason game, which gave some indication of the team's potential. The Irish traveled to Madison Square Garden in early November to take on the USSR National Team, this in the year before the Olympics, when it would be expected to be strongest. And the much younger ND team lost by only one to the defending (although dubious) Olympic champs, 77-76. Actually, however, the best team in the world in 1975-76 may have been ND's fifth opponent, the Indiana Hoosiers. After the Irish beat Kansas there, 72-64, they rolled into Bloomington with a 4-0 record . . . and rolled out with a 4-1 record. Despite a furious late rally, ND lost, 63-60, one of IU's closest shaves all season. The Hoosiers went 32-0 and won the national championship; no NCAA Division I team has finished undefeated since. To close the pre-exam session, ND rolled over St. Francis of Pennsylvania, 103-73, behind Dantley's 37.

Last year's eight-game road string was cut to two for 1975-76. But the Irish lost both—a real heartbreaker to Kentucky, 79-77, and a blowout by UCLA, 86-70, the team's only really bad outing all season. Returning home, ND let its bench strength shine in an 88-71 defeat of Manhattan; the Irish outscored the New Yorkers 41-2 and outrebounded them 25-0 off the bench, and fast-improving 6-11 freshman center Bill Laimbeer, Notre Dame's first varsity player of that height, scored 15 points and earned a start at Civic Arena against Pitt. The Irish got their revenge from the upset of 1974-75, 77-66, behind A.D.'s 34.

Phelps received a jolt when the team returned home. He learned that Laimbeer had failed to make his grades and would be ineligible the rest of the season, just as he was starting to learn the system. But, except for his height, he was hardly missed. Notre Dame went 13-2 the rest of the season, and things started with another awesome display of offense against Ball State, 119-78. They continued at the ancient Cincinnati Gardens against Xavier, 90-79 (35 for Dantley), and back at home against St. Joseph's (IN), 97-60. Then next was what Digger dubbed "The Triple Crown," a three-game-in-eight-days streak against highly-touted opponents, all at home. And he wanted a sweep.

First was UCLA, which had beaten ND by 16 at Pauley. But at the ACC, it was a different story. The Bruins were on their way to a 10th straight berth in the Final Four, but Notre Dame sidetracked them for the third straight year, an unheard-of accomplishment. Adrian Dantley did his usual, scoring 30, and Duck Williams tallied 18 in ND's most lopsided win over the Uclans so far, 95-85. Second was DePaul, which was making a remarkable comeback after nearly demoting its program to Division II in 1971. But the complete return would have to wait a bit longer, as—who else?—Dantley had 31 to pace the 89-68 Irish win. And third was Maryland. But the Irish fell seven lengths short of their Triple Crown; the top-five-ranked Terrapins won down the stretch, 69-63.

However, Notre Dame won its next nine games, and only a couple were close. Both were on the road, and in both the Irish took the lead and then not only held it, but added on to it, by use of a four-corner offense. Four men were positioned high, and Duck Williams was the odd man out. He would use the extra attention paid to Dantley, who could break loose at any time, to work his way behind the defense for a pass—and an easy layup. When it worked, and it usually did, it was a point scoring weapon and helped make close games into more comfortable ones. That is just what happened at South Carolina (90-83) and Dayton—Notre Dame's first regular-season win there since 1910 (85-79). The four-corners wasn't needed in the others. At the Spectrum, Dantley scored 41 and ND coasted over LaSalle 108-89, and back home Davidson fell, 117-74; St. Bonaventure, a late addition to the schedule after the NCAA, in a last-minute decision, allowed teams to schedule a 27th game, did likewise, 95-80; Villanova went down, 84-57, and West Virginia, 95-77.

In the latter game, Dantley scored his 2,000th career point, but didn't lead the team in scoring for that night; that honor was reserved for freshman center/forward Bruce Flowers, who tallied 27. In the other two road games, Butler fell in front of only about 4,500 fans at Indianapolis' new Market Square Arena (an Indiana-Purdue game was on television, and Butler no longer held the interest of the average Indianapolitan, even if playing Notre Dame), 92-79, and Fordham at the Garden, 92-78, behind A.D.'s 33.

The winning streak ended against 22-1 Marquette at home. The Warriors used a balanced scoring attack and took advantage of ND's horrendous first-half shooting (8-for-29) to build up a big lead and then hold on to win, 81-75. Two nights later, the Irish had it no easier with one of the best Western Michigan teams of modern times (also 22-1 coming in). The game went into overtime, but 13-of-14 accuracy from the free throw line during the extra stanza helped ND close its regular season with a 95-88 win.

Notre Dame was sent to the Mideast Regional this time and was supposed to have an easy time with first-round opponent Cincinnati, but far from it. It took a Toby Knight tip-in at the :02 mark after a controversial five-second call to salvage a 79-78 victory after the Bearcats had looked like winners. Then it was off to one of ND's least favorites sites (Freedom Hall) to play a traditional thorn in the side (Michigan). But the Irish looked good; they led by eight twice in the second half. But they began to focus on protecting their lead and their offensive flow slowed. Usually when that happens, disaster lurks nearby. In this case the Wolverines, who went to the NCAA final game to nearly everyone's surprise for an all-Big Ten final, came back after the Irish got careless and upset them, 80-76, a premature end to a really good season otherwise.

For a team without a significant senior in 1975-76, there were several major losses entering the 1976-77 season. First, Adrian Dantley finally did what he had threatened to do in 1975 and put his name into the hardship draft; then again, that move was generally expected. For Digger to lose two-thirds of his last recruiting class was not: Bill Laimbeer, who had sat out the last 19 games because of academic probation, flunked out of school entirely and was enrolled at Owens Technical College in Toledo, Ohio, and not playing basketball at all in an organized fashion; and Bernard Rencher, who was seen as a potential replacement for Ray Martin in the backcourt, transferred to St. John's.

There were a couple of more subtle changes as well. One was in the schedule. No one ever argued about a couple of weaker teams as early-season fodder before the "real" competition began, but when such teams as Vermont and Stonehill crept onto the schedule later in the season, there were questions. "Stone *who*?" asked one critic. While scheduling like that proved the exception (and actually a benefit) in 1976-77, unfortunately it would become less so in not too many more years. The other was in Digger Phelps himself. He was gradually undergoing a change in his court demeanor: he ditched the loud jackets for more conservative three-piece suits, although the lapel carnation stayed, but just as significantly, the man who seemingly used to compete with Al McGuire in ND-Marquette games to see who could get a technical foul whistled on him first went through the entire 1976-77 season without a single one! Along with his changes in looks and actions came a change in philosophy on the court. Now that his "superstar" was gone, balance became the byword. And that there was: all five of his regular starting lineup averaged in double figures, and Bill Paterno, his senior sixth man, averaged 9.6 points per game.

This balance got off to a great start (7-0). Opening at Maryland in the game with the earliest known starting time in Notre Dame history (11 AM), Toby Knight had 19 and Duck Williams 16 plus the game winner in an 80-79 overtime win. The game had been arranged only a few weeks before and it marked the continuation of a series originally meant as a two-shot deal when it began in 1974-75. Following this were three consecutive home blowouts (Cal Poly-Pomona, Valparaiso, and Northwestern were the victims). The most notable happening in the Pomona contest, and eventually of any home blowout (and there were many in a 21-6 season), was the debut of the "SWAT Team."

Always heralded by the pep band's stirring rendition of the "Theme from SWAT," the once-popular TV show, the five men would take the court as one when it was mop-up time and usually entertained the crowd until it was time to go home (or, in some of the more abject blowouts, before halftime activities). The SWAT Team was a chance to shine for "Sergeant" Jeff Carpenter, who, after a great deal less playing time as a sophomore, nearly left Notre Dame for elsewhere, and his "lieutenants"—junior Randy Haefner and three walk-ons, senior Bill Sahm (cousin of the early 1960s star Walt Sahm), sophomore Chris Fabian, and freshman Tim Healy. Not only were they entertaining, but they usually added a few more points to ND's final score.

Of course, there were other things to get excited about — like the next two games, for example. Notre Dame's ninth trip to Pauley Pavilion (December 11, 1976) resulted in something which had never happened before. A team from outside the Pac-8 (now Pac-10) defeated UCLA on its home floor to end the Bruins' 115-game non-conference winning streak at Pauley. Duck Williams' 11-for-16 shooting for 22 points led ND's 66-63 triumph, but perhaps just as important was the presence of freshman guard Rich Branning, a resident of nearby Huntington Beach. In four years on the Irish varsity, he was never on an ND team that lost at Pauley, and only one has won there since he graduated. The other big one was back home again with Indiana, the defending national champion. This time the Irish knocked the Hoosiers down, 78-65, but at a high cost: Ray Martin went down for the season—and his career—with a broken ankle. This forced Phelps to put Branning into the starting lineup much earlier than he would have liked, and some adjustments became necessary. After an easy win over much-maligned Vermont (89-48), Notre Dame spent a *long* Christmas holiday trying to make them.

Four games made up this year's trip; four games in a row went into the loss column. Jack Givens scored 30 points, and the Irish played poorly in a Kentucky win, 102-72, the worst ND defeat in six years. In front of the largest crowd ever to jam into Princeton's home gym, the Irish were upset, 76-62, thanks to 26 turnovers. In another tough place for an opponent, the Palestra, Notre Dame again had turnover fever in the first half, but got its act together in the second. A last-second try for an overtime period failed, and Villanova had a win, 64-62. Finally, at Marquette, the Warriors took a 78-69 decision on the way to their only national championship, a retirement present for Al

McGuire. When the Irish returned home 7-4, most of the early-season critics of the scheduling were now saying, "Thank God for Stonehill!" Dave Batton scored 22 and Toby Knight 18 to lead ND to a 98-70 win. Now there was UCLA—at home—and a chance for a sweep for the first time.

But it wasn't to be. This ND-UCLA game was one of streaks, as so many were, and the Bruins had the last one this time. First, the Irish turned a 12-point deficit into a five-point lead, but the Uclans rebounded for a 70-65 win. Notre Dame had now lost five of its last six games and needed a turnaround—quickly.

How about nine straight wins—seven at home—and only one a contest?

The streak began with Pittsburgh, 88-68, which included the longest non-basket in NCAA history. Right before the half, Notre Dame had the ball, hoping for a last-second basket for the halftime momentum. Bill Paterno was instructed to throw a long pass downcourt, and he did—but the ball swished through the net! Unfortunately, this 94-foot shot didn't count because Paterno was out of bounds, but it didn't matter in the final outcome. Fordham went down in a game moved to Sunday from Saturday for TV, 95-71. Dayton was next, the final ending up 97-64 after a 60-33 first half. In Greensboro, North Carolina, the Irish defeated Davidson; back home, they blew out Xavier and 18-2 Holy Cross (behind 26 by Williams in the latter). Against South Carolina, six Irishmen scored in double figures in an 84-66 win; against Butler, the Irish annexed their 67th victory over the Bulldogs (more than against anyone else) in the two schools' 91st basketball encounter, 97-74. The ninth—and closest—of the string was at Madison Square Garden against Manhattan. Digger gave Toby Knight a chance to shine in front of the home folks, and that he did, scoring 27 hard-earned points as ND edged out the Jaspers, 80-76.

West Virginia proved too much for the Irish as they tried to stretch the string to 10. Of course, ND "aided" its own cause by shooting only 30-of-73 from the floor in its 81-68 loss at Mountaineer Gym. And things didn't look good in the next home game, with Loyola; the Irish trailed by 11 at one point in the first half, but Duck Williams' 30 points overall and the team's 39 in the last 9:18 turned a close game into a 111-86 rout. Next, six players hit in the double-digit mark and the "SWAT Team" made its last appearance in another annihilation, 113-77 over La-Salle. The Irish were ready for the next opponent, San Francisco.

This was supposed to be just another game with a Catholic school, but the Dons had changed that by entering the ACC undefeated with a 29-0 record, the only unblemished mark in the country. The game had already begun to capture the imagination of the country when NBC asked if Notre Dame, San Francisco, and DePaul would agree to move the game from March 1 (Tuesday) to March 5 (Saturday). Why DePaul? Because that was Notre Dame's opponent on the 5th. Fortunately, the key Demon officials (helpfully, two ND grads–Gene Sullivan '53, athletic director and Ray Meyer '38, head coach) realized the importance of the game and agreed to move their game to the 7th. Another group that realized what it was all about was the Notre Dame student section.

Exhorted on by the consummate cheerleader himself, Digger Phelps, the chants began an hour before the game and continued throughout: "29–and One! 29–and One! 29–and One!" As the game went on, the cheers became louder and more incessant, crescendoing to a peak when the Irish went into their four-corner offense and ran the Dons roughshod. Don Williams scored 17 of his 25 points on layups, free throws, and three-point plays out of the four corners. The demoralized San Franciscans didn't have a prayer. Notre Dame answered the students' chants by defeating the Dons, 93-82. In recognition of the crowd's inordinate role in setting the emotional tempo of the game, NBC named the Notre Dame student body as the game's Most Valuable Player, an unprecedented and never-duplicated testimony to fan support anywhere. (The Dons never recovered from the loss. In the first round of the NCAA tournament, the still-first-ranked team was blown out by Nevada-Las Vegas.) And in the game moved aside so that national TV could have the ND-SF matchup, Williams had another 26 as ND beat DePaul, 76-68, at Alumni Hall.

Notre Dame began its fourth straight appearance in the NCAA playoffs (a school record), this time in the East Regional, at a venue already visited once, the Palestra. The Irish defeated upstart Hofstra, 90-83, to get to a familiar stumbling block: the regional semifinals. At another previously-visited haunt in 1976-77, Cole Field House at the University of Maryland, the Irish faced North Carolina. They led at the half, 40-30, but the semifinal jinx continued—even on St. Patrick's Day. The Tar Heels slowly chipped away at the lead, taking full advantage of ND's penchant for turnovers (21-8). Finally, All-American Phil Ford won it with two free throws—North Carolina 79, Notre Dame, 77. For the fourth year in a row and 10th NCAA appearance in a row, the Irish had been eliminated in the regional semifinals or earlier. The word "choke" was becoming associated with Digger Phelps and Notre Dame basketball, and did he ever want to change that!

In 1977-78, he did.

The 75th basketball edition of the Fighting Irish became the first to make it to the exalted Final Four of the NCAA playoffs. The team was blessed with some very talented no-names, at least to much of the rest of the basketball world. There were no superstars, just talent that played Digger's substitution system well enough to get past the big hurdles. In fact, the parts were considered so good that ND was ranked third pre-season, the highest at such an early date since the 1968-69 team. The Irish, however, needed more than strong defense and an occasionally potent offense to make it; they needed some incredible luck early in the season. More than any other, the 1977-78 Irish was a team of destiny.

To set the stage: The Irish have streaked to a 6-0 record. This does not include a 19-point blowout of the Russian team in a pre-season tussle, but it does include a 49-point pasting of Mississippi in an inspired piece of scheduling (Ole Miss was the only football team to defeat Notre Dame in 1977, and this paid the school back, it could be said), 98-57 over Baylor, 89-75 over Valparaiso, 76-42 over Lafayette, 88-48 over Northwestern at McGaw Hall, and—for the second straight year—a defeat of UCLA at Pauley Pavilion behind Dave Batton's heroics (22 points plus the clinching free throws), 69-66. Thanks to a loss by top-ranked Kentucky, ND could move into the top spot on the polls with a win at Indiana's Assembly Hall.

But on the night of December 14, nearly everything was off for the Irish. They shot a dismal 25-of-63 from the floor, and the upset-minded Hoosiers won on a free throw by substitute Wayne

Radford with four seconds left, 67-66—and this after ND had come back from a 64-56 deficit at 3:38 to tie up the ballgame. A long bus ride back to South Bend in the gloom of the night awaited the disappointed Irish.

Originally, Notre Dame had chartered a plane for the official party (team members and officials) so that the team could get to Bloomington in the morning, hold an afternoon practice, play the game that evening, and fly home afterwards and only miss one day of classes before finals. But thick fog at Michiana Regional Airport changed the plans. Unwilling to wait for the weather to clear, the Irish took a bus to the game. Meanwhile, the plane which was to take ND from South Bend to Bloomington ended up in Evansville, to pick up one of the up-and-coming teams in the nation, the University of Evansville Aces, for a trip to Indianapolis to play Butler. The plane never made it to Indy. It crashed shortly after takeoff, killing the entire Evansville party in a terrible tragedy . . . on a charter meant for Notre Dame.

Lady Luck had her eye on the Irish all season, and that incident was certainly the most chilling example. The luck, however, wasn't always good. After a convincing win over St. Joseph's (IN), it was Louisville time again for the annual "neutral court" game with Kentucky. Again the Irish were thwarted in the elusive search for a win over the Wildcats. ND led, but Kyle Macy scored eight straight points to put the game into UK's corner, 73-68. And San Francisco got revenge for that 29-and-1 business by knocking off ND at the Oakland-Alameda County Arena, 79-70. But things began to right themselves; nine wins in a row followed, and not all of them could be fully explained by Notre Dame's play.

First, ND defeated St. Bonaventure at the Rochester, New York War Memorial Auditorium, one-time home of the NBA Rochester Royals, 79-78, without Duck Williams, who had a sprained ankle; Dave Batton had 24 to pick up the slack. To begin a six-game home stand, the Irish beat Manhattan, 81-64. Then Ms. Luck contributed to the next two. Villanova entered its January 19 contest as the top free-throw shooting team in the nation, but hit only 13-of-20 against ND (65 percent). The final score was 70-69. Then UCLA came to town for a Sunday contest (moved from Saturday for NBC) and lost, 75-73, for ND's first sweep of the Bruins, thanks to 19 points from Williams—and a little more luck. Junior Bruce Flowers, who was having a terrible individual year and was averaging only 41 percent from the line, hit two late in the game to put ND ahead; on the next time downcourt, the Bruins' James Wilkes, a 73 percent shooter, had a chance to tie—and missed the front end of the one-and-one. This dropped the Uclans to 13-2; both losses were to the Irish.

Win number five was the next night against Dartmouth, 78-64. And even though Lowes Moore set an individual opponent record at the ACC with 40 points, Notre Dame had no trouble with West Virginia, 103-82. Then the snows came . . . and came . . . and came . . .

The "Blizzard of '78" began the night of that game, and kept going. Had not the Mountaineers checked out of their hotel early, they would have been stranded in South Bend for days. The University was shut down for an unprecedented three consecutive school days while the cleanup of all that snow inched along. Most of northern Indiana was cut off from the rest of the world. But NBC saith, "The game must go on!" Somehow, both the NBC people and the Maryland team got into South Bend (the Terrapins took the vacated hotel rooms of West Virginia's party, the only rooms available anywhere in the area) even though no road east of Chicago was yet completely passable. All the "essentials" were there for the Sunday game; now would anyone show up?

South Bend was still on a snow emergency which prohibited private cars on the streets, the parking lots weren't plowed, and the concessionaires stayed home. So the ACC became a general admission ballpark for the day. As an enticement, students who didn't have a ticket could show their student ID at the door and be admitted free—and then sit anywhere they wanted. A fairly sizable crowd managed to walk, tunnel, showshoe, snowmobile, ski, or sled to the game, most of them Notre Dame and Saint Mary's students; the "sixth man," sensing a rare opportunity, ringed the lower arena to become a cheering force unknown since the days of the Fieldhouse if not in volume, then in its Sensurround effect. With that kind of crowd, how could ND help but win the "Snow Bowl"? Relatively unknown freshman Tracy Jackson, from Silver Springs, Maryland, not far from either UM or Washington, DC, was NBC's Player of the Game in the 69-54 victory.

The eighth and ninth straight wins took place with the outside world almost back to normalcy; at the Palestra, ND outran LaSalle, 95-90, behind 23 by Williams and 21 by Batton, the senior duo, which nicely overcame a 39-point performance by the Explorers' sophomore sensation Michael Brooks. Back home, Davidson fell, 100-76, despite 33 by the opponents' John Gerdy. Then the snows came again in this particularly violent winter, this time to New England. Travel out of the region was rendered impossible, resulting in the cancellation of the February 7 game with Holy Cross when the Crusaders couldn't get out. (No mutually agreeable date was found as a makeup.) The lost game gave the Irish more time to prepare for the best DePaul team since the 1940s, which was coming into the ACC for another Sunday game.

Fickle Lady Luck this time went into the hands of the Blue Demons. The game went into overtime, and the faithful were happy when ND snared a 68-63 lead. Complications set in, however; DePaul scored two straight baskets to come within one. But then sophomore Rich Branning, a 78 percent foul shooter, was fouled. He could have clinched the game here; but he missed the front end of the one-and-one. At the other end, Gary Garland put one up for DePaul at the last second. It went through, and the Demons—and Ray Meyer—had their first win ever at the ACC and first at Notre Dame since 1967, 69-68.

A family reunion of sorts took place at Madison Square Garden when ND defeated Fordham, 95-76. Freshman phenom Kelly Tripucka, who had worked his way into the starting lineup, went up against two older brothers for the Rams. Brother Tracy was coaching Fordham, and another brother, T.K., played for the opposition (Kelly outscored him, 15-14). But the new win streak ended at one against South Carolina. The Gamecocks used 23-for-27 accuracy from the foul line, many of them down the stretch, to give ND its fifth loss, 65-60. A first-time opponent, North Carolina State, fell at the ACC, 70-59, aided by dismal Wolfpack shooting (26-of-74). And still another Sunday game was next, against defending national champion and number-one ranked Marquette.

Every so often Digger would pull out all the stops and come up with a gimmick. He was widely credited with the re-emergence of the 1977 football team as the "Green Machine" against USC (the team took the field wearing green jerseys, and thus inspired,

beat up on the Trojans, 49-19, on the way to the national title).
On February 26, 1978, he came up with another one, but the
reviews were decidedly mixed. "The ugliest things I ever saw,"
remarked Kelly Tripucka later when asked about it. This time—
green socks.

Maybe they were embarrassed at the socks, or maybe the
socks were acting like ankle weights, but the Irish fell behind
by 17 in the first half, and trailed by 14 at halftime. But a halftime
pep talk got things back in order. NBC's MVP, Kelly Tripucka,
scored 15 in the second half; but the real MVP was an obscure
sophomore, Bill Hanzlik. Notre Dame had had great problems
stopping the opposition's top scorers all season, and the Warriors had a great one in Butch Lee. Hanzlik was assigned the
task of defending him, and he succeeded beyond anyone's expectations: the Marquette star shot only 6-of-19 from the floor,
and his frustration mounted to the point that he finally received
a warning and then a technical foul for unnecessary retaliation.
The Irish won going away, 65-59, and virtually cinched a fifth
straight NCAA bid. The green socks stayed for the rest of the
season, much to the chagrin of most.

The University of Dayton Arena again proved unfriendly
as Dayton handed Notre Dame its sixth loss, 66-59, despite
Tripucka's 22 points. Then ND got its 20th win for the third
straight season, over Loyola, 83-68, in preparation for a trip to
the Midwest Regional. Maybe those hideous socks did have some
magic in them, because this NCAA journey ended differently
than any which had preceded it.

Bill Laimbeer, back at Notre Dame for 1977-78 after getting
his grades back up and being assured by Phelps that there was
still a place for him at ND, led a balanced attack with 20 points
as the Irish beat Houston in Tulsa, Oklahoma, 100-77. Now the
Irish were back in the semifinals, for the second straight year
on St. Patrick's Day, but at a site where they hadn't lost in six
years (Kansas University) and with a little wearin' o' the green
to help out. The opponent was Utah, an upset winner over Missouri in the first round. The game was a tight one—until, for
once, ND streaked to an 11-0 binge late in the second half to
win, 69-56. For the first time in 20 years, the Irish were in the
regional finals. And look who the opponent was—DePaul, third-

ranked and both the odds-on and the sentimental favorite to win because Ray Meyer hadn't been this close to the Final Four since his first team made it there in 1943, and he didn't have too many more years left before his inevitable retirement. But Digger Phelps had *never* made it this far, and he wasn't about to stop now.

Using a 47-31 advantage in the second half, Notre Dame destroyed the Demons, 84-64, to make the Final Four. Kelly Tripucka, the Midwest Regional MVP, scored 18 to go with the 20 he had against the Utes. Rich Branning added 15 more and seven assists. And all Irish fans were happy. As the clock ticked down the last seconds, Digger leaped high into the air, players hugged each other, and the faithful joined in the celebration. This is what he had been building for, and finally he got it—a berth in The Greatest Show on Earth, the Final Four. As Digger declared, "The rest is gravy."

Joining ND at the Checkerdome in St. Louis were Arkansas, Duke, and Kentucky. With two teams there with some of the most loyal and rabid fans anywhere (ND, UK), and with the possibility that Notre Dame could become the first team to win both the football and basketball national championships in the same academic year, tickets to the games became very scarce. Prices as high as $200 each were reported for ducats as visions of an ND-Kentucky rematch danced like sugar-plums in fans' (and the network's) heads—and in a real neutral site, for once, too. But it was not to be. The Irish had to get past Duke first, and didn't. To ND's credit, it came from way back in the second half to close within two points of the Blue Devils in the last nine seconds. Duke was the NCAA free-throwing percentage champion, and they showed how it was done, with 32-of-37 accuracy from the charity stripe for the game. That made the difference in the 90-86 decision.

Had Arkansas defeated Kentucky (the final was 64-59), the resulting third-place game likely would have had greater national interest than the finals. But the consolation contest reverted to its almost meaningless status quietly. The ND-Arkansas clash appeared headed for overtime, but Ron Brewer nailed a jumper with but one second left to lift the Razorbacks over the Irish, 71-69.

Despite the disappointment at St. Louis, the fourth-place

finish was the best in Notre Dame history. All 14 team members — seniors Dave Batton, Jeff Carpenter, Randy Haefner, and Don Williams; juniors Bruce Flowers and Bill Laimbeer; sophomores Rich Branning, Bill Hanzlik, and Tim Healy; and freshmen Tracy Jackson, Gilbert Salinas, Kelly Tripucka, Stan Wilcox, and Orlando Woolridge — had played a role in that success. And most of them were coming back for more, assuring continued success and, perhaps, more trips to the Final Four.

# 21

## Almost But Not Quite There

Now that Notre Dame was back among the nation's elite, the next three years were, for the most part, disappointing. Successful, yes—three consecutive 22-5 regular seasons are certainly testimony to that. But in none of those years could the Irish return to the Final Four despite having the horses to get back there. One can look at the seasons as a whole—the tournament preparation, if you will—and see three reasons why things didn't jell in the playoffs: scheduling, recruiting, and offense.

From Day One of ND basketball through the middle 1970s, Irish basketball schedules were ambitious. Usually there were two or three "patsy" games to open the season, but after that almost anything went. The philosophy was, essentially, "To be the best, you've got to play the best." Under Digger Phelps, it changed to "We want to play in as many tough places to play as possible." In that he succeeded admirably, particularly during the often murderous holiday trips; but the home schedule gradually became more and more of an afterthought. While the 1978-81 years featured only two home non-sellouts, that was entirely because individual game tickets for those few worthwhile home games became impossible to get otherwise. (Student demand was so high that lotteries and split-season packages for freshmen became necessary, an expedient not used since some home games were played in the South Bend YMCA in the 1920s.) For most of the rest, the fans stayed away in droves, some to the tune of a half to two-thirds empty student section. There were too many games where the only question was: will the margin be large enough to let the scrubs and walk-ons play? In 1978-79 only two of 16 home games were against eventual NCAA tournament teams; in 1980-81 only three of 17 were. (Home scheduling, believe it or not, actually got worse before it got better, to the point where many students felt it was no longer worthwhile to buy season tickets to see—maybe—half a dozen interesting games a season.)

In today's major-college basketball world, recruiting is essential. Aggressive recruiting got Notre Dame where it was in 1978 and aided in those 22-5 regular seasons. But from 1978 to 1981, the Irish had four straight mediocre recruiting years. While part of the reason was that a couple of highly coveted blue-chippers got away, another contributing factor didn't come out until after Tracy Jackson, Kelly Tripucka, and Orlando Woolridge had finished their Notre Dame careers. Digger didn't try to nab anyone who would give any of those three a real challenge for their starting berths, and that decision hurt in the long run. Some of the depth he had in 1978 was missing by 1981.

Finally, there was a decline in offensive production. More will be said about this relating to the 1980-81 season specifically; suffice it to say for now that as the depth decreased, so did the point totals. In three years, the average per game dropped almost eight points, and also, the average victory margin dropped from an incredible 15.6 in 1978-79 to 9.6 in 1980-81 without a significant improvement in quality of opposition. (In fact, the opposite was true.) Phelps became the target of criticism of his coaching tactics because of the slowdown.

But it was hard to knock the 1978-79 team.

It was a young, hungry squad, and probably was one of Digger's two or three best on paper. For the most part, the same lineup took the floor at the beginning of each game: sophomores Kelly Tripucka and Orlando Woolridge at forwards, senior Bill Laimbeer at center, and juniors Rich Branning and Bill Hanzlik at the guards. Beyond that, however, the customary liberal substitution policy still held. Tracy Jackson served as the team's "sixth man" and played that role as well as anyone in the country in 1978-79; Bruce Flowers usually replaced Laimbeer, and could score when needed—when he wasn't fouling; Stan Wilcox started two games at guard and filled in well for the backcourt artists; and Mike Mitchell, the only scholarship freshman (Digger's worst recruiting year since 1972), finished third on the team in assists despite averaging only 13 minutes per game. This team began the year by overwhelming three less-than-formidable foes—Valparaiso, Rice, and Northwestern—by an average score of 98-58. (Notre Dame rolled over many of its opponents; as mentioned, its average scoring margin was better than 15 points.)

Somehow those games proved ample preparation for the UCLA tussle at Pauley, as it was Irish defense—they held the two top Bruin offensive threats to 11-for-34 shooting—that made ND the first team to beat UCLA at its home arena three years in a row, 81-78. And in this year-after-the-Final-Four season, even the home game during the students' Christmas break sold out; ND showed the "townies" something by destroying St. Francis (PA), 96-43. The 53-point margin was the most lopsided in ACC history.

As proof of how good this team was, for the first time since ND began regularly scheduling a Christmas road trip (1974-75) did the team return home with a winning record to show for it. First, the Irish had to endure another frustrating setback at Freedom Hall. A 12-point lead evaporated behind 17 second-half points by Dwight Anderson, and ND lost for the first time all season, 81-76. After that, it was all uphill; consecutive wins vs. Villanova, Davidson, and Marquette (65-60) put the 8-1 Irish atop the polls for only the second week since 1949.

This time Notre Dame stayed there a little while (four weeks). The cause was aided by wins over Lafayette (91-66), San Francisco (88-69, incredibly lopsided for that series), South Carolina (82-73), and Fordham (85-53) . . . but it wasn't by an inexcusable 67-66 loss to Maryland at College Park. Up 66-64 with but a few seconds left, Digger specifically told his players not to foul anyone; he was willing to let the Terrapins make a shot to send it into overtime if it came to that. So what does Bruce Flowers do? While Larry Gibson makes the game-tying basket, Flowers fouls him. Gibson makes the freebee, and ND has its second loss. Oddly, the team didn't drop from the top spot afterwards, because a couple of other highly-ranked teams lost and no one was taking unbeaten Indiana State very seriously yet.

Back at the ACC, the Irish easily defeated Brown and had a surprisingly close call with Xavier (66-57). And then came Dayton in what was Notre Dame's peak of effort in the 1978-79 season. The Flyers had built a 55-46 lead early in the second half when a legend was born. Orlando Woolridge, who was already known for his dunking ability, executed a reverse 360-degree slam (degree of difficulty 3.0) while ND was coming back. After that, the Flyers could have packed up. The crowd was in a frenzy and never came back down. Kelly Tripucka scored a career-high 37 points thanks to Dayton's hacking defense (he set ND records by canning 23-of-26 free throws), and the Irish won going away, 86-71. After the successful conclusion of another four-game home stand with a win over Loyola of Chicago, 84-66 (ND and Loyola haven't played since), Notre Dame traveled to a hornet's nest— North Carolina State's Reynolds Coliseum, where no visiting non-member of the Atlantic Coast Conference had won since 1968. So the Irish were very happy to leave with a streak-ending 53-52 win iced by two Tripucka free throws; this also was Notre Dame's 1100th men's basketball win.

Following the close shave in Raleigh, the still-top-ranked Irish came up against third-ranked UCLA at the ACC. Hundreds more fans than seats were there (students used forged Brown tickets as UCLA tickets, as the former game was relatively lightly attended and the two ducats were identical in color); the excitement seemed electric before the game, as Digger had the students chanting for a "Grand Slam" (i.e., four wins in a row over the Bruins). Yet the only grand slam in a boring, sloppily-played contest was the one Bill Laimbeer missed early in the second half. That muffed opportunity to turn the momentum cost the Irish; though leading, 28-25, at the half, they went through one 14-minute stretch in the second half with only two field goals after the colossal missed dunk, and lost both the game and the number one ranking to the Bruins, 56-52.

Five straight wins followed to keep the Irish in the top three and stretch their record to 22-3. All were convincing, too. Manhattan fell by 23 at the Garden; West Virginia, in front of a record-breaking crowd at Mountaineer Gym, saw Lowes Moore held to nine points after his 40-point performance at ND in 1978 in a 70-54 Irish win; Oklahoma City, a traditionally strong team which had fallen on hard times, and a late replacement on the slate for Indiana, a temporary victim of conflicting schedules, fell by 28; LaSalle, thanks to ND's 61-point second half barrage, lost by 23; and East Carolina was turned back by 15 in the last home game. But the next two games on the road made it abundantly clear that this team had already peaked.

DePaul and Michigan pulled back-to-back upsets over Notre Dame in widely different environments. The Blue Demon game was ND's last visit to cozy but outdated Alumni Hall, which held 5,556 frenzied DePaul fans who saw their Final Four-bound "miracle" team win, 76-72. Two days later, 37,283 people—the largest crowd ever to see Notre Dame play—watched in the cavernous Pontiac Silverdome as Michigan continued its long-standing hex over the Irish, 62-59.

Not surprisingly, ND went back to the NCAAs for the sixth straight season. But to the surprise of many, the Irish were seeded first in the Mideast Regional ahead of streaking Big Ten champion Michigan State. And their performance seemed to bear out the doubts of the critics. Tennessee came within six points of an upset at "neutral" Murfreesboro, home of Middle Tennessee State, and Toledo came within eight at Market Square Arena. Then came the showdown—Notre Dame vs. Michigan State. On this day, Irish luck was overcome by Magic and a bit too much Special K. Earvin "Magic" Johnson and Greg "Special K" Kelser had a field day. Kelser scored 34 points, mostly on dunks set up by Johnson's feeds, and the Spartans were on their way to the Final Four and the national championship. The final was 80-68.

Michigan State wasn't the only institution to give Notre Dame trouble in 1978-79. During the season, the NCAA probed one of ND's players, wanted to declare him ineligible, and could have forced the Irish to forfeit all the games in which he had played. Marc Kelly, a freshman walk-on from California who seldom played more than a minute or two late in Irish blowouts, served as a basketball-playing extra (along with such stalwarts as Bernard King, Larry Farmer, and Mike Warren) in the movie *Fast Break* starring Gabriel Kaplan to earn some spending money during the summer of 1978. However, using logic unknown to any logician, the NCAA said this movie stint made Kelly a professional. When the powers that be discovered that the young man wasn't even on scholarship, the egg-faced NCAA backed down on its earlier threats, but still made him pay back the money he earned—about $250—in order to retain his amateur status. The incident certainly ranks among the most absurd in NCAA enforcement history.

There was no such absurdity in 1979-80, but instead this version of the Irish did something an ND team hadn't done in over a decade—it lost its first NCAA playoff game. There were also times where it seemed as if the team was blowing leads to make games more exciting for TV viewers. And while such claims may be dubious at best, as criticism of the Phelps regime began to mount, such ideas were used as convenient excuses.

As usual, the team had talent and depth; only Flowers and Laimbeer had graduated and coming in were three potentially talented freshmen, although because of the loss of his two centers, Phelps found it necessary to move Orlando Woolridge to the pivot, a position with which the natural forward was never fully comfortable. But depth elsewhere was borne out early in the season when senior Bill Hanzlik suffered a pre-season injury. Substituting ably for the team's strongest defensive player were junior Stan Wilcox and freshman John Paxson, and during that time ND went 6-0. As usual, most of them were against patsies, but the fifth game, against UCLA, was no such thing. The Bruins led most of the game, but not by much, and as the clock began to wind down, the Irish, down by one, set up for the last shot. UCLA fouled who was thought to be the logical candidate for the big-game choke, the freshman Paxson. But he coolly stepped to the line and sank both free throws to put ND up, 75-74. He then was fouled again and canned two more for the final margin of victory, 77-74. But in between was what was perceived as an ugly incident in what had been an intense but friendly rivalry. Students (and the Irish bench) felt that when, late in the game, Kelly Tripucka was elbowed in the mouth and ended up on the floor, it had been a retaliatory move by a Uclan. Television replays showed, however, that one of the referees had inadvertently done it when calling the foul which resulted in the final victory margin.

Hanzlik returned to the lineup in a 69-59 ho-hummer over Fairfield, and he remained there the rest of the season. He was back just in time for one of the strangest road trips in recent history. There was nothing odd about the first stop, Louisville, for the annual loss to Kentucky (86-80), or the second, Oakland, where the Irish lost to San Francisco, 67-59. But because of Digger Phelps' admirable policy of trying to schedule games near each of his players' hometowns, two cities which seldom see big-time college basketball got to see Notre Dame. Shreveport, Louisiana, near Woolridge's home town of Mansfield, was host to an ND-Tulane game, which ND won, 79-59; and San Antonio, Texas, home of Gilbert Salinas, saw ND defeat Texas Christian, 85-68.

With 12 minutes to go in the next game, a home contest with Villanova, another easy win seemed well at hand; ND led, 51-33. But during the next 11:57, the Irish put on a horrific display of basketball as the horrified fans watched the big lead evaporate into a 69-68 Wildcat edge with three seconds left. After a time out, Tracy Jackson saved the night by swishing a pull-it-out 30-footer with no time left. It was a classic case of playing not to lose which deserved not to work. However, there was no doubt as to who should have won the next one, as for the fourth year in a row, ND won at Pauley Pavilion, this one in convincing fashion. Tripucka scored 17 points in a great second-half team effort, and the Irish won, 80-73, in a game which wasn't that close (even the walk-ons got to play). UCLA eventually surprised the "experts" by going all the way to the NCAA final game.

After another ho-hummer at home, Maryland came in, and while how it happened was a little different, the plot was similar to the Villanova game: Irish take lead; Irish build up lead; Irish think they've got it won; opponent thinks otherwise; Irish fall behind with a few seconds left; Tracy Jackson saves the day. In this case, he got loose underneath for an easy layup as the buzzer sounded, and, well . . . it was exiciting for the national TV audience, anyway. Notre Dame did have something of an excuse this time: Tripucka was sidelined by back spasms. In fact, he missed the next three games as well. He was sorely missed in the next game, a rare mid-week road trip to the Palestra to face LaSalle. ND's only lead was 2-0, and All-America candidate Michael Brooks penetrated the defense for 29 points in a 62-60 upset. Back home, three fairly easy ones followed; first, for the only time all season the Irish cracked the century mark in their 105-71 destruction of Davidson; then a sluggish 67-53 win over Navy and a 93-49 blowout of Manhattan upped ND's record to 16-3.

Thirty-seven percent field goal shooting for a team which averaged over 51 percent for the year contributed to Notre Dame's first home loss of the 1980s, 63-55 against North Carolina State. One couldn't help but feel that the Irish were looking forward to the climactic game of the five-game home stand with San Francisco—the series had become such a classic already that it was now at twice-a-year status. Whether holding back or not, they didn't against the Dons; the team played its best 40 minutes of the year in evening the season series. Jackson scored 23, Tripucka added 20, and ND won easily, 78-66.

The Irish then embarked on a three-game road trip and won all three, but by no means was the sweep easy. At Madison Square Garden, Fordham took a 37-29 lead into the locker room at halftime, 20 minutes away from a major upset. But Orlando Woolridge ended the Rams' upset hopes. During one two-and-a-half minute stretch, he scored 13 points; all told he had 23 and Tripucka scored 24 in the 86-76 comeback win. The only contest of the three never in doubt was a 90-66 drubbing of South Carolina; Tripucka, on his 21st birthday, scored 29 points, hauled in 13 rebounds, and generally displayed the form many felt he seldom got a chance to show while with the Irish. (However, he scored 20 or more points in each of the last eight games of 1979-80.) And in Cincinnati, ND streaked to a 20-2 spurt as the second half commenced, overcoming a four-point deficit and defeating Xavier. The momentum seemed to be with the Irish as they returned home for two big games, with always-tough Marquette and unbeaten DePaul.

Two things happened on Sunday, February 24 to divert the fans' attention from the matter at hand. First, that was the day that the United States ice hockey team completed its "Miracle on Ice" at the 1980 Lake Placid Winter Olympics by defeating Finland, 4-2. The nationalistic fervor inspired by the victory carried over to the ND-Marquette game, which started less than an hour after the medal ceremony. Chants of "U-S-A! U-S-A!"

and American flags filled parts of the student section, and it was obvious that on this day the basketball team was playing second fiddle in students' emotions. Or perhaps even third. For student leaders picked this game to demonstrate students' feelings about a brewing controversy over scholarships for so-called "minor sports," i.e., anything other than football and men's basketball. Ironically, most profoundly affected by the re-evaluation in grant-in-aid priorities was ice hockey, which was fully subsidized yet largely ignored by the student body (attendance had been declining since 1978) and so was a prime candidate for a reduction in scholarships. During any breaks in action, the student section became a sea of signs stating "SAVE HOCKEY and other minor sports." With all this extracurricular activity in the stands, Marquette couldn't help but sneak up on the Irish for a 77-74 upset win.

No such diversion of attention occurred three nights later, for DePaul was in town, and the Blue Demons were number one and 25-0. A sense of destiny prevailed in the crowd; the last time an unbeaten, top-ranked team had invaded the ACC this late was in 1977, and the victim was San Francisco in the now-legendary "29 and One!" game. This time, the chant was altered to "25 and One!" But DePaul wasn't going to make it as easy as a cheer from an overflow crowd (nearly 12,000 people—a few hundred more than capacity—snuck, forged, or cajoled their way in). In fact, it took two free throws from 1979-80's designated hero, Tracy Jackson, to send the game into overtime tied at 64. After one overtime, the matter still wasn't decided, and Notre Dame was in its first double-OT contest since 1970. With 19 seconds left in extra period two, Orlando Woolridge canned two foul shots, and the Irish held for the 76-74 upset. When the result became final, the scene was, as one Chicago newspaper termed it, a "near-riot in (the) 'pit'." Notre Dame had closed its home season with a bang, and DePaul? After Ray Meyer's men defeated Illinois State to close the season, they began a three-year hex in their second-round game in the NCAAs by losing to UCLA—a scenario only slightly different than what had happened to San Francisco three years earlier. To top off the regular season, the Irish won at Dayton, which they didn't do very often, 62-54. This time, momentum surely seemed to be with them as they entered Lincoln, Nebraska for an NCAA Midwest Regional second-round game.

But Big Eight champion Missouri had something to prove. Coach Norm Stewart felt his team was the victim of no press coverage, and felt it was as deserving of a first-round bye (which it didn't get) as Notre Dame, which was often on television and in the top 10 despite its light schedule. The "overrated" Irish led the Tigers, 42-36, at half, but ND spent so much time worrying about freshman phenom Steve Stipanovich (one of those recruits that got away from Digger Phelps) that Mark Dressler broke through for 24 second-half points (32 in all) to force an overtime. And the Tigers wouldn't be denied; they ended ND's season, 87-84, earlier than anyone had ever ousted a Phelps-coached team from tournament play. All that could be done now was to bid the seniors (Rich Branning, Bill Hanzlik, Tim Healy) adieu and try to look ahead to 1980-81, because this was the last chance for tri-captains Jackson, Tripucka, and Woolridge to make another trip to the Final Four.

Unfortunately, it didn't happen.

No season in history raised as much controversy over the way the team was handled than this one. While the AP ranked it 10th preseason, there was a feeling that this team had the potential to win it all. Some people blamed Digger Phelps when it didn't happen.

This season had some bizarre twists off the court. Officials at the ACC banned the band from playing Tchaikovsky's "1812 Overture," Notre Dame students' second-most-popular get-psyched song, because the rocking motion that the bleacher residents performed when it was played was seen as potentially dangerous to the roll-up bleachers and those sitting on them. There were problems with a new program supplier: several late-season editions never made it to campus, and some copies of one that did had four pages of the Northwestern program in it by mistake. "Purdue Pete," the Boilermaker mascot, made an unauthorized appearance at the Irish-Dayton game after the outfit had been stolen from its rightful owners by pranksters from Northwestern the weekend before. But of course, the most bizarre part of the season was the play of this heralded team, which often dropped to the level of its far inferior competition and in one case led students to begin cheering lustily—for the visiting team!

All this began at what had been a kind venue to Notre Dame in the recent past—UCLA's Pauley Pavilion. The Irish leaped to a 24-12 lead after nine minutes, but then the Bruins turned on the speed. "Rocket" Rod Foster scored 18 points in the first half as the Uclans took a five-point lead by intermission and then steadily increased that to a 94-81 win, ND's first loss at Pauley since 1975-76. This game was notable for another reason: thanks to an ankle injury to Tim Andree, 6-11 center Joe Kleine became the first Irish freshman to start his first varsity game since Adrian Dantley.

When the team returned home, it began what was easily the worst home schedule in Notre Dame history to that time. Public disenchantment was so great that even though all but one game (against Valparaiso during holiday break) was a pre-season sellout, very rarely were all the seats occupied. Most notably, the student section remained half empty during most games, and those who were there generally sat on their hands, only erupting with spectacular or streak play. This indifference by the students was often reflected in the team's performance.

Digger didn't win any popularity contests either, and not only because of the soft home slate. During the second home game, against Texas Christian, one of the many patsies on the schedule (even TCU's first-year head coach wondered who had been responsible for this travesty, which was arranged before he arrived), Phelps debuted a tactic always booed by friend and foe alike: the so-called "delay offense." Calling it an offense is stretching things; as opposed to its ancestor, the four-corners offense, the main goal here was to run time off the clock and, well, maybe we'll take a shot if we feel like it. Games became as exciting as elevator music, and ND's point production dropped severely. Even several years later, after Kelly Tripucka had become a major NBA scoring star, this strategy was still a topic of conversation thus:

Q. Who was the last man to hold Kelly Tripucka to less than 15 points?

A. Digger Phelps.

Few people cared that the fringe benefit of the slowdown was one of the highest field-goal percentages in NCAA history (.552). That stat, however, was accomplished with an average of only one shot every 47 seconds.

Anyway, the first home game of note after three straight wins over the likes of Montana State, TCU, and Cal Poly-Pomona (the game with the aforementioned faulty program), was against Bobby Knight's Indiana team. The Hoosiers were on the way to their second national title under the fiery head coach, but were sidetracked at Notre Dame. All eyes were on IU's sensational Isiah Thomas, who scored 22, and Landon Turner, whose career would end tragically in less than a year in a paralyzing auto accident, who had 23, when they weren't on the new blue and gold basketball shoes which were almost as arresting as 1978's green socks. But John Paxson, playing as Thomas's shadow, had 18 of his own to lead the Irish to a 68-64 victory. Following a snoozer over Valpo, ND embarked on a five-game holiday road trip, the first three of which saw the Irish play their longest streak of inspired ball all season.

Thanks to an outstanding game by Kelly Tripucka (8-of-14 from the field, 14-of-15 from the line, 30 points), hated Kentucky, which was ranked on top of the UPI survey and second on the AP poll, fell in Freedom Hall, 67-61. Six of Tripucka's free throws came in the crucial final two minutes, when the Wildcats were fouling in hopes of regaining the ball. This was Notre Dame's first win in Louisville since 1973-74 and only the fourth since the series was resumed in 1958-59. Then the Irish went to Charlotte and destroyed Davidson, 87-67, and following that, they annihilated a good Villanova team at the Palestra, 94-65, in ND's top offensive outburst of 1980-81 (matched twice).

The euphoria quickly turned to disaster at the end of the trip. Marquette took a lesson from buzzer-beaters such as Dwight Clay and Tracy Jackson; freshman Glenn Rivers, not content to allow a 52-52 deadlock go into overtime, heaved a desperation shot from well outside NBA three-point range with one second remaining—and the ball swished through, defeating the disbelieving Irish. Some of the effect of that stunner carried over to three nights later, as San Francisco streaked to a 10-point halftime lead. Notre Dame managed to evaporate that lead and send the contest into overtime, but the cumulative effect of a cold shooting night (under 50 percent from the floor for the first time all season and but 11-of-20 from the stripe) made the difference as the Dons pulled it out, 66-63.

The team sleepwalked through its first two home games of 1981, defeating less-than-imposing opponents Hofstra and Fordham in less-than-exciting—and less-than-convincing—fashion, biding its time until the next big game, the rematch with San Francisco. The Dons took a four-point lead into intermission, but the Irish finally woke up in the second half as, spurred on by one of the few vocal crowds of the season, they stretched to a seemingly comfortable 68-60 edge. But, keeping in the Irish tradition most recently noted in several 1979-80 contests, they blew the lead by playing sloppily and too conservatively, and SF took a 75-74 lead late. But John Paxson played hero by scoring six points in the last eight seconds, including a dramatic outside shot plus two technical foul shots awarded after the Dons tried to call a sixth time out, and ND had kept the unusual pattern of each team winning each game on its home court since the series began, 80-75.

Phelps, with his unusually strong emphasis on academics for a modern big-time coach (every player he has coached to term at Notre Dame has received a degree), had put together a second-semester schedule which resulted in only two total missed class days, an incredible feat. The first of them was the Friday before a Saturday game at Maryland, at which ND used 25 points by Tripucka to overcome the Terrapins, 73-70. Back at the ACC, the Irish rolled over Cornell, 80-57, and then, in a great game for the fan but not for the defense-minded Digger, they defeated South Carolina, 94-84. Three Irishmen (Jackson, Paxson, and Tripucka) hit at least 20, and Woolridge netted another 18 in the top home-court offensive burst of the season, which was tied two nights later against a badly-maligned opponent, St. Mary's of California, with a much better defensive effort to boot (94-63). No game all season rivaled this one for student apathy, as the usual fair-to-middling crowd for non-name opponents was downright sparse that night. Support was better against LaSalle, but the Irish weren't. Down 33-30 at half, they came out with a 16-4 spurt to take the lead for good but—as usual—the amazed fans watched ND nearly blow it. The final was 60-59. The uninspiring win raised Notre Dame to an impressive-on-the-surface 16-3 with the annual visit from UCLA in everyone's mind now, especially since ND had already lost the first meeting.

The Irish strategy was to keep the Bruins from making a track meet out of it, and at that they succeeded. There was only one problem, however; they didn't win. An uncharacteristically poor shooting day from the two guards, Jackson and Paxson (6-for-18), coupled with only 6-for-10 accuracy at the foul line, led ND to its only home loss of 1980-81 and only the 10th in the last eight years, 51-50. The 50 points marked ND's lowest point total since the well-intentioned but inept 1971-72 team scored only 32 against UCLA.

Quickly rebounding, Notre Dame had back-to-back games of truly great floor shooting. A field-goal percentage of .655 helped, for once, put a game away early—ND beat Boston University convincingly, 89-63. Then the Irish utterly shot the lights out of Reynolds Coliseum with an awesome display of combined accuracy (65 percent from the floor, 82 percent from the stripe), and North Carolina State never had a chance; the final was 71-55. The team, for the first time since early January, was hot, and just in time, because a neutral-court game against top-ranked Virginia loomed a week and a day away. All there was in between was a Monday night game against Fairfield which should have been no problem.

It ended up, however, a near-disaster.

Wire-watchers at sports desks around the country probably thought the halftime score was a misprint: Fairfield 32, Notre Dame 31. And things didn't get any better for the home team quickly. With only 8:15 left, the Stags still led, 47-42, primed for the biggest upset in basketball all season. Then the Irish ran off 12 straight points to finally take the lead, 54-47. But that lead was tenuous. ND had numerous attempts to put away the visitors once and for all, but the obviously uninspired Irish missed numerous one-and-the-bonus attempts, giving the psyched Stags continued life.

Meanwhile, Fairfield had gained support in its quest from an unexpected source – the Notre Dame student section. Rebelling, finally, against the patience-taxing ND strategy which had become disparagingly known as "Diggerball," the faithful left the faith. Rather than booing the awful Irish performance, as was not unheard of in the past, for the only known time in any sport in Notre Dame history, *they began cheering for the other team.* And not just a few scattered souls – almost everyone had joined in by the time the game had reached it final minute. Bill Varner, a sophomore standing in for the sorely missed Orlando Woolridge (out with pinkeye), canned 1-of-2 free throws with mere seconds left to make the margin 57-55. The Stags, however, had one more chance. Exhorted on by the crowd, Fairfield drove down the court but, for one rare moment (the visitors shot 69 percent from the floor on this bizarre evening), they missed the outside shot, and a successful followup was ruled to be after the buzzer, much to the genuine disappointment of most of the fans. Notre Dame had won another game it really didn't deserve to; fortunately, there was plenty of time to put this embarrassment behind before Virginia came calling at the previously obscure Chicago suburb of Rosemont, Illinois.

Rosemont was the home of a brand-new, 17,000-seat barn of an arena called the The Horizon, which was the new home of DePaul basketball. But on this Sunday (February 22), Notre Dame and Virginia took over the place. The Cavaliers were top-ranked and unbeaten – and thus the stage was set for another great Irish upset. It was one of the finest games of the year anywhere, even considering the low score, and neither team really deserved to lose. The way this one ended, therefore, was appropriate.

Virginia led by one and, after an Irish turnover, had the ball. But Notre Dame played a tough five-on-four defense and forced the Cavaliers into a five-second call on the ensuing inbounds play. Now the Irish, after presumably blowing their last chance, had another. Both Jackson and Tripucka missed relatively simple shots and the rebound bounced away from the basket . . .

right into the "perfectly positioned" Orlando Woolridge's hands. He immediately heaved a 16-foot prayer in the general direction of the basket just as the obnoxious Horizon air horn sounded – and bingo! Notre Dame 57, Virginia 56. Orlando was also one of the defensive stars of the game, as his double-team with, alternately, Tim Andree and Joe Kleine kept UVA's 7-4 skyscraper Ralph Sampson tied up the entire game; he was held to 10 points. For the second time in 1980-81, ND had knocked off Number One – and oddly, neither time at the ACC and both times at neutral courts.

A predicted letdown against still another clunker, St. Francis (PA), did not materialize (ND won, 87-71). And then the celebrated senior trio plus oft-injured Gilbert Salinas, the all-but-forgotten Stan Wilcox, and walk-on Kevin Hawkins (son of Tom Hawkins, who was a teammate of Mike Ireland, son of George Ireland, thus connecting the only father-son combinations to play varsity ball at Notre Dame) played their last home game, against Dayton. The three biggies excelled: Tracy Jackson and Kelly Tripucka each had 20, and Orlando Woolridge added 18, and ND rolled, 70-57, thus cinching an eighth straight trip to the NCAA tournament, the longest streak in the nation at that time. To close the regular season, the Irish returned to the "scene of the crime," the Rosemont Horizon, to face DePaul. But what a difference! This time the crowd was not the pro-Irish throng which was there two weeks prior. Nonetheless, ND led, 24-15, after 11 minutes of play. But the cold and the butter set in on the fingers. A 34.2 percent second-half shooting clip and 23 total turnovers spelled doom for Notre Dame, 74-64.

Sent to the East Regional, Notre Dame was preparing to meet Georgetown in the second round when Digger got some bad news. First, unknown to anyone but insiders, Woolridge had suffered a thigh bruise in practice the Thursday before the Virginia game (thus explaining the heavy tape on the leg), but had continued to play because there was no one who could adequately replace him – the depth was simply not of the same quality as it had once been. So it came as a blow when tests revealed calcium deposits on the affected limb. There was some doubt that he would play at all in the tournament, but he did, albeit often in great pain. Secondly, upstart ECAC South champion

James Madison upset Georgetown, the first of a couple of unforeseen results which affected Irish preparedness.

The smart money claimed the NCAA had set up the East bracket so that, assuming no upsets (never a sound assumption to make in the tourney, alas), two big-ratings TV games would result: a *third* ND-UCLA game in the semis, and—assuming the third time was the charm—an ND-Virginia rematch for the Final Four berth. However, Brigham Young stunned the Bruins in the second round, and the sluggish Irish bored a regional TV audience by making the fourth president's namesake institution look better than they were, 54-45. What transpired the following Thursday ranks as one of the most infamous games in Notre Dame basketball history (only the 1969 Michigan State "black booing" game ranks in the same league).

The Irish streaked to a 10-point halftime lead, 28-18, and as the second half began, ND threatened to make it a rout, upping it to 32-18. One reason was an effective box-and-one defense with the "one" on the Cougars' high-scoring (25.2 ppg) Danny Ainge. The vaunted senior, shadowed by John Paxson, scored only two points in the first half and was a non-factor for 39 minutes and 52 seconds.

Meanwhile, thanks to Tripucka and an inspired Woolridge, the lead was still 11, 40-29, with 11:49 left. But then the team began playing not to lose rather than to win. The Irish got careless, taking far too long to attempt shots and blowing opportunities (they missed easy layups and one-and-the-bonus attempts), and BYU began, slowly, to make a ballgame out of what shouldn't have been. When the Cougars closed to within one, 48-47, at the 3:34 mark, ND seemed content to hold the ball the rest of the game even though three BYU starters had four fouls. At 1:17 Woolridge was tied up, and the resulting jump ball was nabbed by the Cougars. Fourteen seconds later, Greg Ballif gave the underdogs from Utah their first lead.

Notre Dame set up for the last shot, exhausting its timeouts in the process. With 10 seconds left, Tripucka canned a baseline jumper to give the Irish the edge again, 50-49. The Cougars called time out at :08 and, depending on ND's defensive setup, planned either to throw the ball downcourt and hope for a breakaway or to pass the ball to Ainge and let him do his stuff. When the

Irish pressured the ball, BYU took option two—and it was off to the bullfight. One after another Notre Dame "matador" got out of the way of the raging bull, er, Cougar, in a stunning display of non-defense, and at :02, Ainge was sweet. He arched a shot above the last ND torero, Woolridge, and the helpless Irish could only react with stunned silence as the buzzer at Atlanta's Omni tolled the end of the most controversial season of the Phelps era—51-50.

What was supposed to be the finest season in Irish history was finally over. Now all Digger could do was put everything behind and look ahead, because after the disappointment and, in some quarters, outright anger which resulted from three talented teams not making the Final Four, it was rebuilding time at Notre Dame.

# 22

◆━━◆━━◆━━◆━━◆

# Starting Over

During the three-year span 1981-84, the Irish tried to retain national prominence, but it wasn't easy; the cumulative record over that time was the worst of Phelps' coaching career (50-39). But the ND coach received more praise about his coaching than at any time in the past, because in all three seasons he got far more out of the teams than anyone could have reasonably expected.

Originally Digger felt his 1981-82 team, consisting mainly of substitutes from the 1980-81 season, could "steal" 20 wins. After that goal quickly eluded his grasp, he then felt this "Rat Pack"—a nickname Phelps adopted for this team from a movie called *Ocean's Eleven*, in which a group of old Army buddies, to everyone's surprise, pull off a series of hotel heists—could "steal" an NIT bid. In the end, they were able to "steal" 10 wins and 17 losses, thus becoming only the second Phelps-coached ND team to end with a losing record.

Despite his pre-season optimism, Phelps had to know that the Irish were in for a long season. He had lost three-fifths of his starting lineup—Tracy Jackson, Kelly Tripucka, and Orlando Woolridge—to graduation and the NBA, and his center of the future, Joe Kleine, through transfer to Arkansas. Despite all this, and a bad recruiting year to boot, the Associated Press board of sportswriters felt the Irish could pull off the steal, as its pre-season poll tabbed the team 19th. ND remained there for a week after an 83-53 defeat of St. Joseph's (IN). And then the dreams began to become nightmares.

First came a 26-point home loss to UCLA, the most lopsided Irish defeat ever in the ACC.

Next, another ACC first: the Irish lost to a team not recog-

250

nized as a current or traditional basketball power (Murray State). Five days later, they pulled the same stunt, with Northern Illinois the beneficiary this time.

Then came what a writer for the student newspaper *The Observer* termed "The Death March." Five road games over the Christmas holidays, four of them against rated teams—and five straight losses. The team did manage to take Kentucky into overtime by using a well-executed stallball game. Even with a hostile Freedom Hall crowd booing incessantly, ND stayed in its game plan, at one point making over 200 consecutive passes; they finally lost, 34-28. And they also led San Francisco at half before falling.

Finally, one of the brighter spots of Notre Dame's 2-9 start, the play of sophomore Tom Sluby, was eliminated thanks to academic probation. With an injury to freshman guard Dan Duff, that made only seven scholarship players able to play much of the rest of the season—the worst depth Phelps had had since 1972-73, and with nowhere near the talent.

The rest of the season was a roller-coaster ride of comebacks (a defeat of Idaho after being down by 18 in the first half), upsets (a revenge win over San Francisco, then ranked seventh), tough losses (a 48-47 setback to UCLA at Pauley Pavilion in which the Irish failed to score in the last 11 minutes), and blowout losses (a 71-58 decision by Seton Hall and a 65-50 thrashing by Fordham, the Rams' first win against their old coach in nine years).

Perhaps the most embarrassing moment in a year of many was the decision by NBC not to televise the last game of the season against Michigan; a spokesman for the network termed it "a worthless game between two worthless teams." (Michigan's record was worse than Notre Dame's.) It was the only game on the ND slate not to appear on TV somewhere in the country. The people in Pontiac apparently had the same opinion about this one as NBC, for only 14,445 showed up at the huge Silverdome. And, by the way, Digger finally beat the Wolverines for the first time, 53-52, thanks to John Paxson's 30 points.

But the season wasn't all embarrassment and shame; there were some highlights.

One was the play of Paxson. He came out of the shadows of his better-known upperclass teammates of the last two years to start every game, average 16.9 points, dish off 99 assists, and provide leadership on and off the court. His play was impressive enough, even on a 10-17 team, to earn him All-America status — the first time since Lloyd Aubrey that anyone from a sub-.500 ND team was so honored.

Another was the other guard, Mike Mitchell. The only scholarship senior on the squad, he also served as a leader in his role as captain. For the first time since his freshman year, his knees stayed in place well enough for him to play all but one game, average 6.4 points, and provide 70 assists as Paxson's backcourt running mate.

Also, there was the return of the students. As duly noted previously, in the recent past many ND undergrads bought season tickets but only went to the big games, avoiding the long list of losers otherwise. This season saw the best overall student crowds in years, as the spirit in games, bad and good, played a key role in Irish victories, most notably in games against Davidson and Idaho.

Against Davidson, they braved a near-blizzard to fill the student section while the season-ticket-holding townspeople stayed home a la the 1978 Maryland game. Digger got the crowd going by using the old technical foul ploy early on, and the team rolled. And in the Idaho game, the student body groaned as the Vandals hit shot after shot without a miss. Finally, midway through the first half, one of the Idaho men finally missed a field-goal attempt. That seemingly ordinary event resulted in a standing ovation, one that lasted the rest of the game as a roused crowd exhorted the Irish back into a blowout and finally into the victory column. In this off-year, no game, not even those against the usual nobodies on the home slate, was a sure win; realizing this, the students came out en masse for most ACC contests and helped the Irish to an 8-8 home record.

Finally, there was the knowledge that, like most frustration, it had to end eventually and that things had to get better. And, thanks to an outstanding recruiting year — ND's best in five seasons — they did.

But before the new came around, the old returned for another hurrah. Eighteen of the greatest basketball players Notre Dame has ever known came back to the ACC on September 18,

1982 to play in a benefit game for Logan Center, a South Bend agency for the developmentally disabled. From the latter Johnny Dee stars like Austin Carr and Sid Catlett to the more recent of Digger's graduates like Tripucka and Woolridge, they were all there. And while the White team, made up of mostly recent players, defeated the Blue team of the "older" stars, 105-102, that didn't really matter so much in the scheme of this day. What was more important was the money raised for the Center—nearly $50,000 through game tickets and a jersey auction. This "blast from the past" made Irish fans recall great moments of time past. But after it was over, it was time to push ahead.

A stellar defense (ND's most stingy since 1948-49) and a patient offense which worked for the high-percentage shot (for the fourth time since Digger's arrival, the Irish finished among the top 10 nationally in field-goal accuracy), aided by the steadying influence of John Paxson and a schedule woefully lacking in quality—the latter of which likely cost ND an NCAA tournament bid—added up to a 19-10 record in 1982-83. But it was the freshmen, who made greater contributions more quickly than any previous Notre Dame freshman class, that made it possible: Ken Barlow, Tim Kempton, Joseph Price, Jim Dolan, and Joe Buchanan. Their unprecedented adjustment to the collegiate game landed three of them (Barlow, Kempton, and Price) in the starting lineup in their first game in an Irish uniform, which was won over Stonehill. The Irish also defeated St. Francis (PA) for an 2-0 record going into "The Week."

Not since 1969-70, when the Irish played three of the top five teams on the road in an eight-day span, did Notre Dame play so many high-caliber teams in so short a time as it did December 1-7. Unfortunately, the results were the same as they had been over a decade earlier—all three ended in losses.

Kentucky made its first visit to Notre Dame since 1950, when Adolph Rupp's tirades about winning in the Fieldhouse rendered a return trip impossible during his lifetime. The last 22 games, except for one NCAA tourney matchup in 1970, had been played in Louisville's Freedom Hall, mainly for financial reasons: Notre Dame made more money on its annual visit there than anywhere else outside New York. In 1971, the two schools signed a 10-year agreement to continue the game in its "neutral" site. Phelps soon learned to curse that contract, mainly because he couldn't win there consistently; he often mused that he would like to meet Kentucky in "neutral" Elkhart, Indiana, a few miles east of Notre Dame. When the old contract lapsed, after much difficulty a new two-year pact with the first game at Louisville and the second at Notre Dame was finally agreed upon, after which the series would end. Yet even though the game was played at "Freedom Hall North," as one banner high above the court proclaimed, the result was the same; thanks to 75 percent field-goal accuracy, UK won, 58-45. UCLA beat the Irish on a layup by Ralph Jackson with three seconds left, 65-64, ending a spirited upset bid, and the experienced Indiana Hoosiers took advantage of an inhuman 80 percent from the floor in the second half to romp, 68-52.

The Irish closed their longest home stand since 1914-15 by cranking up the offense. Paxson, Kempton, Barlow, and senior Bill Varner were the main scoring architects as ND defeated a few of the lesser lights on the slate—92-70 over Fairfield, 88-45 over Dartmouth, 108-70 over Valparaiso (the 108 marking the most points for Notre Dame in almost exactly five years), and 83-60 over NIT-bound William and Mary.

The long nine-game home stand had a major drawback: the team had not had the experience of playing on the road. Davidson, for the first time in the school's history, beat the Irish, 54-51 in overtime, and Villanova came from behind in the second half to beat ND at the Palestra, 61-55. And after another home win, over Canisius, the Irish went to Milwaukee to take on Marquette. It was almost an instant replay of the first two road contests; for the third time ND led at the half only to have the home team come from behind and take the lead. But this time, one of the freshmen who had not been heard from much made the difference. Jim Dolan scored only six points, but four of them were ND's last four in a 59-57 thriller.

After two boring home wins, Notre Dame's road show ran amok again. Maryland used a foul-goal advantage of 26-9 to defeat the Irish, 67-66, in a half-empty Cole Field House (everyone else was watching the Washington Redskins on the way to their first Super Bowl appearance). And following a week's layoff, not only to recover from the loss but also from a scare on the flight home (the plane developed trouble right after takeoff but managed to return to the airport safely), the team went to Pauley Pavilion and lost to UCLA for the sixth straight time, 59-53.

Meanwhile, Notre Dame prepared for the tournament. Home wins over LaSalle and South Carolina upped the Irish record to 12-7, but a second straight loss to Fordham, 75-69 in a new but hostile venue for ND, the Brendan Byrne Meadowlands Arena in East Rutherford, New Jersey, derailed the express. The rest of the way, however, the train seemed back on track The defense and ball-control offense, both anchored by the amazing Paxson, who at the season's end became ND's first consensus All-American since Adrian Dantley, were the reasons why. In those contests, Pax averaged 17 by himself, and Varner came on strong as well until injury forced him to miss the last two regular-season games. The work of the seniors helped overcome slumps by some of the freshmen, most notably Kempton and Barlow. Yet there was no slump on defense; the Irish held their last eight opponents on the regular slate to 47.3 points per game.

Notre Dame put together four straight wins for the third time, beginning with a 43-42 defeat of North Carolina State in Raleigh, the lowest point total for ND in a winning cause since a 43-41 defeat of Michigan State on February 23, 1949. It was the last loss of the season for the Wolfpack, who streaked on to the national championship. The Irish also defeated Pittsburgh, Akron, and Hofstra, but more interesting was a game which was almost played the day after the ND-NCSU game in North Carolina.

A record-setting blizzard had hit the Northeast, and there was some doubt whether Villanova would be able to arrive in North Carolina for a nationally-telecast game against the Tar Heels. Phelps and Notre Dame agreed to substitute for the Wildcats if they could not make it—and when the enraged Villanova people heard that, they boarded buses, got down to Chapel Hill in plenty of time, and not only played but upset the top-ranked Tar Heels! (North Carolina has since been scheduled as an Irish opponent in 1985-86.)

Troublesome DePaul was next. The Demons led most of the way in front of a near-capacity crowd in the Rosemont Horizon, but a furious Irish rally tied the game at 53 with five seconds left. In the ensuing time out, Ray Meyer told his young team, "Five seconds is a long time," as they broke the huddle. And it was long enough for Kenny Patterson to put up a miracle 30-footer which swished through the bucket as the horn sounded on another Irish loss to DePaul.

The season closed with three more home wins. The first was 59-40 over Seton Hall to avenge the loss of a year earlier; the Irish held their guests to only 11 points in the first half and coasted from there. Next, what was expected to be the last obstacle to an NCAA tournament bid was hurdled when ND held Dayton to only 14 second-half points to come back for a 53-41 decision. And finally, amidst a tumultuous reception for the seniors unlike any heard since Austin Carr's last home game in 1971, and buoyed by much-abused senior center Tim Andree's best overall game, Northern Iowa fell, 75-51.

When the bids for the tourney came out, only two independents were named to the 52-team field: Southwestern Louisiana and Marquette, the latter likely because coach Hank Raymonds had announced his retirement beforehand. Also likely was that 19-9 Notre Dame was bypassed because of its obviously weak home schedule. Instead, the NIT made Notre Dame one of its first selections, and matched it with Northwestern in the first round.

The NIT people originally wanted to hold this game in the ACC, but Digger declined because the students were on break, reasoning which evoked a strong response from the South Bend community. Instead, the game ended up at the Horizon. Had the Irish won the first game, they would have hosted the next two rounds—an internal memo had already been distributed to that effect. The opponents in those two games would have been Michigan State and (probably) a DePaul rematch. But the Wildcats stood in the way.

A lacklustre performance, especially in the second half, did in the Irish. They may have been bothered by the NIT's shot clock and the red, white, and blue ABA-style ball, but it was more likely they lost to a hungrier team. This was NU's first post-season appearance ever, and ND still felt some letdown about not going to the NCAAs. Northwestern defeated the Irish worse than anyone save Indiana had all year, 71-57.

There was no time to dwell on past woes as 1983-84 preparations got under way. Phelps' first problem was to answer the burning question, "Who will replace John Paxson?" He tabbed senior Tom Sluby as the man; after an impressive series on a summer tour of Yugoslavia, Sluby was chosen captain, a controversial decision considering his past performances and academic record.

Meanwhile, Digger felt he had the horses, albeit young ones, to return to the NCAAs assuming everyone stayed healthy and eligible. But academic deficiencies forced Phelps to raid the football team for a point guard, and injuries cut his available scholarship players to nine for most of the stretch run. Despite the constant lineup changes these events wrought, the Irish surprised more than a few critics by making the finals of the NIT and hitting the 20-win mark (21, to be exact) for the first time in three years.

Phelps planned to revolve the team around, in addition to Sluby, a front line of sophomores Jim Dolan, Tim Kempton, and Ken Barlow and point guard Joe Buchanan, with help from Dan Duff, Joseph Price, and three freshmen: Scott Hicks, a teammate of Barlow's at Indianapolis Cathedral High; Donald Royal, a Louisiana product reminiscent of another bayou biggie, Orlando Woolridge; and John Bowen, the leading rebounder in Pennsylvania high school history. But Duff and little-used Barry Spencer landed on the ineligibility list, so Digger recruited Joe Howard, a 5-9 junior wide receiver, from the football team, who joined the team after January 1. He immediately added quickness and deft passing as a sixth man and at the same time captured the imagination of Irish fans. The shortest regular since 5-7 Gene Duffy in the late 1950s, "Small Wonder" became the first footballer to play basketball since a trio of men did so in 1972-73.

As Digger juggled things around, trying to find a consistent lineup, Notre Dame struggled to a 6-4 start. He thought he had the quickness to play a little faster-paced game, but poor shooting from both the field and the line forced a change in philosophy back to the more controlled methods of the past three seasons. Poor free-throw shooting was especially troublesome, as three of those four losses were directly attributable to the faulty accuracy from the charity stripe . . . all three of which were all but gone until the Irish turned on the toughest zone press seen from a ND team in some time (80-72 vs. Indiana, 51-47 vs. UCLA, and 68-66 vs. LaSalle). The other loss may have been one of the worst displays of basketball by two colleges anywhere in the country all season, a 40-36 overtime loss at Northwestern's new Welch-Ryan Arena (the refurbished McGaw Hall) which neither team deserved to win. And none of the six wins was impressive, primarily because of the caliber of competition on a weak early-season home schedule, although a 104-56 win over St. Joseph's (IN) in the opener proved that ND could run. As for the rest, well . . . Marist was the butt of numerous jokes beforehand, first from the wags who wondered what Notre Dame was doing playing a Chicago high school, and later from those who, considering the relative ineptitude of recent ND football teams, asked if the Poughkeepsie, New York institution had a football team. St. Francis, New York, was one of the worst Division I teams in the country in 1983-84; and the trio of home games consisting of Lehigh, Cornell, and Valparaiso was sarcastically called "The Big Three" by some members of the local media.

But when Howard joined the team on the Christmas road trip, and Sluby began to take charge where he hadn't early on, the Irish went on a 9-2 tear and made fans think about a possible NCAA trip again. In his very first collegiate game, Howard scored 14 points and dished off seven assists in an important 73-61 win over Holy Cross at the "neutral" Centrum in Worcester, Massachusetts – ND's first regular-season trip to New England since 1962-63. And in the team's first trip to the Pacific Northwest ever, it split two games. Missed free throws (again) both prolonged and ended a contest against surprising Washington (eventual Pac-10 champs), which the Huskies won, 63-61 in double overtime, and in one of of only two "pits" ND played in all year (McArthur Court), the Irish used a psychological ploy – they dressed at the hotel and did not arrive at the gym until moments before tipoff to avoid the stomping feet of rabid fans above the locker room – to help beat Oregon, 66-54.

Six straight home wins upped the longest ND win streak in three years to seven. The highlights were two nationally-televised games in which Notre Dame began to earn back some respect. Hot free-throw shooting down the stretch – 33-for-48 overall – on the coldest day in South Bend history (the official low was -21 degrees F. *before* wind chill was factored in, and the day's high wasn't close to zero) turned a close game into a rout; Villanova was the victim, 81-68. Even bigger was a 52-47 win over then-fifth-ranked Maryland a week later. This one was tied at 45 late in the game when Sluby took charge: in the season's most exciting single play, he drove the lane, put the ball up and in, and was fouled in the process. He hit the free one to convert the three-point play, and the Irish were never headed afterwards. Sluby's new-found take-charge attitude and play resulted in his leading the team in scoring in 17 of the last 19 regular-season games. Another noteworthy effort was a 50-35 defeat of Rice, the 35 marking the all-time ACC low point total for an opponent. (Before writing off Rice as just another typical Digger home opponent, note that a few nights later the Owls upset Arkansas and Joe Kleine.)

During this string, Phelps pretty much ditched the liberal substitution policy he had held and found happiness with a seven-man team—Sluby, Buchanan, Kempton, Dolan, and Barlow, with Howard and Price as subs. He would have remained happy with it all year no doubt. Unfortunately, injuries interfered.

Most costly of these was the stress fracture sustained by Tim Kempton. First suspected before the South Carolina game (the end of ND's win streak, a lacklustre 52-42 setback), he sat out a win over Vermont and played Rutgers at Meadowlands Arena (ND's 1980s version of Freedom Hall) in great pain—and then didn't play again until the NIT. His absence proved even to harsh critics (and there were many) that even though his exuberance might occasionally lead to mistakes, his presence clogging the middle was absolutely essential to the team's success. Kempton's injury elevated Donald Royal to a starting berth, in which he performed very well considering his fairly small minutes-played totals before the big center was sidelined. Also, recurring tendinitis finally sidelined Joe Buchanan for the year after the DePaul game (except for a cameo appearance in the NIT final), and Joe Howard was forced into a starting role. The rest of the season, Digger's patchwork lineup—the "Cabbage Patch Kids" he dubbed them—had some troubles, and limped in with a 2-5 record to close the regular season 17-11.

The lack of depth showed itself, as ND led four of its five losses at halftime but couldn't keep up the pace. Most shocking of these was the Rutgers game; the Irish led by eight at the half and held similar leads throughout much of the second half, but a technique thought gone returned—they began to play not to lose rather than to win, and defeat was snatched from the jaws of victory. The Scarlet Knights chipped away, and chipped away, and finally won with a buzzer-beater, 61-59. That commenced a four-game losing streak which resulted in setbacks by DePaul (62-54), Pittsburgh (67-59 in a game not nearly that close, ND's worst game at home in a couple of years), and at Brigham Young (68-64), the latter despite holding Devin Durrant, then the nation's leading scorer, to only eight points.

Before the DePaul game, Notre Dame fans and coaches paid tribute to Ray Meyer, who was retiring after 42 years at the Blue Demons' helm. Each living ND coach who had led the Irish against DePaul gave Meyer a token of his appreciation, and the fans, holding thousands of heart-shaped "We Love You Ray" signs, stood and cheered in tribute in a welcome never before awarded a visiting coach by an Irish crowd. Meyer, of course, had begun his collegiate coaching career at Notre Dame, and he ended his career ledger against his alma mater with his fourth straight win over ND, the longest DePaul streak over the Irish in the 42-year continuous history of the series.

ND finally broke the dry spell by besting Manhattan in Madison Square Garden—Notre Dame's first trip there in three years—by 63-58, and then clinched a bid to the NIT by knocking off Marquette behind—who else—Tom Sluby's 30 points, 65-56. And Sluby closed out with a second straight 30-point performance, against Dayton, but the Irish blew an eight-point halftime lead and lost, 80-70.

After the swan dive at the end of the season, predicting ND's performance in the NIT was difficult at best. Much would depend on how well Kempton was able to come back, how well the deliberate Notre Dame offense would perform under the constraints of a 45-second shot clock, and how well they could play defense, rebound, and perform down the stretch. They did all better than perhaps even Phelps could have envisioned.

Notre Dame was awarded a home game in the first round,

against new opponent Old Dominion. The opponent selection was a mystery; perhaps all the "11,345" capacity crowds listed in past media guides told the NIT people that anyone would fill the ACC although in most cases that figure was nowhere near the number who showed up. Why a team of great local interest, like North Carolina State or Ohio State, was not chosen no one could answer satisfactorily, and neither could the 5,442 who showed up, the smallest paid crowd in ACC history for a Notre Dame men's basketball game. But the Irish won, 67-62, and went back to New England for Round Two, a "neutral court" game at Springfield, Massachusetts, birthplace of basketball, against Boston College, in a "rematch" of the controversial 1983 Liberty Bowl football game. A close game became a rout because ND found something it hadn't had all year: accuracy at the foul line. Shooting a near-miraculous 34-for-39 there, the Irish won, 66-52 for the 1200th basketball win in their history. This entitled Phelps' men to a rematch with Pitt—this time at the Panthers' 6500-seat band box, Fitzgerald Fieldhouse. And what did the Irish do? They continued to rebound, play defense, and shoot fouls better than the opposition, and did at Pittsburgh what they hadn't had a prayer of doing at Notre Dame—beat the Panthers. The 72-64 win put the surprising Irish into the NIT Final Four for the third time in four trips to the invitational.

Southwestern Louisiana, a run-and-gun type team, was held down by the stingy Irish defense, 65-59. This put ND into the final game for the second time in Phelps' tenure, against Michigan, a constant thorn in the side of Notre Dame teams in post-season play. This time was no exception. Irish luck ran out thanks to an Irishman on the Wolverines, Tim McCormick, who scored 28 on 13-of-16 accuracy from the field, and Michigan—a team many thought deserved a bid to the NCAAs rather than the NIT—won its first NIT, or any other basketball title, 83-63.

However, there was nothing to be ashamed of. Notre Dame had made it four games farther than in 1982-83, three games farther than most realists would have expected, and even though faced with long odds in the second half of the final, impressed more than a few observers with its continued intense play until it was over on the clock. And the Irish were losing only Sluby, who scored 616 points in the second-longest season in ND history

(33 games, 21-12), and Cecil Rucker, a crowd favorite if not a Phelps favorite, to graduation, and had four outstanding recruits, including two *Parade* All-Americans, one of which was expected to earn a starting berth immediately, coming in. The future looked bright indeed.

The primary reasons for optimism among the incoming freshmen were a six-foot point guard from Jersey City, New Jersey, David Rivers, and a Yugoslavian shooting guard named Drazen Petrovic. Even before the new school year began, Phelps hyped them heavily. Here was two-fifths of his starting lineup, Digger claimed — before either had participated in an official practice with the Irish! (No doubt this kind of talk contributed to Joe Buchanan's transfer to Cal-Irvine.) In September Petrovic relented to tremendous pressure to stay in Europe, and all the attention centered on Rivers. But there was something to the buildup.

First, however, some misinformation needs to be corrected. When Rivers started his first game at Notre Dame (against Manhattan), he was *not* the first freshman to do so since Adrian Dantley, as many in the national media claimed. Joe Kleine did in 1980-81 against UCLA, and three of Rivers' teammates, juniors Tim Kempton, Ken Barlow, and Joseph Price, did in 1982-83 against Stonehill. Regardless, Phelps did give Rivers more freedom of operation than any of those others; rather than Rivers having to adapt to his teammates, the reverse was true. Because he had such free rein, the freshman didn't always play intelligently, especially in the early season, resulting in forced passes and poor shot selection. But as time went on, this happened less and less often, and he became one of the top freshmen in the country. He also led ND in scoring, the first freshman to do so since Vince Boryla on the war-depleted 1944-45 team. Most crucially, though, Notre Dame won 20 regular-season games and made the NCAA playoffs for the first time in four years.

Rivers was not the only reason the Irish returned to the expanded 64-team national championship round. Barlow was the team's most consistent scorer until the last couple of weeks of the season thanks to a good outside touch for someone 6-10, and sophomore Donald Royal proved a pleasant surprise with his much-improved inside game, both offensively and defensively. When they were hot, both Price and sophomore Scott Hicks had terrific perimeter shots, and the latter also turned in some great defensive performances. Those five men formed the foundation of a strong transition offense and pressing defense, something Phelps had not had at ND since his outstanding 1973-74 team. And though Kempton and Jim Dolan had offensive off-years, their rebounding (along with Barlow's and Royal's) was essential to the Irish success, as the team was among national leaders in out-rebounding the opposition.

Also, for the first time in nine years, Notre Dame had a home schedule worthy of its tradition, and its road slate was no slouch, either; the highlight was a home-and-home series with the other three major Midwest independents—Dayton, DePaul, and Marquette—in what some see as a first step toward a powerful "Vatican Conference." In hopes of filling more seats, a goal also aided by better home games, ND officials moved the starting time of night games from 8 P.M. to 7 P.M., though there were gripes that so soon after dinner was *too* early. Finally, there was the Jeckyll-and-Hyde student section, which at times was among the most vocal and supportive since the days of the Fieldhouse, but at other times was as rude and unsportsmanlike as any since that 1963-64 group that nearly caused that season's DePaul game to be forfeited.

But there were nothing but cheers as the Irish began 4-0, including a big win over then highly regarded Indiana, 74-63. Rivers shone offensively, hitting 23, and Hicks blanketed the Hoosiers' Olympian, Steve Alford, on defense, keeping him from becoming a factor in IU's attack. Earlier, ND had upended Manhattan, Northwestern, and St. Francis. In a bizarre scheduling move, the Manhattan game (67-52) was played on a Sunday night, the first prime-time Sabbath game in Irish history. The win over Northwestern (79-61) finally got ND on the up side of a game with the Wildcats again. In the 85-45 win over St. Francis, Rivers had a collegiate low four points, and the leading scorer and rebounder was another freshman, 6-9 Gary Voce. His 17-point, 15-rebound performance, the latter a one-game Irish high for the season, added to fan dissatisfaction with Tim Kempton; in their eyes, Voce should have been playing more.

After the initial burst at home, Notre Dame was faced with six straight road games—the most in a row in 10 years—and was only able to split them. In the first, the Irish tried to play run-and-gun against a team which reveled in that style of offense—DePaul—and while they scored 83, they gave up 95 in the worst defense by any ND team since December 30, 1976 against Kentucky. One day later, the Irish helped dedicate a new gym at Valparaiso, which they also had done in 1939 and 1962. Just like those other two times, they blew out their hosts, 88-57, behind another strong performance by Gary Voce and a good showing from another freshman, Matt Beeuwsaert.

The next couple of weeks were nail-biters, and that was before the team traveled to Omaha to play Creighton after a 21-day layoff. Rumors flew around campus about the academic standing of David Rivers; supposedly he had a terrible mid-semester report and was a few days away from probation. But he, along with everyone else on the squad managed to get the grades high enough to stay eligible for the second semester.

Notre Dame's unusually long break ended, as it usually does, with a sluggish performance. Against Creighton, an old-time foe back on the schedule after over a decade, Barlow scored 25, but Rivers turned an ankle and missed almost all of the second half. Even without their leader, the Irish had every chance to win this one, but lost, 60-58. Then they easily defeated Davidson, which used to be habit but had not been in recent years, and then fell to Rice, 73-70, in tiny Autry Court in Houston. And another loss nearly followed at Marquette; the Irish blew a big lead late only to have the Warriors go ahead, 62-61. Then Rivers, with six seconds left, took the Irish inbounds pass, drove the length of the court, and put up a jumper from the right corner which went in as the buzzer sounded to save the day.

When ND finally returned home for its first game in the ACC in 43 days, it systematically took care of Holy Cross, 96-63, to move to 8-3 before the DePaul rematch. For this one, Digger pulled out a few stops. He put his team in gold uniforms for the first time since the mid-1970s and had the players enter through the student body section, but these ploys couldn't overcome key mistakes while nursing a three-point lead and 40 percent shooting from the field for the game. DePaul left the ACC with its sixth consecutive win over the Irish, 71-66. Three days later, ND tackled a hot Dayton team, and behind the steady play of Rivers and Barlow, with an assist from a phenomenal and (almost) classy performance by the student section, cooled off the Flyers, 66-61. But then Notre Dame cooled off as well, and played poorly its next three games.

During the course of a season, players will occasionally have off days. On good teams, when one man is cold, someone else is hot and will compensate. It is rare when nearly everyone goes cold at the same time. Well, the Maryland game at College Park was a rarity. Only Barlow among the regulars had his shooting touch; Rivers went 2-for-13, Royal 2-for-10, Price 2-for-5, Hicks 0-for-3, and Kempton 1-for-11, the last of which inspired Maryland fans to chant sarcastically, "We want Kempton! We want Kempton!" The Irish were indeed lucky to leave with only a 12-point loss after all that (77-65). The malaise carried over to the next two home contests, against also-rans Providence and St. Louis; the team shot poorly in both, but a talent advantage led to 70-63 and 48-42 wins, the latter ND's low point mark for the season. Only four other times in 30 games did the Irish score less than 60, and they split them.

One on the positive side was against UCLA. A particularly heads-up play by David Rivers in this game—calling a time out when he had fallen on his stomach rescuing a loose ball from out of bounds—inspired NBC sportscaster Al McGuire, a master of hyperbole, to exclaim his now-famous remark: "He's an Einstein! He's a Michelangelo!" But even though Rivers had 18 points, Jim Dolan's 10 points and Joseph Price's eight keyed the Irish win in Pauley Pavilion for the first time since the Rich Branning days, 53-52. The sluggishness seemed to be gone after their fourth straight win, a romp over LaSalle, just in time for a match-up for the first time in 43 years with Syracuse, arranged partially on the urging of Fr. Theodore Hesburgh, who hailed from that area. The result, however, was an inglorious end to the winning streak.

The Orangemen beat the Irish, 65-62, in controversial fashion: with the score tied at 60, Rivers drove in for what appeared to be the go-ahead basket, but a prone official waved it off, calling charging on the play. The momentum switched to the visitors, who hit five free throws down the stretch from there. This game also was marred by the worst fan behavior at Notre Dame in over two decades. Students rained oranges upon the court during pre-game introductions and were, rightfully, threatened with a technical foul if they continued. The more traditional toilet paper debris stopped action after ND's first basket with another warning. After the game, oranges again were thrown from the stands, most in the general direction of the referees, one of which hit Irish assistant coach Pete Gillen in the back of the head.

Nothing came down onto the court during the next game, a 25-point win over New Orleans played in the midst of the worst South Bend snowstorm since the legendary Blizzard of 1978. Local officials urged anyone who had to drive to get to the ACC to stay home, and they did; only about 4,000 showed up. Another matchup against a highly-ranked opponent followed with the renewal of a series with Duke at Notre Dame's 1980s jinx joint, the Byrne Meadowlands Arena, where the Irish are now 0-4. The Blue Devils jumped out to a 10-0 lead and were never headed as they handed ND its seventh loss, 81-69. The Irish now were faced with the difficult proposition of having to win six of their last seven games to hit the 20-win mark and most likely assure an NCAA bid.

As opposed to the injury-related fold in 1983-84, they came through with flying colors this time.

Their one loss down the stretch came from an unexpected source—Butler, still *another* team back on the ND slate after a long hiatus. The school Notre Dame has defeated in basketball more often than any other came from behind to win in overtime, 70-69. The Irish let an eight-point halftime lead slip away in front of the largest Hinkle Fieldhouse crowd in many years. And they almost lost to upstart Loyola of Maryland, the fourth different Loyola to appear on the Irish schedule over the years. After 10 minutes, ND had a 26-10 lead and appeared to be breezing. The team then stopped playing with the same intensity; at the end, had it not been for several missed shots from close range, not unlike what happened to UCLA in 1974, the Greyhounds would have pulled off the greatest upset in ACC history. The final: 61-60. This marked the last appearance of the gold uniforms, which also had adorned the Irish in losses to DePaul and Syracuse; after this disaster, Digger shelved them for good.

In the other five wins, all against quality teams, Notre

Dame's ability to work inside, especially to Donald Royal, and draw fouls made the difference. Only against Fordham at Madison Square Garden did the Irish score as many two-pointers as the opposition. They were able to win by making lots of foul shots, especially when they were in the bonus situation. Royal and, of course, Rivers were the most productive charity-tossers; the former was 35-for-39 in wins over Washington (57-50), Marquette (66-60), and at Dayton (80-73 in double overtime), and the latter hit 21 of 25 in the same contests. Even Tim Kempton, who had been booed when he was inserted for a fouled-out Jim Dolan in the Washington game (the students chanted for Gary Voce), brought cheers for his inspired play in the second half against Marquette. Finally, when ND played Brigham Young at the ACC (the final was 67-58), poor sportsmanship reared its ugly head at one point; when a Cougar player hobbled off the court with an injury, instead of stunned silence and polite applause, the cheering section let out a big "Awww."

Because of the late-season triumphs, there was little doubt that Notre Dame was heading back to the NCAAs. The question became where—and for the first time the Irish were placed at home for the first and second rounds of the Southeast (formerly Mideast) Regional. (Twice before the ACC had played host to NCAA tourney games, and both times Notre Dame was sent elsewhere.) The smart money suggested that ND would defeat its first-round opponent, Oregon State, and then lose to the expected winner of the other bracket, North Carolina. That is exactly what happened.

David Rivers put on a second-half show, and Joseph Price, starting for the ill Ken Barlow, scored 16 points to lead the Irish past the Beavers, 79-70. But the Tar Heels ended ND's season in the next round with a 60-58 decision. No one could realistically blame Phelps' coaching strategy for the loss; he brilliantly had David Rivers milk the clock with his dribbling until less than 10 seconds were left. Then the freshman began to make his move for the winning basket—and he lost the ball. Carolina grabbed it, passed to a breaking-away Kenny Smith, and he slammed it home to end the game. The two elements of Notre Dame's game which had won so many contests in 1984-85 had gone awry; before Rivers's rare miscue the team had shot only 54 percent from the free throw line, the main reason why his near-heroics were necessary in the first place.

Despite ND's abrupt bow-out, the Irish had taken another step back up the ladder to the elite teams in the country. With basically everyone of significance returning for 1985-86, a continued climb to the Top 20 seemed assured.

# 23

## Women Join the Club

For 130 years, Notre Dame's undergraduate population was all male. But changing times—and a failed merger with neighboring Saint Mary's College—led the University to begin accepting women for the 1972-73 academic year. Of course, with the rich athletic tradition under the Golden Dome, it was natural that the newest members of the University community would want to become part of it. One of the first women's sports to take off was basketball.

During the team's first three years, it was what is known as a "club." Club teams are not funded by the Athletic Department, but by participants themselves through such means as dues or football concession stands. Because of the relative scarcity of funds, club sports usually have volunteer coaches and take few (and short) road trips. Eventually the club members may decide to petition for varsity status and the resulting Athletic Department aid. (Not all clubs want this; Notre Dame's rugby, sailing, and crew teams, for example, have been clubs for years and seem to have no tendencies toward changing their status.) If there has been enough participant interest in a club before its application, the request is usually granted. Nowadays, all new teams must start as clubs before varsity status can be considered. And so it was with women's basketball.

The year after women were admitted, the four women's dorms at the time formed an interhall league, and a closely-contested one at that. Also, at Digger Phelps' annual walk-on tryouts for his men's team, three women showed up. The interest in the sport was obviously there, and so a group of interhall stars including Mary Lou Mulvihill, Mary Clemency, and Patty Coogan found a coach—a graduate student named Jeanne Earley—and formed a club for the 1974-75 season. Mostly because of scheduling dificulties, the team played only seven games in its initial season.

On January 30, 1975, a new team represented Notre Dame for the first time as 15 women trekked to East Lansing, Michigan, to take on Big Ten powerhouse Michigan State. If they had wanted to start on a winning track, this wasn't the place to do it. The Spartans destroyed the Irish women, 84-23. Mulvihill scored eight points to lead the club. Never again would the women score so few points in a game; only once would they lose by such a wide margin.

The women's home debut, against Toledo, also resulted in a loss, 50-31. Two more home losses followed: the first to the team which would become the women's chief rival of the early years, across-the-street Saint Mary's; the second, another slaughter— this time, a 47-point destruction at the hands of Ball State. At 0-4 with three games remaining, the only way to go was up, and that they did.

Kalamazoo College became the first Irish victim in women's basketball. A tough, consistent defensive effort led the women to a 44-36 win. Two days later, the first-ever road win came courtesy of Lewis College, 50-45. Then came the rematch against Saint Mary's to see if the newcomers could even up the score in the "Shuttle Series," as the rivalry became known (a shuttle bus runs between the two campuses most hours of the day and night). The Irish did, eking out a win over the Belles, 38-37.

After the respectable showing for a first-year team (3-4), interest in the club grew; about 50 women tried out for the club in the fall of 1975. Eighteen made the original team (a 19th player was added later), among them the tri-captains, Becky Banasiak, Mary Clemency, and Patty Coogan (all seniors); Bonita Bradshaw, a junior, who became the first black to represent Notre Dame in women's basketball (not until Trena Keys in 1982 would there be another) and proved an intimidating presence on the floor because of her size; and a freshman who was offered athletic scholarships at several schools, but decided to come to Notre

Dame for its pre-med program and play basketball as a sideline. Her name was Carol Lally.

From the western Pennsylvania town of Sharon, Lally immediately became the scoring star of the club team. Four consecutive years she led the team in total points scored. She was also a leader, as evidenced by the fact that she was elected co-captain of the 1976-77 squad as a sophomore—an Irish basketball first—and served as co-captain for three consecutive years—another first.

She started out quickly, putting in 23 points in her second collegiate game, a 58-49 loss to IUPU-Fort Wayne. Notre Dame had begun to schedule teams more in its level of competition at the time—no more Michigan States for a while—and had put together a 13-game slate for 1975-76.

The team's first win of the season after two losses was against Northwestern, another school fairly new in the sport, 43-34. Interestingly, the coach of that Wildcat squad was none other than Mary DiStanislao, who became Notre Dame's coach in 1980. (She was to get things moving at Northwestern so rapidly that the next season her team played an improved Irish squad and won by 19. Notre Dame dropped the Division I Wildcats from the schedule after that.) The first-ever extended road trip followed, with wins at Albion and St. Joseph's (IN) and a loss at Marquette.

The Marquette contest came about because of an important connection. It just so happened that Marquette's head basketball coach, Tat Shiely, is the sister of one of the Notre Dame starters in 1975-76, Judy Shiely. The Warriors were inked for a home-and-home series for that season. After Notre Dame achieved varsity status, Marquette became a constant on the schedule, as the Irish played the Warriors every season from 1977-78 through 1983-84.

Then, of course, there were the games with Saint Mary's.

For the only time, SMC swept the two-game season series. In the first game, the Belles' defense held Lally to three free throws as they defeated the Irish 59-50. In the rematch, ineptitude at the foul line hurt Notre Dame. The team shot a combined 1-for-7 as Saint Mary's won what must be one of the lowest-scoring games in modern women's basketball history—28-27. Saint Mary's eventually finished second in the state in its best-ever basketball season.

Such a defensive effort was not uncommon for this second edition of the Notre Dame women's basketball club; they gave up, on the average, less than 46 points per game. At the same time, however, the offense could muster but 43 a game; as a result, the team finished with a 6-7 record. But things were looking up as women's basketball moved into its third year.

First, the Irish joined the Indiana Women's Intercollegiate Sports Organization (IWISO) for 1976-77. This rendered the team eligible for post-season competition. Second, although losing the senior tri-captains, there was plenty of experienced talent returning (Lally, Shiely, Bradshaw, co-captain Maureen Maloney), plus several newcomers who contributed immediately (Jane Politiski, Carola Cummings, Pat Meyer). As was the pattern from the previous two years, everyone on the 16-woman squad contributed to the team's success. Finally, in Sally Duffy, the team had a sideline coach often reminiscent of a younger Digger Phelps. Duffy had-been co-coach the year before. While not coaching the squad, she found time to complete her graduate studies and serve as rector of Lewis Hall on campus. Add all this together and, for the first time, the sum was a winning season (9-6).

The initial contest of the season was the latest battle in the war against Saint Mary's. Until this time the annual two-game series was merely heated; now it became controversial, thanks to some inflammatory coverage in the Notre Dame *Observer*. Sports Editor Fred Herbst apparently went to the Saturday afternoon game, played after the Notre Dame men had done their usual to Valparaiso, and in his column on Monday performed a hatchet job on both schools' basketball programs and, by extension, the athletes who played for the teams. Dozen of letters commenting on Herbst's diatribe poured into the *Observer* office, almost all critical. Among the bushel of letters published in the paper on the article, the first—and last—word on the entire controversy was this one, a challenge which, unfortunately, was never carried out:

Dear Freddy:

I don't want to waste my time writing you a letter. I'd rather settle the matter where it counts. How about a basketball game someday—I'll spot you six points.

Carol Lally

P.S. You set the time and place.

Oh, by the way, almost lost in the brouhaha—and the *Observer* "coverage"— was that Notre Dame won, 56-35. (Saint Mary's never won another game in the Shuttle Series.)

The team played a schedule more representative of a college program gearing toward local post-season playoffs than any in the past; most of the competition consisted of small Indiana schools, the kind the Irish theoretically would play in the early playoff rounds. Of the 13 regular-season games, 10 were against Indiana colleges; the other three opponents were from Illinois. (Compare this to the helter-skelter 1974-75 slate, of which only three of the seven contests were against Indiana schools.) With this schedule, the Irish women were 6-1 as of February 5, the only loss coming to Mary D's Northwestern squad. One of the wins was the rematch against Saint Mary's, which had more than the usual attention given it because of the unnecessary controversy surrounding the earlier game. This one was much more closely contested; the lead changed hands many times until ND finally went ahead to stay with about a minute left and won by four.

After that 6-1 start—impressive by any standards, but particularly in light of the fact that most of the teams they played enjoyed varsity status—things fell apart somewhat, as four of the next five games ended in losses. One last win, against St. Francis of Fort Wayne, Indiana, secured ND's final regular-season slate at 8-5.

The IWISO Northern District Small College Tournament was the first step on the way to a state championship, but the Irish tripped on it. Notre Dame was facing IUPU-Fort Wayne in the opening game for the third time in 1976-77, and each team had won on.its home court. On the neutral court at Valparaiso, the Irish lost a squeaker, 47-45, effectively ending the season.

They did come back to defeat Grace in what was essentially the consolation game later that day.

Despite the setback in the tournament, the women's basketball club had come a long way in three short years. The next logical step was varsity status, and all involved knew it. The application for elevation was submitted to the athletic director; its acceptance was announced by "Moose" Krause in early October of 1977. Sharon Petro, a physical education instructor, became new coach of the team, replacing the graduated Sally Duffy. The third Notre Dame women's sport to attain varsity status (fencing and tennis were the first two) was on its way.

# 24

## Onward and Upward

Women's basketball now had varsity status and some of the benefits that go along with that, including regular practice space and a paid coach. Otherwise, not much was different in at least two respects: the schedule was similar to the last club schedule in its heavy Indiana emphasis, and the team continued to improve. In fact, the first varsity women's team had a final record of 13-4, still the best of any ND women's hoops squad (by percentage).

Many principals of the last club team were back—high-scoring Carol Lally and Pat Meyer, senior co-captain Marge Meagher, top rebounder Jane Politiski. Add to that three outstanding first-timers—pint-sized (5 feet) freshman Maggie Lally (Carol's sister), sophomore Molly Cashman, and a 5-11 sophomore transfer student from neighboring Saint Mary's, Kelly Hicks—and the solid nucleus of a successful small time program was established.

The 1977-78 squad won its first five contests, most by convincing margins. Valparaiso was the first varsity victim; Hicks had 17 on the way to a 48-41 Irish victory. Carol Lally set a record in the next game, a 79-67 defeat of St. Joseph's (IN), by scoring 27 points on 11-for-16 field goal shooting and 5-of-7 from the line. After the women returned from Christmas break, they were rusty in a 50-46 victory at Purdue-Calumet, but hit the groove in two consecutive blowouts: 68-39 over IUPU-Fort Wayne, the team which had knocked the ND club out of the state playoffs the year before, and 68-25 over Grace, the 25 marking an all-time low score against an Irish women's team.

The progress of the team could have been put on fast forward. Upon the elevation of the women to varsity status, Notre Dame received an invitation to an eight-team tournament hosted by Brown University. Most of the other seven invitees were playing at a higher level of competition than the 1977-78 Irish. Participation in this tourney might have helped the program, but finances and finals—immovable barriers both—made Notre Dame officials decline the offer.

But back in the real world, the five-game streak came to an abrupt end at Marquette by a 66-41 score, perhaps an indication of how the Irish might have fared in Providence. The only other loss in the regular season came at the hands of Northern Illinois, 65-58. Those two squads were the only non-Indiana schools Notre Dame played in 1977-78.

Inside the state, the Irish defeated all comers—Saint Mary's twice, both times by a 10-point margin, Manchester by 25, Indiana Tech by 17, and two schools which had defeated the women the year before, Goshen by five at Goshen, and Marion by 12, the latter a 40-point turnaround in one year. All of the regulars made significant contributions in the victories, especially Jane Politiski. In the last five regular-season games she rebounded like a magnet, averaging an incredible 19.4 rebounds per game during that stretch, including a high of 22 against Goshen, still the Irish women's record for one game. She also scored 22 points in the same game and 20 against Tech while Carol Lally was injured. And after that layoff, Carol returned with a vengeance with 23 in the second St. Mary's game.

Notre Dame finished the regular season 11-2, but it meant little except to show that the team was pretty good. One of the features of the AIAW (Association of Intercollegiate Athletics for Women) playoffs was that every member institution was included. The Irish, however, certainly played up to their record in the Indiana Small College North District playoffs, as they easily won the district title over Huntington (65-52) and St. Francis (61-45), earning a trip to the state playoffs. But back-to-back losses, to Vincennes (73-69) and St. Joseph's (65-64), whom the Irish had defeated by 12 earlier in the season, sent Notre Dame home with a disappointing fourth-place state finish. It was disappointing only in comparison to the record entering the tourney, but not so considering that it was the first season of varsity competition for the Irish.

Of the top seven players in 1977-78, only Marge Meagher

was lost to graduation for 1978-79, and three able freshmen came out for the team and made important contributions to the Irish second varsity year effort: Trish McManus, a 5-11 center/forward whose presence would become essential later in the season; Missy Conboy, a 5-8 forward who spelled Carol Lally and Pat Meyer; and Jan Schlaff, a 5-5 guard whose contributions were limited by late-season injuries which probably aided in making her freshman year her only year as a varsity athlete. With a tougher schedule which included some scholarship-giving institutions and two tournaments, the Irish finished with a strong 16-6 mark.

Carol Lally, now a senior, showed she was going to continue where she had left off the year before, as the team's high scorer put in 25 in an 81-51 defeat of Clarke. That began a string of 10 consecutive games in which she scored at least ten points. During that skein, the Irish went 8-2, losing only to Big Ten teams on the road (Illinois and Michigan). Included in that streak were the women's first two tournament appearances.

The December 9th Huntington, Indiana tournament was first; the Irish defeated Valparaiso (for the second time in eight days; ND had won by 18 at Valpo) and host Huntington to take home the trophy. And before the rest of campus had returned from the holidays, Notre Dame defeated Upper Iowa, host Northern Illinois, and Chicago State to win the Huskie Invitational.

It was about this time that the team received a blow. Kelly Hicks broke her ankle and was sidelined the rest of the season. Fortunately, the play of her replacement, Trish McManus, was impressive. Despite not playing much before Hicks' injury, she finished fourth on the team in scoring and third in rebounds, occasionally leading the team in those categories in individual games.

The scoring string of Carol Lally finally ended in the third game against Valparaiso, this one at Notre Dame. The Valpo defense keyed on her, holding her to four points, but Jane Politiski scored 13 and pulled down 12 boards to lead the Irish to their third win of the year over the Crusaders. Including that game, Notre Dame continued to roll after the start of the second semester, going 5-1, the one loss against another higher-level team, DePaul. The highlight of that stretch was ND's first-ever win over Marquette. The senior Lally canned 23 points as the Irish defeated Tat Shiely's squad, 60-57.

After closing the season with a closer-than-expected 68-64 win over Goshen, the women hit the road and ended the season on a down note by losing to both St. Joseph's and Marion. In the latter game, Politiski broke Carol Lally's one-game scoring record with 29, and came within one of breaking her own record in rebounds, but to no avail. Marion won 65-63, on a 20-foot shot with three seconds left. These were the first times in two years that ND had lost to Indiana schools during the regular season.

As the women entered the district playoffs, they had to contend with—guess who?—Valparaiso, for the *fourth* time. Again the Crusaders held Carol Lally to fewer points than her 13-per-game average—six, to be exact. And again Politiski took up the slack with 13 points and 15 rebounds. And again the Irish won, but by only three, 52-49.

The next night against Saint Mary's—for the third time this season—was no easier. The Irish led only 25-24 at the half thanks to a SMC full-court press. But ND started the second half by outscoring Saint Mary's, 13-2; they coasted the rest of the way, which put Notre Dame into the district finals for the second straight year. But it was against St. Joseph's, on the Pumas' home court, where the Irish had lost just 10 days earlier.

This time, things were to be different.

In the women's first-ever overtime game, Maggie Lally stole the ball from the Pumas, who were holding the ball in the extra stanza with a one-point lead and 10 seconds to play. She drove to the basket, put up a left-handed layup, and missed. But Carola Cummings, a seldom-used player in the game only because Pat Meyer and co-captain Molly Cashman had fouled out, came down with the rebound and put it in. The Irish had their second straight North District championship, 70-69.

For the second straight year, the women lost their first-round game in the state tourney. This time Franklin was the culprit, aided greatly by cold shooting from the Irish. Notre Dame shot 31 percent from the floor and 48 percent from the line; Franklin won, 69-64, to end the Irish season prematurely.

Sharon Petro began her third season at the helm with—again—a great deal of talent. She had lost Carol Lally and Pat

Meyer to graduation, but she had a healthy Kelly Hicks and the usual crop of newcomers, among them Sheila Liebscher, a junior trying out for the varsity for the first time, who occasionally started at guard instead of Maggie Lally or Molly Cashman, and Jan Crowe, a 5-11 freshman forward/center. And then there was Shari Matvey.

Matvey, a 6-1 center, had been an all-state selection for two straight years at Austintown Fitch High School near Youngstown, Ohio, and had been offered basketball scholarships by several schools. Instead, she chose to come to Notre Dame, which did not award grants-in-aid to female athletes. She felt the education she would get toward a future medical career was worth turning down an athletic scholarship at another school. And for that the basketball record book will likely never be the same.

During the 1979-80 season, Matvey broke the one-game scoring record, the season record, and numerous other records for field goals, rebounds, and blocked shots. In fact, her 529 points that year is more than any other freshman, male or female, has scored in a Notre Dame varsity uniform. She also became Notre Dame's first winner of post-season accolades, as she was named to the Division III all-Region V (Midwest) squad.

She started right off in her first varsity contest; coming off the bench, she scored 21 points, snared 14 rebounds, and blocked six shots as the much-taller-than-in-the-past Irish (six players listed at 5-10 or above) defeated Marion in the first round of the Taylor (University) Invitational. They then won the crown by defeating Cedarville (OH) in the finals. After Notre Dame polished off Saint Mary's for the eighth straight time since 1976, the women took on their first Division I opponent of the year, Michigan. The Division III Irish nearly pulled off an upset, but the Wolverines won it in overtime, 66-60.

Several things happened at the Huskie Invitational, where the Irish were defending their championship. First and foremost, they didn't repeat, losing to Northwest Missouri State 77-43 in the finals. Second, Shari Matvey continued her scoring leadership, as she tallied 31 points—an Irish record—against Chicago State and was named to the all-tournament team. Third, Jane Politiski injured an ankle and was forced to miss six games, yet the Irish depth managed to make her absence less noticeable.

After she was able to play again, she served as an off-the-bench sparkplug until she was 100 percent again.

The rest of the regular season was excruciating at times for Petro and her assistant, Bob Scott. While Matvey continued to score and score and rebound and rebound and block one shot after another, and Politiski and Trish McManus added their own scoring punch, as a whole this team seemed to lack a certain killer instinct, and often let teams come from way behind to make matters interesting, sometimes *too* interesting. A few examples:

—Against St. Joseph's, the Irish led 55-33 with 12:25 left in the game. After a few problems showed themselves, not the least of which was that three starters fouled out, the women had won by only eight, 72-64.

—The very next game, against St. Ambrose, they had to come from way behind a weaker team, and then hold on for a two-point victory.

—Versus Mount St. Joseph (OH), again the team had to come from behind, but almost blew it. The Irish led 75-63 with 2:10 left. A comfortable margin, right? Wrong. Notre Dame won 78-76 as Matvey tied her three-week-old scoring record with 31 essential points.

—Then there was the ultimate fold against Marion, which the Irish had already beaten once in 1979-80. With 10 minutes left, the women led 59-40; they were still up 61-44 with 7:42 remaining. After that, well . . . for all intents and purposes, the Titans were playing basketball five-on-zero. As an invisible lid draped over the Irish basket, the Marion five slowly whittled away the ND lead. Finally, with two seconds left, Marion's Monica Brown fired a jumper which marked the 17th and 18th consecutive points for MC and put the Titans up for the only time in the game—when it counted, at the final buzzer. 62-61.

The Irish entered the "second season" with a 14-7 record, not quite up to prior standards; most of the losses, however, were to higher-caliber competition. The women, seeded first in the north district of Indiana, won their sectional for the third straight year, despite—you guessed it—late-game rallies by both Grace and Goshen.

Disappointment had greeted Sharon Petro's squad in the state playoffs each of the last two seasons, but not this time. Notre

Dame first got past Huntington, 52-46, and found itself in the final game for the first time—against Goshen, the same team the Irish had defeated one week earlier. This time, on the Angela Athletic Facility floor at Saint Mary's College, the women won convincingly, 80-66, as Jane Politiski had 24 and Shari Matvey 20.

For the first time, Notre Dame found itself in the AIAW Division III Region V (Midwest) playoffs. In the first-round game, the Irish pulled a stunning upset by defeating seventh-ranked Greenville, the Illinois state champion, 55-51. Then two tough losses, to Adrian and Spring Arbor, presumably ended the Irish season with a fourth-place finish in Region V.

It wasn't to be, as the women's impressive performance in a very tough regional earned them an at-large bid to the 24-team AIAW Nationals. In the first game, against Region VIII runner-up Pacific Lutheran, the Irish reversed their usual trend; they came on in the second half to win going away, 57-48, as Matvey scored 25 of her 30 points in the latter stanza. This win was a landmark in the short history of the women's team, for it was its 20th of the season, the first time the women's basketball team, had accomplished this milestone. However, it was to be the last, as fifth-ranked Wisconsin-LaCrosse outclassed the Irish, 80-57, in the next round. It was the end of their season, but this team had much to be proud of—they finished as one of the top 16 Division III teams in the country, they had gone 20-10 against some tough competition, and their season had lasted longer than their male counterparts'!

But some changes were in the works behind the scenes. While the 1979-80 women's team was breaking records and going farther than anyone could have expected, the University—finally—was preparing to end its long feud with Washington and comply with the controversial Title IX of the Education Amendments of 1972 (tacked onto the landmark Civil Rights Act of 1965), which prohibits sex discrimination in education—and, by extension, the athletic programs in any school receiving federal funds. One of the moves was to immediately elevate the women's basketball program from Division III (unsubsidized) to Division I (for all intents and purposes, fully subsidized) and appoint Digger Phelps as "coordinator of varsity basketball," a move which essentially put both programs under the same umbrella. The first priority was to decide who would coach Notre Dame into the Big Time.

Fifty people applied for the job, and four were interviewed: Sharon Petro, and the head coaches of Penn, Northwestern, and Rutgers. And to the surprise of almost all outsiders, the winner was from the same school which had contributed Ara Parseghian to Notre Dame football—Mary DiStanislao, the head coach of Northwestern University.

DiStanislao had impeccable credentials: she had built a Division I program basically from scratch in Evanston, including back-to-back trips to the final eight of the nationals, at a school with the same emphasis on academics as Notre Dame. For Petro, it marked the end of her association with basketball, but not with the University. She became women's tennis coach and is leading the Irish toward national prominence in that sport. But for the returning basketball players new challenges under a new coach were ahead.

# 25

## Moving with Mary D

Mary DiStanislao was named coach in April 1980. Unfortunately, the first date for recruits to sign letters of intent was a month past, which meant most of the blue-chippers had already been nabbed. Yet before the start of the 1980-81 season, she had inked two players to the first athletic grants-in-aid given to Notre Dame women. As it turned out, neither made significant contributions as players after the first year.

The first of those signed was Jenny Klauke, an all-state performer from Glenview, Illinois; the other, Mary Joan Forbes, was North Carolina Division 4-A Player of the Year as a high school senior. Both, however, were plagued by injuries, and Forbes' knee problems were serious enough to end her basketball career after severely limited action as a freshman. But despite a pre-season stress fracture in her foot (a problem which would recur throughout the next three years), Klauke at times was very impressive her freshman year.

Joining the two scholarship freshman were four freshman walk-ons and a sophomore who saw extensive action in this transitional season—Theresa Mullins, Kara O'Malley, Molly Ryan, Theresa Smith, and Debbi Hensley—along with six returning members of the top-16 Division III squad of the season past: high-scoring Shari Matvey, co-captain guards Maggie Lally and Sheila Liebscher, and forwards Missy Conboy, Trish McManus, and Jan Crowe. Could this team of rookies and women with little experience against Division I competition be molded into a successful patterned offense and hard-nosed defense, as "Mary D" would emphasize, and take on the world?

Well . . . not exactly.

Had the 1980-81 squad played a Division II schedule, a winning season probably would have resulted. But the schedule consisted of an abundance of fairly good Division I opponents, and as a consequence, the first partially subsidized Irish women's team went 10-18.

The first game of the new era was at home against South Dakota. A curious crowd of over 1,000 showed up at the ACC and saw the Irish lead at halftime only to fall, 67-60. Butler, a strong Division II squad, made the women 0-2 nine days later via a 60-51 score, a game in which the Irish again led at the half but shot poorly in the second 20 minutes.

After that, the women hovered around .500 for awhile. Impressive victories over Concordia and Saint Mary's were followed by a loss to St. Francis of Joliet, Illinois (a Division II school). A trip to the Penn Holiday Tournament resulted in a second-place finish after an upset of Iona and a loss to Delaware; and an utter annihilation of Davidson at Charlotte (85-37) followed by a loss at Villanova in which the Irish looked good (70-57) and one to Marquette in which they didn't (62-55) made a 4-6 record at the end of the Christmas holidays.

Easily the best player on the squad as of that time was Jan Crowe, who seemed the epitome of the type of player Mary D wanted on her front line. After the first 10 games, Crowe led the team in scoring and rebounds and was a stalwart on defense, often playing opponents several inches taller than her 5-11 and doing well. The high point of this was in the Concordia game: while she led the team with 27 points and 11 rebounds, she held the 6-2 opposing center scoreless and forced her out on fouls with over 10 minutes left. Maggie Lally and Sheila Liebscher provided much-needed leadership in the backcourt, and the freshman walkons, particularly Molly Ryan and Kara O'Malley, also made significant contributions.

Unfortunately for the immediate future of the squad, Crowe ended up on the academic probation list, which meant that two players who had been disappointing to DiStanislao would have to become less so. In the first 10 games Shari Matvey had been scoring almost as often as Crowe, but her defense left much to be desired in the coach's eyes; and Jenny Klauke at guard had been trying to do too much too soon. Both had found themselves benched frequently as a result.

Both began to play with confidence in the next eight games as the Irish evened their record at 9-9. Five times in eight games Matvey scored at least 20, including 29 in a losing effort against Illinois-Chicago Circle and 25 in another win over Saint Mary's. She also provided a spark against St. Ambrose, as every time the Queen Bees tried to come back, Matvey would go in for two and keep the Irish ahead. As for Klauke, she scored 22 in an 86-44 romp over Goshen as she finally began to show some of the offensive potential for which she had been recruited.

Although Notre Dame's record was 9-9, it was a misleading .500; the Irish still had some distance to go before becoming competitive in Division I. Nothing could illustrate this better than ND's ninth loss, to nationally-ranked South Carolina. Lally literally could not see over the woman assigned to guard her, which effectively stalled the Irish offense; and of the Gamecocks' eight traveling-squad members, six were 5-10 or taller, including a 6-6 freshman. Since ND's tallest woman was 6-1, it didn't take long for South Carolina to shoot over the defense. They did so early and often, and the result was a 124-48 pummelling, the worst defeat ever of a Notre Dame women's basketball team.

The most difficult part of the season—the last six regular-season games, all against quality opposition and five consecutive on the road—ended in an 0-6 ledger as the women tried unsuccessfully to give Mary D her 100th career victory as a head coach. The highlight of these games was the inspired play of Jenny Klauke. Against Ball State on February 11, she put on a display reminiscent of Austin Carr; she put in 27 points—*all in the second half*—but the Irish lost 79-61. She put in another 24 against Michigan and 20 against 16th-ranked Virginia at the Rosemont Horizon to avoid destruction by superior teams.

After the regular season ended with an 88-53 loss to Illinois, it was off to the state playoffs and a rematch against Ball State. And this time the Irish did everything right. Matvey, Klauke, and Molly Ryan scored in double figures; Trish McManus pulled down 13 rebounds despite a severe cold; Missy Conboy stole the ball three times and scored six second-half points; and Notre

Dame turned the ball over but 13 times in the entire game. The one thing they couldn't do was win, as Ball State shot 65 percent from the floor in the second half, mostly from top-of-the-key range, in its 76-69 win, ruining what had been ND's best performance against a Division I team all year.

This interminably long season (or so it seemed) finally ended in, of all places, Alaska, as the Irish, subsidized by Alaska's state government, traveled to Anchorage—the first ND team in any sport to visit the 49th state—while most of the rest of the campus was 5,000 miles away in Florida for spring break. While there, ND participated in the Northern Lights Tournament and finished fourth, defeating host Alaska-Anchorage (for Mary D's 100th win, finally) by one, 59-58, before losing to San Diego State and Hawaii.

Matvey again finished the season as high scorer and rebounder, followed by Klauke in the former and McManus in the latter category. Both Matvey and Lally received accolades as second-team academic All-Americans, Lally for the second straight year. Maggie, one of two graduating seniors from the 1980-81 squad, was the last player left from the first varsity team, and her departure marked the end of an era. Women's basketball no longer would be just a game but a full-time commitment; it would take an intense love of the game to sacrifice most other facets of college life for six months without the benefit of a scholarship.

Few became willing to do so. Of the four freshman walk-ons on the 1980-81 team, only Theresa Mullins returned. Trish McManus also decided to end her varsity career even though she had a year remaining. Overall, only six women of the 14 on the 1980-81 team came back for more. Those coming in, however, would more than compensate.

DiStanislao made up for a next-to-nonexistent recruiting year in 1980 by having an extraordinary one in 1981. Five blue-chippers from all over the nation made immediate contributions to the team. Part of the lure to Notre Dame was the potential to do just that—and the results made ND one of the surprise women's basketball teams in the country in 1981-82.

Had it not been for five straight losses at the end of the season—three of which the Irish could have won—the Irish probably would have arrived in the NCAA tournament in the first year of women's competition in that organization. (The AIAW also had a national tourney in 1981-82, but the exodus into the other group was so great that this women's group was defunct in 1982-83.) As it was, the freshman-dominated squad finished with a fine 16-9 record, and in the process Mary D received a nomination for the annual Stayfree Coach of the Year Award, for which she had been nominated twice while at Northwestern.

She earned the nomination by molding her "finds" — center/forwards Mary Beth Schueth and Carrie Bates, forward Ruth Kaiser, and guards Laura Dougherty and Susan Neville — with returning sophomore Mullins and juniors Debbi Hensley and Shari Matvey into a tough defensive unit which finished third in the nation in scoring defense, giving up but 55.1 points per game, including 10 times when the Irish held opponents to 50 points or less. At the same time, they were molded into a patient offense — as patient as the 30-second clock which is a part of women's basketball will allow — in search of the high-percentage shot. They found it often enough to finish 10th in the nation in field goal percentage (.494). That combination of offense and defense, more than any individual star, tells the story of the 1981-82 Irish.

They started out the year 4-3, beginning with a 78-44 shellacking of St. Joseph's of Indiana, a 54-point turnaround from last season's 20-point loss. Kaiser had 22 and Bates 17 in their debut college games; Matvey added 18. Two days later, the young Irish faced their initial challenge of the season against highly-regarded UCLA. Coming into the game the Bruins had scored over 80 points a contest, but the tough Irish defense held them to only 50. Unfortunately, ND could muster but 45 — but the closeness of this game was somewhat of an upset. Obviously this team had made some progress already toward becoming a factor in Division I.

As if to prove it, Notre Dame promptly went out and beat up on next-door neighbor Saint Mary's by the most lopsided victory margin in Irish women's hoops history. Every healthy player saw action as the Belles were rung, 92-29, in the last meeting between the two schools. (Unless Saint Mary's elevates its program above Division III or Notre Dame demotes its, they'll prob-

ably never meet again.) But two days later, the Irish lost to a
Division II team, albeit one that finished with a 23-3 record—
Butler, 67-58. Over two months would pass until Notre Dame
gave up so many points in a game again.

The surge which vaulted the Irish to the top of the NCAA
defensive stats began in the first ND women's game to be televised live, by the Chicago-area cable station Sportschannel. After
the ND men had lost to Northern Illinois, the TV people stuck
around and beamed the women's 67-52 win over NIU to north-
eastern Illinois. Schueth began a string of eight consecutive
double-digit scoring efforts with 13; three other freshmen also
ended in double figures (Bates, Kaiser, and Dougherty). Then
it was off to the Palestra for a return trip to the Penn Holiday
Tournament, and for the second straight year ND finished second, defeating the host in the opener and losing to Mt. St. Mary's
of Maryland in the finals.

The beginning of 1982 was the beginning of the impressive
play which led to DiStanislao's Coach of the Year nomination,
as her team won 10 consecutive games and went 12-1 over the
next month and a half. What made this more impressive was
that many of the opponents were of Division I caliber. And what
better way to open the new year than with a major upset?

That's just what the Irish pulled off, as Missouri, which concluded the season in the Top 20, fell 60-53 in Kansas City's
Kemper Arena. Bates, Kaiser, and Schueth scored 12 each, and
Matvey scored 11 to become Notre Dame's first female 1,000-point
scorer for a career. A week later, the women again opened some
eyes around the nation by easily winning the Dial Classic in
Minneapolis—Creighton fell, 69-48, and Marquette went down
in the finals, 50-36. Schueth was named the tourney's MVP; as
for the team, it was its first defeat of Marquette since February
3, 1979.

Following a sluggish performance against St. Francis of Joliet, in which the women had to come from behind against an
inferior team, Notre Dame upped its win streak to a school-
record-tying seven with relatively easy wins against Southern
Methodist (76-60), Valparaiso (84-27, 24 by Matvey), and Michigan (71-48, the first time the women's varsity had defeated a Big

Ten team). Had not St. Ambrose been forced to cancel a game because of the omnipresent Indiana snows, the streak might have hit eight earlier than it did.

On January 28, the streak did hit eight as the Irish nosed out old nemesis Ball State to avenge two losses in 1980-81, 60-57. This time, the freshman recruit who had seen the least action made the biggest overall contribution. Susan Neville put in 11 points, seven in the second half, while also snaring four rebounds and dishing out as many assists; as importantly, she made a key steal with time ticking away and the Irish clinging to a two-point lead. Her free throw which resulted from a BSU foul clinched the win.

Game 9 in the streak was an easier-than-the-final score-indicated 60-43 defeat of Marquette in a rematch of the Dial Classic championship, and the 10th win was in Cincinnati against Mount St. Joseph, 70-54, in which Jenny Klauke, who had seen little action because of another pre-season stress fracture, had her best game of the season with 14 points, four rebounds and a steal in 23 minutes.

The next night, at Miami of Ohio, the streak ended. The Irish led by eight late in the first half, but the Redskins outscored them 23-8 over the next 13 minutes and the Irish were unable to catch up, losing 65-61. Upon returning home, a new streak was begun: Taylor and Cincinnati were added to the Irish victim list. At this point the Irish were 16-4, and talk of a post-season tournament bid began to circulate.

As it turned out, that's all it was—talk.

Notre Dame lost its last five contests of the year, starting with two road losses to tough opposition—Illinois (83-53) and South Carolina (76-54). So much for the national lead in scoring defense which the Irish had held for several weeks. They could take some, but not much, solace in their improved showing with the Gamecocks; a 76-point deficit had been reduced to 22 in only one year. But three home games remained, and while tourney talk had hushed, it was not completely silenced.

Three straight home losses did just that, all of which the Irish could, or even should, have won. Mary Beth Schueth's 28-point performance was wasted, as was a comeback from a 13-point deficit to tie Nebraska after 40 minutes; the Irish blew

a five-point lead in the first overtime and finally lost in the second, 98-88. Two days later, DePaul was the spoiler. Notre Dame
led by three with four minutes left but mistakes down the stretch
ruined what had been a fine Irish performance, and the Lady
Demons escaped with a 60-55 win. And finally, another unreal
game from Schueth (29 points and 11 rebounds while playing
all 40 minutes) and a rare start by team captain and lone senior
Missy Conboy in her final game went for naught, as Michigan
State sent ND to its fifth straight downfall, 68-59. Despite the
end-of-season folding act (for the second straight year), one could
only be hopeful of continued progress, as only one senior was
graduating and four more top-notch freshmen were augmenting
the already-existing talent.

An even more ambitious schedule, including both the NCAA
and AIAW national champions, greeted the women cagers in
1982-83. The end result was an even better record of 20-7, including an 8-1 skein at the end of the season—a complete turnaround
from the slumps which had plagued DiStanislao's first two teams.
Despite the record, the Irish stayed home at tournament time,
and there was a simple reason: Notre Dame was unable to defeat
any of its Top 20 opponents. Of the seven losses, six were at
the hands of teams ranked when ND faced them.

The first two of those teams were UCLA and Rutgers, the
Irish opponents in the inaugural Orange Crush Classic. Played
in the Rosemont Horizon in suburban Chicago, it was the first
tourney to feature both men's and women's squads. In the opening round, Notre Dame lost to a quite different Bruin team from
the one the Irish nearly upset a year earlier; UCLA found it could
play run-and-gun against them this time, and won 82-54. The
next night's consolation game was the closest the women came
to upsetting a top opponent. Two freshmen played key roles in
the halftime tie between ND and Rutgers—Trena Keys, a 6-1 forward who had been Indiana's "Miss Basketball" in 1982, who
started and went 4-of-4 from the floor until her ankle was stepped
on by a Rutgers player late in the half, and Lynn Ebben, a 5-11
guard/forward who led the team at the end with 21 points. But
the loss of Keys marked the end of the upset bid over the AIAW
national champion; ND lost 81-74. The loss tied a record, as it
was the seventh in a row over two years.

Right after that, the women came within one of tying the opposite record, as they rattled off nine straight wins against the "weaker" part of their schedule. Some of the highlights included the first ND wins over Butler and Miami of Ohio. A small but vocal "sixth man"—part of which originally stationed itself behind the Miami bench until asked to move—aided the Irish in the latter contest, as they came from behind late in the contest to knock off the team which had ended 1981-82's long winning streak. Also, a St. Francis team which had lost to ND by only four a year past lost by 44 this time around, an indication of improvement over the year; later, though, the Irish played two inferior teams unnecessarily close on the road (Western Michigan went down by six, Michigan by four). And by defeating East Carolina on December 30, Notre Dame won its 100th women's basketball game.

The best game of the streak may have been the ninth, when ND defeated Georgetown by 10 at Washington, DC, although the Irish did lead by 21 late in the game. Another significant road win was over Villanova (72-68) at the Villanova Fieldhouse, only the seventh Wildcat home loss in five years.

A loss to a ranked team marked the end of the string. Maryland, which entered the game unbeaten, left it the same way. Eventually they were able to take advantage of offensive rebounds, and Notre Dame was doomed, 84-62. Again the big win had eluded the Irish.

After a defeat of the only Division III team on the schedule (Augustana, 87-66, in which Carrie Bates scored an Irish season-high 24 points), the Alabama women rolled into the ACC and rolled out with a win, the only unranked team to defeat ND all season. The Crimson Tide contest, witnessed by the largest crowd to see an Irish women's basketball game, was one of three games included in the men's basketball season-ticket package. The 1,575 there went home disappointed, however. Notre Dame couldn't buy baskets at crucial moments and failed to take advantage of its depth; the Tide finished on top, 71-56, and thus became the first Alabama team in any sport to defeat the Irish.

ND used hot shooting to defeat Detroit next, and then utilized mass substitution to turn a contest against Illinois-Chicago into a rout. Mary D inserted her "White Team"—Carrie Bates,

Trena Keys, Lynn Ebben, Denise Basford, and Jenny Klauke—
to spell the starting "Blue Team" with the Irish up only 15-11.
When they finally were relieved, Notre Dame led 40-18 and
coasted from there to an 88-61 victory, the high offensive output of the season.

Again the Irish tried to defeat a ranked opponent, this time
on a road trip to Arizona State (in Tempe, Ruth Kaiser's hometown) and UCLA. And *again* they were embarrassed twice.
Arizona State used the all-around play of 5-6 Cassandra Lander,
whose 24 points, 13 rebounds, six steals and four assists almost
singlehandedly defeated the Irish. Cold shooting at inopportune
times, a lack of rebounding, and a career-low two points for Mary
Beth Schueth didn't help matters any in ASU's 82-57 win. And
things weren't much better against the Bruins in a Crush Classic
rematch. As had happened in late November, the Irish, unable
to control the tempo, were forced into a running game, and
UCLA's nine-point halftime lead became a rout, 84-53. The four-
day road trip which must have seemed like four weeks was the
low point of the season.

But the rest of the way, Notre Dame went 8-1 in a frantic
late-season attempt to secure a bid to either the NCAA championships or the National Women's Invitational Tournament. In
the process, ND defeated two conference champions, played
some clutch basketball by pulling games out with little time left,
and held teams to their lowest point totals of the season.

First, however, the women showed some offensive punch
by taking out their West Coast frustrations on Loyola of Illinois.
Aided by Shari Matvey's 12 points in the first 11 minutes, the
Irish held off the Ramblers 80-61. And the Irish put together a
balanced scoring attack (Schueth and Kaiser had 14, Keys and
Laura Dougherty had 13) to defeat Iowa State, 69-58. The two-
game winning streak abruptly ended the next Friday night, but
nearly everyone expected it.

In the second most hyped sporting event at Notre Dame
in 1982-83 (only the Michigan night football game was more
played up), the Irish took on two-time defending national champion and number-one ranked Louisiana Tech in the ACC. In front
of by far the largest crowd for women's hoops in Notre Dame
history (over 3,500), and an extremely enthusiastic one at that,

Tech took some time getting its offense in gear without its all-American guard Kim Mulkey, who did not suit up because of illness. At the half, the Irish were closer than anyone could have expected, trailing the Lady Techsters by 14, 31-17. But 13 straight points to open the second half ended any hopes for a major upset and took the vociferous "sixth man" out of the game once and for all. LTU ended up rolling, 81-39, as one major Irish weakness – the lack of a tall center to clog the middle – showed to a fault. Again the Irish had failed in its efforts at upsetting a ranked team.

After that setback, the march toward a bid continued. At Bradley, the Irish played, in DiStanislao's words, "Swiss cheese" defense for most of the first half as the Braves rolled up a 39-21 advantage and appeared on the verge of an upset. But Laura Dougherty signlehandedly, through points and assists, cut the deficit to 10 at the half. Then the Irish defense held the potent Bradley offense (86 points per game) to 18 points in the *entire* second half while the offense caught up and pulled ahead; ND eventually won, 68-57. The next night, against Gateway Conference leader Illinois State, the Irish fell behind 41-32 midway through the second half, but frantically managed to close to within three, 47-44, with :44 remaining. Then it was Dougherty's turn again: first she hit two free throws, then, surrounded by three ISU players, hit a miracle jumper which bounced on the rim three times before finally going through the hoop with nine seconds left. For the first time all season ND had defeated someone it wasn't suppposed to beat, 48-47, and in the process held ISU to its lowest point total of the season (as had been done against Bradley).

Marquette and an unexpectedly stubborn DePaul squad were the next victims. The win over the Warriors was Notre Dame's first-ever at MU, and the DePaul game was their first win at the Rosemont Horizon. And Mary D's Traveling Salvation Show returned home to close the regular season in two of the most exciting games played in the ACC in the 1980s.

Strong Division II-level Dayton and the Irish took alternating big leads, only to have the opponent catch up and pass. But with 41 seconds left, the Flyers took a one-point lead, and with :08 on the clock, the Irish set up a potential game-winning play only to have a pass stolen by Debra Yingling. Had she made both ends of the two-shot intentional foul which resulted, the game would have been over. Only one went in, however, which set the stage for DiStanislao's answer to Dwight Clay again. Dougherty put up a 12-footer while surrounded by three players (sound familiar?) . . . and it swished through as the buzzer sounded. The resulting overtime period was anticlimactic, as the Irish had the momentum and never lost it. The final was 68-64.

Coming off the first overtime win for an ND women's team since 1979, the Irish found themselves in another OT thriller against Indiana. Again a miracle play was needed to take the game there, but this time it was a Ruth Kaiser inbounds pass to Carrie Bates, who muscled in for the layup with two seconds left in regulation. Then Kaiser took control in the extra stanza, and the women had done it again, defeating the eventual Big Ten champs, 63-61. Now it was sit and wait time for some sort of post-season bid with a 20-7 record.

Saturday, March 12 – Bid Day – came and went, and the phone never rang. Neither the NCAA nor the NWIT – the latter to which the Irish supposedly had a bid in the bag the week before invitation day if the NCAA didn't want them, and which was roundly criticized for some of the suspect teams it *did* take – was interested. The women's fine season came to a crashing halt on the same day as the Old Fieldhouse came to a similar end after a 15-year reprieve. But the Irish women's basketball team had tasted some success in Division I, and had built a program to be reckoned with in the future.

# 26

---

## Oops!

The past two seasons had been little steps forward for the women's basketball program. The 1983-84 season, however, proved to be, at least, a little step in the wrong direction.

Hopes were high for continued improvement; only two players had graduated, and three good recruits had come in to replace them. Also, after the non-bid one year earlier, Notre Dame had joined a new women's sports league, the North Star Conference, with seven other schools (Butler, Dayton, DePaul, Detroit, Evansville, Loyola, and Xavier), with the hope of eventually securing an automatic bid to the NCAA tournament for the conference winner. There are much fewer at-large spots available in the women's tourney than in the men's, and there is currently a perception that women's college basketball in the Midwest is somehow inferior to that in most other parts of the country, so teams from there stay home—even with good records and tough schedules—unless they win a conference. Opinion from insiders on the league was generally favorable; it was seen as a necessary step to take for the women to have a real shot at a bid. Others saw the joining of a conference as a step down for the young program on the road to national respectability.

But the 1983-84 team stepped down in national respect all by itself.

When the last second had elapsed from the last half of the last game, the women had finished with an extremely disappointing 14-14 record—and only a 6-4 record in the conference, good for a second-place tie with Detroit. (Loyola won with a 9-1 ledger.) What made things worse was that not only did this team have much talent on paper, but at times it looked like a world-beater. But when the women were bad, they were awful.

The big highlights of the season came exactly three months apart. On December 3, the Irish, still with high hopes for the season ahead, defeated a "name" team for the first time in almost two years; they played a great overall game in topping UCLA, 70-61. On March 3, the season a bitter disappointment, the women went into Dayton Arena a decided underdog against Dayton, the top-ranked team in Division II and preparing for a move to Division I in 1984-85. But, behind strong performances by Mary Beth Schueth and Trena Keys, among others, Notre Dame pulled the upset, 63-57.

So what happened in between?

Well, start a week before the UCLA game with the Notre Dame Classic, the first college basketball tournament to be held at the University during the season. This was the re-named and moved Orange Crush Classic, revised after the corporate sponsor pulled out. The tournament nearly bit the dust until Mary DiStanislao and athletic director Gene Corrigan stepped in to keep the great field—Maryland, Tennessee, and defending national champion Southern California, along with ND—intact. Few expected the Irish to have a chance, and they didn't; they finished fourth. But the performance varied. They actually looked good against Tennessee, but the Lady Vols were too good and won, 71-56. But in the consolation against Maryland, they played like losers and lost by 18. DiStanislao spent all season trying to find out which team was the *real* 1983-84 Irish, but as the record shows, she never really found out.

The women generally played well against the big-name teams. As mentioned, they beat UCLA and Dayton; and they also knocked off Villanova, 85-79, to start a 6-2 surge in the last eight games to salvage the .500 season. And while they couldn't defeat any of the three teams on the schedule which finished in the top 10 on the Division I poll, they did close the gap: in addition to the decent showing against Tennessee, the women lost to Old Dominion by 71-57, and to Louisiana Tech in Ruston, 83-56, the latter an improvement over the 81-39 loss at LTU's hands at ND one year earlier. In the Tech game, Laura Dougherty had a fine individual game with 23 points, the high mark for anyone on the team all season.

However, the 1983-84 squad couldn't win the close ones, and that was its downfall. In games decided by less than five points, Notre Dame was 0-7. (Compare that to 1982-83, when the Irish were 7-0 in the same category.) And all seven of those were against teams in the same or a slightly lower level as ND. In those seven contests, the team was plagued by inconsistency, disorganization, and the lack of a real floor leader to take charge when the occasion merited it.

The first of these close ones was against Northwestern in DiStanislao's first visit to Evanston as ND coach since she left the Wildcats' coaching job in 1980. And the Wildcats, fresh off a double-overtime loss to eventual national champion USC, dumped the Irish, 78-74. And two weeks later—after less-than-inspired wins against Michigan and Western Michigan—an unheralded but good Central Michigan team (Mid-American Conference champions-to-be) topped ND, 72-69.

Then, after the loss to Old Dominion in the first round of the Nike Christmas Classic, the team played poorly against host Boston College in the consolation and lost another nail-biter, 59-55. Two convincing wins (East Carolina and Xavier) followed, and then the loss to Tech mentioned earlier.

Easily the nadir of the season was a three-game stretch after the loss to the Lady Techsters (January 15-21) in which ND looked as bad as any time since Mary D's first season. The women lost a Sunday game to Southern Methodist by one, 64-63, and then three nights later dropped a 59-56 contest to Loyola, a league opponent, in a performance so lacklustre and disorganized that immediately after the game a frustrated DiStanislao had the team change into its practice clothes and return to the court for a post-game workout. Alas, it didn't help: on Saturday the demoralized team went to Alumni Hall to face an almost equally up-and-down DePaul team and were beaten horribly, 62-46, thanks to a 36-16 halftime deficit. Everyone, including seldom-used seniors and walk-ons, got into this one in a futile search for a working combination. The game was also noteworthy because Mary Beth Schueth, who had started 62 consecutive games going back to the sixth game of her freshman year, did not start—a result of her season-long slump to that time. The loss dropped ND to 6-10 and without a prayer for post-season play.

The women then came back to beat Evansville and then settle the score with the Lady Demons. Keys and Schueth keyed one of the better ND performances of the year, and the Irish had a 78-62 win, a 32-point turnaround in a little over a week. But the close-game bugaboo returned: ND lost to Michigan State, 73-72, and Illinois State, 61-59. Then came the strong game against Villanova and the 6-2 finish.

Along with the win over Villanova, the women defeated Illinois-Chicago, Detroit, Dayton, Xavier in the home finale, and Evansville in the overall finale. The last of those was the key, because that win finally evened their record after a second loss to Loyola (64-53) ruined any hope for a winning mark. And that one wasn't easy for much of the first half, until Jenny Klauke entered the game. In her last contest as a collegian, she scored 12 points and generally served as the spark to the Notre Dame win over the Aces, 80-68. The other loss was of the close nature again, at Detroit, 85-80.

But all was not lost. The 1983-84 team featured some strong individual performances by Schueth and Keys down the stretch, and both Carrie Bates and Laura Dougherty added good performances. Bates was the most consistent game-to-game performer; she quietly became a force in the front line, leading the team in scoring and free-throw percentage (finishing among the top 20 in the nation in the latter) and finishing second in field-goal accuracy. Dougherty actually led the nation—both men and women—in charity-stripe accuracy for several weeks in January while the rest of the team was fading; although slumping late in the season, she still finished with an excellent .821 mark.

Also important was the play of sophomores Lynn Ebben and Denise Basford and junior Ruth Kaiser, plus two of the three freshmen. Vonnie Thompson, a point guard, adapted well to the college game and started her first varsity contest, but—like nearly everyone else—faded in January before regaining a starting berth for the stretch run; and Lavetta Willis, whose aggressive play eventually earned her six starts and many trips to the foul line. In the MSU loss, she set a team record by going 10-for-10 from the line.

Overall, the team was extremely talented, but the nine front-liners only seldom coalesced into the working unit necessary for a successful year. In the case of the 1983-84 season, the whole was much less than the sum of its parts.

Making a whole of the parts in 1984-85 seemed like it would be no easier. There were 15 scholarship players to try and balance among five starting spots, and it took a while to find the right lineup. The team, at various points, was 1-3 and 5-6 and had already played itself out of any trip to postseason play, but once league play began the Irish were overwhelming. They proved the class of the North Star Conference, finishing 13-1; of the wins, only two were close, and their average winning margin was 21 points. With that performance some, especially Mary DiStanislao, began talking tournament, but the 20-8 Irish stayed home.

That lackluster performance out of the gate was the costliest in terms of acquiring a postseason bid. A season-opening 62-57 loss to Tennessee, the NCAA runnerup in 1983-84, at Tennessee was encouraging in its closeness and also in the play of two-fifths of an outstanding freshman class, 5-6 point guard Mary Gavin and 6-2 forward Sandy Botham. Both proved pleasant surprises as the year went on. A not-so-pleasant surprise, though, awaited ND in its home opener.

Purdue, a perennial Big Ten second-division resident, came back from a 15-point second-half deficit to defeat the Irish, 62-59. Spearheading the Boilermaker comeback was a freshman in whom Notre Dame showed shockingly little interest in recruiting, although she would have provided something the Irish have never had—a gate attraction. No further evidence is needed than the 1,445—the largest home crowd for the women all season—who showed up, most of whom wanted to see Sharon Versyp, 1984 Indiana "Miss Basketball" from nearby Mishawaka High School, in her college debut for Purdue. And when she almost singlehandedly led her team to victory in the final minutes, with eight points and a key assist during that time, the most pro-visitor crowd in arena history made its delight known; the Irish now found themselves essentially playing a road game at home. This loss as much as any of ND's eight probably cost the women the chance to continue the season beyond game 28. A road loss to another nearly-permanent resident of the Big Ten's lower echelon, Michigan, didn't help, either. Sandwiched between those two embarrassments was—finally—the team's first win, 70-59 over Eastern Michigan. Notre Dame's problem? Too many turnovers, a lack of production from the guards, and a rebounding deficit despite a sizable front line.

The women started to show signs of what was to come once the NSC schedule began with four straight romps, starting with a 76-46 rout of Western Michigan, a school which made the NCAA tournament because it won the Mid-American Conference. They continued with a 72-49 defeat of Georgetown, 71-60 at Northern Illinois, and 71-59 over previously unbeaten Michigan State, ND's first win over the Spartans in its 11-year women's basketball history. The key to the four wins was the play of seniors Carrie Bates, Mary Beth Schueth, and Laura Dougherty. The latter two, who also served as co-captains, spent an inordinate amount of time on the bench during the 1-3 stretch, but once they finally got onto the floor, they showed why they didn't belong on the sidelines as much as Mary D kept them there. Bates was the most consistent inside threat during the stretch, averaging 18 points per game over the four contests.

After Christmas, however, Bates went into a major slump and junior Trena Keys began to emerge as the team's top scorer, but the Irish lost three straight games on opposite ends of the continent. The West Coast, where the women have yet to win, again proved inhospitable. UCLA, which finished the season in the top 20, decimated ND, 78-51, to make up for a year earlier, and USC, aided by the 21-rebound performance of the best-known female player in the nation, Cheryl Miller, and a poor Irish shooting night (38 percent), held on to win, 69-53, in a contest which was much closer than the score indicates. Three thousand miles away, in Philadelphia, LaSalle took full advantage of one-sided officiating (the Explorers took 38 foul shots to ND's 13) to win, 71-66. Though they were playing better now, the women's record had dropped to 5-6; they were going to have to turn around soon if the season wasn't to end up a second straight disaster.

But from here on, Notre Dame was nearly invincible; 15 of the last 17 games were Irish victories, and in both of the losses, the women led in the second half only to fall behind. The turning point of the season came after that LaSalle debacle when the women traveled down to College Park to play Maryland. The Terrapins, who had defeated ND easily two years in a row, fell without much difficulty, 49-40. The Irish defense was the story here; in the first half, the fierce ND man-to-man held Maryland to seven points, which if not a Division I defensive record is awfully close to one. (And this with a 30-second shot clock!) And when they finally got home, the team, behind 24 by Keys and a slump-ending 19 from Bates, easily swamped Illinois-Chicago, 70-49, in preparation for the conference slate.

By this time, DiStanislao had fewer problems keeping people happy, because there were fewer people to keep happy. Her entire sophomore class was no longer playing; two of the women transferred and the other ended up on academic probation. At the end of January, she would lose another player—Carrie Bates, who decided it was no longer in her best interest to remain on the team. Had Bates left before Christmas, her loss would have been devastating. But her heir apparent at power forward, Sandy Botham, had developed into a bona fide college player faster than anyone expected, and another tall freshman, 6-3 Kathy Brommeland, proved she could come off the bench and perform well, so Bates, at least in terms of the team's performance, was hardly missed.

Meanwhile, the Irish began their conference season 1-1. They controlled the tempo effectively against pre-season NSC favorite Detroit and beat the Titans in Detroit, 76-62. Eight days later, after a game at Loyola was postponed because of snow, ND took on DePaul at Alumni Hall and, despite a 30-25 lead at half, fell, 72-64, after a 23-6 Blue Demon tear early in the second half. This would be the women's last loss to a league opponent.

Their only other loss came to Alabama at Tuscaloosa on February 13, 67-62. Again the Irish led at the half but couldn't hold on thanks to a poor (40 percent) shooting performance after intermission. A win over the Crimson Tide, who spent several weeks in the Top 20 during the season, could have been a major boost to ND's already slim tournament hopes.

Instead, the women had to be content with their utter domination of the fellow conference schools. After they had blitzed all comers into submission, they had won the title; Mary

D was named North Star Conference coach of the year; Keys added Player of the Year accolades; Schueth joined Keys on the first team all-NSC; and the ever-improving Botham was named to the second team. The team or its individual members broke roughly three dozen school records and was among NCAA leaders in field-goal percentage (.500), field-goal percentage defense (.399), and scoring margin (11.8). And of course, since most of the North Star games were blowouts, all 11 remaining players saw much action, thus keeping everybody happy.

Most of the destruction took place against the two worst teams in the league, Butler and Xavier. The game at Butler ended up 79-40 and the rematch was worse (99-36, tying a margin of victory record – 63 points – set when Saint Mary's was still on the Irish slate). Against Xavier, the women scored in triple digits for the first time ever in the home game, 107-61, and then won in Cincinnati, 78-50. More vitally, Notre Dame dominated those teams which were supposed to be the biggest threats to Irish title hopes.

Against Loyola, the 1983-84 NSC champion, and its spark-plug, national assists leader Faith Mimnaugh, the Irish effectively shut down the Lady Ramblers by holding Mimnaugh to five assists; they then ran away with the home contest in the second half behind 28 from Keys for an 84-59 victory. Less than a week later, the two schools made up their earlier snowed-out game, and for the first time in two years ND won a close one – 64-63. Botham scored 24, and Mary Gavin made two important hoops late in the game and came up with a key steal to send Loyola to only the second home loss in its last 28 games in tiny Alumni Gym. Notre Dame would win another close one in Evansville, 72-70, after the Irish had beaten the Aces more easily at the ACC. And against Dayton, the last team with a shot to catch the hot Irish, Trena Keys became only the second woman for ND to score 30 points in a game when the team defeated the Flyers there, 81-66; when the two played at the ACC, the Irish closed the door on the slim Dayton hopes by winning, 72-57. After the game, the happy players and coaches cut down the net in celebration.

One of the most satisfying wins, to players, coaches, and fans alike, was the February 24 DePaul rematch. Not only did the Irish win, 68-57, to avenge their only conference loss, but junior Lynn Ebben, by canning two free throws with one second left, not only annexed a season-high 17 points for herself, but rewarded 1,143 fans with a coupon good for a free "Big Gulp" (extra large soft drink) at any nearby 7-11 store. (If the women led by seven or 11 at the end of either half, everyone in attendance received a free drink coupon.) The 7-11 people weren't the only corporate supporters of women's basketball in 1984-85; Domino's Pizza and Lee Jeans also sponsored contests.

The one contest, though, that eluded the Irish again was a post-season game. Because the North Star Conference is seen nationally as weak, rightly or wrongly (ND's 7-7 non-conference record is seen as confirmation of this), the only way Notre Dame might ever make the NCAA or NWIT is to lobby for an expansion of the former to 48 teams (from the current 32) so that the league champion will receive an automatic bid. Until that happens—or the Irish beat a blockbuster team in a blockbuster year—Mary DiStanislao and her players will have to read the newspapers or buy tickets to find out what post-season play is all about.

# Section II
# *The Statistics*

# Men's All-Time Game-By-Game Scores

This listing includes every official game a team representing Notre Dame has played in varsity competition. Games not included were considered as scrimmages (two games against South Bend High 1912-13, one against the Michigan City YMCA 1922-23) or as "unofficial" by NCAA rules which consider all competition against non-collegiate opposition after 1951-52 as such.

Scores listed in *italics* are those which have been unable to be corroborated by obtaining a box score. This does *not* mean that the score is necessarily incorrect; it only means that a complete player-by-player statistical breakdown is so far unavailable. Any help in confirming these scores through local newspaper accounts would be greatly appreciated.

1896-97 (Won 2, Lost 1, .667)
Coach: Frank Hering
Captain: John Shillington

| Feb. 24 | Fort Wayne YMCA | (H) | W | 26 | 11 |
|---------|-----------------|-----|---|----|----|
| Mar. 18 | Fort Wayne YMCA | (A) | W | 21 | 5 |
| Mar. 27 | Central YMCA | (H) | L | 22 | 25 |
| | | | | 69 | 41 |

1897-98 (Won 1, Lost 2, .333)
Coach: Frank Hering
Captain: Martin O'Shaughnessy

| Jan. 29 | First Regiment | (H) | L | 8 | 64 |
|---------|----------------|-----|---|----|----|
| Feb. 5 | Clybornes | (H) | L | 13 | 19 |
| Feb. 16 | Rush Medical | (H) | W | 16 | 13 |
| | | | | 37 | 96 |

1898-99 (Won 2, Lost 0, 1.000)
Coach: J. Fred Powers
Captain: J. Fred Powers

| Jan. 25 | South Bend Commercial A.C. | (H) | W | *19* | *6* |
|---------|----------------------------|-----|---|------|------|
| Feb. 4 | Rush Medical | (H) | W | *21* | *11* |
| | | | | *40* | *17* |

307

**1899-1900; 1900-01 — NO TEAM**

**1901-02 (Won 2, Lost 2, .500)**
Coach: Dominic Groogan
Captain: Dominic Groogan

| | | | | | |
|---|---|---|---|---|---|
| Feb. 19 | Indianapolis YMCA | (A) | L | 22 | 42 |
| Feb. 20 | Anderson YMCA | (A) | W | 29 | 23 |
| Feb. 21 | Anderson YMCA | (A) | W | 22 | 11 |
| Feb. 22 | Logansport Commercial College | (A) | L | 14 | 17 |
| | | | | 87 | 93 |

**1902-03 through 1906-07 — NO TEAM**

**1907-08 (Won 12, Lost 4, .750)**
Coach: Bert Maris
Captain: Raymond Scanlon

| | | | | | |
|---|---|---|---|---|---|
| Jan. 15 | South Bend Commercial A.C. | (H) | W | 66 | 2 |
| Jan. 18 | Kalamazoo YMCA | (H) | W | 78 | 8 |
| Jan. 24 | Wabash | (H) | L | 18 | 26 |
| Jan. 29 | Hartford City | (H) | W | 32 | 14 |
| Jan. 31 | Michigan State | (A) | L | 20 | 33 |
| Feb. 1 | Michigan State | (N) | W | 23 | 16 |
| Feb. 3 | Detroit YMCA | (A) | L | 22 | 38 |
| Feb. 5 | Lewis Institute | (H) | W | 28 | 17 |
| Feb. 8 | Lake Forest | (H) | W | 38 | 18 |
| Feb. 13 | Baker U. | (H) | W | 46 | 13 |
| Feb. 15 | Indianapolis YMCA | (H) | W | 61 | 12 |
| Feb. 18 | Wabash | (A) | L | 15 | 32 |
| Feb. 19 | Indiana | (A) | W | 21 | 20 |
| Feb. 20 | St. Mary's (KY) | (A) | W | 36 | 22 |
| Feb. 22 | Indianapolis YMCA | (A) | W | 43 | 22 |
| Feb. 27 | Michigan State | (H) | W | 39 | 20 |
| | | | | 586 | 313 |

N—Lansing, Mich.

**1908-09 (Won 33, Lost 7, .825)**
Coach: Bert Maris
Captain: Raymond Scanlon

| | | | | | |
|---|---|---|---|---|---|
| Dec. 2 | Lewis Institute | (H) | W | 37 | 14 |
| Dec. 10 | Marion Club | (H) | W | 30 | 10 |
| Dec. 18 | Armour Institute | (A) | W | 46 | 20 |
| Dec. 19 | Central YMCA (OT) | (A) | L | 22 | 26 |
| Dec. 21 | Morrison YMCA | (A) | W | 24 | 20 |
| Dec. 22 | Company C, Muscatine, IA | (A) | L | 23 | 30 |
| Dec. 23 | Company M, Fairfield (IA) | (A) | W | 49 | 22 |

| Dec. 24 | Peoria YMCA | (A) | W | 43 | 27 |
|---------|-------------|-----|---|----|----|
| Dec. 25 | Shelby College | (A) | W | *64* | *14* |
| Dec. 26 | Christian Brothers | (A) | W | 60 | 15 |
| Dec. 29 | Nashville A.C. | (A) | W | *30* | *15* |
| Dec. 30 | Birmingham A.C. | (A) | W | 38 | 20 |
| Dec. 31 | Montgomery YMCA | (A) | W | 55 | 21 |
| Jan. 1 | Mobile YMCA | (A) | W | 41 | 18 |
| Jan. 1 | Mobile YMCA | (A) | W | 23 | 14 |
| Jan. 2 | New Orleans YMCA | (A) | W | 28 | 9 |
| Jan. 4 | Birmingham A.C. | (A) | W | 30 | 22 |
| Jan. 5 | Marion Club | (A) | W | 38 | 24 |
| Jan. 16 | Central YMCA | (H) | W | 25 | 8 |
| Jan. 23 | Michigan State | (H) | W | 26 | 10 |
| Jan. 27 | Butler | (A) | W | 47 | 11 |
| Jan. 29 | Dayton | (A) | W | 30 | 13 |
| Jan. 30 | Varsity Club (Dayton) | (A) | W | 48 | 16 |
| Feb. 3 | Oregons (Dallas) | (H) | W | 31 | 20 |
| Feb. 5 | Wabash | (A) | W | 31 | 23 |
| Feb. 6 | Battery A | (H) | W | 34 | 12 |
| Feb. 8 | Michigan State | (A) | W | 34 | 18 |
| Feb. 9 | Detroit A.C. | (A) | W | 31 | 24 |
| Feb. 10 | Buffalo Germans | (A) | L | *22* | *34* |
| Feb. 11 | Buffalo Germans | (A) | L | *18* | *31* |
| Feb. 12 | Syracuse Pastime A.C. | (A) | L | 25 | 26 |
| Feb. 13 | Cornell | (A) | W | 32 | 13 |
| Feb. 15 | Niagara | (A) | W | 28 | 20 |
| Feb. 16 | Company M, Grove City, PA. | (A) | W | *41* | *20* |
| Feb. 18 | Pittsburgh Lyceum | (A) | W | 34 | 19 |
| Feb. 19 | Tiffin A.C. | (A) | L | 26 | 40 |
| Feb. 20 | Miami (OH) | (H) | W | 29 | 12 |
| Feb. 22 | Detroit A.C. | (H) | L | 15 | 25 |
| Feb. 25 | Armour Institute | (H) | W | 21 | 8 |
| Feb. 27 | Wabash | (H) | W | 33 | 24 |
| | | | | *1342* | *770* |

1909-10 (Won 10, Lost 4, .714)
Coach: Bert Maris
Captain: Chester Freeze

| Dec. 8 | Lewis Institute | (H) | W | 29 | 17 |
|--------|-----------------|-----|---|----|----|
| Dec. 11 | Rochester A.C. | (H) | W | 60 | 15 |
| Jan. 12 | Marion Club | (H) | W | 23 | 16 |
| Jan. 29 | Michigan State | (H) | L | 21 | 28 |
| Jan. 31 | Rose Polytechnical | (A) | W | 33 | 15 |
| Feb. 1 | Wabash | (A) | L | 17 | 19 |
| Feb. 2 | Dayton | (A) | W | 31 | 10 |

| Feb. 3 | Dayton Turners | (A) | W | 31 | 30 |
| Feb. 9 | Butler | (H) | W | 49 | 16 |
| Feb. 14 | Lincoln College | (H) | W | 45 | 20 |
| Feb. 17 | Michigan State | (A) | L | 23 | 43 |
| Feb. 18 | Hope College | (A) | L | 26 | 37 |
| Feb. 23 | Olivet | (H) | W | 35 | 15 |
| Mar. 5 | Wabash | (H) | W | 28 | 19 |
| | | | | 451 | 300 |

541

1910-11 (Won 7, Lost 3, .700)
Coach: Bert Maris
Captain: James Fish

| Dec. 10 | Lewis Institute | (H) | W | 25 | 17 |
| Dec. 17 | Hull House | (H) | W | 25 | 14 |
| Jan. 14 | Olivet | (H) | W | 43 | 8 |
| Jan. 21 | Wabash | (H) | L | 21 | 39 |
| Jan. 28 | North Central | (H) | W | 16 | 9 |
| Feb. 9 | Detroit YMCA | (A) | W | 30 | 24 |
| Feb. 20 | Wabash | (A) | W | 23 | 15 |
| Feb. 21 | Rose Polytechnical | (A) | W | 31 | 23 |
| Feb. 22 | Dayton | (A) | L | 21 | 27 |
| Feb. 23 | Dayton Turners | (A) | L | 22 | 25 |
| | | | | 257 | 201 |

1911-12 (Won 16, Lost 2, .889)
Coach: Bert Maris
Captain: William Granfield

| Dec. 6 | South Bend Commercial A.C | (H) | W | 24 | 9 |
| Dec. 9 | Lewis Institute | (H) | W | 25 | 7 |
| Jan. 15 | All-Collegians | (H) | W | 36 | 5 |
| Jan. 20 | North Central | (H) | L | 19 | 23 |
| Jan. 27 | Wabash | (H) | W | 28 | 25 |
| Jan. 30 | Lane Tech | (H) | W | 26 | 12 |
| Feb. 2 | Wabash | (A) | W | 20 | 18 |
| Feb. 5 | Rose Polytechnical | (H) | W | 31 | 14 |
| Feb. 8 | Detroit | (H) | W | 32 | 19 |
| Feb. 14 | South Bend Commercial A.C. | (A) | L | 18 | 24 |
| Feb. 16 | Earlham | (A) | W | 17 | 14 |
| Feb. 17 | Ohio State | (A) | W | 24 | 23 |
| Feb. 19 | Heidelberg U. | (A) | W | 36 | 23 |
| Feb. 20 | St. John's (OH) | (A) | W | 33 | 18 |
| Feb. 21 | Detroit | (A) | W | 28 | 19 |
| Feb. 24 | DePaul | (H) | W | 58 | 11 |
| Mar. 7 | DePaul | (A) | W | 32 | 20 |
| Mar. 9 | South Bend Commercial A.C. | (A) | W | 38 | 22 |
| | | | | 525 | 306 |

1912-13 (Won 13, Lost 2, .867)
Coach: Bill Nelson
Captain: Albert Feeney

| Dec. 13 | Lewis Institute | (H) | W | 38 | 5 |
|---|---|---|---|---|---|
| Jan. 11 | Company H, Illinois Nat'l Guard | (H) | W | 52 | 8 |
| Jan. 18 | North Central | (H) | W | 34 | 17 |
| Jan. 25 | Wabash | (H) | W | 28 | 21 |
| Jan. 28 | St. Viator | (H) | W | 36 | 11 |
| Feb. 5 | Rose Polytechnical | (A) | W | 54 | 10 |
| Feb. 6 | Wabash | (A) | W | 33 | 23 |
| Feb. 7 | Earlham | (A) | W | 28 | 18 |
| Feb. 8 | Marshall | (A) | W | 27 | 9 |
| Feb. 10 | Denison | (A) | L | 13 | 47 |
| Feb. 11 | Ohio Wesleyan | (A) | W | 26 | 24 |
| Feb. 12 | St. John's (OH) | (A) | W | 33 | 24 |
| Feb. 13 | Michigan State | (A) | L | 7 | 40 |
| Feb. 28 | Earlham | (H) | W | 31 | 12 |
| Mar. 7 | Beloit | (H) | W | 38 | 18 |
| | | | | 478 | 287 |

1913-14 (Won 11, Lost 5, .688)
Coach: Jesse Harper
Captain: James Cahill

| Dec. 13 | Lewis Institute | (H) | W | 36 | 18 |
|---|---|---|---|---|---|
| Jan. 10 | Beloit* | (H) | W | 35 | 9 |
| Jan. 13 | Polish Seminary | (H) | W | 38 | 20 |
| Jan. 17 | Lake Forest | (H) | W | 33 | 15 |
| Jan. 24 | Michigan State | (H) | W | 28 | 16 |
| Jan. 27 | Wabash | (A) | W | 23 | 16 |
| Jan. 31 | Wabash | (H) | W | 34 | 27 |
| Feb. 4 | Michigan State | (A) | L | 22 | 44 |
| Feb. 7 | Ohio State | (H) | L | 20 | 22 |
| Feb. 9 | St. John's (OH) | (A) | W | 28 | 22 |
| Feb. 10 | Cornell | (A) | L | 14 | 41 |
| Feb. 11 | Colgate | (A) | W | 31 | 26 |
| Feb. 12 | Syracuse | (A) | L | 14 | 50 |
| Feb. 13 | Clarkson Institute | (A) | L | 22 | 32 |
| Feb. 14 | St. Lawrence (OT) | (A) | W | 25 | 23 |
| Feb. 20 | West Virginia Wesleyan | (H) | W | 35 | 34 |
| | | | | 438 | 415 |

* Notre Dame's 100th victory

1914-15 (Won 14, Lost 3, .824)
Coach: Jesse Harper
Captain: Joseph Kenny

| Dec. 12 | Lewis Institute | (H) | W | 36 | 14 |
|---|---|---|---|---|---|
| Dec. 16 | Arkansas | (H) | W | 29 | 10 |
| Jan. 9 | Lake Forest | (H) | L | 24 | 34 |
| Jan. 13 | North Central | (H) | W | 24 | 21 |
| Jan. 16 | Beloit | (H) | W | 42 | 21 |
| Jan. 20 | South Bend YMCA | (A) | W | 59 | 30 |
| Jan. 23 | Indiana Dental | (H) | W | 70 | 13 |
| Jan. 27 | Polish Seminary | (H) | W | 36 | 20 |
| Jan. 30 | St. Ignatius | (H) | W | 41 | 18 |
| Feb. 2 | Michigan State | (A) | L | 13 | 14 |
| Feb. 5 | Wabash | (H) | W | 19 | 17 |
| Feb. 10 | Olivet | (H) | W | 38 | 21 |
| Feb. 11 | Battery A | (A) | W | 31 | 28 |
| Feb. 13 | Michigan State | (H) | W | 24 | 19 |
| Feb. 17 | West Virginia Wesleyan | (H) | W | 55 | 30 |
| Feb. 19 | Wabash (2 OT) | (A) | L | 25 | 29 |
| Feb. 20 | Rose Polytechnical | (A) | W | 47 | 38 |
| | | | | 613 | 377 |

1915-16 (Won 9, Lost 3, .750)
Coach: Jesse Harper
Captain: Richard Daley

| Dec. 15 | Lewis Institute | (H) | W | 56 | 19 |
|---|---|---|---|---|---|
| Jan. 12 | Kalamazoo | (H) | W | 23 | 21 |
| Jan. 15 | Lake Forest | (H) | L | 24 | 30 |
| Jan. 18 | Michigan State | (H) | W | 19 | 18 |
| Jan. 22 | Dubuque | (H) | W | 31 | 16 |
| Jan. 26 | Western Michigan | (H) | W | 35 | 25 |
| Jan. 29 | St. Ignatius | (H) | W | 24 | 15 |
| Feb. 2 | Michigan State | (A) | W | 24 | 23 |
| Feb. 5 | Beloit | (H) | W | 31 | 20 |
| Feb. 9 | St. Viator | (H) | W | 24 | 15 |
| Feb. 11 | Wabash | (H) | L | 19 | 41 |
| Feb. 18 | Wabash | (A) | L | 34 | 42 |
| | | | | 344 | 285 |

1916-17 (Won 8, Lost 5, .615)
Coach: Jesse Harper
Captain: Joseph McKenna

| Dec. 15 | Purdue | (A) | L | 18 | 21 |
|---|---|---|---|---|---|
| Jan. 11 | West Virginia Wesleyan | (H) | W | 37 | 16 |
| Jan. 13 | South Bend YMCA | (A) | W | 32 | 16 |
| Jan. 17 | Kalamazoo | (H) | L | 30 | 32 |
| Jan. 20 | Lake Forest | (H) | W | 17 | 11 |

| | | | | | |
|---|---|---|---|---|---|
| Jan. 24 | Western Michigan | (H) | W | 27 | 15 |
| Jan. 27 | Michigan State | (A) | L | 25 | 31 |
| Feb. 6 | St. Viator | (H) | W | 46 | 26 |
| Feb. 9 | Wabash | (H) | L | 18 | 25 |
| Feb. 14 | Michigan State | (H) | W | 33 | 19 |
| Feb. 22 | DePauw | (A) | W | 17 | 15 |
| Feb. 23 | Wabash | (A) | L | 17 | 27 |
| Feb. 24 | Franklin | (A) | W | 27 | 16 |
| | | | | 344 | 270 |

1917-18 (Won 2, Lost 4, .333)
Coach: Jesse Harper (Knute Rockne Dec. 15)
Captain: Peter Ronchetti (Thomas King named captain before season but was
  called to duty in World War I)

| | | | | | |
|---|---|---|---|---|---|
| Dec. 15 | Purdue | (A) | L | 12 | 48 |
| Jan. 19 | Western Michigan | (H) | W | 17 | 14 |
| Jan. 26 | Wabash | (H) | L | 16 | 34 |
| Feb. 1 | Michigan State | (A) | L | 12 | 27 |
| Feb. 7 | Michigan State | (H) | W | 25 | 23 |
| Feb. 15 | Wabash | (A) | L | 14 | 18 |
| | | | | 96 | 164 |

1918-19 (Won 2, Lost 10, .167)
Coach: Charles Dorais
Captain: Leonard Bahan

| | | | | | |
|---|---|---|---|---|---|
| Jan. 14 | Purdue | (A) | L | 13 | 31 |
| Jan. 22 | Kalamazoo | (H) | W | 23 | 12 |
| Jan. 25 | Western Michigan | (H) | L | 29 | 31 |
| Feb. 1 | Michigan State | (H) | L | 28 | 32 |
| Feb. 8 | Wabash | (H) | L | 26 | 34 |
| Feb. 11 | DePauw | (H) | L | 23 | 39 |
| Feb. 21 | Western Michigan | (A) | L | 9 | 29 |
| Feb. 22 | Michigan State | (A) | W | 17 | 16 |
| Feb. 27 | DePauw | (A) | L | 20 | 41 |
| Feb. 28 | Wabash | (A) | L | 15 | 45 |
| Mar. 1 | Franklin | (A) | L | 22 | 32 |
| Mar. 3 | Indiana | (A) | L | 11 | 29 |
| | | | | 236 | 371 |

1919-20 (Won 5, Lost 13, .278)
Coach: Charles Dorais (Knute Rockne Jan. 14-28, 1920)
Captains: Joseph Brandy and Harry Mehre (honorary)

| | | | | | |
|---|---|---|---|---|---|
| Dec. 17 | Purdue | (A) | L | 22 | 40 |
| Dec. 18 | Fort Wayne K of C | (A) | L | 12 | 41 |

| Jan. 14 | Kalamazoo | (H) | W | 44 | 17 |
|---|---|---|---|---|---|
| Jan. 19 | Western Michigan | (H) | L | 22 | 23 |
| Jan. 23 | Western Michigan | (A) | L | 21 | 37 |
| Jan. 24 | Michigan State | (A) | L | 20 | 23 |
| Jan. 28 | South Bend YMCA | (A) | L | 25 | 30 |
| Jan. 31 | Marquette | (H) | L | 22 | 23 |
| Feb. 4 | South Bend YMCA | (A) | L | 9 | 25 |
| Feb. 7 | Wabash | (H) | W | 24 | 14 |
| Feb. 9 | Michigan State | (H) | W | 30 | 23 |
| Feb. 14 | Detroit | (H) | W | 29 | 26 |
| Feb. 17 | DePauw (OT) | (H) | L | 33 | 38 |
| Feb. 19 | Dubuque | (A) | W | 29 | 18 |
| Feb. 20 | Nebraska | (A) | L | 18 | 25 |
| Feb. 21 | Nebraska | (A) | L | 15 | 31 |
| Feb. 25 | DePauw | (A) | L | 20 | 31 |
| Feb. 26 | Wabash | (A) | L | 26 | 28 |
| | | | | 421 | 493 |

1920-21 (Won 9, Lost 14, .391)
Coach: Walter Halas
Captain: Harry Mehre

| Jan. 3 | Detroit Rayls | (A) | L | 11 | 19 |
|---|---|---|---|---|---|
| Jan. 4 | St. John's (OH) | (A) | L | 11 | 17 |
| Jan. 5 | Mount Union | (A) | W | 27 | 25 |
| Jan. 6 | Akron Firestones | (A) | L | 15 | 20 |
| Jan. 7 | Huntington American Legion | (A) | L | 21 | 31 |
| Jan. 12 | Armour Institute | (A) | W | 46 | 28 |
| Jan. 13 | Valparaiso | (A) | W | 21 | 17 |
| Jan. 18 | Kalamazoo | (H) | W | 49 | 22 |
| Jan. 21 | Dayton | (H) | W | 44 | 19 |
| Jan. 22 | Michigan State | (H) | W | 36 | 23 |
| Jan. 27 | Wabash | (A) | L | 15 | 30 |
| Jan. 28 | DePauw | (A) | L | 25 | 26 |
| Jan. 31 | Western Michigan | (A) | L | 23 | 30 |
| Feb. 1 | Michigan State | (A) | L | 25 | 37 |
| Feb. 3 | DePauw | (H) | L | 25 | 31 |
| Feb. 5 | Marquette | (A) | L | 19 | 26 |
| Feb. 10 | Western Michigan | (H) | W | 24 | 19 |
| Feb. 11 | Armour Institute | (H) | W | 59 | 15 |
| Feb. 17 | Creighton | (A) | L | 20 | 24 |
| Feb. 18 | Nebraska | (A) | L | 18 | 25 |
| Feb. 19 | Nebraska | (A) | L | 21 | 39 |
| Feb. 23 | Valparaiso | (H) | L | 26 | 32 |
| Feb. 25 | Wabash | (H) | W | 31 | 30 |
| | | | | 613 | 585 |

1921-22 (Won 6, Lost 13, .316)
Coach: Walter Halas
Captain: Roger Kiley (Ineligible as of Jan. 28, 1922); Frank McDermott

| Dec. 15 | DePauw | (A) | L | 21 | 51 |
|---|---|---|---|---|---|
| Dec. 16 | Armour Institute | (A) | W | 33 | 17 |
| Dec. 17 | Northwestern | (A) | L | 16 | 18 |
| Jan. 2 | Illinois | (A) | L | 38 | 49 |
| Jan. 3 | Illinois | (A) | L | 27 | 40 |
| Jan. 5 | Butler | (A) | L | 21 | 37 |
| Jan. 11 | Kalamazoo | (H) | L | 30 | 41 |
| Jan. 16 | Butler | (N) | L | 23 | 28 |
| Jan. 20 | Creighton | (A) | W | 28 | 25 |
| Jan. 21 | Creighton | (A) | L | 22 | 25 |
| Jan. 25 | Armour Institute | (H) | W | 44 | 18 |
| Jan. 31 | Michigan State | (H) | W | 31 | 22 |
| Feb. 3 | Wabash | (N) | L | 25 | 27 |
| Feb. 7 | Columbia College (IA) | (H) | W | 32 | 20 |
| Feb. 11 | Northwestern | (N) | W | 30 | 20 |
| Feb. 16 | Michigan State | (A) | L | 24 | 30 |
| Feb. 17 | Kalamazoo | (A) | L | 13 | 25 |
| Feb. 24 | DePauw | (H) | L | 24 | 45 |
| Feb. 27 | Wabash | (A) | L | 26 | 38 |
| | | | | 508 | 576 |

N—South Bend, Ind. (YMCA)

1922-23 (Won 10, Lost 12, .455)
Coach: Walter Halas
Captain: Michael Kane

| Dec. 8 | Michigan | (A) | L | 23 | 41 |
|---|---|---|---|---|---|
| Dec. 9 | Michigan State | (A) | W | 40 | 15 |
| Dec. 14 | Lewis Institute | (H) | W | 40 | 15 |
| Dec. 18 | Illinois Wesleyan | (A) | W | 32 | 25 |
| Dec. 19 | Bradley | (A) | W | 29 | 18 |
| Dec. 20 | Millikin | (A) | L | 20 | 23 |
| Dec. 21 | Illinois (OT) | (A) | L | 38 | 41 |
| Jan. 2 | Northwestern | (A) | W | 20 | 13 |
| Jan. 3 | Iowa | (A) | W | 24 | 23 |
| Jan. 4 | Armour Institute | (A) | W | 40 | 20 |
| Jan. 8 | Butler | (A) | L | 16 | 29 |
| Jan. 9 | Purdue | (A) | L | 21 | 39 |
| Jan. 15 | Armour Institute | (H) | W | 29 | 14 |
| Jan. 18 | Western Michigan | (H) | W | 28 | 23 |
| Jan. 29 | Butler | (N) | L | 18 | 41 |
| Feb. 7 | Indiana | (A) | L | 18 | 33 |

| Feb. 8  | DePauw          | (A) | L | 31  | 32  |
|---------|-----------------|-----|---|-----|-----|
| Feb. 14 | Kalamazoo       | (H) | W | 34  | 33  |
| Feb. 19 | Wabash          | (N) | L | 21  | 26  |
| Feb. 23 | DePauw          | (N) | L | 28  | 29  |
| Feb. 28 | Michigan State  | (N) | L | 21  | 22  |
| Mar. 5  | Wabash          | (A) | L | 15  | 40  |
|         |                 |     |   | 586 | 595 |

N – South Bend, IN. (YMCA)

1923-24 (Won 15, Lost 8, .652)
Coach: George Keogan
Captain: Eugene Mayl

| Dec. 8  | Minnesota          | (A) | L | 21  | 22  |
|---------|--------------------|-----|---|-----|-----|
| Dec. 10 | Minnesota          | (A) | W | 16  | 14  |
| Dec. 15 | Armour Institute   | (N) | W | 29  | 17  |
| Dec. 19 | Northwestern       | (N) | W | 25  | 16  |
| Jan. 2  | Illinois           | (A) | L | 21  | 29  |
| Jan. 5  | Michigan (OT)      | (N) | W | 29  | 25  |
| Jan. 10 | Western Michigan   | (N) | W | 22  | 21  |
| Jan. 12 | Loyola (IL)        | (N) | W | 24  | 23  |
| Jan. 16 | Loyola (IL)        | (A) | W | 21  | 16  |
| Jan. 19 | Franklin           | (N) | L | 12  | 19  |
| Jan. 25 | Michigan State     | (N) | W | 35  | 18  |
| Feb. 5  | Wabash             | (N) | L | 22  | 27  |
| Feb. 9  | Concordia          | (A) | W | 38  | 34  |
| Feb. 12 | Indiana            | (A) | L | 20  | 21  |
| Feb. 13 | Wabash             | (A) | W | 23  | 16  |
| Feb. 19 | Adrian             | (N) | W | 48  | 12  |
| Feb. 22 | Creighton          | (A) | L | 22  | 29  |
| Feb. 23 | Creighton          | (A) | L | 12  | 23  |
| Feb. 25 | St. Viator         | (N) | W | 36  | 19  |
| Feb. 29 | Michigan State     | (A) | W | 23  | 21  |
| Mar. 1  | Western Michigan   | (A) | W | 33  | 23  |
| Mar. 6  | Wittenberg         | (A) | W | 39  | 16  |
| Mar. 7  | Franklin           | (A) | L | 29  | 40  |
|         |                    |     |   | 600 | 501 |

N – South Bend, IN. (YMCA)

1924-25 (Won 11, Lost 11, .500)
Coach: George Keogan
Captain: Noble Kizer

| Dec. 8  | Armour Institute | (N) | W | 34 | 13 |
|---------|------------------|-----|---|----|----|
| Dec. 13 | St. Thomas       | (A) | W | 27 | 26 |
| Dec. 15 | Minnesota        | (A) | L | 12 | 25 |
| Dec. 19 | Northwestern     | (A) | W | 22 | 13 |
| Dec. 30 | Northwestern     | (N) | W | 36 | 15 |

| Jan. 5 | Mercer | (N) | W | 44 | 17 |
|--------|--------|-----|---|----|----|
| Jan. 9 | Butler | (A) | L | 16 | 31 |
| Jan. 10 | Franklin | (A) | L | 22 | 26 |
| Jan. 16 | Michigan State | (N) | W | 37 | 14 |
| Jan. 23 | Creighton | (A) | L | 21 | 34 |
| Jan. 24 | Creighton | (A) | L | 17 | 26 |
| Jan. 31 | Loyola (IL) | (N) | W | 40 | 21 |
| Feb. 3 | Wabash | (A) | L | 30 | 40 |
| Feb. 7 | Illinois | (N) | W | 29 | 18 |
| Feb. 10 | Butler | (N) | L | 23 | 32 |
| Feb. 14 | Wabash | (N) | L | 28 | 37 |
| Feb. 21 | Penn State | (A) | L | 22 | 33 |
| Feb. 23 | Carnegie Tech | (A) | L | 31 | 36 |
| Feb. 28 | Franklin | (N) | L | 27 | 31 |
| Mar. 3 | Michigan State | (A) | W | 42 | 10 |
| Mar. 6 | Columbia College (IA) | (A) | W | 44 | 26 |
| Mar. 7 | Loyola (IL)* | (A) | W | 19 | 11 |
| | | | | 623 | 535 |

N–South Bend, IN. (YMCA)
*Notre Dame's 200th victory

1925-26 (Won 19, Lost 1, .950)
Coach: George Keogan
Captain: Vincent McNally (Joseph Dienhart named captain at end of 1924-25
   season but unable to play in 1925-26)

| Dec. 7 | Armour Institute | (H) | W | 53 | 26 |
|--------|------------------|-----|---|----|----|
| Dec. 12 | Minnesota | (H) | W | 36 | 14 |
| Dec. 15 | Northwestern | (A) | W | 30 | 20 |
| Dec. 18 | Iowa | (H) | W | 17 | 16 |
| Dec. 30 | Northwestern | (H) | W | 38 | 21 |
| Jan. 2 | Mercer | (H) | W | 48 | 31 |
| Jan. 5 | Kansas State | (H) | W | 38 | 23 |
| Jan. 8 | Franklin | (A) | L | 22 | 33 |
| Jan. 15 | Detroit | (A) | W | 31 | 14 |
| Jan. 16 | City College of Detroit | (A) | W | 24 | 17 |
| Jan. 20 | Wabash | (A) | W | 41 | 29 |
| Jan. 22 | Michigan State | (H) | W | 33 | 14 |
| Jan. 30 | Detroit (OT) | (H) | W | 31 | 26 |
| Feb. 6 | Illinois | (A) | W | 26 | 14 |
| Feb. 13 | Wabash | (H) | W | 25 | 23 |
| Feb. 16 | Michigan State | (A) | W | 40 | 25 |
| Feb. 20 | Carnegie Tech | (H) | W | 60 | 26 |
| Feb. 27 | Franklin | (H) | W | 40 | 19 |
| Mar. 5 | Creighton | (H) | W | 23 | 17 |
| Mar. 6 | Creighton | (H) | W | 29 | 18 |
| | | | | 685 | 426 |

1926-27 (Won 19, Lost 1, .950)
Coach: George Keogan
Captain: John Nyikos

| Dec. 6 | Armour Institute | (H) | W | 51 | 14 |
|---|---|---|---|---|---|
| Dec. 11 | Earlham | (H) | W | 42 | 12 |
| Dec. 18 | Minnesota | (A) | W | 24 | 19 |
| Dec. 20 | Iowa | (A) | W | 19 | 18 |
| Dec. 30 | Northwestern | (H) | W | 28 | 20 |
| Jan. 3 | Northwestern | (A) | W | 27 | 21 |
| Jan. 8 | Detroit | (H) | W | 41 | 24 |
| Jan. 14 | Franklin | (A) | L | 22 | 34 |
| Jan. 22 | Wabash | (H) | W | 37 | 26 |
| Jan. 29 | Michigan State | (H) | W | 36 | 15 |
| Feb. 4 | Marquette | (A) | W | 27 | 21 |
| Feb. 8 | Wisconsin | (A) | W | 19 | 14 |
| Feb. 12 | Franklin | (H) | W | 36 | 16 |
| Feb. 16 | Wabash | (A) | W | 35 | 25 |
| Feb. 19 | Pittsburgh | (H) | W | 33 | 17 |
| Feb. 22 | Detroit | (A) | W | 24 | 23 |
| Feb. 23 | Michigan State | (A) | W | 34 | 22 |
| Feb. 26 | Marquette | (H) | W | 33 | 13 |
| Mar. 4 | Creighton | (A) | W | 31 | 20 |
| Mar. 5 | Creighton | (A) | W | 31 | 16 |
| | | | | 630 | 390 |

1927-28 (Won 18, Lost 4, .818)
Coach: George Keogan (Michael Nyikos Dec. 9-12, 1927)
Captain: Joseph Jachym

| Dec. 5 | Armour Institute | (H) | W | 37 | 12 |
|---|---|---|---|---|---|
| Dec. 9 | Illinois Wesleyan | (H) | W | 40 | 23 |
| Dec. 12 | Iowa | (A) | W | 23 | 20 |
| Dec. 20 | Northwestern | (H) | W | 28 | 22 |
| Dec. 23 | Minnesota | (A) | W | 26 | 18 |
| Dec. 29 | Northwestern | (A) | L | 23 | 25 |
| Dec. 31 | Princeton | (H) | W | 35 | 24 |
| Jan. 7 | Pennsylvania (OT) | (A) | W | 30 | 28 |
| Jan. 13 | Franklin | (H) | W | 36 | 24 |
| Jan. 17 | Wabash | (H) | W | 30 | 19 |
| Jan. 21 | Drake | (A) | W | 29 | 19 |
| Jan. 28 | Michigan State (3 OT) | (H) | W | 29 | 25 |
| Feb. 3 | Michigan State | (A) | L | 16 | 26 |
| Feb. 7 | Wisconsin | (A) | W | 21 | 14 |
| Feb. 11 | Butler | (H) | W | 32 | 24 |
| Feb. 17 | Carnegie Tech | (A) | W | 31 | 19 |
| Feb. 18 | Pittsburgh | (A) | L | 22 | 24 |

| | | | | | |
|---|---|---|---|---|---|
| Feb. 23 | Marquette | (A) | W | 21 | 13 |
| Feb. 25 | Drake | (H) | W | 33 | 12 |
| Feb. 29 | Wabash | (A) | W | 30 | 26 |
| Mar. 3 | Marquette | (H) | W | 24 | 19 |
| Mar. 7 | Butler | (A) | L | 13 | 21 |
| | | | | 609 | 457 |

1928-29 (Won 15, Lost 5, .750)
Coach: George Keogan
Captains: Joseph Jachym and Francis Crowe

| | | | | | |
|---|---|---|---|---|---|
| Dec. 10 | Armour Institute | (H) | W | 54 | 14 |
| Dec. 15 | Albion | (H) | W | 15 | 8 |
| Dec. 18 | Northwestern | (H) | L | 14 | 18 |
| Dec. 21 | Indiana | (H) | L | 17 | 29 |
| Dec. 28 | Kansas | (N) | W | 32 | 21 |
| Dec. 29 | Kansas | (N) | W | 29 | 17 |
| Jan. 5 | Detroit | (H) | W | 49 | 14 |
| Jan. 9 | Wabash | (A) | W | 42 | 19 |
| Jan. 12 | Kentucky | (H) | L | 16 | 19 |
| Jan. 19 | Pennsylvania | (A) | W | 31 | 19 |
| Jan. 23 | Michigan State | (H) | W | 29 | 24 |
| Jan. 26 | Northwestern | (A) | L | 24 | 27 |
| Feb. 2 | Wabash | (H) | W | 26 | 23 |
| Feb. 5 | Marquette | (A) | W | 29 | 17 |
| Feb. 9 | Pittsburgh | (H) | W | 33 | 23 |
| Feb. 15 | Butler | (A) | W | 24 | 21 |
| Feb. 22 | Michigan State (2 OT) | (A) | W | 28 | 27 |
| Feb. 23 | Detroit | (A) | W | 19 | 16 |
| Mar. 2 | Marquette | (H) | W | 19 | 16 |
| Mar. 8 | Butler | (H) | L | 16 | 35 |
| | | | | 546 | 407 |

N—Kansas City, KS

1929-30 (Won 14, Lost 6, .700)
Coach: George Keogan
Captain: Clarence Donovan

| | | | | | |
|---|---|---|---|---|---|
| Dec. 2 | Kalamazoo | (H) | W | 40 | 16 |
| Dec. 7 | Lake Forest | (H) | W | 49 | 20 |
| Dec. 13 | Albion | (H) | W | 59 | 11 |
| Dec. 19 | Northwestern (OT) | (H) | L | 28 | 30 |
| Dec. 23 | Iowa | (H) | W | 32 | 19 |
| Dec. 28 | Ohio State | (A) | L | 22 | 29 |
| Dec. 31 | Northwestern | (A) | W | 22 | 18 |
| Jan. 7 | Indiana | (A) | W | 30 | 29 |
| Jan. 11 | Marquette | (H) | W | 44 | 28 |

| | | | | | |
|---|---|---|---|---|---|
| Jan. 18 | Pittsburgh | (A) | L | 13 | 33 |
| Jan. 20 | Fal (Mexico City) | (H) | W | 29 | 23 |
| Jan. 22 | Michigan State | (A) | L | 21 | 28 |
| Jan. 31 | Wabash | (H) | W | 26 | 10 |
| Feb. 4 | Marquette | (A) | W | 20 | 18 |
| Feb. 8 | Pittsburgh | (H) | L | 16 | 25 |
| Feb. 14 | Butler | (A) | W | 28 | 20 |
| Feb. 18 | Michigan State | (H) | W | 29 | 17 |
| Feb. 22 | Wabash | (A) | L | 16 | 21 |
| Feb. 28 | Butler | (H) | W | 29 | 16 |
| Mar. 8 | Pennsylvania | (A) | W | 24 | 17 |
| | | | | 577 | 428 |

1930-31 (Won 12, Lost 8, .600)
Coach: George Keogan
Captain: Joseph Gavin (honorary)

| | | | | | |
|---|---|---|---|---|---|
| Dec. 8 | Kalamazoo | (H) | W | 26 | 15 |
| Dec. 12 | Northwestern | (H) | L | 29 | 44 |
| Dec. 15 | Purdue | (A) | L | 22 | 34 |
| Dec. 19 | Pennsylvania | (H) | W | 31 | 19 |
| Dec. 30 | Illinois Wesleyan | (A) | W | 24 | 17 |
| Jan. 3 | Northwestern | (A) | L | 17 | 20 |
| Jan. 6 | Ohio State | (H) | W | 27 | 24 |
| Jan. 9 | Wabash | (A) | W | 29 | 19 |
| Jan. 13 | Marquette | (H) | W | 30 | 23 |
| Jan. 17 | Pennsylvania | (A) | W | 21 | 20 |
| Jan. 24 | Pittsburgh (OT) | (H) | L | 20 | 28 |
| Feb. 3 | Indiana | (A) | W | 25 | 20 |
| Feb. 7 | Pittsburgh (OT) | (A) | L | 32 | 35 |
| Feb. 13 | Wabash | (H) | W | 18 | 17 |
| Feb. 21 | Butler | (H) | W | 27 | 19 |
| Feb. 28 | Army | (A) | W | 26 | 25 |
| Mar. 2 | Syracuse (OT) | (A) | L | 23 | 28 |
| Mar. 6 | Marquette | (A) | W | 26 | 25 |
| Mar. 10 | Butler | (A) | L | 15 | 20 |
| Mar. 14 | Iowa | (A) | L | 17 | 23 |
| | | | | 485 | 475 |

1931-32 (Won 18, Lost 2, .900)
Coach: George Keogan
Captain: Norbert Crowe

| | | | | | |
|---|---|---|---|---|---|
| Dec. 4 | Kalamazoo | (H) | W | 37 | 7 |
| Dec. 8 | Adrian | (H) | W | 37 | 14 |
| Dec. 12 | Indiana | (H) | L | 18 | 23 |
| Dec. 15 | Purdue | (H) | L | 24 | 32 |

| Dec. 21 | Northwestern * | (H) | W | 32 | 25 |
|---------|----------------|-----|---|----|----|
| Dec. 31 | Northwestern | (A) | W | 22 | 21 |
| Jan. 5 | St. Thomas | (H) | W | 34 | 19 |
| Jan. 9 | Michigan State | (A) | W | 28 | 25 |
| Jan. 12 | Marquette | (H) | W | 43 | 31 |
| Jan. 16 | Pennsylvania | (A) | W | 32 | 25 |
| Jan. 23 | Pittsburgh | (H) | W | 25 | 12 |
| Feb. 1 | Iowa | (H) | W | 33 | 18 |
| Feb. 6 | Pittsburgh | (A) | W | 26 | 19 |
| Feb. 10 | Syracuse | (H) | W | 26 | 18 |
| Feb. 13 | Western Reserve | (A) | W | 32 | 25 |
| Feb. 19 | Butler | (A) | W | 37 | 32 |
| Feb. 23 | Michigan State | (H) | W | 28 | 20 |
| Feb. 27 | Army | (H) | W | 41 | 23 |
| Mar. 4 | Marquette | (A) | W | 37 | 26 |
| Mar. 10 | Butler | (H) | W | 28 | 23 |
| | | | | 620 | 437 |

*Notre Dame's 300th victory

1932-33 (Won 16, Lost 6, .727)
Coach: George Keogan
Captain: John Baldwin

| Dec. 9 | Albion | (H) | W | 41 | 20 |
|---------|--------|-----|---|----|----|
| Dec. 15 | Illinois Wesleyan | (H) | W | 24 | 12 |
| Dec. 19 | Northwestern | (H) | W | 28 | 25 |
| Dec. 23 | Purdue | (A) | L | 31 | 36 |
| Dec. 28 | Ohio State | (A) | L | 24 | 30 |
| Dec. 31 | Northwestern | (A) | L | 29 | 33 |
| Jan. 7 | Marquette (OT) | (H) | L | 32 | 35 |
| Jan. 9 | Michigan State | (A) | W | 36 | 19 |
| Jan. 14 | Butler | (H) | L | 25 | 27 |
| Jan. 17 | Minnesota | (H) | W | 30 | 22 |
| Jan. 21 | Pittsburgh | (A) | L | 35 | 39 |
| Jan. 23 | Toledo | (A) | W | 42 | 14 |
| Feb. 1 | Carnegie Tech | (H) | W | 37 | 35 |
| Feb. 4 | Chicago | (A) | W | 39 | 26 |
| Feb. 11 | Pittsburgh | (H) | W | 38 | 31 |
| Feb. 18 | Pennsylvania | (A) | W | 36 | 24 |
| Feb. 20 | Western Reserve | (A) | W | 40 | 35 |
| Feb. 24 | Michigan State | (H) | W | 30 | 25 |
| Mar. 1 | Butler (OT) | (A) | W | 42 | 41 |
| Mar. 4 | Wabash | (H) | W | 43 | 29 |
| Mar. 7 | Marquette | (A) | W | 36 | 34 |
| Mar. 11 | Minnesota | (A) | W | 31 | 27 |
| | | | | 749 | 618 |

1933-34 (Won 20, Lost 4, .833)
Coach: George Keogan
Captain: Edward Krause

| Dec. 4 | Kalamazoo | (H) | W | 30 | 22 |
|---|---|---|---|---|---|
| Dec. 9 | Northwestern | (H) | W | 28 | 24 |
| Dec. 13 | Ball State | (H) | W | 43 | 22 |
| Dec. 15 | Albion | (H) | W | 48 | 25 |
| Dec. 19 | Purdue | (H) | W | 39 | 28 |
| Dec. 22 | Bradley | (A) | W | 34 | 27 |
| Dec. 30 | Northwestern | (A) | W | 37 | 21 |
| Jan. 4 | Arizona | (H) | W | 46 | 24 |
| Jan. 6 | Michigan State (3 OT) | (A) | W | 34 | 33 |
| Jan. 9 | Marquette | (H) | W | 30 | 28 |
| Jan. 13 | Butler | (H) | W | 37 | 17 |
| Jan. 20 | Pittsburgh | (A) | L | 34 | 39 |
| Jan. 24 | Chicago | (H) | W | 37 | 26 |
| Jan. 31 | Valparaiso | (H) | W | 27 | 25 |
| Feb. 3 | Detroit | (A) | W | 36 | 17 |
| Feb. 6 | Minnesota | (H) | W | 43 | 34 |
| Feb. 10 | Xavier | (A) | W | 25 | 15 |
| Feb. 12 | Temple | (A) | W | 42 | 33 |
| Feb. 17 | Pittsburgh | (H) | L | 17 | 21 |
| Feb. 21 | Michigan State | (H) | W | 28 | 19 |
| Feb. 24 | Butler | (A) | W | 34 | 24 |
| Mar. 3 | Ohio State | (H) | W | 33 | 21 |
| Mar. 10 | Marquette | (A) | L | 20 | 21 |
| Mar. 12 | Minnesota (OT) | (A) | L | 41 | 43 |
| | | | | 823 | 609 |

1934-35 (Won 13, Lost 9, .591)
Coach: George Keogan (Joe Boland and Tom Conley Jan. 31)
Captain: John Jordan

| Dec. 7 | Kalamazoo | (H) | W | 35 | 18 |
|---|---|---|---|---|---|
| Dec. 15 | Albion | (H) | W | 37 | 11 |
| Dec. 18 | Northwestern | (H) | L | 25 | 26 |
| Dec. 26 | Stanford | (H) | W | 29 | 19 |
| Dec. 29 | New York U. * | (N1) | L | 18 | 25 |
| Dec. 31 | Holy Cross | (N2) | W | 45 | 19 |
| Jan. 5 | Minnesota | (A) | L | 28 | 30 |
| Jan. 8 | Marquette | (H) | W | 23 | 20 |
| Jan. 12 | Butler | (H) | W | 30 | 29 |
| Jan. 19 | Pittsburgh | (A) | L | 22 | 26 |
| Jan. 21 | Detroit | (A) | W | 41 | 28 |
| Jan. 26 | Chicago | (H) | W | 32 | 20 |

| Jan. 31 | Ohio State | (A) | L | 22 | 31 |
|---|---|---|---|---|---|
| Feb. 2 | Washington (MO) | (H) | W | 38 | 15 |
| Feb. 5 | Illinois | (A) | L | 26 | 27 |
| Feb. 9 | Northwestern | (A) | W | 28 | 26 |
| Feb. 16 | Pittsburgh** | (H) | L | 25 | 27 |
| Feb. 23 | Butler | (A) | W | 27 | 23 |
| Mar. 1 | Marquette | (A) | L | 21 | 36 |
| Mar. 4 | Minnesota | (H) | W | 38 | 27 |
| Mar. 9 | Xavier | (A) | W | 42 | 34 |
| Mar. 11 | Temple | (N3) | L | 26 | 34 |
| | | | | 658 | 551 |

N1—New York, NY. (Madison Square Garden); N2 — Boston, MA.; N3 — Philadelphia, PA. (Convention Hall)
* First regular college basketball doubleheader in Madison Square Garden (Game 2)
** Game lasted approximately 52½ minutes as a result of timekeeper's error

1935-36 (Won 22, Lost 2, Tied 1, .900)
Coach: George Keogan
Captains: John Ford and Martin Peters

| Nov. 30 | Albion | (H) | W | 62 | 26 |
|---|---|---|---|---|---|
| Dec. 4 | St. Mary's (MN) | (H) | W | 45 | 22 |
| Dec. 4 | Kalamazoo | (H) | W | 65 | 17 |
| Dec. 7 | Millikin | (N1) | W | 58 | 30 |
| Dec. 7 | St. Joseph's (IN) | (N1) | W | 71 | 22 |
| Dec. 10 | Washington (MO) | (A) | W | 35 | 27 |
| Dec. 16 | Northwestern | (H) | W | 40 | 29 |
| Dec. 23 | Purdue | (A) | L | 40 | 54 |
| Dec. 31 | Northwestern* | (A) | T | 20 | 20 |
| Jan. 4 | Minnesota | (A) | W | 29 | 27 |
| Jan. 10 | Pittsburgh | (A) | W | 43 | 35 |
| Jan. 14 | Marquette | (H) | W | 37 | 22 |
| Jan. 18 | Pennsylvania | (A) | W | 37 | 27 |
| Jan. 20 | Syracuse | (A) | W | 46 | 43 |
| Jan. 25 | Butler | (H) | W | 35 | 27 |
| Feb. 1 | St. Benedict's | (H) | W | 53 | 17 |
| Feb. 5 | Illinois | (H) | W | 33 | 23 |
| Feb. 10 | Kentucky | (H) | W | 41 | 20 |
| Feb. 14 | New York U. | (N2) | W | 38 | 27 |
| Feb. 22 | Pittsburgh | (H) | W | 43 | 27 |
| Feb. 25 | Minnesota | (H) | W | 37 | 15 |
| Feb. 29 | Butler | (A) | W | 34 | 30 |
| Mar. 4 | Ohio State | (H) | L | 23 | 28 |

| Mar. 7 | Marquette | (A) | W | 37 | 34 |
|--------|-----------|-----|---|-----|-----|
| Mar. 10 | Detroit | (A) | W | 51 | 28 |
| | | | | 1053 | 677 |

N1–South Bend, IN. (Studebaker Gym); N2 – New York, NY. (Madison Square Garden)
* Scorer's error not discovered until after game completed

1936-37 (Won 20, Lost 3, .870)
Coach: George Keogan
Captain: Ray Meyer

| Dec. 5 | Kalamazoo | (H) | W | 41 | 27 |
|--------|-----------|-----|---|-----|-----|
| Dec. 8 | St. Mary's (MN) | (H) | W | 39 | 27 |
| Dec. 12 | Western Illinois | (H) | W | 37 | 22 |
| Dec. 16 | Northwestern | (H) | L | 19 | 38 |
| Dec. 19 | Illinois | (A) | L | 29 | 44 |
| Dec. 31 | Northwestern | (A) | W | 24 | 23 |
| Jan. 2 | Chicago | (A) | W | 30 | 27 |
| Jan. 5 | Kentucky | (N1) | W | 41 | 28 |
| Jan. 9 | Butler | (H) | W | 25 | 24 |
| Jan. 13 | Pittsburgh | (A) | L | 31 | 34 |
| Jan. 18 | Syracuse | (H) | W | 52 | 31 |
| Jan. 23 | Pennsylvania | (A) | W | 41 | 36 |
| Jan. 25 | Western Reserve | (A) | W | 55 | 20 |
| Feb. 3 | Purdue | (H) | W | 47 | 40 |
| Feb. 6 | Illinois | (H) | W | 41 | 33 |
| Feb. 13 | New York U. | (N2) | W | 52 | 26 |
| Feb. 15 | Canisius* | (A) | W | 40 | 36 |
| Feb. 20 | Pittsburgh | (H) | W | 29 | 18 |
| Feb. 23 | Marquette | (H) | W | 41 | 24 |
| Feb. 27 | Butler | (A) | W | 42 | 17 |
| Mar. 6 | Marquette | (A) | W | 39 | 35 |
| Mar. 8 | Minnesota | (H) | W | 44 | 18 |
| Mar. 12 | Detroit | (A) | W | 36 | 18 |
| | | | | 875 | 646 |

N1–Louisville, KY.; N2–New York, NY. (Madison Square Garden)
* Notre Dame's 400th victory

1937-38 (Won 20, Lost 3, .870)
Coach: George Keogan
Captain: Ray Meyer

| Dec. 1 | Columbia College (IA) | (H) | W | 49 | 18 |
|--------|-----------------------|-----|---|-----|-----|
| Dec. 4 | Ball State | (H) | W | 43 | 28 |
| Dec. 8 | Western Michigan | (H) | W | 60 | 21 |
| Dec. 13 | Wisconsin | (H) | W | 33 | 31 |

| Dec. 18 | Northwestern | (H) | W | 30 | 27 |
|---|---|---|---|---|---|
| Dec. 22 | Xavier | (A) | W | 45 | 26 |
| Dec. 28 | Illinois (OT) | (A) | L | 32 | 33 |
| Dec. 31 | Northwestern | (A) | W | 40 | 29 |
| Jan. 4 | Minnesota | (A) | L | 25 | 37 |
| Jan. 8 | Pennsylvania | (A) | W | 45 | 25 |
| Jan. 10 | Canisius | (A) | W | 57 | 33 |
| Jan. 15 | Kentucky | (H) | W | 47 | 37 |
| Jan. 19 | Pittsburgh | (A) | W | 51 | 41 |
| Jan. 22 | Butler | (H) | W | 39 | 26 |
| Feb. 1 | St. Louis | (H) | W | 50 | 25 |
| Feb. 5 | Pittsburgh | (H) | W | 51 | 17 |
| Feb. 9 | Marquette | (A) | L | 43 | 45 |
| Feb. 14 | Butler | (A) | W | 45 | 22 |
| Feb. 21 | Michigan State | (H) | W | 48 | 32 |
| Feb. 25 | New York U. | (N1) | W | 50 | 38 |
| Feb. 26 | Colgate | (N2) | W | 49 | 38 |
| Mar. 4 | Marquette | (H) | W | 39 | 28 |
| Mar. 11 | Detroit | (A) | W | 45 | 31 |
| | | | | 1016 | 688 |

N1—New York, NY. (Madison Square Garden); N2—Albany, NY.

**1938-39 (Won 15, Lost 6, .714)**
Coach: George Keogan
Captain: Earl Brown

| Dec. 1 | Kalamazoo | (H) | W | 64 | 13 |
|---|---|---|---|---|---|
| Dec. 3 | Ball State | (H) | W | 70 | 30 |
| Dec. 10 | Wisconsin | (A) | L | 39 | 45 |
| Dec. 15 | Michigan | (H) | L | 38 | 40 |
| Dec. 22 | Northwestern | (H) | W | 48 | 30 |
| Dec. 31 | Northwestern | (A) | L | 39 | 43 |
| Jan. 2 | Cornell | (H) | W | 48 | 18 |
| Jan. 7 | Butler | (H) | W | 37 | 35 |
| Jan. 14 | Kentucky | (N1) | W | 42 | 37 |
| Jan. 16 | Western Reserve | (H) | W | 59 | 36 |
| Jan. 21 | Canisius | (A) | W | 72 | 36 |
| Jan. 23 | John Carroll | (A) | W | 74 | 37 |
| Jan. 28 | Minnesota | (H) | W | 55 | 33 |
| Feb. 3 | Illinois | (H) | W | 38 | 24 |
| Feb. 11 | New York U. | (N2) | W | 34 | 30 |
| Feb. 13 | Syracuse (OT) | (A) | W | 35 | 34 |
| Feb. 18 | Marquette | (H) | L | 22 | 47 |
| Feb. 25 | Marquette | (A) | L | 50 | 58 |
| Mar. 1 | Butler | (A) | L | 27 | 35 |

| Mar. 7 | Detroit | (A) | W | 48 | 42 |
| Mar. 12 | New York U. | (H) | W | 46 | 42 |
| | | | | 985 | 745 |

N1—Louisville, KY.; N2—New York, NY. (Madison Square Garden)

1939-40 (Won 15, Lost 6, .714)
Coach: George Keogan
Captain: Mark Ertel

| Nov. 30 | Kalamazoo | (H) | W | 62 | 34 |
| Dec. 4 | Valparaiso | (A) | W | 63 | 26 |
| Dec. 6 | Cincinnati | (H) | W | 54 | 17 |
| Dec. 12 | Wisconsin | (H) | W | 51 | 33 |
| Dec. 16 | Michigan | (A) | L | 39 | 41 |
| Dec. 22 | Southern California | (H) | L | 38 | 55 |
| Dec. 27 | Illinois | (A) | L | 29 | 42 |
| Dec. 30 | Northwestern | (A) | L | 37 | 47 |
| Jan. 6 | Syracuse | (H) | W | 33 | 29 |
| Jan. 13 | Kentucky | (H) | W | 52 | 47 |
| Jan. 16 | Butler | (H) | W | 55 | 39 |
| Jan. 20 | Pennsylvania | (A) | W | 55 | 35 |
| Jan. 27 | Northwestern | (H) | W | 56 | 27 |
| Feb. 3 | Illinois | (H) | W | 58 | 40 |
| Feb. 10 | New York U. | (N) | L | 43 | 52 |
| Feb. 12 | Toledo | (A) | W | 38 | 30 |
| Feb. 17 | John Carroll | (H) | W | 46 | 27 |
| Feb. 20 | Marquette | (H) | W | 56 | 39 |
| Feb. 26 | Butler | (A) | L | 38 | 39 |
| Mar. 2 | Marquette | (A) | W | 36 | 32 |
| Mar. 9 | Detroit | (A) | W | 47 | 40 |
| | | | | 986 | 771 |

N—New York, NY. (Madison Square Garden)

1940-41 (Won 17, Lost 5, .773)
Coach: George Keogan (Ray Meyer from Feb. 8, 1941 to end of season)
Captain: Edward Riska

| Nov. 30 | Monmouth | (H) | W | 81 | 34 |
| Nov. 30 | Kalamazoo | (H) | W | 73 | 37 |
| Dec. 7 | Illinois Wesleyan | (H) | W | 34 | 28 |
| Dec. 14 | Wisconsin | (A) | L | 43 | 44 |
| Dec. 19 | Michigan | (H) | W | 37 | 27 |
| Dec. 23 | Illinois (OT) | (H) | L | 39 | 41 |
| Dec. 31 | Northwestern | (A) | L | 36 | 46 |
| Jan. 4 | Kentucky | (N1) | W | 48 | 47 |
| Jan. 6 | Wabash | (H) | W | 53 | 38 |

| Jan. 11 | Butler | (H) | W | 45 | 35 |
|---|---|---|---|---|---|
| Jan. 18 | Pennsylvania | (A) | W | 53 | 37 |
| Jan. 20 | Syracuse (OT) | (A) | W | 54 | 49 |
| Jan. 25 | Michigan State | (H) | W | 46 | 39 |
| Feb. 1 | Marquette | (H) | W | 58 | 40 |
| Feb. 4 | North Dakota | (H) | W | 46 | 38 |
| Feb. 8 | Northwestern | (H) | W | 47 | 36 |
| Feb. 14 | New York U. | (N2) | W | 41 | 38 |
| Feb. 22 | Carnegie Tech | (H) | W | 53 | 42 |
| Feb. 24 | Butler | (A) | L | 40 | 54 |
| Mar. 1 | Michigan State | (A) | L | 35 | 44 |
| Mar. 8 | Marquette | (A) | W | 44 | 39 |
| Mar. 12 | Detroit | (A) | W | 56 | 42 |
| | | | | 1062 | 875 |

N1—Louisville, KY.; N2—New York, NY. (Madison Square Garden)

1941-42 (Won 16, Lost 6, .727)
Coach: George Keogan (Ray Meyer all away/neutral games except Feb. 9)
Captain: Arthur Pope

| Nov. 29 | Franklin | (H) | W | 49 | 30 |
|---|---|---|---|---|---|
| Dec. 3 | Great Lakes | (H) | L | 46 | 52 |
| Dec. 6 | St. Louis | (H) | W | 51 | 22 |
| Dec. 13 | Wisconsin | (A) | L | 35 | 43 |
| Dec. 19 | Michigan | (A) | W | 46 | 40 |
| Dec. 23 | Illinois | (A) | L | 29 | 48 |
| Dec. 31 | Northwestern | (A) | W | 40 | 36 |
| Jan. 3 | Harvard | (H) | W | 39 | 31 |
| Jan. 7 | Washington (MO) | (H) | W | 34 | 31 |
| Jan. 12 | Syracuse | (H) | W | 51 | 35 |
| Jan. 17 | Butler | (A) | L | 43 | 49 |
| Jan. 21 | Northwestern | (H) | W | 61 | 43 |
| Jan. 24 | Michigan State | (H) | W | 52 | 49 |
| Jan. 31 | Marquette | (H) | W | 66 | 42 |
| Feb. 7 | Kentucky | (H) | W | 46 | 43 |
| Feb. 9 | Great Lakes | (N1) | W | 46 | 43 |
| Feb. 14 | New York U. | (N2) | W | 55 | 43 |
| Feb. 21 | Western Reserve | (H) | W | 70 | 39 |
| Feb. 24 | Butler | (H) | W | 57 | 54 |
| Feb. 28 | Michigan State | (A) | L | 43 | 46 |
| Mar. 7 | Marquette | (A) | L | 43 | 46 |
| Mar. 12 | Detroit | (A) | W | 43 | 41 |
| | | | | 1045 | 906 |

N1—Chicago, IL. (Stadium); N2—New York, NY. (Madison Square Garden)

**1942-43 (Won 18, Lost 2, .900)**
Coach: George Keogan (Died Feb. 17, 1943)
 Edward Krause
Captain: Charles Butler

| Nov. 28 | Ball State | (H) | W | 56 | 42 |
|---|---|---|---|---|---|
| Dec. 4 | Western Michigan | (H) | W | 53 | 35 |
| Dec. 12 | Northwestern | (N1) | W | 53 | 44 |
| Dec. 14 | Wisconsin (OT) | (H) | W | 61 | 59 |
| Dec. 19 | Purdue | (H) | W | 46 | 43 |
| Jan. 16 | Northwestern | (N1) | W | 49 | 36 |
| Jan. 23 | Kentucky | (N2) | L | 55 | 60 |
| Jan. 25 | Butler | (A) | W | 45 | 34 |
| Jan. 30 | DePaul | (N1) | W | 50 | 47 |
| Feb. 2 | Marquette | (H) | W | 50 | 45 |
| Feb. 6 | Michigan State | (H) | W | 45 | 34 |
| Feb. 13 | New York U. * | (N3) | W | 74 | 43 |
| Feb. 15 | Canisius | (A) | W | 55 | 37 |
| Feb. 20 | Great Lakes (OT) | (N1) | L | 56 | 60 |
| Feb. 23 | Butler | (H) | W | 64 | 32 |
| Feb. 27 | Michigan State | (A) | W | 45 | 42 |
| Mar. 2 | Wabash | (H) | W | 69 | 42 |
| Mar. 6 | Marquette | (A) | W | 49 | 47 |
| Mar. 8 | Great Lakes (OT) | (A) | W | 44 | 42 |
| Mar. 12 | Detroit | (H) | W | 52 | 43 |
| | | | | 1071 | 867 |

N1–Chicago, IL. (Stadium); N2–Louisville, KY.; N3–New York, NY.
 (Madison Square Garden)
* Notre Dame's 500th victory

**1943-44 (Won 10, Lost 9, .526)**
Coach: Edward Krause (Wally Ziemba Mar. 3)
Captain: Bernard Rutledge

| Dec. 1 | Alma | (H) | W | 56 | 32 |
|---|---|---|---|---|---|
| Dec. 4 | Western Michigan | (H) | L | 42 | 46 |
| Dec. 18 | Wisconsin | (H) | W | 41 | 31 |
| Dec. 8 | Northwestern | (N1) | L | 32 | 48 |
| Dec. 23 | Purdue | (H) | W | 47 | 40 |
| Dec. 31 | Wisconsin | (N2) | L | 45 | 47 |
| Jan. 3 | Purdue | (A) | W | 35 | 32 |
| Jan. 18 | Kentucky | (N3) | L | 54 | 55 |
| Jan. 11 | Marquette | (H) | W | 52 | 46 |
| Jan. 21 | Northwestern | (N1) | L | 36 | 43 |
| Jan. 26 | Valparaiso | (H) | W | 57 | 44 |
| Jan. 29 | Marquette | (A) | L | 43 | 60 |
| Feb. 2 | Bunker Hill | (H) | W | 65 | 55 |

| Feb. 5 | DePaul | (N1) | L | 45 | 61 |
|--------|--------|------|---|----|----|
| Feb. 9 | Great Lakes | (A) | L | 48 | 84 |
| Feb. 14 | New York U. | (N4) | W | 59 | 53 |
| Feb. 19 | Great Lakes | (N1) | W | 54 | 51 |
| Feb. 26 | Iowa | (H) | W | 66 | 42 |
| Mar. 3 | Camp Grant | (N1) | L | 47 | 63 |
| | | | | 924 | 933 |

N1—Chicago, IL. (Stadium); N2—Milwaukee, WI.; N3—Louisville, KY.;
N4—New York, NY. (Madison Square Garden)

**1944-45 (Won 15, Lost 5, .750)**
Coach: Clem Crowe
Captain: Vince Boryla (honorary)

| Dec. 6 | Kellogg Field | (H) | W | 89 | 28 |
|--------|---------------|-----|---|----|----|
| Dec. 9 | Miami (OH) | (H) | W | 68 | 34 |
| Dec. 12 | Alma | (H) | W | 71 | 30 |
| Dec. 16 | Wisconsin | (A) | W | 57 | 46 |
| Dec. 19 | Loras | (H) | W | 91 | 44 |
| Dec. 23 | Iowa | (A) | L | 46 | 63 |
| Dec. 30 | Purdue | (H) | W | 49 | 47 |
| Jan. 2 | Purdue | (A) | L | 32 | 44 |
| Jan. 6 | Great Lakes | (A) | L | 58 | 59 |
| Jan. 10 | Iowa Pre-Flight | (A) | W | 49 | 44 |
| Jan. 16 | Marquette | (H) | W | 79 | 56 |
| Jan. 20 | Great Lakes | (N1) | W | 55 | 51 |
| Jan. 27 | Kentucky (OT) | (N2) | W | 59 | 58 |
| Feb. 2 | DePaul | (N1) | L | 52 | 56 |
| Feb. 3 | Northwestern | (N1) | W | 56 | 37 |
| Feb. 10 | New York U. | (N3) | W | 66 | 60 |
| Feb. 14 | Iowa Pre-Flight | (H) | W | 51 | 38 |
| Feb. 17 | Marquette | (A) | L | 55 | 56 |
| Feb. 27 | Northwestern | (H) | W | 71 | 66 |
| Mar. 6 | Detroit | (H) | W | 87 | 43 |
| | | | | 1241 | 960 |

N1—Chicago, IL. (Stadium); N2—Louisville, KY.; N3—New York, NY.
(Madison Square Garden)

**1945-46 (Won 17, Lost 4, .810)**
Coach: Elmer Ripley
Captain: William Hassett

| Dec. 8 | Camp Atterbury | (H) | W | 56 | 37 |
|--------|----------------|-----|---|----|----|
| Dec. 11 | Chanute Field | (H) | W | 52 | 45 |
| Dec. 15 | Wisconsin | (H) | W | 65 | 51 |
| Dec. 19 | St. Louis | (H) | W | 60 | 45 |
| Dec. 22 | Purdue | (H) | W | 49 | 47 |

| Jan. 2 | Purdue | (A) | W | 50 | 48 |
|--------|--------|-----|---|-----|-----|
| Jan. 5 | DePaul | (H) | W | 43 | 42 |
| Jan. 11 | Great Lakes | (A) | W | 72 | 50 |
| Jan. 14 | St. Louis | (A) | W | 51 | 48 |
| Jan. 18 | Great Lakes | (N1) | W | 56 | 54 |
| Jan. 22 | Marquette | (H) | W | 69 | 67 |
| Jan. 26 | Kentucky | (N2) | W | 56 | 47 |
| Jan. 31 | Michigan State | (H) | W | 62 | 57 |
| Feb. 2 | Northwestern | (N1) | L | 55 | 56 |
| Feb. 7 | Canisius | (A) | W | 69 | 47 |
| Feb. 9 | New York U. | (N3) | L | 58 | 62 |
| Feb. 16 | Marquette | (A) | L | 59 | 68 |
| Feb. 20 | Michigan State | (A) | W | 56 | 54 |
| Feb. 23 | DePaul | (N1) | L | 47 | 63 |
| Feb. 26 | Northwestern | (H) | W | 57 | 50 |
| Mar. 2 | Detroit | (A) | W | 66 | 39 |
| | | | | 1208 | 1077 |

N1—Chicago, IL. (Stadium); N2—Louisville, KY.; N3—New York, NY. (Madison Square Garden)

1946-47 (Won 20, Lost 4, .833)
Coach: Edward Krause
Captain: Francis Curran

| Dec. 4 | Franklin | (H) | W | 86 | 38 |
|--------|----------|-----|---|-----|-----|
| Dec. 7 | Ball State | (H) | W | 80 | 31 |
| Dec. 9 | Indiana | (A) | W | 70 | 60 |
| Dec. 14 | Wisconsin (OT) | (A) | L | 49 | 53 |
| Dec. 21 | Drake | (H) | W | 59 | 56 |
| Dec. 27 | Dartmouth | (N1) | W | 66 | 55 |
| Jan. 3 | St. Louis | (A) | W | 48 | 46 |
| Jan. 7 | Butler | (H) | W | 86 | 40 |
| Jan. 11 | Purdue | (A) | L | 56 | 60 |
| Jan. 14 | Michigan State | (A) | W | 74 | 56 |
| Jan. 18 | Detroit | (A) | W | 81 | 40 |
| Jan. 25 | Purdue | (H) | W | 74 | 43 |
| Jan. 28 | Marquette | (H) | W | 87 | 61 |
| Feb. 1 | Kentucky | (N2) | L | 30 | 60 |
| Feb. 3 | Butler | (A) | W | 73 | 60 |
| Feb. 8 | Michigan State | (H) | W | 70 | 54 |
| Feb. 11 | Northwestern | (N3) | W | 52 | 44 |
| Feb. 17 | DePaul | (H) | W | 80 | 45 |
| Feb. 22 | Canisius | (A) | W | 45 | 39 |
| Feb. 24 | New York U. | (N4) | W | 64 | 60 |
| Feb. 28 | DePaul | (N3) | L | 50 | 61 |
| Mar. 1 | Northwestern | (N3) | W | 55 | 53 |

| | | | | | |
|---|---|---|---|---|---|
| Mar. 5 | St. Louis | (H) | W | 65 | 43 |
| Mar. 8 | Marquette | (A) | W | 73 | 68 |
| | | | | 1573 | 1226 |

N1—Cleveland, OH.; N2—Louisville, KY.; N3—Chicago, IL. (Stadium);
N4—New York, NY. (Madison Square Garden)

1947-48 (Won 17, Lost 7, .708)
Coach: Edward Krause (John Brennan Dec. 6)
Captain: John Hiller

| | | | | | |
|---|---|---|---|---|---|
| Dec. 6 | Indiana State | (H) | W | 66 | 49 |
| Dec. 8 | Illinois | (A) | L | 38 | 40 |
| Dec. 13 | Northwestern | (N1) | W | 61 | 55 |
| Dec. 20 | Denver | (A) | L | 60 | 61 |
| Dec. 23 | Kansas | (A) | W | 51 | 49 |
| Jan. 1 | Indiana—(Hoosier Classic) | (N2) | L | 46 | 72 |
| Jan. 2 | Purdue—(Hoosier Classic) | (N2) | W | 42 | 40 |
| Jan. 5 | Georgetown | (H) | W | 77 | 69 |
| Jan. 7 | Butler | (H) | W | 71 | 47 |
| Jan. 10 | DePaul | (H) | W | 52 | 46 |
| Jan. 17 | St. Louis | (A) | L | 40 | 42 |
| Jan. 24 | Northwestern (OT) | (N1) | W | 59 | 48 |
| Feb. 2 | Kentucky | (H) | W | 64 | 55 |
| Feb. 4 | Butler | (A) | W | 53 | 52 |
| Feb. 5 | Detroit | (A) | W | 55 | 30 |
| Feb. 9 | St. Louis | (H) | L | 51 | 68 |
| Feb. 14 | DePaul | (N1) | L | 46 | 50 |
| Feb. 17 | Michigan State | (A) | W | 51 | 44 |
| Feb. 24 | Michigan State | (H) | L | 50 | 54 |
| Feb. 25 | Marquette | (H) | W | 72 | 55 |
| Feb. 28 | Canisius | (A) | W | 64 | 53 |
| Mar. 1 | New York U. | (N3) | W | 64 | 59 |
| Mar. 3 | Pennsylvania | (A) | W | 60 | 56 |
| Mar. 6 | Marquette | (A) | W | 76 | 62 |
| | | | | 1369 | 1256 |

N1—Chicago, IL. (Stadium); N2—Indianapolis, IN.; N3—New York, NY.
(Madison Square Garden)

1948-49 (Won 17, Lost 7, .708)
Coach: Edward Krause
Captain: Paul Gordon

| | | | | | |
|---|---|---|---|---|---|
| Dec. 8 | Illinois (OT) | (H) | L | 58 | 59 |
| Dec. 11 | Northwestern | (N1) | W | 55 | 44 |
| Dec. 13 | Wisconsin | (H) | W | 60 | 54 |
| Dec. 20 | Pennsylvania | (H) | W | 55 | 42 |
| Dec. 22 | Navy | (N1) | W | 70 | 62 |

| Dec. 27 | Purdue – (Hoosier Classic) | (N2) | W | 51 | 50 |
| Dec. 28 | Indiana – (Hoosier Classic) | (N2) | L | 47 | 50 |
| Dec. 30 | Southern Methodist | (A) | W | 58 | 45 |
| Jan. 3 | St. Mary's (CA) | (N3) | W | 70 | 66 |
| Jan. 11 | DePaul | (H) | L | 38 | 59 |
| Jan. 18 | Butler | (H) | W | 60 | 58 |
| Jan. 22 | Denver | (H) | W | 49 | 46 |
| Jan. 29 | Kentucky | (N4) | L | 38 | 62 |
| Jan. 31 | Butler | (A) | L | 54 | 68 |
| Feb. 3 | Michigan State | (H) | W | 63 | 47 |
| Feb. 8 | Marquette | (A) | W | 71 | 64 |
| Feb. 12 | St. Louis | (A) | L | 44 | 61 |
| Feb. 16 | Marquette | (H) | W | 59 | 42 |
| Feb. 19 | DePaul | (N1) | W | 54 | 49 |
| Feb. 23 | Michigan State* | (A) | W | 43 | 41 |
| Feb. 26 | Canisius | (A) | W | 59 | 51 |
| Feb. 28 | New York U. | (N5) | W | 71 | 66 |
| Mar. 5 | Northwestern | (N1) | W | 59 | 56 |
| Mar. 7 | St. Louis | (H) | L | 59 | 68 |
| | | | | 1345 | 1310 |

N1 – Chicago, IL. (Stadium); N2 – Indianapolis, IN.; N3 – San Francisco, CA.;
    N4 – Louisville, KY.; N5 – New York, NY (Madison Square Garden)
* Notre Dame's 600th victory

1949-50 (Won 15, Lost 9, .625)
Coach: Edward Krause
Captain: Kevin O'Shea

| Dec. 8 | Creighton | (H) | W | 57 | 50 |
| Dec. 13 | Wisconsin | (A) | L | 48 | 56 |
| Dec. 17 | Northwestern | (N1) | L | 56 | 66 |
| Dec. 19 | Iowa | (H) | L | 62 | 64 |
| Dec. 29 | Indiana – (Hoosier Classic) | (N2) | L | 69 | 79 |
| Dec. 30 | Purdue – (Hoosier Classic) | (N2) | W | 59 | 41 |
| Jan. 4 | Butler | (H) | W | 54 | 33 |
| Jan. 7 | Michigan State | (A) | W | 76 | 65 |
| Jan. 11 | DePaul | (H) | W | 58 | 53 |
| Jan. 13 | John Carroll | (A) | W | 73 | 66 |
| Jan. 14 | Canisius | (A) | L | 50 | 53 |
| Jan. 18 | Michigan State | (H) | W | 71 | 65 |
| Jan. 23 | Kentucky | (H) | W | 64 | 51 |
| Jan. 28 | Northwestern | (N1) | W | 64 | 57 |
| Jan. 31 | Butler | (A) | L | 57 | 63 |
| Feb. 4 | Marquette | (H) | W | 79 | 61 |
| Feb. 7 | Loyola (IL) | (N1) | W | 56 | 41 |
| Feb. 11 | St. Louis | (A) | L | 45 | 55 |

| Feb. 14 | Loyola (IL) | (H) | W | 67 | 60 |
| Feb. 18 | DePaul | (N1) | L | 58 | 68 |
| Feb. 23 | St. Louis | (H) | W | 55 | 52 |
| Feb. 25 | Navy | (A) | W | 65 | 59 |
| Feb. 27 | New York U. | (N3) | L | 63 | 66 |
| Mar. 4 | Marquette | (A) | W | 65 | 58 |
| | | | | 1471 | 1382 |

N1–Chicago, IL. (Stadium); N2–Indianapolis, IN.; N3–New York, NY. (Madison Square Garden)

1950-51 (Won 13, Lost 11, .542)
Coach: Edward Krause
Captains: Daniel Bagley and Martin O'Connor

| Dec. 6 | Franklin | (H) | W | 67 | 44 |
| Dec. 9 | Anderson | (H) | W | 72 | 46 |
| Dec. 11 | Wisconsin | (H) | W | 67 | 61 |
| Dec. 16 | Northwestern | (N1) | W | 82 | 76 |
| Dec. 18 | Iowa | (A) | L | 60 | 63 |
| Dec. 22 | Purdue–(Hoosier Classic) | (N2) | W | 83 | 70 |
| Dec. 23 | Indiana–(Hoosier Classic) | (N2) | L | 56 | 64 |
| Dec. 30 | Northwestern | (A) | W | 76 | 73 |
| Jan. 3 | St. Louis | (A) | L | 47 | 56 |
| Jan. 5 | Butler | (H) | W | 55 | 48 |
| Jan. 9 | Loyola (IL) | (H) | W | 78 | 67 |
| Jan. 13 | Xavier | (A) | L | 52 | 60 |
| Jan. 15 | Kentucky | (A) | L | 44 | 69 |
| Jan. 25 | Michigan State | (A) | L | 43 | 60 |
| Jan. 30 | Butler | (A) | W | 75 | 65 |
| Feb. 3 | Marquette | (H) | W | 82 | 56 |
| Feb. 10 | DePaul | (N1) | L | 54 | 68 |
| Feb. 13 | St. Louis | (H) | W | 77 | 70 |
| Feb. 16 | DePaul | (H) | W | 61 | 55 |
| Feb. 19 | Michigan State | (H) | W | 56 | 46 |
| Feb. 24 | Canisius | (A) | L | 53 | 60 |
| Feb. 26 | New York U. | (N3) | L | 72 | 87 |
| Feb. 27 | Pennsylvania | (A) | L | 60 | 71 |
| Mar. 3 | Marquette | (A) | L | 50 | 55 |
| | | | | 1522 | 1490 |

N1–Chicago, IL. (Stadium); N2–Indianapolis, IN.; N3–New York, NY. (Madison Square Garden)

1951-52 (Won 16, Lost 10, .615)
Coach: John Jordan
Captain: Leroy Leslie (Donald Strasser was captain at beginning of season but forced to relinquish captaincy because of academic problems)

*Hooping It Up*

| Dec. 1 | St. Thomas | (A) | W | 71 | 37 |
|--------|-----------|-----|---|----|----|
| Dec. 4 | Wabash | (H) | W | 75 | 46 |
| Dec. 8 | Wisconsin | (A) | W | 63 | 53 |
| Dec. 11 | Northwestern | (H) | W | 65 | 54 |
| Dec. 17 | Loyola (IL) | (H) | W | 77 | 57 |
| Dec. 22 | Pennsylvania | (H) | W | 83 | 78 |
| Dec. 28 | Indiana—(Hoosier Classic) | (N1) | L | 54 | 67 |
| Dec. 29 | Purdue—(Hoosier Classic) | (N1) | W | 64 | 54 |
| Jan. 2 | Michigan State | (H) | L | 52 | 66 |
| Jan. 5 | Louisville | (A) | L | 59 | 65 |
| Jan. 8 | Butler | (H) | W | 55 | 49 |
| Jan. 12 | Marquette | (A) | W | 74 | 56 |
| Jan. 15 | Michigan State | (A) | W | 56 | 48 |
| Jan. 26 | Canisius | (A) | W | 72 | 59 |
| Jan. 28 | Pittsburgh | (A) | L | 55 | 62 |
| Feb. 2 | Kentucky | (N2) | L | 66 | 71 |
| Feb. 4 | Northwestern | (A) | W | 75 | 69 |
| Feb. 7 | Marquette | (H) | L | 50 | 57 |
| Feb. 9 | St. Louis | (A) | L | 58 | 80 |
| Feb. 11 | Butler | (A) | W | 52 | 48 |
| Feb. 14 | DePaul | (H) | W | 76 | 70 |
| Feb. 18 | Pittsburgh | (H) | L | 60 | 62 |
| Feb. 23 | Navy | (A) | L | 58 | 67 |
| Feb. 25 | New York U. (OT) | (N3) | W | 75 | 74 |
| Feb. 26 | Pennsylvania | (A) | L | 66 | 67 |
| Mar. 1 | DePaul | (N2) | W | 78 | 77 |
| | | | | 1689 | 1593 |

N1—Indianapolis, IN.; N2—Chicago, IL. (Stadium); N3—New York, NY. (Madison Square Garden)

1952-53 (Won 19, Lost 5, .792)
Coach: John Jordan
Captain: Norbert Lewinski

| Dec. 3 | Creighton | (H) | W | 80 | 59 |
|--------|-----------|-----|---|----|----|
| Dec. 6 | Indiana | (H) | W | 71 | 70 |
| Dec. 13 | Marquette | (A) | W | 84 | 64 |
| Dec. 17 | Loyola (IL) | (H) | W | 53 | 45 |
| Dec. 19 | Kansas State —(Michigan State Classic) | (N1) | L | 64 | 80 |
| Dec. 20 | UCLA—(Michigan State Classic) | (N1) | W | 68 | 60 |
| Dec. 27 | Butler | (A) | W | 63 | 49 |
| Dec. 31 | Northwestern | (A) | W | 62 | 57 |
| Jan. 5 | Holy Cross | (N2) | W | 73 | 71 |
| Jan. 6 | New York U. (OT) | (N3) | W | 78 | 77 |
| Jan. 14 | Purdue | (A) | W | 71 | 55 |

| Jan. 17 | St. Louis | (A) | L | 81 | 86 |
| Jan. 19 | Bradley | (H) | W | 74 | 64 |
| Jan. 31 | DePaul | (N4) | L | 56 | 83 |
| Feb. 4 | Butler | (H) | W | 80 | 58 |
| Feb. 11 | Louisville | (H) | W | 73 | 62 |
| Feb. 14 | St. Louis | (N4) | L | 77 | 78 |
| Feb. 16 | Michigan State | (H) | W | 72 | 64 |
| Feb. 18 | Marquette | (H) | W | 74 | 68 |
| Feb. 21 | Northwestern | (H) | W | 83 | 67 |
| Feb. 25 | DePaul | (H) | W | 93 | 67 |
| Mar. 10 | Eastern Kentucky —(NCAA Mideast Regional) | (N5) | W | 72 | 57 |
| Mar. 13 | Pennsylvania —(NCAA Mideast Regional) | (N4) | W | 69 | 57 |
| Mar. 14 | Indiana —(NCAA Mideast Regional) | (N4) | L | 66 | 79 |
| | | | | 1737 | 1577 |

N1—East Lansing, MI.; N2—Boston, MA.; N3—New York, NY. (Madison Square Garden); N4—Chicago, IL. (Stadium); N5—Fort Wayne, IN.

1953-54 (Won 22, Lost 3, .880)
Coach: John Jordan
Captain: Richard Rosenthal

| Dec. 3 | Ball State | (H) | W | 84 | 63 |
| Dec. 8 | Northwestern | (H) | W | 75 | 66 |
| Dec. 10 | Detroit | (H) | W | 72 | 45 |
| Dec. 14 | Indiana | (A) | L | 55 | 66 |
| Dec. 17 | Loyola (IL) | (H) | W | 81 | 65 |
| Dec. 23 | Bradley | (A) | L | 72 | 74 |
| Dec. 31 | Northwestern | (A) | W | 52 | 50 |
| Jan. 6 | Louisville | (H) | W | 72 | 53 |
| Jan. 9 | New York U. | (H) | W | 99 | 64 |
| Jan. 15 | Holy Cross | (N1) | W | 83 | 61 |
| Jan. 16 | Canisius | (A) | W | 78 | 59 |
| Jan. 19 | Purdue | (H) | W | 95 | 74 |
| Feb. 3 | Butler | (H) | W | 95 | 58 |
| Feb. 6 | DePaul | (N2) | W | 59 | 54 |
| Feb. 9 | Michigan State | (A) | W | 74 | 71 |
| Feb. 15 | DePaul | (H) | W | 86 | 71 |
| Feb. 17 | Butler | (A) | W | 81 | 56 |
| Feb. 20 | Navy | (A) | W | 84 | 72 |
| Feb. 22 | Pennsylvania | (A) | W | 62 | 47 |
| Feb. 25 | Marquette | (H) | W | 79 | 66 |
| Feb. 27 | Loyola (IL) | (N2) | W | 71 | 65 |

| Mar. 6 | Marquette | (A) | W | 79 | 68 |
| Mar. 9 | Loyola (LA) | | | | |
| | −(NCAA Mideast Regional) | (N3) | W | 80 | 70 |
| Mar. 12 | Indiana | | | | |
| | −(NCAA Mideast Regional) | (N4) | W | 65 | 64 |
| Mar. 13 | Penn State | | | | |
| | −(NCAA Mideast Regional) | (N4) | L | 63 | 71 |
| | | | | 1896 | 1573 |

N1−Boston, MA.; N2−Chicago, IL. (Stadium); N3−Fort Wayne, IN.; N4−Iowa City, IA.


1954-55 (Won 14, Lost 10, .583)
Coach: John Jordan
Captain: Jack Stephens

| Dec. 3 | Wisconsin | (H) | W | 72 | 61 |
| Dec. 8 | Northwestern | (H) | W | 79 | 69 |
| Dec. 11 | Indiana | (H) | L | 70 | 73 |
| Dcc. 13 | Loyola (IL) | (H) | W | 89 | 76 |
| Dec. 15 | Purdue | (A) | L | 58 | 78 |
| Dec. 18 | Illinois | (A) | L | 57 | 66 |
| Dec. 23 | Minnesota | (A) | L | 66 | 77 |
| Dec. 29 | Loyola (LA) | | | | |
| | −(Sugar Bowl Tournament) | (N1) | W | 66 | 45 |
| Dec. 30 | Holy Cross | | | | |
| | −(Sugar Bowl Tournament) | (N1) | W | 74 | 69 |
| Jan. 3 | Louisville | (A) | L | 69 | 73 |
| Jan. 5 | Butler | (H) | W | 83 | 58 |
| Jan. 8 | New York U. | (N2) | W | 93 | 74 |
| Jan. 10 | Holy Cross | (N3) | L | 57 | 93 |
| Jan. 15 | Northwestern | (A) | W | 82 | 74 |
| Feb. 5 | Loyola (IL) | (N4) | W | 91 | 83 |
| Feb. 7 | Michigan State | (H) | L | 79 | 93 |
| Feb. 10 | Bradley | (H) | W | 87 | 63 |
| Feb. 14 | Butler | (A) | W | 81 | 71 |
| Feb. 19 | Tulsa | (A) | L | 59 | 74 |
| Feb. 21 | Kansas State* | (A) | W | 76 | 74 |
| Feb. 24 | Marquette | (H) | L | 74 | 84 |
| Feb. 26 | DePaul | (N4) | L | 77 | 81 |
| Mar. 1 | DePaul | (H) | W | 72 | 61 |
| Mar. 5 | Marquette | (A) | W | 85 | 64 |
| | | | | 1796 | 1734 |

N1−New Orleans, LA.; N2−New York, NY. (Madison Square Garden);
    N3−Boston, MA.; N4−Chicago, IL. (Stadium)
* Notre Dame's 700th victory

1955-56 (Won 9, Lost 15, .375)
Coach: John Jordan
Captain: John Fannon

| Dec. 1 | Detroit | (A) | L | 71 | 77 |
|---|---|---|---|---|---|
| Dec. 5 | Wisconsin | (H) | L | 66 | 70 |
| Dec. 7 | Loyola (IL) (OT) | (H) | W | 85 | 84 |
| Dec. 10 | Northwestern | (A) | W | 71 | 61 |
| Dec. 13 | Illinois | (H) | L | 93 | 103 |
| Dec. 16 | Minnesota | (A) | L | 75 | 83 |
| Dec. 21 | Michigan State (OT) | (A) | L | 78 | 84 |
| Dec. 29 | Alabama | | | | |
| | −(Sugar Bowl Tournament) | (N1) | W | 86 | 80 |
| Dec. 30 | Utah | | | | |
| | −(Sugar Bowl Tournament) | (N1) | W | 70 | 65 |
| Jan. 4 | Butler | (H) | W | 83 | 69 |
| Jan. 7 | DePaul (OT) | (H) | L | 74 | 77 |
| Jan. 11 | Louisville (OT) | (H) | L | 75 | 80 |
| Jan. 16 | Northwestern | (H) | W | 86 | 72 |
| Jan. 30 | Indiana | (A) | L | 76 | 81 |
| Feb. 4 | Loyola (IL) | (N2) | L | 65 | 71 |
| Feb. 7 | Butler | (A) | L | 74 | 81 |
| Feb. 11 | Navy | (A) | W | 70 | 63 |
| Feb. 12 | Holy Cross | (N3) | L | 72 | 84 |
| Feb. 14 | Providence (OT) | (A) | L | 83 | 85 |
| Feb. 18 | Purdue | (H) | L | 68 | 80 |
| Feb. 20 | Marquette | (H) | W | 88 | 85 |
| Feb. 25 | DePaul | (N2) | L | 74 | 80 |
| Feb. 29 | Marquette | (A) | W | 87 | 69 |
| Mar. 3 | Bradley | (A) | L | 63 | 69 |
| | | | | 1833 | 1853 |

N1−New Orleans, LA.; N2−Chicago, IL. (Stadium); N3−Boston, MA.

1956-57 (Won 20, Lost 8, .714)
Coach: John Jordan
Captain: John Smyth

| Dec. 5 | St. Joseph's (IN) | (H) | W | 98 | 55 |
|---|---|---|---|---|---|
| Dec. 8 | Wisconsin | (A) | W | 75 | 55 |
| Dec. 10 | Northwestern | (H) | L | 60 | 75 |
| Dec. 15 | Purdue | (A) | L | 72 | 85 |
| Dec. 17 | Valparaiso | (H) | W | 86 | 74 |
| Dec. 22 | Louisville | (A) | L | 75 | 85 |
| Dec. 26 | New York U. | | | | |
| | −(ECAC Holiday Festival) | (N1) | W | 72 | 71 |
| Dec. 28 | Brigham Young | | | | |
| | −(ECAC Holiday Festival) | (N1) | W | 91 | 66 |

| Dec. 29 | Manhattan | | | | |
|---|---|---|---|---|---|
| | –(ECAC Holiday Festival) | (N1) | L | 79 | 86 |
| Jan. 5 | Butler | (H) | L | 84 | 86 |
| Jan. 7 | Northwestern | (A) | W | 82 | 61 |
| Jan. 12 | Loyola (IL) | (H) | W | 90 | 76 |
| Jan. 15 | Michigan State | (H) | W | 86 | 76 |
| Jan. 26 | Illinois | (N2) | L | 81 | 99 |
| Jan. 29 | Indiana | (H) | W | 94 | 82 |
| Feb. 2 | Canisius (2 OT) | (A) | L | 89 | 94 |
| Feb. 4 | Holy Cross | (N3) | W | 99 | 82 |
| Feb. 7 | Portland | (H) | W | 78 | 64 |
| Feb. 9 | Loyola (IL) | (N2) | W | 96 | 64 |
| Feb. 13 | Butler | (A) | W | 70 | 65 |
| Feb. 20 | Detroit | (H) | W | 99 | 88 |
| Feb. 23 | DePaul | (H) | W | 95 | 80 |
| Feb. 26 | Marquette | (A) | W | 76 | 56 |
| Mar. 2 | DePaul | (A) | W | 85 | 73 |
| Mar. 6 | Marquette | (H) | W | 94 | 55 |
| Mar. 12 | Miami (OH) | | | | |
| | –(NCAA Mideast Regional) | (N4) | W | 89 | 77 |
| Mar. 15 | Michigan State | | | | |
| | –(NCAA Mideast Regional) | (N5) | L | 83 | 85 |
| Mar. 16 | Pittsburgh | | | | |
| | –(NCAA Mideast Regional) | (N5) | W | 86 | 85 |
| | | | | 2364 | 2100 |

N1–New York, NY (Madison Square Garden); N2–Chicago, IL. (Stadium); N3–Boston, MA.; N4–Columbus, OH.; N5–Lexington, KY.

1957-58 (Won 24, Lost 5, .828)
Coach: John Jordan (Jim Gibbons Jan 25–Feb 1)
Captains: Robert Devine and John McCarthy

| Dec. 3 | St. Ambrose | (H) | W | 82 | 63 |
|---|---|---|---|---|---|
| Dec. 7 | Wisconsin | (A) | W | 75 | 53 |
| Dec. 9 | Nebraska | (H) | W | 69 | 56 |
| Dec. 14 | Marquette | (A) | L | 64 | 78 |
| Dec. 17 | Loyola (IL) | (H) | W | 82 | 63 |
| Dec. 21 | Michigan State | (A) | L | 72 | 79 |
| Dec. 27 | Purdue–(Hoosier Classic) | (N1) | W | 68 | 61 |
| Dec. 28 | Indiana–(Hoosier Classic) | (N1) | W | 89 | 74 |
| Dec. 31 | Northwestern | (A) | W | 71 | 66 |
| Jan. 6 | Butler | (H) | W | 83 | 72 |
| Jan. 10 | Valparaiso | (N2) | W | 94 | 69 |
| Jan. 15 | DePaul | (H) | W | 79 | 61 |
| Jan. 18 | Louisville | (A) | L | 83 | 94 |
| Jan. 25 | Illinois | (N3) | W | 81 | 67 |

| Jan. 29 | Louisville | (H) | W | 73 | 53 |
|---|---|---|---|---|---|
| Feb. 1 | Bradley | (N3) | L | 70 | 81 |
| Feb. 4 | Canisius | (H) | W | 71 | 59 |
| Feb. 8 | Air Force | (H) | W | 98 | 70 |
| Feb. 10 | Marquette | (H) | W | 106 | 74 |
| Feb. 12 | Butler | (A) | W | 90 | 81 |
| Feb. 15 | North Carolina | (N3) | W | 89 | 70 |
| Feb. 20 | New York U. | (N4) | W | 93 | 77 |
| Feb. 22 | Navy | (A) | W | 85 | 63 |
| Feb. 28 | Holy Cross | (H) | W | 86 | 58 |
| Mar. 1 | Detroit | (A) | W | 102 | 96 |
| Mar. 4 | DePaul | (A) | W | 75 | 71 |
| Mar. 11 | Tennessee Tech | | | | |
| | –(NCAA Mideast Regional) | (N5) | W | 94 | 61 |
| Mar. 14 | Indiana | | | | |
| | –(NCAA Mideast Regional) | (N6) | W | 94 | 87 |
| Mar. 15 | Kentucky | | | | |
| | –(NCAA Mideast Regional) | (A) | L | 56 | 89 |
| | | | | 2374 | 2046 |

N1–Indianapolis, IN.; N2–Fort Wayne, IN; N3–Chicago, IL. (Stadium); N4–New York, NY. (Madison Square Garden); N5–Evanston, IL.; N6–Lexington, KY.

1958-59 (Won 12, Lost 13, .480)
Coach: John Jordan
Captains: Tom Hawkins and Eugene Duffy

| Dec. 3 | Bellarmine | (H) | W | 87 | 55 |
|---|---|---|---|---|---|
| Dec. 8 | Northwestern | (H) | L | 63 | 68 |
| Dec. 13 | Wisconsin | (A) | L | 54 | 56 |
| Dec. 17 | Michigan State | (H) | L | 56 | 74 |
| Dec. 19 | North Carolina | | | | |
| | –(Bluegrass Festival) | (N1) | L | 77 | 81 |
| Dec. 20 | Louisville | | | | |
| | –(Bluegrass Festival) | (A) | W | 61 | 53 |
| Dec. 26 | Indiana–(Hoosier Classic) | (N2) | W | 73 | 67 |
| Dec. 27 | Purdue–(Hoosier Classic) | (N2) | L | 59 | 74 |
| Dec. 31 | Northwestern | (A) | L | 67 | 102 |
| Jan. 3 | North Carolina | (N3) | L | 54 | 69 |
| Jan. 6 | Butler | (H) | L | 60 | 62 |
| Jan. 10 | Detroit | (H) | W | 73 | 62 |
| Jan. 13 | DePaul | (A) | L | 66 | 69 |
| Jan. 17 | Loyola (IL) | (H) | W | 88 | 61 |
| Jan. 24 | Illinois | (N4) | W | 85 | 75 |
| Jan. 31 | Xavier | (N4) | L | 71 | 73 |
| Feb. 2 | St. John's (NY) | (H) | W | 72 | 70 |

| Feb. 7 | Canisius | (A) | W | 76 | 59 |
|--------|----------|-----|---|----|----|
| Feb. 9 | Army | (A) | W | 76 | 60 |
| Feb. 14 | Kentucky | (N4) | L | 52 | 71 |
| Feb. 16 | Butler (3 OT) | (A) | L | 89 | 92 |
| Feb. 21 | DePaul | (H) | W | 76 | 67 |
| Feb. 24 | Marquette | (A) | L | 76 | 95 |
| Mar. 2 | Valparaiso | (H) | W | 93 | 65 |
| Mar. 7 | Marquette | (H) | W | 51 | 35 |
|  |  |  |  | 1755 | 1715 |

N1–Louisville, KY.; N2–Indianapolis, IN.; N3–Charlotte, NC.; N4–Chicago, IL. (Stadium)

1959-60 (Won 17, Lost 9, .654)
Coach: John Jordan
Captain: Michael Graney

| Dec. 3 | Western Illinois | (H) | W | 77 | 59 |
|--------|------------------|-----|---|----|----|
| Dec. 5 | Michigan State (OT) | (A) | L | 56 | 61 |
| Dec. 7 | Wisconsin | (H) | W | 78 | 58 |
| Dec. 9 | Northwestern (2 OT) | (A) | W | 93 | 88 |
| Dec. 12 | Air Force | (A) | W | 67 | 52 |
| Dec. 14 | Nebraska | (A) | W | 70 | 62 |
| Dec. 18 | Loyola (IL) | (H) | W | 67 | 45 |
| Dec. 22 | Purdue–(Hoosier Classic) | (N1) | W | 82 | 79 |
| Dec. 23 | Indiana–(Hoosier Classic) | (N1) | L | 60 | 71 |
| Jan. 2 | North Carolina | (N2) | L | 65 | 75 |
| Jan. 5 | Butler | (H) | W | 76 | 51 |
| Jan. 9 | Detroit | (H) | W | 75 | 63 |
| Jan. 12 | DePaul | (A) | W | 73 | 70 |
| Jan. 16 | St. Francis (PA) | (H) | W | 75 | 56 |
| Jan. 19 | Detroit | (A) | L | 61 | 68 |
| Jan. 22 | Bradley | (N3) | L | 65 | 86 |
| Jan. 30 | Illinois | (N3) | L | 67 | 71 |
| Feb. 2 | Canisius | (H) | W | 71 | 65 |
| Feb. 6 | Army | (H) | W | 87 | 55 |
| Feb. 13 | Kentucky | (A) | L | 65 | 68 |
| Feb. 16 | Butler | (A) | W | 79 | 62 |
| Feb. 20 | DePaul | (H) | W | 70 | 58 |
| Feb. 23 | Evansville | (A) | L | 87 | 92 |
| Feb. 27 | Louisville | (N3) | W | 65 | 54 |
| Feb. 29 | Creighton | (H) | W | 76 | 64 |
| Mar. 8 | Ohio |  |  |  |  |
|  | –(NCAA Mideast Regional) | (N4) | L | 66 | 74 |
|  |  |  |  | 1873 | 1707 |

N1–Indianapolis, IN.; N2–Charlotte, NC.; N3–Chicago, IL. (Stadium); N4–Lexington, KY.

1960-61 (Won 12, Lost 14, .462)
Coach: John Jordan
Captain: William Crosby

| Dec. 1 | Western Illinois | (H) | W | 79 | 56 |
|---|---|---|---|---|---|
| Dec. 5 | Evansville | (H) | W | 83 | 68 |
| Dec. 7 | Kentucky | (N1) | L | 62 | 68 |
| Dec. 10 | Bowling Green | (H) | W | 61 | 50 |
| Dec. 16 | UCLA | (A) | L | 54 | 85 |
| Dec. 17 | Southern California | (A) | L | 63 | 93 |
| Dec. 20 | Indiana | (N2) | L | 69 | 74 |
| Dec. 27 | Purdue – (Hoosier Classic) | (N3) | L | 58 | 78 |
| Dec. 28 | Illinois – (Hoosier Classic) | (N3) | W | 69 | 66 |
| Dec. 31 | Northwestern | (A) | L | 56 | 59 |
| Jan. 4 | Butler | (H) | W | 72 | 56 |
| Jan. 7 | North Carolina | (N4) | L | 71 | 73 |
| Jan. 12 | St. Francis (PA) | (H) | W | 76 | 54 |
| Jan. 14 | Detroit | (H) | W | 66 | 62 |
| Jan. 17 | DePaul | (H) | W | 61 | 58 |
| Jan. 28 | Illinois | (N5) | L | 62 | 77 |
| Jan. 30 | Butler | (A) | W | 74 | 69 |
| Feb. 2 | St. John's (NY) | (H) | W | 64 | 63 |
| Feb. 4 | Canisius | (A) | L | 72 | 79 |
| Feb. 6 | Michigan State | (H) | L | 74 | 89 |
| Feb. 11 | Detroit | (A) | L | 71 | 82 |
| Feb. 14 | Bradley (OT) | (N5) | L | 81 | 84 |
| Feb. 18 | Portland | (H) | W | 80 | 49 |
| Feb. 20 | St. Louis | (H) | L | 60 | 74 |
| Feb. 25 | DePaul | (A) | L | 57 | 78 |
| Mar. 1 | Creighton | (H) | W | 61 | 54 |
| | | | | 1756 | 1798 |

N1 – Louisville, KY.; N2 – Fort Wayne, IN.; N3 – Indianapolis, IN.; N4 – Charlotte, NC.; N5 – Chicago, Ill. (Stadium)

1961-62 (Won 7, Lost 16, .304)
Coach: John Jordan
Captain: Armand Reo

| Dec. 1 | Bellarmine | (H) | W | 71 | 52 |
|---|---|---|---|---|---|
| Dec. 4 | Northwestern (OT) | (H) | W | 59 | 58 |
| Dec. 9 | Creighton | (A) | L | 71 | 73 |
| Dec. 11 | Nebraska | (A) | L | 61 | 65 |
| Dec. 16 | Michigan State | (A) | W | 73 | 72 |
| Dec. 18 | New York U. | (H) | L | 73 | 81 |
| Dec. 27 | St. Louis | (A) | L | 72 | 81 |
| Dec. 30 | Kentucky | (N1) | L | 53 | 100 |
| Jan. 2 | Indiana | (N2) | L | 95 | 122 |

| Jan. 6 | North Carolina | (N3) | L | 80 | 99 |
| Jan. 9 | Butler | (H) | L | 67 | 83 |
| Jan. 13 | Detroit* | (H) | W | 77 | 59 |
| Jan. 16 | DePaul | (H) | W | 88 | 80 |
| Jan. 27 | Illinois | (N4) | L | 77 | 85 |
| Jan. 29 | St. John's (NY) (2 OT) | (H) | L | 72 | 78 |
| Feb. 6 | Canisius | (H) | W | 88 | 72 |
| Feb. 10 | Creighton | (H) | L | 71 | 74 |
| Feb. 12 | Butler | (A) | L | 77 | 86 |
| Feb. 17 | Detroit | (A) | L | 87 | 105 |
| Feb. 19 | Purdue | (N2) | L | 90 | 115 |
| Feb. 24 | Bradley | (N4) | L | 87 | 93 |
| Feb. 27 | Evansville | (A) | W | 99 | 91 |
| Mar. 3 | DePaul | (A) | L | 80 | 87 |
| | | | | 1768 | 1911 |

N1–Louisville, KY.; N2–Fort Wayne, IN.; N3–Charlotte, NC.; N4–Chicago, IL. (Stadium)
* Notre Dame's 800th victory

1962-63 (Won 17, Lost 9, .654)
Coach: John Jordan
Captains: John Andreoli and John Matthews

| Dec. 1 | St. Joseph's (IN) | (H) | W | 87 | 73 |
| Dec. 4 | Michigan State | (H) | W | 92 | 85 |
| Dec. 6 | St. Francis (PA) | (H) | W | 101 | 70 |
| Dec. 8 | Valparaiso | (A) | W | 102 | 90 |
| Dec. 11 | Western Michigan | (H) | W | 82 | 68 |
| Dec. 13 | Creighton | (H) | W | 74 | 48 |
| Dec. 22 | Butler | (A) | L | 59 | 66 |
| Dec. 29 | Kentucky | (N1) | L | 70 | 78 |
| Dec. 31 | Illinois | (N2) | W | 90 | 88 |
| Jan. 2 | Indiana | (N3) | W | 73 | 70 |
| Jan. 5 | North Carolina (OT) | (H) | L | 68 | 76 |
| Jan. 9 | DePaul | (H) | W | 82 | 62 |
| Jan. 12 | Detroit | (H) | W | 105 | 70 |
| Jan. 14 | Butler | (H) | W | 80 | 54 |
| Jan. 16 | DePaul | (A) | L | 69 | 83 |
| Jan. 21 | Purdue | (N3) | W | 96 | 86 |
| Feb. 7 | Boston College | (A) | W | 74 | 66 |
| Feb. 9 | St. John's (NY) | (A) | L | 52 | 57 |
| Feb. 13 | Gannon College | (H) | W | 82 | 47 |
| Feb. 16 | Navy | (H) | W | 68 | 56 |
| Feb. 18 | Bowling Green | (A) | L | 58 | 67 |
| Feb. 21 | New York U. | (N4) | L | 79 | 80 |
| Feb. 23 | Detroit | (A) | W | 83 | 79 |

| Feb. 27 | Evansville | (H) | W | 78 | 72 |
|---------|-----------|-----|---|------|------|
| Mar. 2 | Bradley | (N2) | L | 66 | 72 |
| Mar. 11 | Bowling Green | | | | |
| | −(NCAA Mideast Regional) | (N5) | L | 72 | 77 |
| | | | | 2042 | 1840 |

N1−Louisville, KY.; N2−Chicago, IL. (Stadium); N3−Fort Wayne, IN.;
N4−New York, NY. (Madison Square Garden); N5−Evanston, IL.

1963-64 (Won 10, Lost 14, .417)
Coach: John Jordan
Captain: Richard Erlenbaugh

| Dec. 2 | Christian Brothers | (H) | W | 98 | 65 |
|--------|-------------------|-----|---|------|------|
| Dec. 4 | Indiana | (N1) | L | 102 | 108 |
| Dec. 10 | Bowling Green | (H) | W | 79 | 65 |
| Dec. 12 | Valparaiso | (H) | W | 107 | 60 |
| Dec. 14 | Illinois | (A) | L | 68 | 79 |
| Dec. 17 | Western Michigan | (A) | L | 89 | 92 |
| Dec. 21 | Northwestern | (A) | W | 70 | 68 |
| Dec. 28 | Kentucky | (N2) | L | 81 | 101 |
| Dec. 31 | Illinois | (N3) | L | 73 | 87 |
| Jan. 4 | North Carolina | (N4) | L | 68 | 78 |
| Jan. 8 | DePaul | (H) | L | 73 | 86 |
| Jan. 11 | Creighton | (A) | L | 81 | 95 |
| Jan. 13 | Detroit (OT) | (H) | L | 104 | 114 |
| Jan. 18 | Michigan State | (A) | W | 95 | 80 |
| Jan. 21 | Purdue (2 OT) | (N1) | L | 103 | 112 |
| Feb. 3 | Butler | (A) | W | 72 | 64 |
| Feb. 5 | DePaul | (A) | L | 75 | 90 |
| Feb. 8 | Detroit | (A) | L | 89 | 100 |
| Feb. 15 | St. Louis | (H) | W | 82 | 73 |
| Feb. 17 | St. John's (NY) | (H) | W | 89 | 83 |
| Feb. 19 | Butler | (H) | W | 90 | 73 |
| Feb. 22 | Bradley | (N3) | L | 72 | 82 |
| Feb. 25 | Evansville | (H) | W | 91 | 75 |
| Feb. 29 | Creighton | (H) | L | 71 | 84 |
| | | | | 2027 | 2014 |

N1−Fort Wayne, IN.: N2−Louisville, KY.; N3−Chicago, IL. (Stadium);
N4−Greensboro, NC.

1964-65 (Won 15, Lost 12, .556)
Coach: Johnny Dee
Captains: Jay Miller and Walter Sahm

| Dec. 1 | Lewis College | (H) | W | 99 | 87 |
|--------|--------------|-----|---|------|------|
| Dec. 4 | Ball State | (H) | W | 116 | 82 |

| Dec. 8 | Michigan State | (H) | W | 100 | 93 |
|---|---|---|---|---|---|
| Dec. 10 | Detroit | (H) | W | 107 | 86 |
| Dec. 12 | Evansville | (A) | L | 82 | 89 |
| Dec. 19 | St. John's (NY) | (A) | L | 72 | 76 |
| Dec. 21 | Indiana | (N1) | L | 81 | 107 |
| Dec. 29 | Kentucky | (N2) | W | 111 | 97 |
| Dec. 31 | Bradley | (N3) | L | 72 | 74 |
| Jan. 4 | Western Michigan | (H) | W | 115 | 87 |
| Jan. 9 | Houston | (A) | W | 110 | 80 |
| Jan. 11 | St. Louis | (A) | L | 67 | 75 |
| Jan. 16 | Butler | (H) | W | 94 | 57 |
| Jan. 19 | Purdue | (A) | L | 74 | 78 |
| Jan. 23 | Toledo | (H) | W | 113 | 65 |
| Jan. 30 | Illinois | (N3) | L | 87 | 101 |
| Feb. 1 | Wisconsin | (H) | L | 90 | 98 |
| Feb. 6 | Detroit | (A) | L | 74 | 77 |
| Feb. 8 | Butler | (A) | W | 94 | 72 |
| Feb. 10 | DePaul | (H) | W | 62 | 59 |
| Feb. 13 | Ohio | (H) | W | 94 | 86 |
| Feb. 17 | Bowling Green | (A) | W | 88 | 72 |
| Feb. 20 | Duke | (N3) | L | 88 | 101 |
| Feb. 24 | New York U. | (N4) | L | 54 | 60 |
| Feb. 27 | DePaul | (A) | W | 83 | 67 |
| Mar. 1 | Creighton | (H) | W | 92 | 74 |
| Mar. 8 | Houston (OT) | | | | |
| | —(NCAA Midwest Regional) | (N5) | L | 98 | 99 |
| | | | | 2417 | 2199 |

N1—Fort Wayne, IN.; N2—Louisville, KY.; N3—Chicago, IL. (Stadium); N4—New York, NY. (Madison Square Garden); N5—Lubbock, TX.

1965-66 (Won 5, Lost 21, .192)
Coach: Johnny Dee
Captain: James McGann

| Dec. 1 | Lewis College | (H) | W | 75 | 69 |
|---|---|---|---|---|---|
| Dec. 4 | Wisconsin | (A) | L | 79 | 97 |
| Dec. 7 | St. Norbert | (H) | W | 110 | 77 |
| Dec. 11 | Michigan State | (A) | L | 69 | 93 |
| Dec. 15 | Bowling Green | (H) | W | 85 | 77 |
| Dec. 18 | Boston College | (H) | L | 89 | 93 |
| Dec. 21 | Indiana | (N1) | L | 58 | 80 |
| Dec. 29 | Kentucky | (N2) | L | 69 | 103 |
| Dec. 31 | Duke | (N3) | L | 73 | 95 |
| Jan. 4 | Purdue | (H) | L | 92 | 109 |
| Jan. 8 | Air Force | (N4) | L | 57 | 68 |

| | | | | | |
|---|---|---|---|---|---|
| Jan. 10 | Creighton | (A) | L | 59 | 72 |
| Jan. 13 | Detroit | (H) | L | 84 | 97 |
| Jan. 15 | DePaul | (A) | L | 71 | 97 |
| Jan. 19 | Loyola (CA) | (H) | L | 86 | 96 |
| Jan. 28 | Illinois | (N5) | L | 92 | 120 |
| Jan. 31 | Butler | (A) | L | 67 | 90 |
| Feb. 5 | Georgia Tech | (H) | L | 61 | 75 |
| Feb. 9 | Butler | (H) | W | 84 | 61 |
| Feb. 12 | Detroit | (A) | W | 76 | 67 |
| Feb. 15 | St. John's (NY) | (H) | L | 59 | 77 |
| Feb. 17 | New York U. | (N6) | L | 78 | 102 |
| Feb. 19 | Bradley (2 OT) | (N5) | L | 44 | 55 |
| Feb. 23 | DePaul | (H) | L | 71 | 79 |
| Feb. 28 | Western Michigan | (A) | L | 76 | 82 |
| Mar. 2 | Creighton | (H) | L | 68 | 72 |
| | | | | 1932 | 2203 |

N1–Fort Wayne, IN.; N2–Louisville, KY.; N3–Greensboro, NC.; N4–Denver, CO.; N5–Chicago, IL. (Stadium); N6–New York, NY. (Madison Square Garden)

1966-67 (Won 14, Lost 14, .500)
Coach: Johnny Dee
Captain: James Monahan

| | | | | | |
|---|---|---|---|---|---|
| Dec. 1 | Lewis College | (H) | W | 100 | 77 |
| Dec. 3 | Toledo | (A) | L | 80 | 98 |
| Dec. 7 | Detroit | (H) | L | 73 | 74 |
| Dec. 10 | Evansville (OT) | (A) | L | 99 | 105 |
| Dec. 14 | St. Norbert | (H) | W | 97 | 72 |
| Dec. 17 | St. John's (NY) | (A) | L | 62 | 65 |
| Dec. 20 | Indiana | (N1) | L | 91 | 94 |
| Dec. 23 | UCLA | (A) | L | 67 | 96 |
| Dec. 27 | California–(Rainbow Classic) | (N2) | L | 63 | 69 |
| Dec. 28 | Montana–(Rainbow Classic) | (N2) | L | 69 | 70 |
| Dec. 31 | Kentucky | (N3) | L | 85 | 96 |
| Jan. 7 | Air Force | (H) | W | 68 | 56 |
| Jan. 11 | King's College | (H) | W | 93 | 54 |
| Jan. 14 | DePaul | (A) | W | 76 | 72 |
| Jan. 21 | Detroit | (A) | W | 87 | 71 |
| Jan. 28 | Illinois | (N4) | W | 90 | 75 |
| Jan. 30 | Butler | (A) | W | 101 | 80 |
| Feb. 1 | Michigan State (OT) | (H) | L | 80 | 85 |
| Feb. 4 | Georgia Tech | (A) | L | 87 | 102 |
| Feb. 6 | Hawaii | (H) | W | 90 | 58 |
| Feb. 8 | DePaul | (H) | L | 49 | 56 |

| Feb. 11 | Houston | (H) | W | 87 | 78 |
|---------|---------|-----|---|----|----|
| Feb. 13 | Butler | (H) | W | 57 | 48 |
| Feb. 18 | Bradley | (N4) | L | 89 | 94 |
| Feb. 20 | Western Michigan | (H) | W | 73 | 68 |
| Feb. 23 | New York U. | (N5) | W | 79 | 66 |
| Feb. 25 | Duke | (N6) | L | 65 | 77 |
| Mar. 4 | Creighton | (H) | W | 84 | 59 |
| | | | | 2241 | 2115 |

N1—Fort Wayne, IN.; N2—Honolulu, HI; N3—Louisville, KY.; N4—Chicago, IL. (Stadium); N5—New York, NY. (Madison Square Garden); N6—Charlotte, NC.

1967-68 (Won 21, Lost 9, .700)
Coach: Johnny Dee
Captain: Bob Arnzen

| Dec. 2 | St. Joseph's (IN) | (H) | W | 97 | 72 |
|--------|-------------------|-----|---|-----|-----|
| Dec. 5 | Wisconsin | (A) | W | 81 | 73 |
| Dec. 9 | Lewis College | (H) | W | 97 | 59 |
| Dec. 11 | Southern Methodist | (H) | W | 79 | 59 |
| Dec. 14 | St. Norbert | (H) | W | 102 | 70 |
| Dec. 19 | Indiana | (N1) | L | 91 | 96 |
| Dec. 21 | Utah State | (A) | W | 73 | 72 |
| Dec. 23 | UCLA | (A) | L | 63 | 114 |
| Dec. 28 | Villa Madonna | (H) | W | 64 | 59 |
| Dec. 30 | Kentucky | (N2) | L | 73 | 81 |
| Jan. 3 | King's College | (H) | W | 105 | 68 |
| Jan. 6 | Air Force | (N3) | W | 58 | 45 |
| Jan. 8 | Creighton | (A) | W | 72 | 63 |
| Jan. 10 | Detroit | (H) | W | 83 | 63 |
| Jan. 13 | DePaul | (A) | W | 75 | 68 |
| Jan. 17 | Butler | (H) | W | 82 | 77 |
| Jan. 27 | Illinois | (N4) | L | 67 | 68 |
| Jan. 30 | Michigan State | (A) | L | 68 | 89 |
| Feb. 3 | Detroit | (A) | L | 79 | 82 |
| Feb. 6 | DePaul (OT) | (H) | W | 91 | 85 |
| Feb. 10 | Duke | (N4) | L | 67 | 73 |
| Feb. 13 | St. John's (NY) | (H) | L | 81 | 83 |
| Feb. 17 | Bradley | (N4) | W | 64 | 61 |
| Feb. 22 | New York U. | (N5) | W | 70 | 67 |
| Feb. 27 | Valparaiso | (H) | W | 87 | 75 |
| Mar. 2 | Creighton | (H) | W | 73 | 68 |
| Mar. 16 | Army—(NIT) | (N5) | W | 62 | 58 |
| Mar. 19 | Long Island—(NIT) | (N5) | W | 62 | 60 |

| Mar. 21 | Dayton (OT)–(NIT) | (N5) | L | 74 | 76 |
|---|---|---|---|---|---|
| Mar. 23 | St. Peter's–(NIT) | (N5) | W | 81 | 78 |
| | | | | 2321 | 2162 |

N1–Fort Wayne, IN.; N2–Louisville, KY.; N3–Denver, CO.; N4–Chicago, IL. (Stadium); N5–New York, NY. (Madison Square Garden)

1968-69 (Won 20, Lost 7, .741)
Coach: Johnny Dee
Captain: Bob Arnzen

| Dec. 3 | King's College | (A) | W | 84 | 54 |
|---|---|---|---|---|---|
| Dec. 7 | UCLA* | (H) | L | 75 | 88 |
| Dec. 11 | Wisconsin | (H) | W | 57 | 56 |
| Dec. 14 | St. Louis | (A) | W | 101 | 76 |
| Dec. 16 | Minnesota | (H) | W | 69 | 65 |
| Dec. 21 | Indiana | (H) | W | 104 | 94 |
| Dec. 28 | Kentucky | (N1) | L | 90 | 110 |
| Dec. 30 | American U. | (N2) | W | 92 | 67 |
| Jan. 4 | St. Peter's | (H) | W | 85 | 71 |
| Jan. 6 | Fordham | (H) | W | 84 | 65 |
| Jan. 9 | Butler | (H) | W | 76 | 73 |
| Jan. 11 | DePaul | (H) | W | 66 | 60 |
| Jan. 13 | Air Force | (H) | W | 88 | 53 |
| Jan. 15 | Detroit | (H) | W | 84 | 77 |
| Jan. 25 | Illinois | (N3) | L | 57 | 91 |
| Jan. 30 | Georgia Tech | (H) | W | 71 | 52 |
| Feb. 1 | Houston | (N4) | L | 82 | 89 |
| Feb. 5 | DePaul | (A) | W | 85 | 73 |
| Feb. 8 | Detroit** | (A) | W | 79 | 72 |
| Feb. 11 | Michigan State | (H) | L | 59 | 71 |
| Feb. 15 | Utah State | (H) | W | 108 | 82 |
| Feb. 17 | Butler | (A) | W | 94 | 90 |
| Feb. 20 | New York U. | (N5) | W | 98 | 88 |
| Feb. 25 | Valparaiso | (H) | W | 89 | 72 |
| Mar. 1 | St. John's (NY) (OT) | (A) | W | 71 | 67 |
| Mar. 3 | Creighton | (H) | L | 74 | 79 |
| Mar. 8 | Miami (OH) –(NCAA Mideast Regional) | (N6) | L | 60 | 63 |
| | | | | 2182 | 1998 |

N1–Louisville, KY.; N2–Baltimore, MD.; N3–Chicago, IL. (Stadium); N4–Houston, TX. (Astrodome); N5–New York, NY. (Madison Square Garden); N6–Carbondale, IL.
* Athletic and Convocation Center Dedication Game
** Notre Dame's 900th victory

**1969-70 (Won 21, Lost 8, .724)**
Coach: Johnny Dee
Captain: Austin Carr

| Dec. 1 | Minnesota | (A) | W | 84 | 75 |
|--------|-----------|-----|---|-----|-----|
| Dec. 3 | Michigan | (H) | W | 87 | 86 |
| Dec. 6 | Valparaiso | (A) | W | 98 | 82 |
| Dec. 10 | Northern Illinois | (H) | W | 111 | 92 |
| Dec. 13 | St. Louis | (H) | W | 65 | 53 |
| Dec. 15 | Kansas | (H) | L | 63 | 75 |
| Dec. 20 | Indiana | (A) | W | 89 | 88 |
| Dec. 27 | Kentucky | (N1) | L | 100 | 102 |
| Dec. 29 | West Virginia —(Sugar Bowl Tournament) | (N2) | W | 84 | 80 |
| Dec. 30 | South Carolina (OT) —(Sugar Bowl Tournament) | (N2) | L | 83 | 84 |
| Jan. 3 | UCLA | (A) | L | 77 | 108 |
| Jan. 7 | Fordham | (H) | W | 91 | 76 |
| Jan. 10 | Villanova (OT) | (H) | W | 94 | 92 |
| Jan. 14 | DePaul | (H) | W | 96 | 73 |
| Jan. 17 | Duquesne | (N3) | W | 82 | 66 |
| Jan. 20 | Michigan State | (A) | L | 82 | 85 |
| Jan. 31 | Illinois | (N3) | W | 86 | 83 |
| Feb. 4 | St. Peter's | (H) | W | 135 | 88 |
| Feb. 7 | Marquette (2 OT) | (H) | W | 96 | 95 |
| Feb. 10 | St. John's (NY) | (H) | W | 90 | 76 |
| Feb. 14 | Detroit (OT) | (A) | W | 95 | 93 |
| Feb. 16 | Tulane | (H) | W | 115 | 80 |
| Feb. 19 | New York U. | (N4) | W | 77 | 65 |
| Feb. 21 | West Virginia | (H) | W | 114 | 78 |
| Feb. 23 | Butler | (A) | W | 121 | 114 |
| Feb. 28 | Dayton | (A) | L | 79 | 95 |
| Mar. 7 | Ohio —(NCAA Mideast Regional) | (N5) | W | 112 | 82 |
| Mar. 12 | Kentucky —(NCAA Mideast Regional) | (N6) | L | 99 | 109 |
| Mar. 14 | Iowa —(NCAA Mideast Regional) | (N6) | L | 106 | 121 |
| | | | | 2711 | 2496 |

N1—Louisville, KY.; N2—New Orleans, LA.; N3—Chicago, IL. (Stadium); N4—New York, NY. (Madison Square Garden); N5—Dayton, OH.; N6—Columbus, OH.

**1970-71 (Won 20, Lost 9, .690)**
Coach: Johnny Dee
Captain: Austin Carr

| Dec. 1 | Michigan | (A) | W | 94 | 81 |
|--------|----------|-----|---|-----|-----|

| Dec. 5 | South Carolina | (H) | L | 82 | 85 |
|---|---|---|---|---|---|
| Dec. 10 | Northwestern | (N1) | W | 94 | 88 |
| Dec. 12 | St. Louis | (A) | W | 68 | 67 |
| Dec. 15 | Indiana | (H) | L | 103 | 106 |
| Dec. 29 | Kentucky | (N2) | W | 99 | 92 |
| Dec. 31 | Santa Clara (OT) | (H) | W | 85 | 83 |
| Jan. 2 | Minnesota | (H) | W | 97 | 73 |
| Jan. 10 | Air Force | (A) | W | 75 | 71 |
| Jan. 12 | Marquette | (A) | L | 66 | 71 |
| Jan. 14 | Detroit | (H) | W | 93 | 79 |
| Jan. 18 | Duquesne (OT) | (A) | L | 78 | 81 |
| Jan. 23 | UCLA | (H) | W | 89 | 82 |
| Jan. 26 | Michigan State | (H) | W | 104 | 80 |
| Jan. 30 | Illinois (OT) | (N1) | L | 66 | 68 |
| Feb. 6 | Creighton | (H) | W | 102 | 91 |
| Feb. 8 | Butler | (H) | W | 93 | 81 |
| Feb. 11 | Villanova | (N3) | L | 81 | 99 |
| Feb. 13 | DePaul | (A) | W | 107 | 76 |
| Feb. 15 | Valparaiso | (H) | W | 100 | 75 |
| Feb. 18 | Fordham | (N4) | L | 88 | 94 |
| Feb. 20 | West Virginia | (A) | W | 107 | 98 |
| Feb. 23 | New York U. | (H) | W | 106 | 68 |
| Feb. 27 | St. John's (NY) | (A) | W | 92 | 79 |
| Mar. 1 | Dayton | (H) | W | 83 | 82 |
| Mar. 4 | Western Michigan | (H) | W | 110 | 79 |
| Mar. 13 | Texas Christian —(NCAA Midwest Regional) | (N5) | W | 102 | 94 |
| Mar. 18 | Drake (OT) —(NCAA Midwest Regional) | (N6) | L | 72 | 79 |
| Mar. 20 | Houston —(NCAA Midwest Regional) | (N6) | L | 106 | 119 |
| | | | | 2642 | 2422 |

N1–Chicago, IL. (Stadium); N2–Louisville, KY.; N3–Philadelphia, PA. (Palestra); N4–New York, NY. (Madison Square Garden); N5–Houston, TX (Hofheinz Pavilion); N6–Wichita, KS.

1971-72 (Won 6, Lost 20, .231)
Coach: Digger Phelps
Captain: Doug Gemmell (non-playing; injured in off-season and out for the season)

| Dec. 1 | Michigan | (H) | L | 83 | 101 |
|---|---|---|---|---|---|
| Dec. 4 | Valparaiso | (A) | W | 81 | 71 |
| Dec. 6 | Western Michigan | (H) | W | 83 | 77 |
| Dec. 8 | Kansas | (A) | L | 72 | 88 |
| Dec. 11 | St. Louis | (H) | L | 80 | 92 |
| Dec. 18 | Indiana | (A) | L | 29 | 94 |

| Dec. 22 | UCLA | (A) | L | 56 | 114 |
|---------|------|-----|---|----|----|
| Dec. 28 | Kentucky | (N1) | L | 67 | 83 |
| Jan. 15 | Tulane | (A) | W | 87 | 78 |
| Jan. 17 | Georgia Tech | (A) | L | 62 | 82 |
| Jan. 20 | Duquesne | (H) | L | 79 | 84 |
| Jan. 24 | Marquette | (H) | L | 62 | 71 |
| Jan. 28 | Illinois | (N2) | L | 59 | 81 |
| Jan. 29 | UCLA | (H) | L | 32 | 57 |
| Feb. 1 | Michigan State | (A) | L | 74 | 98 |
| Feb. 3 | West Virginia | (H) | L | 87 | 97 |
| Feb. 5 | LaSalle | (A) | W | 97 | 71 |
| Feb. 8 | St. John's (NY) | (H) | L | 75 | 86 |
| Feb. 12 | DePaul | (H) | W | 93 | 78 |
| Feb. 14 | Bowling Green | (H) | W | 92 | 65 |
| Feb. 19 | North Carolina | (N3) | L | 74 | 99 |
| Feb. 22 | Fordham | (H) | L | 72 | 89 |
| Feb. 26 | Creighton | (A) | L | 77 | 104 |
| Feb. 28 | South Carolina | (A) | L | 83 | 109 |
| Mar. 1 | Villanova | (H) | L | 75 | 78 |
| Mar. 4 | Dayton | (A) | L | 74 | 86 |
| | | | | 1905 | 2233 |

N1 – Louisville, KY.; N2 – Chicago, IL. (Stadium); N3 – New York, NY. (Madison Square Garden)

1972-73 (Won 18, Lost 12, .600)
Coach: Digger Phelps
Captains: Game Captains; later, Gary Novak and John Shumate

| Dec. 2 | Michigan | (A) | L | 87 | 96 |
|--------|----------|-----|---|----|----|
| Dec. 4 | Ohio State (OT) | (H) | L | 75 | 81 |
| Dec. 6 | Valparaiso | (H) | W | 82 | 72 |
| Dec. 9 | St. Louis | (A) | L | 58 | 60 |
| Dec. 12 | Indiana | (H) | L | 67 | 69 |
| Dec. 23 | UCLA | (A) | L | 56 | 82 |
| Dec. 30 | Kentucky | (N1) | L | 63 | 65 |
| Jan. 7 | Kansas (OT) | (H) | W | 66 | 64 |
| Jan. 11 | DePaul | (A) | W | 72 | 67 |
| Jan. 13 | Marquette | (A) | W | 71 | 69 |
| Jan. 17 | Pittsburgh (OT) | (H) | W | 85 | 76 |
| Jan. 20 | Dayton | (H) | W | 94 | 58 |
| Jan. 22 | Duquesne | (A) | L | 72 | 81 |
| Jan. 25 | Illinois | (N2) | L | 84 | 87 |
| Jan. 27 | UCLA | (H) | L | 63 | 82 |
| Feb. 1 | Villanova | (N3) | W | 82 | 66 |
| Feb. 3 | Xavier | (H) | W | 94 | 68 |
| Feb. 5 | Butler | (H) | W | 89 | 62 |

| Feb. 7 | Michigan State | (H) | W | 85 | 72 |
|---|---|---|---|---|---|
| Feb. 10 | LaSalle | (H) | W | 87 | 71 |
| Feb. 15 | Fordham | (N4) | L | 69 | 70 |
| Feb. 17 | Duke | (A) | L | 74 | 86 |
| Feb. 22 | West Virginia | (A) | W | 92 | 73 |
| Feb. 24 | St. John's (NY) | (N5) | W | 75 | 71 |
| Feb. 28 | Western Michigan | (H) | W | 76 | 65 |
| Mar. 3 | South Carolina | (H) | W | 73 | 69 |
| Mar. 17 | Southern California – (NIT) | (N4) | W | 69 | 65 |
| Mar. 20 | Louisville – (NIT) | (N4) | W | 79 | 71 |
| Mar. 24 | North Carolina – (NIT) | (N4) | W | 78 | 71 |
| Mar. 25 | Virginia Tech (OT) – (NIT) | (N4) | L | 91 | 92 |
| | | | | 2308 | 2181 |

N1 – Louisville,KY.; N2 – Chicago, IL. (Stadium); N3 – Philadelphia, PA (Palestra); N4 – New York, NY. (Madison Square Garden); N5 – Uniondale, N.Y.

1973-74 (Won 26, Lost 3, .897)
Coach: Digger Phelps
Captains: Gary Novak and John Shumate

| Dec. 1 | Valparaiso | (H) | W | 112 | 62 |
|---|---|---|---|---|---|
| Dec. 3 | Ohio State (OT) | (A) | W | 76 | 72 |
| Dec. 6 | Northwestern | (A) | W | 98 | 74 |
| Dec. 8 | St. Louis | (H) | W | 94 | 65 |
| Dec. 11 | Indiana | (A) | W | 73 | 67 |
| Dec. 20 | Denver | (H) | W | 99 | 59 |
| Dec. 29 | Kentucky | (N1) | W | 94 | 79 |
| Jan. 12 | Xavier | (H) | W | 87 | 44 |
| Jan. 15 | Georgetown | (H) | W | 104 | 77 |
| Jan. 19 | UCLA* | (H) | W | 71 | 70 |
| Jan. 22 | Kansas | (A) | W | 76 | 74 |
| Jan. 24 | St. Francis (PA) | (H) | W | 78 | 58 |
| Jan. 26 | UCLA | (A) | L | 75 | 94 |
| Jan. 29 | Marquette | (H) | W | 69 | 63 |
| Jan. 31 | DePaul | (H) | W | 101 | 72 |
| Feb. 2 | Davidson | (H) | W | 95 | 84 |
| Feb. 4 | Michigan State | (A) | W | 91 | 89 |
| Feb. 6 | LaSalle | (A) | W | 98 | 78 |
| Feb. 9 | Duke | (H) | W | 87 | 68 |
| Feb. 14 | Fordham | (N2) | W | 79 | 69 |
| Feb. 16 | South Carolina | (A) | W | 72 | 68 |
| Feb. 18 | Western Michigan | (H) | W | 85 | 68 |
| Feb. 23 | West Virginia | (H) | W | 108 | 80 |
| Feb. 26 | Ball State | (H) | W | 93 | 69 |
| Mar. 2 | Villanova | (H) | W | 115 | 85 |

| Mar. 4 | Dayton | (A) | L | 82 | 97 |
|---|---|---|---|---|---|
| Mar. 9 | Austin Peay | | | | |
| | −(NCAA Mideast Regional) | (N3) | W | 108 | 66 |
| Mar. 14 | Michigan | | | | |
| | −(NCAA Mideast Regional) | (N4) | L | 68 | 77 |
| Mar. 16 | Vanderbilt | | | | |
| | −(NCAA Mideast Regional) | (N4) | W | 118 | 88 |
| | | | | 2606 | 2116 |

N1−Louisville, KY.; N2−New York, NY. (Madison Square Garden); N3−Terre Haute, IN.; N4−Tuscaloosa, AL.
* End of UCLA's 88-game winning streak, longest in college basketball history

1974-75 (Won 19, Lost 10, .655)
Coach: Digger Phelps
Captains: Dwight Clay and Peter Crotty

| Nov. 30 | Valparaiso | (A) | W | 91 | 80 |
|---|---|---|---|---|---|
| Dec. 4 | Northwestern | (H) | W | 100 | 84 |
| Dec. 7 | Princeton | (H) | W | 80 | 66 |
| Dec. 9 | Kansas* | (H) | W | 75 | 59 |
| Dec. 11 | Indiana | (H) | L | 84 | 94 |
| Dec. 21 | UCLA | (A) | L | 72 | 85 |
| Dec. 28 | Kentucky | (N1) | L | 96 | 113 |
| Dec. 30 | Butler | (A) | W | 93 | 83 |
| Jan. 4 | Maryland | (A) | L | 82 | 90 |
| Jan. 8 | Davidson | (N2) | W | 89 | 73 |
| Jan. 11 | Villanova | (N3) | W | 125 | 90 |
| Jan. 13 | Pittsburgh (OT) | (N4) | L | 77 | 84 |
| Jan. 18 | Marquette | (A) | L | 68 | 71 |
| Jan. 20 | Holy Cross | (H) | W | 96 | 91 |
| Jan. 25 | UCLA | (H) | W | 84 | 78 |
| Jan. 28 | Western Michigan | (A) | W | 73 | 71 |
| Feb. 1 | Xavier | (H) | W | 96 | 58 |
| Feb. 5 | Michigan State | (H) | L | 73 | 76 |
| Feb. 8 | South Carolina (OT) | (H) | W | 66 | 65 |
| Feb. 10 | Air Force | (H) | W | 99 | 66 |
| Feb. 13 | St. John's (NY) | (N5) | W | 68 | 67 |
| Feb. 15 | LaSalle | (H) | W | 91 | 75 |
| Feb. 17 | St. Joseph's (IN) | (H) | W | 97 | 81 |
| Feb. 22 | DePaul | (A) | L | 70 | 75 |
| Feb. 25 | Fordham | (H) | W | 98 | 61 |
| Mar. 1 | Dayton | (H) | W | 102 | 69 |
| Mar. 15 | Kansas | | | | |
| | −(NCAA Midwest Regional) | (N6) | W | 77 | 71 |
| Mar. 20 | Maryland | | | | |
| | −(NCAA Midwest Regional) | (N7) | L | 71 | 83 |

Mar. 22   Cincinnati (OT)

| | | | | |
|---|---|---|---|---|
|     –(NCAA Midwest Regional) | (N7) | L | 87 | 95 |
| | | | 2480 | 2254 |

N1–Louisville, KY.; N2–Charlotte, NC; N3–Philadelphia, PA. (Palestra); N4–Pittsburgh, PA. (Civic Arena); N5–New York, NY. (Madison Square Garden); N6–Tulsa, OK,; N7–Las Cruces, NM.

\* Notre Dame's 1000th victory

## 1975-76 (Won 23, Lost 6, .793)
Coach: Digger Phelps
Captains: Adrian Dantley and Bill Paterno

| Date | Opponent | | | | |
|---|---|---|---|---|---|
| Nov. 29 | Kent State | (H) | W | 90 | 61 |
| Dec. 2 | Valparaiso | (H) | W | 117 | 83 |
| Dec. 6 | Texas Tech | (H) | W | 88 | 63 |
| Dec. 8 | Kansas | (A) | W | 72 | 64 |
| Dec. 11 | Indiana | (A) | L | 60 | 63 |
| Dec. 13 | St. Francis (PA) | (H) | W | 103 | 73 |
| Dec. 30 | Kentucky | (N1) | L | 77 | 79 |
| Jan. 3 | UCLA | (A) | L | 70 | 86 |
| Jan. 10 | Manhattan | (H) | W | 88 | 71 |
| Jan. 12 | Pittsburgh | (N2) | W | 77 | 66 |
| Jan. 14 | Ball State | (H) | W | 119 | 78 |
| Jan. 17 | Xavier | (A) | W | 90 | 79 |
| Jan. 21 | St. Joseph's (IN) | (H) | W | 97 | 60 |
| Jan. 24 | UCLA | (H) | W | 95 | 85 |
| Jan. 28 | DePaul | (H) | W | 89 | 68 |
| Jan. 31 | Maryland | (H) | L | 63 | 69 |
| Feb. 4 | LaSalle | (N3) | W | 108 | 89 |
| Feb. 7 | Davidson | (H) | W | 117 | 74 |
| Feb. 9 | St. Bonaventure | (H) | W | 95 | 80 |
| Feb. 11 | Villanova | (H) | W | 84 | 57 |
| Feb. 14 | West Virginia | (H) | W | 97 | 77 |
| Feb. 16 | Butler | (N6) | W | 92 | 79 |
| Feb. 19 | Fordham | (N4) | W | 91 | 78 |
| Feb. 21 | South Carolina | (A) | W | 90 | 83 |
| Feb. 25 | Dayton | (A) | W | 85 | 79 |
| Feb. 28 | Marquette | (H) | L | 75 | 81 |
| Mar. 1 | Western Michigan (OT) | (H) | W | 95 | 88 |
| Mar. 13 | Cincinnati | | | | |
| |     –(NCAA Mideast Regional) | (N5) | W | 79 | 78 |
| Mar. 18 | Michigan | | | | |
| |     –(NCAA Mideast Regional) | (N1) | L | 76 | 80 |
| | | | | 2579 | 2171 |

N1–Louisville, KY.: N2–Pittsburgh, Pa. (Civic Arena); N3–Philadelphia, PA.

354     *Hooping It Up*

(Spectrum); N4—New York, NY. (Madison Square Garden); N5—Lawrence, KS.; N6—Indianapolis, IN. (Market Square Arena)

1976-77 (Won 22, Lost 7, .759)
Coach: Digger Phelps
Captains: Bill Paterno, Ray Martin, and Toby Knight

| Nov. 27 | Maryland (OT) | (A) | W | 80 | 79 |
|---|---|---|---|---|---|
| Dec. 1 | Cal Poly-Pomona | (H) | W | 93 | 67 |
| Dec. 4 | Valparaiso | (H) | W | 93 | 56 |
| Dec. 7 | Northwestern | (H) | W | 105 | 78 |
| Dec. 11 | UCLA | (A) | W | 66 | 63 |
| Dec. 14 | Indiana | (H) | W | 78 | 65 |
| Dec. 21 | Vermont | (H) | W | 89 | 48 |
| Dec. 30 | Kentucky | (N1) | L | 72 | 102 |
| Jan. 3 | Princeton | (A) | L | 62 | 76 |
| Jan. 5 | Villanova | (N2) | L | 62 | 64 |
| Jan. 16 | Marquette | (A) | L | 69 | 78 |
| Jan. 18 | Stonehill | (H) | W | 98 | 70 |
| Jan. 23 | UCLA | (H) | L | 65 | 70 |
| Jan. 26 | Pittsburgh | (H) | W | 88 | 68 |
| Jan. 30 | Fordham | (H) | W | 93 | 71 |
| Feb. 1 | Dayton | (H) | W | 97 | 64 |
| Feb. 5 | Davidson | (N3) | W | 88 | 57 |
| Feb. 7 | Xavier | (H) | W | 94 | 63 |
| Feb. 9 | Holy Cross | (H) | W | 91 | 73 |
| Feb. 12 | South Carolina | (H) | W | 84 | 66 |
| Feb. 14 | Butler | (H) | W | 97 | 74 |
| Feb. 17 | Manhattan | (N4) | W | 80 | 76 |
| Feb. 19 | West Virginia | (A) | L | 68 | 81 |
| Feb. 23 | Loyola (IL) | (H) | W | 111 | 86 |
| Feb. 26 | LaSalle | (H) | W | 113 | 77 |
| Mar. 1 | San Francisco | (H) | W | 93 | 82 |
| Mar. 5 | DePaul | (A) | W | 76 | 68 |
| Mar. 12 | Hofstra | | | | |
| | —(NCAA East Regional) | (N2) | W | 90 | 83 |
| Mar. 17 | North Carolina | | | | |
| | —(NCAA East Regional) | (N5) | L | 77 | 79 |
| | | | | 2472 | 2084 |

N1—Louisville, KY.; N2—Philadelphia, PA. (Palestra); N3—Greensboro, NC.; N4—New York, NY. (Madison Square Garden); N5—College Park, MD.

1977-78 (Won 23, Lost 8, .742)
Coach: Digger Phelps
Captains: Dave Batton and Don Williams

| Date | Opponent | | | | |
|------|----------|------|------|------|------|
| Nov. 26 | Mississippi | (H) | W | 111 | 62 |
| Nov. 30 | Baylor | (H) | W | 98 | 57 |
| Dec. 3 | Valparaiso | (H) | W | 89 | 75 |
| Dec. 5 | Lafayette | (H) | W | 76 | 42 |
| Dec. 7 | Northwestern | (A) | W | 88 | 48 |
| Dec. 10 | UCLA | (A) | W | 69 | 66 |
| Dec. 14 | Indiana | (A) | L | 66 | 67 |
| Dec. 23 | St. Joseph's (IN) | (H) | W | 108 | 72 |
| Dec. 31 | Kentucky | (N1) | L | 68 | 73 |
| Jan. 10 | San Francisco | (N2) | L | 70 | 79 |
| Jan. 14 | St. Bonaventure | (N3) | W | 79 | 78 |
| Jan. 17 | Manhattan | (H) | W | 81 | 64 |
| Jan. 19 | Villanova | (H) | W | 70 | 69 |
| Jan. 22 | UCLA | (H) | W | 75 | 73 |
| Jan. 23 | Dartmouth | (H) | W | 78 | 64 |
| Jan. 25 | West Virginia | (H) | W | 103 | 82 |
| Jan. 29 | Maryland | (H) | W | 69 | 54 |
| Feb. 1 | LaSalle | (A) | W | 95 | 90 |
| Feb. 4 | Davidson | (H) | W | 100 | 76 |
| Feb. 12 | DePaul (OT) | (H) | L | 68 | 69 |
| Feb. 16 | Fordham | (N4) | W | 95 | 76 |
| Feb. 18 | South Carolina | (A) | L | 60 | 65 |
| Feb. 21 | North Carolina State | (H) | W | 70 | 59 |
| Feb. 26 | Marquette | (H) | W | 65 | 59 |
| Mar. 4 | Dayton | (A) | L | 59 | 66 |
| Mar. 6 | Loyola (IL) | (H) | W | 83 | 68 |
| Mar. 12 | Houston –(NCAA Midwest Regional) | (N5) | W | 100 | 77 |
| Mar. 17 | Utah –(NCAA Midwest Regional) | (N6) | W | 69 | 56 |
| Mar. 19 | DePaul –(NCAA Midwest Regional) | (N6) | W | 84 | 64 |
| Mar. 25 | Duke–(NCAA Final Round) | (N7) | L | 86 | 90 |
| Mar. 27 | Arkansas –(NCAA Final Round) | (N7) | L | 69 | 71 |
| | | | | 2501 | 2111 |

N1–Louisville, KY.; N2–Oakland, CA.; N3–Rochester, NY.; N4–New York, NY. (Madison Square Garden); N5–Tulsa, OK.; N6–Lawrence, KS.; N7–St. Louis, MO.

**1978-79 (Won 24, Lost 6, .800)**
Coach: Digger Phelps
Captains: Bruce Flowers and Bill Laimbeer

| Date | Opponent | | | | |
|------|----------|------|------|------|------|
| Dec. 2 | Valparaiso | (H) | W | 87 | 57 |
| Dec. 4 | Rice | (H) | W | 105 | 61 |

| Dec. 6 | Northwestern | (H) | W | 101 | 57 |
|---|---|---|---|---|---|
| Dec. 9 | UCLA | (A) | W | 81 | 78 |
| Dec. 27 | St. Francis (PA) | (H) | W | 96 | 43 |
| Dec. 30 | Kentucky | (N1) | L | 76 | 81 |
| Jan. 6 | Villanova | (N2) | W | 75 | 64 |
| Jan. 8 | Davidson | (N3) | W | 95 | 63 |
| Jan. 13 | Marquette | (A) | W | 65 | 60 |
| Jan. 16 | Lafayette | (H) | W | 91 | 66 |
| Jan. 18 | San Francisco | (H) | W | 88 | 69 |
| Jan. 20 | South Carolina | (H) | W | 82 | 73 |
| Jan. 24 | Fordham | (H) | W | 85 | 53 |
| Jan. 27 | Maryland | (A) | L | 66 | 67 |
| Jan. 30 | Brown | (H) | W | 80 | 53 |
| Feb. 1 | Xavier | (H) | W | 66 | 57 |
| Feb. 3 | Dayton | (H) | W | 86 | 71 |
| Feb. 5 | Loyola (IL) | (H) | W | 84 | 66 |
| Feb. 7 | North Carolina State* | (A) | W | 53 | 52 |
| Feb. 11 | UCLA | (H) | L | 52 | 56 |
| Feb. 15 | Manhattan | (N4) | W | 86 | 63 |
| Feb. 17 | West Virginia | (A) | W | 70 | 54 |
| Feb. 21 | Oklahoma City | (H) | W | 88 | 60 |
| Feb. 24 | LaSalle | (H) | W | 93 | 70 |
| Feb. 26 | East Carolina | (H) | W | 89 | 72 |
| Mar. 2 | DePaul | (A) | L | 72 | 76 |
| Mar. 4 | Michigan | (N5) | L | 59 | 62 |
| Mar. 11 | Tennessee −(NCAA Mideast Regional) | (N6) | W | 73 | 67 |
| Mar. 16 | Toledo −(NCAA Mideast Regional) | (N7) | W | 79 | 71 |
| Mar. 18 | Michigan State −(NCAA Mideast Regional) | (N7) | L | 68 | 80 |
| | | | | 2391 | 1922 |

N1−Louisville, KY.; N2−Philadelphia, PA. (Palestra); N3−Charlotte, NC.; N4−New York, NY. (Madison Square Garden); N5−Pontiac, MI.; N6− Murfreesboro, TN.; N7−Indianapolis, IN.

* Notre Dame's 1100th victory

1979-80 (Won 22, Lost 6, .786)
Coach: Digger Phelps
Captains: Rich Branning and Bill Hanzlik

| Dec. 1 | Valparaiso | (H) | W | 92 | 66 |
|---|---|---|---|---|---|
| Dec. 3 | Iowa State | (H) | W | 87 | 77 |
| Dec. 5 | Northwestern | (A) | W | 73 | 56 |
| Dec. 8 | St. Louis | (H) | W | 93 | 65 |
| Dec. 11 | UCLA | (H) | W | 77 | 74 |

| Dec. 13 | St. Joseph's (IN) | (H) | W | 79 | 58 |
|---|---|---|---|---|---|
| Dec. 22 | Fairfield (CT) | (H) | W | 69 | 59 |
| Dec. 29 | Kentucky | (N1) | L | 80 | 86 |
| Jan. 8 | San Francisco | (N2) | L | 59 | 67 |
| Jan. 10 | Tulane | (N3) | W | 79 | 59 |
| Jan. 13 | Texas Christian | (N4) | W | 85 | 68 |
| Jan. 15 | Villanova | (H) | W | 70 | 69 |
| Jan. 19 | UCLA | (A) | W | 80 | 73 |
| Jan. 23 | Canisius | (H) | W | 84 | 63 |
| Jan. 26 | Maryland | (H) | W | 64 | 63 |
| Jan. 30 | LaSalle | (A) | L | 60 | 62 |
| Feb. 2 | Davidson | (H) | W | 105 | 71 |
| Feb. 4 | Navy | (H) | W | 67 | 53 |
| Feb. 6 | Manhattan | (H) | W | 93 | 49 |
| Feb. 9 | North Carolina State | (H) | L | 55 | 63 |
| Feb. 11 | San Francisco | (H) | W | 78 | 66 |
| Feb. 14 | Fordham | (N5) | W | 86 | 76 |
| Feb. 16 | South Carolina | (A) | W | 90 | 66 |
| Feb. 20 | Xavier | (A) | W | 85 | 72 |
| Feb. 24 | Marquette | (H) | L | 74 | 77 |
| Feb. 27 | DePaul (2 OT) | (H) | W | 76 | 74 |
| Mar. 1 | Dayton | (A) | W | 62 | 54 |
| Mar. 8 | Missouri (OT) | | | | |
| | –(NCAA Midwest Regional) | (N6) | L | 84 | 87 |
| | | | | 2186 | 1873 |

N1–Louisville, KY.; N2–Oakland, CA.; N3–Shreveport, LA.; N4–San Antonio, TX.; N5–New York, NY. (Madison Square Garden); N6–Lincoln, NB.

1980-81 (Won 23, Lost 6, .793)
Coach: Digger Phelps
Captains: Tracy Jackson, Kelly Tripucka, and Orlando Woolridge

| Nov. 29 | UCLA | (A) | L | 81 | 94 |
|---|---|---|---|---|---|
| Dec. 2 | Montana State | (H) | W | 89 | 68 |
| Dec. 4 | Texas Christian | (H) | W | 79 | 63 |
| Dec. 6 | Cal Poly-Pomona | (H) | W | 76 | 50 |
| Dec. 9 | Indiana | (H) | W | 68 | 64 |
| Dec. 22 | Valparaiso | (H) | W | 69 | 56 |
| Dec. 27 | Kentucky | (N1) | W | 67 | 61 |
| Jan. 4 | Davidson | (N2) | W | 87 | 67 |
| Jan. 6 | Villanova | (N3) | W | 94 | 65 |
| Jan. 10 | Marquette | (A) | L | 52 | 54 |
| Jan. 13 | San Francisco (OT) | (N4) | L | 63 | 66 |
| Jan. 17 | Hofstra | (H) | W | 65 | 55 |
| Jan. 19 | Fordham | (H) | W | 67 | 61 |

| Jan. 21 | San Francisco | (H) | W | 80 | 75 |
| Jan. 24 | Maryland | (A) | W | 73 | 70 |
| Jan. 27 | Cornell | (H) | W | 80 | 57 |
| Jan. 31 | South Carolina | (H) | W | 94 | 84 |
| Feb. 2 | St. Mary's (CA) | (H) | W | 94 | 63 |
| Feb. 4 | LaSalle | (H) | W | 60 | 59 |
| Feb. 8 | UCLA | (H) | L | 50 | 51 |
| Feb. 10 | Boston U. | (H) | W | 89 | 63 |
| Feb. 14 | North Carolina State | (A) | W | 71 | 55 |
| Feb. 16 | Fairfield (CT) | (H) | W | 57 | 55 |
| Feb. 22 | Virginia | (N5) | W | 57 | 56 |
| Feb. 26 | St. Francis (PA) | (H) | W | 87 | 71 |
| Feb. 28 | Dayton | (H) | W | 70 | 57 |
| Mar. 8 | DePaul | (A) | L | 64 | 74 |
| Mar. 14 | James Madison | | | | |
| | −(NCAA East Regional) | (N6) | W | 54 | 45 |
| Mar. 19 | Brigham Young | | | | |
| | −(NCAA East Regional) | (N7) | L | 50 | 51 |
| | | | | 2087 | 1810 |

N1−Louisville, KY.; N2−Charlotte, NC.; N3−Philadelphia, PA. (Palestra); N4−Oakland, CA.; N5−Rosemont, IL.; N6−Providence, RI.; N7−Atlanta, GA.

1981-82 (Won 10, Lost 17, .370)
Coach: Digger Phelps
Captain: Mike Mitchell

| Nov. 28 | St. Joseph's (IN) | (H) | W | 82 | 52 |
| Dec. 1 | Indiana | (A) | L | 55 | 69 |
| Dec. 5 | UCLA | (H) | L | 49 | 75 |
| Dec. 7 | Murray State | (H) | L | 54 | 56 |
| Dec. 12 | Northern Illinois | (H) | L | 65 | 70 |
| Dec. 22 | Valparaiso | (H) | W | 75 | 60 |
| Dec. 29 | Kentucky (OT) | (N1) | L | 28 | 34 |
| Jan. 2 | Missouri | (N2) | L | 70 | 92 |
| Jan. 4 | LaSalle | (A) | L | 61 | 66 |
| Jan. 6 | Virginia | (N3) | L | 54 | 87 |
| Jan. 12 | San Francisco | (N4) | L | 55 | 57 |
| Jan. 16 | Davidson | (H) | W | 59 | 45 |
| Jan. 19 | Villanova | (H) | L | 46 | 48 |
| Jan. 23 | Maryland | (H) | W | 55 | 51 |
| Jan. 25 | Idaho (OT) | (H) | W | 50 | 48 |
| Jan. 27 | Maine | (H) | W | 79 | 55 |
| Jan. 30 | Marquette | (H) | L | 62 | 70 |
| Feb. 2 | San Francisco | (H) | W | 75 | 66 |

| Feb. 7 | UCLA | (A) | L | 47 | 48 |
|--------|------|-----|---|----|----|
| Feb. 13 | North Carolina State | (H) | L | 42 | 62 |
| Feb. 18 | Seton Hall | (N5) | L | 58 | 71 |
| Feb. 20 | South Carolina | (A) | W | 59 | 55 |
| Feb. 23 | Fordham | (H) | L | 50 | 65 |
| Feb. 28 | DePaul | (H) | L | 69 | 81 |
| Mar. 2 | Northern Iowa | (H) | W | 86 | 56 |
| Mar. 6 | Dayton | (A) | L | 72 | 79 |
| Mar. 7 | Michigan | (N6) | W | 53 | 52 |
| | | | | 1610 | 1670 |

N1−Louisville, KY.; N2−Kansas City, MO.; N3−Landover, MD.; N4−Oakland, CA.; N5−East Rutherford, NJ.; N6−Pontiac, MI.

1982-83 (Won 19, Lost 10, .655)
Coach: Digger Phelps
Captain: John Paxson

| Nov. 26 | Stonehill | (H) | W | 74 | 60 |
|---------|-----------|-----|---|----|----|
| Nov. 27 | St. Francis (PA) | (H) | W | 74 | 49 |
| Dec. 1 | Kentucky | (H) | L | 45 | 58 |
| Dec. 4 | UCLA | (H) | L | 64 | 65 |
| Dec. 7 | Indiana | (H) | L | 52 | 68 |
| Dec. 9 | Fairfield (CT) | (H) | W | 92 | 70 |
| Dec. 11 | Dartmouth | (H) | W | 88 | 45 |
| Dec. 22 | Valparaiso | (H) | W | 108 | 70 |
| Dec. 30 | William and Mary | (H) | W | 83 | 60 |
| Jan. 4 | Davidson (OT) | (N1) | L | 51 | 54 |
| Jan. 7 | Villanova | (N2) | L | 55 | 61 |
| Jan. 12 | Canisius | (H) | W | 78 | 47 |
| Jan. 15 | Marquette | (A) | W | 59 | 57 |
| Jan. 17 | Lafayette | (H) | W | 51 | 40 |
| Jan. 19 | Bucknell | (H) | W | 64 | 52 |
| Jan. 22 | Maryland | (A) | L | 67 | 68 |
| Jan. 30 | UCLA | (A) | L | 53 | 59 |
| Feb. 2 | LaSalle | (H) | W | 68 | 56 |
| Feb. 5 | South Carolina | (H) | W | 66 | 56 |
| Feb. 10 | Fordham | (N3) | L | 69 | 75 |
| Feb. 12 | North Carolina State | (A) | W | 43 | 42 |
| Feb. 16 | Pittsburgh | (N4) | W | 60 | 54 |
| Feb. 21 | Akron | (H) | W | 80 | 45 |
| Feb. 22 | Hofstra | (H) | W | 61 | 50 |
| Feb. 26 | DePaul | (A) | L | 53 | 55 |
| Mar. 3 | Seton Hall | (H) | W | 59 | 40 |
| Mar. 7 | Dayton | (H) | W | 53 | 41 |

| Mar. 10 | Northern Iowa | (H) | W | 75 | 51 |
| Mar. 17 | Northwestern–(NIT) | (N5) | L | 57 | 71 |
| | | | | 1902 | 1619 |

N1–Charlotte, NC.; N2–Philadelphia, PA. (Palestra); N3–East Rutherford, NJ.; N4–Pittsburgh, PA. (Civic Arena); N5–Rosemont, IL.

1983-84 (Won 21, Lost 12, .636)
Coach: Digger Phelps
Captain: Tom Sluby

| Nov. 25 | St. Joseph's (IN) | (H) | W | 104 | 56 |
| Nov. 26 | Marist | (H) | W | 75 | 68 |
| Nov. 29 | Indiana | (A) | L | 72 | 80 |
| Dec. 3 | UCLA | (H) | L | 47 | 51 |
| Dec. 5 | St. Francis (NY) | (H) | W | 71 | 49 |
| Dec. 7 | Northwestern (OT) | (A) | L | 36 | 40 |
| Dec. 10 | Lehigh | (H) | W | 68 | 46 |
| Dec. 13 | Cornell | (H) | W | 55 | 48 |
| Dec. 21 | Valparaiso | (H) | W | 80 | 48 |
| Jan. 4 | LaSalle | (N1) | L | 66 | 68 |
| Jan. 6 | Holy Cross | (N2) | W | 73 | 61 |
| Jan. 9 | Washington (2 OT) | (N3) | L | 61 | 63 |
| Jan. 11 | Oregon | (A) | W | 66 | 54 |
| Jan. 16 | Lafayette | (H) | W | 65 | 39 |
| Jan. 21 | Villanova | (H) | W | 81 | 68 |
| Jan. 23 | Rice | (H) | W | 50 | 35 |
| Jan. 25 | Davidson (OT) | (H) | W | 59 | 56 |
| Jan. 28 | Maryland | (H) | W | 52 | 47 |
| Feb. 1 | Fordham | (H) | W | 79 | 59 |
| Feb. 4 | South Carolina | (A) | L | 42 | 52 |
| Feb. 6 | Vermont | (H) | W | 63 | 49 |
| Feb. 9 | Rutgers | (N4) | L | 59 | 61 |
| Feb. 11 | DePaul | (H) | L | 54 | 62 |
| Feb. 15 | Pittsburgh | (H) | L | 59 | 67 |
| Feb. 18 | Brigham Young | (A) | L | 64 | 68 |
| Feb. 22 | Manhattan | (N5) | W | 63 | 58 |
| Feb. 25 | Marquette | (H) | W | 65 | 56 |
| Mar. 3 | Dayton | (A) | L | 70 | 80 |
| Mar. 14 | Old Dominion–(NIT) | (H) | W | 67 | 62 |
| Mar. 19 | Boston College*–(NIT) | (N6) | W | 66 | 52 |
| Mar. 23 | Pittsburgh–(NIT) | (A) | W | 72 | 64 |
| Mar. 26 | Southwestern Louisiana–(NIT) | (N5) | W | 65 | 59 |
| Mar. 28 | Michigan–(NIT) | (N5) | L | 63 | 83 |
| | | | | 2132 | 1909 |

N1–Philadelphia, PA. (Spectrum); N2–Worcester, MA. (Centrum); N3–

Seattle, WA. (Kingdome); N4—East Rutherford, NJ.; N5—New York, NY. (Madison Square Garden); N6—Springfield, MA.
* Notre Dame's 1200th victory

1984-85 (Won 21, Lost 9, .700)
Coach: Digger Phelps
Captains: Ken Barlow, Jim Dolan, and Tim Kempton

| | | | | | |
|---|---|---|---|---|---|
| Nov. 25 | Manhattan | (H) | W | 67 | 52 |
| Nov. 29 | Northwestern | (H) | W | 79 | 61 |
| Dec. 1 | St. Francis (PA) | (H) | W | 85 | 45 |
| Dec. 4 | Indiana | (H) | W | 74 | 63 |
| Dec. 8 | DePaul | (A) | L | 83 | 95 |
| Dec. 9 | Valparaiso | (A) | W | 88 | 57 |
| Dec. 30 | Creighton | (A) | L | 58 | 60 |
| Jan. 5 | Davidson | (A) | W | 79 | 62 |
| Jan. 7 | Rice | (A) | L | 70 | 73 |
| Jan. 12 | Marquette | (A) | W | 63 | 62 |
| Jan. 16 | Holy Cross | (H) | W | 96 | 61 |
| Jan. 20 | DePaul | (H) | L | 66 | 71 |
| Jan. 23 | Dayton | (H) | W | 66 | 61 |
| Jan. 26 | Maryland | (A) | L | 65 | 77 |
| Jan. 28 | Providence | (H) | W | 70 | 63 |
| Jan. 30 | St. Louis | (H) | W | 48 | 42 |
| Feb. 3 | UCLA | (A) | W | 53 | 52 |
| Feb. 6 | LaSalle | (H) | W | 71 | 58 |
| Feb. 9 | Syracuse | (H) | L | 62 | 65 |
| Feb. 13 | New Orleans | (H) | W | 79 | 54 |
| Feb. 16 | Duke | (N1) | L | 69 | 81 |
| Feb. 18 | Loyola (MD) | (H) | W | 61 | 60 |
| Feb. 20 | Fordham | (N2) | W | 65 | 54 |
| Feb. 23 | Brigham Young | (H) | W | 67 | 58 |
| Feb. 28 | Butler (OT) | (A) | L | 69 | 70 |
| Mar. 3 | Washington | (H) | W | 57 | 50 |
| Mar. 6 | Marquette | (H) | W | 66 | 60 |
| Mar. 9 | Dayton (2 OT) | (A) | W | 80 | 73 |
| Mar. 14 | Oregon State | | | | |
| | —(NCAA Southeast Regional) | (H) | W | 79 | 70 |
| Mar. 16 | North Carolina | | | | |
| | —(NCAA Southeast Regional) | (H) | L | 58 | 60 |
| | | | | 2093 | 1870 |

N1—East Rutherford, N.J.; N2—New York, NY. (Madison Square Garden)

*Hooping It Up*

# Men's Basketball Coaching Records

| Season(s) | Coach | W | L | T | Pct. |
|---|---|---|---|---|---|
| 1896-98 | Frank Hering | 3 | 3 | 0 | .500 |
| 1898-99 | J. Fred Powers | 2 | 0 | 0 | 1.000 |
| 1901-02 | Dominic Groogan | 2 | 2 | 0 | .500 |
| 1907-12 | Bert Maris | 78 | 20 | 0 | .796 |
| 1912-13 | Bill Nelson | 13 | 2 | 0 | .867 |
| 1913-18 | Jesse Harper | 44 | 20 | 0 | .698 |
| 1918-20 | Charles Dorais | 7 | 23 | 0 | .233 |
| 1920-23 | Walter Halas | 25 | 39 | 0 | .391 |
| 1923-43 | George Keogan | 327 | 97 | 1 | .771 |
| 1943-44; | | | | | |
| 1946-51 | Edward Krause | 98 | 48 | 0 | .671 |
| 1944-45 | Clem Crowe | 15 | 5 | 0 | .750 |
| 1945-46 | Elmer Ripley | 17 | 4 | 0 | .810 |
| 1951-64 | John Jordan | 199 | 131 | 0 | .603 |
| 1964-71 | Johnny Dee | 116 | 80 | 0 | .592 |
| 1971-85 | Digger Phelps | 277 | 132 | 0 | .677 |
| All-Time Record (82 seasons) | | 1223 | 606 | 1 | .699 |

# Men's All-Time Register and Season Records

Included in this list are all men who played in at least one varsity basketball game from 1896-97 through 1984-85 and what is known of their season statistics. Blank spaces indicate missing or incomplete information; those games for which a box score is unavailable at present are listed in italics in the All-Time Game-By-Game Scores section. Any help would be greatly appreciated in filling in the gaps. The same also goes for missing heights, birth dates, and death dates.

FORMAT:

LAST NAME, FIRST NAME HGT. DATE OF BIRTH  DATE OF DEATH
(if applicable)

Season GP FGM-FGA Pct. FTM-FTA Pct. Reb Avg. PF PTS. PPG.

**AFFELDT, JAMES**     6-0     b. 10-22-1943

| Season | G | FG | FG% | FT | FT% | Reb | Avg | Ast | Pts | Avg |
|---|---|---|---|---|---|---|---|---|---|---|
| 1962-63 | 2 | 0-2 | .000 | 0-0 | .000 | 2 | 1.0 | 2 | 0 | 0.0 |

**ALBERTS, EDWARD**     6-2

| Season | G | FG | FG% | FT | FT% | Reb | Avg | Ast | Pts | Avg |
|---|---|---|---|---|---|---|---|---|---|---|
| 1931-32 | 4 | 0 | | 0-0 | .000 | | | 0 | 0 | 0.0 |
| 1932-33 | 18 | 13-65 | .200 | 5-11 | .455 | | | 15 | 31 | 1.7 |
| 1933-34 | 8 | 2 | | 1-1 | 1.000 | | | 3 | 5 | 0.6 |
| | 30 | 15 | | 6-12 | .500 | | | 18 | 36 | 1.2 |

**ALLEN, DONALD**     6-1     b. 11-27-1914

| Season | G | FG | FG% | FT | FT% | Reb | Avg | Ast | Pts | Avg |
|---|---|---|---|---|---|---|---|---|---|---|
| 1933-34 | 18 | 4 | | 1-3 | .333 | | | 8 | 9 | 0.5 |
| 1935-36 | 9 | 3 | | 1 | | | | 5 | 7 | 0.8 |
| 1936-37 | 9 | 2 | | 0-0 | .000 | | | 5 | 4 | 0.4 |
| | 36 | 9 | | 2 | | | | 18 | 20 | 0.6 |

**ALLOCCO, FRANK**     6-1     b. 3-1-1953

| Season | G | FG | FG% | FT | FT% | Reb | Avg | Ast | Pts | Avg |
|---|---|---|---|---|---|---|---|---|---|---|
| 1972-73 | 6 | 1-5 | .200 | 0-0 | .000 | 3 | 0.5 | 4 | 6 | 1.0 |

**ANDERSON, EDWARD**     5-10     d.4-26-1974

| Season | G | FG | FG% | FT | FT% | Reb | Avg | Ast | Pts | Avg |
|---|---|---|---|---|---|---|---|---|---|---|
| 1919-20 | 17 | 5 | | 0 | | | | | 10 | 0.6 |
| 1920-21 | | | | | | | | | | |
| 1921-22 | 10 | 7 | | 0 | | | | | 14 | 1.4 |

**ANDERSON, ROGER**     6-9     b. 2-5-1954

| Season | G | FG | FG% | FT | FT% | Reb | Avg | Ast | Pts | Avg |
|---|---|---|---|---|---|---|---|---|---|---|
| 1972-73 | 3 | 1-2 | .500 | 1-1 | 1.000 | 1 | 0.3 | 0 | 3 | 1.0 |
| 1973-74 | 10 | 3-9 | .333 | 3-6 | .500 | 8 | 0.8 | 1 | 9 | 0.9 |
| 1974-75 | 8 | 4-9 | .444 | 0-1 | .000 | 3 | 0.4 | 4 | 8 | 1.0 |
| 1975-76 | 12 | 5-7 | .714 | 7-10 | .700 | 11 | 0.9 | 3 | 17 | 1.5 |
| | 33 | 13-27 | .481 | 11-18 | .611 | 23 | 0.7 | 8 | 37 | 1.1 |

**ANDREE, TIM**     6-10     b. 4-28-1961

| Season | G | FG | FG% | FT | FT% | Reb | Avg | Ast | Pts | Avg |
|---|---|---|---|---|---|---|---|---|---|---|
| 1979-80 | 25 | 30-66 | .455 | 31-51 | .544 | 59 | 2.4 | 51 | 91 | 3.8 |
| 1980-81 | 28 | 30-58 | .517 | 16-29 | .552 | 58 | 2.1 | 64 | 76 | 2.7 |
| 1981-82 | 25 | 69-141 | .489 | 45-71 | .634 | 104 | 4.2 | 86 | 183 | 7.3 |
| 1982-83 | 27 | 25-46 | .543 | 17-26 | .654 | 60 | 2.2 | 23 | 67 | 2.5 |
| | 105 | 154-311 | .495 | 109-177 | .616 | 281 | 2.7 | 224 | 417 | 4.0 |

**ANDREOLI, JOHN**     6-3     b. 7-10-1941

| Season | G | FG | FG% | FT | FT% | Reb | Avg | Ast | Pts | Avg |
|---|---|---|---|---|---|---|---|---|---|---|
| 1960-61 | 16 | 19-53 | .358 | 13-18 | .722 | 46 | 2.9 | 20 | 51 | 3.2 |
| 1961-62 | 23 | 119-267 | .446 | 64-87 | .736 | 150 | 6.5 | 59 | 298 | 13.0 |
| 1962-63 | 26 | 158-380 | .416 | 75-98 | .765 | 138 | 5.3 | 71 | 391 | 15.0 |
| | 65 | 296-700 | .423 | 152-203 | .749 | 334 | 5.1 | 150 | 740 | 11.4 |

**ANDREWS, FRANC**

| Season | G | FG | FG% | FT | FT% | Reb | Avg | Ast | Pts | Avg |
|---|---|---|---|---|---|---|---|---|---|---|
| 1926-27 | 1 | 0 | | 0 | | | | 0 | 0 | 0.0 |

## ANGSTEN, EDWARD

| 1931-32 | 1 | 0 | | 0-0 | .000 | | | 0 | 0 | 0.0 |
|---|---|---|---|---|---|---|---|---|---|---|
| 1932-33 | 1 | 1-3 | .333 | 0-0 | .000 | | | 0 | 2 | 2.0 |
| | 2 | 1 | | 0-0 | .000 | | | 0 | 2 | 1.0 |

## ARNZEN, BOB          6-5    b. 11-3-1947

| 1966-67 | 28 | 225-488 | .461 | 147-177 | .831 | 355 | 12.7 | 59 | 597 | 21.4 |
|---|---|---|---|---|---|---|---|---|---|---|
| 1967-68 | 30 | 269-527 | .510 | 106-134 | .791 | 310 | 10.3 | 49 | 644 | 21.5 |
| 1968-69 | 24 | 172-359 | .479 | 80-103 | .767 | 279 | 11.6 | 50 | 424 | 17.7 |
| | 82 | 666-1374 | .485 | 333-414 | .804 | 944 | 11.5 | 158 | 1665 | 20.3 |

## ATTLEY, GEORGE

| 1909-10 | 6 | 2 | | 0 | | | | | 4 | 0.7 |
|---|---|---|---|---|---|---|---|---|---|---|

## AUBREY, LLOYD          6-5    b. 8-29-1934

| 1953-54 | 11 | 10-22 | .455 | 6-15 | .400 | | | 10 | 26 | 2.4 |
|---|---|---|---|---|---|---|---|---|---|---|
| 1954-55 | 24 | 160-423 | .378 | 85-120 | .708 | | | 94 | 405 | 16.9 |
| 1955-56 | 24 | 197-466 | .423 | 145-201 | .721 | | | 88 | 539 | 22.5 |
| | 59 | 367-911 | .403 | 236-336 | .702 | | | 192 | 970 | 16.4 |

## AYOTTE, LEE          6-4    b. 12-1-1934

| 1954-55 | 22 | 41-124 | .331 | 5-23 | .217 | | | 30 | 87 | 4.0 |
|---|---|---|---|---|---|---|---|---|---|---|
| 1955-56 | 16 | 13-42 | .310 | 8-17 | .471 | | | 19 | 34 | 2.1 |
| 1957-58 | 7 | 5-13 | .385 | 0-1 | .000 | 9 | 1.3 | 8 | 10 | 1.4 |
| | 45 | 59-179 | .330 | 13-41 | .317 | | | 57 | 131 | 2.9 |

## BACH, JOSEPH          5-11    b.          d. 10-24-1966

| 1923-24 | 3 | 0 | | 0 | | | | 1 | 0 | 0.0 |
|---|---|---|---|---|---|---|---|---|---|---|

## BADER, CLARENCE          d. 10-21-1973

| 1917-18 | 6 | 3 | | 1 | | | | | 7 | 1.2 |
|---|---|---|---|---|---|---|---|---|---|---|
| 1918-19 | 10 | 10 | | 2 | | | | | 22 | 2.2 |
| | 16 | 13 | | 3 | | | | | 29 | 1.8 |

## BAGARUS, STEPHEN          5-11    b. 6-19-1919

| 1939-40 | 11 | 7 | | 6 | | | | 9 | 20 | 1.8 |
|---|---|---|---|---|---|---|---|---|---|---|
| 1940-41 | 3 | 0 | | 0-1 | .000 | | | 1 | 0 | 0.0 |
| | 14 | 7 | | 6 | | | | 10 | 20 | 1.4 |

## BAGLEY, DANIEL          6-4    b. 10-24-1929

| 1949-50 | 23 | 84-270 | .348 | 67-117 | .573 | | | 93 | 255 | 11.1 |
|---|---|---|---|---|---|---|---|---|---|---|
| 1950-51 | 24 | 120-340 | .353 | 78-118 | .661 | | | 88 | 318 | 13.3 |
| | 47 | 214-610 | .351 | 145-235 | .617 | | | 181 | 573 | 12.2 |

### BAHAN, LEONARD  5-9

| | | | | | | | | |
|---|---|---|---|---|---|---|---|---|
| 1917-18 | 5 | 10 | | 3 | | | 23 | 4.6 |
| 1918-19 | 12 | 42 | | 1 | | | 85 | 7.1 |
| | 17 | 52 | | 4 | | | 108 | 6.4 |

### BALDWIN, JOHN  5-8

| | | | | | | | | | |
|---|---|---|---|---|---|---|---|---|---|
| 1930-31 | 17 | 23 | | 12-22 | .545 | | 25 | 58 | 3.4 |
| 1931-32 | 9 | 17 | | 5-10 | .500 | | 14 | 39 | 4.3 |
| 1932-33 | 21 | 46-156 | .295 | 13-26 | .500 | | 49 | 105 | 5.0 |
| | 47 | 86 | | 30-58 | .517 | | 88 | 202 | 4.3 |

### BARLOW, KEN  6-10  b. 10-20-1964

| | | | | | | | | | | |
|---|---|---|---|---|---|---|---|---|---|---|
| 1982-83 | 29 | 85-148 | .574 | 22-35 | .629 | 120 | 4.1 | 72 | 192 | 6.6 |
| 1983-84 | 33 | 121-221 | .548 | 54-71 | .761 | 183 | 5.5 | 96 | 296 | 9.0 |
| 1984-85 | 30 | 179-363 | .493 | 80-105 | .762 | 194 | 6.5 | 91 | 438 | 14.6 |
| | 92 | 385-732 | .526 | 156-211 | .739 | 497 | 5.4 | 259 | 926 | 10.1 |

### BARNHORST, LEO  6-4  b. 5-17-1924

| | | | | | | | | | |
|---|---|---|---|---|---|---|---|---|---|
| 1946-47 | 24 | 88-280 | .314 | 29-62 | .468 | | 71 | 205 | 8.5 |
| 1947-48 | 24 | 116-290 | .400 | 58-88 | .659 | | 77 | 290 | 12.1 |
| 1948-49 | 24 | 113-318 | .355 | 57-91 | .626 | | 81 | 283 | 11.8 |
| | 72 | 317-888 | .357 | 144-241 | .598 | | 229 | 778 | 10.8 |

### BARRETT, ORDO

1901-02

### BATTON, DAVE  6-9

| | | | | | | | | | | |
|---|---|---|---|---|---|---|---|---|---|---|
| 1974-75 | 28 | 80-153 | .523 | 26-42 | .619 | 112 | 4.0 | 56 | 186 | 6.6 |
| 1975-76 | 28 | 115-236 | .487 | 25-41 | .610 | 162 | 5.8 | 59 | 255 | 9.1 |
| 1976-77 | 27 | 137-255 | .537 | 55-74 | .743 | 173 | 6.4 | 67 | 329 | 12.2 |
| 1977-78 | 31 | 188-332 | .566 | 59-79 | .747 | 210 | 6.8 | 66 | 434 | 14.0 |
| | 114 | 520-976 | .533 | 165-236 | .699 | 657 | 5.8 | 248 | 1205 | 10.6 |

### BAUJAN, HARRY  5-8

| | | | | | | | |
|---|---|---|---|---|---|---|---|
| 1914-15 | 3 | 0 | | 0 | | | 0 | 0.0 |
| 1916-17 | 2 | 0 | | 0 | | | 0 | 0.0 |
| | 5 | 0 | | 0 | | | 0 | 0.0 |

### BAUR, ADELBERT

| | | | | | | |
|---|---|---|---|---|---|---|
| 1934-35 | 1 | 0 | | 0 | | 0 | 0 | 0.0 |

### BEDAN, JACK  6-8  b. 2-18-1936

| | | | | | | | | |
|---|---|---|---|---|---|---|---|---|
| 1954-55 | 11 | 3-19 | .158 | 7-12 | .583 | | 12 | 13 | 1.2 |
| 1955-56 | 8 | 5-20 | .250 | 4-9 | .444 | | 9 | 14 | 1.8 |

| 1956-57 | 13 | 21-53 | .396 | 9-14 | .643 | 30 | 2.3 | 16 | 51 | 3.9 |
|---------|----|-------|------|------|------|----|-----|----|----|-----|
|         | 32 | 29-92 | .315 | 20-35 | .571 |   |     | 37 | 78 | 2.4 |

BEEUWSAERT, MATT       6-6    b. 3-6-1966

| 1984-85 | 20 | 28-53 | .528 | 10-18 | .556 | 44 | 2.2 | 28 | 66 | 3.3 |

BEKELJA, MICKEY       6-4

| 1957-58 | 6 | 2-6 | .333 | 1-2 | .500 | 2 | 0.3 | 2 | 5 | 0.8 |
|---------|----|-----|------|-----|------|----|-----|----|----|-----|
| 1958-59 | 12 | 14-39 | .359 | 5-8 | .625 | 28 | 2.3 | 20 | 33 | 2.8 |
| 1959-60 | 15 | 29-78 | .372 | 16-19 | .842 | 71 | 4.7 | 22 | 74 | 4.9 |
|         | 33 | 45-123 | .366 | 22-29 | .759 | 101 | 3.1 | 44 | 112 | 3.4 |

BENIGNI, GEORGE

| 1944-45 | 13 | 9 |  | 4-11 | .364 |  |  | 17 | 22 | 1.7 |

BENSBERG, WILLIAM

1912-13

BENTLEY, ROBERT       6-2    b. 10-22-1944

| 1964-65 | 16 | 8-24 | .333 | 5-11 | .455 | 13 | 0.8 | 11 | 21 | 1.3 |
|---------|----|------|------|------|------|----|-----|----|----|-----|
| 1965-66 | 4 | 17-40 | .425 | 13-14 | .929 | 15 | 3.8 | 9 | 47 | 11.8 |
| 1966-67 | 14 | 25-66 | .379 | 6-13 | .462 | 14 | 1.0 | 21 | 56 | 4.0 |
|         | 34 | 50-130 | .385 | 24-38 | .632 | 42 | 1.2 | 41 | 124 | 3.6 |

BERGMAN, ALFRED       5-8    b.          d. 6- -1961

| 1913-14 | 10 | 12 |  | 9 |  |  |  |  | 33 | 3.3 |
|---------|----|----|--|---|--|--|--|--|----|-----|
| 1914-15 | 4 | 11 |  | 0 |  |  |  |  | 22 | 5.5 |
|         | 14 | 23 |  | 9 |  |  |  |  | 55 | 3.9 |

BERNARDI, JOHN       5-11    b. 7-21-1945

| 1965-66 | 17 | 14-47 | .298 | 12-17 | .706 | 11 | 0.6 | 21 | 40 | 2.4 |
|---------|----|-------|------|-------|------|----|-----|----|----|-----|
| 1966-67 | 2 | 0-0 | .000 | 0-0 | .000 | 0 | 0.0 | 1 | 0 | 0.0 |
|         | 19 | 14-47 | .298 | 12-17 | .706 | 11 | 0.6 | 22 | 40 | 2.1 |

BERTRAND, JOE       6-3

| 1951-52 | 23 | 116-277 | .419 | 61-111 | .550 |  |  | 83 | 293 | 12.7 |
|---------|----|---------|------|--------|------|--|--|----|-----|------|
| 1952-53 | 24 | 130-298 | .436 | 87-144 | .604 |  |  | 74 | 347 | 14.5 |
| 1953-54 | 25 | 144-340 | .424 | 124-188 | .660 |  |  | 83 | 412 | 16.5 |
|         | 72 | 390-915 | .426 | 272-443 | .614 |  |  | 240 | 1052 | 14.6 |

BESTEN, ELMER

| 1925-26 | 10 | 0 |  | 2 |  |  |  |  | 2 | 0.2 |
|---------|----|---|--|---|--|--|--|--|---|-----|
| 1926-27 | 1 | 0 |  | 1 |  |  |  | 1 | 1 | 1.0 |
|         | 11 | 0 |  | 3 |  |  |  |  | 3 | 0.3 |

BJOIN, ANDREW
1912-13

| BOLAND, RAY | | | | 5-7 | b. 7-21-1911 | | | | |
|---|---|---|---|---|---|---|---|---|---|
| 1932-33 | 1 | 0-0 | .000 | 0-0 | .000 | | 0 | 0 | 0.0 |

| BONICELLI, ORLANDO | | | | 6-0 | b. 2-6-1922 | | | | |
|---|---|---|---|---|---|---|---|---|---|
| 1941-42 | 16 | 13 | | 13-19 | .684 | | 12 | 39 | 2.4 |
| 1942-43 | 19 | 15 | | 6 | | | 13 | 36 | 1.9 |
| | 35 | 28 | | 19 | | | 25 | 75 | 2.1 |

| BONNER, JOHN | | | | | | | | | |
|---|---|---|---|---|---|---|---|---|---|
| 1934-35 | 12 | 2 | | 5 | | | 3 | 9 | 0.8 |
| 1935-36 | 3 | 1 | | 1 | | | 2 | 3 | 1.0 |
| | 15 | 3 | | 6 | | | 5 | 12 | 0.8 |

| BOROWSKI, CHUCK | | | | 5-11 | | | | | |
|---|---|---|---|---|---|---|---|---|---|
| 1935-36 | 3 | 1 | | 1 | | | 2 | 3 | 1.0 |

| BORNHORST, THOMAS | | | | 6-4 | b. 1-28-1944 | | | | | |
|---|---|---|---|---|---|---|---|---|---|---|
| 1963-64 | 4 | 3-5 | .600 | 0-0 | .000 | 3 | 0.8 | 4 | 6 | 1.5 |
| 1964-65 | 15 | 8-28 | .286 | 0-3 | .000 | 16 | 1.1 | 9 | 16 | 1.1 |
| 1965-66 | 22 | 56-115 | .415 | 17-29 | .586 | 79 | 3.6 | 37 | 129 | 5.9 |
| | 41 | 67-168 | .399 | 17-32 | .531 | 98 | 2.4 | 50 | 151 | 3.7 |

| BORYLA, VINCE | | | | 6-4 | b. 3-11-1927 | | | | |
|---|---|---|---|---|---|---|---|---|---|
| 1944-45 | 20 | 130 | | 62-94 | .660 | | 66 | 322 | 16.1 |
| 1945-46 | 21 | 128-369 | .347 | 65-93 | .699 | | 75 | 321 | 15.3 |
| | 41 | 258 | | 127-187 | .679 | | 141 | 643 | 15.7 |

| BOWEN, JOHN | | | | 6-8 | b. 3-15-1965 | | | | | |
|---|---|---|---|---|---|---|---|---|---|---|
| 1983-84 | 23 | 12-23 | .522 | 2-3 | .667 | 25 | 1.1 | 7 | 26 | 1.1 |
| 1984-85 | 4 | 2-4 | .500 | 0.0 | .000 | 4 | 1.0 | 3 | 4 | 0-0 |
| | 27 | 14-27 | .519 | 2-3 | .667 | 29 | 1.1 | 10 | 30 | 1.1 |

BOYLE, JOSEPH
1907-08

| BRADTKE, ROBERT | | | | 6-1 | b. 12-23-1938 | | | | | |
|---|---|---|---|---|---|---|---|---|---|---|
| 1957-58 | 10 | 2-11 | .182 | 9-14 | .643 | 7 | 0.7 | 9 | 13 | 1.3 |
| 1958-59 | 21 | 65-196 | .332 | 16-28 | .571 | 79 | 3.8 | 33 | 146 | 7.0 |
| 1959-60 | 12 | 39-125 | .312 | 24-32 | .750 | 54 | 4.5 | 16 | 102 | 8.5 |
| | 43 | 106-332 | .319 | 49-74 | .662 | 140 | 3.3 | 58 | 261 | 6.1 |

### BRANDY, JOSEPH　　　　5-8

| | | | | | |
|---|---|---|---|---|---|
| 1917-18 | 14 | 0 | 0 | 0 | 0.0 |
| 1918-19 | 11 | 21 | 16 | 58 | 5.3 |
| 1919-20 | 12 | 20 | 5 | 45 | 3.8 |
| | 27 | 41 | 21 | 103 | 3.8 |

### BRANNING, RICH　　　　6-3　　b. 8-4-1957

| | | | | | | | | | | |
|---|---|---|---|---|---|---|---|---|---|---|
| 1976-77 | 29 | 108-227 | .476 | 95-119 | .798 | 64 | 2.2 | 71 | 311 | 10.7 |
| 1977-78 | 30 | 129-277 | .466 | 71-97 | .752 | 55 | 1.8 | 65 | 329 | 11.0 |
| 1978-79 | 29 | 125-267 | .468 | 47-77 | .610 | 31 | 1.1 | 66 | 297 | 10.2 |
| 1979-80 | 26 | 120-226 | .531 | 55-82 | .671 | 45 | 1.7 | 60 | 295 | 11.3 |
| | 114 | 482-997 | .483 | 261-375 | .715 | 193 | 1.7 | 262 | 1232 | 10.8 |

### BRAY, JAMES

| | | | | | | |
|---|---|---|---|---|---|---|
| 1926-27 | 12 | 3 | 1 | | 7 | 0.6 |
| 1927-28 | 18 | 11 | 12 | 18 | 34 | 1.9 |
| 1928-29 | 8 | 1 | 1 | 8 | 3 | 0.4 |
| | 38 | 15 | 14 | | 44 | 1.2 |

### BRENNAN, JOHN　　　　6-4　　b. 7-13-1925

| | | | | | | | | |
|---|---|---|---|---|---|---|---|---|
| 1946-47 | 24 | 114-341 | .334 | 61-109 | .560 | 88 | 289 | 12.0 |
| 1947-48 | 9 | 46-121 | .380 | 24-39 | .615 | 31 | 116 | 12.9 |
| 1948-49 | 11 | 40-137 | .292 | 41-60 | .683 | 42 | 121 | 11.0 |
| | 44 | 200-599 | .334 | 126-208 | .606 | 161 | 526 | 12.0 |

### BRENNAN, THOMAS　　　　6-3　　b. 3-21-1922

| | | | | | | | | |
|---|---|---|---|---|---|---|---|---|
| 1941-42 | 3 | 3 | | 0-0 | .000 | 2 | 6 | 2.0 |
| 1942-43 | 20 | 34 | | 20 | | 41 | 88 | 4.4 |
| | 23 | 37 | | 20 | | 43 | 93 | 4.1 |

### BRISLIN, JOHN
1908-09

### BROKAW, GARY　　　　6-3　　b. 1-11-1954

| | | | | | | | | | | |
|---|---|---|---|---|---|---|---|---|---|---|
| 1972-73 | 30 | 209-481 | .435 | 105-145 | .724 | 142 | 4.7 | 86 | 523 | 17.4 |
| 1973-74 | 28 | 201-361 | .557 | 76-109 | .697 | 124 | 4.4 | 73 | 478 | 17.1 |
| | 58 | 410-842 | .487 | 181-254 | .713 | 266 | 4.6 | 159 | 1001 | 17.3 |

### BROWN, EARL　　　　6-0　　b. 10-23-1915

| | | | | | | | |
|---|---|---|---|---|---|---|---|
| 1936-37 | 21 | 28 | | 18-34 | .529 | 40 | 74 | 3.5 |
| 1937-38 | 23 | 33 | | 20 | | 86 | 3.7 |
| 1938-39 | 19 | 31 | | 20 | | 82 | 4.3 |
| | 63 | 92 | | 58 | | 242 | 3.8 |

**BROWN, HARVEY**     d. 1-13-1957

|  | | | | | | | | | | |
|---|---|---|---|---|---|---|---|---|---|---|
| 1921-22 | 1 | 0 | | 0 | | | | 1 | 0 | 0.0 |

**BROWN,**

|  | | | | | | | | | | |
|---|---|---|---|---|---|---|---|---|---|---|
| 1928-29 | 1 | 0 | | 0 | | | | 1 | 0 | 0.0 |

**BROWNING, ROBERT**

|  | | | | | | | | | | |
|---|---|---|---|---|---|---|---|---|---|---|
| 1940-41 | 1 | 0 | | 0 | | | | 0 | 0 | 0.0 |

**BUCHANAN, JOE**     6-2   b. 2-10-1964

|  | | | | | | | | | | |
|---|---|---|---|---|---|---|---|---|---|---|
| 1982-84 | 24 | 8-18 | .444 | 8-12 | .667 | 17 | 0.7 | 26 | 24 | 1.0 |
| 1983-84 | 18 | 24-59 | .407 | 7-16 | .438 | 31 | 1.7 | 30 | 55 | 3.1 |
| | 42 | 32-77 | .416 | 15-28 | .536 | 48 | 1.1 | 56 | 79 | 1.9 |

**BURKE, CHESTER**     6-0
1907-08

**BURKE, JOHN**
1908-09

|  | | | | | | | | | | |
|---|---|---|---|---|---|---|---|---|---|---|
| 1909-10 | 11 | 12 | | 0 | | | | | 24 | 2.2 |
| 1910-11 | 4 | 6 | | 0 | | | | | 12 | 3.0 |

**BURNS, JAMES**

|  | | | | | | | | | | |
|---|---|---|---|---|---|---|---|---|---|---|
| 1921-22 | 9 | 3 | | 0 | | | | | 6 | 0.7 |

**BURNS, THOMAS**

|  | | | | | | | | | | |
|---|---|---|---|---|---|---|---|---|---|---|
| 1929-30 | 8 | 1 | | 0-0 | .000 | | | 4 | 2 | 0.3 |
| 1930-31 | 17 | 10 | | 6-15 | .400 | | | 35 | 26 | 1.5 |
| 1931-32 | 20 | 13 | | 11-20 | .550 | | | 39 | 37 | 1.9 |
| | 45 | 24 | | 17-35 | .486 | | | 78 | 65 | 1.4 |

**BURNS, THOMAS D.**

|  | | | | | | | | | | |
|---|---|---|---|---|---|---|---|---|---|---|
| 1896-97 | 2 | 0 | | 0 | | | | 0 | 0 | 0.0 |
| 1897-98 | 3 | 1 | | 0 | | | | | 2 | 0.7 |
| | 5 | 1 | | 0 | | | | | 2 | 0.4 |

**BUSCH, VINCENT**

|  | | | | | | | | | | |
|---|---|---|---|---|---|---|---|---|---|---|
| 1928-29 | 8 | 4 | | 4 | | | | 7 | 12 | 1.5 |
| 1929-30 | 14 | 3 | | 3-4 | .750 | | | 8 | 9 | 0.6 |
| | 22 | 7 | | 7 | | | | 15 | 21 | 1.0 |

**BUTLER, CHARLES**     6-2   b. 8-15-1920

|  | | | | | | | | | | |
|---|---|---|---|---|---|---|---|---|---|---|
| 1940-41 | 21 | 44 | | 29 | | | | | 117 | 5.6 |
| 1941-42 | 21 | 41 | | 40-69 | .580 | | | 26 | 122 | 5.8 |
| 1942-43 | 20 | 60 | | 60 | | | | 37 | 180 | 9.0 |
| | 62 | 145 | | 129 | | | | | 419 | 6.8 |

## BUTORAC, FRANK 6-1

| Year | G | FG | FG% | FT | FT% | | | | Pts | Avg |
|---|---|---|---|---|---|---|---|---|---|---|
| 1928-29 | 4 | 4 | | 2 | | | | 2 | 10 | 2.5 |
| 1929-30 | 8 | 0 | | 1-1 | 1.000 | | | 3 | 1 | 0.1 |
| | 12 | 4 | | 3 | | | | 5 | 11 | 0.9 |

## BYRNE, JOSEPH

| Year | G | FG | FG% | FT | FT% | | | | Pts | Avg |
|---|---|---|---|---|---|---|---|---|---|---|
| 1911-12 | 6 | 4 | | 0 | | | | | 8 | 1.3 |
| 1912-13 | | | | | | | | | | |

## CAHILL, JAMES

| Year | G | FG | FG% | FT | FT% | | | | Pts | Avg |
|---|---|---|---|---|---|---|---|---|---|---|
| 1911-12 | | | | | | | | | | |
| 1912-13 | 14 | 44 | | 29 | | | | | 117 | 8.4 |
| 1913-14 | 12 | 26 | | 22 | | | | | 74 | 6.2 |

## CALDWELL, THOMAS 6-5 b. 8-15-1945

| Year | G | FG | FG% | FT | FT% | Reb | Avg | | Pts | Avg |
|---|---|---|---|---|---|---|---|---|---|---|
| 1965-66 | 18 | 73-177 | .412 | 63-88 | .716 | 161 | 8.9 | 51 | 209 | 11.6 |
| 1966-67 | 28 | 85-173 | .491 | 70-94 | .745 | 119 | 4.3 | 68 | 240 | 8.6 |
| | 46 | 158-350 | .451 | 133-182 | .731 | 280 | 6.1 | 119 | 449 | 9.8 |

## CARIDEO, FRANK 5-7 b. 6-4-1908

| Year | G | FG | FG% | FT | FT% | | | | Pts | Avg |
|---|---|---|---|---|---|---|---|---|---|---|
| 1928-29 | 2 | 0 | | 0 | | | | 1 | 0 | 0.0 |
| 1929-30 | 2 | 1 | | 0-0 | .000 | | | 0 | 2 | 1.0 |
| | 4 | 1 | | 0 | | | | 1 | 2 | 0.5 |

## CARNES, JAMES

| Year | G | FG | FG% | FT | FT% | | | | Pts | Avg |
|---|---|---|---|---|---|---|---|---|---|---|
| 1939-40 | 13 | 4 | | 5 | | | | 2 | 13 | 1.0 |
| 1940-41 | 21 | 35 | | 12 | | | | | 82 | 3.9 |
| | 34 | 39 | | 17 | | | | | 95 | 2.8 |

## CARPENTER, JEFF 6-0

| Year | G | FG | FG% | FT | FT% | Reb | Avg | | Pts | Avg |
|---|---|---|---|---|---|---|---|---|---|---|
| 1974-75 | 25 | 14-48 | .212 | 14-17 | .824 | 27 | 1.1 | 41 | 42 | 1.7 |
| 1975-76 | 24 | 15-40 | .375 | 6-12 | .500 | 23 | 1.0 | 38 | 36 | 1.5 |
| 1976-77 | 24 | 13-40 | .325 | 14-18 | .778 | 29 | 1.2 | 33 | 40 | 1.7 |
| 1977-78 | 26 | 13-35 | .371 | 5-12 | .417 | 15 | 0.6 | 29 | 31 | 1.2 |
| | 99 | 55-163 | .337 | 39-59 | .661 | 94 | 0.9 | 141 | 149 | 1.5 |

## CARR, AUSTIN 6-3 b. 3-10-1948

| Year | G | FG | FG% | FT | FT% | Reb | Avg | | Pts | Avg |
|---|---|---|---|---|---|---|---|---|---|---|
| 1968-69 | 16 | 143-294 | .486 | 67-85 | .788 | 84 | 5.3 | 31 | 353 | 22.0 |
| 1969-70 | 29 | 444-799 | .556 | 218-264 | .826 | 240 | 8.3 | 41 | 1106 | 38.1 |
| 1970-71 | 29 | 430-852 | .515 | 241-297 | .811 | 214 | 7.4 | 56 | 1101 | 37.9 |
| | 74 | 1017-1925 | .528 | 526-646 | .814 | 538 | 7.3 | 128 | 2560 | 34.6 |

## CARSON, JAMES 5-9 b. 7-14-1916

| Year | G | FG | FG% | FT | FT% | | | | Pts | Avg |
|---|---|---|---|---|---|---|---|---|---|---|
| 1935-36 | 3 | 3 | | 0 | | | | 0 | 6 | 2.0 |
| 1936-37 | 7 | 5 | | 0-0 | .000 | | | 1 | 10 | 1.4 |

| 1937-38 | 8 | 4 | | 4 | | | | | | 12 | 1.5 |
|---|---|---|---|---|---|---|---|---|---|---|---|
| | 18 | 12 | | 4 | | | | | | 28 | 1.6 |

**CASSIDY, CLIFFORD**

| 1914-15 | 13 | 12 | | 0 | | | | | | 24 | 1.8 |
|---|---|---|---|---|---|---|---|---|---|---|---|
| 1915-16 | 7 | 5 | | 2 | | | | | | 12 | 1.7 |
| 1916-17 | 6 | 6 | | 0 | | | | | | 12 | 2.0 |
| | 26 | 23 | | 2 | | | | | | 48 | 1.8 |

**CATLETT, SID**　　　　6-8　　b. 4-8-1948

| 1968-69 | 25 | 54-172 | .314 | 14-38 | .368 | 171 | 6.8 | 45 | 122 | 4.9 |
|---|---|---|---|---|---|---|---|---|---|---|
| 1969-70 | 28 | 104-253 | .411 | 33-71 | .465 | 214 | 7.6 | 73 | 241 | 8.6 |
| 1970-71 | 29 | 119-296 | .402 | 47-63 | .746 | 298 | 10.3 | 78 | 285 | 9.8 |
| | 82 | 277-721 | .384 | 94-172 | .547 | 683 | 8.3 | 196 | 648 | 7.9 |

**CHAPMAN, FRANCIS**　　　　6-3　　b. 1-5-1921

| 1940-41 | 2 | 0 | | 0 | | | | 0 | 0 | 0.0 |
|---|---|---|---|---|---|---|---|---|---|---|

**CLANCY, RICHARD**　　　　6-2　　　　d. 1-20-1972

| 1949-50 | 3 | 0-1 | .000 | 0-0 | .000 | | | 0 | 0 | 0.0 |
|---|---|---|---|---|---|---|---|---|---|---|

**CLAY, DWIGHT**　　　　6-0　　b.1-29-1953

| 1972-73 | 30 | 151-392 | .385 | 49-69 | .710 | 86 | 2.9 | 64 | 351 | 11.7 |
|---|---|---|---|---|---|---|---|---|---|---|
| 1973-74 | 28 | 89-223 | .389 | 23-29 | .793 | 61 | 2.2 | 47 | 201 | 7.2 |
| 1974-75 | 29 | 108-253 | .427 | 29-39 | .744 | 75 | 2.6 | 46 | 245 | 8.4 |
| | 87 | 348-868 | .401 | 101-137 | .737 | 222 | 2.6 | 157 | 797 | 9.2 |

**COFFEY, DONALD**

| 1922-23 | 4 | 1 | | 0-0 | .000 | | | 0 | 2 | 0.5 |
|---|---|---|---|---|---|---|---|---|---|---|

**COLERICK, JOHN**　　　　6-2　b.　　　　d. 2-15-1948

| 1926-27 | 16 | 12 | | 6 | | | | | 30 | 1.9 |
|---|---|---|---|---|---|---|---|---|---|---|
| 1927-28 | 16 | 36 | | 22 | | | | | 94 | 5.9 |
| 1928-29 | 14 | 38 | | 18 | | | | | 94 | 6.7 |
| | 46 | 86 | | 46 | | | | | 218 | 4.7 |

**COLLINS, CHUCK**

| 1922-23 | 1 | 0 | | 0-0 | .000 | | | 0 | 0 | 0.0 |
|---|---|---|---|---|---|---|---|---|---|---|

**CONDON, EDWARD**　　　　6-4　　b. 6-18-1931

| 1950-51 | 5 | 4-11 | .364 | 2-3 | .667 | | | 6 | 10 | 2.0 |
|---|---|---|---|---|---|---|---|---|---|---|
| 1952-53 | 7 | 5-10 | .500 | 3-6 | .500 | | | 3 | 13 | 1.9 |
| | 12 | 9-21 | .429 | 5-9 | .556 | | | 9 | 23 | 1.9 |

**CONLEY, TOM**　　　　5-11　　b. 5-7-1908

| 1929-30 | 12 | 3 | | 0-1 | .000 | | | 6 | 6 | 0.5 |
|---|---|---|---|---|---|---|---|---|---|---|

**CONNELL, JAMES**
1908-09

| | | | | | | | | | |
|---|---|---|---|---|---|---|---|---|---|
| **CONNOR, GEORGE** | | | | 6-3 | b. 1-21-1925 | | | | |
| 1946-47 | 16 | 15-33 | .455 | 10-25 | .400 | | 19 | 40 | 2.5 |

| | | | | | | | | | |
|---|---|---|---|---|---|---|---|---|---|
| **CONRAD, FRANK** | | | | | | | | | |
| 1936-37 | 2 | 0 | | 1-2 | .500 | | 0 | 1 | 0.5 |

| | | | | | | | | |
|---|---|---|---|---|---|---|---|---|
| **CONROY, LOUIS** | | | | | | | | |
| 1924-25 | 22 | 25 | | 15-25 | .600 | 39 | 65 | 3.0 |
| 1925-26 | 20 | 17 | | 13 | | | 47 | 2.4 |
| 1926-27 | 20 | 32 | | 24 | | | 88 | 4.4 |
| | 62 | 74 | | 52 | | | 200 | 3.2 |

| | | | | | | | |
|---|---|---|---|---|---|---|---|
| **COPPS, GORDON** | | | | | d. 12-5-1972 | | |
| 1927-28 | 2 | 1 | | 1 | | 1 | 3 | 1.5 |

| | | | | | | |
|---|---|---|---|---|---|---|
| **CORCORAN, CHARLES** | | | | | | |
| 1914-15 | 2 | 1 | | 0 | | 2 | 1.0 |

| | | | | | | | | | |
|---|---|---|---|---|---|---|---|---|---|
| **CORLEY, RAYMOND** | | | | 6-0 | b. 1-1-1928 | | | | |
| 1945-46 | 18 | 6-36 | .167 | 5-7 | .714 | | 19 | 17 | 0.9 |

| | | | | | | | |
|---|---|---|---|---|---|---|---|
| **CORNELL, FRANK** | | | 5-5 | | | | |
| 1896-97 | 3 | 11 | | 0 | | 1 | 22 | 7.3 |
| 1897-98 | 2 | 2 | | 0 | | | 4 | 2.0 |
| | 5 | 13 | | 0 | | | 26 | 5.2 |

| | | | | | | |
|---|---|---|---|---|---|---|
| **COUGHLIN, DAN** | | | 5-9 | | | |
| 1919-20 | 5 | 0 | | 0 | | 0 | 0.0 |
| 1920-21 | | | | | | | |
| 1921-22 | 9 | 7 | | 0 | | 14 | 1.6 |

| | | | | | | | |
|---|---|---|---|---|---|---|---|
| **CRADDOCK, JOHN** | | | | | | | |
| 1942-43 | 2 | 1 | | 0-0 | .000 | 0 | 2 | 1.0 |

| | | | | | | | | |
|---|---|---|---|---|---|---|---|---|
| **CREEVY, RICHARD** | | | | 6-1 | b. 12-7-1920 | | | |
| 1940-41 | 2 | 1 | | 0-0 | .000 | 1 | 2 | 1.0 |

| | | | | | | |
|---|---|---|---|---|---|---|
| **CRILLY, JAMES** | | | | | | |
| 1913-14 | 1 | 0 | | 0 | | 0 | 0.0 |

| | | | | | | | | |
|---|---|---|---|---|---|---|---|---|
| **CRIMMINS, BERNARD** | | | | 5-11 | b. 4-14-1919 | | | |
| 1939-40 | 3 | 1 | | 1 | | 4 | 3 | 1.0 |
| 1940-41 | 3 | 1 | | 0-0 | .000 | 0 | 2 | 0.7 |
| | 6 | 2 | | 1 | | 4 | 5 | 0.8 |

### CROSBY, WILLIAM    6-4    b. 8-6-1939    d. 8- -1983

| | | | | | | | | | |
|---|---|---|---|---|---|---|---|---|---|
| 1958-59 | 19 | 31-112 | .277 | 23-27 | .852 | 55 | 2.9 | 35 | 85 | 4.5 |
| 1959-60 | 26 | 50-154 | .325 | 34-53 | .642 | 169 | 6.5 | 75 | 134 | 5.2 |
| 1960-61 | 26 | 80-213 | .376 | 64-83 | .771 | 154 | 5.2 | 87 | 224 | 8.6 |
| | 71 | 161-479 | .336 | 121-163 | .742 | 358 | 5.0 | 197 | 443 | 6.2 |

### CROTTY, PETER    6-8    b. 5-3-1953

| | | | | | | | | | |
|---|---|---|---|---|---|---|---|---|---|
| 1972-73 | 30 | 87-202 | .431 | 66-118 | .559 | 203 | 6.8 | 99 | 240 | 8.0 |
| 1973-74 | 22 | 10-32 | .313 | 18-25 | .720 | 33 | 1.5 | 19 | 38 | 1.7 |
| 1974-75 | 28 | 46-106 | .434 | 13-23 | .565 | 91 | 3.3 | 68 | 105 | 3.8 |
| | 80 | 143-340 | .421 | 87-166 | .584 | 327 | 4.1 | 186 | 383 | 4.8 |

### CROWE, CLEM    5-9    b.    d. 4-13-1983

| | | | | | | | |
|---|---|---|---|---|---|---|---|
| 1923-24 | 23 | 70 | | 19 | | | | 159 | 6.9 |
| 1924-25 | 16 | 41 | | 12-25 | .480 | | 26 | 94 | 5.9 |
| 1925-26 | 19 | 49 | | 33 | | | | 131 | 6.9 |
| | 58 | 160 | | 64 | | | | 384 | 6.6 |

### CROWE, EDWARD    5-11

| | | | | | | | | |
|---|---|---|---|---|---|---|---|---|
| 1924-25 | 5 | 0 | | 0-0 | .000 | | 1 | 0 | 0.0 |

### CROWE, EMMETT    5-9    b. 9-14-1917

| | | | | | | | | |
|---|---|---|---|---|---|---|---|---|
| 1936-37 | 2 | 0 | | 0-1 | .000 | | 0 | 0 | 0.0 |
| 1937-38 | 1 | 0 | | 0.0 | .000 | | 0 | 0 | 0.0 |
| | 3 | 0 | | 0-1 | .000 | | 0 | 0 | 0.0 |

### CROWE, FRANCIS

| | | | | | | |
|---|---|---|---|---|---|---|
| 1926-27 | 19 | 45 | | 20 | | | 110 | 5.8 |
| 1927-28 | 22 | 48 | | 27 | | | 123 | 5.6 |
| 1928-29 | 19 | 44 | | 18 | | | 106 | 5.6 |
| | 60 | 137 | | 65 | | | 339 | 5.7 |

### CROWE, LEO    5-10    b.    d. 4-24-1966

| | | | | | | | |
|---|---|---|---|---|---|---|---|
| 1931-32 | 15 | 14 | | 4-7 | .571 | 9 | 32 | 2.1 |
| 1932-33 | 21 | 20-95 | .211 | 30-44 | .682 | 45 | 70 | 3.3 |
| 1933-34 | 23 | 42 | | 22-39 | .564 | 37 | 106 | 4.6 |
| | 59 | 76 | | 56-90 | .622 | 91 | 208 | 3.5 |

### CROWE, MICHAEL    5-8    b. 1-15-1916    d. 5-11-1972

| | | | | | | | |
|---|---|---|---|---|---|---|---|
| 1935-36 | 8 | 7 | | 3 | | 3 | 17 | 2.1 |
| 1936-37 | 16 | 7 | | 7-16 | .438 | 12 | 21 | 1.3 |
| 1937-38 | 21 | 13 | | 11 | | | 37 | 1.8 |
| | 45 | 27 | | 21 | | | 75 | 1.7 |

### CROWE, NORBERT

| | | | | | | | | |
|---|---|---|---|---|---|---|---|---|
| 1929-30 | 20 | 22 | | 8-23 | .348 | 19 | 52 | 2.6 |
| 1930-31 | 20 | 29 | | 10-19 | .526 | 27 | 68 | 3.4 |
| 1931-32 | 20 | 36 | | 9-21 | .429 | 34 | 81 | 4.1 |
| | 60 | 87 | | 27-63 | .429 | 80 | 201 | 3.4 |

### CROWLEY, JOHN

| | | | | | | | | |
|---|---|---|---|---|---|---|---|---|
| 1926-27 | 2 | 0 | | 0 | | 0 | 0 | 0.0 |

### CUNHA, DANIEL                    d. 7-2-1968

| | | | | | | | | |
|---|---|---|---|---|---|---|---|---|
| 1934-35 | 5 | 2 | | 0 | | 5 | 4 | 0.8 |

### CURRAN, FRANCIS          6-2     b. 7-4-1922

| | | | | | | | | |
|---|---|---|---|---|---|---|---|---|
| 1941-42 | 18 | 23 | | 3-9 | .333 | 23 | 49 | 2.7 |
| 1942-43 | 20 | 75 | | 36 | | 36 | 186 | 9.3 |
| 1946-47 | 24 | 96-271 | .354 | 47-72 | .653 | 57 | 239 | 10.0 |
| | 62 | 194 | | 86 | | 116 | 474 | 7.6 |

### DAHMAN, RAYMOND          5-8

| | | | | | | | | |
|---|---|---|---|---|---|---|---|---|
| 1924-25 | 20 | 21 | | 4-12 | .333 | 22 | 46 | 2.3 |
| 1925-26 | 20 | 32 | | 13 | | | 77 | 3.9 |
| 1926-27 | 19 | 25 | | 13 | | | 63 | 3.3 |
| | 59 | 78 | | 30 | | | 186 | 3.2 |

### DALEY, RICHARD

| | | | | | | |
|---|---|---|---|---|---|---|
| 1914-15 | 17 | 38 | | 2 | 78 | 4.6 |
| 1915-16 | 7 | 26 | | 0 | 52 | 7.4 |
| 1916-17 | 9 | 13 | | 0 | 26 | 2.9 |
| | 33 | 77 | | 2 | 156 | 4.7 |

### DALY, CHARLES          5-7
1898-99

### DANTLEY, ADRIAN          6-5     b. 2-28-1955

| | | | | | | | | | | |
|---|---|---|---|---|---|---|---|---|---|---|
| 1973-74 | 28 | 189-339 | .558 | 133-161 | .826 | 255 | 9.1 | 74 | 511 | 18.3 |
| 1974-75 | 29 | 315-581 | .542 | 253-314 | .806 | 296 | 10.2 | 86 | 883 | 30.4 |
| 1975-76 | 29 | 300-510 | .588 | 229-294 | .779 | 292 | 10.1 | 73 | 829 | 28.6 |
| | 86 | 804-1430 | .562 | 615-769 | .800 | 843 | 9.8 | 233 | 2223 | 25.8 |

### DAVIS, DICK

| | | | | | | | | |
|---|---|---|---|---|---|---|---|---|
| 1931-32 | 11 | 11 | | 3-5 | .600 | 11 | 25 | 2.3 |

### DAVIS, WILLIAM          6-3     b. 10-3-1921

| | | | | | | |
|---|---|---|---|---|---|---|
| 1942-43 | 16 | 14 | | 4 | 27 | 32 | 2.0 |

### DEARIE, JOHN                    6-6     b. 3-23-1940

| | | | | | | | | | | |
|---|---|---|---|---|---|---|---|---|---|---|
| 1959-60 | 25 | 133-310 | .429 | 59-109 | .541 | 230 | 9.2 | 64 | 325 | 13.0 |
| 1960-61 | 25 | 86-220 | .391 | 70-127 | .551 | 188 | 7.5 | 62 | 242 | 9.7 |
| 1961-62 | 22 | 74-202 | .366 | 30-78 | .385 | 156 | 7.1 | 77 | 178 | 8.1 |
| | 72 | 293-732 | .400 | 159-314 | .506 | 574 | 8.0 | 203 | 745 | 10.3 |

### DeCOOK, RAYMOND

| | | | | | | | | |
|---|---|---|---|---|---|---|---|---|
| 1929-30 | 19 | 38 | | 19-35 | .543 | 37 | 95 | 5.0 |
| 1930-31 | 20 | 52 | | 27-53 | .509 | 37 | 131 | 6.6 |
| 1931-32 | 17 | 35 | | 16-28 | .571 | 18 | 86 | 5.1 |
| | 56 | 125 | | 62-116 | .534 | 92 | 312 | 5.6 |

### DEE, JOHNNY                    5-9     b. 9-12-1923

| | | | | | | | | |
|---|---|---|---|---|---|---|---|---|
| 1944-45 | 20 | 109 | | 33-71 | .465 | 53 | 251 | 12.6 |
| 1945-46 | 21 | 47-175 | .269 | 27-43 | .628 | 49 | 121 | 5.8 |
| | 41 | 156 | | 60-114 | .526 | 102 | 372 | 9.1 |

### DEL ZOPPO, ALBERT

| | | | | | | | | |
|---|---|---|---|---|---|---|---|---|
| 1938-39 | 6 | 1 | | 1 | | 4 | 3 | 0.5 |
| 1939-40 | 12 | 6 | | 2 | | 4 | 14 | 1.2 |
| 1940-41 | 9 | 5 | | 4-4 | 1.000 | 5 | 14 | 1.6 |
| | 27 | 12 | | 7 | | 13 | 31 | 1.1 |

### DeMOTS, JOHN

| | | | | | | | | |
|---|---|---|---|---|---|---|---|---|
| 1934-35 | 7 | 2 | | 4 | | 3 | 8 | 1.1 |
| 1935-36 | 9 | 7 | | 2 | | 4 | 16 | 1.8 |
| 1936-37 | 7 | 3 | | 1-3 | .333 | 2 | 7 | 1.0 |
| | 23 | 12 | | 7 | | 9 | 31 | 1.3 |

### DERRIG, JAMES                    6-2     b. 12-15-1946

| | | | | | | | | | | |
|---|---|---|---|---|---|---|---|---|---|---|
| 1966-67 | 22 | 44-90 | .489 | 30-36 | .833 | 46 | 2.1 | 27 | 118 | 5.4 |
| 1967-68 | 30 | 93-212 | .439 | 86-110 | .782 | 110 | 3.7 | 42 | 272 | 9.1 |
| 1968-69 | 9 | 5-22 | .227 | 10-18 | .556 | 12 | 1.3 | 3 | 20 | 2.2 |
| | 61 | 142-324 | .438 | 126-164 | .768 | 168 | 2.8 | 72 | 410 | 6.7 |

### DEVINE, ROBERT                    6-0     b. 2-8-1935

| | | | | | | | | | | |
|---|---|---|---|---|---|---|---|---|---|---|
| 1955-56 | 24 | 115-284 | .405 | 88-121 | .727 | | | 62 | 318 | 13.3 |
| 1956-57 | 28 | 142-364 | .390 | 72-96 | .750 | 133 | 4.8 | 71 | 356 | 12.7 |
| 1957-58 | 29 | 138-389 | .355 | 93-126 | .738 | 122 | 4.2 | 73 | 369 | 12.7 |
| | 81 | 395-1037 | .381 | 253-343 | .738 | | | 206 | 1043 | 12.9 |

### DEW, WILLIAM                    5-11                    d. 6-30-1972

| | | | | | | | |
|---|---|---|---|---|---|---|---|
| 1927-28 | 1 | 0 | | 0-0 | .000 | 2 | 0 | 0.0 |
| 1928-29 | 1 | 0 | | 0 | | 1 | 0 | 0.0 |
| | 2 | 0 | | 0 | | 3 | 0 | 0.0 |

### DIENHART, JOSEPH

| | | | | | | | | | |
|---|---|---|---|---|---|---|---|---|---|
| 1923-24 | 11 | 14 | | 4 | | | | 32 | 2.9 |
| 1924-25 | 20 | 19 | | 15-24 | .625 | | 15 | 53 | 2.7 |
| | 31 | 33 | | 19 | | | | 85 | 2.7 |

### DOAR, JAMES          5-11
1901-02

### DOLAN, JIM          6-8     b. 9-23-1964

| | | | | | | | | | | |
|---|---|---|---|---|---|---|---|---|---|---|
| 1982-83 | 28 | 60-117 | .513 | 56-76 | .739 | 131 | 4.7 | 72 | 176 | 6.3 |
| 1983-84 | 33 | 96-193 | .497 | 50-79 | .633 | 245 | 7.4 | 103 | 242 | 7.3 |
| 1984-85 | 27 | 44-86 | .512 | 27-41 | .659 | 124 | 4.6 | 61 | 115 | 4.3 |
| | 88 | 200-396 | .505 | 133-196 | .679 | 500 | 5.7 | 236 | 533 | 6.1 |

### DOMBROSKY, JOSEPH          6-4     b. 9-13-1931

| | | | | | | | | | |
|---|---|---|---|---|---|---|---|---|---|
| 1950-51 | 2 | 0-0 | .000 | 0-0 | .000 | | | 4 | 0 | 0.0 |

### DONAHUE, MATTHEW

| | | | | | |
|---|---|---|---|---|---|
| 1897-98 | 3 | 0 | 0 | 0 | 0.0 |

### DONAPHIN, ROBERT          6-5     b. 3-10-1945

| | | | | | | | | | |
|---|---|---|---|---|---|---|---|---|---|
| 1963-64 | 1 | 0-1 | .000 | 0-0 | .000 | 2 | 2.0 | 0 | 0 | 0.0 |

### DONOVAN, CLARENCE

| | | | | | | | |
|---|---|---|---|---|---|---|---|
| 1927-28 | 20 | 23 | | 12 | | | 58 | 2.9 |
| 1928-29 | 19 | 25 | | 14 | | | 64 | 3.4 |
| 1929-30 | 20 | 24 | | 16-24 | .667 | 34 | 64 | 3.2 |
| | 59 | 72 | | 42 | | | 186 | 3.2 |

### DONOVAN, JOHN

| | | | | | | |
|---|---|---|---|---|---|---|
| 1896-97 | 3 | 3 | 0 | | 3 | 6 | 2.0 |
| 1897-98 | 2 | 2 | 3 | | | 7 | 3.5 |
| | 5 | 5 | 3 | | | 13 | 2.6 |

### DOUGHERTY, CLEMENT

| | | | | | |
|---|---|---|---|---|---|
| 1911-12 | 2 | 1 | 0 | 2 | 1.0 |

### DOWD, OWEN          6-2     b. 10-27-1942

| | | | | | | | | | |
|---|---|---|---|---|---|---|---|---|---|
| 1962-63 | 2 | 1-2 | .500 | 2-5 | .400 | 4 | 2.0 | 1 | 4 | 2.0 |

### DREW, BILL          6-5     b. 5-27-1955

| | | | | | | | | | |
|---|---|---|---|---|---|---|---|---|---|
| 1973-74 | 13 | 15-31 | .484 | 4-7 | .571 | 10 | 0.8 | 3 | 34 | 2.8 |
| 1974-75 | 11 | 9-43 | .209 | 3-4 | .750 | 14 | 1.3 | 2 | 21 | 1.9 |
| | 24 | 24-74 | .324 | 7-11 | .636 | 24 | 1.0 | 5 | 55 | 2.3 |

### DUBUC, JOHN          5-10     b. 9-17-1888     d. 8-29-1958
1907-08

### DUCHARME, PAUL  5-10  b. 8-27-1917

| | | | | | | | | | | |
|---|---|---|---|---|---|---|---|---|---|---|
| 1936-37 | 4 | 0 | | 0-0 | .000 | | | 0 | 0 | 0.0 |
| 1937-38 | 18 | 10 | | 16 | | | | | 36 | 2.0 |
| 1938-39 | 21 | 69 | | 39 | | | | | 177 | 8.4 |
| | 43 | 79 | | 55 | | | | | 213 | 5.0 |

### DUDGEON, PATRICK  6-2  b. 2-28-1943

| | | | | | | | | | | |
|---|---|---|---|---|---|---|---|---|---|---|
| 1962-63 | 3 | 3-9 | .333 | 0-0 | .000 | 3 | 1.0 | 2 | 6 | 2.0 |
| 1963-64 | 12 | 11-34 | .324 | 2-2 | 1.000 | 14 | 1.2 | 14 | 24 | 2.0 |
| 1964-65 | 7 | 0-3 | .000 | 0-0 | .000 | 4 | 0.6 | 4 | 0 | 0.0 |
| | 22 | 14-46 | .304 | 2-2 | 1.000 | 21 | 1.0 | 20 | 30 | 1.4 |

### DUFF, DAN  6-0  b. 12-27-1962

| | | | | | | | | | | |
|---|---|---|---|---|---|---|---|---|---|---|
| 1981-82 | 15 | 6-20 | .300 | 7-13 | .538 | 9 | 0.6 | 24 | 19 | 1.3 |
| 1982-83 | 24 | 4-14 | .286 | 22-26 | .846 | 19 | 0.8 | 31 | 30 | 1.3 |
| 1983-84 | 10 | 11-24 | .458 | 11-17 | .647 | 19 | 1.9 | 11 | 33 | 3.3 |
| 1984-85 | 28 | 4-12 | .333 | 21-32 | .656 | 14 | 0.5 | 33 | 29 | 1.0 |
| | 77 | 25-70 | .357 | 61-88 | .693 | 61 | 0.8 | 99 | 111 | 1.4 |

### DUFFY, EUGENE  5-7  b.        d. 3-25-1971

| | | | | | | | | | | |
|---|---|---|---|---|---|---|---|---|---|---|
| 1956-57 | 22 | 29-59 | .492 | 21-37 | .568 | 24 | 1.1 | 26 | 77 | 3.6 |
| 1957-58 | 29 | 63-177 | .356 | 64-90 | .711 | 102 | 3.5 | 52 | 190 | 6.6 |
| 1958-59 | 25 | 67-192 | .349 | 37-58 | .638 | 107 | 4.3 | 33 | 171 | 6.8 |
| | 76 | 159-428 | .371 | 122-185 | .659 | 233 | 3.1 | 111 | 440 | 5.8 |

### DUFFY,
1920-21

### DUMONT, WILLIAM  6-3  b. 1-5-1926

| | | | | | | | | | | |
|---|---|---|---|---|---|---|---|---|---|---|
| 1943-44 | 4 | 0 | | 2-2 | 1.000 | | | 3 | 2 | 0.5 |

### DUWAN, GERALD

| | | | | | | | | | | |
|---|---|---|---|---|---|---|---|---|---|---|
| 1929-30 | 2 | 1 | | 2-2 | 1.000 | | | 2 | 4 | 2.0 |

### EATON, LAWRENCE  6-2  b. 2-14-1931

| | | | | | | | | | | |
|---|---|---|---|---|---|---|---|---|---|---|
| 1950-51 | 18 | 2-13 | .154 | 3.3 | 1.000 | | | 11 | 7 | 0.4 |

### EDWARDS, GENE  6-1

| | | | | | | | | | | |
|---|---|---|---|---|---|---|---|---|---|---|
| 1924-25 | 3 | 0 | | 2-2 | 1.000 | | | 0 | 2 | 0.7 |

### EGART, JOHN  5-11  b. 3-9-1950

| | | | | | | | | | | |
|---|---|---|---|---|---|---|---|---|---|---|
| 1970-71 | 15 | 9-24 | .375 | 8-13 | .615 | 5 | 0.3 | 13 | 26 | 1.7 |
| 1971-72 | 26 | 63-199 | .317 | 35-55 | .636 | 65 | 2.5 | 91 | 161 | 6.2 |
| | 41 | 72-227 | .323 | 43-68 | .632 | 70 | 1.6 | 104 | 187 | 4.6 |

### EGGEMAN, JOHN  6-4
1898-99

**ELLIS, HOWARD**

| | | | | | | |
|---|---|---|---|---|---|---|
| 1915-16 | 6 | 9 | 0 | | 18 | 3.0 |

**ELLIS, REX**  6-3  b. 7-8-1919

| | | | | | | |
|---|---|---|---|---|---|---|
| 1937-38 | 18 | 13 | 8 | | 34 | 1.9 |
| 1938-39 | 20 | 28 | 24 | | 80 | 4.0 |
| 1939-40 | 21 | 45 | 29 | 33 | 119 | 5.7 |
| | 59 | 86 | 61 | | 233 | 3.9 |

**ELSER, DON**  6-3  b. 8-4-1913  d. 10-18-1968

| | | | | | | | |
|---|---|---|---|---|---|---|---|
| 1933-34 | 2 | 0 | 0-0 | .000 | 1 | 0 | 0.0 |
| 1934-35 | 16 | 15 | 15 | | 14 | 45 | 2.8 |
| 1935-36 | 1 | 2 | 0 | | 0 | 4 | 4.0 |
| | 19 | 17 | 15 | | 15 | 49 | 2.6 |

**ELY, JOHN**

| | | | | | | |
|---|---|---|---|---|---|---|
| 1909-10 | 2 | 0 | 0 | | 0 | 0.0 |

**ENGEL, JAMES**  6-2  b. 12-24-1920

| | | | | | | | |
|---|---|---|---|---|---|---|---|
| 1940-41 | 11 | 8 | 2 | | | 18 | 1.6 |
| 1941-42 | 4 | 4 | 0-2 | .000 | 0 | 8 | 2.0 |
| | 15 | 12 | 2 | | | 26 | 1.7 |

**ENRIGHT, REX**  d. 4-6-1960

| | | | | | | | |
|---|---|---|---|---|---|---|---|
| 1922-23 | 22 | 48 | 19-37 | .514 | | 115 | 5.2 |
| 1923-24 | 22 | 48 | 36 | | | 132 | 6.0 |
| 1925-26 | 1 | 0 | 0-1 | .000 | 1 | 0 | 0.0 |
| | 45 | 96 | 55 | | | 247 | 5.5 |

**ERLENBAUGH, RICHARD**  6-4  b. 1-20-1942

| | | | | | | | | | |
|---|---|---|---|---|---|---|---|---|---|
| 1961-62 | 7 | 6-17 | .353 | 2-7 | .286 | 8 | 1.1 | 7 | 14 | 2.0 |
| 1962-63 | 17 | 14-61 | .230 | 9-15 | .600 | 42 | 2.5 | 24 | 37 | 2.2 |
| 1963-64 | 21 | 23-71 | .324 | 14-18 | .778 | 46 | 2.2 | 27 | 60 | 2.9 |
| | 45 | 43-149 | .289 | 25-40 | .625 | 96 | 2.1 | 58 | 111 | 2.5 |

**ERTEL, MARK**  6-4  b. 2-26-1919

| | | | | | | |
|---|---|---|---|---|---|---|
| 1937-38 | 15 | 7 | 3 | | 17 | 1.1 |
| 1938-39 | 21 | 42 | 16 | | 100 | 4.8 |
| 1939-40 | 21 | 52 | 31 | 46 | 135 | 6.4 |
| | 57 | 101 | 50 | | 252 | 4.4 |

**FABIAN, CHRIS**  6-2  b. 6-19-1957

| | | | | | | | | | |
|---|---|---|---|---|---|---|---|---|---|
| 1976-77 | 13 | 4-12 | .333 | 5-9 | .556 | 5 | 0.4 | 4 | 13 | 1.0 |

**FANNON, JOHN**  6-5  b. 2-19-1934

| | | | | | | | |
|---|---|---|---|---|---|---|---|
| 1953-54 | 25 | 89-271 | .328 | 44-73 | .603 | | 99 | 222 | 8.9 |

| | | | | | | | | | | |
|---|---|---|---|---|---|---|---|---|---|---|
| 1954-55 | 24 | 76-268 | .284 | 62-98 | .633 | | | 92 | 214 | 8.9 |
| 1955-56 | 15 | 34-108 | .315 | 22-37 | .595 | | | 48 | 90 | 6.0 |
| | 64 | 199-647 | .308 | 128-208 | .615 | | | 239 | 526 | 8.2 |

### FARRELL, DANIEL    6-2    b. 4-2-1931

| | | | | | | | | | | |
|---|---|---|---|---|---|---|---|---|---|---|
| 1950-51 | 1 | 0-1 | .000 | 1-2 | .500 | | | 1 | 1 | 1.0 |

### FARRELL, MICHAEL    6-5    b. 7-14-1938

| | | | | | | | | | | |
|---|---|---|---|---|---|---|---|---|---|---|
| 1958-59 | 7 | 4-12 | .333 | 0-0 | .000 | 16 | 2.3 | 7 | 8 | 1.1 |
| 1959-60 | 1 | 0-1 | .000 | 0-0 | .000 | 0 | 0.0 | 0 | 0 | 0.0 |
| | 8 | 4-13 | .308 | 0-0 | .000 | 16 | 2.0 | 7 | 8 | 1.0 |

### FARRIS, CHARLES    6-2

| | | | | | | | | | | |
|---|---|---|---|---|---|---|---|---|---|---|
| 1930-31 | 3 | 0 | | 0-0 | .000 | | | 3 | 0 | 0.0 |
| 1932-33 | 5 | 0-14 | .000 | 0-1 | .000 | | | 6 | 0 | 0.0 |
| | 8 | 0 | | 0-1 | .000 | | | 9 | 0 | 0.0 |

### FAUGHT, ROBERT    6-5    b. 9-2-1921

| | | | | | | | | | | |
|---|---|---|---|---|---|---|---|---|---|---|
| 1941-42 | 22 | 84 | | 41-61 | .672 | | | 45 | 209 | 9.5 |
| 1942-43 | 20 | 74 | | 48 | | | | 42 | 196 | 9.8 |
| | 42 | 158 | | 89 | | | | 87 | 405 | 9.6 |

### FEENEY, ALBERT    5-11    b.    d. 11- -1950

| | | | | | | | | | | |
|---|---|---|---|---|---|---|---|---|---|---|
| 1910-11 | 9 | 0 | | 0 | | | | | 0 | 0.0 |
| 1911-12 | 18 | 2 | | 0 | | | | | 4 | 0.2 |
| 1912-13 | | | | | | | | | | |

### FEHLIG, VINCENT

| | | | | | | | | | | |
|---|---|---|---|---|---|---|---|---|---|---|
| 1931-32 | 1 | 1 | | 0-1 | .000 | | | 0 | 2 | 2.0 |
| 1932-33 | 5 | 2-7 | .286 | 0-0 | .000 | | | 1 | 4 | 0.8 |
| | 6 | 3 | | 0-1 | .000 | | | 1 | 6 | 1.0 |

### FENNESSEY, JOHN

| | | | | | | | | | | |
|---|---|---|---|---|---|---|---|---|---|---|
| 1897-98 | 3 | 0 | | 0 | | | | | 0 | 0.0 |
| 1898-99 | | | | | | | | | | |

### FICHTEL, NEAL    6-2    b. 1-25-1927

| | | | | | | | | | | |
|---|---|---|---|---|---|---|---|---|---|---|
| 1948-49 | 11 | 2-7 | .286 | 3-3 | 1.000 | | | 6 | 7 | 0.6 |
| 1949-50 | 14 | 7-24 | .292 | 5-12 | .417 | | | 15 | 19 | 1.4 |
| 1950-51 | 16 | 8-26 | .308 | 11-16 | .688 | | | 35 | 27 | 1.7 |
| | 41 | 17-57 | .298 | 19-31 | .613 | | | 56 | 53 | 1.3 |

### FINEGAN, CHARLES    5-11

| | | | | | | | | | | |
|---|---|---|---|---|---|---|---|---|---|---|
| 1911-12 | 5 | 1 | | 0 | | | | | 2 | 0.4 |
| 1912-13 | | | | | | | | | | |

| 1913-14 | 14 | 3 | | 1 | | | | | 7 | 0.5 |
|---|---|---|---|---|---|---|---|---|---|---|
| 1914-15 | 15 | 2 | | 0 | | | | | 4 | 0.3 |

### FINNEGAN, THOMAS          6-2    b. 3-29-1942

| 1961-62 | 12 | 9-36 | .250 | 9-13 | .692 | 16 | 1.3 | 9 | 27 | 2.3 |
|---|---|---|---|---|---|---|---|---|---|---|

### FINNEGAN, WALES                              d. 8-5-1971

| 1909-10 | 9 | 14 | | 0 | | | | | 28 | 3.1 |
|---|---|---|---|---|---|---|---|---|---|---|

### FISCHER, ROBERT          6-0    b. 8-15-1921    d. 11-17-194

| 1940-41 | 5 | 1 | | 0-0 | .000 | | | 0 | 2 | 0.4 |
|---|---|---|---|---|---|---|---|---|---|---|
| 1941-42 | 3 | 0 | | 0-0 | .000 | | | 1 | 0 | 0.0 |
| | 8 | 1 | | 0-0 | .000 | | | 1 | 2 | 0.3 |

### FISH, JAMES                              b. 2-20-1890

| 1907-08 | | | | | | | | | | |
|---|---|---|---|---|---|---|---|---|---|---|
| 1908-09 | | | | | | | | | | |
| 1909-10 | 12 | 39 | | 5 | | | | | 83 | 6.9 |
| 1910-11 | 10 | 29 | | 3 | | | | | 61 | 6.1 |

### FITZGERALD, FREEMAN          6-0    b.          d. 5-6-1942

| 1912-13 | | | | | | | | | | |
|---|---|---|---|---|---|---|---|---|---|---|
| 1913-14 | 13 | 12 | | 35 | | | | | 59 | 4.5 |
| 1914-15 | 15 | 42 | | 41 | | | | | 125 | 8.3 |
| 1915-16 | 11 | 49 | | 59 | | | | | 157 | 14.3 |

### FITZGERALD, RAY          5-10    b. 11-27-1926

| 1944-45 | 2 | 0 | | 0-0 | .000 | | | 0 | 0 | 0.0 |
|---|---|---|---|---|---|---|---|---|---|---|

### FITZGERALD, ROBERT

| 1938-39 | 1 | 0 | | 0-0 | .000 | | | 0 | 0 | 0.0 |
|---|---|---|---|---|---|---|---|---|---|---|

### FITZPATRICK, GEORGE

| 1916-17 | 11 | 2 | | 0 | | | | | 4 | 0.4 |
|---|---|---|---|---|---|---|---|---|---|---|

### FLEMING, CHARLES

| 1898-99 | | | | | | | | | | |
|---|---|---|---|---|---|---|---|---|---|---|

### FLOWERS, BRUCE          6-9    b. 6-13-1957

| 1975-76 | 29 | 100-166 | .602 | 28-45 | .662 | 166 | 5.7 | 95 | 228 | 7.9 |
|---|---|---|---|---|---|---|---|---|---|---|
| 1976-77 | 27 | 134-236 | .586 | 36-60 | .600 | 206 | 7.6 | 96 | 304 | 11.3 |
| 1977-78 | 31 | 86-179 | .480 | 41-64 | .641 | 149 | 4.8 | 93 | 213 | 6.9 |
| 1978-79 | 30 | 107-163 | .656 | 70-84 | .833 | 147 | 4.9 | 94 | 284 | 9.5 |
| | 117 | 427-744 | .574 | 175-253 | .692 | 668 | 5.7 | 378 | 1029 | 8.8 |

### FOLEY, JOHN          6-5    b. 3-14-1924

| 1946-47 | 17 | 14-56 | .250 | 14-24 | .583 | | | 16 | 42 | 2.5 |
|---|---|---|---|---|---|---|---|---|---|---|

| Year | G | FG-FGA | FG% | FT-FTA | FT% | | | | | |
|------|---|--------|-----|--------|-----|---|---|----|-----|-----|
| 1947-48 | 24 | 81-236 | .343 | 46-80 | .575 | | | 70 | 208 | 8.7 |
| 1948-49 | 24 | 44-146 | .301 | 31-47 | .660 | | | 65 | 119 | 5.0 |
| 1949-50 | 24 | 63-183 | .344 | 36-52 | .692 | | | 80 | 162 | 6.8 |
| | 89 | 202-621 | .325 | 127-203 | .626 | | | 231 | 531 | 6.0 |

### FOLEY, THOMAS

| Year | G | FG-FGA | FG% | FT-FTA | FT% | | | | | |
|------|---|--------|-----|--------|-----|---|---|---|---|-----|
| 1942-43 | 1 | 0 | | 0-0 | .000 | | | 0 | 0 | 0.0 |

### FORD, JOHN          6-2

| Year | G | FG | | FT-FTA | FT% | | | | | |
|------|---|----|---|--------|-----|---|---|----|-----|-----|
| 1933-34 | 22 | 15 | | 10-15 | .667 | | | 23 | 40 | 1.8 |
| 1934-35 | 22 | 40 | | 26 | | | | 34 | 106 | 4.8 |
| 1935-36 | 24 | 45 | | 23 | | | | | 113 | 4.7 |
| | 68 | 100 | | 59 | | | | | 259 | 3.8 |

### FORSEE, JOHN

| Year | G | FG | | FT | | | | | | |
|------|---|----|---|-----|-----|---|---|---|---|-----|
| 1927-28 | 1 | 1 | | 1 | | | | 0 | 3 | 3.0 |
| 1929-30 | 3 | 2 | | 0-0 | .000 | | | 0 | 4 | 1.3 |
| | 4 | 3 | | 1 | | | | 0 | 7 | 1.8 |

### FRANGER, MICHAEL          5-11

| Year | G | FG-FGA | FG% | FT-FTA | FT% | | | | | |
|------|---|--------|-----|--------|------|----|-----|----|----|-----|
| 1966-67 | 16 | 21-81 | .259 | 10-24 | .417 | 31 | 1.4 | 23 | 52 | 3.3 |
| 1967-68 | 15 | 5-23 | .217 | 1-1 | 1.000 | 6 | 0.4 | 1 | 11 | 0.7 |
| | 31 | 26-104 | .250 | 11-25 | .440 | 37 | 1.2 | 24 | 63 | 2.0 |

### FREEZE, CHESTER          6-2

| Year | G | FG | | FT | | | | | | |
|------|---|----|---|----|---|---|---|---|----|-----|
| 1908-09 | | | | | | | | | | |
| 1909-10 | 13 | 5 | | 0 | | | | | 10 | 0.8 |

### FRITSCH, JAMES          6-2      b. 6-4-1925

| Year | G | FG-FGA | FG% | FT-FTA | FT% | | | | | |
|------|---|--------|-----|--------|------|---|---|---|---|-----|
| 1946-47 | 2 | 1-5 | .200 | 0-0 | .000 | | | 1 | 2 | 1.0 |
| 1947-48 | 3 | 0-2 | .000 | 0-0 | .000 | | | 1 | 0 | 0.0 |
| 1948-49 | 6 | 0-3 | .000 | 4-4 | 1.000 | | | 4 | 4 | 0.7 |
| | 11 | 1-10 | .100 | 4-4 | 1.000 | | | 6 | 6 | 0.5 |

### FURMAN, THADDEUS          6-2      b. 8-29-1923

| Year | G | FG | | FT-FTA | FT% | | | | | |
|------|---|----|---|--------|------|---|---|---|----|-----|
| 1943-44 | 7 | 4 | | 6-8 | .750 | | | 3 | 14 | 2.0 |

### GAGLIONE, FRANK          5-10      b. 12-28-1915

| Year | G | FG | | FT-FTA | FT% | | | | | |
|------|---|----|---|--------|------|---|---|---|----|-----|
| 1936-37 | 8 | 1 | | 0-1 | .000 | | | 5 | 2 | 0.3 |
| 1937-38 | 6 | 3 | | 2 | | | | | 8 | 1.3 |
| 1938-39 | 11 | 4 | | 3 | | | | | 11 | 1.0 |
| | 25 | 8 | | 5 | | | | | 21 | 0.8 |

### GALLAGHER, JOHN          6-5      b. 1-3-1948

| Year | G | FG-FGA | FG% | FT-FTA | FT% | | | | | |
|------|---|--------|-----|--------|------|----|-----|---|----|-----|
| 1967-68 | 11 | 8-14 | .571 | 10-14 | .714 | 18 | 1.6 | 7 | 26 | 2.4 |

| | | | | | | | | | | |
|---|---|---|---|---|---|---|---|---|---|---|
| 1968-69 | 13 | 6-8 | .750 | 2-5 | .400 | 8 | 0.6 | 2 | 14 | 1.1 |
| 1969-70 | 19 | 26-56 | .464 | 11-16 | .688 | 22 | 1.2 | 10 | 63 | 3.3 |
| | 43 | 40-78 | .513 | 23-35 | .657 | 48 | 1.1 | 19 | 103 | 2.4 |

GALLAGHER,

| | | | | | | | | | | |
|---|---|---|---|---|---|---|---|---|---|---|
| 1923-24 | 3 | 0 | | 0 | | | | 1 | 0 | 0.0 |

GARVEY, ARTHUR        6-1   b.              d. 9-22-1973
1920-21

GASPARELLA, JOSEPH

| | | | | | | | | | | |
|---|---|---|---|---|---|---|---|---|---|---|
| 1943-44 | 1 | 0 | | 0-0 | .000 | | | 1 | 0 | 0.0 |

GAVIN, JOSEPH

| | | | | | | | | | | |
|---|---|---|---|---|---|---|---|---|---|---|
| 1928-29 | 12 | 9 | | 3 | | | | 3 | 21 | 1.8 |
| 1929-30 | 18 | 18 | | 6-13 | .462 | | | 14 | 42 | 2.3 |
| 1930-31 | 20 | 24 | | 12-22 | .545 | | | 26 | 60 | 3.0 |
| | 50 | 51 | | 21 | | | | 43 | 123 | 2.5 |

GEBERT, ALBERT                            d. 12-4-1980

| | | | | | | | | | | |
|---|---|---|---|---|---|---|---|---|---|---|
| 1926-27 | 4 | 1 | | 0 | | | | 0 | 2 | 0.5 |

GEMMELL, DOUG        6-3   b. 1-8-1950

| | | | | | | | | | | |
|---|---|---|---|---|---|---|---|---|---|---|
| 1969-70 | 16 | 27-52 | .519 | 9-16 | .563 | 43 | 2.7 | 14 | 63 | 3.9 |
| 1970-71 | 27 | 44-121 | .364 | 13-26 | .500 | 104 | 3.4 | 41 | 101 | 3.7 |
| | 43 | 71-173 | .410 | 22-42 | .524 | 147 | 3.4 | 55 | 164 | 3.8 |

GEOGHEGAN, WALTER

| | | | | | | | | | | |
|---|---|---|---|---|---|---|---|---|---|---|
| 1897-98 | 2 | 0 | | 0 | | | | | 0 | 0.0 |

GIBBONS, JAMES        6-2   b. 8-19-1930

| | | | | | | | | | | |
|---|---|---|---|---|---|---|---|---|---|---|
| 1950-51 | 23 | 25-72 | .347 | 30-50 | .600 | | | 77 | 80 | 3.5 |
| 1951-52 | 22 | 18-65 | .277 | 23-35 | .657 | | | 60 | 59 | 2.7 |
| 1952-53 | 21 | 19-71 | .268 | 31-47 | .660 | | | 65 | 69 | 3.3 |
| | 66 | 62-208 | .298 | 84-132 | .636 | | | 202 | 208 | 3.2 |

GIBSON, FRANK

1908-09

GIEDLIN, RICHARD        6-2   b. 12-19-1929

| | | | | | | | | | | |
|---|---|---|---|---|---|---|---|---|---|---|
| 1948-49 | 15 | 3-26 | .115 | 0-1 | .000 | | | 3 | 6 | 0.4 |

GILFILLAN, EARL

| | | | | | | | | | | |
|---|---|---|---|---|---|---|---|---|---|---|
| 1918-19 | 3 | 9 | | 13 | | | | | 31 | 10.3 |

GILHOOLEY,FRANK        6-0   b. 6-15-1924

| | | | | | | | | | | |
|---|---|---|---|---|---|---|---|---|---|---|
| 1943-44 | 7 | 2 | | 0-0 | .000 | | | 5 | 4 | 0.6 |
| 1944-45 | 20 | 26 | | 11-25 | .440 | | | 45 | 63 | 3.2 |

| 1945-46 | 20 | 9-44 | .205 | 6-11 | .545 | | | 23 | 24 | 1.2 |
|---|---|---|---|---|---|---|---|---|---|---|
| | 47 | 37 | | 17-36 | .472 | | | 73 | 91 | 1.9 |

GILLESPIE, JOE          6-3     b. 9-20-1919

| 1938-39 | 4 | 3 | | 1 | | | | | 7 | 1.8 |
|---|---|---|---|---|---|---|---|---|---|---|
| 1939-40 | 12 | 6 | | 2 | | | | 6 | 14 | 1.2 |
| | 16 | 9 | | 3 | | | | | 21 | 1.3 |

GILLIGAN, JOSEPH

| 1921-22 | 10 | 3 | | 0 | | | | | 6 | 0.6 |
|---|---|---|---|---|---|---|---|---|---|---|

GIPP, GEORGE          6-0     b. 2-8-1895          d. 12-14-1920

| 1918-19 | 4 | 6 | | 0 | | | | | 12 | 3.0 |
|---|---|---|---|---|---|---|---|---|---|---|

GLEASON, EDWARD          6-1     b. 2-16-1936

| 1955-56 | 15 | 14-46 | .304 | 31-47 | .660 | | | 17 | 59 | 3.9 |
|---|---|---|---|---|---|---|---|---|---|---|
| 1956-57 | 17 | 30-80 | .375 | 38-49 | .776 | 30 | 1.8 | 25 | 98 | 5.8 |
| 1957-58 | 20 | 12-38 | .316 | 18-24 | .750 | 25 | 1.3 | 17 | 42 | 2.1 |
| | 52 | 56-164 | .341 | 87-120 | .725 | | | 59 | 199 | 3.8 |

GLEASON, JOE          6-0     b. 8-30-1914

| 1935-36 | 4 | 1 | | 0 | | | | 1 | 2 | 0.5 |
|---|---|---|---|---|---|---|---|---|---|---|

GLEASON, ROBERT          6-0     b. 6-10-1922

| 1943-44 | 2 | 0 | | 0-0 | .000 | | | 0 | 0 | 0.0 |
|---|---|---|---|---|---|---|---|---|---|---|

GLENN, EDWARD

1901-02

GOHEEN, HARRY          6-0     b. 11-20-1926

| 1944-45 | 2 | 2 | | 0-0 | .000 | | | 1 | 4 | 2.0 |
|---|---|---|---|---|---|---|---|---|---|---|

GOLDSMITH, EDMUND

| 1935-36 | 1 | 0 | | 0 | | | | | 0 | 0.0 |
|---|---|---|---|---|---|---|---|---|---|---|

GOONEN, JOHN          5-9     b. 9-28-1921

| 1945-46 | 3 | 0-2 | .000 | 1-1 | 1.000 | | | 5 | 1 | 0.3 |
|---|---|---|---|---|---|---|---|---|---|---|
| 1946-47 | 8 | 2-5 | .400 | 4-6 | .667 | | | 6 | 8 | 1.0 |
| 1947-48 | 23 | 13-44 | .295 | 13-21 | .619 | | | 37 | 39 | 1.7 |
| | 34 | 15-51 | .294 | 18-28 | .643 | | | 48 | 48 | 1.4 |

GORDON, PAUL          6-0     b. 4-8-1927

| 1944-45 | 18 | 26 | | 13-24 | .542 | | | 32 | 65 | 3.6 |
|---|---|---|---|---|---|---|---|---|---|---|
| 1946-47 | 19 | 29-115 | .252 | 15-30 | .500 | | | 46 | 73 | 3.8 |
| 1947-48 | 23 | 64-212 | .302 | 32-48 | .667 | | | 65 | 160 | 7.0 |
| 1948-49 | 21 | 64-217 | .295 | 54-79 | .684 | | | 59 | 182 | 8.7 |
| | 81 | 183 | | 114-181 | .630 | | | 202 | 480 | 5.9 |

GRADY, WILLIAM                                      d. 6-10-1973
1914-15   9    13                    1                        27    3.0

GRANEY, MICHAEL                    6-5     b. 12-6-1938
1957-58   16   66-173   .382   26-52   .500   206   12.9   58   158    9.9
1958-59   25   104-342  .304   50-82   .610   337   13.5   89   258   10.3
1959-60   26   179-463  .387   92-146  .630   350   13.5   99   450   17.3
          67   349-978  .357   168-280 .600   893   13.3  246   866   12.9

GRANFIELD, PATRICK                                  d. 1-31-1974
1919-20   12    3                    0                         6    0.5

GRANFIELD, WILLIAM
1910-11   9    16                    0                        32    3.6
1911-12   17   79                    0                       158    9.3
1912-13

GRANT, CHET               5-7     b. 2-22-1892    d. 7-24-1985
1916-17   9    9                     0                        18    2.0
1920-21

GRASSEY, GARY                      6-8     b. 6-21-1960
1981-82   11   2-7      .286   1-2     .500     2    0.2    1     5    0.5

GRINAGER, PAUL
1919-20   4    6                     0                        12    3.0

GROOGAN, DOMINIC
1901-02

GUSHURST, FRED             5-10    b. 7-22-1890    d. 12-28-1977
1913-14   1    0                     0                         0    0.0

HAEFNER, RANDY                     6-6
1974-75   7    8-14     .571   6-8     .750     8    1.1    1    22    3.1
1975-76   8    9-26     .346   1-2     .500     5    0.6    5    19    2.4
1976-77   17   9-21     .429   5-6     .833    24    1.4    7    23    1.4
1977-78   12   1-5      .200   0-1     .000     3    0.3    4     2    0.2
          44   27-66    .409   12-17   .706    40    0.9   17    66    1.5

HAMILTON, ROBERT                                    d. 12-2-1983
1926-27   3    1                     1                         3    1.0
1927-28   15   14                    8                        36    2.4
          18   15                    9                        39    2.2

HANSEN, THOMAS                     6-2     b. 5-5-1952
1971-72   25   25-67    .373   10-17   .588    24    1.0   24    60    2.4

| | | | | | | | | | | |
|---|---|---|---|---|---|---|---|---|---|---|
| 1972-73 | 9 | 1-2 | .500 | 0-1 | .000 | 0 | 0.0 | 2 | 2 | 0.2 |
| 1973-74 | 1 | 0-0 | .000 | 0-0 | .000 | 1 | 1.0 | 1 | 0 | 0.0 |
| | 35 | 26-69 | .377 | 10-18 | .556 | 25 | 0.7 | 27 | 62 | 1.8 |

### HANZLIK, BILL  6-7  b. 12-6-1957

| | | | | | | | | | | |
|---|---|---|---|---|---|---|---|---|---|---|
| 1967-77 | 28 | 38-91 | .418 | 39-55 | .710 | 51 | 1.8 | 60 | 115 | 4.1 |
| 1977-78 | 30 | 40-78 | .513 | 30-38 | .789 | 57 | 1.9 | 63 | 110 | 3.7 |
| 1978-79 | 29 | 95-164 | .579 | 63-77 | .818 | 84 | 2.9 | 70 | 253 | 8.7 |
| 1979-80 | 22 | 61-135 | .452 | 44-60 | .733 | 74 | 3.4 | 80 | 166 | 7.5 |
| | 109 | 234-468 | .500 | 176-230 | .765 | 266 | 2.4 | 273 | 644 | 5.9 |

### HARDY, KEVIN  6-5  b. 7-28-1945

| | | | | | | | | | | |
|---|---|---|---|---|---|---|---|---|---|---|
| 1964-65 | 18 | 20-45 | .444 | 2-8 | .250 | 38 | 2.1 | 18 | 42 | 2.3 |

### HARVEY, DONALD

| | | | | | | | |
|---|---|---|---|---|---|---|---|
| 1925-26 | 4 | 10 | | 3 | | | 23 | 5.8 |

### HASSETT, WILLIAM  5-10  b. 10-21-1921

| | | | | | | | |
|---|---|---|---|---|---|---|---|
| 1944-45 | 19 | 69 | | 26-45 | .578 | | 49 | 164 | 8.6 |
| 1945-46 | 21 | 66-208 | .317 | 37-61 | .607 | | 52 | 169 | 8.0 |
| | 40 | 135 | | 63-106 | .594 | | 101 | 333 | 8.3 |

### HAWKINS, KEVIN  6-5  b. 10-2-1959

| | | | | | | | | | | |
|---|---|---|---|---|---|---|---|---|---|---|
| 1978-79 | 12 | 3-9 | .333 | 3-5 | .600 | 8 | 0.7 | 5 | 9 | 0.8 |
| 1979-80 | 12 | 2-2 | 1.000 | 3-4 | .750 | 7 | 0.6 | 6 | 7 | 0.6 |
| 1980-81 | 8 | 0-1 | .000 | 2-2 | 1.000 | 2 | 0.3 | 1 | 2 | 0.3 |
| | 32 | 5-12 | .417 | 8-11 | .727 | 17 | 0.5 | 12 | 18 | 0.6 |

### HAWKINS, TOM  6-5  b. 12-22-1936

| | | | | | | | | | | |
|---|---|---|---|---|---|---|---|---|---|---|
| 1956-57 | 28 | 227-527 | .431 | 122-186 | .656 | 484 | 17.3 | 64 | 576 | 20.6 |
| 1957-58 | 29 | 286-623 | .459 | 158-224 | .705 | 499 | 17.2 | 80 | 730 | 25.2 |
| 1958-59 | 22 | 197-486 | .455 | 120-173 | .694 | 335 | 15.2 | 69 | 514 | 23.4 |
| | 79 | 710-1636 | .440 | 400-583 | .686 | 1318 | 16.7 | 213 | 1820 | 23.0 |

### HAYES, ARTHUR

1898-99

### HAYES, FRANK

| | | | | | |
|---|---|---|---|---|---|
| 1917-18 | 6 | 6 | | 0 | | 12 | 2.0 |
| 1918-19 | 4 | 0 | | 0 | | 0 | 0.0 |
| | 10 | 6 | | 0 | | 12 | 1.2 |

### HEALY, TIM  6-1  b. 2-24-1958

| | | | | | | | | | | |
|---|---|---|---|---|---|---|---|---|---|---|
| 1976-77 | 12 | 2-6 | .333 | 2-3 | .667 | 9 | 0.8 | 3 | 6 | 0.5 |
| 1977-78 | 12 | 1-5 | .200 | 0-1 | .000 | 3 | 0.3 | 4 | 2 | 0.2 |
| 1978-79 | 18 | 7-20 | .350 | 6-11 | .545 | 12 | 0.7 | 5 | 20 | 1.1 |

| 1979-80 | 15 | 5-9 | .556 | 1-5 | .200 | 3 | 0.2 | 3 | 11 | 0.7 |
|---|---|---|---|---|---|---|---|---|---|---|
|  | 57 | 15-40 | .375 | 9-20 | .450 | 27 | 0.5 | 15 | 39 | 0.7 |

**HEENAN, DENNIS**

| 1929-30 | 6 | 3 | | 2-5 | .400 | | | 0 | 8 | 1.3 |
|---|---|---|---|---|---|---|---|---|---|---|

**HERRON, EDWARD** 6-0

| 1896-97 | 3 | 0 | | 0 | | | | 6 | 0 | 0.0 |
|---|---|---|---|---|---|---|---|---|---|---|

**HEYL, WILLIAM**    b. 1-21-1889

1907-08
1908-09

**HICKS, SCOTT** 6-3 b. 1-18-1965

| 1983-84 | 30 | 48-134 | .358 | 47-67 | .701 | 82 | 2.7 | 34 | 143 | 4.8 |
|---|---|---|---|---|---|---|---|---|---|---|
| 1984-85 | 28 | 95-205 | .463 | 57-86 | .663 | 104 | 3.7 | 62 | 247 | 8.8 |
|  | 58 | 143-339 | .442 | 104-153 | .680 | 186 | 3.2 | 96 | 390 | 6.7 |

**HIGGINS, THOMAS** 6-3 b. 10-23-1935

| 1954-55 | 2 | 0-0 | .000 | 2-2 | 1.000 | | | 2 | 2 | 1.0 |
|---|---|---|---|---|---|---|---|---|---|---|
| 1955-56 | 1 | 0-0 | .000 | 0-0 | .000 | | | 0 | 0 | 0.0 |
|  | 3 | 0-0 | .000 | 2-2 | 1.000 | | | 2 | 2 | 0.7 |

**HILLER, JOHN** 6-0 b. 1-12-1921

| 1941-42 | 16 | 34 | | 18-25 | .720 | | | 39 | 86 | 5.4 |
|---|---|---|---|---|---|---|---|---|---|---|
| 1946-47 | 11 | 6-26 | .231 | 0-3 | .000 | | | 8 | 12 | 1.1 |
| 1947-48 | 23 | 41-145 | .283 | 9-24 | .375 | | | 53 | 91 | 4.0 |
|  | 50 | 81 | | 27-52 | .519 | | | 100 | 189 | 3.8 |

**HINGA, JAMES** 6-4 b. 12-29-1948

| 1968-69 | 16 | 10-23 | .439 | 10-17 | .588 | 16 | 1.0 | 20 | 30 | 1.9 |
|---|---|---|---|---|---|---|---|---|---|---|
| 1969-70 | 27 | 30-85 | .353 | 24-36 | .667 | 63 | 2.3 | 60 | 84 | 3.1 |
| 1970-71 | 2 | 0-0 | .000 | 0-0 | .000 | 0 | 0.0 | 1 | 0 | 0.0 |
|  | 45 | 40-108 | .370 | 34-53 | .642 | 79 | 1.8 | 81 | 114 | 2.6 |

**HINGA, WILLIAM** 6-7 b. 11-15-1950

| 1970-71 | 10 | 0-5 | .000 | 2-4 | .500 | 4 | 0.4 | 6 | 2 | 0.2 |
|---|---|---|---|---|---|---|---|---|---|---|
| 1971-72 | 7 | 3-9 | .333 | 2-2 | 1.000 | 8 | 1.1 | 5 | 8 | 1.1 |
|  | 17 | 3-14 | .214 | 4-6 | .667 | 12 | 0.7 | 11 | 10 | 0.6 |

**HINGER, RALPH** 6-2 b. 11-9-1927

| 1948-49 | 2 | 1-2 | .500 | 2-2 | 1.000 | | | 2 | 4 | 2.0 |
|---|---|---|---|---|---|---|---|---|---|---|

**HOGAN, PAUL** 5-9

| 1917-18 | 1 | 0 | | 0 | | | | 0 | 0.0 |
|---|---|---|---|---|---|---|---|---|---|

HOLLAND, JERRY

| 1932-33 | 2 | 0-2 | .000 | 0-0 | .000 | | | 0 | 0 | 0.0 |
|---|---|---|---|---|---|---|---|---|---|---|

HONINGFORD, RICHARD    6-6    b. 2-22-1932

| 1952-53 | 1 | 0-0 | .000 | 0-0 | .000 | | | 1 | 0 | 0.0 |
|---|---|---|---|---|---|---|---|---|---|---|
| 1953-54 | 13 | 1-19 | .053 | 4-10 | .400 | | | 12 | 6 | 0.5 |
| | 14 | 1-19 | .053 | 4-10 | .400 | | | 13 | 6 | 0.4 |

HOPKINS, JOHN    6-0

| 1933-34 | 6 | 4 | | 1-2 | .500 | | | 1 | 9 | 1.5 |
|---|---|---|---|---|---|---|---|---|---|---|
| 1934-35 | 20 | 20 | | 4 | | | | 14 | 44 | 2.2 |
| 1935-36 | 22 | 32 | | 20 | | | | | 84 | 3.8 |
| | 48 | 56 | | 25 | | | | | 137 | 2.9 |

HORNUNG, PAUL    6-2    b. 12-23-1935

| 1954-55 | 10 | 27-79 | .342 | 7-15 | .467 | | | 8 | 11 | 1.1 |
|---|---|---|---|---|---|---|---|---|---|---|

HOST, PAUL    5-11    b. 1-2-1910

| 1929-30 | 5 | 2 | | 3-5 | .600 | | | 1 | 7 | 1.4 |
|---|---|---|---|---|---|---|---|---|---|---|

HOUSER, MAX    6-1    b.    d. 8-5-1928

| 1922-23 | 1 | 0 | | 0-0 | .000 | | | 0 | 0 | 0.0 |
|---|---|---|---|---|---|---|---|---|---|---|

HOWARD, JOE    5-9    b. 12-21-1962

| 1983-84 | 23 | 34-77 | .442 | 59-98 | .602 | 32 | 1.4 | 49 | 127 | 5.5 |
|---|---|---|---|---|---|---|---|---|---|---|

HUGHES,

| 1926-27 | 10 | 2 | | 0 | | | | | 4 | 0.4 |
|---|---|---|---|---|---|---|---|---|---|---|

HUNSINGER, ED    d. 8-24-1960

| 1922-23 | 1 | 0 | | 0-0 | .000 | | | 0 | 0 | 0.0 |
|---|---|---|---|---|---|---|---|---|---|---|

IRELAND, GEORGE    5-11    b. 6-15-1913

| 1933-34 | 24 | 27 | | 14-26 | .538 | | | 41 | 68 | 2.8 |
|---|---|---|---|---|---|---|---|---|---|---|
| 1934-35 | 22 | 32 | | 23 | | | | 46 | 87 | 4.0 |
| 1935-36 | 23 | 40 | | 16 | | | | | 96 | 4.2 |
| | 69 | 99 | | 53 | | | | | 251 | 3.6 |

IRELAND, MICHAEL    6-7    b. 9-29-1937

| 1956-57 | 5 | 2-10 | .200 | 3-7 | .429 | 11 | 2.2 | 3 | 7 | 1.4 |
|---|---|---|---|---|---|---|---|---|---|---|
| 1957-58 | 16 | 10-37 | .270 | 11-14 | .786 | 45 | 2.8 | 23 | 31 | 1.9 |
| 1958-59 | 7 | 6-20 | .300 | 3-4 | .750 | 15 | 2.1 | 9 | 15 | 2.1 |
| | 28 | 18-67 | .269 | 17-25 | .680 | 71 | 2.5 | 35 | 53 | 1.9 |

JACHYM, JOSEPH

| 1926-27 | 19 | 29 | | 14 | | | | | 72 | 3.8 |
|---|---|---|---|---|---|---|---|---|---|---|

| | | | | | | | | | | |
|---|---|---|---|---|---|---|---|---|---|---|
| 1927-28 | 20 | 26 | | 18 | | | | | 70 | 3.5 |
| 1928-29 | 20 | 27 | | 25 | | | | | 79 | 4.0 |
| | 59 | 82 | | 57 | | | | | 221 | 3.7 |

### JACKOWSKI, RALPH     5-10    b. 5-9-1915

| | | | | | | | | | | |
|---|---|---|---|---|---|---|---|---|---|---|
| 1935-36 | 4 | 1 | | 0 | | | | | 5 | 2 | 0.5 |

### JACKSON, TRACY     6-6    b. 4-21-1959

| | | | | | | | | | | |
|---|---|---|---|---|---|---|---|---|---|---|
| 1977-78 | 28 | 66-120 | .550 | 26-40 | .650 | 91 | 3.3 | 31 | 158 | 5.6 |
| 1978-79 | 30 | 141-274 | .515 | 68-96 | .708 | 124 | 4.1 | 44 | 350 | 11.7 |
| 1979-80 | 28 | 162-315 | .514 | 99-141 | .702 | 198 | 7.1 | 54 | 423 | 15.1 |
| 1980-81 | 28 | 157-282 | .557 | 48-65 | .738 | 156 | 5.6 | 48 | 362 | 12.9 |
| | 114 | 526-941 | .531 | 241-342 | .705 | 569 | 5.0 | 177 | 1293 | 11.3 |

### JAEKELS, MICHAEL     6-5    b. 3-7-1930

| | | | | | | | | | | |
|---|---|---|---|---|---|---|---|---|---|---|
| 1949-50 | 4 | 0-5 | .000 | 1-1 | 1.000 | | | 2 | 1 | 0.3 |

### JASKWHICH, CHUCK     5-11    b. 3-4-1911

| | | | | | | | | | | |
|---|---|---|---|---|---|---|---|---|---|---|
| 1930-31 | 6 | 1 | | 0-1 | .000 | | | 6 | 2 | 0.3 |

### JASTRAB, ROBERT     6-3    b. 4-13-1934

| | | | | | | | | | | |
|---|---|---|---|---|---|---|---|---|---|---|
| 1953-54 | 5 | 1-5 | .200 | 0-0 | .000 | | | 4 | 2 | 0.4 |
| 1954-55 | 4 | 2-6 | .333 | 1-2 | .500 | | | 1 | 5 | 1.3 |
| | 9 | 3-11 | .273 | 1-2 | .500 | | | 5 | 7 | 0.8 |

### JESEWITZ, LARRY     6-8    b. 5-20-1943

| | | | | | | | | | | |
|---|---|---|---|---|---|---|---|---|---|---|
| 1962-63 | 18 | 45-143 | .315 | 18-40 | .450 | 120 | 6.7 | 36 | 108 | 6.0 |
| 1963-64 | 23 | 70-192 | .365 | 37-51 | .725 | 169 | 7.3 | 68 | 177 | 7.7 |
| 1964-65 | 23 | 62-139 | .446 | 25-40 | .625 | 133 | 5.8 | 58 | 149 | 6.5 |
| | 64 | 177-474 | .373 | 80-131 | .611 | 422 | 6.6 | 162 | 434 | 6.8 |

### JOHNSON, CLAY

| | | | | | | | | | | |
|---|---|---|---|---|---|---|---|---|---|---|
| 1929-30 | 4 | 0 | | 2-3 | .667 | | | 3 | 2 | 0.5 |
| 1930-31 | 15 | 15 | | 6-21 | .286 | | | 26 | 36 | 2.4 |
| 1931-32 | 11 | 1 | | 1-5 | .200 | | | 9 | 3 | 0.4 |
| | 30 | 16 | | 9-29 | .310 | | | 38 | 41 | 1.4 |

### JOHNSON, TOM     6-2    b. 10-19-1924

| | | | | | | | | | | |
|---|---|---|---|---|---|---|---|---|---|---|
| 1947-48 | 6 | 2-4 | .500 | 1-2 | .500 | | | 1 | 5 | 0.8 |
| 1949-50 | 8 | 1-4 | .250 | 1-1 | 1.000 | | | 5 | 3 | 0.4 |
| | 14 | 3-8 | .375 | 2-3 | .667 | | | 6 | 8 | 0.6 |

### JONES, COLLIS     6-7    b. 7-3-1949

| | | | | | | | | | | |
|---|---|---|---|---|---|---|---|---|---|---|
| 1968-69 | 27 | 61-161 | .379 | 35-59 | .695 | 143 | 5.3 | 41 | 157 | 5.9 |
| 1969-70 | 29 | 232-502 | .462 | 75-125 | .600 | 359 | 12.4 | 98 | 539 | 18.6 |

| 1970-71 | 29 | 274-579 | .473 | 123-176 | .699 | 382 | 13.2 | 95 | 671 | 23.1 |
|---|---|---|---|---|---|---|---|---|---|---|
|  | 85 | 567-1242 | .457 | 233-360 | .647 | 884 | 10.4 | 234 | 1367 | 16.0 |

JORDAN, JOHN            6-0     b. 10-23-1910

| 1932-33 | 22 | 34-161 | .211 | 18-34 | .529 |  |  | 28 | 86 | 3.9 |
|---|---|---|---|---|---|---|---|---|---|---|
| 1933-34 | 23 | 29 |  | 16-32 | .500 |  |  | 22 | 74 | 3.2 |
| 1934-35 | 21 | 15 |  | 14 |  |  |  | 17 | 44 | 2.1 |
|  | 66 | 78 |  | 48 |  |  |  | 67 | 204 | 3.1 |

JORDAN, THOMAS            6-0     b. 10-5-1914

| 1935-36 | 16 | 9 |  | 2 |  |  |  | 6 | 20 | 1.3 |
|---|---|---|---|---|---|---|---|---|---|---|
| 1936-37 | 17 | 17 |  | 11-13 | .846 |  |  | 19 | 45 | 2.6 |
| 1937-38 | 21 | 17 |  | 5 |  |  |  |  | 39 | 1.9 |
|  | 54 | 43 |  | 18 |  |  |  |  | 104 | 1.9 |

KANE, MICHAEL            5-8

| 1920-21 |  |  |  |  |  |  |  |  |  |  |
|---|---|---|---|---|---|---|---|---|---|---|
| 1921-22 | 16 | 25 |  | 3 |  |  |  |  | 53 | 3.3 |
| 1922-23 | 14 | 13 |  | 0-0 | .000 |  |  |  | 26 | 1.9 |

KARTHOLL, JAMES

| 1944-45 | 14 | 11 |  | 7-10 | .700 |  |  | 19 | 29 | 2.1 |
|---|---|---|---|---|---|---|---|---|---|---|

KAUFMANN, FRANK            6-2     b. 4-16-1926

| 1943-44 | 10 | 5 |  | 1-1 | 1.000 |  |  | 7 | 11 | 1.1 |
|---|---|---|---|---|---|---|---|---|---|---|
| 1946-47 | 16 | 5-27 | .185 | 5-6 | .833 |  |  | 17 | 15 | 0.9 |
| 1947-48 | 15 | 3-10 | .300 | 1-2 | .500 |  |  | 15 | 7 | 0.5 |
| 1948-49 | 22 | 21-76 | .276 | 18-26 | .692 |  |  | 45 | 60 | 2.7 |
|  | 63 | 34 |  | 25-35 | .714 |  |  | 84 | 93 | 1.5 |

KEARNEY, WILLIAM

| 1953-54 | 1 | 0-0 | .000 | 0-0 | .000 |  |  | 0 | 0 | 0.0 |
|---|---|---|---|---|---|---|---|---|---|---|
| 1954-55 | 2 | 0-0 | .000 | 0-2 | .000 |  |  | 1 | 0 | 0.0 |
|  | 3 | 0-0 | .000 | 0-2 | .000 |  |  | 1 | 0 | 0.0 |

KEATING, LEO            d. 1-3-1978

| 1932-33 | 10 | 7-24 | .292 | 1-8 | .125 |  |  | 5 | 15 | 1.5 |
|---|---|---|---|---|---|---|---|---|---|---|

KEEFE, EMMETT            5-10   b.        d. 9-11-1965

| 1914-15 | 3 | 2 |  | 0 |  |  |  |  | 4 | 1.3 |
|---|---|---|---|---|---|---|---|---|---|---|
| 1915-16 | 7 | 3 |  | 0 |  |  |  |  | 6 | 0.9 |
|  | 10 | 5 |  | 0 |  |  |  |  | 10 | 1.0 |

KEGLER, WILLIAM

| 1896-97 | 2 | 0 |  | 0 |  |  |  | 0 | 0 | 0.0 |
|---|---|---|---|---|---|---|---|---|---|---|

### KELLEHER, WILLIAM          5-8

| | | | | | | | | | |
|---|---|---|---|---|---|---|---|---|---|
| 1911-12 | 11 | 2 | | 0 | | | | 4 | 0.4 |
| 1913-14 | 13 | 16 | | 0 | | | | 32 | 2.5 |
| 1914-15 | 5 | 2 | | 0 | | | | 4 | 0.8 |
| | 29 | 20 | | 0 | | | | 40 | 1.4 |

### KELLER, BRIAN          6-5    b. 4-19-1946

| | | | | | | | | | |
|---|---|---|---|---|---|---|---|---|---|
| 1965-66 | 26 | 123-300 | .410 | 51-72 | .708 | 198 | 7.6 | 80 | 297 | 11.4 |
| 1966-67 | 14 | 15-37 | .405 | 1-5 | .200 | 20 | 1.4 | 11 | 31 | 2.2 |
| 1967-68 | 6 | 3-8 | .375 | 0-0 | .000 | 10 | 1.7 | 1 | 6 | 1.0 |
| | 46 | 141-345 | .409 | 52-77 | .675 | 228 | 5.0 | 92 | 334 | 7.3 |

### KELLEY, JIM

| | | | | | | | | | |
|---|---|---|---|---|---|---|---|---|---|
| 1940-41 | 2 | 0 | | 1-3 | .333 | | | 3 | 1 | 0.5 |

### KELLY, HERBERT          d. 5-18-1973

| | | | | | | |
|---|---|---|---|---|---|---|
| 1911-12 | 7 | 5 | | 0 | 10 | 1.4 |
| 1912-13 | | | | | | |
| 1913-14 | 1 | 5 | | 0 | 10 | 10.0 |

### KELLY, JOHN

| | | | | | | |
|---|---|---|---|---|---|---|
| 1938-39 | 1 | 0 | | 0 | 0 | 0 | 0.0 |

### KELLY, JOHN          6-2    b. 2-15-1924

| | | | | | | | | |
|---|---|---|---|---|---|---|---|---|
| 1943-44 | 19 | 57 | | 26-54 | .481 | 33 | 140 | 7.4 |
| 1946-47 | 22 | 69-189 | .365 | 28-48 | .583 | 29 | 166 | 7.5 |
| | 41 | 126 | | 54-102 | .529 | 62 | 306 | 7.5 |

### KELLY, MARC          5-10    b. 6-28-1960

| | | | | | | | | | |
|---|---|---|---|---|---|---|---|---|---|
| 1978-79 | 13 | 5-10 | .500 | 0-1 | .000 | 3 | 0.2 | 3 | 10 | 0.8 |
| 1979-80 | 11 | 2-9 | .222 | 0-1 | .000 | 5 | 0.5 | 0 | 4 | 0.4 |
| 1980-81 | 10 | 0-0 | .000 | 0-1 | .000 | 1 | 0.1 | 2 | 0 | 0.0 |
| 1981-82 | 11 | 2-6 | .333 | 2-5 | .400 | 4 | 0.4 | 3 | 6 | 0.5 |
| | 45 | 9-23 | .360 | 2-8 | .250 | 13 | 0.3 | 8 | 20 | 0.4 |

### KEMPTON, TIM          6-9    b. 1-25-1964

| | | | | | | | | | |
|---|---|---|---|---|---|---|---|---|---|
| 1982-83 | 27 | 101-168 | .601 | 83-113 | .735 | 159 | 5.9 | 74 | 285 | 10.6 |
| 1983-84 | 26 | 78-165 | .473 | 113-148 | .764 | 165 | 6.3 | 80 | 269 | 10.3 |
| 1984-85 | 27 | 62-141 | .440 | 68-87 | .782 | 130 | 4.8 | 71 | 192 | 7.1 |
| | 80 | 241-474 | .508 | 264-348 | .759 | 454 | 5.8 | 225 | 746 | 9.3 |

### KENNEDY, EUGENE          d. 1-15-1973

| | | | | | | |
|---|---|---|---|---|---|---|
| 1919-20 | 16 | 18 | | 1 | 37 | 2.3 |
| 1920-21 | | | | | | |
| 1921-22 | 18 | 17 | | 0 | 34 | 1.9 |

### KENNEDY, JAMES     6-1    b. 12-9-1924
| 1946-47 | 1 | 0-1 | .000 | 3-3 | 1.000 | | 0 | 3 | 3.0 |
|---|---|---|---|---|---|---|---|---|---|

### KENNEDY, TOM
| 1944-45 | 1 | 0 | | 0-0 | .000 | | 0 | 0 | 0.0 |
|---|---|---|---|---|---|---|---|---|---|

### KENNY, GENE     5-11    b. 6-3-1927    d. 8-2-1959
| 1948-49 | 4 | 1-5 | .200 | 0-0 | .000 | | 1 | 2 | 0.5 |
|---|---|---|---|---|---|---|---|---|---|
| 1949-50 | 4 | 4-11 | .364 | 3-6 | .500 | | 2 | 11 | 2.8 |
| | 8 | 5-16 | .313 | 3-6 | .500 | | 3 | 13 | 1.6 |

### KENNY, JOSEPH     d. 1-4-1968
| 1911-12 | 10 | 26 | | 9 | | | | 61 | 6.1 |
|---|---|---|---|---|---|---|---|---|---|
| 1912-13 | | | | | | | | | |
| 1913-14 | 15 | 71 | | 0 | | | | 102 | 6.8 |
| 1914-15 | 17 | 77 | | 0 | | | | 154 | 9.1 |

### KILEY, ROGER     6-0    b. 10-23-1900    d. 9-6-1974
| 1919-20 | 15 | 24 | | 0 | | | | 48 | 3.2 |
|---|---|---|---|---|---|---|---|---|---|
| 1920-21 | | | | | | | | | |
| 1921-22 | 11 | 21 | | 3 | | | | 45 | 4.1 |

### KING, PAUL     5-11    b. 2-12-1934
| 1953-54 | 1 | 0-1 | .000 | 0-0 | .000 | | 1 | 0 | 0.0 |
|---|---|---|---|---|---|---|---|---|---|
| 1954-55 | 4 | 1-5 | .200 | 0-0 | .000 | | 3 | 2 | 0.5 |
| | 5 | 1-6 | .167 | 0-0 | .000 | | 4 | 2 | 0.4 |

### KING, THOMAS     5-10    b.    d. 1-4-1972
| 1915-16 | 10 | 4 | | 0 | | | | 8 | 0.8 |
|---|---|---|---|---|---|---|---|---|---|
| 1916-17 | 13 | 16 | | 0 | | | | 32 | 2.5 |
| | 23 | 20 | | 0 | | | | 40 | 1.7 |

### KIRKLAND, FRANCIS
| 1914-15 | 6 | 2 | | 0 | | | | 4 | 0.7 |
|---|---|---|---|---|---|---|---|---|---|

### KIVISTO, ERNEST     6-0    b. 8-31-1921
| 1943-44 | 16 | 26 | | 7-14 | .500 | | 11 | 59 | 3.7 |
|---|---|---|---|---|---|---|---|---|---|

### KIZER, MARSHALL
| 1927-28 | 5 | 0 | | 0 | | | 2 | 0 | 0.0 |
|---|---|---|---|---|---|---|---|---|---|
| 1928-29 | 3 | 0 | | 0 | | | 1 | 0 | 0.0 |
| 1929-30 | 8 | 4 | | 0-0 | .000 | | 1 | 8 | 1.0 |
| | 16 | 4 | | 0 | | | 4 | 8 | 0.5 |

### KIZER, NOBLE     5-8    b. 3-11-1900    d. 6-13-1940
| 1922-23 | 21 | 47 | | 162 | | | | 256 | 12.2 |
|---|---|---|---|---|---|---|---|---|---|

| | | | | | | | | | | |
|---|---|---|---|---|---|---|---|---|---|---|
| 1923-24 | 20 | 46 | | 13 | | | | | 105 | 5.3 |
| 1924-25 | 17 | 16 | | 7-12 | .583 | | | 20 | 39 | 2.3 |
| | 58 | 109 | | 182 | | | | | 400 | 6.9 |
| KLEINE, JOE | | | | 6-11 | b. 1-4-1962 | | | | | |
| 1980-81 | 29 | 32-50 | .640 | 12-16 | .750 | 71 | 2.4 | 44 | 76 | 2.6 |
| KLIER, GENE | | | | 6-1 | b. 1-4-1919 | | | | | |
| 1937-38 | 19 | 11 | | 6 | | | | | 28 | 1.5 |
| 1938-39 | 20 | 22 | | 4 | | | | | 48 | 2.4 |
| 1939-40 | 21 | 29 | | 7 | | | | 35 | 65 | 3.1 |
| | 60 | 62 | | 17 | | | | | 141 | 2.4 |
| KLIER, LEO | | | | 6-1 | b. 5-21-1923 | | | | | |
| 1942-43 | 3 | 4-4 | 1.000 | 0-0 | .000 | | | 0 | 8 | 2.7 |
| 1943-44 | 19 | 117 | | 59-98 | .602 | | | 39 | 293 | 15.4 |
| 1945-46 | 21 | 147-513 | .287 | 61-115 | .530 | | | 54 | 355 | 16.9 |
| | 43 | 268 | | 120-213 | .563 | | | 93 | 656 | 15.3 |
| KLUCK, RICHARD | | | | 6-2 | b. 8-18-1927 | | | | | |
| 1945-46 | 15 | 0-1 | .000 | 2-2 | 1.000 | | | 3 | 2 | 0.4 |
| 1946-47 | 14 | 8-30 | .267 | 5-7 | .714 | | | 12 | 21 | 1.5 |
| 1947-48 | 14 | 12-30 | .400 | 3-8 | .375 | | | 14 | 27 | 1.9 |
| 1948-49 | 18 | 17-62 | .279 | 7-16 | .438 | | | 22 | 41 | 2.3 |
| | 51 | 37-123 | .301 | 17-33 | .515 | | | 51 | 91 | 1.8 |
| KNIGHT, TOBY | | | | 6-9 | b. 5-3-1955 | | | | | |
| 1973-74 | 18 | 18-38 | .474 | 12-15 | .800 | 37 | 2.1 | 18 | 48 | 2.7 |
| 1974-75 | 26 | 114-235 | .485 | 25-39 | .641 | 203 | 7.8 | 83 | 253 | 9.7 |
| 1975-76 | 28 | 90-196 | .459 | 29-44 | .659 | 192 | 6.9 | 85 | 209 | 7.5 |
| 1976-77 | 29 | 187-331 | .585 | 67-94 | .713 | 306 | 10.6 | 87 | 441 | 15.2 |
| | 101 | 409-800 | .511 | 133-192 | .692 | 738 | 7.3 | 273 | 951 | 9.4 |
| KNOBEL, GEORGE | | | | | | | | | | |
| 1936-37 | 5 | 3 | | 0-1 | .000 | | | 3 | 6 | 1.2 |
| KOCMALSKI, ROBERT | | | | 6-0 | | | | | | |
| 1966-67 | 2 | 0-0 | .000 | 0-0 | .000 | 0 | 0.0 | 1 | 0 | 0.0 |
| KOHIN, RAYMOND | | | | | | | | | | |
| 1922-23 | 1 | 0 | | 0-0 | .000 | | | 2 | 0 | 0.0 |
| KOKEN, MIKE | | | | 5-9 | b. 4-6-1909 | | | | | |
| 1930-31 | 4 | 0 | | 0-0 | .000 | | | 1 | 0 | 0.0 |
| KRAFT, WILLIAM | | | | 6-4 | b. 11-26-1944 | | | | | |
| 1963-64 | 13 | 13-38 | .342 | 4-7 | .571 | 27 | 2.1 | 14 | 30 | 2.3 |

### KRAUSE, EDWARD     6-3   b. 2-2-1913

| | | | | | | | | | | |
|---|---|---|---|---|---|---|---|---|---|---|
| 1931-32 | 18 | 48 | | 42-72 | .583 | | | 33 | 138 | 7.7 |
| 1932-33 | 21 | 77-240 | .321 | 59-116 | .509 | | | 54 | 213 | 10.1 |
| 1933-34 | 23 | 76 | | 44-75 | .587 | | | 45 | 196 | 8.5 |
| | 62 | 201 | | 145-263 | .551 | | | 132 | 547 | 8.8 |

### KUKA, RAPHAEL     6-3   b. 2-17-1922

| | | | | | | | | | | |
|---|---|---|---|---|---|---|---|---|---|---|
| 1941-42 | 20 | 15 | | 5-13 | .385 | | | 40 | 35 | 1.8 |
| 1942-43 | 12 | 17 | | 3 | | | | 26 | 37 | 3.1 |
| | 32 | 32 | | 8 | | | | 66 | 72 | 2.3 |

### KURZ, WILLIAM     6-8   b. 8-13-1941

| | | | | | | | | | | |
|---|---|---|---|---|---|---|---|---|---|---|
| 1960-61 | 8 | 10-30 | .333 | 5-6 | .833 | 25 | 3.1 | 3 | 25 | 3.1 |

### KUZMICZ, DAVE     6-3   b. 1-16-1955

| | | | | | | | | | | |
|---|---|---|---|---|---|---|---|---|---|---|
| 1973-74 | 18 | 9-21 | .321 | 11-16 | .688 | 10 | 0.6 | 14 | 29 | 1.6 |
| 1974-75 | 21 | 20-40 | .500 | 11-13 | .846 | 11 | 0.5 | 9 | 51 | 2.4 |
| 1975-76 | 16 | 4-20 | .200 | 8-12 | .667 | 14 | 0.9 | 6 | 16 | 1.0 |
| 1976-77 | 24 | 22-44 | .500 | 4-11 | .364 | 20 | 0.8 | 9 | 48 | 2.0 |
| | 79 | 55-125 | .440 | 36-54 | .667 | 55 | 0.7 | 38 | 144 | 1.8 |

### KYLE,

| | | | | | | | | | | |
|---|---|---|---|---|---|---|---|---|---|---|
| 1932-33 | 1 | 0-0 | .000 | 0-0 | .000 | | | 0 | 0 | 0.0 |

### LAIMBEER, BILL     6-11   b. 5-19-1957

| | | | | | | | | | | |
|---|---|---|---|---|---|---|---|---|---|---|
| 1975-76 | 10 | 32-65 | .492 | 18-23 | .783 | 79 | 7.9 | 22 | 82 | 8.2 |
| 1977-78 | 29 | 97-175 | .554 | 42-62 | .677 | 190 | 6.6 | 81 | 236 | 8.1 |
| 1978-79 | 30 | 78-145 | .538 | 35-50 | .700 | 164 | 5.5 | 88 | 191 | 6.4 |
| | 69 | 207-385 | .538 | 95-135 | .704 | 433 | 6.3 | 191 | 509 | 7.4 |

### LAMMERS, PAUL     6-2   b. 1-28-1925

| | | | | | | | | | | |
|---|---|---|---|---|---|---|---|---|---|---|
| 1943-44 | 1 | 0 | | 0-0 | .000 | | | 0 | 0 | 0.0 |
| 1944-45 | 7 | 3 | | 2-2 | 1.000 | | | 1 | 8 | 1.1 |
| | 8 | 3 | | 2-2 | 1.000 | | | 1 | 8 | 1.0 |

### LARSON, JOHN

| | | | | | | | | | | |
|---|---|---|---|---|---|---|---|---|---|---|
| 1911-12 | 3 | 0 | | 0 | | | | | 0 | 0.0 |

### LATTNER, JOHN     6-2   b. 10-24-1932

| | | | | | | | | | | |
|---|---|---|---|---|---|---|---|---|---|---|
| 1951-52 | 4 | 6-10 | .600 | 0-1 | .000 | | | 5 | 12 | 3.0 |

### LAYDEN, ELMER     6-0   b. 5-4-1903   d. 6-30-1973

| | | | | | | | | | | |
|---|---|---|---|---|---|---|---|---|---|---|
| 1922-23 | 10 | 3 | | 1-1 | 1.000 | | | 8 | 7 | 0.7 |

### LEAHY, BERNARD     5-10   b.     d. 3- -1978

| | | | | | | | | | | |
|---|---|---|---|---|---|---|---|---|---|---|
| 1928-29 | 4 | 3 | | 0 | | | | 0 | 6 | 1.5 |

### LESLIE, LEROY   6-2   b. 5-23-1930

| Year | G | FG | Pct | FT | Pct | Reb | Pts | Avg |
|---|---|---|---|---|---|---|---|---|
| 1949-50 | 24 | 114-327 | .349 | 62-107 | .579 | 78 | 290 | 12.1 |
| 1950-51 | 24 | 123-393 | .313 | 70-112 | .625 | 91 | 316 | 13.2 |
| 1951-52 | 26 | 145-405 | .358 | 77-111 | .694 | 100 | 367 | 14.1 |
| | 74 | 382-1125 | .340 | 209-330 | .633 | 269 | 973 | 13.1 |

### LEWINSKI, NORBERT   6-5   b. 6-14-1930

| Year | G | FG | Pct | FT | Pct | Reb | Pts | Avg |
|---|---|---|---|---|---|---|---|---|
| 1950-51 | 24 | 92-295 | .312 | 55-95 | .579 | 92 | 239 | 10.0 |
| 1951-52 | 26 | 87-214 | .407 | 39-71 | .549 | 59 | 213 | 8.2 |
| 1952-53 | 24 | 143-424 | .337 | 73-135 | .541 | 95 | 359 | 15.0 |
| | 74 | 322-933 | .345 | 167-301 | .555 | 246 | 811 | 11.0 |

### LEY, THEODORE

| Year | G | FG | Pct | FT | Pct | Reb | Pts | Avg |
|---|---|---|---|---|---|---|---|---|
| 1923-24 | 1 | 1 | | 0 | | 0 | 2 | 2.0 |
| 1924-25 | 6 | 1 | | 0-2 | .000 | 0 | 2 | 0.3 |
| 1925-26 | 14 | 8 | | 3 | | | 19 | 1.3 |
| | 21 | 10 | | 3 | | | 23 | 1.1 |

### LOFTUS, JOHN   6-0   b. 2-12-1926

| Year | G | FG | Pct | FT | Pct | Reb | Pts | Avg |
|---|---|---|---|---|---|---|---|---|
| 1943-44 | 2 | 0 | | 0-0 | .000 | 1 | 0 | 0.0 |
| 1947-48 | 5 | 0-2 | .000 | 0-0 | .000 | 1 | 0 | 0.0 |
| 1948-49 | 16 | 4-25 | .160 | 1-2 | .500 | 8 | 9 | 0.6 |
| | 23 | 4 | | 1-2 | .500 | 10 | 9 | 0.4 |

### LOGAN, LESLIE   5-9   b.     d. 2-29-1968

| Year | G | FG | Pct | FT | Pct | Reb | Pts | Avg |
|---|---|---|---|---|---|---|---|---|
| 1920-21 | | | | | | | | |
| 1921-22 | 17 | 17 | | 3 | | | 37 | 2.2 |
| 1922-23 | 19 | 29 | | 3-11 | .273 | | 61 | 3.2 |

### LOVE, KARL   6-4   b. 3-4-1961

| Year | G | FG | Pct | FT | Pct | Reb | Avg | Ast | Pts | Avg |
|---|---|---|---|---|---|---|---|---|---|---|
| 1981-82 | 11 | 5-9 | .556 | 0-0 | .000 | 3 | 0.3 | 0 | 10 | 0.9 |
| 1982-83 | 9 | 4-9 | .444 | 2-2 | 1.000 | 1 | 0.1 | 1 | 10 | 1.1 |
| | 20 | 9-18 | .500 | 2-2 | 1.000 | 4 | 0.2 | 1 | 20 | 1.0 |

### LOYD, CARL   5-11   b. 11-24-1925

| Year | G | FG | Pct | FT | Pct | Reb | Pts | Avg |
|---|---|---|---|---|---|---|---|---|
| 1943-44 | 9 | 36 | | 2-8 | .250 | 8 | 74 | 8.2 |
| 1946-47 | 19 | 21-89 | .236 | 2-9 | .222 | 4 | 44 | 2.3 |
| | 28 | 57 | | 4-17 | .235 | 12 | 118 | 4.2 |

### LUCAS, WILLIAM   6-4   b. 2-16-1951

| Year | G | FG | Pct | FT | Pct | Reb | Avg | Ast | Pts | Avg |
|---|---|---|---|---|---|---|---|---|---|---|
| 1970-71 | 2 | 0-0 | .000 | 0-0 | .000 | 0 | 0.0 | 0 | 0 | 0.0 |
| 1971-72 | 7 | 0-8 | .000 | 4-4 | 1.000 | 7 | 1.0 | 0 | 4 | 0.6 |
| | 9 | 0-8 | .000 | 4-4 | 1.000 | 7 | 0.8 | 0 | 4 | 0.4 |

### LUEPKE, HENRY 6-8 b. 5-12-1935

|  | | | | | | | | | | |
|---|---|---|---|---|---|---|---|---|---|---|
| 1954-55 | 2 | 0-3 | .000 | 0-0 | .000 | | | 1 | 0 | 0.0 |
| 1956-57 | 3 | 1-5 | .200 | 0-0 | .000 | 3 | 1.0 | 3 | 2 | 0.7 |
| | 5 | 1-8 | .125 | 0-0 | .000 | | | 4 | 2 | 0.4 |

### LUJACK, JOHNNY 6-0 b. 1-4-1925

|  | | | | | | | | | | |
|---|---|---|---|---|---|---|---|---|---|---|
| 1943-44 | 17 | 23 | | 11-17 | .647 | | | 43 | 57 | 3.4 |
| 1946-47 | 2 | 0-1 | .000 | 0-0 | .000 | | | 1 | 0 | 0.0 |
| | 19 | 23 | | 11-17 | .647 | | | 44 | 57 | 3.4 |

### LUSH, LOUIS
1912-13

### MAGNUSSON, FLOYD

|  | | | | | | | | |
|---|---|---|---|---|---|---|---|---|
| 1944-45 | 5 | 6 | | 0-0 | .000 | | 6 | 12 | 2.4 |

### MAHONEY, PHILIP

|  | | | | | | | |
|---|---|---|---|---|---|---|---|
| 1922-23 | 11 | 4 | | 0-0 | .000 | 8 | 0.7 |
| 1923-24 | 23 | 23 | | 14 | | 60 | 2.6 |
| 1924-25 | 21 | 16 | | 13-38 | .342 | 31 | 45 | 2.1 |
| | 55 | 43 | | 27 | | | 113 | 2.1 |

### MALLOY, ED 6-4 b. 5-3-1941

|  | | | | | | | | | | |
|---|---|---|---|---|---|---|---|---|---|---|
| 1960-61 | 3 | 1-4 | .250 | 0-0 | .000 | 2 | 0.7 | 1 | 2 | 0.7 |
| 1961-62 | 11 | 9-18 | .500 | 1-5 | .200 | 9 | 0.8 | 10 | 19 | 1.7 |
| 1962-63 | 7 | 3-16 | .188 | 0-1 | .000 | 4 | 0.6 | 7 | 6 | 0.9 |
| | 21 | 13-38 | .342 | 1-6 | .167 | 15 | 0.7 | 18 | 27 | 1.3 |

### MARTIN, RAY 6-1 b. 2-7-1955

|  | | | | | | | | | | |
|---|---|---|---|---|---|---|---|---|---|---|
| 1973-74 | 27 | 32-68 | .471 | 22-35 | .628 | 30 | 1.1 | 42 | 86 | 3.2 |
| 1974-75 | 28 | 39-103 | .379 | 28-47 | .596 | 51 | 1.8 | 75 | 106 | 3.8 |
| 1975-76 | 29 | 60-136 | .441 | 29-46 | .644 | 51 | 1.8 | 73 | 149 | 5.1 |
| 1976-77 | 6 | 14-23 | .609 | 8-12 | .667 | 11 | 1.8 | 9 | 36 | 6.0 |
| | 90 | 145-330 | .439 | 87-140 | .621 | 143 | 1.6 | 199 | 377 | 4.2 |

### MARTIN, THOMAS

|  | | | | | | | |
|---|---|---|---|---|---|---|---|
| 1896-97 | 2 | 0 | | 0 | | 1 | 0 | 0.0 |

### MATHEWS, LEE 5-10 b. d. 9- -1947

|  | | | | | | |
|---|---|---|---|---|---|---|
| 1909-10 | 10 | 21 | | 1 | | 43 | 4.3 |
| 1910-11 | 1 | 3 | | 0 | | 6 | 6.0 |
| | 11 | 24 | | 1 | | 49 | 4.5 |

## MATTHEWS, JOHN   6-0   b. 10-2-1941

| Year | G | FG | Pct | FT | Pct | | | | Pts | Avg |
|---|---|---|---|---|---|---|---|---|---|---|
| 1960-61 | 24 | 24-91 | .264 | 20-35 | .571 | 28 | 1.2 | 17 | 68 | 2.8 |
| 1961-62 | 23 | 105-271 | .387 | 70-92 | .761 | 66 | 2.9 | 66 | 280 | 12.2 |
| 1962-63 | 26 | 121-328 | .369 | 73-94 | .777 | 50 | 1.9 | 61 | 315 | 12.1 |
| | 73 | 250-610 | .362 | 163-221 | .738 | 144 | 2.0 | 144 | 663 | 9.1 |

## MAY, SHERMAN     d. 4-14-1969

| Year | G | | | | | | | | Pts | Avg |
|---|---|---|---|---|---|---|---|---|---|---|
| 1915-16 | 3 | 0 | | 0 | | | | | 0 | 0.0 |

## MAYL, EUGENE   6-1

| Year | G | FG | | FT | Pct | | | | Pts | Avg |
|---|---|---|---|---|---|---|---|---|---|---|
| 1921-22 | 19 | 18 | | 0 | | | | | 36 | 1.8 |
| 1922-23 | 22 | 11 | | 0-0 | .000 | | | | 22 | 1.0 |
| 1923-24 | 23 | 10 | | 6 | | | | | 26 | 1.1 |
| | 64 | 39 | | 6 | | | | | 84 | 1.3 |

## McCARTHY, EMMETT   6-3   b. 7-11-1938

| Year | G | FG | Pct | FT | Pct | | | | Pts | Avg |
|---|---|---|---|---|---|---|---|---|---|---|
| 1958-59 | 19 | 44-132 | .333 | 10-20 | .500 | 76 | 4.0 | 20 | 98 | 5.2 |
| 1959-60 | 26 | 152-383 | .397 | 69-103 | .670 | 177 | 6.8 | 50 | 373 | 14.3 |
| | 45 | 196-515 | .381 | 79-123 | .642 | 253 | 5.6 | 70 | 471 | 10.5 |

## McCARTHY, JOHN     d. 5-6-1974

| Year | G | FG | | FT | Pct | | | | Pts | Avg |
|---|---|---|---|---|---|---|---|---|---|---|
| 1927-28 | 18 | 17 | | 6 | | | | | 40 | 2.2 |
| 1928-29 | 19 | 15 | | 20 | | | | | 50 | 2.6 |
| 1929-30 | 19 | 34 | | 37-60 | .617 | | | 28 | 105 | 5.5 |
| | 56 | 66 | | 63 | | | | | 195 | 3.5 |

## McCARTHY, JOHN   6-3   b. 12-23-1936

| Year | G | FG | Pct | FT | Pct | | | | Pts | Avg |
|---|---|---|---|---|---|---|---|---|---|---|
| 1955-56 | 20 | 48-154 | .312 | 25-44 | 586 | | | 32 | 121 | 6.1 |
| 1956-57 | 28 | 155-378 | .410 | 121-157 | .771 | 286 | 10.2 | 71 | 431 | 15.4 |
| 1957-58 | 29 | 212-543 | .390 | 132-156 | .846 | 314 | 10.8 | 75 | 556 | 19.2 |
| | 77 | 415-1075 | .386 | 278-357 | .779 | | | 178 | 1108 | 14.4 |

## McCARTHY, WILLIAM     d. 6-15-1978

| Year | G | FG | | FT | Pct | | | | Pts | Avg |
|---|---|---|---|---|---|---|---|---|---|---|
| 1928-29 | 1 | 0 | | 0 | | | | 0 | 0 | 0.0 |
| 1929-30 | 4 | 0 | | 0-0 | .000 | | | 4 | 0 | 0.0 |
| | 5 | 0 | | 0 | | | | 4 | 0 | 0.0 |

## McCLOSKEY, GERALD   6-3   b. 5-7-1931

| Year | G | FG | Pct | FT | Pct | | | | Pts | Avg |
|---|---|---|---|---|---|---|---|---|---|---|
| 1950-51 | 17 | 43-121 | .355 | 16-24 | .667 | | | 49 | 102 | 6.0 |
| 1951-52 | 19 | 66-187 | .353 | 7-12 | 583 | | | 40 | 139 | 7.3 |
| 1952-53 | 15 | 19-64 | .297 | 7-9 | .777 | | | 15 | 45 | 3.0 |
| | 51 | 128-372 | .344 | 30-45 | .667 | | | 104 | 286 | 5.6 |

## McDERMOTT, FRANK

| Year | G | FG | | FT | | | | | Pts | Avg |
|---|---|---|---|---|---|---|---|---|---|---|
| 1916-17 | 13 | 69 | | 56 | | | | | 194 | 14.9 |

| | | | | | | | | | | |
|---|---|---|---|---|---|---|---|---|---|---|
| 1920-21 | | | | | | | | | | |
| 1921-22 | 19 | 72 | | 99 | | | | | 243 | 12.8 |

### McDONALD, PAUL      6-0
1908-09

### McGANN, DONALD      6-3    b. 6-19-1938

| | | | | | | | | | | |
|---|---|---|---|---|---|---|---|---|---|---|
| 1957-58 | 1 | 0-0 | .000 | 0-0 | .000 | 0 | 0.0 | 0 | 0 | 0.0 |
| 1958-59 | 8 | 5-24 | .208 | 6-8 | .750 | 11 | 1.4 | 6 | 16 | 2.0 |
| 1959-60 | 20 | 26-52 | .500 | 18-37 | .486 | 29 | 1.5 | 18 | 70 | 3.5 |
| | 29 | 31-76 | .408 | 24-45 | .537 | 40 | 1.4 | 24 | 86 | 3.0 |

### McGANN, JAMES      6-3    b. 4-1-1944

| | | | | | | | | | | |
|---|---|---|---|---|---|---|---|---|---|---|
| 1963-64 | 18 | 29-82 | .354 | 10-16 | .625 | 50 | 2.8 | 31 | 68 | 3.8 |
| 1964-65 | 27 | 87-207 | .420 | 42-59 | .712 | 112 | 4.1 | 76 | 216 | 12.1 |
| 1965-66 | 25 | 98-278 | .353 | 59-91 | .648 | 98 | 3.9 | 80 | 255 | 10.2 |
| | 70 | 214-567 | .377 | 111-166 | .669 | 260 | 3.7 | 187 | 539 | 7.7 |

### McGINN, EDWARD      6-4    b. 11-13-1930

| | | | | | | | | | |
|---|---|---|---|---|---|---|---|---|---|
| 1951-52 | 4 | 0-0 | .000 | 1-2 | .500 | | 5 | 1 | 0.3 |
| 1952-53 | 10 | 2-13 | .154 | 1-8 | .125 | | 2 | 5 | 0.5 |
| 1953-54 | 21 | 12-46 | .261 | 8-16 | .500 | | 20 | 32 | 1.5 |
| | 35 | 14-59 | .237 | 10-26 | .385 | | 27 | 38 | 1.1 |

### McGRAIN, FRANCIS

| | | | | | | |
|---|---|---|---|---|---|---|
| 1917-18 | 2 | 2 | | 1 | 5 | 2.5 |

### McGRAW, THOMAS      5-11    b. 9-6-1950

| | | | | | | | | | | |
|---|---|---|---|---|---|---|---|---|---|---|
| 1971-72 | 16 | 10-31 | .323 | 2-3 | .667 | 6 | 0.4 | 7 | 22 | 1.3 |

### McGUFF, ALBERT      5-10    b. 4-7-1911    d.12-6-1971

| | | | | | | | |
|---|---|---|---|---|---|---|---|
| 1932-33 | 9 | 6-28 | .214 | 0-1 | .000 | 9 | 12 | 1.3 |

### McINTOSH, ROBERT

| | | | | | |
|---|---|---|---|---|---|
| 1911-12 | 2 | 0 | | 0 | 0 | 0.0 |

### McKENNA, GERALD

| | | | | | |
|---|---|---|---|---|---|
| 1921-22 | 1 | 0 | | 0 | 0 | 0 | 0.0 |

### McKENNA, JOSEPH

| | | | | | |
|---|---|---|---|---|---|
| 1915-16 | 11 | 10 | | 0 | 20 | 1.8 |
| 1916-17 | 13 | 16 | | 2 | 34 | 2.6 |
| | 24 | 26 | | 2 | 54 | 2.3 |

### McKIRCHY, JAMES      6-4    b. 9-25-1945

| | | | | | | | | | | |
|---|---|---|---|---|---|---|---|---|---|---|
| 1965-66 | 21 | 39-92 | .424 | 30-44 | .682 | 55 | 2.6 | 46 | 108 | 5.1 |
| 1966-67 | 19 | 28-59 | .475 | 15-26 | .577 | 39 | 2.1 | 24 | 71 | 3.7 |

| | | | | | | | | | | |
|---|---|---|---|---|---|---|---|---|---|---|
| 1967-68 | 24 | 24-62 | .387 | 20-29 | .690 | 43 | 1.8 | 36 | 68 | 2.8 |
| | 64 | 91-213 | .427 | 65-99 | .657 | 137 | 2.1 | 106 | 247 | 3.9 |

**McNALLY, VINCENT**  6-1

| | | | | | | | | |
|---|---|---|---|---|---|---|---|---|
| 1924-25 | 22 | 41 | | 19-34 | .559 | | 32 | 101 | 4.6 |
| 1925-26 | 20 | 54 | | 37 | | | | 145 | 7.3 |
| 1926-27 | 19 | 22 | | 15 | | | | 59 | 3.1 |
| | 61 | 117 | | 71 | | | | 305 | 5.0 |

**McNALLY,**

| | | | | | | | |
|---|---|---|---|---|---|---|---|
| 1929-30 | 3 | 0 | | 0-0 | .000 | 2 | 0 | 0.0 |

**McNICHOLS, DANIEL**  d. 11-24-1923

| | | | | | | |
|---|---|---|---|---|---|---|
| 1909-10 | 5 | 3 | | 2 | | 8 | 1.6 |
| 1910-11 | 7 | 2 | | 2 | | 6 | 0.9 |
| 1911-12 | 15 | 37 | | 25 | | 99 | 6.6 |
| | 27 | 42 | | 29 | | 113 | 4.2 |

**McNICHOLS, WILLIAM**

| | | | | | | |
|---|---|---|---|---|---|---|
| 1897-98 | 2 | 1 | | 0 | | 2 | 1.0 |
| 1898-99 | | | | | | | |

**MEAGHER, JAMES**  6-0  b. 4-8-1922

| | | | | | | | | |
|---|---|---|---|---|---|---|---|---|
| 1941-42 | 1 | 0 | | 0-0 | .000 | 0 | 0 | 0.0 |
| 1942-43 | 4 | 0 | | 2-2 | 1.000 | 1 | 2 | 0.5 |
| | 5 | 0 | | 2-2 | 1.000 | 1 | 2 | 0.4 |

**MEDLEY, BENJAMIN**
1901-02

**MEEHAN, JACKIE**  6-1  b. 7-20-1949

| | | | | | | | | | | |
|---|---|---|---|---|---|---|---|---|---|---|
| 1968-69 | 19 | 25-55 | .455 | 11-14 | .786 | 30 | 1.6 | 32 | 61 | 3.2 |
| 1969-70 | 27 | 34-77 | .442 | 18-27 | .667 | 47 | 1.7 | 39 | 86 | 3.2 |
| 1970-71 | 28 | 41-120 | .342 | 18-33 | .545 | 62 | 2.2 | 86 | 100 | 3.5 |
| | 74 | 100-252 | .397 | 47-74 | .635 | 139 | 1.9 | 157 | 247 | 3.3 |

**MEHRE, HARRY**  6-1  b.  d. 9- -1978

| | | | | | | | |
|---|---|---|---|---|---|---|---|
| 1919-20 | 18 | 80 | | 60 | | | 220 | 12.2 |
| 1920-21 | | | | | | | | |
| 1921-22 | 3 | 10 | | 0 | | 3 | 20 | 6.7 |

**MELODY, FELIX**

| | | | | | | | |
|---|---|---|---|---|---|---|---|
| 1922-23 | 1 | 1 | | 0-0 | .000 | 0 | 2 | 2.0 |

### METTLER, VICTOR  5-10  b. 9-26-1912  d. 6-14-1981

|  | | | | | | | | |
|---|---|---|---|---|---|---|---|---|
| 1932-33 | 6 | 1-5 | .200 | 0-1 | .000 | 6 | 2 | 0.3 |
| 1933-34 | 7 | 4 | | 0-0 | .000 | 5 | 8 | 1.1 |
| 1934-35 | 4 | 0 | | 0 | | 1 | 0 | 0.0 |
| | 17 | 5 | | 0 | | 12 | 10 | 0.6 |

### MEYER, RAY  5-10  b. 12-18-1913

|  | | | | | | |
|---|---|---|---|---|---|---|
| 1935-36 | 15 | 24 | 8 | 12 | 56 | 3.7 |
| 1936-37 | 23 | 39 | 23-38 .605 | 29 | 101 | 4.4 |
| 1937-38 | 13 | 7 | 2 | | 16 | 1.2 |
| | 51 | 70 | 33 | | 173 | 3.4 |

### MEYERS, JOSEPH

|  | | | | | |
|---|---|---|---|---|---|
| 1915-16 | 11 | 24 | 0 | 48 | 4.4 |
| 1916-17 | 1 | 0 | 0 | 0 | 0.0 |
| | 12 | 24 | 0 | 48 | 4.0 |

### MEYERS, STEPHEN

1912-13

### MILLER, DONALD  5-11  b. 3-30-1902  d. 7-28-1979

|  | | | | | | |
|---|---|---|---|---|---|---|
| 1922-23 | 17 | 20 | 0-0 | .000 | 40 | 2.4 |
| 1923-24 | 15 | 6 | 5 | | 17 | 1.1 |
| | 32 | 26 | 5 | | 57 | 1.8 |

### MILLER, JAY  6-4  b. 7-19-1943

|  | | | | | | | | | | |
|---|---|---|---|---|---|---|---|---|---|---|
| 1962-63 | 26 | 85-226 | .376 | 83-125 | .664 | 226 | 8.7 | 75 | 253 | 9.7 |
| 1963-64 | 23 | 97-246 | .394 | 68-96 | .708 | 178 | 7.7 | 66 | 262 | 11.4 |
| 1964-65 | 27 | 192-409 | .469 | 89-133 | .669 | 276 | 10.2 | 88 | 473 | 17.5 |
| | 76 | 374-881 | .425 | 240-354 | .678 | 680 | 8.9 | 229 | 988 | 13.0 |

### MILLS, RUPERT  6-2  b.  d. 7-20-1929

|  | | | | | |
|---|---|---|---|---|---|
| 1912-13 | | | | | |
| 1913-14 | 16 | 46 | 1 | 93 | 5.8 |
| 1914-15 | 17 | 63 | 16 | 142 | 8.4 |

### MIRRINGTON, NORMAN  6-1  b. 9-24-1926

|  | | | | | | | | |
|---|---|---|---|---|---|---|---|---|
| 1944-45 | 2 | 1 | 0-0 | .000 | | 0 | 2 | 1.0 |

### MITCHELL, MIKE  6-2  b. 11-3-1959

|  | | | | | | | | | | |
|---|---|---|---|---|---|---|---|---|---|---|
| 1978-79 | 29 | 34-69 | .493 | 18-23 | .783 | 26 | 0.9 | 20 | 86 | 3.0 |
| 1979-80 | 24 | 26-62 | .419 | 7-14 | .500 | 30 | 1.3 | 24 | 59 | 2.5 |
| 1980-81 | 13 | 7-13 | .538 | 3-5 | .600 | 3 | 0.2 | 4 | 17 | 1.3 |
| 1981-82 | 26 | 72-138 | .522 | 23-27 | .852 | 43 | 1.7 | 64 | 167 | 6.4 |
| | 92 | 139-282 | .493 | 51-69 | .739 | 102 | 1.1 | 112 | 329 | 3.6 |

### MOCK, RAYMOND

| | | | | | | | |
|---|---|---|---|---|---|---|---|
| 1925-26 | 2 | 1 | | 0 | | 1 | 2 | 1.0 |
| 1926-27 | 1 | 1 | | 0 | | 0 | 2 | 2.0 |
| | 3 | 2 | | 0 | | 1 | 4 | 1.3 |

### MOIR, JOHN    6-2    b. 5-22-1915    d. 11-16-1975

| | | | | | | | |
|---|---|---|---|---|---|---|---|
| 1935-36 | 23 | 112 | | 36 | | | 260 | 11.3 |
| 1936-37 | 22 | 113 | | 64-99 | .646 | 32 | 290 | 13.2 |
| 1937-38 | 22 | 92 | | 46 | | | 230 | 10.5 |
| | 67 | 317 | | 146 | | | 780 | 11.6 |

### MOLONEY, JUSTIN    b. 10-3-1887

| | | | | | | |
|---|---|---|---|---|---|---|
| 1907-08 | | | | | | |
| 1908-09 | | | | | | |
| 1909-10 | 12 | 59 | | 52 | | 170 | 14.2 |
| 1910-11 | 10 | 33 | | 42 | | 108 | 10.8 |

### MONAHAN, JAMES    6-3    b. 6-5-1945

| | | | | | | | | | |
|---|---|---|---|---|---|---|---|---|---|
| 1964-65 | 26 | 27-71 | .380 | 15-22 | .682 | 77 | 3.0 | 24 | 69 | 2.7 |
| 1965-66 | 26 | 140-389 | .360 | 113-162 | .698 | 253 | 9.7 | 78 | 393 | 15.1 |
| 1966-67 | 28 | 83-197 | .421 | 70-106 | .660 | 120 | 4.3 | 78 | 236 | 8.4 |
| | 80 | 250-657 | .381 | 198-290 | .683 | 450 | 5.6 | 180 | 698 | 8.7 |

### MOORE, DANIEL

| | | | | | | |
|---|---|---|---|---|---|---|
| 1925-26 | 7 | 2 | | 0 | | 3 | 4 | 0.6 |

### MOORE, JOHN    6-2    b. 9-20-1920

| | | | | | | | |
|---|---|---|---|---|---|---|---|
| 1941-42 | 1 | 0 | | 0-0 | .000 | 0 | 0 | 0.0 |

### MORAN, JOHN    d. 3-27-1973

| | | | | | | |
|---|---|---|---|---|---|---|
| 1928-29 | 1 | 1 | | 0 | | 0 | 2 | 2.0 |

### MORELLI, JOSEPH    6-1    b. 7-2-1934

| | | | | | | | | |
|---|---|---|---|---|---|---|---|---|
| 1954-55 | 14 | 6-13 | .462 | 2-4 | .500 | | 7 | 14 | 1.0 |
| 1955-56 | 14 | 40-115 | .348 | 29-47 | .617 | | 29 | 109 | 7.8 |
| 1956-57 | 22 | 52-154 | .338 | 48-69 | .696 | 67 | 3.0 | 37 | 152 | 6.9 |
| | 50 | 98-282 | .348 | 79-120 | .658 | | 73 | 275 | 5.5 |

### MORGAN, STEVE

| | | | | | | |
|---|---|---|---|---|---|---|
| 1910-11 | 1 | 0 | | 0 | | 0 | 0.0 |

### MORITZ, CHRIS

| | | | | | | |
|---|---|---|---|---|---|---|
| 1935-36 | 4 | 3 | | 2 | | 1 | 8 | 2.0 |

### MOYNIHAN, TIMOTHY    6-1    b.    d. 4-3-1952

| | | | | | | |
|---|---|---|---|---|---|---|
| 1926-27 | 5 | 0 | | 0 | | 1 | 0 | 0.0 |

| | | | | | | | | | |
|---|---|---|---|---|---|---|---|---|---|
| 1927-28 | 11 | 4 | | 4 | | | 11 | 12 | 1.1 |
| 1928-29 | 7 | 3 | | 1 | | | 3 | 7 | 1.0 |
| | 23 | 7 | | 5 | | | 15 | 19 | 0.8 |

### MULCAHY, HAROLD
1920-21

### MULLEN, JOHN      6-1   b. 5-17-1925

| | | | | | | | | | |
|---|---|---|---|---|---|---|---|---|---|
| 1944-45 | 8 | 9 | | 1-5 | .200 | | 3 | 19 | 2.4 |
| 1945-46 | 1 | 0-0 | .000 | 0-0 | .000 | | 0 | 0 | 0.0 |
| | 9 | 9 | | 1-5 | .200 | | 3 | 19 | 2.1 |

### MURPHY, DWIGHT      6-3   b. 7-28-1947

| | | | | | | | | | | |
|---|---|---|---|---|---|---|---|---|---|---|
| 1966-67 | 28 | 121-303 | .399 | 49-76 | .645 | 121 | 4.3 | 89 | 291 | 10.4 |
| 1967-68 | 30 | 146-352 | .415 | 62-82 | .756 | 196 | 6.5 | 93 | 354 | 11.8 |
| 1968-69 | 26 | 108-226 | .478 | 41-56 | .732 | 92 | 3.5 | 54 | 257 | 9.9 |
| | 84 | 375-881 | .426 | 152-214 | .710 | 409 | 4.9 | 236 | 902 | 10.7 |

### MURPHY, GENE

| | | | | | | | | |
|---|---|---|---|---|---|---|---|---|
| 1919-20 | 1 | 0 | | 0 | | | 0 | 0.0 |

### MURPHY, JEREMIAH

| | | | | | | | |
|---|---|---|---|---|---|---|---|
| 1915-16 | 5 | 1 | | 0 | | 2 | 0.4 |
| 1916-17 | 7 | 3 | | 0 | | 6 | 0.8 |
| | 12 | 4 | | 0 | | 8 | 0.7 |

### MURPHY, JOHN      b. 4-25-1887

| | | | | | | |
|---|---|---|---|---|---|---|
| 1911-12 | 1 | 0 | | 0 | 0 | 0.0 |

### MURPHY, LEO

| | | | | | | | |
|---|---|---|---|---|---|---|---|
| 1944-45 | 2 | 0 | | 0-0 | .000 | 1 | 0 | 0.0 |

### MURPHY, TIM

| | | | | | | | |
|---|---|---|---|---|---|---|---|
| 1922-23 | 4 | 0 | | 0-0 | .000 | 0 | 0 | 0.0 |

### MURPHY, WILLIAM
1908-09

| | | | | | |
|---|---|---|---|---|---|
| 1909-10 | 6 | 4 | | 0 | 8 | 1.3 |

### NAUGHTON, JOSEPH      5-8

| | | | | | | | |
|---|---|---|---|---|---|---|---|
| 1896-97 | 3 | 6 | | 0 | | 3 | 12 | 4.0 |
| 1897-98 | 1 | 1 | | 0 | | 2 | 2.0 |
| | 4 | 7 | | 0 | | 14 | 3.5 |

### NEUMAYR, JOHN      6-3   b. 5-11-1930

| | | | | | | | |
|---|---|---|---|---|---|---|---|
| 1949-50 | 20 | 34-125 | .272 | 13-23 | .565 | 47 | 81 | 4.1 |

| | | | | | | | | | | |
|---|---|---|---|---|---|---|---|---|---|---|
| 1950-51 | 24 | 58-180 | .322 | 38-59 | .644 | | | 60 | 154 | 6.4 |
| 1951-52 | 13 | 8-26 | .308 | 3-4 | .750 | | | 16 | 19 | 1.5 |
| | 57 | 100-331 | .302 | 54-86 | .628 | | | 123 | 254 | 4.5 |

### NEWBOLD, JAMES

| | | | | | | | | | | |
|---|---|---|---|---|---|---|---|---|---|---|
| 1932-33 | 15 | 1-12 | .083 | 3-7 | .429 | | | 13 | 5 | 0.3 |
| 1933-34 | 11 | 2 | | 2-4 | .500 | | | 4 | 6 | 0.5 |
| | 26 | 3 | | 5-11 | .455 | | | 17 | 11 | 0.4 |

### NEWBOLD, ROBERT

| | | | | | | | | | | |
|---|---|---|---|---|---|---|---|---|---|---|
| 1926-27 | 10 | 7 | | 2 | | | | | 16 | 1.6 |
| 1927-28 | 21 | 18 | | 19 | | | | | 55 | 2.6 |
| 1928-29 | 12 | 3 | | 3 | | | | 5 | 9 | 0.8 |
| | 43 | 28 | | 24 | | | | | 80 | 1.9 |

### NEWBOLD, WILLIAM

| | | | | | | | | | | |
|---|---|---|---|---|---|---|---|---|---|---|
| 1929-30 | 18 | 33 | | 19-41 | .463 | | | 28 | 85 | 4.7 |
| 1930-31 | 20 | 32 | | 29-42 | .690 | | | 30 | 93 | 4.7 |
| 1931-32 | 20 | 34 | | 21-35 | .600 | | | 43 | 89 | 4.5 |
| | 58 | 99 | | 69-118 | .585 | | | 101 | 267 | 4.6 |

### NEWELL, CASEY    6-1    b. 5-8-1963

| | | | | | | | | | | |
|---|---|---|---|---|---|---|---|---|---|---|
| 1983-84 | 10 | 1-10 | .100 | 2-4 | .500 | 1 | 0.1 | 0 | 4 | 0.4 |
| 1984-85 | 6 | 0-10 | .000 | 2-7 | .286 | 1 | 0.2 | 1 | 2 | 0.3 |
| | 16 | 1-20 | .050 | 4-11 | .364 | 2 | 0.1 | 1 | 6 | 0.4 |

### NIEMIERA, JOHN    6-1

| | | | | | | | | | | |
|---|---|---|---|---|---|---|---|---|---|---|
| 1941-42 | 19 | 50 | | 37-49 | .755 | | | 26 | 137 | 7.2 |
| 1942-43 | 20 | 38 | | 27 | | | | 43 | 103 | 5.2 |
| | 39 | 88 | | 64 | | | | 69 | 240 | 6.2 |

### NOLAN, ROGER    d. 1-3-1983

| | | | | | | | | | | |
|---|---|---|---|---|---|---|---|---|---|---|
| 1924-25 | 5 | 1 | | 1-2 | .500 | | | 2 | 3 | 0.6 |

### NOONAN, WILLIAM    6-1    b. 3-31-1940

| | | | | | | | | | | |
|---|---|---|---|---|---|---|---|---|---|---|
| 1958-59 | 15 | 15-60 | .250 | 0-3 | .000 | 19 | 1.3 | 13 | 30 | 2.0 |
| 1959-60 | 14 | 8-23 | .348 | 8-13 | .615 | 22 | 1.6 | 11 | 24 | 1.7 |
| 1960-61 | 11 | 6-16 | .375 | 2-5 | .400 | 8 | 0.7 | 1 | 14 | 1.3 |
| | 40 | 29-99 | .293 | 10-21 | .476 | 49 | 1.2 | 25 | 68 | 1.7 |

### NOVAK, GARY    6-7    b. 6-9-1952

| | | | | | | | | | | |
|---|---|---|---|---|---|---|---|---|---|---|
| 1971-72 | 26 | 217-496 | .438 | 74-114 | .622 | 269 | 10.3 | 48 | 508 | 19.5 |
| 1972-73 | 30 | 173-347 | .499 | 39-73 | .534 | 293 | 9.8 | 71 | 385 | 12.8 |
| 1973-74 | 29 | 97-186 | .522 | 16-39 | .410 | 174 | 6.0 | 49 | 210 | 7.2 |
| | 85 | 487-1029 | .473 | 129-231 | .557 | 736 | 8.7 | 168 | 1103 | 12.9 |

NOWAK, PAUL    6-6   b. 3-15-1914   d. 12- -1982

| | | | | | | | | | | |
|---|---|---|---|---|---|---|---|---|---|---|
| 1935-36 | 23 | 65 | 31 | | | | | | 161 | 7.0 |
| 1936-37 | 21 | 56 | 40-62 | .645 | | | 49 | | 152 | 7.2 |
| 1937-38 | 23 | 68 | 37 | | | | | | 173 | 7.5 |
| | 67 | 189 | 108 | | | | | | 486 | 7.3 |

NOWERS, PAUL    5-11

| | | | | | |
|---|---|---|---|---|---|
| 1911-12 | 12 | 26 | 0 | 52 | 4.3 |
| 1912-13 | | | | | |
| 1913-14 | 15 | 13 | 0 | 26 | 1.7 |

NOWICKI, SEBASTIAN

| | | | | | | | |
|---|---|---|---|---|---|---|---|
| 1939-40 | 4 | 0 | 1-2 | .500 | 0 | 1 | 0.3 |

NYIKOS, JOHN    5-10

| | | | | | | | |
|---|---|---|---|---|---|---|---|
| 1924-25 | 22 | 67 | 39-70 | .570 | 36 | 173 | 7.9 |
| 1925-26 | 20 | 68 | 27 | | | 163 | 8.2 |
| 1926-27 | 19 | 72 | 19 | | | 163 | 8.6 |
| | 61 | 207 | 85 | | | 499 | 8.2 |

NYIKOS, MICHAEL

| | | | | | |
|---|---|---|---|---|---|
| 1925-26 | 7 | 15 | 3 | 33 | 4.7 |

OBERBRUNER, KENNETH    5-11   b. 10-5-1918

| | | | | | | |
|---|---|---|---|---|---|---|
| 1938-39 | 14 | 20 | 6 | | 46 | 3.3 |
| 1939-40 | 20 | 29 | 15 | 37 | 73 | 3.7 |
| | 34 | 49 | 21 | | 119 | 3.5 |

O'BOYLE, FRANK

| | | | | | | | |
|---|---|---|---|---|---|---|---|
| 1922-23 | 5 | 0 | 0-0 | .000 | 0 | 0 | 0.0 |

O'CONNELL, MICHAEL    6-1   b. 3-15-1948

| | | | | | | | | | | |
|---|---|---|---|---|---|---|---|---|---|---|
| 1967-68 | 23 | 51-144 | .354 | 57-84 | .679 | 93 | 4.0 | 60 | 159 | 6.9 |
| 1968-69 | 23 | 32-73 | .438 | 55-67 | .821 | 33 | 1.4 | 39 | 119 | 5.2 |
| 1969-70 | 26 | 58-141 | .411 | 46-66 | .697 | 69 | 2.7 | 67 | 162 | 6.2 |
| | 72 | 141-358 | .394 | 158-217 | .728 | 195 | 2.7 | 166 | 440 | 6.1 |

O'CONNELL,

| | | | | | | | |
|---|---|---|---|---|---|---|---|
| 1929-30 | 9 | 0 | 1-4 | .250 | 2 | 1 | 0.0 |

O'CONNOR, JOHN    6-0   b. 5-11-1915

| | | | | | | | |
|---|---|---|---|---|---|---|---|
| 1935-36 | 2 | 1 | 3 | | 1 | 5 | 2.5 |
| 1936-37 | 6 | 2 | 0-0 | .000 | 2 | 4 | 0.7 |
| 1937-38 | 3 | 1 | 0 | | | 2 | 0.7 |
| | 11 | 4 | 3 | | | 11 | 1.0 |

O'CONNOR, MARTIN

| | | | | | | | | |
|---|---|---|---|---|---|---|---|---|
| 1948-49 | 20 | 11-41 | .268 | 11-16 | .688 | 16 | 33 | 1.7 |
| 1949-50 | 23 | 7-46 | .152 | 24-30 | .800 | 28 | 38 | 1.7 |
| 1950-51 | 24 | 59-190 | .311 | 62-99 | .626 | 83 | 180 | 7.5 |
| | 67 | 77-277 | .278 | 97-145 | .669 | 127 | 251 | 3.7 |

O'CONNOR, MICHAEL

| | | | | | | | |
|---|---|---|---|---|---|---|---|
| 1934-35 | 2 | 0 | 1 | | 3 | 1 | 0.5 |

O'CONNOR, THOMAS

1912-13

O'CONNOR, WILLIAM          6-4     b. 5-2-1926

| | | | | | | | | |
|---|---|---|---|---|---|---|---|---|
| 1943-44 | 1 | 0 | | 0-0 | .000 | 0 | 0 | 0.0 |
| 1944-45 | 9 | 8 | | 2-2 | 1.000 | 9 | 18 | 2.0 |
| | 10 | 8 | | 2-2 | 1.000 | 9 | 18 | 1.8 |

O'CONNOR,

| | | | | | | |
|---|---|---|---|---|---|---|
| 1917-18 | 2 | 0 | 0 | | 0 | 0.0 |

OELRICK, DICK          5-11

| | | | | | | | |
|---|---|---|---|---|---|---|---|
| 1931-32 | 1 | 0 | 0-0 | .000 | 1 | 0 | 0.0 |

O'HALLORAN, JAMES          5-11

| | | | | | | | | |
|---|---|---|---|---|---|---|---|---|
| 1946-47 | 21 | 41-106 | .387 | 14-27 | .519 | 32 | 96 | 4.6 |
| 1947-48 | 24 | 56-186 | .301 | 38-68 | .559 | 62 | 150 | 6.3 |
| 1948-49 | 24 | 82-213 | .385 | 78-106 | .736 | 66 | 242 | 10.1 |
| | 69 | 179-505 | .354 | 130-201 | .647 | 160 | 488 | 7.1 |

O'KANE, JOSEPH          6-1

| | | | | | | | | |
|---|---|---|---|---|---|---|---|---|
| 1932-33 | 4 | 1-4 | .250 | 0-1 | .000 | 0 | 2 | 0.5 |
| 1933-34 | 14 | 9 | | 3-7 | .429 | 8 | 21 | 1.5 |
| 1934-35 | 22 | 54 | | 26 | | 23 | 134 | 6.1 |
| | 40 | 64 | | 29 | | 31 | 157 | 3.9 |

O'KEEFE, THOMAS          6-2     b. 6-3-1928

| | | | | | | | | |
|---|---|---|---|---|---|---|---|---|
| 1945-46 | 1 | 0-0 | .000 | 0-0 | .000 | 0 | 0 | 0.0 |

O'LEARY, CHARLES          6-0     b. 2-6-1921

| | | | | | | | |
|---|---|---|---|---|---|---|---|
| 1940-41 | 18 | 10 | | 6 | | 26 | 1.4 |
| 1941-42 | 5 | 1 | | 1-2 | .500 | 4 | 3 | 0.6 |
| 1942-43 | 1 | 1 | | 0-0 | .000 | 0 | 2 | 2.0 |
| | 24 | 12 | | 7 | | 31 | 1.3 |

O'MARA, THOMAS          6-6     b. 4-25-1952

| | | | | | | | | | | |
|---|---|---|---|---|---|---|---|---|---|---|
| 1971-72 | 26 | 176-401 | .434 | 90-126 | .714 | 137 | 5.3 | 77 | 442 | 17.0 |

O'NEAL, FRED

| | | | | | | | | |
|---|---|---|---|---|---|---|---|---|
| 1910-11 | 4 | 5 | | 0 | | | 10 | 2.5 |

O'NEAL, WILLIAM　　　　　5-11　b. 5-2-1944

| | | | | | | | | | | |
|---|---|---|---|---|---|---|---|---|---|---|
| 1964-65 | 8 | 4-12 | .333 | 0-0 | .000 | 4 | 0.5 | 4 | 8 | 1.0 |

O'NEIL,

| | | | | | | | |
|---|---|---|---|---|---|---|---|
| 1927-28 | 1 | 0 | | 0-0 | .000 | | 1 | 0 | 0.0 |

O'NEILL, KEVIN　　　　　6-2　b. 9-7-1944

| | | | | | | | | | | |
|---|---|---|---|---|---|---|---|---|---|---|
| 1963-64 | 3 | 1-2 | .500 | 0-0 | .000 | 3 | 1.0 | 0 | 2 | 0.7 |
| 1964-65 | 3 | 0-2 | .000 | 0-0 | .000 | 2 | 0.7 | 0 | 0 | 0.0 |
| 1965-66 | 18 | 22-55 | .400 | 8-15 | .533 | 15 | 0.8 | 26 | 52 | 2.9 |
| | 24 | 23-59 | .390 | 8-15 | .533 | 20 | 0.8 | 26 | 54 | 2.3 |

O'NEILL, LAWRENCE　　　　　　　d. 3-5-1977

| | | | | | | | | | |
|---|---|---|---|---|---|---|---|---|---|
| 1932-33 | 4 | 2-2 | 1.000 | 0-0 | .000 | | 1 | 4 | 1.0 |
| 1933-34 | 2 | 0 | | 0-1 | .000 | | 0 | 0 | 0.0 |
| | 6 | 2 | | 0-1 | .000 | | 1 | 4 | 0.7 |

O'NEILL, PHILIP　　　　　　　　d. 8-2-1955

1901-02

O'SHAUGHNESSY, MARTIN

| | | | | | | |
|---|---|---|---|---|---|---|
| 1897-98 | 3 | 1 | | 6 | | 8 | 2.7 |
| 1898-99 | | | | | | |

O'SHEA, KEVIN　　　　　6-1　b. 7-10-1925

| | | | | | | | | |
|---|---|---|---|---|---|---|---|---|
| 1946-47 | 22 | 91-261 | .349 | 28-57 | .491 | 40 | 210 | 9.5 |
| 1947-48 | 23 | 100-316 | .316 | 65-109 | .613 | 47 | 265 | 11.5 |
| 1948-49 | 22 | 85-265 | .321 | 62-99 | .626 | 67 | 232 | 10.5 |
| 1949-50 | 24 | 133-390 | .341 | 92-141 | .652 | 67 | 358 | 14.9 |
| | 91 | 409-1232 | .332 | 247-403 | .612 | 221 | 1065 | 11.7 |

OSTERMAN, HARRY　　　　　6-4　b. 1-9-1932

| | | | | | | | | |
|---|---|---|---|---|---|---|---|---|
| 1950-51 | 1 | 2-6 | .333 | 0-0 | .000 | 3 | 4 | 4.0 |

OSTERMAN, ROBERT　　　　　6-3　b. 2-11-1919

| | | | | | | | |
|---|---|---|---|---|---|---|---|
| 1939-40 | 3 | 0 | | 0-2 | .000 | 0 | 0 | 0.0 |

PATERNO, BILL　　　　　6-5　b. 3-24-1955

| | | | | | | | | | | |
|---|---|---|---|---|---|---|---|---|---|---|
| 1973-74 | 29 | 95-190 | .500 | 33-46 | .717 | 99 | 3.4 | 59 | 223 | 7.7 |
| 1974-75 | 29 | 166-344 | .483 | 55-78 | .705 | 197 | 6.8 | 84 | 387 | 13.3 |
| 1975-76 | 29 | 103-232 | .444 | 40-57 | .702 | 116 | 4.0 | 62 | 246 | 8.5 |
| 1976-77 | 29 | 110-249 | .442 | 58-82 | .707 | 135 | 4.7 | 83 | 278 | 9.6 |
| | 116 | 474-1015 | .467 | 186-263 | .707 | 547 | 4.7 | 288 | 1134 | 9.8 |

PAVELA, STEVE    5-9    b. 9-25-1923

| | | | | | | | | |
|---|---|---|---|---|---|---|---|---|
| 1942-43 | 1 | 0 | | 0-0 | .000 | | 0 | 0 | 0.0 |

PAXSON, JOHN    6-2    b. 9-29-1960

| | | | | | | | | | | |
|---|---|---|---|---|---|---|---|---|---|---|
| 1979-80 | 27 | 42-87 | .483 | 41-55 | .745 | 34 | 1.3 | 41 | 125 | 4.6 |
| 1980-81 | 29 | 113-218 | .518 | 61-89 | .685 | 53 | 1.8 | 61 | 287 | 9.9 |
| 1981-82 | 27 | 185-346 | .535 | 72-93 | .774 | 55 | 2.0 | 66 | 442 | 16.4 |
| 1982-83 | 29 | 219-411 | .533 | 74-100 | .740 | 63 | 2.2 | 60 | 512 | 17.7 |
| | 112 | 559-1062 | .526 | 248-337 | .736 | 205 | 1.8 | 228 | 1366 | 12.2 |

PEARSON, DUDLEY

| | | | | | |
|---|---|---|---|---|---|
| 1917-18 | 1 | 0 | 0 | | 0 | 0.0 |
| 1918-19 | 9 | 5 | 0 | | 10 | 1.1 |
| | 10 | 5 | 0 | | 10 | 1.0 |

PETERS, JEFF    6-4    b. 3-6-1966

| | | | | | | | | | | |
|---|---|---|---|---|---|---|---|---|---|---|
| 1984-85 | 15 | 11-29 | .379 | 4-6 | .667 | 8 | 0.5 | 9 | 26 | 1.7 |

PETERS, MARTIN    6-3    b. 12-27-1912

| | | | | | | | |
|---|---|---|---|---|---|---|---|
| 1933-34 | 22 | 50 | 20-40 | .500 | 40 | 120 | 5.5 |
| 1934-35 | 20 | 53 | 31 | | 39 | 137 | 6.9 |
| 1935-36 | 23 | 16 | 17 | | 49 | 2.1 |
| | 65 | 119 | 68 | | 306 | 4.7 |

PIERCE, ROBERT    6-2    b. 8-25-1922

| | | | | | | | |
|---|---|---|---|---|---|---|---|
| 1943-44 | 11 | 6 | 4-4 | 1.000 | 3 | 16 | 1.5 |

PLEICK, JOHN    6-8    b. 2-27-1949

| | | | | | | | | | | |
|---|---|---|---|---|---|---|---|---|---|---|
| 1968-69 | 22 | 30-62 | .484 | 15-22 | .682 | 62 | 2.8 | 25 | 75 | 3.4 |
| 1969-70 | 16 | 61-135 | .452 | 24-42 | .571 | 107 | 6.7 | 54 | 146 | 9.1 |
| 1970-71 | 27 | 81-197 | .411 | 50-72 | .694 | 165 | 6.1 | 104 | 212 | 7.8 |
| | 65 | 172-394 | .437 | 89-136 | .654 | 334 | 5.1 | 183 | 433 | 6.7 |

PLISKA, JOSEPH    5-10    b. 10-17-1890

| | | | | | | |
|---|---|---|---|---|---|---|
| 1911-12 | 1 | 1 | 0 | | 2 | 2.0 |
| 1912-13 | | | | | | |
| 1913-14 | 2 | 1 | 0 | | 2 | 1.0 |

POPE, ARTHUR    b. 6-1-1919

| | | | | | | | |
|---|---|---|---|---|---|---|---|
| 1939-40 | 4 | 0 | 0-0 | .000 | 2 | 0 | 0.0 |
| 1940-41 | 19 | 11 | 3 | | 25 | 1.3 |
| 1941-42 | 16 | 5 | 9-10 | .900 | 14 | 19 | 1.2 |
| | 39 | 16 | 12 | | 44 | 1.1 |

POWERS, J. FRED

| | | | | | | | | | | |
|---|---|---|---|---|---|---|---|---|---|---|
| 1897-98 | 2 | 6 | | 0 | | | | | 12 | 6.0 |
| 1898-99 | | | | | | | | | | |

PRICE, JOSEPH     6-5    b. 7-18-1963

| | | | | | | | | | | |
|---|---|---|---|---|---|---|---|---|---|---|
| 1982-83 | 29 | 49-110 | .445 | 14-26 | .538 | 39 | 1.3 | 49 | 112 | 3.9 |
| 1983-84 | 33 | 79-170 | .465 | 34-50 | .680 | 73 | 2.2 | 67 | 192 | 5.8 |
| 1984-85 | 25 | 54-122 | .443 | 25-31 | .806 | 45 | 1.8 | 49 | 133 | 5.3 |
| | 87 | 182-402 | .453 | 73-107 | .682 | 157 | 1.8 | 165 | 437 | 5.0 |

PURCELL, TOM

| | | | | | | | | | | |
|---|---|---|---|---|---|---|---|---|---|---|
| 1925-26 | 7 | 6 | | 3 | | | | | 15 | 2.1 |

QUINLAN, JOHN

1901-02

QUINN, DANIEL     6-4    b. 3-14-1947

| | | | | | | | | | | |
|---|---|---|---|---|---|---|---|---|---|---|
| 1966-67 | 6 | 3-9 | .333 | 3-6 | .500 | 8 | 1.3 | 2 | 9 | 1.5 |
| 1967-68 | 10 | 5-18 | .278 | 8-8 | 1.000 | 15 | 1.5 | 10 | 18 | 1.8 |
| 1968-69 | 13 | 3-7 | .429 | 0-2 | .000 | 10 | 0.8 | 6 | 6 | 0.5 |
| | 29 | 11-34 | .324 | 11-16 | .688 | 33 | 1.1 | 18 | 33 | 1.1 |

QUINN, FRANCIS     6-2    b. 3-20-1920

| | | | | | | | | | | |
|---|---|---|---|---|---|---|---|---|---|---|
| 1939-40 | 11 | 3 | | 0 | | | | 3 | 6 | 0.5 |
| 1940-41 | 21 | 34 | | 14 | | | | | 82 | 3.9 |
| 1941-42 | 22 | 33 | | 10-17 | .588 | | | 47 | 76 | 3.5 |
| | 54 | 70 | | 24 | | | | | 164 | 3.0 |

RATTERMAN, GEORGE     6-0    b. 11-12-1926

| | | | | | | | | | | |
|---|---|---|---|---|---|---|---|---|---|---|
| 1944-45 | 20 | 99 | | 36-51 | .706 | | | 30 | 234 | 11.7 |
| 1945-46 | 21 | 72-256 | .281 | 36-60 | .600 | | | 45 | 180 | 8.6 |
| 1946-47 | 17 | 36-132 | .273 | 11-21 | .524 | | | 21 | 83 | 4.9 |
| | 58 | 207 | | 83-132 | .629 | | | 96 | 497 | 8.6 |

REARDON, THOMAS

| | | | | | | | | | | |
|---|---|---|---|---|---|---|---|---|---|---|
| 1922-23 | 21 | 22 | | 1-3 | .333 | | | | 45 | 2.1 |
| 1923-24 | 20 | 19 | | 5 | | | | | 43 | 2.2 |
| | 41 | 41 | | 6 | | | | | 88 | 2.1 |

REBORA, STEVEN     5-10

| | | | | | | | | | | |
|---|---|---|---|---|---|---|---|---|---|---|
| 1952-53 | 2 | 1-1 | 1.000 | 0-0 | .000 | | | 2 | 2 | 1.0 |
| 1953-54 | 10 | 4-11 | .364 | 3-6 | .500 | | | 6 | 11 | 1.1 |
| 1954-55 | 14 | 2-7 | .286 | 3-6 | .500 | | | 8 | 7 | 0.5 |
| | 26 | 7-19 | .368 | 6-12 | .500 | | | 16 | 20 | 0.8 |

### REED, RON      6-6    b. 11-2-1942

| | | | | | | | | | | |
|---|---|---|---|---|---|---|---|---|---|---|
| 1962-63 | 16 | 92-217 | .424 | 43-59 | .729 | 197 | 12.3 | 39 | 227 | 14.2 |
| 1963-64 | 18 | 154-375 | .411 | 52-91 | .571 | 318 | 17.7 | 61 | 360 | 20.0 |
| 1964-65 | 27 | 242-565 | .428 | 82-119 | .689 | 357 | 13.2 | 90 | 566 | 21.0 |
| | 61 | 488-1157 | .422 | 177-269 | .658 | 872 | 14.3 | 190 | 1153 | 18.9 |

### REGELEAN, JAMES      6-8    b. 8-26-1950

| | | | | | | | | | | |
|---|---|---|---|---|---|---|---|---|---|---|
| 1970-71 | 15 | 10-21 | .476 | 8-11 | .727 | 22 | 1.5 | 13 | 28 | 1.8 |
| 1971-72 | 9 | 6-31 | .194 | 1-2 | .500 | 18 | 2.0 | 10 | 13 | 1.4 |
| | 24 | 16-52 | .308 | 9-13 | .692 | 40 | 1.7 | 23 | 41 | 1.7 |

### REHME, FRANK

| | | | | | | | | | | |
|---|---|---|---|---|---|---|---|---|---|---|
| 1938-39 | 1 | 0 | | 0-0 | .000 | | | 0 | 0 | 0.0 |

### REILLY, MICHAEL      6-0    b. 2-8-1941

| | | | | | | | | | | |
|---|---|---|---|---|---|---|---|---|---|---|
| 1960-61 | 2 | 0-1 | .000 | 0-0 | .000 | 0 | 0.0 | 0 | 0 | 0.0 |

### REINHART, THOMAS      6-5    b. 10-18-1937

| | | | | | | | | | | |
|---|---|---|---|---|---|---|---|---|---|---|
| 1956-57 | 1 | 1-3 | .333 | 0-2 | .000 | 3 | 3.0 | 0 | 2 | 2.0 |
| 1957-58 | 29 | 102-287 | 355 | 32-56 | .571 | 196 | 6.8 | 85 | 236 | 8.1 |
| 1958-59 | 23 | 97-302 | .321 | 30-50 | .600 | 150 | 6.5 | 57 | 224 | 9.7 |
| | 53 | 200-592 | .338 | 62-108 | .574 | 349 | 6.6 | 142 | 462 | 8.7 |

### RENCHER, BERNARD      6-2    b. 3-9-1957

| | | | | | | | | | | |
|---|---|---|---|---|---|---|---|---|---|---|
| 1975-76 | 28 | 59-139 | .424 | 13-27 | .481 | 42 | 1.5 | 34 | 131 | 4.7 |

### RENSBERGER, ROBERT      6-3    b. 3-7-1921

| | | | | | | | | | | |
|---|---|---|---|---|---|---|---|---|---|---|
| 1940-41 | 13 | 8 | | 4 | | | | | 20 | 1.5 |
| 1941-42 | 21 | 55 | | 30-41 | .732 | | | 33 | 140 | 6.7 |
| 1942-43 | 20 | 78 | | 29 | | | | 44 | 185 | 9.3 |
| | 54 | 141 | | 63 | | | | | 345 | 6.4 |

### REO, ARMAND      6-6    b. 2-19-1940

| | | | | | | | | | | |
|---|---|---|---|---|---|---|---|---|---|---|
| 1959-60 | 13 | 13-41 | .317 | 6-7 | .857 | 34 | 2.6 | 20 | 32 | 2.5 |
| 1960-61 | 26 | 166-400 | 415 | 46-70 | .657 | 277 | 10.7 | 86 | 378 | 14.5 |
| 1961-62 | 23 | 165-431 | .383 | 84-100 | .840 | 265 | 11.5 | 84 | 414 | 18.0 |
| | 62 | 344-872 | .394 | 136-177 | .768 | 576 | 9.3 | 190 | 824 | 13.3 |

### RESTOVICH, GEORGE      6-1    b. 4-12-1946

| | | | | | | | | | | |
|---|---|---|---|---|---|---|---|---|---|---|
| 1965-66 | 26 | 75-211 | .355 | 71-86 | .826 | 120 | 4.6 | 90 | 221 | 8.5 |
| 1966-67 | 23 | 26-68 | .382 | 21-32 | .656 | 48 | 2.1 | 41 | 73 | 3.2 |
| 1967-68 | 29 | 33-64 | .516 | 17-23 | .739 | 50 | 1.7 | 36 | 83 | 2.9 |
| | 78 | 134-343 | .391 | 109-141 | .773 | 218 | 2.8 | 167 | 377 | 4.8 |

### REYNOLDS, JACK 6-1 b. 1-19-1932

| | | | | | | | | | |
|---|---|---|---|---|---|---|---|---|---|
| 1951-52 | 7 | 3-15 | .200 | 2-8 | .250 | | 10 | 8 | 1.1 |
| 1952-53 | 14 | 12-29 | .414 | 7-16 | .438 | | 16 | 31 | 2.2 |
| 1953-54 | 17 | 6-22 | .273 | 8-11 | .727 | | 15 | 20 | 1.2 |
| | 38 | 21-66 | .318 | 17-35 | .486 | | 41 | 59 | 1.6 |

### RILEY, GEORGE 6-8

| | | | | | | | | | |
|---|---|---|---|---|---|---|---|---|---|
| 1945-46 | 7 | 1-4 | .250 | 2-4 | .500 | | 0 | 4 | 0.6 |

### RISKA, EDWARD 6-0 b. 10-4-1919

| | | | | | | | |
|---|---|---|---|---|---|---|---|
| 1938-39 | 21 | 70 | | 62 | | 202 | 9.6 |
| 1939-40 | 21 | 85 | | 62 | 46 | 232 | 11.0 |
| 1940-41 | 17 | 61 | | 52 | | 174 | 10.2 |
| | 59 | 216 | | 176 | | 608 | 10.3 |

### RIVERS, DAVID 6-0 b. 1-20-1965

| | | | | | | | | | |
|---|---|---|---|---|---|---|---|---|---|
| 1984-85 | 30 | 168-398 | .422 | 138-173 | .798 | 78 | 2.6 | 68 | 474 | 15.8 |

### ROBERTS, WILLIAM 6-7 b. 3-13-1925

| | | | | | | | |
|---|---|---|---|---|---|---|---|
| 1944-45 | 8 | 8 | | 1-3 | .333 | 7 | 17 | 2.1 |

### ROESLER, KARL 6-7 b. 4-2-1941

| | | | | | | | | | | |
|---|---|---|---|---|---|---|---|---|---|---|
| 1959-60 | 8 | 9-22 | .409 | 6-8 | .750 | 21 | 2.6 | 10 | 24 | 3.0 |
| 1960-61 | 24 | 51-139 | .367 | 25-36 | .694 | 88 | 3.7 | 47 | 127 | 5.3 |
| 1961-62 | 23 | 83-238 | .349 | 49-64 | .766 | 183 | 8.0 | 86 | 215 | 9.3 |
| | 55 | 143-399 | .358 | 80-108 | .741 | 292 | 5.3 | 143 | 366 | 6.7 |

### ROMANOWSKI, THEODORE 6-5 b. 8-27-1939

| | | | | | | | | | | |
|---|---|---|---|---|---|---|---|---|---|---|
| 1960-61 | 2 | 0-1 | .000 | 0-1 | .000 | 2 | 1.0 | 2 | 0 | 0.0 |
| 1961-62 | 8 | 0-4 | .000 | 2-4 | .500 | 7 | 0.9 | 3 | 2 | 0.3 |
| | 10 | 0-5 | .000 | 2-5 | .400 | 9 | 0.9 | 5 | 2 | 0.2 |

### ROMEO, ANTHONY d. 8-28-1977

| | | | | | | | | |
|---|---|---|---|---|---|---|---|---|
| 1939-40 | 1 | 0 | | 0-0 | .000 | 0 | 0 | 0.0 |

### RONCHETTI, PETER 5-11

| | | | | | | |
|---|---|---|---|---|---|---|
| 1915-16 | 8 | 8 | | 1 | 17 | 2.1 |
| 1916-17 | 8 | 7 | | 4 | 18 | 2.3 |
| 1917-18 | 6 | 9 | | 21 | 39 | 6.5 |
| | 22 | 24 | | 26 | 74 | 3.4 |

### ROSENTHAL, RICHARD 6-5 b. 1-20-1933

| | | | | | | | | |
|---|---|---|---|---|---|---|---|---|
| 1951-52 | 26 | 133-425 | .313 | 63-109 | .578 | 104 | 329 | 12.7 |
| 1952-53 | 24 | 148-476 | .311 | 96-141 | .681 | 77 | 392 | 16.3 |
| 1953-54 | 25 | 176-507 | .347 | 154-203 | .759 | 78 | 506 | 20.2 |
| | 75 | 457-1408 | .325 | 313-452 | .692 | 259 | 1227 | 16.4 |

### ROWAN, RON — 6-5 — b. 4-23-1963

| | | | | | | | | | | |
|---|---|---|---|---|---|---|---|---|---|---|
| 1981-82 | 23 | 52-114 | .456 | 31-42 | .738 | 46 | 2.0 | 40 | 135 | 5.9 |
| 1982-83 | 13 | 17-35 | .486 | 5-7 | .714 | 17 | 1.3 | 9 | 39 | 3.0 |
| | 36 | 69-149 | .463 | 36-49 | .735 | 63 | 1.8 | 49 | 174 | 4.8 |

### ROYAL, DONALD — 6-7 — b. 5-2-1966

| | | | | | | | | | | |
|---|---|---|---|---|---|---|---|---|---|---|
| 1983-84 | 31 | 38-64 | .594 | 28-45 | .622 | 72 | 2.3 | 49 | 104 | 3.4 |
| 1984-85 | 30 | 75-151 | .497 | 122-156 | .782 | 164 | 5.5 | 72 | 272 | 9.1 |
| | 61 | 113-215 | .526 | 150-201 | .746 | 236 | 3.9 | 121 | 376 | 6.2 |

### RUCKER, CECIL — 6-8 — b. 3-6-1962

| | | | | | | | | | | |
|---|---|---|---|---|---|---|---|---|---|---|
| 1980-81 | 14 | 13-22 | .591 | 4-8 | .500 | 9 | 0.6 | 2 | 30 | 2.1 |
| 1981-82 | 26 | 64-122 | .525 | 26-38 | .684 | 108 | 4.2 | 53 | 154 | 5.9 |
| 1982-83 | 15 | 7-19 | .368 | 6-9 | .667 | 11 | 0.7 | 2 | 20 | 1.3 |
| 1983-84 | 15 | 6-16 | .375 | 9-11 | .818 | 23 | 1.5 | 12 | 21 | 1.4 |
| | 70 | 90-179 | .503 | 45-66 | .682 | 151 | 2.2 | 69 | 225 | 3.2 |

### RUTLEDGE, BERNARD — 6-1 — b. 10-1-1923 — d. 4-19-1954

| | | | | | | | | | | |
|---|---|---|---|---|---|---|---|---|---|---|
| 1942-43 | 2 | 0 | | 1-1 | 1.000 | | | 1 | 1 | 0.5 |
| 1943-44 | 18 | 54 | | 2-8 | .250 | | | 57 | 110 | 6.1 |
| | 20 | 54 | | 3-9 | .333 | | | 58 | 111 | 5.6 |

### RYAN, LARRY — 6-1 — b. 9-4-1918

| | | | | | | | | | | |
|---|---|---|---|---|---|---|---|---|---|---|
| 1938-39 | 8 | 7 | | 3 | | | | | 17 | 1.1 |
| 1939-40 | 21 | 31 | | 12 | | | | 30 | 74 | 3.5 |
| 1940-41 | 22 | 24 | | 26 | | | | | 74 | 3.4 |
| | 51 | 62 | | 41 | | | | | 165 | 3.2 |

### RYDZEWSKI, FRANK — 6-1

| | | | | | | | | | | |
|---|---|---|---|---|---|---|---|---|---|---|
| 1915-16 | 1 | 0 | | 0 | | | | | 0 | 0.0 |

### SADOWSKI, EDWARD — 5-11 — b. 2-2-1915

| | | | | | | | | | | |
|---|---|---|---|---|---|---|---|---|---|---|
| 1936-37 | 23 | 24 | | 8-25 | .320 | | | 31 | 56 | 2.4 |
| 1937-38 | 23 | 56 | | 22 | | | | | 134 | 5.8 |
| 1938-39 | 21 | 46 | | 25 | | | | | 117 | 5.6 |
| | 67 | 126 | | 55 | | | | | 307 | 4.6 |

### SAHM, BILL — 6-2 — b. 3-7-1955

| | | | | | | | | | | |
|---|---|---|---|---|---|---|---|---|---|---|
| 1976-77 | 17 | 2-22 | .091 | 4-12 | .333 | 11 | 0.6 | 13 | 8 | 0.5 |

### SAHM, WALTER — 6-9 — b. 1-1-1943

| | | | | | | | | | | |
|---|---|---|---|---|---|---|---|---|---|---|
| 1962-63 | 26 | 155-362 | .428 | 62-110 | .564 | 438 | 16.8 | 84 | 372 | 14.3 |
| 1963-64 | 18 | 135-304 | .444 | 43-71 | .606 | 315 | 17.5 | 65 | 313 | 17.4 |
| 1964-65 | 24 | 156-341 | .457 | 80-130 | .615 | 393 | 16.4 | 80 | 392 | 16.3 |
| | 68 | 446-1067 | .443 | 185-311 | .595 | 1146 | 16.9 | 229 | 1077 | 15.8 |

SALINAS, GILBERT 6-11 b. 7-13-1959

| | | | | | | | | | | |
|---|---|---|---|---|---|---|---|---|---|---|
| 1977-78 | 17 | 14-33 | .424 | 14-19 | .737 | 28 | 1.6 | 14 | 42 | 2.5 |
| 1978-79 | 8 | 12-28 | .429 | 13-17 | .765 | 22 | 2.8 | 18 | 37 | 4.8 |
| 1979-80 | 26 | 40-74 | .541 | 25-35 | .714 | 52 | 2.0 | 57 | 105 | 4.0 |
| 1980-81 | 13 | 14-32 | .438 | 10-17 | .588 | 14 | 1.1 | 16 | 38 | 2.9 |
| | 64 | 80-167 | .479 | 62-88 | .705 | 116 | 1.8 | 105 | 222 | 3.5 |

SALMON, LOUIS 5-10 b. d. 9-27-1965

1901-02

SANFORD, JOSEPH

| | | | | | | | |
|---|---|---|---|---|---|---|---|
| 1919-20 | 4 | 3 | 0 | | | 6 | 1.5 |

SCANLON, RAYMOND 5-11

1907-08
1908-09

SCHAFER, OSCAR

| | | | | | | | |
|---|---|---|---|---|---|---|---|
| 1911-12 | 2 | 0 | 2 | | | 2 | 1.0 |

SCHEER, ARTHUR

| | | | | | | | |
|---|---|---|---|---|---|---|---|
| 1924-25 | 2 | 0 | 0-0 | .000 | | 2 | 0 | 0.0 |

SCHMELZER, GREG 6-6 b. 12-27-1952

| | | | | | | | | | | |
|---|---|---|---|---|---|---|---|---|---|---|
| 1971-72 | 12 | 8-22 | .364 | 5-8 | .625 | 15 | 1.3 | 9 | 21 | 1.7 |
| 1972-73 | 3 | 0-0 | .000 | 0-0 | .000 | 0 | 0.0 | 2 | 0 | 0.0 |
| 1973-74 | 9 | 4-13 | .308 | 0-0 | .000 | 6 | 0.7 | 4 | 8 | 0.8 |
| | 24 | 12-35 | .343 | 5-8 | .625 | 21 | 0.9 | 15 | 29 | 1.2 |

SCHNURR, EDWARD 6-0 b. 11-21-1940

| | | | | | | | | | | |
|---|---|---|---|---|---|---|---|---|---|---|
| 1959-60 | 9 | 26-69 | .377 | 29-39 | .744 | 21 | 2.3 | 12 | 81 | 9.0 |
| 1960-61 | 26 | 114-275 | .415 | 90-112 | .804 | 87 | 3.3 | 39 | 318 | 12.2 |
| 1961-62 | 23 | 118-305 | .387 | 82-104 | .788 | 153 | 6.7 | 41 | 318 | 13.8 |
| | 58 | 258-649 | .398 | 201-255 | .788 | 261 | 4.5 | 92 | 717 | 12.4 |

SCHRAEDER, WILLIAM 6-6 b. d. 10-19-1968

| | | | | | | | | | | |
|---|---|---|---|---|---|---|---|---|---|---|
| 1930-31 | 3 | 1 | | 0-0 | .000 | | | 1 | 2 | 0.7 |
| 1931-32 | 2 | 0 | | 0-0 | .000 | | | 2 | 0 | 0.0 |
| | 5 | 1 | | 0-0 | .000 | | | 3 | 2 | 0.4 |

SCHUCKMAN, MYRON 6-9 b. 1-4-1954

| | | | | | | | | | | |
|---|---|---|---|---|---|---|---|---|---|---|
| 1972-73 | 7 | 1-6 | .167 | 1-3 | .333 | 6 | 0.9 | 3 | 3 | 0.4 |
| 1973-74 | 13 | 3-6 | .500 | 2-4 | .500 | 7 | 0.5 | 4 | 8 | 0.6 |
| 1974-75 | 5 | 1-4 | .250 | 2-5 | .400 | 2 | 0.4 | 4 | 4 | 0.8 |
| 1975-76 | 15 | 3-6 | .500 | 5-5 | 1.000 | 12 | 0.8 | 6 | 11 | 0.8 |
| | 40 | 8-22 | .364 | 10-17 | .588 | 27 | 0.7 | 17 | 26 | 0.7 |

### SCHUMACHER, ALLAN

| | | | | | | | |
|---|---|---|---|---|---|---|---|
| 1930-31 | 16 | 3 | 1-6 | .167 | 11 | 7 | 0.4 |
| 1931-32 | 12 | 5 | 3-5 | .600 | 5 | 13 | 1.1 |
| | 28 | 8 | 4-11 | .364 | 16 | 20 | 0.7 |

### SHAW, LAWRENCE          d. 3-19-1977

| | | | | | | |
|---|---|---|---|---|---|---|
| 1919-20 | 2 | 0 | 0 | | 0 | 0.0 |

### SHEEHAN, THOMAS          6-2

| | | | | | | | |
|---|---|---|---|---|---|---|---|
| 1943-44 | 6 | 1 | 1-1 | 1.000 | 13 | 3 | 0.5 |

### SHEEHAN, WILLIAM          d. 6-21-1972

| | | | | | | |
|---|---|---|---|---|---|---|
| 1922-23 | 13 | 1 | 0-1 | .000 | 2 | 0.2 |

### SHEFFIELD, LARRY          6-1

| | | | | | | | | | |
|---|---|---|---|---|---|---|---|---|---|
| 1962-63 | 16 | 100-218 | .459 | 57-71 | .803 | 53 | 3.3 | 27 | 257 | 16.1 |
| 1963-64 | 24 | 214-496 | .431 | 107-142 | .754 | 86 | 3.6 | 49 | 535 | 22.3 |
| 1964-65 | 27 | 185-426 | .434 | 93-128 | .727 | 114 | 4.2 | 65 | 463 | 17.1 |
| | 67 | 499-1140 | .438 | 257-341 | .754 | 253 | 3.8 | 141 | 1255 | 18.7 |

### SHIELDS, LYMAN          6-2     b. 1-5-1915

| | | | | | | | |
|---|---|---|---|---|---|---|---|
| 1936-37 | 4 | 3 | 1-1 | 1.000 | 2 | 7 | 1.8 |
| 1937-38 | 2 | 1 | 0-0 | .000 | 0 | 2 | 1.0 |
| | 6 | 4 | 1-1 | 1.000 | 2 | 9 | 1.5 |

### SHILLINGTON, JOHN          d. 2-15-1898

| | | | | | | |
|---|---|---|---|---|---|---|
| 1896-97 | 3 | 10 | 7 | 5 | 27 | 9.0 |

### SHINE, ENTEE          6-2     b. 12-15-1930

| | | | | | | | |
|---|---|---|---|---|---|---|---|
| 1951-52 | 13 | 30-108 | .278 | 22-47 | .468 | 47 | 82 | 6.3 |

### SHUMATE, JOHN          6-9     b. 4-6-1952

| | | | | | | | | | |
|---|---|---|---|---|---|---|---|---|---|
| 1972-73 | 30 | 257-434 | .592 | 117-179 | .654 | 365 | 12.2 | 76 | 631 | 22.0 |
| 1973-74 | 29 | 281-448 | .627 | 141-196 | .719 | 319 | 11.0 | 65 | 703 | 24.2 |
| | 59 | 538-882 | .610 | 258-375 | .688 | 684 | 11.6 | 141 | 1334 | 22.6 |

### SILINSKI, DONALD          6-3     b. 5-19-1951

| | | | | | | | | | |
|---|---|---|---|---|---|---|---|---|---|
| 1970-71 | 11 | 10-15 | .667 | 2-2 | 1.000 | 14 | 1.3 | 6 | 22 | 2.0 |
| 1971-72 | 25 | 60-165 | .364 | 31-53 | .585 | 116 | 4.6 | 45 | 151 | 6.0 |
| 1972-73 | 24 | 34-83 | .410 | 15-26 | .576 | 44 | 1.8 | 39 | 83 | 3.5 |
| | 60 | 104-263 | .395 | 48-81 | .593 | 174 | 2.9 | 90 | 256 | 4.3 |

### SINGER, CYRINES          6-2     b. 5-7-1917

| | | | | | | | |
|---|---|---|---|---|---|---|---|
| 1940-41 | 22 | 63 | 19 | | 145 | 6.6 |
| 1941-42 | 19 | 41 | 10-18 | .556 | 23 | 92 | 4.8 |
| | 41 | 104 | 29 | | 237 | 5.8 |

### SINNOTT, THOMAS     6-4    b. 6-2-1949

| | | | | | | | | | | | |
|---|---|---|---|---|---|---|---|---|---|---|---|
| 1968-69 | 24 | 31-64 | .487 | 19-25 | .760 | 42 | 1.8 | 37 | 81 | 3.4 |
| 1969-70 | 27 | 59-133 | .444 | 19-30 | .633 | 92 | 3.4 | 61 | 137 | 5.1 |
| 1970-71 | 29 | 40-104 | .385 | 14-28 | .500 | 58 | 2.0 | 59 | 94 | 3.2 |
| | 80 | 130-301 | .432 | 52-83 | .627 | 192 | 2.4 | 157 | 312 | 3.9 |

### SITKO, STEVE     6-0    b. 11-16-1917

| | | | | | | |
|---|---|---|---|---|---|---|
| 1937-38 | 4 | 1 | 0 | | 2 | 0.5 |

### SKARICH, SAMUEL     6-4    b. 12-2-1942

| | | | | | | | | | | |
|---|---|---|---|---|---|---|---|---|---|---|
| 1961-62 | 3 | 1-8 | .125 | 1-1 | 1.000 | 5 | 1.7 | 0 | 3 | 1.0 |
| 1962-63 | 18 | 26-59 | .441 | 14-17 | .824 | 41 | 2.3 | 10 | 66 | 3.7 |
| 1963-64 | 22 | 83-181 | .459 | 24-37 | .649 | 56 | 2.5 | 20 | 190 | 8.6 |
| | 43 | 110-248 | .444 | 39-55 | .709 | 102 | 2.4 | 30 | 259 | 6.0 |

### SKRZYCKI, ROBERT     b. 10-12-1938

| | | | | | | | | | | |
|---|---|---|---|---|---|---|---|---|---|---|
| 1958-59 | 2 | 0-3 | .000 | 0-0 | .000 | 2 | 1.0 | 1 | 0 | 0.0 |
| 1959-60 | 2 | 1-3 | .333 | 2-2 | 1.000 | 0 | 0.0 | 1 | 4 | 2.0 |
| | 4 | 1-6 | .167 | 2-2 | 1.000 | 2 | 0.5 | 2 | 4 | 1.0 |

### SLACKFORD, FRED     6-0

| | | | | | | |
|---|---|---|---|---|---|---|
| 1915-16 | 3 | 1 | 0 | | 2 | 0.7 |

### SLUBY, TOM     6-4    b. 2-18-1962

| | | | | | | | | | | |
|---|---|---|---|---|---|---|---|---|---|---|
| 1980-81 | 27 | 36-70 | .514 | 14-21 | .667 | 38 | 1.4 | 51 | 86 | 3.2 |
| 1981-82 | 11 | 35-86 | .407 | 16-33 | .485 | 23 | 2.1 | 35 | 86 | 7.8 |
| 1982-83 | 27 | 57-110 | .518 | 22-26 | .846 | 47 | 1.7 | 63 | 136 | 5.0 |
| 1983-84 | 33 | 254-505 | .503 | 108-166 | .651 | 90 | 2.7 | 83 | 616 | 18.7 |
| | 98 | 382-771 | .495 | 160-246 | .650 | 198 | 2.0 | 241 | 924 | 9.4 |

### SMID, PATRICK     6-2    b. 2-10-1924

| | | | | | | | | | |
|---|---|---|---|---|---|---|---|---|---|
| 1943-44 | 1 | 0 | | 1-1 | 1.000 | | 0 | 1 | 1.0 |
| 1946-47 | 2 | 0-1 | .000 | 0-0 | .000 | | 1 | 0 | 0.0 |
| | 3 | 0 | | 1-1 | 1.000 | | 1 | 1 | 0.3 |

### SMITH, DON     6-2    b. 8-21-1918

| | | | | | | |
|---|---|---|---|---|---|---|
| 1938-39 | 1 | 0 | 4 | | 4 | 4.0 |
| 1939-40 | 19 | 11 | 4 | 21 | 26 | 1.4 |
| | 20 | 11 | 8 | | 30 | 1.5 |

### SMITH, EDWARD

| | | | | | | |
|---|---|---|---|---|---|---|
| 1927-28 | 21 | 27 | 19 | | 73 | 3.5 |
| 1928-29 | 19 | 23 | 21 | | 67 | 3.5 |
| 1929-30 | 20 | 33 | 15-25 | .600 | 31 | 81 | 4.1 |
| | 60 | 83 | 55 | | 221 | 3.7 |

### SMITH, FRANK

| | | | | | | | |
|---|---|---|---|---|---|---|---|
| 1935-36 | 2 | 0 | 0 | | | 0 | 0 | 0.0 |

### SMITH, MAURICE 5-10

| | | | | | | |
|---|---|---|---|---|---|---|
| 1917-18 | 4 | 0 | 0 | | 0 | 0.0 |
| 1918-19 | 9 | 2 | 0 | | 4 | 0.4 |
| 1920-21 | | | | | | |

### SMITH, ROBERT 6-1 b. 2-24-1920

| | | | | | | |
|---|---|---|---|---|---|---|
| 1938-39 | 10 | 5 | 2 | | | 12 | 1.2 |
| 1939-40 | 19 | 26 | 2 | | 21 | 54 | 2.8 |
| 1940-41 | 22 | 59 | 16 | | | 134 | 6.1 |
| | 51 | 90 | 20 | | | 200 | 3.9 |

### SMITH, WILLIAM 6-7 b. 5-28-1924

| | | | | | | | |
|---|---|---|---|---|---|---|---|
| 1943-44 | 5 | 4 | 2-8 | .250 | | 7 | 10 | 2.0 |

### SMITH,

| | | | | | | |
|---|---|---|---|---|---|---|
| 1911-12 | 4 | 0 | 0 | | 0 | 0.0 |
| 1912-13 | | | | | | |

### SMYTH, JOHN 6-5 b. 6-5-1934

| | | | | | | | | | | |
|---|---|---|---|---|---|---|---|---|---|---|
| 1954-55 | 24 | 122-368 | .332 | 70-108 | .649 | | | 97 | 314 | 13.1 |
| 1955-56 | 24 | 155-419 | .370 | 78-123 | .634 | | | 90 | 388 | 16.2 |
| 1956-57 | 28 | 208-463 | .449 | 118-156 | .756 | 423 | 15.1 | 101 | 534 | 19.1 |
| | 76 | 485-1250 | .388 | 266-387 | .687 | | | 288 | 1236 | 16.3 |

### SOBEK, ANDY 6-1 b. 7-1-1926

| | | | | | | | | |
|---|---|---|---|---|---|---|---|---|
| 1944-45 | 8 | 5 | | 1-4 | .250 | | 6 | 11 | 1.4 |
| 1947-48 | 1 | 0-1 | .000 | 0-0 | .000 | | 1 | 0 | 0.0 |
| | 9 | 5 | | 1-4 | .250 | | 7 | 11 | 1.2 |

### SOBEK, GEORGE 6-0 b. 2-10-1920

| | | | | | | | |
|---|---|---|---|---|---|---|---|
| 1939-40 | 17 | 46 | 37 | | | 31 | 129 | 7.6 |
| 1940-41 | 20 | 34 | 38 | | | | 106 | 5.3 |
| 1941-42 | 12 | 5 | 3-7 | .429 | | 10 | 13 | 1.1 |
| | 49 | 85 | 78 | | | | 248 | 5.1 |

### SOBEK, JOSEPH 5-11 b. 3-19-1923

| | | | | | | | | |
|---|---|---|---|---|---|---|---|---|
| 1945-46 | 7 | 5-24 | .208 | 4-5 | .800 | | 5 | 14 | 2.0 |
| 1946-47 | 7 | 6-19 | .316 | 5-8 | .625 | | 8 | 17 | 2.4 |
| | 14 | 11-43 | .256 | 9-13 | .692 | | 13 | 31 | 2.2 |

### SPENCER, BARRY 6-7 b. 7-3-1962

| | | | | | | | | | | |
|---|---|---|---|---|---|---|---|---|---|---|
| 1980-81 | 15 | 7-24 | .292 | 6-12 | .500 | 18 | 1.2 | 11 | 20 | 1.3 |

| | | | | | | | | | | |
|---|---|---|---|---|---|---|---|---|---|---|
| 1981-82 | 25 | 55-123 | .447 | 34-60 | .567 | 113 | 4.5 | 63 | 144 | 5.8 |
| 1983-84 | 5 | 1-4 | .250 | 2-4 | 500 | 8 | 1.6 | 3 | 4 | 0.8 |
| 1984-85 | 13 | 14-27 | .519 | 7-12 | .583 | 20 | 1.5 | 9 | 35 | 2.7 |
| | 58 | 77-178 | .433 | 49-88 | .557 | 159 | 2.7 | 86 | 203 | 3.5 |

**STAAB, FRED**     5-11   b. 10-10-1909

| | | | | | | | | | | |
|---|---|---|---|---|---|---|---|---|---|---|
| 1930-31 | 5 | 0 | | 1-1 | 1.000 | | | 1 | 1 | 0.2 |

**STALL, ROBERT**

| | | | | | | | | | | |
|---|---|---|---|---|---|---|---|---|---|---|
| 1940-41 | 1 | 0 | | 0 | | | | 0 | 0 | 0.0 |

**STEINER, THOMAS**

| | | | | | | | | | | |
|---|---|---|---|---|---|---|---|---|---|---|
| 1896-97 | 3 | 1 | | 0 | | | | 3 | 2 | 0.7 |
| 1897-98 | 3 | 0 | | 0 | | | | | 0 | 0.0 |
| | 6 | 1 | | 0 | | | | | 2 | 0.3 |

**STEPHENS, JACK**     6-3   b. 5-18-1933

| | | | | | | | | | |
|---|---|---|---|---|---|---|---|---|---|
| 1951-52 | 12 | 25-75 | .333 | 13-30 | .433 | | 16 | 63 | 5.3 |
| 1952-53 | 24 | 109-306 | .356 | 111-192 | .578 | | 49 | 329 | 13.7 |
| 1953-54 | 25 | 155-399 | .388 | 111-194 | .572 | | 60 | 421 | 16.8 |
| 1954-55 | 24 | 155-429 | .361 | 191-270 | .707 | | 54 | 501 | 20.9 |
| | 85 | 444-1209 | .368 | 426-686 | .592 | | 179 | 1314 | 15.5 |

**STEPHENSON, JOSEPH**

| | | | | | | | |
|---|---|---|---|---|---|---|---|
| 1910-11 | 2 | 1 | | 0 | | 2 | 1.0 |

**STEVENS, CHRIS**     6-6   b. 9-12-1952

| | | | | | | | | | | |
|---|---|---|---|---|---|---|---|---|---|---|
| 1971-72 | 25 | 44-132 | .333 | 34-52 | .654 | 117 | 4.7 | 46 | 122 | 4.8 |
| 1972-73 | 13 | 2-12 | .167 | 1-3 | .333 | 8 | 0.6 | 4 | 5 | 0.4 |
| 1973-74 | 9 | 6-12 | .500 | 0-1 | .000 | 5 | 0.6 | 3 | 12 | 1.3 |
| | 47 | 52-156 | .333 | 35-56 | .625 | 130 | 2.8 | 53 | 139 | 3.0 |

**STEVENSON, JAMES**

| | | | | | | | | |
|---|---|---|---|---|---|---|---|---|
| 1947-48 | 10 | 5-15 | .333 | 1-4 | .250 | | 7 | 11 | 1.1 |

**STINE, RALEIGH**       d. 8-27-1935

| | | | | | | | |
|---|---|---|---|---|---|---|---|
| 1917-18 | 6 | 5 | | 0 | | 10 | 1.7 |
| 1918-19 | 12 | 3 | | 0 | | 6 | 0.5 |
| | 18 | 8 | | 0 | | 16 | 0.9 |

**STRASSER, DONALD**     6-0   b. 7-20-1929

| | | | | | | | | | |
|---|---|---|---|---|---|---|---|---|---|
| 1949-50 | 24 | 88-273 | .322 | 39-68 | .574 | | 53 | 215 | 9.0 |
| 1950-51 | 3 | 7-34 | .206 | 9-10 | .900 | | 7 | 23 | 7.7 |
| 1951-52 | 15 | 36-118 | .305 | 14-25 | .570 | | 46 | 86 | 5.7 |
| | 42 | 131-425 | .308 | 62-103 | .602 | | 106 | 324 | 7.7 |

### STURM, OMER  6-0  b. 1-11-1922

| | | | | | | | | |
|---|---|---|---|---|---|---|---|---|
| 1941-42 | 3 | 0 | | 2-2 | 1.000 | | 0 | 2 | 0.7 |
| 1942-43 | 1 | 0 | | 0-0 | .000 | | 0 | 0 | 0.0 |
| | 4 | 0 | | 2-2 | 1.000 | | 0 | 2 | 0.5 |

### SUGARMAN, LOUIS
1908-09

### SULLIVAN, THOMAS  6-0  b. 1-21-1933

| | | | | | | | | | | |
|---|---|---|---|---|---|---|---|---|---|---|
| 1951-52 | 2 | 0-1 | .000 | 0-0 | .000 | | | 1 | 0 | 0.0 |
| 1952-53 | 8 | 9-20 | .450 | 1-2 | .500 | | | 8 | 19 | 2.4 |
| 1956-57 | 19 | 23-69 | .333 | 9-16 | .563 | 47 | 2.5 | 30 | 55 | 2.9 |
| | 29 | 32-90 | .356 | 10-18 | .556 | | | 39 | 74 | 2.6 |

### SULLIVAN, WILLIAM  6-0  b. 6-10-1932

| | | | | | | | | | |
|---|---|---|---|---|---|---|---|---|---|
| 1951-52 | 11 | 7-22 | .318 | 1-6 | .167 | | 15 | 15 | 1.4 |
| 1952-53 | 23 | 42-108 | .389 | 27-46 | .587 | | 45 | 111 | 4.8 |
| 1953-54 | 25 | 62-205 | .362 | 45-79 | .570 | | 73 | 169 | 6.8 |
| | 59 | 111-335 | .331 | 73-131 | .557 | | 133 | 295 | 5.0 |

### SWEENEY, CHARLES  6-0  b. 5-5-1914

| | | | | | | |
|---|---|---|---|---|---|---|
| 1935-36 | 7 | 5 | 2 | 2 | 12 | 1.7 |

### SWIFT, JAMES

| | | | | | | |
|---|---|---|---|---|---|---|
| 1921-22 | 1 | 0 | 0 | 0 | 0 | 0.0 |

### TEDERS, VINCENT

| | | | | | | | |
|---|---|---|---|---|---|---|---|
| 1928-29 | 6 | 4 | 2 | | 2 | 10 | 1.7 |
| 1929-30 | 1 | 0 | 0-0 | .000 | 0 | 0 | 0.0 |
| 1930-31 | 1 | 0 | 0-0 | .000 | 0 | 0 | 0.0 |
| | 8 | 4 | 2 | | 2 | 10 | 1.3 |

### TOBIN, JOHN  5-8

| | | | | | | | |
|---|---|---|---|---|---|---|---|
| 1931-32 | 1 | 0 | 0-0 | .000 | 0 | 0 | 0.0 |

### TODOROVICH, MARKO  6-4  b. 6-11-1923

| | | | | | | | |
|---|---|---|---|---|---|---|---|
| 1943-44 | 18 | 54 | 19-45 | .422 | 55 | 127 | 7.1 |

### TOWNSEND, MICHAEL  6-3  b. 3-19-1952

| | | | | | | | | | | |
|---|---|---|---|---|---|---|---|---|---|---|
| 1971-72 | 24 | 35-86 | .407 | 17-33 | .515 | 84 | 3.5 | 38 | 87 | 3.6 |
| 1972-73 | 7 | 2-10 | .200 | 0-1 | .000 | 4 | 0.6 | 3 | 4 | 0.6 |
| | 31 | 37-96 | .385 | 17-34 | .500 | 88 | 2.8 | 41 | 91 | 2.9 |

### TOWNSEND, WILLIE  6-3  b. 11-9-1949

| | | | | | | | | | | |
|---|---|---|---|---|---|---|---|---|---|---|
| 1971-72 | 26 | 108-245 | .437 | 26-50 | .520 | 177 | 6.8 | 86 | 242 | 9.3 |

| 1972-73 | 16 | 16-24 | .667 | 1-4 | .250 | 13 | 0.8 | 14 | 33 | 2.1 |
|---|---|---|---|---|---|---|---|---|---|---|
| | 42 | 124-269 | .461 | 27-54 | .500 | 190 | 4.5 | 100 | 275 | 6.5 |

TRACY, JOHN    6-3    b. 1-22-1946

| 1965-66 | 14 | 12-37 | .324 | 11-17 | .647 | 15 | 1.1 | 5 | 35 | 2.5 |
|---|---|---|---|---|---|---|---|---|---|---|
| 1966-67 | 7 | 4-13 | .308 | 1-1 | 1.000 | 6 | 0.9 | 2 | 9 | 1.3 |
| | 21 | 16-50 | .320 | 12-18 | .667 | 21 | 1.0 | 7 | 44 | 2.1 |

TRAFTON, GEORGE    6-2    d. 9-5-1971

| 1919-20 | 2 | 4 | | 1 | | | | | 9 | 4.5 |
|---|---|---|---|---|---|---|---|---|---|---|

TRIPUCKA, KELLY    6-6    b. 2-16-1959

| 1977-78 | 31 | 141-247 | .571 | 80-108 | .741 | 161 | 5.2 | 52 | 362 | 11.7 |
|---|---|---|---|---|---|---|---|---|---|---|
| 1978-79 | 29 | 143-277 | .516 | 129-151 | .854 | 125 | 4.3 | 59 | 415 | 14.3 |
| 1979-80 | 23 | 150-270 | .556 | 115-151 | .762 | 151 | 6.6 | 66 | 415 | 18.0 |
| 1980-81 | 29 | 195-354 | .551 | 137-168 | .815 | 169 | 5.8 | 81 | 527 | 18.2 |
| | 112 | 629-1148 | .548 | 461-578 | .798 | 606 | 5.4 | 258 | 1719 | 15.8 |

TRUMP, DEAN    6-8    b. 9-6-1925

| 1943-44 | 8 | 1 | | 1-1 | 1.000 | | | 0 | 3 | 0.4 |
|---|---|---|---|---|---|---|---|---|---|---|

TULLY, JOHN    6-7    b. 6-3-1939

| 1958-59 | 18 | 56-134 | .418 | 44-70 | .629 | 131 | 7.3 | 55 | 156 | 8.7 |
|---|---|---|---|---|---|---|---|---|---|---|
| 1959-60 | 22 | 67-177 | .379 | 44-67 | .657 | 137 | 6.2 | 54 | 178 | 8.1 |
| 1960-61 | 25 | 106-264 | .402 | 66-119 | .555 | 215 | 8.6 | 86 | 278 | 11.1 |
| | 65 | 229-575 | .398 | 154-256 | .602 | 483 | 7.4 | 195 | 612 | 9.4 |

ULATOWSKI, CLEMENT    b. 11-21-1887

| 1909-10 | 14 | 15 | | 3 | | | | | 33 | 2.4 |
|---|---|---|---|---|---|---|---|---|---|---|
| 1910-11 | 10 | 9 | | 0 | | | | | 18 | 1.8 |
| | 24 | 24 | | 3 | | | | | 51 | 2.1 |

VALES, JOSEPH    6-2

| 1964-65 | 3 | 1-1 | 1.000 | 0-0 | .000 | 0 | 0.0 | 0 | 2 | 0.7 |
|---|---|---|---|---|---|---|---|---|---|---|
| 1965-66 | 4 | 4-19 | .211 | 3-4 | .750 | 10 | 2.5 | 10 | 11 | 2.8 |
| | 7 | 5-20 | .250 | 3-4 | .750 | 10 | 1.4 | 10 | 13 | 1.9 |

VALES, RAY    6-1    b. 3-8-1939

| 1958-59 | 1 | 0-0 | .000 | 1-1 | 1.000 | 0 | 0.0 | 1 | 1 | 1.0 |
|---|---|---|---|---|---|---|---|---|---|---|
| 1959-60 | 3 | 0-1 | .000 | 0-0 | .000 | 0 | 0.0 | 0 | 0 | 0.0 |
| 1960-61 | 9 | 6-14 | .429 | 0-3 | .000 | 6 | 0.7 | 2 | 12 | 1.3 |
| | 13 | 6-15 | .400 | 1-4 | .250 | 6 | 0.5 | 3 | 13 | 1.0 |

VALIBUS, ROBERT    6-3    b. 5-7-1952

| 1971-72 | 6 | 20-68 | .294 | 14-21 | .667 | 12 | 2.0 | 33 | 54 | 9.0 |
|---|---|---|---|---|---|---|---|---|---|---|

VANCE, ROBERT

| 1909-10 | 2 | 18 | | 0 | | | | | 36 | 18.0 |
|---|---|---|---|---|---|---|---|---|---|---|

VAN DYKE, LEWIS

| 1919-20 | 1 | 0 | | 0 | | | | | 0 | 0.0 |
|---|---|---|---|---|---|---|---|---|---|---|

VARGA, THOMAS          5-11   b. 7-5-1953

| 1972-73 | 5 | 6-7 | .857 | 0-2 | .000 | 3 | 0.6 | 4 | 12 | 2.4 |
|---|---|---|---|---|---|---|---|---|---|---|
| 1973-74 | 2 | 2-3 | .667 | 0-0 | .000 | 0 | 0.0 | 0 | 4 | 2.0 |
| 1974-75 | 7 | 5-8 | .625 | 0-0 | .000 | 4 | 0.6 | 2 | 10 | 1.4 |
| | 14 | 13-18 | .722 | 0-2 | .000 | 7 | 0.5 | 6 | 26 | 1.9 |

VARNER, BILL          6-6   b. 8-1-1960

| 1979-80 | 24 | 36-76 | .474 | 16-23 | .696 | 44 | 1.8 | 23 | 88 | 3.7 |
|---|---|---|---|---|---|---|---|---|---|---|
| 1980-81 | 29 | 53-100 | .530 | 36-58 | .621 | 60 | 2.1 | 30 | 142 | 4.9 |
| 1981-82 | 26 | 113-238 | .475 | 33-46 | .717 | 160 | 6.2 | 70 | 259 | 10.0 |
| 1982-83 | 27 | 134-222 | .604 | 31-47 | .660 | 129 | 4.8 | 59 | 299 | 11.1 |
| | 106 | 336-636 | .528 | 116-174 | .667 | 393 | 3.7 | 182 | 788 | 7.4 |

VAUGHAN, JAMES

| 1926-27 | 1 | 0 | | 0 | | | | 0 | 0 | 0.0 |
|---|---|---|---|---|---|---|---|---|---|---|

VAUGHAN, ROBERT          d. 2-17-1969
1908-09

VIGNALI, ANTHONY          6-6   b. 12-9-1946

| 1965-66 | 20 | 40-120 | .333 | 55-71 | .775 | 90 | 4.5 | 36 | 135 | 6.8 |
|---|---|---|---|---|---|---|---|---|---|---|
| 1966-67 | 3 | 0-2 | .000 | 0-0 | .000 | 2 | 0.7 | 0 | 0 | 0.0 |
| 1967-68 | 10 | 3-16 | .188 | 5-7 | .714 | 15 | 1.5 | 4 | 11 | 1.1 |
| | 33 | 43-138 | .312 | 60-78 | .769 | 107 | 3.2 | 40 | 146 | 4.4 |

VIKTORYN, JOHN

| 1925-26 | 10 | 10 | | 4 | | | | | 24 | 2.4 |
|---|---|---|---|---|---|---|---|---|---|---|
| 1926-27 | 1 | 0 | | 0 | | | | 1 | 0 | 0.0 |
| 1927-28 | 2 | 0 | | 0 | | | | 0 | 0 | 0.0 |
| | 13 | 10 | | 4 | | | | | 24 | 1.8 |

VINCIGUERRA, RALPH          6-0   b. 5-24-1922

| 1940-41 | 7 | 1 | | 2-2 | 1.000 | | | 2 | 4 | 0.6 |
|---|---|---|---|---|---|---|---|---|---|---|
| 1941-42 | 4 | 4 | | 1-1 | 1.000 | | | 1 | 9 | 2.3 |
| 1942-43 | 13 | 6 | | 1 | | | | 9 | 13 | 1.0 |
| | 24 | 11 | | 4 | | | | 12 | 26 | 1.1 |

VOCE, GARY          6-9   b. 11-24-1965

| 1984-85 | 27 | 25-41 | .610 | 10-19 | .526 | 64 | 2.4 | 22 | 60 | 2.2 |
|---|---|---|---|---|---|---|---|---|---|---|

**VOEDISCH, JOHN**    6-1   b.     d. 11- -1972

| | | | | | | | |
|---|---|---|---|---|---|---|---|
| 1925-26 | 3 | 0 | 0-0 | .000 | 0 | 0 | 0.0 |
| 1926-27 | 1 | 0 | 0 | | 2 | 0 | 0.0 |
| | 4 | 0 | 0 | | 2 | 0 | 0.0 |

**VOEGELE, JOSEPH**    6-1

| | | | | | | | | |
|---|---|---|---|---|---|---|---|---|
| 1931-32 | 18 | 28 | | 19-39 | .487 | 19 | 75 | 3.8 |
| 1932-33 | 22 | 74-254 | .291 | 50-96 | .521 | 51 | 198 | 9.0 |
| 1933-34 | 23 | 57 | | 45-89 | .506 | 51 | 159 | 6.9 |
| | 63 | 159 | | 114-224 | .509 | 121 | 432 | 6.9 |

**VOGLEWEDE, ROBERT**

| | | | | | | |
|---|---|---|---|---|---|---|
| 1926-27 | 6 | 4 | 2 | | 10 | 1.7 |
| 1927-28 | 13 | 4 | 0 | 3 | 8 | 0.6 |
| 1928-29 | 4 | 2 | 2 | 6 | 6 | 1.5 |
| | 23 | 10 | 4 | | 24 | 1.0 |

**VOHS, DALE**

| | | | | | |
|---|---|---|---|---|---|
| 1918-19 | 7 | 4 | 0 | 8 | 1.1 |

**WADE, FRANK**    6-0

| | | | | | | | |
|---|---|---|---|---|---|---|---|
| 1933-34 | 2 | 1 | 0-1 | .000 | 1 | 2 | 0.7 |
| 1934-35 | 21 | 13 | 7 | | 32 | 33 | 1.6 |
| 1935-36 | 23 | 26 | 17 | | | 69 | 3.0 |
| | 47 | 40 | 24 | | | 104 | 2.2 |

**WAGNER, LEWIS**    6-0   b. 9-6-1918

| | | | | | | |
|---|---|---|---|---|---|---|
| 1937-38 | 3 | 0 | 0 | | 0 | 0.0 |
| 1938-39 | 2 | 0 | 3 | | 3 | 1.5 |
| 1939-40 | 1 | 0 | 0-0 | .000 | 0 | 0 | 0.0 |
| | 6 | 0 | 3 | | 3 | 0.5 |

**WALKER, THOMAS**    6-2   b. 2- -1918

| | | | | | | | |
|---|---|---|---|---|---|---|---|
| 1936-37 | 1 | 0 | 0-0 | .000 | 0 | 0 | 0.0 |
| 1937-38 | 1 | 0 | 0-0 | .000 | 0 | 0 | 0.0 |
| | 2 | 0 | 0-0 | .000 | 0 | 0 | 0.0 |

**WALLJASPER, DENNIS**    6-5   b. 2-25-1939

| | | | | | | | | | | |
|---|---|---|---|---|---|---|---|---|---|---|
| 1958-59 | 1 | 0-0 | .000 | 0-1 | .000 | 0 | 0.0 | 1 | 0 | 0.0 |
| 1959-60 | 2 | 0-0 | .000 | 2-2 | 1.000 | 2 | 1.0 | 2 | 2 | 1.0 |
| 1960-61 | 10 | 7-21 | .333 | 3-8 | .375 | 30 | 3.0 | 11 | 17 | 1.7 |
| | 13 | 7-21 | .333 | 5-11 | .455 | 32 | 2.5 | 14 | 19 | 1.5 |

**WALSH, ADAM**    6-0   b. 12-4-1901    d. 1-13-1985

| | | | | | |
|---|---|---|---|---|---|
| 1923-24 | 8 | 0 | 0 | 0 | 0.0 |

### WALSH, ROBERT

| | | | | | | | |
|---|---|---|---|---|---|---|---|
| 1909-10 | 4 | 2 | | 0 | | 4 | 1.0 |
| 1910-11 | 6 | 1 | | 0 | | 2 | 0.3 |
| | 10 | 3 | | 0 | | 6 | 0.6 |

### WARD, GILBERT                          6-1

| | | | | | | | |
|---|---|---|---|---|---|---|---|
| 1914-15 | 8 | 10 | | 3 | | 23 | 2.9 |
| 1915-16 | 2 | 1 | | 0 | | 2 | 1.0 |
| | 10 | 11 | | 3 | | 25 | 2.5 |

### WARD, LEO

| | | | | | | | |
|---|---|---|---|---|---|---|---|
| 1918-19 | 10 | 14 | | 0 | | 28 | 2.8 |
| 1919-20 | 4 | 0 | | 0 | | 0 | 0.0 |
| | 14 | 14 | | 0 | | 28 | 2.0 |

### WARD,

| | | | | | | | |
|---|---|---|---|---|---|---|---|
| 1923-24 | 14 | 9 | | 6 | | 24 | 1.7 |

### WEIMAN, WILLIAM                 6-2      b. 9-30-1934

| | | | | | | | | | |
|---|---|---|---|---|---|---|---|---|---|
| 1953-54 | 22 | 27-76 | .355 | 15-36 | .417 | | 60 | 69 | 3.1 |
| 1954-55 | 24 | 65-214 | .304 | 41-80 | .513 | | 91 | 171 | 7.1 |
| 1955-56 | 24 | 60-201 | .299 | 41-72 | .569 | | 87 | 161 | 6.7 |
| | 70 | 152-491 | .310 | 97-188 | .516 | | 238 | 401 | 5.7 |

### WENTWORTH, GEORGE

| | | | | | | | | | |
|---|---|---|---|---|---|---|---|---|---|
| 1933-34 | 1 | 0 | | 0-0 | .000 | | 0 | 0 | 0.0 |
| 1934-35 | 5 | 3 | | 0 | | | 1 | 6 | 1.2 |
| 1935-36 | 2 | 2 | | 0 | | | 0 | 4 | 2.0 |
| | 8 | 5 | | 0 | | | 1 | 10 | 1.3 |

### WHITE, JIM                          6-2      b. 2-8-1921

| | | | | | | | | |
|---|---|---|---|---|---|---|---|---|
| 1940-41 | 3 | 3 | | 0-1 | .000 | | 1 | 6 | 2.0 |

### WHITMORE, ROBERT             6-7      b. 9-3-1946

| | | | | | | | | | | | |
|---|---|---|---|---|---|---|---|---|---|---|---|
| 1966-67 | 28 | 173-354 | .489 | 112-187 | .599 | 384 | 13.7 | 90 | 458 | 16.4 |
| 1967-68 | 30 | 252-524 | .481 | 157-219 | .717 | 414 | 13.8 | 85 | 661 | 22.0 |
| 1968-69 | 26 | 184-403 | .457 | 93-137 | .679 | 245 | 9.4 | 90 | 461 | 17.7 |
| | 84 | 609-1281 | .475 | 362-543 | .667 | 1043 | 12.4 | 265 | 1580 | 18.8 |

### WILCOX, HUGHES                  6-6      b. 9-10-1930

| | | | | | | | | | |
|---|---|---|---|---|---|---|---|---|---|
| 1949-50 | 12 | 5-17 | .294 | 3-6 | .500 | | 13 | 13 | 1.1 |
| 1950-51 | 16 | 3-20 | .150 | 3-5 | .600 | | 19 | 9 | 0.6 |
| | 28 | 8-37 | .216 | 6-11 | .545 | | 32 | 22 | 0.8 |

WILCOX, PERCY

| | | | | | | | | | |
|---|---|---|---|---|---|---|---|---|---|
| 1920-21 | | | | | | | | | |
| 1921-22 | 2 | 0 | | 0 | | | | 0 | 0.0 |

WILCOX, STAN      6-3    b. 3-22-1959

| | | | | | | | | | |
|---|---|---|---|---|---|---|---|---|---|
| 1977-78 | 29 | 30-61 | .492 | 12-18 | .667 | 23 | 0.8 | 38 | 72 | 2.5 |
| 1978-79 | 28 | 46-107 | .430 | 16-19 | .842 | 26 | 0.9 | 32 | 108 | 3.9 |
| 1979-80 | 24 | 28-69 | .406 | 12-15 | .800 | 14 | 0.6 | 26 | 68 | 2.8 |
| 1980-81 | 19 | 11-28 | .393 | 0-4 | .000 | 3 | 0.2 | 7 | 22 | 1.2 |
| | 100 | 115-265 | .434 | 40-56 | .714 | 66 | 0.7 | 103 | 270 | 2.7 |

WILLIAMS, DON      6-3    b. 8-2-1956

| | | | | | | | | | |
|---|---|---|---|---|---|---|---|---|---|
| 1974-75 | 27 | 67-170 | .394 | 23-32 | .719 | 36 | 1.3 | 38 | 157 | 5.8 |
| 1975-76 | 29 | 146-300 | .487 | 59-83 | .711 | 63 | 2.2 | 61 | 351 | 12.1 |
| 1976-77 | 29 | 212-414 | .512 | 102-132 | .773 | 74 | 2.6 | 55 | 526 | 18.1 |
| 1977-78 | 30 | 165-337 | .490 | 69-91 | .758 | 48 | 1.6 | 71 | 399 | 13.3 |
| | 115 | 590-1221 | .483 | 253-338 | .749 | 221 | 1.9 | 225 | 1433 | 12.5 |

WILLIAMS, FRED                    d. 4-23-1974

| | | | | | | | |
|---|---|---|---|---|---|---|---|
| 1909-10 | 1 | 0 | | 0 | | | 0 | 0.0 |

WILLIAMS, JAMES      6-3    b. 1-15-1937

| | | | | | | | | | |
|---|---|---|---|---|---|---|---|---|---|
| 1956-57 | 5 | 7-11 | .636 | 1-2 | .500 | 7 | 1.4 | 5 | 15 | 3.0 |
| 1957-58 | 14 | 14-35 | .400 | 6-8 | .750 | 27 | 1.9 | 17 | 34 | 2.4 |
| | 19 | 21-46 | .457 | 7-10 | .700 | 34 | 1.8 | 22 | 49 | 2.6 |

WILSON,

| | | | | | | | |
|---|---|---|---|---|---|---|---|
| 1935-36 | 1 | 0 | | 0 | | | 0 | 0 | 0.0 |

WISE, RICHARD      6-9    b. 6-25-1933

| | | | | | | | | |
|---|---|---|---|---|---|---|---|---|
| 1951-52 | 2 | 1-2 | .500 | 0-0 | .000 | | 0 | 2 | 1.0 |
| 1952-53 | 14 | 6-17 | .353 | 3-14 | .214 | | 17 | 15 | 1.1 |
| | 16 | 7-19 | .368 | 3-14 | .214 | | 17 | 17 | 1.1 |

WITTENBURG, CHARLES      6-3    b. 4-24-1935

| | | | | | | | | | |
|---|---|---|---|---|---|---|---|---|---|
| 1955-56 | 1 | 0-0 | .000 | 0-0 | .000 | | | 0 | 0 | 0.0 |
| 1956-57 | 2 | 2-3 | .667 | 2-2 | 1.000 | 0 | 0.0 | 0 | 6 | 3.0 |
| | 3 | 2-3 | .667 | 2-2 | 1.000 | | | 0 | 6 | 2.0 |

WOLBECK, KEN      6-7    b. 10-15-1951

| | | | | | | | | | |
|---|---|---|---|---|---|---|---|---|---|
| 1971-72 | 6 | 3-10 | .300 | 4-5 | .800 | 4 | 0.7 | 4 | 10 | 1.7 |
| 1972-73 | 13 | 10-31 | .323 | 7-8 | .875 | 11 | 0.8 | 9 | 27 | 2.0 |
| 1973-74 | 2 | 2-5 | .400 | 0-0 | .000 | 0 | 0.0 | 0 | 4 | 2.0 |
| | 21 | 15-46 | .326 | 11-13 | .846 | 15 | 0.7 | 13 | 41 | 2.0 |

### WOLF, CHARLES

| | | | | | | | | |
|---|---|---|---|---|---|---|---|---|
| 1946-47 | 6 | 3-12 | .250 | 2-3 | .667 | 5 | 8 | 1.3 |

### WOOD, FAY    6-0   b.        d. 5-5-1925
1907-08
1908-09

### WOOLRIDGE, ORLANDO    6-9   b. 12-16-1959

| | | | | | | | | | |
|---|---|---|---|---|---|---|---|---|---|
| 1977-78 | 24 | 41-78 | .526 | 16-33 | .485 | 51 | 2.1 | 24 | 98 | 4.1 |
| 1978-79 | 30 | 145-253 | .573 | 41-56 | .732 | 145 | 4.8 | 56 | 331 | 11.0 |
| 1979-80 | 27 | 124-212 | .585 | 81-117 | .692 | 186 | 6.9 | 76 | 329 | 12.2 |
| 1980-81 | 28 | 156-240 | .650 | 90-135 | .667 | 168 | 6.0 | 67 | 402 | 14.4 |
| | 109 | 466-783 | .595 | 228-341 | .669 | 550 | 5.0 | 223 | 1160 | 10.6 |

### WRAY, ROBERT    6-4   b. 7-10-1930

| | | | | | | | | |
|---|---|---|---|---|---|---|---|---|
| 1949-50 | 17 | 10-39 | .256 | 5-14 | .357 | 23 | 25 | 1.5 |
| 1950-51 | 18 | 18-60 | .300 | 16-28 | .571 | 39 | 52 | 2.9 |
| 1951-52 | 3 | 0-4 | .000 | 1-2 | .500 | 6 | 1 | 0.3 |
| | 38 | 28-103 | .272 | 22-44 | .500 | 68 | 78 | 2.1 |

### WUKOVITS, THOMAS    6-0

| | | | | | | | |
|---|---|---|---|---|---|---|---|
| 1935-36 | 20 | 25 | | 6 | | 56 | 2.8 |
| 1936-37 | 23 | 34 | | 27-41 | .659 | 29 | 95 | 4.1 |
| 1937-38 | 23 | 60 | | 40 | | 160 | 7.0 |
| | 66 | 119 | | 73 | | 311 | 4.7 |

### YEZERSKI, SAM

| | | | | | | |
|---|---|---|---|---|---|---|
| 1938-39 | 10 | 12 | 2 | | 26 | 2.6 |
| 1939-40 | 8 | 2 | 4 | 0 | 8 | 1.0 |
| 1940-41 | 8 | 3 | 2 | 1 | 8 | 1.0 |
| | 26 | 17 | 8 | | 42 | 1.6 |

### ZGODZINSKI, LEO    d. 1-17-1978

| | | | | | |
|---|---|---|---|---|---|
| 1911-12 | 2 | 2 | 0 | 4 | 2.0 |

### ZIEGENHORN, MAURICE

| | | | | | |
|---|---|---|---|---|---|
| 1938-39 | 17 | 19 | 12 | 50 | 2.9 |

### ZIEMBA, WALT    6-3   b. 7-19-1919

| | | | | | | |
|---|---|---|---|---|---|---|
| 1940-41 | 1 | 0 | 1 | 4 | 1 | 1.0 |

### ZIZNEWSKI, JAY    6-6   b. 3-6-1949

| | | | | | | | | | |
|---|---|---|---|---|---|---|---|---|---|
| 1967-68 | 3 | 3-9 | .333 | 2-6 | .333 | 10 | 3.3 | 3 | 8 | 2.7 |
| 1968-69 | 4 | 1-2 | .500 | 0-1 | .000 | 3 | 0.8 | 1 | 2 | 0.5 |
| 1969-70 | 23 | 34-66 | .515 | 16-40 | .400 | 88 | 3.8 | 36 | 84 | 3.7 |
| | 30 | 38-77 | .494 | 18-47 | .383 | 101 | 3.4 | 40 | 94 | 3.1 |

# Women's All-Time Game-By-Game Scores

**1974-75** (Won 3, Lost 4, .429)
Coach: Jeanne Earley
Captain: Mary Clemency and Patty Coogan

| Jan. 30 | Michigan State | (A) | L | 23 | 84 |
|---|---|---|---|---|---|
| Feb. 1 | Toledo | (H) | L | 31 | 50 |
| Feb. 6 | Saint Mary's | (H) | L | 46 | 53 |
| Feb. 8 | Ball State | (H) | L | 31 | 78 |
| Feb. 13 | Kalamazoo | (H) | W | 44 | 36 |
| Feb. 15 | Lewis College | (A) | W | 50 | 45 |
| Feb. 22 | Saint Mary's | (H) | W | 38 | 37 |
| | | | | 263 | 383 |

**1975-76** (Won 6, Lost 7, .462)
Coaches: Jeanne Earley and Sally Duffy
Captains: Becky Banasiak, Mary Clemency and Patty Coogan

| Dec. 13 | Grace | (H) | L | 37 | 62 |
|---|---|---|---|---|---|
| Jan. 17 | IUPU-Fort Wayne | (A) | L | 49 | 58 |
| Jan. 24 | Saint Mary's | (H) | L | 50 | 59 |
| Jan. 31 | Northwestern | (H) | W | 43 | 34 |
| Feb. 5 | Albion | (A) | W | 42 | 33 |
| Feb. 7 | Marquette | (A) | L | 47 | 52 |
| Feb. 10 | St. Joseph's (IN) | (A) | W | 47 | 32 |
| Feb. 13 | IUPU-Fort Wayne | (H) | W | 56 | 49 |
| Feb. 14 | Northern Illinois | (H) | L | 26 | 52 |
| Feb. 19 | St. Joseph's (IN) | (H) | W | 51 | 47 |
| Feb. 21 | St. Francis (IN) | (A) | W | 49 | 44 |
| Feb. 25 | Saint Mary's | (H) | L | 27 | 28 |
| Feb. 28 | Marquette | (H) | L | 41 | 45 |
| | | | | 565 | 595 |

**1976-77** (Won 9, Lost 6, .600)
Coach: Sally Duffy
Captains: Carol Lally and Maureen Maloney

| Dec. 4 | Saint Mary's | (H) | W | 56 | 35 |
|---|---|---|---|---|---|
| Dec. 9 | Grace | (A) | W | 75 | 48 |
| Jan. 19 | Northwestern | (H) | L | 44 | 63 |
| Jan. 21 | IUPU-Fort Wayne | (H) | W | 52 | 44 |
| Jan. 31 | Saint Mary's | (H) | W | 63 | 59 |
| Feb. 4 | St. Joseph's (IN) | (H) | W | 57 | 43 |

| Feb. 5 | Northern Illinois | (H) | W | 54 | 43 |
|---|---|---|---|---|---|
| Feb. 9 | Marion | (A) | L | 48 | 76 |
| Feb. 12 | Goshen | (H) | L | 42 | 49 |
| Feb. 15 | Bethel | (A) | W | 50 | 29 |
| Feb. 17 | Chicago State | (H) | L | 39 | 63 |
| Feb. 19 | IUPU-Fort Wayne | (A) | L | 55 | 67 |
| Feb. 22 | St. Francis (IN) | (A) | W | 71 | 62 |
| Feb. 25 | IUPU-Fort Wayne–(IWISO N. District Tournament) | (N) | L | 45 | 47 |
| Feb. 25 | Grace–(IWISO N. District Tournament) | (N) | W | 61 | 57 |
| | | | | 812 | 785 |

N–Valparaiso, IN.

1977-78 (Won 13, Lost 4, .765)
Coach: Sharon Petro
Captains: Carol Lally and Marge Meagher

| Dec. 3 | Valparaiso | (H) | W | 48 | 41 |
|---|---|---|---|---|---|
| Dec. 6 | St. Joseph's (IN) | (A) | W | 79 | 67 |
| Jan. 18 | Purdue-Calumet | (A) | W | 50 | 46 |
| Jan. 24 | IUPU-Fort Wayne | (H) | W | 68 | 39 |
| Jan. 31 | Grace | (H) | W | 68 | 25 |
| Feb. 3 | Marquette | (A) | L | 41 | 66 |
| Feb. 6 | Saint Mary's | (H) | W | 61 | 51 |
| Feb. 9 | Manchester | (A) | W | 74 | 49 |
| Feb. 11 | Northern Illinois | (H) | L | 58 | 65 |
| Feb. 13 | Goshen | (A) | W | 62 | 57 |
| Feb. 15 | Indiana Tech | (A) | W | 68 | 51 |
| Feb. 18 | Marion | (H) | W | 62 | 50 |
| Feb. 20 | Saint Mary's | (A) | W | 69 | 59 |
| Feb. 24 | Huntington–(IAIAW N. District Tournament) | (N) | W | 65 | 52 |
| Feb. 25 | St. Francis (IN)–(IAIAW N. District Tournament) | (N) | W | 61 | 45 |
| Mar. 4 | Vincennes–(IAIAW State Tournament) | (N) | L | 69 | 73 |
| Mar. 5 | St. Joseph's (IN)–(IAIAW State Tournament) | (A) | L | 64 | 65 |
| | | | | 1067 | 901 |

N–Rensselaer, IN.

1978-79 (Won 16, Lost 6, .727)
Coach: Sharon Petro
Captains: Carol Lally and Molly Cashman

| Nov. 18 | Clarke | (H) | W | 81 | 51 |
|---|---|---|---|---|---|
| Nov. 28 | Illinois | (A) | L | 60 | 81 |

| Dec. 1 | Valparaiso | (A) | W | 74 | 56 |
|---|---|---|---|---|---|
| Dec. 19 | Valparaiso – (Huntington Tournament) | (N1) | W | 66 | 52 |
| Dec. 9 | Huntington – (Huntington Tournament) | (A) | W | 74 | 66 |
| Dec. 11 | Saint Mary's | (H) | W | 71 | 54 |
| Jan. 12 | Upper Iowa – (Huskie Invitational) | (N2) | W | 71 | 49 |
| Jan. 12 | Northern Illinois – (Huskie Invitational) | (A) | W | 62 | 60 |
| Jan. 13 | Chicago State – (Huskie Invitational) | (N2) | W | 78 | 55 |
| Jan. 20 | Michigan | (A) | L | 66 | 93 |
| Jan. 22 | Valparaiso | (H) | W | 57 | 43 |
| Jan. 24 | IUPU-Fort Wayne | (A) | W | 49 | 41 |
| Jan. 27 | Saint Mary's | (A) | W | 70 | 43 |
| Jan. 30 | DePaul | (A) | L | 53 | 82 |
| Feb. 3 | Marquette | (H) | W | 60 | 57 |
| Feb. 10 | Goshen | (H) | W | 68 | 64 |
| Feb. 13 | St. Joseph's (IN) | (A) | L | 62 | 67 |
| Feb. 16 | Marion | (A) | L | 63 | 65 |
| Feb. 22 | Valparaiso – (IAIAW N. District Tournament) | (N3) | W | 52 | 49 |
| Feb. 23 | Saint Mary's – (IAIAW N. District Tournament) | (N3) | W | 61 | 49 |
| Feb. 24 | St. Joseph's (IN) (OT) – (IAIAW N. District Tournament) | (A) | W | 70 | 69 |
| Mar. 1 | Franklin – (IAIAW State Tournament) | (N4) | L | 64 | 69 |
| | | | | 1432 | 1315 |

N1 – Huntington, IN.; N2 – DeKalb, IL.; N3 – Rensselaer, IN.; N4 – Terre Haute, IN.

1979-80 (Won 20, Lost 10, .667)
Coach: Sharon Petro
Captains: Molly Cashman and Jane Politiski

| Nov. 30 | Marion – (Taylor Invitational) | (N1) | W | 68 | 60 |
|---|---|---|---|---|---|
| Dec. 1 | Cedarville – (Taylor Invitational) | (N1) | W | 73 | 60 |
| Dec. 4 | Saint Mary's | (A) | W | 81 | 45 |
| Dec. 8 | Michigan (OT) | (H) | L | 60 | 66 |
| Jan. 11 | SIU-Edwardsville – (Huskie Invitational) | (N2) | W | 65 | 51 |
| Jan. 11 | Chicago State – (Huskie Invitational) | (N2) | W | 68 | 61 |
| Jan. 12 | Northeast Missouri State – (Huskie Invitational) | (N2) | L | 43 | 77 |

| Jan. 14 | South Dakota | (A) | L | 61 | 76 |
|---------|--------------|-----|---|----|----|
| Jan. 16 | St. Joseph's (IN) | (H) | W | 72 | 64 |
| Jan. 18 | St. Ambrose | (H) | W | 54 | 52 |
| Jan. 20 | St. Louis | (H) | L | 49 | 65 |
| Jan. 22 | Valparaiso | (A) | W | 65 | 55 |
| Jan. 24 | Chicago | (A) | W | 70 | 61 |
| Jan. 26 | Mount St. Joseph | (H) | W | 78 | 76 |
| Jan. 30 | Saint Mary's | (H) | W | 73 | 56 |
| Feb. 2 | Marquette | (H) | L | 46 | 67 |
| Feb. 7 | Purdue-Calumet | (H) | W | 79 | 38 |
| Feb. 9 | Goshen | (A) | W | 52 | 49 |
| Feb. 12 | Huntington | (A) | W | 70 | 64 |
| Feb. 15 | Marion | (H) | L | 61 | 62 |
| Feb. 19 | Illinois-Chicago | (A) | L | 59 | 71 |
| Feb. 22 | Grace – (IAIAW N. District Tournament) | (N3) | W | 73 | 65 |
| Feb. 23 | Goshen – (IAIAW N. District Tournament) | (N3) | W | 61 | 54 |
| Feb. 29 | Huntington – (IAIAW State Tournament) | (N4) | W | 52 | 46 |
| Mar. 1 | Goshen – (IAIAW State Tournament) | (N4) | W | 61 | 54 |
| Mar. 6 | Greenville – (AIAW Midwest Regional) | (N1) | W | 55 | 51 |
| Mar. 7 | Adrian – (AIAW Midwest Regional) | (N1) | L | 59 | 73 |
| Mar. 8 | Spring Arbor – (AIAW Midwest Regional) | (N1) | L | 56 | 61 |
| Mar. 12 | Pacific Lutheran – (AIAW Nationals, Division III) | (A) | W | 57 | 48 |
| Mar. 15 | Wisconsin-LaCrosse – (AIAW Nationals, Division III) | (A) | L | 57 | 80 |
| | | | | 1897 | 1825 |

N1 – Upland, IN.; N2 – DeKalb, IL.; N3 – Angola, IN.; N4 – Notre Dame, IN. (Saint Mary's College)

1980-81 (Won 10, Lost 18, .357)
Coach: Mary DiStanislao
Captains: Maggie Lally and Sheila Liebscher

| Nov. 22 | South Dakota | (H) | L | 60 | 67 |
|---------|--------------|-----|---|----|----|
| Dec. 1 | Butler | (H) | L | 51 | 60 |
| Dec. 6 | Concordia | (H) | W | 82 | 51 |
| Dec. 8 | Saint Mary's | (H) | W | 71 | 52 |
| Dec. 11 | St. Francis (IL) | (H) | L | 54 | 57 |
| Dec. 19 | Iona – (Penn Holiday Tournament) | (N1) | W | 69 | 65 |

| Dec. 20 | Delaware | | | | |
| | −(Penn Holiday Tournament) | (N1) | L | 56 | 70 |
| Jan. 4 | Davidson | (N2) | W | 85 | 37 |
| Jan. 6 | Villanova | (A) | L | 57 | 70 |
| Jan. 10 | Marquette | (A) | L | 55 | 62 |
| Jan. 14 | Taylor | (H) | W | 77 | 71 |
| Jan. 17 | Miami (OH) | (H) | L | 53 | 93 |
| Jan. 18 | Illinois-Chicago | (H) | L | 61 | 78 |
| Jan. 22 | Valparaiso | (H) | W | 57 | 48 |
| Jan. 28 | Saint Mary's | (A) | W | 59 | 44 |
| Jan. 31 | South Carolina | (H) | L | 48 | 124 |
| Feb. 5 | Goshen | (H) | W | 86 | 44 |
| Feb. 7 | St. Ambrose | (H) | W · | 56 | 49 |
| Feb. 11 | Ball State | (A) | L | 61 | 79 |
| Feb. 17 | St. Joseph's (IN) | (A) | L | 64 | 84 |
| Feb. 20 | Michigan | (A) | L | 65 | 96 |
| Feb. 22 | Virginia | (N3) | L | 40 | 68 |
| Feb. 26 | Michigan State | (A) | L | 45 | 76 |
| Feb. 28 | Illinois | (H) | L | 53 | 88 |
| Mar. 6 | Ball State | | | | |
| | −(IAIAW State Tournament) | (N4) | L | 69 | 76 |
| Mar. 20 | Alaska-Anchorage | | | | |
| | −(Northern Lights | | | | |
| | Tournament) | (A) | W | 59 | 58 |
| Mar. 21 | San Diego State | | | | |
| | −(Northern Lights Tournament) | (N5) | L | 34 | 71 |
| Mar. 22 | Hawaii | | | | |
| | −(Northern Lights Tournament) | (N5) | L | 55 | 61 |
| | | | | 1682 | 1899 |

N1−Philadelphia, PA. (Palestra); N2−Charlotte, NC.; N3−Rosemont, IL.; N4−Bloomington, IN.; N5−Anchorage, AK

1981-82 (Won 16, Lost 9, .640)
Coach: Mary DiStanislao
Captain: Missy Conboy

| Dec. 3 | St. Joseph's (IN) | (H) | W | 78 | 44 |
| Dec. 5 | UCLA | (H) | L | 45 | 50 |
| Dec. 8 | Saint Mary's | (H) | W | 92 | 29 |
| Dec. 10 | Butler | (A) | L | 58 | 67 |
| Dec. 12 | Northern Illinois | (H) | W | 67 | 52 |
| Dec. 18 | Pennsylvania | | | | |
| | −(Penn Holiday Tournament) | (A) | W | 62 | 47 |
| Dec. 19 | Mount St. Mary's | | | | |
| | −(Penn Holiday Tournament) | (N1) | L | 44 | 57 |
| Jan. 2 | Missouri | (N2) | W | 60 | 53 |
| Jan. 9 | Creighton−(Dial Classic) | (N3) | W | 69 | 48 |

| Jan. 10 | Marquette—(Dial Classic) | (N3) | W | 50 | 36 |
|---|---|---|---|---|---|
| Jan. 13 | St. Francis (IL) | (A) | W | 61 | 57 |
| Jan. 17 | Southern Methodist | (H) | W | 76 | 60 |
| Jan. 21 | Valparaiso | (A) | W | 84 | 27 |
| Jan. 24 | Michigan | (H) | W | 71 | 48 |
| Jan. 28 | Ball State | (H) | W | 60 | 57 |
| Jan. 30 | Marquette | (H) | W | 60 | 43 |
| Feb. 5 | Mount St. Joseph | (A) | W | 70 | 54 |
| Feb. 6 | Miami (OH) | (A) | L | 61 | 65 |
| Feb. 10 | Taylor | (H) | W | 79 | 41 |
| Feb. 13 | Cincinnati | (H) | W | 67 | 58 |
| Feb. 16 | Illinois | (A) | L | 53 | 83 |
| Feb. 20 | South Carolina | (A) | L | 54 | 76 |
| Feb. 25 | Nebraska (2 OT) | (H) | L | 88 | 98 |
| Feb. 27 | DePaul | (H) | L | 55 | 60 |
| Mar. 6 | Michigan State | (H) | L | 59 | 68 |
| | | | | 1623 | 1378 |

N1—Philadelphia, PA. (Palestra); N2—Kansas City, MO.; N3—Minneapolis, MN.

1982-83 (Won 20, Lost 7, .741)
Coach: Mary DiStanislao
Captain: Debbi Hensley and Theresa Mullins

| Nov. 26 | UCLA | | | | |
|---|---|---|---|---|---|
| | —(Orange Crush Classic) | (N) | L | 54 | 82 |
| Nov. 27 | Rutgers | | | | |
| | —(Orange Crush Classic) | (N) | L | 74 | 81 |
| Dec. 2 | Butler | (H) | W | 80 | 73 |
| Dec. 4 | St. Francis (IL) | (H) | W | 86 | 42 |
| Dec. 8 | Western Michigan | (A) | W | 68 | 62 |
| Dec. 10 | Miami (OH) | (H) | W | 64 | 59 |
| Dec. 12 | Michigan | (A) | W | 62 | 58 |
| Dec. 15 | Eastern Michigan | (H) | W | 75 | 58 |
| Dec. 30 | East Carolina* | (H) | W | 52 | 50 |
| Jan. 3 | Villanova | (A) | W | 72 | 68 |
| Jan. 6 | Georgetown | (A) | W | 78 | 68 |
| Jan. 8 | Maryland | (A) | L | 62 | 84 |
| Jan. 13 | Augustana | (H) | W | 87 | 66 |
| Jan. 16 | Alabama | (H) | L | 56 | 71 |
| Jan. 21 | Detroit | (H) | W | 78 | 61 |
| Jan. 27 | Arizona State | (A) | L | 57 | 82 |
| Jan. 30 | UCLA | (A) | L | 53 | 84 |
| Feb. 4 | Loyola (IL) | (H) | W | 80 | 61 |
| Feb. 6 | Iowa State | (H) | W | 69 | 58 |
| Feb. 11 | Louisiana Tech | (H) | L | 39 | 81 |
| Feb. 18 | Bradley | (A) | W | 68 | 57 |

| Feb. 19 | Illinois State | (A) | W | 48 | 47 |
|---------|----------------|-----|---|----|----|
| Feb. 25 | Marquette | (A) | W | 74 | 50 |
| Feb. 26 | DePaul | (N) | W | 52 | 50 |
| Mar. 6 | Dayton (OT) | (H) | W | 68 | 64 |
| Mar. 9 | Indiana (OT) | (H) | W | 63 | 61 |
| | | | | 1807 | 1739 |

N—Rosemont, IL.
* Notre Dame's 100th victory

1983-84 (Won 14, Lost 14, .500)
Coach: Mary DiStanislao
Captains: Theresa Mullins and Mary Beth Schueth

| Nov. 22 | Marquette | (H) | W | 96 | 63 |
|---------|-----------|-----|---|----|----|
| Nov. 25 | Tennessee—(Notre Dame Classic) | (H) | L | 56 | 71 |
| Nov. 26 | Maryland—(Notre Dame Classic) | (H) | L | 57 | 75 |
| Dec. 3 | UCLA | (H) | W | 70 | 61 |
| Dec. 7 | Northwestern | (A) | L | 74 | 78 |
| Dec. 9 | Michigan | (H) | W | 66 | 50 |
| Dec. 14 | Western Michigan | (H) | W | 75 | 54 |
| Dec. 21 | Central Michigan | (H) | L | 69 | 72 |
| Dec. 29 | Old Dominion —(Nike Christmas Classic) | (N) | L | 57 | 71 |
| Dec. 30 | Boston College —(Nike Christmas Classic) | (A) | L | 55 | 59 |
| Jan. 5 | East Carolina | (A) | W | 66 | 50 |
| Jan. 7 | Xavier | (A) | W | 85 | 68 |
| Jan. 12 | Louisiana Tech | (A) | L | 56 | 83 |
| Jan. 15 | Southern Methodist | (A) | L | 63 | 64 |
| Jan. 18 | Loyola (IL) | (H) | L | 56 | 59 |
| Jan. 21 | DePaul | (A) | L | 46 | 62 |
| Jan. 27 | Evansville | (H) | W | 77 | 56 |
| Jan. 30 | DePaul | (H) | W | 78 | 62 |
| Feb. 3 | Michigan State | (A) | L | 72 | 73 |
| Feb. 8 | Illinois State | (H) | L | 59 | 61 |
| Feb. 11 | Villanova | (H) | W | 85 | 79 |
| Feb. 14 | Detroit | (H) | W | 72 | 67 |
| Feb. 18 | Detroit | (A) | L | 80 | 85 |
| Feb. 25 | Xavier | (H) | W | 91 | 77 |
| Feb. 27 | Illinois-Chicago | (A) | W | 77 | 58 |
| Mar. 3 | Dayton | (A) | W | 63 | 57 |
| Mar. 8 | Loyola (IL) | (A) | L | 53 | 64 |
| Mar. 10 | Evansville | (A) | W | 80 | 68 |
| | | | | 1934 | 1847 |

N—Chestnut Hill, MA.

1984-85 (Won 20, Lost 8, .714)
Coach: Mary DiStanislao
Captains: Laura Dougherty and Mary Beth Schueth

| Nov. 24 | Tennessee | (A) | L | 57 | 62 |
|---|---|---|---|---|---|
| Nov. 26 | Purdue | (H) | L | 59 | 62 |
| Nov. 30 | Eastern Michigan | (A) | W | 70 | 59 |
| Dec. 2 | Michigan | (A) | L | 64 | 75 |
| Dec. 5 | Western Michigan | (H) | W | 76 | 46 |
| Dec. 8 | Georgetown | (H) | W | 72 | 49 |
| Dec. 12 | Northern Illinois | (A) | W | 71 | 60 |
| Dec. 20 | Michigan State | (H) | W | 71 | 59 |
| Dec. 30 | UCLA | (A) | L | 51 | 78 |
| Jan. 2 | Southern California | (N) | L | 53 | 69 |
| Jan. 6 | LaSalle | (A) | L | 66 | 71 |
| Jan. 9 | Maryland | (A) | W | 49 | 40 |
| Jan. 14 | Illinois-Chicago | (H) | W | 70 | 49 |
| Jan. 19 | Detroit | (A) | W | 76 | 62 |
| Jan. 27 | DePaul | (A) | L | 64 | 72 |
| Jan. 30 | Butler | (A) | W | 79 | 40 |
| Feb. 1 | Evansville | (H) | W | 74 | 53 |
| Feb. 5 | Dayton | (A) | W | 81 | 66 |
| Feb. 9 | Xavier | (H) | W | 107 | 61 |
| Feb. 13 | Alabama | (A) | L | 62 | 67 |
| Feb. 17 | Detroit | (H) | W | 66 | 53 |
| Feb. 20 | Loyola (IL) | (H) | W | 84 | 59 |
| Feb. 24 | DePaul | (H) | W | 68 | 57 |
| Feb. 26 | Loyola (IL) | (A) | W | 64 | 63 |
| Feb. 28 | Butler | (H) | W | 99 | 36 |
| Mar. 3 | Evansville | (A) | W | 72 | 70 |
| Mar. 6 | Dayton | (H) | W | 72 | 57 |
| Mar. 9 | Xavier | (A) | W | 78 | 50 |
|  |  |  |  | 1975 | 1645 |

N—Fullerton, CA.

# Women's Basketball Coaching Records

| Season(s) | Coach | W | L | Pct. |
|---|---|---|---|---|
| 1974-76 | Jeanne Earley* | 9 | 11 | .450 |
| 1975-77 | Sally Duffy* | 15 | 13 | .536 |
| 1977-80 | Sharon Petro | 49 | 20 | .710 |
| 1980-84 | Mary DiStanislao | 60 | 48 | .556 |
| All Time Record (11 seasons) |  | 147 | 93 | .613 |

* Includes 1975-76 season in record of both coaches

# Women's All-Time Register and Season Records

Note: Statistics on players prior to 1977-78 are quite scarce. Information reflects compilation from the best available sources.

FORMAT

LAST NAME, FIRST NAME  HGT  DATE OF BIRTH  DATE OF DEATH
(if applicable)

Season  GP  FGM-FGA  Pct.  FTM-FTA  Pct.  Reb  Avg.  PF  PTS.  PPG.

ADAMS, ANN MARIE
1975-76

ADAMSON, LIZ
1974-75

ANDERSON, KATHY
1974-75
1975-76

| ANTOLIK, RENEE | | | | | | 5-5 | b. 6-19-1960 | | | | |
|---|---|---|---|---|---|---|---|---|---|---|---|
| 1978-79 | 12 | 8-28 | .286 | 2-5 | .400 | 4 | 0.3 | 5 | 18 | 1.5 |
| 1979-80 | 19 | 6-46 | .130 | 2-14 | .143 | 11 | 0.6 | 6 | 14 | 0.7 |
| | 31 | 14-74 | .189 | 4-19 | .211 | 15 | 0.5 | 11 | 32 | 1.0 |

BANASIAK, BECKY
1974-75
1975-76

| BARRON, KATHY | | | | | | 5-9 | b. 6-2-1966 | | | | |
|---|---|---|---|---|---|---|---|---|---|---|---|
| 1984-85 | 17 | 9-15 | .600 | 12-16 | .750 | 13 | 0.8 | 6 | 30 | 1.8 |

| BASFORD, DENISE | | | | | | 5-9 | b. 3-28-1964 | | | | |
|---|---|---|---|---|---|---|---|---|---|---|---|
| 1982-83 | 26 | 27-62 | .435 | 14-24 | .583 | 35 | 1.3 | 48 | 68 | 2.6 |
| 1983-84 | 26 | 27-66 | .409 | 9-20 | .450 | 45 | 1.7 | 45 | 63 | 2.4 |
| 1984-85 | 27 | 16-44 | .364 | 6-9 | .667 | 46 | 1.7 | 41 | 38 | 1.4 |
| | 79 | 70-172 | .407 | 29-53 | .547 | 126 | 1.6 | 134 | 169 | 2.1 |

| BATES, CARRIE | | | | | | 6-1 | b. 5-20-1963 | | | | |
|---|---|---|---|---|---|---|---|---|---|---|---|
| 1981-82 | 25 | 136-231 | .589 | 39-59 | .661 | 164 | 6.6 | 39 | 311 | 12.4 |
| 1982-83 | 27 | 86-168 | .512 | 44-56 | .786 | 127 | 4.7 | 36 | 216 | 8.0 |

| | | | | | | | | | | |
|---|---|---|---|---|---|---|---|---|---|---|
| 1983-84 | 28 | 129-234 | .551 | 75-91 | .824 | 155 | 5.5 | 44 | 333 | 11.9 |
| 1984-85 | 16 | 88-161 | .547 | 24-44 | .545 | 78 | 4.9 | 17 | 200 | 12.5 |
| | 96 | 439-794 | .553 | 182-250 | .728 | 524 | 5.5 | 136 | 1060 | 11.0 |

### BATTEL, CYNTHIA          5-5    b. 12-31-195

| | | | | | | | | | | |
|---|---|---|---|---|---|---|---|---|---|---|
| 1978-79 | 12 | 8-25 | .320 | 5-12 | .417 | 10 | 0.8 | 11 | 21 | 1.8 |

### BERGES, ANN
1974-75
1975-76
1976-77

### BERRY, LIZ
1975-76

### BORKOWSKI, MARY          5-5    b. 12-3-1964

| | | | | | | | | | | |
|---|---|---|---|---|---|---|---|---|---|---|
| 1983-84 | 4 | 3-6 | .500 | 0-0 | .000 | 2 | 0.5 | 3 | 6 | 1.5 |

### BOTHAM, SANDY          6-2    b. 12-12-1965

| | | | | | | | | | | |
|---|---|---|---|---|---|---|---|---|---|---|
| 1984-85 | 28 | 108-204 | .529 | 46-66 | .697 | 142 | 5.1 | 82 | 262 | 9.4 |

### BRADSHAW, BONITA          5-10
1975-76
1976-77

### BROMMELAND, KATHY          6-3    b. 2-5-1966

| | | | | | | | | | | |
|---|---|---|---|---|---|---|---|---|---|---|
| 1984-85 | 21 | 41-76 | .539 | 15-19 | .789 | 56 | 2.7 | 33 | 97 | 4.8 |

### BROWN, LISA          5-5    b. 4-7-1964

| | | | | | | | | | | |
|---|---|---|---|---|---|---|---|---|---|---|
| 1982-83 | 11 | 6-12 | .500 | 3-4 | .750 | 3 | 0.3 | 9 | 15 | 1.4 |
| 1983-84 | 13 | 6-14 | .429 | 1-5 | .200 | 10 | 0.8 | 8 | 13 | 1.0 |
| | 24 | 12-26 | .462 | 4-9 | .444 | 13 | 0.5 | 17 | 28 | 1.2 |

### BURNS, ERIN
1976-77

### CASHMAN, MOLLY          5-4    b. 9-20-1957

| | | | | | | | | | | |
|---|---|---|---|---|---|---|---|---|---|---|
| 1977-78 | 17 | 63 | | 26-54 | .481 | | | 49 | 152 | 8.9 |
| 1978-79 | 22 | 68-163 | .417 | 34-64 | .531 | 45 | 2.0 | 46 | 170 | 7.7 |
| 1979-80 | 29 | 54-163 | .331 | 30-53 | .556 | 65 | 2.2 | 80 | 138 | 4.3 |
| | 68 | 185 | | 90-171 | .526 | | | 175 | 460 | 6.8 |

### CLEMENCY, MARY
1974-75
1975-76

### CONBOY, MISSY  5-8  b. 4-19-1960

| Year | G | FG | FG% | FT | FT% | | | | | |
|---|---|---|---|---|---|---|---|---|---|---|
| 1978-79 | 20 | 31-85 | .365 | 11-20 | .550 | 53 | 2.7 | 20 | 73 | 3.7 |
| 1979-80 | 30 | 83-221 | .376 | 29-55 | .527 | 115 | 3.8 | 50 | 195 | 6.5 |
| 1980-81 | 28 | 33-115 | .287 | 14-26 | .538 | 73 | 2.6 | 47 | 80 | 2.9 |
| 1981-82 | 15 | 5-23 | .217 | 7-12 | .583 | 16 | 1.1 | 21 | 17 | 1.1 |
| | 93 | 152-444 | .342 | 61-113 | .540 | 257 | 2.8 | 138 | 365 | 3.9 |

### CONLISK, BETH  5-8  b. 3-13-1958

| Year | G | FG | FG% | FT | FT% | | | | | |
|---|---|---|---|---|---|---|---|---|---|---|
| 1976-77 | | | | | | | | | | |
| 1977-78 | 8 | 3 | | 1-4 | .250 | | | 5 | 7 | 0.9 |

### COOGAN, PATTY

|  |
|---|
| 1974-75 |
| 1975-76 |

### CROWE, JAN  5-11  b. 7-28-1961

| Year | G | FG | FG% | FT | FT% | | | | | |
|---|---|---|---|---|---|---|---|---|---|---|
| 1979-80 | 4 | 11-18 | .611 | 10-19 | .526 | 19 | 4.8 | 5 | 32 | 8.0 |
| 1980-81 | 10 | 47-106 | .443 | 40-83 | .482 | 102 | 10.2 | 19 | 134 | 13.4 |
| 1981-82 | 6 | 14-27 | .519 | 6-14 | .429 | 26 | 4.3 | 9 | 34 | 5.7 |
| | 20 | 72-151 | .477 | 56-116 | .483 | 147 | 7.4 | 33 | 200 | 10.0 |

### CUMMINGS, CAROLA  5-4  b. 6-15-1958

| Year | G | FG | FG% | FT | FT% | | | | | |
|---|---|---|---|---|---|---|---|---|---|---|
| 1976-77 | | | | | | | | | | |
| 1977-78 | 8 | 9 | | 6-13 | .462 | | | 6 | 24 | 3.0 |
| 1978-79 | 15 | 15-43 | .349 | 10-22 | .455 | 9 | 0.6 | 8 | 40 | 2.7 |

### CURLISS, LAURA  5-11  b. 1-17-1962

| Year | G | FG | FG% | FT | FT% | | | | | |
|---|---|---|---|---|---|---|---|---|---|---|
| 1980-81 | 1 | 0-1 | .000 | 0-0 | .000 | 0 | 0.0 | 0 | 0 | 0.0 |

### DODGE, LAURA

|  |
|---|
| 1975-76 |

### DOUGHERTY, LAURA  5-10  b. 5-29-1963

| Year | G | FG | FG% | FT | FT% | | | | | |
|---|---|---|---|---|---|---|---|---|---|---|
| 1981-82 | 25 | 89-175 | .509 | 41-53 | .774 | 33 | 1.3 | 53 | 219 | 8.8 |
| 1982-83 | 27 | 125-283 | .442 | 43-64 | .672 | 56 | 2.1 | 74 | 293 | 10.9 |
| 1983-84 | 27 | 104-229 | .454 | 55-67 | .821 | 40 | 1.5 | 52 | 263 | 9.7 |
| 1984-85 | 27 | 75-149 | .503 | 34-42 | .810 | 27 | 1.0 | 41 | 184 | 6.8 |
| | 106 | 393-836 | .470 | 173-226 | .765 | 156 | 1.5 | 220 | 959 | 9.0 |

### EBBEN, LYNN  5-11  b. 1-30-1964

| Year | G | FG | FG% | FT | FT% | | | | | |
|---|---|---|---|---|---|---|---|---|---|---|
| 1982-83 | 22 | 72-157 | .459 | 26-37 | .703 | 79 | 3.6 | 29 | 170 | 7.7 |
| 1983-84 | 28 | 88-176 | .500 | 17-24 | .708 | 66 | 2.4 | 45 | 193 | 6.9 |
| 1984-85 | 27 | 64-131 | .489 | 19-26 | .731 | 62 | 2.3 | 46 | 147 | 5.4 |
| | 77 | 224-464 | .483 | 62-87 | .713 | 207 | 2.7 | 120 | 510 | 6.6 |

### FONDI, SUE
1975-76
1976-77

---

### FORBES, MARY JOAN  5-10  b. 7-24-1962

| | | | | | | | | | | |
|---|---|---|---|---|---|---|---|---|---|---|
| 1980-81 | 9 | 1-9 | .111 | 2-2 | 1.000 | 14 | 1.6 | 4 | 4 | 0.4 |

### FREY, BARB
1974-75
1975-76

---

### GAVIN, MARY  5-6  b. 4-30-66

| | | | | | | | | | | |
|---|---|---|---|---|---|---|---|---|---|---|
| 1984-85 | 26 | 31-77 | .403 | 23-38 | .605 | 56 | 2.2 | 53 | 85 | 3.3 |

### HENSLEY, DEBBI  5-6  b. 2-3-1961

| | | | | | | | | | | |
|---|---|---|---|---|---|---|---|---|---|---|
| 1980-81 | 23 | 8-30 | .267 | 5-11 | .455 | 33 | 1.4 | 34 | 21 | 0.9 |
| 1981-82 | 25 | 14-51 | .275 | 8-16 | .500 | 29 | 1.2 | 47 | 36 | 1.4 |
| 1982-83 | 27 | 8-33 | .242 | 14-27 | .519 | 48 | 1.8 | 53 | 30 | 1.1 |
| | 75 | 30-114 | .263 | 27-54 | .500 | 110 | 1.5 | 134 | 87 | 1.2 |

### HICKS, KELLY  5-10  b. 7-7-1958

| | | | | | | | | | | |
|---|---|---|---|---|---|---|---|---|---|---|
| 1977-78 | 17 | 56 | | 19-40 | .475 | | | 54 | 131 | 7.7 |
| 1978-79 | 9 | 31-85 | .365 | 14-22 | .636 | 45 | 5.0 | 28 | 76 | 8.4 |
| 1979-80 | 30 | 52-158 | .329 | 26-43 | .605 | 111 | 3.7 | 77 | 130 | 4.3 |
| | 56 | 139 | | 59-105 | .562 | | | 159 | 337 | 6.0 |

### JERGESEN, JANE  5-8  b. 12-30-1960

| | | | | | | | | | | |
|---|---|---|---|---|---|---|---|---|---|---|
| 1979-80 | 12 | 9-24 | .375 | 6-10 | .600 | 16 | 1.3 | 5 | 24 | 2.0 |

### KAISER, RUTH  5-10  b. 1-11-1963

| | | | | | | | | | | |
|---|---|---|---|---|---|---|---|---|---|---|
| 1981-82 | 24 | 99-196 | .505 | 33-46 | .717 | 132 | 5.7 | 44 | 231 | 9.6 |
| 1982-83 | 27 | 82-174 | .471 | 29-41 | .707 | 108 | 4.0 | 57 | 193 | 7.1 |
| 1983-84 | 28 | 70-151 | .464 | 19-29 | .655 | 109 | 3.9 | 52 | 159 | 5.7 |
| 1984-85 | 26 | 26-53 | .491 | 6-18 | .333 | 61 | 2.3 | 41 | 58 | 2.2 |
| | 105 | 277-574 | .483 | 87-134 | .649 | 410 | 3.9 | 194 | 641 | 6.1 |

### KEYS, TRENA  6-1  b. 9-30-1964

| | | | | | | | | | | |
|---|---|---|---|---|---|---|---|---|---|---|
| 1982-83 | 25 | 117-243 | .481 | 28-36 | .778 | 39 | 3.6 | 48 | 262 | 10.5 |
| 1983-84 | 28 | 111-269 | .413 | 35-51 | .686 | 88 | 3.1 | 57 | 257 | 9.2 |
| 1984-85 | 28 | 212-410 | .517 | 59-84 | .702 | 157 | 5.6 | 63 | 483 | 17.2 |
| | 81 | 440-922 | .477 | 122-177 | .713 | 324 | 4.0 | 168 | 1002 | 12.4 |

### KLAUKE, JENNY  5-10  b. 7-7-1962

| | | | | | | | | | | |
|---|---|---|---|---|---|---|---|---|---|---|
| 1980-81 | 26 | 103-226 | .456 | 58-81 | .716 | 130 | 5.0 | 70 | 264 | 10.2 |
| 1981-82 | 12 | 14-29 | .483 | 9-10 | .900 | 13 | 1.1 | 12 | 37 | 3.1 |

| | | | | | | | | | | | |
|---|---|---|---|---|---|---|---|---|---|---|---|
| 1982-83 | 10 | 12-26 | .462 | 8-16 | .500 | 15 | 1.5 | 18 | 32 | 3.2 |
| 1983-84 | 12 | 15-33 | .455 | 16-20 | .800 | 25 | 2.1 | 18 | 46 | 3.8 |
| | 60 | 144-314 | .459 | 91-127 | .717 | 183 | 3.1 | 118 | 379 | 6.3 |

KUNKEL, SUE

1976-77

LALLY, CAROL    5-6    b. 7-8-1957

| | | | | | | | | | | |
|---|---|---|---|---|---|---|---|---|---|---|
| 1975-76 | | | | | | | | | | |
| 1976-77 | | | | | | | | | | |
| 1977-78 | 16 | 82 | | 17-35 | .472 | | | 46 | 181 | 11.3 |
| 1978-79 | 22 | 117-322 | .363 | 47-96 | .490 | 139 | 6.3 | 59 | 281 | 12.8 |

LALLY, MAGGIE    5-1    b. 4-3-1959

| | | | | | | | | | | |
|---|---|---|---|---|---|---|---|---|---|---|
| 1977-78 | 17 | 47 | | 16-29 | .552 | | | 37 | 110 | 6.5 |
| 1978-79 | 22 | 61-165 | .370 | 25-38 | .658 | 34 | 1.5 | 44 | 147 | 6.7 |
| 1979-80 | 30 | 77-204 | .377 | 32-55 | .582 | 48 | 1.6 | 73 | 186 | 6.2 |
| 1980-81 | 28 | 22-71 | .310 | 9-17 | .529 | 25 | 0.9 | 55 | 53 | 1.9 |
| | 97 | 207 | | 82-139 | .590 | | | 209 | 496 | 5.1 |

LEW, KATHY    5-9    b. 10-11-1959

| | | | | | | | | | | |
|---|---|---|---|---|---|---|---|---|---|---|
| 1977-78 | 14 | 2 | | 6-20 | .300 | | | 18 | 10 | 0.7 |

LIEBSCHER, SHEILA    5-8    b. 4-1-1959

| | | | | | | | | | | |
|---|---|---|---|---|---|---|---|---|---|---|
| 1979-80 | 29 | 37-119 | .311 | 19-34 | .559 | 85 | 2.9 | 34 | 93 | 3.2 |
| 1980-81 | 28 | 34-98 | .347 | 14-21 | .667 | 78 | 2.8 | 37 | 82 | 2.9 |
| | 57 | 71-217 | .327 | 33-55 | .600 | 163 | 2.9 | 71 | 175 | 3.1 |

MALONEY, MAUREEN    5-9

1974-75
1975-76
1976-77

MATVEY, SHARI    6-1    b. 10-8-1961

| | | | | | | | | | | |
|---|---|---|---|---|---|---|---|---|---|---|
| 1979-80 | 30 | 237-407 | .582 | 55-93 | .591 | 305 | 10.2 | 85 | 529 | 17.6 |
| 1980-81 | 28 | 184-379 | .485 | 46-68 | .676 | 213 | 7.6 | 50 | 414 | 14.8 |
| 1981-82 | 25 | 109-203 | .537 | 14-24 | .583 | 119 | 4.8 | 45 | 232 | 9.3 |
| 1982-83 | 26 | 86-167 | .515 | 26-35 | .743 | 105 | 4.0 | 57 | 198 | 7.6 |
| | 109 | 616-1156 | .533 | 141-220 | .641 | 745 | 6.8 | 237 | 1373 | 12.6 |

MAZENEC, MARY BETH

1974-75

McGUIRE, MOLLY

1975-76

### McLEAN, MARTHA   5-8   b. 8-2-1958

| | | | | | | | | | | |
|---|---|---|---|---|---|---|---|---|---|---|
| 1978-79 | 10 | 5-19 | .263 | 0-4 | .000 | 9 | 0.9 | 7 | 10 | 1.0 |

### McMANUS, TRICIA   5-11   b. 10-31-1960

| | | | | | | | | | | |
|---|---|---|---|---|---|---|---|---|---|---|
| 1978-79 | 22 | 63-168 | .375 | 26-57 | .456 | 124 | 5.6 | 47 | 152 | 6.9 |
| 1979-80 | 30 | 102-272 | .376 | 62-99 | .626 | 189 | 6.3 | 102 | 266 | 8.9 |
| 1980-81 | 28 | 76-211 | .360 | 38-76 | .500 | 169 | 6.0 | 97 | 190 | 6.8 |
| | 80 | 241-651 | .370 | 126-232 | .543 | 482 | 6.0 | 246 | 608 | 7.6 |

### McMENAMIN, MARGARET
1976-77

### McRAE, KATHY
1974-75
1976-77

### MEAGHER, MARGE   5-9   b. 8-16-1956
1975-76
1976-77

| | | | | | | | | | | |
|---|---|---|---|---|---|---|---|---|---|---|
| 1977-78 | 17 | 61 | | 17-31 | .578 | | | 39 | 139 | 8.1 |

### MEYER, PAT   5-9   b. 3-6-1958
1976-77

| | | | | | | | | | | |
|---|---|---|---|---|---|---|---|---|---|---|
| 1977-78 | 15 | 37 | | 13-26 | .500 | | | 41 | 87 | 5.8 |
| 1978-79 | 22 | 52-155 | .385 | 12-19 | .632 | 89 | 4.0 | 73 | 116 | 5.3 |

### MONAGLE, JANICE   5-5   b. 6-10-1963

| | | | | | | | | | | |
|---|---|---|---|---|---|---|---|---|---|---|
| 1981-82 | 8 | 4-9 | .444 | 0-0 | .000 | 3 | 0.4 | 2 | 8 | 1.0 |
| 1982-83 | 4 | 1-1 | 1.000 | 0-1 | .000 | 0 | 0.0 | 2 | 2 | 0.5 |
| | 12 | 5-10 | .500 | 0-1 | .000 | 3 | 0.3 | 4 | 10 | 0.8 |

### MOONEY, JO ANN
1974-75

### MORRISON, BETH   6-5   b. 11-5-1966

| | | | | | | | | | | |
|---|---|---|---|---|---|---|---|---|---|---|
| 1984-85 | 14 | 13-33 | .394 | 6-9 | .667 | 23 | 1.6 | 17 | 32 | 2.3 |

### MULLINS, THERESA   5-6   b. 7-6-1962

| | | | | | | | | | | |
|---|---|---|---|---|---|---|---|---|---|---|
| 1980-81 | 28 | 52-166 | .313 | 6-12 | .500 | 37 | 1.3 | 42 | 110 | 3.9 |
| 1981-82 | 25 | 49-124 | .395 | 7-9 | .778 | 29 | 1.2 | 47 | 105 | 4.2 |
| 1982-83 | 11 | 5-15 | .333 | 1-1 | 1.000 | 6 | 0.5 | 8 | 11 | 1.0 |
| 1983-84 | 4 | 0-2 | .000 | 3-4 | .750 | 1 | 0.3 | 1 | 3 | 0.8 |
| | 68 | 106-307 | .345 | 17-26 | .654 | 73 | 1.1 | 98 | 229 | 3.4 |

### MULVIHILL, MARY LOU
1974-75

### MURPHY, BYRNE    5-6   b. 3-18-1957

| | | | | | | | | | | |
|---|---|---|---|---|---|---|---|---|---|---|
| 1974-75 | | | | | | | | | | |
| 1975-76 | | | | | | | | | | |
| 1977-78 | 10 | 3 | | 0-2 | .000 | | | 3 | 6 | 0.6 |

### MYLER, ELLEN

| | |
|---|---|
| 1974-75 | |

### NEVILLE, SUSAN    5-9   b. 6-29-1963

| | | | | | | | | | | |
|---|---|---|---|---|---|---|---|---|---|---|
| 1981-82 | 21 | 26-77 | .338 | 15-25 | .600 | 27 | 1.3 | 31 | 67 | 3.2 |

### NEWMAN, DAVA    5-5   b. 8-11-1964

| | | | | | | | | | | |
|---|---|---|---|---|---|---|---|---|---|---|
| 1983-84 | 4 | 2-3 | .667 | 2-4 | .500 | 0 | 0.0 | 3 | 6 | 1.5 |

### O'BRIEN, PATTI    5-7   b. 3-24-1960

| | | | | | | | | | | |
|---|---|---|---|---|---|---|---|---|---|---|
| 1978-79 | 17 | 10-30 | .333 | 4-7 | .571 | 44 | 2.6 | 17 | 24 | 1.4 |
| 1979-80 | 14 | 9-39 | .231 | 4-6 | .667 | 32 | 2.3 | 13 | 22 | 1.6 |
| | 31 | 19-69 | .275 | 8-13 | .615 | 76 | 2.5 | 30 | 46 | 1.5 |

### O'HAREN, MICHELLE    5-3   b. 6-28-1958

| | | | | | | | | | | |
|---|---|---|---|---|---|---|---|---|---|---|
| 1977-78 | 14 | 9 | | 5-8 | .625 | | | 11 | 23 | 1.6 |

### O'MALLEY, KARA    5-8   b. 3-6-1962

| | | | | | | | | | | |
|---|---|---|---|---|---|---|---|---|---|---|
| 1980-81 | 24 | 23-89 | .258 | 14-26 | .538 | 89 | 3.7 | 34 | 60 | 2.5 |

### O'REILLY, JAYNE

| | |
|---|---|
| 1975-76 | |
| 1976-76 | |

### POLITISKI, JANE    5-11   b. 3-7-1958

| | | | | | | | | | | |
|---|---|---|---|---|---|---|---|---|---|---|
| 1976-77 | | | | | | | | | | |
| 1977-78 | 17 | 62 | | 35-67 | .522 | | | 45 | 159 | 9.4 |
| 1978-79 | 22 | 94-243 | .387 | 57-104 | .548 | 206 | 9.4 | 59 | 245 | 11.1 |
| 1979-80 | 24 | 111-271 | .410 | 46-78 | .590 | 189 | 7.9 | 54 | 268 | 11.2 |

### RICKHOFF, NANCY

| | |
|---|---|
| 1974-75 | |

### ROBILLARD, REGINA    5-6   b. 5-10-1958

| | | | | | | | | | | |
|---|---|---|---|---|---|---|---|---|---|---|
| 1977-78 | 13 | 5 | | 8-14 | .571 | | | 18 | 18 | 1.4 |

### ROONEY, CARRIE    5-5   b. 7-10-1959

| | | | | | | | | | | |
|---|---|---|---|---|---|---|---|---|---|---|
| 1977-78 | 9 | 4 | | 1-5 | .200 | | | 9 | 9 | 1.0 |

### RYAN, MOLLY    5-6   b. 7-30-1962

| | | | | | | | | | | |
|---|---|---|---|---|---|---|---|---|---|---|
| 1980-81 | 28 | 84-233 | .361 | 48-77 | .623 | 56 | 2.0 | 51 | 216 | 7.7 |

### SCHLAFF, JANET    5-5   b. 4-7-1960

| | | | | | | | | | | |
|---|---|---|---|---|---|---|---|---|---|---|
| 1978-79 | 16 | 26-68 | .382 | 7-11 | .636 | 20 | 1.3 | 9 | 59 | 3.7 |

### SCHUETH, MARY BETH    6-0   b. 4-1-1963

| | | | | | | | | | | |
|---|---|---|---|---|---|---|---|---|---|---|
| 1981-82 | 25 | 137-265 | .517 | 52-105 | .495 | 227 | 9.1 | 64 | 326 | 13.0 |
| 1982-83 | 27 | 128-267 | .479 | 61-101 | .604 | 241 | 8.9 | 71 | 317 | 11.7 |
| 1983-84 | 27 | 114-222 | .514 | 69-108 | .639 | 186 | 6.9 | 55 | 297 | 11.0 |
| 1984-85 | 26 | 108-214 | .505 | 77-107 | .720 | 199 | 7.7 | 62 | 293 | 11.3 |
| | 105 | 487-968 | .503 | 259-421 | .615 | 853 | 8.1 | 252 | 1233 | 11.7 |

### SHIELY, JUDY    5-7

| | | | | | | | | | | |
|---|---|---|---|---|---|---|---|---|---|---|
| 1974-75 | | | | | | | | | | |
| 1975-76 | | | | | | | | | | |
| 1976-77 | | | | | | | | | | |

### SKIERESZ, MICKEY    6-0   b. 12-17-1964

| | | | | | | | | | | |
|---|---|---|---|---|---|---|---|---|---|---|
| 1983-84 | 15 | 14-28 | .500 | 17-24 | .708 | 22 | 1.5 | 16 | 45 | 3.0 |
| 1984-85 | 4 | 3-6 | .500 | 3-4 | .750 | 10 | 2.5 | 3 | 9 | 2.2 |
| | 19 | 17-34 | .500 | 20-28 | .714 | 32 | 1.7 | 19 | 54 | 2.8 |

### SMITH, ANN    5.5   b. 1-20-1959

| | | | | | | | | | | |
|---|---|---|---|---|---|---|---|---|---|---|
| 1977-78 | 8 | 3 | | 0-0 | .000 | | | 2 | 6 | 0.8 |

### SMITH, THERESA    5-10   b. 1-6-1962

| | | | | | | | | | | |
|---|---|---|---|---|---|---|---|---|---|---|
| 1980-81 | 21 | 17-78 | .218 | 20-29 | .690 | 61 | 2.9 | 28 | 54 | 2.6 |

### SULLIVAN, EUNICE    5-3   b. 10-24-1957

| | | | | | | | | | | |
|---|---|---|---|---|---|---|---|---|---|---|
| 1977-78 | 10 | 2 | | 1-2 | .500 | | | 4 | 5 | 0.5 |

### THOMPSON, VONNIE    5-7   b. 8-8-1965

| | | | | | | | | | | |
|---|---|---|---|---|---|---|---|---|---|---|
| 1983-84 | 28 | 53-136 | .390 | 16-26 | .615 | 50 | 1.8 | 42 | 122 | 4.4 |
| 1984-85 | 7 | 5-19 | .263 | 4-4 | 1.000 | 12 | 1.7 | 3 | 14 | 2.0 |
| | 35 | 58-155 | .374 | 20-30 | .667 | 62 | 1.8 | 45 | 136 | 3.9 |

### WILLIS, LAVETTA    5-11   b. 10-1-1965

| | | | | | | | | | | |
|---|---|---|---|---|---|---|---|---|---|---|
| 1983-84 | 28 | 45-72 | .625 | 38-65 | .585 | 114 | 4.1 | 74 | 128 | 4.6 |
| 1984-85 | 13 | 14-34 | .412 | 15-25 | .600 | 45 | 3.5 | 22 | 43 | 3.3 |
| | 41 | 59-106 | .557 | 53-90 | .589 | 159 | 3.9 | 96 | 171 | 4.2 |

# Men's Season Scoring Leaders

Based on total points scored
Any who finished among NCAA leaders is so designated with position in parentheses

| Season | Name | GP | FG | FT | Pts | Avg. |
|--------|------|-----|-----|-----|-----|------|
| 1896-97 | John Shillington | 3 | 10 | 7 | 27 | 9.0 |
| 1897-98 | J. Fred Powers | 2 | 5 | 0 | 10 | 5.0 |
| 1898-99 | J. Fred Powers | 2 | | | | |
| 1901-02 | | | | | | |
| 1907-08 | | | | | | |
| 1908-09 | | | | | | |
| 1909-10 | Justin Moloney | 12 | 59 | 52 | 170 | 14.2 |
| 1910-11 | Justin Moloney | 10 | 33 | 42 | 102 | 10.2 |
| 1911-12 | William Granfield | 17 | 79 | 0 | 158 | 9.3 |
| 1912-13 | | | | | | |
| 1913-14 | Joseph Kenny | 15 | 51 | 0 | 102 | 6.8 |
| 1914-15 | Joseph Kenny | 17 | 77 | 0 | 154 | 9.1 |
| 1915-16 | Freeman Fitzgerald | 11 | 49 | 59 | 157 | 14.3 |
| 1916-17 | Frank McDermott | 13 | 69 | 56 | 194 | 14.9 |
| 1917-18 | Peter Ronchetti | 6 | 9 | 21 | 39 | 6.5 |
| 1918-19 | Leonard Bahan | 12 | 42 | 1 | 85 | 7.1 |
| 1919-20 | Harry Mehre | 18 | 80 | 60 | 220 | 12.2 |
| 1920-21 | | | | | | |
| 1921-22 | Frank McDermott | 19 | 72 | 99 | 243 | 12.8 |
| 1922-23 | Noble Kizer | 21 | 47 | 162 | 256 | 12.2 |
| 1923-24 | Clem Crowe | 23 | 70 | 19 | 159 | 6.9 |
| 1924-25 | John Nyikos | 22 | 67 | 39 | 173 | 7.9 |
| 1925-26 | John Nyikos | 20 | 68 | 27 | 163 | 8.2 |
| 1926-27 | John Nyikos | 19 | 72 | 19 | 163 | 8.6 |
| 1927-28 | Francis Crowe | 22 | 48 | 27 | 123 | 5.6 |
| 1928-29 | Francis Crowe | 19 | 44 | 18 | 106 | 5.6 |
| 1929-30 | John McCarthy | 19 | 34 | 37 | 105 | 5.5 |
| 1930-31 | Raymond DeCook | 20 | 52 | 27 | 131 | 6.6 |
| 1931-32 | Edward Krause | 18 | 48 | 42 | 138 | 7.7 |
| 1932-33 | Edward Krause | 21 | 77 | 59 | 213 | 10.1 |
| 1933-34 | Edward Krause | 23 | 76 | 44 | 196 | 8.5 |
| 1934-35 | Martin Peters | 20 | 53 | 31 | 137 | 6.9 |
| 1935-36 | John Moir | 23 | 112 | 36 | 260 | 11.3 |
| 1936-37 | John Moir | 22 | 113 | 64 | 290 | 13.2 |
| 1937-38 | John Moir | 22 | 92 | 46 | 230 | 10.5 |
| 1938-39 | Edward Riska | 21 | 70 | 62 | 202 | 9.6 |

| | | | | | |
|---|---|---|---|---|---|
| 1939-40 | Edward Riska | 21 | 85 | 62 | 232 | 11.0 |
| 1940-41 | Edward Riska | 17 | 61 | 52 | 174 | 10.2 |
| 1941-42 | Robert Faught | 22 | 84 | 41 | 209 | 9.5 |
| 1942-43 | Robert Faught | 20 | 74 | 48 | 196 | 9.8 |
| 1943-44 | Leo Klier | 19 | 117 | 59 | 293 | 15.4 |
| 1944-45 | Vince Boryla | 20 | 130 | 62 | 322 | 16.1 |
| 1945-46 | Leo Klier | 21 | 147 | 61 | 355 | 16.9 |
| 1946-47 | John Brennan | 24 | 114 | 61 | 289 | 12.0 |
| 1947-48 | Leo Barnhorst | 24 | 116 | 58 | 290 | 12.1 |
| 1948-49 | Leo Barnhorst | 24 | 113 | 57 | 283 | 11.8 |
| 1949-50 | Kevin O'Shea | 24 | 133 | 92 | 358 | 14.9 |
| 1950-51 | Daniel Bagley | 24 | 120 | 78 | 318 | 13.3 |
| 1951-52 | Leroy Leslie | 26 | 145 | 77 | 367 | 14.1 |
| 1952-53 | Richard Rosenthal | 24 | 148 | 96 | 392 | 16.3 |
| 1953-54 | Richard Rosenthal | 25 | 176 | 154 | 506 | 20.2 |
| 1954-55 | Jack Stephens | 24 | 155 | 191 | 501 | 20.9 |
| 1955-56 | Lloyd Aubrey | 24 | 197 | 145 | 539 | 22.5 |
| 1956-57 | Tom Hawkins | 28 | 227 | 122 | 576 | 20.6 |
| 1957-58 | Tom Hawkins (11) | 29 | 286 | 158 | 730 | 25.2 |
| 1958-59 | Tom Hawkins (10) | 22 | 197 | 120 | 514 | 23.4 |
| 1959-60 | Michael Graney | 26 | 179 | 92 | 450 | 17.3 |
| 1960-61 | Armand Reo | 26 | 166 | 46 | 378 | 14.5 |
| 1961-62 | Armand Reo | 23 | 165 | 84 | 414 | 18.0 |
| 1962-63 | John Andreoli | 26 | 158 | 75 | 391 | 15.0 |
| 1963-64 | Larry Sheffield | 24 | 214 | 107 | 535 | 22.3 |
| 1964-65 | Ron Reed | 27 | 242 | 82 | 566 | 21.0 |
| 1965-66 | James Monahan | 26 | 140 | 113 | 393 | 15.1 |
| 1966-67 | Bob Arnzen | 28 | 225 | 147 | 597 | 21.4 |
| 1967-68 | Robert Whitmore | 30 | 252 | 157 | 661 | 22.0 |
| 1968-69 | Robert Whitmore | 26 | 184 | 93 | 461 | 17.7 |
| 1969-70 | Austin Carr (2) | 29 | 444 | 218 | 1106 | 38.1 |
| 1970-71 | Austin Carr (2) | 29 | 430 | 241 | 1101 | 37.9 |
| 1971-72 | Gary Novak | 26 | 217 | 74 | 508 | 19.5 |
| 1972-73 | John Shumate | 30 | 257 | 117 | 631 | 22.0 |
| 1973-74 | John Shumate (10) | 29 | 281 | 141 | 703 | 24.2 |
| 1974-75 | Adrian Dantley (2) | 29 | 315 | 253 | 883 | 30.4 |
| 1975-76 | Adrian Dantley (4) | 29 | 300 | 229 | 829 | 28.6 |
| 1976-77 | Don Williams | 29 | 212 | 102 | 526 | 18.1 |
| 1977-78 | Dave Batton | 31 | 188 | 59 | 435 | 14.0 |
| 1978-79 | Kelly Tripucka | 29 | 143 | 129 | 415 | 14.3 |
| 1979-80 | Tracy Jackson | 28 | 162 | 99 | 423 | 15.1 |
| 1980-81 | Kelly Tripucka | 29 | 195 | 137 | 527 | 18.2 |
| 1981-82 | John Paxson | 27 | 185 | 72 | 442 | 16.4 |
| 1982-83 | John Paxson | 29 | 219 | 74 | 512 | 17.7 |
| 1983-84 | Tom Sluby | 33 | 254 | 108 | 616 | 18.7 |
| 1984-85 | David Rivers | 30 | 168 | 138 | 474 | 15.8 |

# Women's Season Scoring Leaders

Based on total points scored

| | | | | | | |
|---|---|---|---|---|---|---|
| 1974-75 | | | | | | |
| 1975-76 | Carol Lally | | | | | |
| 1976-77 | Carol Lally | | | | | |
| 1977-78 | Carol Lally | 16 | 82 | 17 | 181 | 11.3 |
| 1978-79 | Carol Lally | 22 | 111 | 47 | 281 | 12.8 |
| 1979-80 | Shari Matvey | 30 | 237 | 55 | 529 | 17.6 |
| 1980-81 | Shari Matvey | 28 | 184 | 46 | 414 | 14.8 |
| 1981-82 | Mary Beth Schueth | 25 | 137 | 52 | 326 | 13.0 |
| 1982-83 | Mary Beth Schueth | 27 | 128 | 61 | 317 | 11.7 |
| 1983-84 | Carrie Bates | 28 | 129 | 75 | 333 | 11.9 |
| 1984-85 | Trena Keys | 28 | 212 | 59 | 483 | 17.2 |

# Individual Records—Men

*In a Game*

Points—61, Austin Carr vs. Ohio., Mar. 7, 1970 at Dayton, OH, NCAA
    Mideast Regional First Round (NCAA Tournament Record)
Points at Home—55, Austin Carr vs. West Virginia, Feb. 21, 1970
Points in a Half—38, Austin Carr vs. Detroit, Jan. 14, 1971 at ACC.
Field Goals Attempted—44, Austin Carr vs. Ohio, Mar. 7, 1970 at
    Dayton, OH
    44, Austin Carr vs. Butler, Feb. 23, 1970 at
    Butler
Field Goals Made—25, Austin Carr vs. Ohio, Mar. 7, 1970 at Dayton, OH.
Field Goals Made Consecutively—14, Austin Carr vs. South Carolina, Dec.
    30, 1969 at New Orleans, LA.,
    Sugar Bowl Tournament
Free Throws Attempted—26, Kelly Tripucka vs. Dayton, Feb. 3, 1979
    at ACC
Free Throws Made—23, Kelly Tripucka vs. Dayton, Feb. 3, 1979 at ACC
Free Throws Made Consecutively— 15, Bob Arnzen vs. N.Y.U., Feb. 23,
    1967 at Madison Square
    Garden
Rebounds—30, Bob Whitmore vs. St. Norbert, Dec. 14, 1967 at ND
    30, Walter Sahm vs. Ball State, Dec. 4, 1964 at ND

Assists—17, Jackie Meehan vs. Ohio., Mar. 7, 1970 at Dayton, OH.
　　17, Jackie Meehan vs. Creighton, Feb. 6, 1971 at ACC
Fouls—9, Chester Freeze vs. Mobile YMCA, Jan. 1, 1909, first game,
　　at Mobile, AL.

*In a Season*

Points—1106, Austin Carr, 1969-70
Points per Game—38.1, Austin Carr, 1969-70
Field Goals Attempted—832, Austin Carr, 1970-71
Field Goals Made—444, Austin Carr, 1969-70
Field Goals Made Consecutively—20, John Shumate, 1972-73 (Mar. 20, 24)
Field Goal Percentage—.656, Bruce Flowers, 1978-79 (107-163)
Free Throws Attempted—314, Adrian Dantley, 1974-75
Free Throws Made—253, Adrian Dantley, 1974-75
Free Throws Made Consecutively—36, Austin Carr, 1969-70 (Feb. 7, 10,
　　　　　　　　　　　　　　　　14, 16, 19)
Free Throw Percentage—.854, Kelly Tripucka, 1978-79 (129-151)
Rebounds—499, Tom Hawkins, 1957-58
Rebounds per Game—17.7, Ron Reed, 1963-64
Assists—214, Jackie Meehan, 1970-71
Fouls—104, Dick Rosenthal, 1951-52
　　　　104, John Pleick, 1970-71
Times Fouled Out—11, Daniel Bagley, 1949-50
　　　　　　　　　11, Leroy Leslie, 1951-52
　　　　　　　　　11, John Pleick, 1970-71
Games Played—39, Robert Vaughan, 1908-09
Games Started—39, Robert Vaughan, 1908-09
Games Started Consecutively—38, Robert Vaughan, 1908-09

*In a Career*

Points—2560, Austin Carr, 1968-71
Points per Game—34.6, Austin Carr, 1968-71
Field Goals Attempted—1923, Austin Carr, 1968-71
Field Goals Made—1107, Austin Carr, 1968-71
Field Goal Percentage—.610, John Shumate, 1972-74 (538-882)
Free Throws Attempted—769, Adrian Dantley, 1973-76
Free Throws Made—615, Adrian Dantley, 1973-76
Free Throw Percentage—.814, Austin Carr, 1968-71 (526-646)
Rebounds—1318, Tom Hawkins, 1956-59
Rebounds per Game—16.9, Walter Sahm, 1962-65

Assists—466, Rich Branning, 1976-80
Fouls—378, Bruce Flowers, 1975-79
Times Fouled Out—25, Leroy Leslie, 1949-52
Games Played—117, Bruce Flowers, 1975-79
Games Started—104, Rich Branning, 1976-80
Games Started Consecutively—85, Gary Novak, 1971-74
                                    85, John Paxson, 1980-83

# Team Records—Men

*In a Game*

Points—135, vs. St. Peter's, Feb. 4, 1970 at ACC
Points at Home—135, vs. St. Peter's, Feb. 4, 1970
Points in a Half—75, vs. Villanova, Jan. 11, 1975 at Palestra, Philadelphia,
        PA.
Field Goals Attempted—112, vs. St. Peter's, Feb. 4, 1970
Field Goals Made—60, vs. St. Peter's, Feb. 4, 1970
Field Goal Percentage—.724, vs. Butler, Jan. 30, 1967 at Butler (42-58)
Free Throws Attempted—50, vs. Kansas, Mar. 15, 1975 at Tulsa, Okla.,
                                NCAA Midwest Regional First Round
Free Throws Made—39, vs. Wisconsin, Dec. 4, 1965 at Wisconsin
Rebounds—91, vs. St. Norbert, Dec. 7, 1965 at ND
Assists—31, vs. Valparaiso, Dec. 1, 1973 at ACC;
            vs. Fordham, Feb. 16, 1978 at Madison Square Garden
Attendance—37,283, vs. Michigan, Mar. 4, 1979 at Pontiac Silverdome
Attendance at Home—12,000 vs. UCLA, Dec. 7, 1968 at ACC
Victory Margin—70, vs. Kalamazoo YMCA, Jan. 18, 1908 at ND
Defeat Margin—65, Indiana, Dec. 18, 1971 at Indiana
Fewest Points—7, vs. Michigan Agricultural College (MSU), Feb. 13,
            1913 at MAC

*In a Season*

Points—2711, 1969-70
Points per Game—93.5, 1969-70
Field Goals Attempted—2332, 1957-58
Field Goals Made—1109, 1969-70
Field Goal Percentage—.552, 1980-81 (824-1492)
Free Throws Attempted—793, 1956-57
Free Throws Made—571, 1984-85
Free Throw Percentage—.763, 1978-79 (509-667)
Rebounds—1722, 1964-65

Rebounds per Game—63.8, 1964-65
Assists—544, 1977-78
Fouls—665, 1950-51
Games Played—40, 1908-09
Games Won—33, 1908-09
Games Lost—21, 1965-66
Fewest Games Played—2, 1898-99
Fewest Games Won—1, 1897-98 (3 games played)
                   2, 1918-19 (12 games played)
                   2, 1917-18 (6 games played)
                   2, 1901-02 (4 games played)
                   2, 1896-97 (3 games played)
                   2, 1898-99 (2 games played)
                   5, 1965-66 (26 games played)
                   5, 1919-20 (18 games played)
Fewest Games Lost—0, 1898-99 (2 games played)
                   1, 1926-27 (20 games played)
                   1, 1925-26 (20 games played)
                   1, 1896-97 (3 games played)
Won-Lost Percentage—1.000, 1898-99 (2-0)
                   .950, 1925-26, 1926-27 (both 19-1)
Worst Won-Lost Percentage—.167, 1918-19 (2-10)
                   .192, 1965-66 (5-21)
Attendance—386,230, 1978-79
Attendance at Home—204,807, 1982-83
Attendance per Game, Home—11,345, 1978-79
Scoring Margin—16.9, 1973-74

*In a Career*

Consecutive Wins—22, last 11 games of 1932-33 and first 11 of 1933-34
                   22, 1908-09
Consecutive Wins, Home—38, Dec. 4, 1943 to Feb. 9, 1948
Consecutive Wins, Road—18, 1908-09
Consecutive Losses—13, 1965-66
Consecutive Losses, Home—6, 1971-72
Consecutive Losses, Road—11, Mar. 8, 1965 to Feb. 12, 1966
                   11, Feb. 17, 1966 to Jan. 14, 1967

# Individual Records—Women

*In a Game*

Points—31, Shari Matvey vs. Mount St. Joseph, Jan. 26, 1980 at ACC
    31, Shari Matvey vs. Chicago State, Jan. 11, 1980 at DeKalb,
    IL., Huskie Invitational
Points at Home—31, Shari Matvey vs. Mount St. Joseph, Jan. 26, 1980
Points in a Half—27, Jenny Klauke vs. Ball State, Feb. 11, 1981 at Ball
    State
Field Goals Attempted—30, Shari Matvey vs. Chicago State, Jan. 11, 1980
    at DeKalb, IL.
Field Goals Made—14, Shari Matvey vs. Mount St. Joseph, Jan. 26, 1980
    at ACC.
    14, Shari Matvey vs. Chicago State, Jan. 11, 1980
    at DeKalb, IL.
Free Throws Attempted—18, Janice Crowe vs. Concordia, Dec. 6, 1980
    at ACC
Free Throws Made—12, Trena Keys vs. Dayton, Feb. 5, 1985 at Dayton
Rebounds—22, Jane Politiski vs. Goshen, Feb. 13, 1978 at Goshen
Assists—13, Denise Basford vs. Detroit, Feb 18, 1984 at Detroit

*In a Season*

Points—529, Shari Matvey, 1979-80
Points per Game—17.6, Shari Matvey, 1979-80
Field Goals Attempted—410, Trena Keys, 1984-85
Field Goals Made—237, Shari Matvey, 1979-80
Field Goal Percentage—.589, Carrie Bates, 1981-82 (136-231)
Free Throws Attempted—108, Mary Beth Schueth, 1983-84
Free Throws Made—77, Mary Beth Schueth, 1984-85
Free Throw Percentage—.765, Laura Dougherty, 1981-85 (75-91)
Rebounds—305, Shari Matvey, 1979-80
Rebounds per Game—11.9, Jane Politiski, 1977-78
Assists—116, Mary Gavin, 1984-85
Fouls—102, Trish McManus, 1979-80
Times Fouled Out—5, Trish McManus, 1979-80
Games Played—30, Kelly Hicks, 1979-80
    30, Maggie Lally, 1979-80
    30, Trish McManus, 1979-80
    30, Missy Conboy, 1979-80
    30, Shari Matvey, 1979-80

Games Started—29, Kelly Hicks, 1979-80
Games Started Consecutively—28, Trena Keys, 1984-85


*In a Career*

Points—1373, Shari Matvey, 1979-83
Points per Game—12.6, Shari Matvey, 1979-83
Field Goals Attempted—1156, Shari Matvey, 1979-83
Field Goals Made—616, Shari Matvey, 1979-83
Field Goal Percentage—.553, Carrie Bates, 1981-85 (439-794)
Free Throws Attempted—421, Mary Beth Schueth, 1981-85
Free Throws Made—259, Mary Beth Schueth, 1981-85
Free Throw Percentage—.765, Laura Dougherty, 1981-85 (173-226)
Rebounds—853, Mary Beth Schueth, 1981-85
Rebounds per Game—9.5, Jane Politiski, 1977-80
Assists—326, Laura Dougherty, 1981-85
Fouls—252, Mary Beth Schueth, 1981-85
Times Fouled Out—12, Trish McManus, 1978-81
Games Played—109, Shari Matvey, 1979-83
Games Started—95, Mary Beth Schueth, 1981-85
Games Started Consecutively—62, Mary Beth Schueth, 1981-84


# Team Records—Women

*In a Game*

Points—107, vs. Xavier, Feb. 9, 1985 at ACC
Points at Home—107, vs. Xavier, Feb. 9, 1985
Points in a Half—55, vs. Xavier, Feb. 9, 1985
Field Goals Attempted—97, vs. Grace, Jan. 31, 1978 at ND
Field Goals Made—44, vs. Butler, Feb. 28, 1985 at ACC.
Field Goal Percentage—.702, vs. Xavier, Feb. 9, 1985 at ACC (40-57)
Free Throws Attempted—38, vs. Xavier, Feb. 9, 1985
Free Throws Made—27, vs. Dayton, Feb. 5, 1985
                    27, vs. Xavier, Feb. 9, 1985
Rebounds—74, vs. IUPU-Fort Wayne, Jan. 24, 1978 at ND
Assists—26, vs. Detroit, Feb. 18, 1984 at Detroit
          26, vs. Butler, Feb. 28, 1985
Attendance—4,325, vs. Louisiana Tech, Jan. 12, 1984 at Louisiana Tech

Attendance, Home—3,420, vs. Louisiana Tech, Feb. 11, 1983
Victory Margin—63, vs. Saint Mary's, Dec. 8, 1981 at ACC
          63, vs. Butler, February 28, 1985
Defeat Margin—76, vs. South Carolina, Jan. 31, 1981 at ACC
Fewest Points—23, vs. Michigan State, Jan. 30, 1975 at Michigan State

*In a Season*

Points—1975, 1984-85
Points per Game—70.5, 1984-85
Field Goals Attempted—1941, 1979-80
Field Goals Made—813, 1984-85
Field Goal Percentage—.500, 1984-85 (813-1626)
Free Throws Attempted—559, 1979-80
Free Throws Made—372, 1983-84
Free Throw Percentage—.691, 1983-84 (372-538)
Rebounds—1355, 1979-80
Rebounds per Game—48.5, 1977-78
Assists—435, 1982-83
Fouls—584, 1979-80
Games Played—30, 1979-80
Games Won—20, 1982-83
          20, 1979-80
          20, 1984-85
Games Lost—18, 1980-81
Fewest Games Played—7, 1974-75
Fewest Games Won—3, 1974-75 (7 games played)
          6, 1975-76 (13 games played)
          9, 1976-77 (14 games played)
          10, 1980-81 (28 games played)
Fewest Games Lost—4, 1977-78 (17 games played)
          4, 1974-75 (7 games played)
Won-Lost Percentage—.765, 1977-78 (13-4)
          .741, 1982-83 (20-7)
Worst Won-Lost Percentage—.357, 1980-81 (10-18)
Scoring Margin—11.8, 1984-85

*In a Career*

Consecutive Wins—10, 1981-82
Consecutive Wins, Home—11, 1984-85 (current)

Consecutive Wins, Road—6, 1977-78
                         6, 1978-79
                         6, 1981-82
Consecutive Losses—7, last 5 games of 1981-82 and first 2 of 1982-83
                       7, 1980-81
Consecutive Losses at Home—3, 1981-82
                               3, Feb. 15, 1980 to Dec. 6, 1980
                               3, 1974-75
Consecutive Losses, Road—6, 1980-81

# Notre Dame Men in the Naismith Memorial Basketball Hall of Fame

Listed chronologically
Each listing is followed by the category and year of election

George Keogan, Coach, 1961.

Elmer Ripley, Contributor, 1972. A successful professional ballplayer in the teens and 20s, Ripley also served as coach at Yale, Army and Georgetown as well as his one season at Notre Dame. Later, he also coached the Israel and Canada Olympic basketball teams.

Edward "Moose" Krause, Player, 1975.

Ray Meyer, Coach, 1978. Elected for his success and longevity at the helm of DePaul, he began his collegiate coaching career as an assistant to Keogan and served as *de facto* head coach for part of two seasons during Keogan's illness (1940-42). Also a two-time captain during his ND playing days.

Walter Kennedy, Contributor, 1980. Best known as publicist and later commissioner of the NBA, Kennedy, a 1934 graduate of ND, served his alma mater as sports information director during World War II (1943-45).

# Notre Dame Basketball Olympians

Listed chronologically

Vince Boryla, 1948. Elected to a team composed primarily of University of Kentucky and Phillips 66 Oilers AAU players, he scored 28 points in the gold medal effort. At the time he was a member of the Denver Nuggets AAU team during a stint in the service; he returned to school in 1948-49, but to the University of Denver rather than ND.

Adrian Dantley, 1976. Led U.S. Olympic team in scoring, both overall and in the championship game, as team won its eighth gold medal in nine Olympiads. It was his last triumph as an amateur—he had already decided to forego his senior year to turn pro.

Bill Hanzlik, 1980. Named to team but never played against international competition because of U.S. boycott of Moscow Olympics.

Joe Kleine, 1984. Played at Notre Dame as a freshman before transferring to Arkansas, where he became a star. Member of U.S. team which convincingly won the gold medal and was ranked with the 1960 American squad as the greates in Olympic history.